Phil Edmonston

LEMON-AID

2012

NEW CARS
and TRUCKS

Phil Edmonston

LEMON-AID

2012

NEW CARS and TRUCKS

DUNDURN

TORONTO

Editing: Jade Colbert, Andrea Douglas, Greg Ioannou
Design: Jack Steiner
Printer: Webcom

1   2   3   4   5   15   14   13   12   11

 Conseil des Arts du Canada   Canada Council for the Arts    Canadä   ONTARIO ARTS COUNCIL CONSEIL DES ARTS DE L'ONTARIO

We acknowledge the support of the **Canada Council for the Arts** and the **Ontario Arts Council** for our publishing program. We also acknowledge the financial support of the **Government of Canada** through the **Canada Book Fund** and **Livres Canada Books**, and the **Government of Ontario** through the **Ontario Book Publishing Tax Credit program**, and the **Ontario Media Development Corporation**.

Care has been taken to trace the ownership of copyright material used in this book. The author and the publisher welcome any information enabling them to rectify any references or credits in subsequent editions.
J. Kirk Howard, President

Printed and bound in Canada.
www.dundurn.com

Dundurn Press
3 Church Street, Suite 500
Toronto, Ontario, Canada
M5E 1M2

Gazelle Book Services Limited
White Cross Mills
High Town, Lancaster, England
LA1 4XS

Dundurn Press
2250 Military Road
Tonawanda, NY
U.S.A. 14150

 MIX
Paper from
responsible sources
FSC
www.fsc.org   FSC® C004071

CONTENTS

KEY DOCUMENTS

MORE PROFIT, LESS CAR

Paint delamination is a common defect that automakers often blame on everything from bird droppings to ultraviolet light—or they simply say the warranty has expired. The courts haven't been very receptive to these kinds of excuses.

No-Haggle Hubris

I'm going to sell more for less and make it up in volume? That's like burning in hell. We're not interested.

JOE LATHAM, CHRYSLER DEALER
AUTOMOTIVE NEWS, MAY 2, 2011

Here, Honey. Take the Steering Wheel

A motorist driving a new Chevrolet Cruze says he was driving down a highway when the steering wheel came off in his hands. Seriously.

General Motors said it believes it was an isolated incident, but is recalling 2,100 of the cars nonetheless ....

You'll be cruising for a bruising in a steering-wheel-less Chevy Cruze.

1

Here's what GM says it thinks happened: when this particular car was in production, the wrong steering wheel was installed. Inspectors caught the mistake, and the correct wheel replaced the incorrect one, but it was not properly secured. It was just a matter of time before it came off the steering column.

MARK HUFFMAN
CONSUMERAFFAIRS.COM, APRIL 12, 2011

Best of Times and Worst of Times

What a difference a month of earthquakes, a tsunami, and multiple nuclear reactor meltdowns can make for car sales. Detroit automakers are suddenly awash in profits, car buyers are actually *visiting* Chrysler/Fiat showrooms, and the South Koreans and Europeans have gained important market share with new restyled and high-tech products.

More important, the Japanese are now considering pairing up with Chinese automakers in running joint-owned auto plants in China, all the more remarkable given the two countries' longstanding hostility towards one another.

A good car turns sour

Honda and Toyota are on the ropes, having suffered (along with their main suppliers) the most tsunami damage. Production fell to one-half of normal capacity for both automakers, both in Japan and in North America. Nissan/Infiniti has also been hurt, by two earthquakes that struck near its new Iwaki engine plant, located just 56 kilometres from the Fukushima power plant. Last year, that facility built over 560,000 engines and remains key to Nissan's future V6 production. The earthquakes almost wiped it out—twice.

Shortly after they were completely destroyed by atomic bomb attacks in the last days of the Second World War, Hiroshima and Nagasaki were predicted to be atomic wastelands for hundreds of years. It's ironic, then, that today Mazda's Hiroshima plant is one of the largest single-site automobile manufacturing plants in the world, with an annual production capacity of around 480,000 radiation-free cars.

A good car goes bad—*Consumer Reports* says Honda's Civic is no longer rated "Recommended" because of problems found with its 2012 redesign. The car has been a Canadian sales leader for the past 13 years.

Just as Honda was recovering from one tsunami, last July it was hit by a wave of bad publicity following the decision by *Consumer Reports* to drop its long-time "Recommended" rating of the Honda Civic. The non-profit consumer magazine blames the lower rating on the redesigned 2012 Honda Civic's poor performance. *Lemon-Aid* dropped its rating years ago for the same reason.

Detroit could not have had a more providential act of God. Japanese new car shortages and supplier disruptions will push car prices through the roof beginning in September 2011 and lasting through the first quarter of 2012. Plus, double-digit sales increases in China and Europe will breathe new life into the American automobile industry. Already, Chrysler, Ford, and General Motors have reported record profits through the first half of 2011.

Most European automakers are also doing quite well this year, led by Audi, BMW, Mercedes-Benz, and Volkswagen. Indian-owned Jaguar and Rover are defying the dire predictions of poor auto sales and making some money (Rover more than Jaguar) after decades of red ink. Saab, Volvo, and Morris/MGs, on the other hand, have had dismal sales and are now owned by the Chinese, who, in the spirit of world democracy, have the sacred right to pour their Renminbi down these rabbit holes as well.

European auto manufacturers will soon end Lexus' reign as the top-selling European luxury car due to the limited supply of Lexus product following the March 11 Japanese earthquake and the added competition of less-expensive and more fuel-efficient small cars from Mercedes and BMW. Additionally, a record number of Lexus leaseholders are coming off three-year leases this year and are expected to buy out their leases because off-lease Lexus and other higher-end models have begun to appreciate more than their contracted residual value.

2012 Buying Strategies

Fewer new cars mean higher new and used car prices for buyers of small and family-sized vehicles, who will be at a disadvantage due to the weakened competition. Insiders expect the Detroit Three to raise 2012 retail prices about 10 percent and continue to offer meager sales incentives until they are faced with real competition next year. By that time, Chrysler/Fiat, Ford, and GM will have built up a hefty cash reserve to feed new rounds of rebates and discounts and keep their sales momentum going.

What should the savvy buyer do?

1. Buy out the lease, and sell your vehicle privately for much more next year.
2. Look for some privately sold three-year-old bargains with some of the original warranty left.
3. Shop in the States for fully loaded trucks, SUVs, and sports cars.
4. Consider only vehicles recommended by *Lemon-Aid*, and steer clear of Fukushima-imported Japanese new cars and trucks until their radiation safety has been assured.
5. Buy during the first quarter of 2012 when more competition from the Japanese will ease prices and offer more models to choose from.

Forget Japanese car bargains in the short term. There won't be any. Instead, consider the South Korean makes. They are expected to rake in big sales numbers by retailing their 2012 vehicles with about half the increase predicted for Detroit-based automakers. Take note that Hyundai and Kia models have become even more popular as a result of the *Consumer Reports* 2011 Annual Auto Issue, which gives a "Recommended" green light to most of Hyundai's 2011 lineup and (incredible, but true) to a few Kia offerings.

Lemon-Aid's Mission: A Cheap New Vehicle That Lasts 15 Years

Lemon-Aid is approaching its 41st year of publication with the same goal with which it started: to help readers find cheap, reliable, safe vehicles that can be kept a minimum of 15 years.

During the past decade, car-buying attitudes have changed dramatically. At one time, you were judged by what you drove. And, what you drove was traded in every three to five years. That's no longer the case. We are now more environmentally sensitive and cost-conscious. Buyers expect their new cars to burn less fuel, and they want their vehicles to last much longer than the finance payments.

It's easy to see why. Canadians are keeping their cars for up to 10 years (particularly in eastern and western Canada); expecting it to last another five years isn't all that unreasonable. In fact, reliable vehicles in rural areas often stay in the family nest for several decades. They become the "second car" when both parents work; they go off to college with the children; and they return to provide transportation for graduates going to their first jobs, or for grandma and grandpa's around-town excursions.

Every time I go on my annual *Lemon-Aid* cross-country book tour, readers invariably tell me, "Phil, my parents used *Lemon-Aid* when they bought their first car—a 1975 Dodge Dart."

Yes, the years have passed quickly. Yet many of the same sales scams and quality issues continue to plague car buyers. On the other hand, consumer rights have been reinforced throughout Canada. No longer do I have to beat down $2 million libel lawsuits from automakers (Honda and Nissan were the first and last), and I haven't picketed a dealership or auto show in decades (although I did get thrown out of the Edmonton Auto Show a few years back after I went in front of the Mercedes-Benz kiosk and told CBC TV that the "C" in Mercedes' C-class cars stood for "crappy").

It's hard to believe that *Lemon-Aid,* which had just over a hundred pages 40 years ago, now requires 500 or so pages to give car buyers the info they need to buy a reliable and safe vehicle.

What's New in Lemon-Aid 2012?

- There are more vehicles rated, and we have made some surprising downgrades and upgrades relative to some redesigned models. Many newly designed vehicles don't perform as well as previous iterations, like the BMW X5, Honda Civic and Odyssey, Hyundai Sonata and Elantra, Mercedes-Benz E350, and Toyota 4Runner and Sienna.

- We have included more roof crashworthiness ratings and updated our cross-border shopping guide, so you can buy for less in the States or ask your Canadian dealer to match the *Lemon-Aid*-listed price.
- Revised summaries of safety- and performance-related defects that are likely to affect 2011 and 2012 vehicles. This information is gleaned from internal service bulletins, government-posted consumer complaints, and *Lemon-Aid* reader feedback.
- In Appendix I, "Mini-Reviews and 2013 Previews," we rate vehicles that have been on the market for only a short time or are sold in small numbers, as well as give previews of some 2013 models that may be more hype than hope.

As always, this year's guide combines test results with owner feedback to provide a critical comparison of 2011 and 2012 vehicles as to their real fuel-economy and crashworthiness.

If new features are "more show than go," or improvements and additional safety features don't justify the higher costs of newer models (like run-flat tires), we say so and suggest you buy the less-loaded, safer, more reliable, cheaper alternative. Front, offset, side, rear, rollover, and roof strength crash test results are also included, along with an exhaustive list of accessories and optional safety features; we'll tell you which are useful and which are useless. We show how much profit dealers make on each vehicle, and what should be considered a fair price on both sides of the border. We are also carefully watching cross-border prices. We know most new- and used-car prices in the States beat the Canadian MSRP by 10–30 percent.

Lemon-Aid is still the comprehensive, practical owner's manual millions of Canadians know and trust. We don't want you to get stuck with a lemon or own a vehicle that can't be serviced, and we don't think you should pay for repairs that are the automaker's fault. That's why every guide includes the latest "secret" automaker warranties that manufacturer bigwigs don't want you to use to buttress your claim for a refund.

Phil Edmonston

October 2011

Part One
"HOT" WHEELS AND GOOD DEALS

"Green" cars may not be as green as they seem.

Chevrolet Volt: An Electric Edsel?

After years of media hype and presidential accolades, Chevrolet has rolled out its new electric car, the Volt, to one of the coolest receptions since Ford began production of the Edsel; in fact, the only way that sales figures for Chevy's new electric car can appear positive is by comparing them to the even more abysmal sales experienced by the Nissan Leaf.

Sales of the Volt appear bleak, and seem to be falling. According to GM's sales figures for February, the Volt accounted for a mere 281 of the 142,919 Chevrolets sold that month; when considering total sales for 2011, the sale of 602 Volts accounts for approximately one-fifth of one percent of the 268,308 Chevrolets sold. (During the same time period, Nissan has sold a stunning 173 of its new Leaf.)

JAMES HEISTER
WWW.THENEWAMERICAN.COM, MARCH 11, 2011

Detroit: Three Times Lucky

First cripple Japanese auto production and supplier support with a devastating earthquake, tsunami, and nuclear plant meltdown (wait for the late-night TV jokesters bragging that Japanese cars will now be easier to find in parking lots at night because they glow). Then, take advantage of a red-hot Chinese market where Buicks are seen as Cadillacs. Top it off with pent-up buyer demand fuelled by greater credit availability, and you have the makings of a dazzling Detroit sales turnaround. In fact, GM, Ford, and Chrysler are now earning more profit while selling far fewer vehicles—except for the Volt. (Sorry, I couldn't resist.) According to Steve Rattner, who helped the White House restructure GM and Chrysler, each Volt costs $40,000 to build and sells for $40,000+ (less a 8,500–$10,000 rebate from the provinces).

Ford and GM Revival

In a desperate effort to cut costs, a lot of makes have been culled from the Detroit herd within the last few years, much to the relief of *Lemon-Aid* staff who said their purchase was a huge mistake in the first place. Those divisions that weren't shut down (Pontiac, Mercury, and Saturn) were sold to other auto manufacturers for barely one-third what they originally cost to acquire (Jaguar, Land Rover, Saab, and Volvo).

In its Perceived Quality Study, the U.S.-based *Automotive Lease Guide* says Ford posted the largest increase of any automaker between fall 2009 and spring 2010. Honda was number one in perceived quality, while Toyota fell from first place to sixth, largely due to its recall of almost 14 million vehicles early this year to fix unintended acceleration, hybrid brake failures, and corrosion-cankered pickup trucks.

Ford's higher scores mean higher residual values for its vehicles. For example, its average car resale value was up by $2,400 U.S. from 2009 to 2010. Market watchers attribute the higher resale values and quality perception to Ford's refusal to accept government handouts, *Consumer Reports*' higher quality ratings, and the allure of new products like the 2012 Fiesta and the redesigned Focus, Fusion, and Taurus models.

Ford's Fiesta, top-ranked for crashworthiness, starts at $12,999, but the more versatile hatchback costs $3,800 more. Why? Less Japanese competition.

Ford recently shuttered Mercury after selling Jaguar, Land Rover, and Aston Martin to Tata Motors, an Indian automaker that builds the world's cheapest car, the Nano. Tata says Jaguar and Land Rover manufacturing will be subcontracted out to China. Thus two British icons, which became Ford "trophy cars," were snapped up by Tata and then shipped off to China. Is it risky trusting a company that's had so many owners? Think of it as getting married four times.

Chrysler: Born Again?

GM's extensive restructuring accomplishments make Chrysler's roll of the dice with a Fiat partnership look extremely risky and short-sighted. With Chrysler hitching its wagon (and minivan) to Fiat, it will be like two drunks propping each other up on the street corner, waiting for the Grand Caravan bus to pick them up.

With less competition from Japan, Chrysler/Fiat could sell egg crates and still make money. That's it, Let's hear it for the 100 hp Fiat Egg Crate 500. No rusting...

What we have with the Chrysler-Fiat partnership is two automakers known for making crappy cars combining into one huge company to make more crappy cars and SUVs.

Fiat's 500 series econoboxes are frugal—and feeble. They have just come on the North American market and local mechanics have no idea how to repair them. Until they do, you are in Guido's hands. Parts, er, they're coming, too. I think.

Chrysler is barely a viable entity, no matter whom it's partnered with. (Remember, not even Mercedes could afford to support Chrysler's cash burn, and that's the main reason why it dumped its 19 percent stake in the company.) Crafty Fiat didn't risk one euro on Chrysler for its first 35 percent of the company, and it will probably end up with a majority stake in the restructured automaker before year's end.

2011 AND 2012 HITS AND MISSES

HITS

1. Ford Edge, Escape, Escape Hybrid, Fiesta, Flex, Focus, Fusion, Fusion Hybrid, and Mustang
2. GM Acadia, Cruze, Enclave, Equinox, Savana, Tahoe, Terrain, TraverseExpress, and Yukon
3. Honda (all models except 2012 Civic)
4. Hyundai (all models except 2012 Sonata)
5. Infiniti (all models)
6. Lincoln MKZ and Town Car
7. Mazda2, Mazda3, Mazda6 B-Series, Miata, and Tribute
8. Nissan Frontier, Rogue, Sentra, and X-Trail
9. Suzuki SX4
10. Subaru Forester and Legacy

MISSES

1. Chrysler (all models)
2. Ford "orphans": Aston Martin, Jaguar, Land Rover, and Volvo
3. GM "orphans": Hummer, Pontiac, Saab, and Saturn
4. GM Canyon and Colorado
5. GM Volt
6. Nissan Quest
7. Nissan Leaf
8. Smart Fortwo
9. Suzuki Equator
10. Volkswagen Routan

Ford's V6-powered Mustang is powerful, handles well, and sips fuel.

Under Chinese ownership, Saab's future is unclear.

 **Best Buy Tips**

Now's a good time to be a contrarian. For example, higher oil prices are driving down prices for large, fully loaded trucks and SUVs. Savings of 30 percent or more are commonplace and will probably increase as we go into the winter months. With the money saved, the fuel penalty is softened and depreciation isn't as steep because of the discounted purchase price.

1. Buy a new or used vehicle that is relatively uncomplicated, is easy to service, and has been sold in large numbers. This will ensure that cheaper, independent garages can provide service and parts.

2. Look for a vehicle that's finishing its model run. But steer clear of models that were axed because of poor reliability or mediocre performance, like GM's front-drive minivans or Smart cars.

3. Stay away from European offerings, especially their SUVs. Dealership networks are weak, parts are inordinately expensive and hard to find, and few garages will invest in the expensive equipment needed to service complicated emissions and fuel-delivery systems. The old axiom that there is a right way, a wrong way, and a European way to troubleshoot a car still holds true.

4. Don't buy a hybrid, electric, or diesel model. They are complicated to service and dealer-dependent, and they don't provide the fuel economy or savings they hype. The recent Fukushima earthquake destroyed many of the hybrid component suppliers and has forced automakers to cut back hybrid production. Electric cars lack a recharging infrastructure; they don't run well in cold weather or over hilly terrain; and the Chevrolet Volt four-seater is known for low heater output...brr. Diesel complexity has increased due to more stringent emissions regulations that require frequent expensive urea fill-ups.

5. Don't buy Chrysler, Dodge, Jeep, or Fiat models. Chrysler is the weakest of the Detroit Three, its lineup has a sad history of serious safety- and performance-related defects, and its automatic transmissions, brakes, and air conditioners are particularly troublesome. This may all change by next year if this year's new powertrains and assorted other improvements correct two decades of design deficiencies. The Dodge 200 and Grand Cherokee refinements will tell us if Chrysler quality has improved. The same holds true for the recently arrived, overpriced Fiat 500. Let the mechanics learn on someone else's car, and wait for owner and fleet feedback. This is how we discovered that Chevy's Volt keeps a chilly interior and that electric cars may get only half their hyped fuel economy in real-world cold-weather driving in Canada.

6. Don't buy GM or Chrysler front-drive models or vehicles made in China. Crash test ratings for many China-made vehicles are listed as "Poor," and their assembly quality is crude, at best. Jacob George, vice-president of China operations for J.D. Power Asia Pacific says China-built vehicles won't match U.S. average initial quality before 2016. As a rule, GM front-drives are less reliable than the rear-drives and have poorly performing powertrains and brakes. Start shopping for a GM car or truck in the first quarter of 2012, when the auto show hoopla has died down and prices continue their downward slide.

7. Consider Ford—the automaker has offered more reliable and better-performing buys since it started cutting costs and selling off large chunks of the company several years ago. The added cash was invested in new models and better quality control that has made some Not Recommended models (such as the 2000–04 Focus) into Above Average (2005–2012 Focus) buys.
8. Don't buy from dual dealerships. Parts inventories at many dealerships may have been depleted due to slow sales, and qualified mechanics may be in short supply. The auto companies represented by a dual dealership see the dealership as less than loyal and will cut the dealership little slack in vehicle deliveries and warranty assistance.
9. Don't buy any vehicle that requires an extended warranty due to a reputation for past failures. Choose a better car instead.
10. Use your credit card for the down payment, and put down as little money as possible. Use credit instead of cash to pay for repairs and maintenance charges. If you want to cancel a sales contract or work order, it's easier to do with a credit card than with cash.

Whom Can You Trust?

No one. Not even *Lemon-Aid*. And be especially wary of "friendly advice." One study carried out by the Sauder School of Business at the University of British Columbia says that friends with expertise in a certain field may provide inaccurate advice when recalling complex or nuanced facts.

Check facts out with several other independent sources. On the Internet, there's always *www.thetruthaboutcars.com*, *www.jalopnik.com*, and *www.safercar.gov*. On the following page is what the NHTSA complaint website looks like—pay particular attention to the tabs running down the left side of the page.

NHTSA is useful when dealer service managers lie and say your problem isn't safety-related or isn't a common failure. For example, here is what one owner experienced with her 2011 Jeep Grand Cherokee 4×4:

> I purchased a 2011 Jeep Grand Cherokee X Package on 1/18/2011. Two weeks after purchasing vehicle I was stopped at a light, while my foot was on the brake the car surged forward almost hitting the car in front of me. Car continued to accelerate on its own. I had to ride the brake home. Dealer said he never had this problem before and had no clue what to do so he had to wait for Chrysler to call him to tell him what to do. Should have red flagged this answer. [A number] of days later dealer called said car was fixed, it was a bad sensor on the gas pedal, replaced, and assured me it was safe to drive. A week later, I was stopped at a stop sign waiting to make a right turn on the way home from dropping off my kids at school.... Suddenly, electronic throttle light and engine light came on, the car accelerated forward, skidding out onto the sidewalk, almost hitting a pole. Due to my quick thinking I avoided death twice

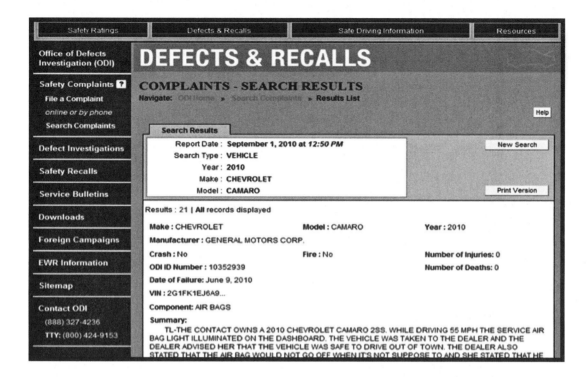

DEFECTS & RECALLS

Office of Defects
Investigation (ODI)

Safety Complaints ❓
  File a Complaint
  online or by phone
  Search Complaints

Defect Investigations

Safety Recalls

Service Bulletins

Downloads

Foreign Campaigns

EWR Information

Sitemap

Contact ODI
  (888) 327-4236
  TTY: (800) 424-9153

COMPLAINTS - SEARCH RESULTS

Navigate: ODI Home » Search Complaints » Results List

Help

Search Results

Report Date :	September 1, 2010 at *12:50 PM*
Search Type :	VEHICLE
Year :	2010
Make :	CHEVROLET
Model :	CAMARO

New Search

Print Version

Results : 21 | All records displayed

Make : CHEVROLET	Model : CAMARO	Year : 2010
Manufacturer : GENERAL MOTORS CORP.		
Crash : No	Fire : No	Number of Injuries: 0
ODI ID Number : 10352939		Number of Deaths: 0
Date of Failure: June 9, 2010		
VIN : 2G1FK1EJ6A9...		
Component: AIR BAGS		

Summary:
    TL-THE CONTACT OWNS A 2010 CHEVROLET CAMARO 2SS. WHILE DRIVING 55 MPH THE SERVICE AIR BAG LIGHT ILLUMINATED ON THE DASHBOARD. THE VEHICLE WAS TAKEN TO THE DEALER AND THE DEALER ADVISED HER THAT THE VEHICLE WAS SAFE TO DRIVE OUT OF TOWN. THE DEALER ALSO STATED THAT THE AIR BAG WOULD NOT GO OFF WHEN ITS NOT SUPPOSE TO AND SHE STATED THAT HE

in this car. My husband and I bought this as a first car for my daughter. The thought of a new driver driving this deathtrap is scary. I will never put myself or anyone in my family in this car. It is seriously a death threat to drivers and pedestrians. Chrysler better man up before more people lose their lives.

Publications you can trust are *Consumer Reports* and the British Consumers Association's *Which?* In Canada, the *Toronto Star*'s long-time consumer columnist Ellen Roseman is a tough advocate for consumer rights and often scoops the motoring press in exposing scams and defects.

The *Toronto Star*'s Saturday "Wheels" section has come a long way during the past three decades. It no longer relies so much on auto industry puff pieces, free press junkets, and the free product "souvenirs" that garnish automaker press conferences. Originally an apologist for the automakers with kissy-kissy car reviews and a weekly "say nothing" column from the president of the Toronto Automobile Dealers Association (TADA), "Wheels" has been improved by its increased use of young freelance journalists and female writers. Yes—female writers! They sweat the details more, are less likely to be intimidated by Oshawa and Oakville suits, and take into account (when necessary) what families need in terms of vehicle performance.

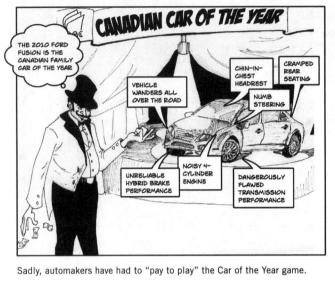

Sadly, automakers have had to "pay to play" the Car of the Year game.

I particularly like the practical articles written by Mark Toljagic (such as "If the warranty runs out, who ya gonna call?"—an article about good places to repair Hondas, Saabs, and Volvos in Toronto, which can be found at *www.wheels.ca/Article Category/article/784979*) and independent-minded Jil McIntosh, an antique car and hot rod hobbyist with knowledge of custom cars and restored vehicles (such as "Prius-like Lexus hardly worth premium," which can be found at *www.wheels. ca/Hybrid/article/785978*).

An example of the "Wheels" section's new tough reporting style is John LeBlanc's May 15, 2010, exposé of the Automobile Journalists Association of Canada (AJAC) and that group's annual Canadian Car of the Year awards. In a large header, LeBlanc asks a simple question: "Should Automakers Pay for Awards?"

His article begins by rehashing the *Wall Street Journal*'s report blasting *Consumers Digest* magazine (not to be confused with *Consumer Reports*) for asking automakers to pay them $35,000 for the right to advertise that they've received *CD*'s "Best Buy" rating, and $25,000 for each lower rating ("Auto Awards Clouded by Fees," *Wall Street Journal*, May 10, 2010).

Before the entry was rewritten with an advertorial slant, Wikipedia had this to say about *Consumers Digest*:

> Founded in 1960 and published by Consumers Digest Communications, LLC, *Consumers Digest* is an American for-profit magazine that allows companies to use its reviews for marketing purposes for a fee. Many car makers have financial ties to the publication. The magazine chose 15 General Motors vehicles for its 2010 "Best Buy" awards—and then GM paid the magazine for the right to mention those awards. According to *Consumers Digest*, the magazine awards its *Consumers Digest* Best Buy seal to products its staff judges to be of the best quality for the most reasonable price.
>
> The magazine charges a $35,000 annual fee for use of its green and gold *Consumers Digest* Best Buy seal. Some of the brands that have licensed the seal include Cal Spas hot tubs, Bridgestone Tires, Brinks Home Security, Multi-Pure Drinking Water Systems, McKleinUSA Business Cases and Mercury Automobiles.... The magazine is sold at newsstands only and does not reveal its sales figures. In 2001, when it ceased subscription distribution, it listed 700,000 subscribers....

The publication has no connection to the *Consumer Reports* magazine published by Consumers Union (which, unlike *Consumers Digest*, is an independent non-profit organization). It also has no relationship to the defunct *Consumers Digest* published by the pioneering Consumers' Research, Inc., 1910–1983, from which Consumers Union sprang.

But how's this for an example of Canadian car columnists' ingenuity: LeBlanc discovered that AJAC doesn't charge a fee for publicizing its 56 or so annual vehicle ratings (hurray!). Instead, AJAC demands that the automakers simply pay the Association $6,900 for each of the 56 vehicles tested, after supplying the vehicle *gratis*.

Writes LeBlanc:

> Although AJAC says on its site the purpose of its event is to "provide consumers with sound, comparative information on vehicles that are new to the market," not all "new" cars are evaluated.... Brands like Aston Martin, Bentley, Chrysler Group, Ferrari, Maserati, Maybach, Lamborghini, Lotus and Rolls-Royce did not participate at all.
>
> So, the question is: Should there be a clear separation of church (automotive award organizers) and state (automaker PR departments) when it comes to automotive awards?

Lemon-Aid says the real question to ask should be this one: If you take bribes (money, trips, computers, clothes, etc.) from companies to extol their products, are you a journalist or a prostitute with a keyboard?

We first answered that question in the 1995 edition of *Lemon-Aid* when we denounced the AJAC and car columnists for taking money from the industry whose cars they were testing.

The "Wheels" article alleges that AJAC is possibly charging automakers 56 times $6,900 annually, or $386,400, not counting the 125 or so individual journalist memberships at $320 each, $3,000 corporate dues, $935 associate corporate dues, and $175 affiliate dues. That's a lot of gas money, and it certainly merits investigation as to where the money goes, who pays what, how elections are carried out, and what family relationships the directors and employees have with the auto writers.

I assume everything is on the up and up with AJAC, but then, when dealing with the auto industry and its apologists, keep in mind that their credibility is only a notch or so above that of British Petroleum (BP) in Louisiana.

For an exceptionally well-written and thoroughly researched update on "Wheels" junkets and more, go to Joe Clark's personal blog at *blog.fawny.org/2008/05/18/wheels-ethics*.

The American "Car of the Year" Scam

After nearly 41 years writing *Lemon-Aid*, I know that car manufacturers run from the truth and look upon independent critics with hostile suspicion. That's why independent car critics have such a difficult time rating new and used vehicles without selling out to the car industry.

Yet the road to "auto-censorship" is so subtle that few writers or broadcasters can resist compromising their integrity: The kids need private schooling; the mortgage must be paid. The smooth-talking executive car pimps are always there to say how much the company admires your work, but then they tell your editor or program director how much better your stories would be with more "balance." And then these hustlers invite you on their trips to Asia and Europe, where they give you geishas, hats, jackets, laptop computers, specially prepared vehicles, and interviews with the top brass. They even sponsor annual journalism awards to make sure their coterie of friendly scribes spouts the party line.

Once you've established a budget and selected some vehicles that interest you, the next step is to ascertain which ones have high safety and reliability ratings. Be wary of the "Car of the Year" ratings found in American car enthusiast magazines and on most websites; their supposedly independent tests are a lot of baloney. Frank Williams, a Canadian auto journalist agrees. Williams says:

You'd be forgiven for thinking COTY awards are little more than a gift to car advertisers, who provide a self-appointed number of "elite" journalists with priority access to press cars, and then co-promote a new product with an old publication. It's certainly an excellent excuse for carmakers like Renault (Alliance), Chevrolet (Citation), Plymouth (RIP, Volare) and Ford (Probe) to sell cars by touting their COTY award like they'd won the Nobel Prize.

If not pissing off your paymasters is the priority, it is perhaps significant that *Car and Driver's* 2006 "10 Best" awards considered 52 cars in new categories, including "Best Luxury Sports Car," "Best Sports Coupe," "Best Roadster," "Best Sports Car" and "Best Muscle Car." Perhaps *C&D* hopes persnickety pistonheads will spend so much time debating which car belongs in what category they'll be too tired to dispute the winners.

Imagine: *Car and Driver* rated the Ford Focus as a "Best Buy" during its first three model years, while government and consumer groups decried the car's dozen or so recall campaigns and the huge number of owners' safety and reliability complaints.

Motor Trend, another American car buff magazine, has been giving out annual COTY awards since the late 1940s. At first the publication recognized automakers only, and then branched out to individual models. Most of the models were heavily publicized in *MT*'s text and ads. Also, many of the highly rated vehicles became infamous for poor reliability and mediocre performance.

Through the years an entire lemon orchard has grown in *Motor Trend*'s Car of the Year lists. Can you see someone trying to sell their AMC/Renault Alliance, Chrysler Omni, Volare, or Aspen, Ford Taurus/Sable, or GMs Vega/Astre as COTY "classics"?

In the final analysis, new car buyers would be better served by a Ouija board's buying recommendation than a "Car of the Year" designation put out by any publication.

Credible Auto Info

Most investigative stories done on the auto industry in Canada (such as exposés on secret car warranties, dangerous airbags, and car company shenanigans) have been written by business columnists, freelancers, or "action line" troubleshooters rather than by reporters on the auto beat. Also, many full-time auto writers have been fired as ad revenues have dried up over the past few years. Most media outlets are now using syndicated, homogenized articles from the States or Toronto that may be only marginally relevant to the rest of Canada.

Again, it bears repeating that those auto reporters who still have a job are regularly beaten into submission by myopic, "kiss-butt" editors and greedy publishers who don't give them the time or the encouragement to do hard-hitting investigative exposés. In fact, it's quite impressive that we do have a small cadre of reporters who won't be cowed.

Canada also has a number of auto experts and consumer advocates who aren't afraid to take on the auto industry and follow good stories, no matter where they lead. Here are some of my favourites:

- Jeremy Cato and Michael Vaughan are two of Canada's best-known automotive and business journalists. This duo is the epitome of auto journalism and business reporting excellence because they ask the tough questions automakers hate to answer. They appear regularly on the Canadian television Business News Network and freelance for a number of national newspapers, including the Toronto *Globe and Mail*.

- Mohamed Bouchama, president of Car Help Canada, shakes up the auto industry by rating new and used cars, providing legal advice, and teaching consumers the art of complaining on *AutoShop* every Sunday at 8 p.m. on Toronto's CP24.
- I have known and respected the Toronto Star's Ellen Roseman for more than 30 years. She is one of Canada's foremost consumer advocates and business columnists, and never pulls back from an important story—no matter how loudly advertisers squeal. She teaches, does TV and radio, and maintains a blog to give her readers current information on all types of consumer issues.
- Phil Bailey is a Lachine, Quebec, garage owner with almost five decades of experience with European, Japanese, and American cars. In his insightful comments on the car industry, he's as skillful with his pen as he is with a wrench, and he's got the everyday garage experience to make him and Toronto AM740 Zoomer Radio broadcaster Alan Gelman such unimpeachable auto industry critics. Alan co-hosts Dave Redinger's *Dave's Corner Garage* on Saturdays at 10 a.m.

These reporters and consumer advocates represent the exception, not the rule. Even the most ardent reporters frequently have to jump through hoops to get their stories out, simply because their editors or station managers have bought into many of the fraudulent practices so common to the auto industry. Haranguing staff for more "balance" is the pretext du jour for squelching hard-hitting stories that implicate dealers and automakers. News editors don't want truth; they want copy and comfort. They'll spend weeks sifting through Prime Minister Stephen Harper's trash bins looking for conflicts of interest while ignoring the auto industry scams threaded throughout their own advertisers' ads and commercials.

Want proof? Try to decipher the fine print in *The Globe and Mail*'s or the *Toronto Star*'s new car ads, or better yet, tell me what the fine print scrolled at breakneck speeds on television car commercials really says. Where is the investigative reporter who will submit these ads to an optometrists' group to confirm that the message is unreadable?

Think about this: Dealers posing as private parties and selling used cars from residences ("curbsiders") are periodically exposed by dealer associations and "crusading" auto journalists. Yet these scam artists place dozens or more ads every week in the classified sections of local newspapers that employ these same muckraking reporters. The same phone numbers and billing addresses reappear in the ads, sometimes days after the scam has been featured in local news reports. The ad order-takers know who these crooks are. News editors know that their own papers are promoting these scammers. Why isn't there an ad exposé by reporters working for these papers? Why don't they publish the fact that it's mostly new-vehicle dealers who supply curbsiders with their cars? That's what I'd call balanced reporting.

Two of my favourite auto journalists—Dan Neil, automotive writer for the liberal *Los Angeles Times*, and Robert Farago, a long-time columnist, auto critic, and creator of *The Truth About Cars* (a British-based website)—were both punished for writing the truth.

Neil's paper was hit with a $10 million (U.S.) loss after General Motors and its dealers pulled their ads in response to his sharp criticism of GM for a series of poor management decisions that lead to the flop of its 2005 G6 model:

> GM is a morass of a business case, but one thing seems clear enough, and Lutz's mistake was to state the obvious and then recant: The company's multiplicity of divisions and models is turning into a circular firing squad, someone's head ought to roll, and the most likely candidate would be the luminous white noggin of Lutz. [The G6] is not an awful car. It's entirely adequate. But plainly, adequate is not nearly enough.
>
> *LOS ANGELES TIMES*, APRIL 6, 2005

The *Times* stood by Neil, a Pulitzer Prize–winning automobile columnist. GM's ads eventually returned after a hiatus of several months.

Farago didn't fare as well. In late August 2005, he was canned and stayed canned. His column was permanently axed, without explanation, by the uber-liberal *San Francisco Chronicle* after his criticism of Subaru's Tribeca, an SUV wannabe that never will be:

> I'm not sure if the *Chronicle* removed my description of the SUV's front end as a "flying vagina" ....In fact, the Subaru B9 Tribeca is both subjectively (to the best of my knowledge and experience) and empirically a dreadful machine that besmirches the reputation of its manufacturer. Sure, the B9 handles well. The review pointed this out. But to suggest that it's an SUV worthy of its manufacturer's hype ("The end of the SUV as we know it" and "The ideal balance of power and refinement") is to become a co-conspirator in Subaru's attempts to mislead the public...I believe the media in general, and newspapers in particular, have an obligation to tell the truth about cars. You know all those puff pieces that fill up the odd blank spot in every single automotive section in this great country of ours? ... And that's why so many car enthusiasts have turned to the web. Other than Dan Neil at the *Los Angeles Times*, there are no print journalists ready, willing and able to directly challenge the auto manufacturers' influence with the plain, unvarnished truth (including the writers found in the happy clappy buff books). Car lovers yearn for the truth about cars. Sites like *www.jalopnik.com* are dedicated to providing it. And that's why the mainstream press' cozy little Boys' Club is doomed.

Other Information Sources

Funny, as soon as they hear that you're shopping for a new car, all your relatives, co-workers, and friends want to tell you what to buy.

After a while, you'll get so many conflicting opinions that it'll seem as if any choice you make will be wrong. Before making your decision, remember that you should invest a month of research into your $15,000–$30,000 new-car-buying project. This includes two weeks for basic research and another two weeks to actually bargain with dealers to get the right price and equipment. The following sources provide a variety of useful information that will help you ferret out what vehicle best suits your needs and budget.

Auto shows

Auto shows are held from January through March across Canada, starting in Montreal and ending in Vancouver. Although you can't buy or drive a car at the show, you can easily compare prices and the interior and exterior styling of different vehicles. In fact, show officials estimate that about 20 percent of auto show visitors are actively seeking info for an upcoming new-car purchase. Interestingly, while the shows are open, dealer traffic nosedives, making for much more generous deals in showrooms. Business usually picks up following the auto shows.

Online services

Anyone with access to the Internet can now obtain useful information about the auto industry in a matter of minutes at little or no cost. Simply go to a search engine like Google and type in a few keywords to find thousands of relevant sites.

 ### Shopping on the Internet

The key word here is "shopping," because *Consumer Reports* magazine has found that barely 2 percent of Internet surfers actually buy a new or used car online. Yet over 80 percent of buyers admit to using the Internet to get prices and specifications before visiting the dealership. Apparently, few buyers want to purchase a new or used vehicle without first seeing what's offered and knowing all money paid will be accounted for.

New-vehicle shopping through automaker and independent websites is a quick and easy way to compare prices and model specifications, but you will have to be careful. Many so-called independent sites are merely fronts for dealers and automakers, tailoring their information to steer you into their showroom or convince you to buy a certain brand of car.

Shoppers now have access to information they once were routinely denied or had trouble finding, such as dealers' price markups and incentive programs, the book value for trade-ins, and considerable safety data. Canadian shoppers can get

Canadian invoice prices and specs by contacting the Automobile Protection Agency (APA) by phone or fax, or online by visiting *www.apa.ca*.

Other advantages to online shopping? Some dealers offer a lower price to online shoppers; the entire transaction, including financing, can be done on the Internet; and buyers don't have to haggle—they merely electronically post their best offers to a number of dealers in their area code (for more convenient servicing of the vehicle) and then await counteroffers. But here are three caveats: (1) You will have to go to a dealer to finalize the contract, and be preyed upon by the financing and insurance (F&I) sales agents; (2) as far as bargains are concerned, *Consumer Reports* says its test shoppers obtained lower prices more frequently by visiting the dealer's showroom and concluding the sale there; and (3) only one-third of online dealers respond to customer queries.

Auto Quality Rankings

Consumer groups and non-profit auto associations like APA (www.apa.ca) and Car Help Canada (www.carhelpcanada.com) are your best bets for the least biased auto ratings for Canadians. They're not perfect, though, so it's a good idea to consult both groups and look for ratings that agree with each other.

Consumer Reports (CR) is an American publication that once had a tenuous affiliation with the Consumers' Association of Canada before their relationship went sour in the '80s.

CR's ratings mostly reflect the Consumers Union's annual U.S. member survey; the responses don't quite mirror the Canadian experience. Components that are particularly vulnerable to our harsh climate usually don't perform as well as the CR reliability ratings indicate, and poor servicing caused by a weak dealer body in Canada can make some service-dependent vehicles a nightmare to own here, whereas the American experience may be less problematic.

Based on more than one million responses from subscribers to *Consumer Reports* and *ConsumerReports.org*, *CR*'s annual auto reliability findings are impressively comprehensive, though they may not always be correct. Statisticians agree that *CR*'s sampling method leaves some room for error, but, with a few notable exceptions, the ratings are fair, conservative, and consistent guidelines for buying a reliable vehicle. Not so for child safety seats. A January 2007 CR report said that 10 out of 12 seats it tested failed disastrously at impact speeds of 56–61 km/h. NHTSA checked *CR*'s findings and discovered that the side-impact speeds actually exceeded 112 km/h. CR admitted it made a mistake.

My only criticism of the CR auto ratings is that many Asian models, like ones by Toyota and Honda, haven't always been as harshly scrutinized as their American counterparts, yet service bulletins and extended "goodwill" warranties have shown for years that they also have serious engine, transmission, brake, and electrical problems. *Consumer Reports* confirmed this anomaly in its April 2006 edition, where it admitted that Asian vehicle quality improvement has "slowed" since 2002—one incredible understatement when one considers that Toyota especially has been coasting on its reputation for quality since the mid-'90s. Toyota owner reports of sudden, unintended acceleration incidents started to climb in 2002.

When and Where to Buy

When to Buy

Shop in the first quarter of 2012 to get a reasonable price. Shoppers who wait until next summer or early fall can double-dip from additional automakers' dealer incentive and buyer rebate programs. Honda, Nissan, and Toyota will likely pour the most money into sales incentives in an effort to recapture market share lost through reduced production in 2011. Remember, too, that vehicles made between March and August offer the most factory upgrades and fewer factory-related glitches.

Visit the showroom at the end of the month, just before closing, when the salesperson will want to make that one last sale to meet the month's quota. If sales have been terrible, the sales manager may be willing to do some extra negotiating in order to boost sales staff morale.

Where to Buy

Large cities have greater selection, and dealers offer a variety of payment plans that will likely suit your budget. Prices in cities are also very competitive as dealers use sales volume to make most of their profit.

But price isn't everything, and good dealers aren't always the ones with the lowest prices. Buying from someone who you know gives honest and reliable service is just as important as getting a low price. Check a dealer's honesty and reliability by talking with motorists in your community who drive vehicles purchased from the local dealer (identified by the nameplate on the vehicle's trunk). If these customers have been treated fairly, they'll be glad to recommend their dealer. You can also check the dealer's thoroughness in new-vehicle preparation and servicing by renting one a dealership vehicle for a weekend, or by getting your trade-in serviced.

How can you tell which dealers are the most honest and competent? Well, judging from the thousands of reports I receive each year, dealerships in small suburban and rural communities are often fairer than big-city dealers because they're more vulnerable to negative word-of-mouth testimonials and to poor sales—when their vehicles aren't selling, good service picks up the slack. Their prices may also be more competitive, but don't count on it. Unfortunately, as part of their bankruptcy restructuring, Chrysler and General Motors closed down many dealerships in suburban and rural areas because the dealers couldn't generate sufficient sales volume to meet the automakers' profit targets.

Dealers that sell more than one manufacturer's product line present special problems. Their overhead can be quite high, and the cancellation of a dual dealership by an automaker in favour of setting up an exclusive franchise elsewhere is an ever-present threat. Parts availability may also be a problem because dealers with two separate vehicle lines must split their inventory and may, therefore, have an inadequate supply on hand (Read: Smart/Mercedes and former Mitsubishi/Chrysler partnership).

The quality of new-vehicle service is directly linked to the number and competence of dealerships within the network. If the network is weak, some parts will likely be unavailable, repair costs can go through the roof, and the skill level of the mechanics may be subpar, since better mechanics command higher salaries. Among foreign manufacturers, Asian automakers have the best overall dealer representation across Canada, except for Mitsubishi and Kia.

Kia's dealer network is adequate and growing through strong sales after having been left by its former owner, Hyundai, to fend on its own for many years. Mitsubishi, on the other hand, was floundering last year, despite having a good array of quality products. Its major problems have always been an insufficient product and a weak dealer network paired with outlets that sold other makes. After many dealers closed their doors when Chrysler and GM went bankrupt, Mitsubishi had to scurry around looking for new dealers who hadn't been gobbled up by Hyundai, Kia, and Mazda. Nevertheless, a surge in 2011 small car sales has helped Mitsu's bottom line tremendously, forcing the automaker to rethink its North American strategy.

European automaker profits are expected to grow throughout 2011 as pent up buyer demand, higher fuel prices, and the quest for better highway performance drives shoppers to small European imports like the BMW 1 Series and the European-based Ford Fiesta. Servicing, however, will continue to be problematic, inasmuch as many good mechanics left the business during the 2008–09 economic downturn.

Although it sells well in Canada, the $42,800 ($39,050 in the States) BMW 135i series has had some serious reliability problems relative to the fuel and electrical systems, engine, and body fit and finish. Fuel and electrical deficiencies seem to be a common complaint among owners of other BMWs, as well.

Despite these drawbacks, you can always get better treatment by going to dealerships that are accredited by auto clubs, such as the Canadian Automobile Association (CAA), or consumer groups like the Automobile Protection Association (APA) and Car Help Canada. Auto club accreditation is no ironclad guarantee that a dealership will be honest or competent; however, if you're insulted, cheated, or given bad service by one of their recommended garages (look for the accreditation symbol in a dealer's phone book ads, on the Internet, or on their shop windows), the accrediting agency is one more place to take your complaint to apply additional mediation pressure. And, as you'll see in Part Two, plaintiffs have won substantial refunds by pleading that an auto club is legally responsible for the actions of a garage it recommends.

Automobile Brokers and Vehicle-Buying Services

Brokers are independent agents who act as intermediaries to find the new or used vehicle you want at a price below what you'd normally pay. They have their Rolodex of contacts, speak the sales lingo, know all the angles and scams, and can generally cut through the bull to find a fair price—usually within days. Their services may cost a few hundred dollars, but you may save a few thousand. Additionally, you save the stress and hassle associated with the dealership experience, which for many people is like a trip to the dentist.

Brokers get new vehicles through dealers, while used vehicles may come from dealers, auctions, private sellers, and leasing companies. The broker's job is to find a vehicle that meets a client's expressed needs and then to negotiate its purchase (or lease) on behalf of that client. The majority of brokers tend to deal exclusively in new vehicles, with a small percentage dealing in both new and used vehicles. Ancillary services vary among brokers and may include such things as comparative vehicle analysis and price research.

The cost of hiring a broker can be charged either as a flat fee of a few hundred dollars or as a percentage of the value of the vehicle (usually 1–2 percent). The flat fee is usually best because it encourages the broker to keep the selling price low. Reputable brokers are not beholden to any particular dealership or make, and they'll disclose their flat fee up front or tell you the percentage amount they'll charge on a specific vehicle. Brokers used to purchasing cars in the States may charge a few thousand dollars, seriously cutting into the savings you may get from a lower purchase price. Seriously consider doing the transaction without a broker. It's that easy.

 Finding the right broker

Good brokers are hard to find, particularly in western Canada. Buyers who are looking for a broker should first ask friends and acquaintances if they can recommend one. Word-of-mouth referrals are often the best because people won't refer others to a service with which they were dissatisfied. Your local credit union or the regional CAA office is a good place to get a broker referral. For instance, Alterna Savings recommends a car-buying service called Dealfinder.

Dealfinder

For most buyers, going into a dealer showroom to negotiate a fair price is intimidating and confusing. Numbers are thrown at you, promises are made and broken, and after getting the "lowest price possible," you realize your neighbour paid a couple thousand dollars less for the same vehicle.

No wonder smart consumers are turning away from the "showroom shakedown" and letting professional buyers, like Ottawa-based Dealfinder Inc. (*www.dealfinder.ca*), separate the steak from the sizzle and real prices from "come-ons." In fact, simply by dealing with the dealership directly, Dealfinder can automatically save you the $200+ sales agent's commission before negotiations even begin.

For a $159 (plus tax) flat fee, Dealfinder acts as a price consultant after you have chosen the vehicle you want. The agency then shops dealers for the new car or truck of your choice in any geographic area you indicate. It gets no kickbacks from retailers or manufacturers, and if you can negotiate and document a lower price than Dealfinder gets, the fee will be refunded. What's more, you're under no obligation to buy the vehicle they recommend, since there is absolutely no collusion between Dealfinder and any manufacturer or dealership.

Dealfinder is a small operation that has been run by Bob Prest for over 17 years. He knows the ins and outs of automobile price negotiation and has an impressive list of clients, including some of Canada's better-known credit unions. His reputation is spread by word-of-mouth recommendations and the occasional media report. He can be reached by phone at 1-800-331-2044, or by email at *dealfinder@magma.ca*.

Buying a New Car, Truck, SUV, or Van

I remember in the '70s, American Motors gave away free TVs with each new car purchase, just before shutting its doors. In the past decade, GM gave away free Dell computers and VW hawked free guitars with its cars. The Detroit Three automakers continue to build poor-quality cars and trucks, although there appears to be some improvement over the past three years, mainly by Ford. The gap between Asian and American automobile quality has narrowed; however, this may reflect only a lowered benchmark following recent glitches with Honda, Nissan, and Toyota powertrains, electrical systems, and body fits. Nevertheless, Ford and Japanese makes continue to dominate J.D. Power and Associates' dependability surveys, while other American and European makes are mostly ranked below the industry average, but are trending upward.

Toyota has done extraordinarily well, even in light of its sudden unintended acceleration and brake failure safety problems that resulted in a $48 million government-imposed fine last year and $10 billion spent in recall campaigns and investigations. Although profits plummeted 77 percent during the first three months of 2011, principally due to the March 2011 earthquake, the company still has $30 billion in cash reserves.

Step 1: Keep It Simple

First, keep in mind that you are going to spend much more money than you may have anticipated—almost $31,000 for the average vehicle transaction, according to Dennis DesRosiers, a Toronto-based auto consultant. This is because of the many hidden fees, like freight charges and so-called administrative costs, that are added to the bottom line. But, with cut-throat discounts and armed with tips from this guide, you can bring that amount down considerably.

According to the Canadian Automobile Association (CAA), the average household owns two vehicles, which are each driven about 20,000 km annually and cost an average of $800 a year for maintenance; DesRosiers estimates $1,100.

Do Toyota hybrids really save you money over a similar gasoline-engine-equipped small car? Not according to the CAA. In its 2010 *Driving Costs* brochure the auto association says that Toyota's Prius hybrid costs more to drive than an equivalent Chevrolet Cobalt. Total cost of driving 32,000 kilometers in a 2010 Toyota Prius is $10,783, while the 2010 Chevrolet Cobalt LT would cost slightly less at $10,694. The cost rises to $14,363 for a 2010 Dodge Grand Caravan.

Keep in mind that it's practically impossible to buy a bare-bones car or truck, because automakers know this is a seller's market until early 2012, so they cram new cars with costly, non-essential performance and convenience features in order to maximize their profits. Nevertheless, money-wasting features like electronic navigation, self-parking, camera vision, digital screens, and voice-command capability can easily be passed up with little impact on safety or convenience. In fact, voice command and in-dash computer screens can be very distracting while driving—producing a negative safety effect. Full-torso side curtain airbags and electronic stability control, however, are important safety options that are well worth the extra expense.

Our driving needs are influenced by where we live, our lifestyle, and our age (see pages 42–44 for a discussion of vehicles best suited to mature drivers). The ideal car should be crashworthy and easy to drive, have minimal high-tech features to distract and annoy, and not cost much to maintain.

In the city, a small wagon or hatchback is more practical and less expensive than a mid-sized car like the Honda Accord or Toyota Camry. Furthermore, have you seen the newer Civic and Elantra? What once were small cars are now quite large, relatively fuel-efficient, and equipped with more horsepower than you'll ever likely need. Nevertheless, if you're going to be doing a lot of highway driving, transporting small groups of people, or loading up on accessories, a medium-sized sedan, wagon, or small sport-utility could be the best choice for price, comfort, and reliability.

Don't let spikes in fuel prices stampede you into buying a vehicle unsuitable to your driving needs. If you travel less than 20,000 km per year, mostly in the city, choose a small car or SUV equipped with a 4-cylinder engine that produces about

140 hp to get the best fuel economy without sacrificing performance. Anything more powerful is just a waste. Extensive highway driving, however, demands the cruising performance, extra power for additional accessories, and durability of a larger, 6-cylinder engine. Believe me, fuel savings will be the last thing on your mind if you buy an underpowered vehicle.

Be especially wary of the towing capabilities bandied about by automakers. They routinely exaggerate towing capability and seldom mention the need for expensive optional equipment, or that the top safe towing speed may be only 72 km/h (45 mph). Generally, 3.0L to 3.8L V6 engines will safely accommodate most towing needs. The 4-cylinder engines may handle light loads but will likely offer a white-knuckle experience when merging with highway traffic or travelling over hilly terrain.

Remember, you may have to change your driving habits to accommodate the type of vehicle you purchase. Front-drive braking is quite different from braking with a rear-drive, and braking efficiency on ABS-equipped vehicles is compromised if you pump the brakes. Also, rear-drive vans handle like trucks, and you may scrub the right rear tire during sharp right-hand turns until you get the hang of making wider turns. Limited rear visibility is another problem with larger vans, forcing drivers to carefully survey side and rear traffic before changing lanes or merging.

Step 2: Be Realistic

Don't confuse styling with needs (do you have a bucket bottom to conform to those bucket seats?) or trendy with essential (will a cheaper downsized SUV like a Hyundai Tucson or Subaru Forester suit you as well as, or better than, a mid-sized car?). Visiting the showroom with your spouse, a level-headed relative, or a sensible friend will help you steer a truer course through all the non-essential options you'll be offered.

Oftentimes, getting a female perspective can be really helpful. Women don't generally receive the same welcome at auto showrooms as men do, but that's because they make the salesmen (yes, usually less than 10 percent of the sales staff are women) work too hard to make a sale. Most sales agents admit that female shoppers are far more knowledgeable about what they want and more patient in negotiating the contract's details than men, who tend to be mesmerized by many of the techno-toys available.

In increasing numbers, women have discovered that minivans, SUVs, and small pickups are more versatile than passenger cars and station wagons. And, having spotted a profitable trend, automakers are offering increased versatility combined with unconventional styling in so-called "crossover" vehicles. These blended cars are part sedan and part station wagon, with a touch of sport-utility added for function and fun. For example, the 2012 Ford Flex is a smaller, sporty crossover vehicle that looks like a miniature SUV. First launched as a 2009 model, the Flex comes in an entry-level SE trim line that brings down the starting price a bit.

Ford's $32,699 ($29,355 in the States) Flex is somewhat pricey, but it does offer car-like performance, SUV versatility, and excellent crashworthiness. A perusal of Ford service bulletins (see the following page) shows long-term reliability is still a question mark.

Women ask the important questions. Men, take your mother, wife, or sister along next time!

Step 3: What Can I Afford?

Determine how much money you can spend, and then decide which vehicles in that price range interest you. Have several models in mind so that the overpriced one won't tempt you too much. As your benchmarks, use the ratings, alternative models, estimated purchase costs, and residual value figures shown in Part Three of this guide. Remember, logic and prudence are the first casualties of showroom hype, so carefully consider what you actually need and how these things will fit into your budget before you compare models and prices at a dealership. Write down your first, second, and third choices relative to each model and the equipment offered. Browse the automaker websites both in Canada and in the States to find the manufacturer's suggested retail price (MSRP), promotions, and package discounts. Look for special low prices that may apply only to Internet-generated referrals. Once you get a good idea of the price variations, get out the fax machine or computer at home or work (a company letterhead is always impressive) and then make the dealers bid against each other (see page 82). Call the lowest-bidding dealership, ask for an appointment to be assured of getting a sales agent's complete attention, and take along the downloaded price info from the Canadian and American automaker websites to prevent arguments.

Sometimes a cheaper "twin" will fit the bill. Twins are nameplates made by different auto manufacturers, or by different divisions of the same company, that are virtually identical in body design and mechanical components, like the Chevrolet Silverado and GMC Sierra pickups; Chrysler minivans; and the 2012

2010 FORD TRUCK FLEX AWD 3.5L-V6 TURBO

All Technical Service Bulletins

NUMBER	DATE	TITLE
11-1-8	01/25/2011	Interior—Squeak/Rattle from Dash Area
10-25-12	12/23/2010	SYNC(R) System—Poor Cell Phone Audio Quality
10-25-10	12/23/2010	Engine Controls—Reduced Heater Output in Cold Temps
10-22-4	11/22/2010	Drivetrain—Shudder/Chatter on Turns/Ckunk on Accel.
10-21-2	11/08/2010	A/T Controls—Slipping/5th Gear Start/Other Issues
10-20-8	10/25/2010	Engine Controls—Tip-in Delayed Shift Between 15–20 mph
10-20-11	10/25/2010	Navigation Radio—Sirius Radio Update Process Failure
10-17-10	09/13/2010	Ignition System—Runs Rough/Hesitates/Misfire DTCs
10-17-3	09/13/2010	Brakes—Front Brake Grunting/Grinding Noise
10-13-3	07/19/2010	Audio System—Poor Radio Reception/Sound Quality
10-13-4	07/19/2010	SYNC(R) System—No Turn-by-Turn Directions
10-9-9	05/24/2010	A/T—DTC P0751/Harsh/No Engagement/Slip on Accel.
10-9-5	05/24/2010	Entertainment System—Rapid Click from Glove Box Area
10-7-2	04/26/2010	Brakes—Rear Brake Drag/Cyclic Noises
10-6-1	04/12/2010	Steering—Fluid Leak at Reservoir Cap in Cold Temps.
10-6-4	04/12/2010	Engine Controls—A/T 3–1 Downshift Bump
10-6-3	04/12/2010	Navigation Radio—Various Navigation/Audio Concerns
10-4-3	03/15/2010	Engine, A/T Controls—2–3 Shift Flare/3–1 Shift Bump
10B14	03/05/2010	Campaign—A/T Intermediate Clutch/Piston Repair
10-2-6	02/15/2010	Engine Controls—Aftermarket Modification Information
10-2-8	02/15/2010	SYNC(R) System—Defaults To "Privacy Mode"
09-25-7	12/28/2009	Drivetrain—PTU R/H Intermediate Shaft Leaks Svc. Tips
09-25-2	12/28/2009	Interior—First Row Center Console Latch Broken
09-23-9	11/30/2009	Drivetrain—Fluid Leaks Between A/T and PTU
09-23-8	11/30/2009	Engine Controls—DTC P0096 After Warm Engine Restart
09-21-5	11/02/2009	Wipers/Washers—Liftgate Window Washer Inoperative
09-20-9	10/19/2009	Interior—Power 2nd Row Seats Won't Fold Forward/Flat

turbocharged Hyundai Sonata and Kia Optima—both cars have practically the same equipement.

Let's look at the savings possible with "twinned" Chrysler minivans. A 2006 Grand Caravan SXT that was originally listed for $35,735 is now worth about $6,000. An upscale 2006 Town & Country Limited that performs similarly to the Grand Caravan, with just a few additional gizmos, first sold for $47,905 and is now worth about $9.500 Where once almost $12,000 separated the two minivans, the price difference is now only $3,500—and you can expect the gap to close to almost nil over the next few years. Did the little extras really justify the Town & Country's higher price, or make it a better buy than the Grand Caravan? Obviously, the marketplace thinks not.

And don't get taken in by the "Buy Canadian!" chanting from Chrysler, Ford, General Motors, and the Canadian Auto Workers. It's pure hokum. While Detroit-based automakers are beating their chests over the need to buy American, they buy Japanese and South Korean companies and then market the foreign imports from Asian factories as their own. This practice has resulted in bastardized name-plates whose parentage isn't always easy to nail down. For example, is the Aveo a Chevy or a Daewoo? (For the record, it's a Daewoo, and not that reliable, to boot.)

Vehicles that are produced through co-ventures between Detroit automakers and Asian manufacturers have better quality control than vehicles manufactured by companies that were bought outright, and this looks like one of the factors that may save the American auto industry. For example, Toyota and Pontiac churned out identical Matrix and Vibe compacts in Ontario and the United States; however, the cheaper, Ontario-built Matrix has the better reputation for quality. On the other hand, Jaguar and Volvo quality have stagnated or declined since Ford bought the companies, and GM-owned Saab didn't do much better. As for Daimler's takeover of Chrysler, what innovative, high-quality products did we see as a result? Very few.

Sometimes choosing a higher trim line that packages many options as standard features will cost you less when you take all the features into account separately. In Canada it's hard to compare these bundled prices with the manufacturer's base price and added options, though U.S. automaker websites often provide more details. All of the separate prices are inflated and must be individually negotiated down, while fully equipped vehicles don't allow for options to be deleted or priced separately. Furthermore, many of the bundled options are superfluous, and you probably wouldn't have chosen them to begin with.

Minivans, for example, often come in two versions: a base commercial (or cargo) version and a more luxurious model for private use. The commercial version doesn't have as many bells and whistles, but it's more likely to be in stock and will probably cost much less. And if you're planning to convert it, there's a wide choice of independent customizers that will likely do a better—and less expensive—job than the dealer. Of course, you will want a written guarantee from the dealer or customizer, or sometimes both, that no changes will invalidate the manufacturer's warranty. Also, look on the lot for a low-mileage (less than 10,000 km) 2011 demonstrator that is carried over unchanged as a 2012 version. You will get an end-of-model-year rebate, a lower price for the extra mileage, and sundry other sales incentives that apply. Remember, if the vehicle has been registered to another company or individual, it is not a demo and should be considered used and be discounted accordingly (by at least 25 percent). You will also want to carry out a CarProof VIN search and get a complete printout of the vehicle's service history.

 **Fraud by Freight**

Lemon-Aid has always cautioned new-car buyers against paying transportation and PDI (pre-delivery inspection) fees, or suggested that these fees can be whittled down by about half. This advice worked well up until last year, when charges ballooned to $1,400–$2,000 and automakers started making them part of the MSRP (manufacturer's suggested retail price) instead of listing the item separately or not at all. This impacts the final price in two ways—one good, the other bad. As part of the MSRP, this extra charge is hidden from the customer and is seen as part of the vehicle's overall cost. On the other hand, when rolled into the MSRP the freight charge/PDI can be more easily negotiated downward with the car's price, since they are no longer touted as sacrosanct "must pay" items.

Leasing without Losing

Why Leasing Costs More

There are many reasons why leasing is a bad idea. It's often touted as an alternative that can make high-cost vehicles more affordable, but for most people, it's really more expensive than buying outright. Lessees usually pay the full MSRP on a vehicle loaded with costly options, plus hidden fees and interest charges that wouldn't be included if the vehicle was purchased instead of leased. Researchers have found that some fully loaded entry-level cars leased with high interest rates and deceptive "special fees" could cost more than what some luxury models would cost to buy. A useful website that takes the mystery out of leasing is *www.federal-reserve.gov/pubs/leasing* (Keys to Vehicle Leasing), run by the U.S. Federal Reserve Board. It goes into incredible detail comparing leasing versus buying, and has a handy dictionary of the terms you're most likely to encounter.

Decoding "Lease-Talk"

Take a close look at the small print found in most leasing ads. Pay particular attention to words relating to the model year, condition of the vehicle ("demonstration" or "used"), equipment, warranty, interest rate, buy-back amount, down payment, security payment, monthly payment, transportation and preparation charges, administration fees ("acquisition" and "disposal" fees), insurance premiums, number of free kilometres, and excess-kilometre charges.

Leasing Advantages

Leasing in Canada once made up almost 35 percent of all motor vehicle sales transactions because of then-rising interest rates and prices. Now, hard-to-find credit and the economic recession have driven leasing down to about 20 percent of all auto transactions. Detroit automakers have backed away from leases, leaving the market to the Asians and Europeans. But leasing is still a fairly popular option, leading to 60-month leases and a proliferation of leasing deals on luxury models. Insiders say that almost all vehicles costing $60,000 or more are leased vehicles.

Experts agree: If you must lease, keep your costs to a minimum by leasing for the shortest time possible, by assuming the unexpired portion of an existing lease, and by making sure that the lease is close-ended (meaning that you walk away from the vehicle when the lease period ends)—this last option is used by 75 percent of lessees, according to the CAA.

Leasing does have a few advantages, though. First, it saves some of your capital, which you can invest to get a return greater than the leasing interest charges. Second, if you are taking a chance on a new model that hasn't been proven, you know that yours can be dumped at the dealer when the lease expires.

But taking a chance on an unproven model raises several questions: What are you doing choosing such a risky venture in the first place? And will you have the patience to wait in the service bay while your luxury lemon waits for parts or a mechanic who's ahead of the learning curve?

Some Precautions and an Alternative

On both new and used purchases and leases, be wary of unjustified hidden costs, like a $495 "administrative" or "disposal" fee, an "acquisition" charge, or boosted transport and freight costs that can collectively add several thousand dollars to a vehicle's retail price. Also, look at the lease transfer fee charged by the leasing company, the dealer, or both. This fee can vary considerably.

Instead of leasing, consider purchasing used. Look for a three- to five-year-old off-lease vehicle with 60,000–100,000 km on the clock and some of the original warranty left. Such a vehicle will be just as reliable for less than half the cost of one bought new or leased. Parts will be easier to find, independent servicing should be a breeze, insurance premiums will come down from the stratosphere, and your financial risk will be lessened considerably if you end up with a lemon.

Breaking a Lease

Not an easy thing to do, and you may wind up paying $3,000–$8,000 in cancellation fees.

The last thing you want to do is stop your payments, especially if you've leased a lemon: The dealer can easily sue you for the remaining money owed, and you will have to pay the legal fees for both sides. You won't be able to prove the vehicle was defective or unreliable, because it will have been seized after the lease payments stopped. So there you are, without the vehicle to make your proof and on the receiving end of a costly lawsuit.

There are several ways a lease can be broken. First, you can ask for free Canadian Motor Vehicle Arbitration Plan (CAMVAP) arbitration (see page 118) if you believe you have leased a lemon. A second recourse, if there's a huge debt remaining, is to send a lawyer's letter cancelling the contract by putting the leasing agency and automaker on notice that the vehicle is unacceptable. This should lead to some negotiation. If this fails, inspect the vehicle, have it legally tendered back to the dealer, and then sue for what you owe plus your inconvenience and assorted sundry expenses. You can use the small claims court on your own if the amount in litigation is less than the court's claim limit.

The leasing agency or dealer may claim extra money when the lease expires, because the vehicle may miss some original equipment or show "unreasonable" wear and tear (dings, paint problems, and excessive tire wear are the most common reasons for extra charges). Protect yourself from these dubious claims by having the vehicle inspected by an independent retailer and taking pictures of the vehicle prior to returning it.

Buying the Right Car or Truck

Front-Drives

Front-drives direct engine power to the front wheels, which pull the vehicle forward while the rear wheels simply support the rear. The biggest benefit of front-drives is foul-weather traction. With the engine and transmission up front, there's lots of extra weight pressing down on the front-drive wheels, increasing tire grip in snow and on wet pavement. But when you drive up a steep hill, or tow a boat or trailer, the weight shifts and you lose the traction advantage.

Although I recommend a number of front-drive vehicles in this guide, I don't like them as much as rear-drives. Granted, front-drives provide a bit more interior room (no transmission hump), more car-like handling, and better fuel economy than do rear-drives. But damage from potholes and fender-benders is usually more extensive, and maintenance costs (especially premature suspension, tire, and brake wear) are much higher than with rear-drives.

Rear-Drives

Rear-drives direct engine power to the rear wheels, which push the vehicle forward. The front wheels steer and also support the front of the vehicle. With the engine up front, the transmission in the middle, and the drive axle in the rear, there's plenty of room for larger and more durable drivetrain components. This makes for less crash damage, lower maintenance costs, and higher towing capacities than with front-drives.

On the downside, rear-drives don't have as much weight over the front wheels as do the

Ford's reengineered, rear-drive 2011 and 2012 Mustang ($26,999; $22,310 in the States) comes with a V6 that's almost as powerful as its earlier V8.

front-drives, and therefore, they can't provide as much traction on wet or icy roads and tend to fishtail unless they're equipped with an expensive traction-control system.

Four-Wheel Drive (4×4)

Four-wheel drive (4×4) directs engine power through a transfer case to all four wheels, which pull and push the vehicle forward, giving you twice as much traction. On most models, the vehicle reverts to rear-drive when four-wheel drive isn't engaged. The large transfer-case housing makes the vehicle sit higher, giving you additional ground clearance.

Keep in mind that extended driving over dry pavement with 4×4 engaged will cause the driveline to bind and result in serious damage. Some buyers are turning instead to rear-drive pickups equipped with winches and large, deep-lugged rear tires.

Many 4×4 customers driving SUVs set on truck platforms have been turned off by the typically rough and noisy driveline, a tendency for the vehicle to tip over when cornering at moderate speeds, vague or truck-like handling, high repair costs, and poor fuel economy.

All-Wheel Drive (AWD)

A standard feature on all Subarus beginning with the 1999 lineup, AWD is four-wheel drive that's on all the time. Used mostly in sedans and minivans, AWD never needs to be deactivated when running over dry pavement and doesn't require the heavy transfer case that raises ground clearance and cuts fuel economy. AWD-equipped vehicles aren't recommended for off-roading because of their lower ground clearance and fragile driveline parts, which aren't as rugged as 4×4 components. But anyhow, you shouldn't be off-roading in a car or minivan in the first place.

Safety and Comfort

Do You Feel Comfortable in the Vehicle?

The advantages of many sports cars and minivans pale in direct proportion to your tolerance for a harsh ride, noise, a claustrophobic interior, and limited visibility. Minivan owners often have to deal with a high step-up, a cold interior, lots of buffeting from wind and passing trucks, and poor rear visibility. With these drawbacks, many buyers find that after falling in love with the showroom image, they end up hating their purchase—all the more reason to test drive your choice over a period of several days to get a real feel for its positive and negative characteristics.

Check to see if the vehicle's interior is user-friendly. For example, can you reach the sound system and AC controls without straining or taking your eyes off the road? Are the controls just as easy to operate by feel as by sight? What about dash glare onto the front windshield, and headlight aim and brightness? Can you drive with the window or sunroof open and not be subjected to an ear-splitting roar? Do rear-seat passengers have to be contortionists to enter or exit, as is the case with many two-door vehicles?

To answer these questions, you need to drive the vehicle over a period of time to test how well it responds to the diversity of your driving needs, without having some impatient sales agent yapping in your ear. If this isn't possible, you may find out too late that the handling is less responsive than you'd wanted.

You can conduct the following showroom tests: Adjust the seat to a comfortable setting, buckle up, and settle in. Can you sit 25 cm away from the steering wheel and still reach the accelerator and brake pedals? Do the head restraints force your chin into your chest? When you look out the windshield and use the rear- and side-view mirrors, do you detect any serious blind spots? Will optional mirrors give you an unobstructed view? Does the seat feel comfortable enough for long trips? Can you reach important controls without moving your back from the seat-back, or taking your eyes off the road? If not, shop for something that better suits your needs.

Which Safety Features Are Best?

Automakers have loaded 2011–12 models with features that wouldn't have been imagined several decades ago, because safety devices appeal to families and some features, like airbags, can be marked up by 500 percent. Yet some safety innovations, such as anti-lock brake systems (ABS) and adaptive cruise control (ACC), don't deliver the safety payoffs promised by automakers and may create additional dangers. For example, anti-lock breaks often fail and are expensive to maintain, while adaptive cruise control may slow the vehicle down when passing another car on the highway. Some of the more-effective safety features are head-protecting side airbags, electronic stability control (ESC), adjustable brake and accelerator pedals, standard integrated child safety seats, seat belt pretensioners, adjustable head restraints, and sophisticated navigation and communication systems.

Seat belts provide the best means of reducing the severity of injury arising from both low- and high-speed frontal collisions. In order to be effective, though, seat belts must be adjusted properly and feel comfortably tight without undue slack. Owners often complain that seat belts don't retract enough for a snug fit, are too tight, chafe the neck, or don't fit children properly. Some automakers have corrected these problems with adjustable shoulder-belt anchors that allow both tall and short drivers to raise or lower the belt for a snug, more comfortable fit. Another important seat belt innovation is the pretensioner (not found on all seat belts), a device that automatically tightens the safety belt in the event of a crash.

Crashworthiness

A vehicle with a high crash protection rating is a lifesaver. In fact, crashworthiness is the one safety improvement over the past 40 years that everyone agrees has paid off handsomely without presenting any additional risks to drivers or passengers. By surrounding occupants with a protective cocoon and deflecting crash forces away from the interior, auto engineers have successfully created safer vehicles without increasing vehicle size or cost. And it is not unreasonable to assume that you'll be involved in an accident someday. According to IIHS, the average car will likely have two accidents before ending up as scrap, and it's twice as likely to be in a severe front-impact crash as a side-impact crash.

Since some vehicles are more crashworthy than others, and since size doesn't always guarantee crash safety, it's important to buy a vehicle that gives you the best protection from frontal, frontal offset, side, and rear collisions while keeping its rollover and roof-collapse potential to a minimum.

 Two Washington-based agencies monitor how vehicle design affects crash safety: the National Highway Traffic Safety Administration (NHTSA) and the Insurance Institute for Highway Safety (IIHS). Crash information from these two groups doesn't always correspond because tests and testing methods vary. NHTSA's crash tests performed on 2011 models are much tougher than the tests previously performed, resulting in dropped star ratings for many vehicles. For example, in the first batch of 30 cars tested last fall, only the BMW 5 Series and Hyundai Sonata kept their five-star safety ratings. Two surprising losers were the Toyota Camry, which went from five stars to three, and the Nissan Versa, which earned an overall rating of only two stars while the previous model had earned four stars.

NHTSA crash-test results for 1990–2011 vehicles and tires are available at *www.safercar.gov/Safety+Ratings*. Information relating to safety complaints, recalls, defect investigations, and service bulletins can be found at *www.safercar.gov/Vehicle+Owners*. IIHS results may be found at *www.iihs.org/ratings*.

Don't get taken in by the five-star crash rating hoopla touted by automakers. There isn't any one vehicle that can claim a prize for being the safest. Vehicles that do well in NHTSA side and front crash tests may not do very well in IIHS offset crash tests, or may have poorly designed head restraints that can increase the severity of neck injuries. Or a vehicle may have a high number of airbag failures, such as the bags deploying when they shouldn't or not deploying when they should.

Before making a final decision on the vehicle you want, look up its crashworthiness and overall safety profile in Part Three.

Cars versus trucks

Occupants of large vehicles have fewer severe injury claims than do occupants of small vehicles. This was proven conclusively in a 1996 NHTSA study that showed that collisions between light trucks or vans and small cars resulted in car occupants having an 81 percent higher fatality rate than the occupants of the light trucks or vans did.

Vehicle weight offers the most protection in two-vehicle crashes. In a head-on crash, for example, the heavier vehicle drives the lighter one backward, which decreases forces inside the heavy vehicle and increases forces in the lighter one. All heavy vehicles, even poorly designed ones, offer this advantage in two-vehicle collisions. However, they may not offer good protection in single-vehicle crashes.

Crash test figures show that SUVs, vans, and trucks also offer more protection to adult occupants than do passenger cars in most crashes because their higher set-up allows them to ride over other vehicles (Ford's 2002 4×4 Explorer lowered its bumper height to prevent this hazard). Conversely, because of their high centre of gravity, easily overloaded tires, and unforgiving suspensions, these vehicles have a disproportionate number of single-vehicle rollovers, which are far deadlier than frontal or side collisions. In the case of the early Ford Explorer, Bridgestone/Firestone CEO John Lampe testified in August 2001 that 42 of the 43 rollovers involving Ford Explorers in Venezuela were on competitors' tires—shifting the rollover blame to the Explorer's design and crashworthiness.

Interestingly, a vehicle's past crashworthiness rating doesn't always guarantee that subsequent model years will be just as safe or safer. Take Ford's Escort as an example. It earned five stars for front-passenger collision protection in 1991 and then earned fewer stars every year thereafter, until the model was discontinued in 2002. The Dodge Caravan is another example. It was given five stars for driver-side protection in 2000, but has earned four stars ever since.

Rollover ratings

Although rollovers represent only 3 percent of crashes (out of 10,000 annual U.S. road accidents), they cause one-third of all traffic deaths from what are usually single-vehicle accidents.

Rollovers occur less frequently with passenger cars and minivans than with SUVs, trucks, and full-sized vans (especially the 15-passenger variety). That's why electronic vehicle stability systems aren't as important a safety feature on passenger cars as on minivans, vans, pickups, and SUVs.

Auto safety experts once thought that SUVs were safer to drive than cars because sport utility vehicles were heavier, larger, and generally sat higher off of the ground. But the Ford Explorer changed that thinking forever.

It all started in the late '90s with a stream of reports from Saudi Arabia, Venezuala, and the southern United States regarding deadly rollovers involving Ford Explorers equipped with faulty Firestone tires. Product liability lawyers made millions in secret settlements, Ford and Firestone accused each other of negligence and paid millions in compensation to victims, and automobile engineers, while denying

Standard electronic stability control and more-stable designs make SUVs like the Honda CR-V (above) twice as safe as the average-sized car. Which vehicles had the highest and lowest driver fatality rates in the IIHS study? The Nissan 350Z was the most dangerous, and several minivans were least likely to flip over.

they were ever at fault, quietly set out to install safety features that would make SUV rollovers less likely.

The engineers succeeded. From the 1999 to 2002 model years, SUVs recorded an average of 82 driver deaths per million registered vehicle years. For model years 2005 to 2008, that rate had plummeted to just 28 per million. SUVs of 2006–09 model years are now much less likely to be involved in rollover crashes than are ordinary cars.

In fact, someone driving a 2009 model year car is almost twice as likely to die in a rollover accident as someone driving a 2009 model year SUV, says the Insurance Institute for Highway Safety in its June report comparing real-world auto accident death rates for various types of 2006–09 vehicles.

The Institute credits the increased used of electronic stability control (ESC) and more-stable car-based designs for the overall declining frequency of SUV rollover accidents. ESC is a computer-based system, used with anti-lock brakes, that helps drivers maintain control during abrupt manoeuvres and on slippery roads.

IIHS statistics list rollover deaths by specific vehicles. For example, the nine safest vehicles were (starting with the safest) the Audi A6, Mercedes-Benz E-Class 4Matic, Toyota Sienna, Ford Edge, Nissan Armada, Land Rover Range Rover Sport, Land Rover LR3, Honda CR-V, and Jeep Grand Cherokee; seven of those are SUVs.

The most deadly vehicles, with the highest fatality rates, were (starting with the most deadly) the Nissan 350Z, Nissan Titan crew cab, Chevrolet Aveo, Chevrolet Cobalt, Nissan Titan extended cab, Kia Spectra, Chevrolet Malibu Classic, Hyundai Tiburon, Nissan Versa, and Chevrolet Colorado extended cab.

Broken down into vehicle classes, the IIHS picked minivans as the safest (25 fatalities per million registered vehicle years), followed by SUVs (28 per million), then pickup trucks (52 per million), with the "cars" class rated most deadly (56 deaths per million).

Starting with the 2012 model year, all new passenger vehicles sold in North America are now required to have stability control.

More Safety Considerations

Unfortunately, there will never be enough easy safety solutions to protect us from ourselves. According to NHTSA's figures, seat belts prevented 75,000 deaths between 2004 and 2008, while over 40 percent of passengers killed in accidents in 2007 were not wearing seat belts. NHTSA has also discovered that kids wear seat belts 87 percent of the time if their parents do, and that 60 percent of children killed on the roads in 2005 were not wearing a seat belt.

Although there has been a dramatic reduction in automobile accident fatalities and injuries over the past three decades, safety experts feel that additional safety features will henceforth pay small dividends, and they expect the highway death and injury rate to start trending upward. They say it's time to target the driver. NHTSA believes that automobile accident fatalities would be cut by half if everyone wore a seat belt and we eliminated of drunk driving. The entirely preventable epidemic of drunk driving is responsible for 33.8 percent of motor vehicle fatalities in Canada, according to a 2002 Transport Canada study (*www. tc.gc.ca/media/documents/roadsafety/tp11759e_2000.pdf*).

This means that safety programs that concentrate primarily on motor vehicle standards won't be as effective as measures that target both the driver and the vehicle—such as more-sophisticated "black box" data recorders; more-stringent licensing requirements, including graduated licensing and de-licensing programs directed at teens and seniors; and stricter law enforcement.

Incidentally, police studies have shown that there's an important benefit to arresting traffic-safety scofflaws: netting dangerous career criminals or seriously impaired drivers before they have the chance to harm others. Apparently, sociopaths and substance abusers don't care which laws they break.

Beware of unsafe designs

Although it sounds hard to believe, automakers will deliberately manufacture a vehicle that will kill or maim simply because, in the long run, it costs less to stonewall complaints and pay off victims than to make a safer vehicle. I learned this lesson after listening to the court testimony of GM engineers—who deliberately placed fire-prone "sidesaddle" gas tanks in millions of pickups to save $3 per vehicle—and after reading the court transcripts of *Grimshaw v. Ford* (fire-prone Pintos) from 1981. Reporter Anthony Prince wrote the following assessment of Ford's indifference in an article titled "Lessons of the Ford/Firestone scandal: Profit motive turns consumers into road kill," *People's Tribune* (Online Edition); Vol. 26, No. 11, November 2000:

> Rejecting safety designs costing between only $1.80 and $15.30 per Pinto, Ford had calculated the damages it would likely pay in wrongful death and injury cases and pocketed the difference. In a cold and calculating "costs/benefits" analysis, Ford projected that the Pinto would probably cause 180 burn deaths, 180 serious burn injuries, [and] 2,100 burned vehicles each year. Also, Ford estimated civil suits of

$200,000 per death, $67,000 per injury, [and] $700 per vehicle for a grand total of $49.5 million. The costs for installing safety features would cost approximately $137 million per year. As a result, the Pinto became a moving target, its unguarded fuel tank subject to rupture by exposed differential bolts shoved into it by rear-end collisions at speeds of as little as 21 miles per hour [34 km/h]. Spewing gasoline into the passenger compartment, the car and its passengers became engulfed in a raging inferno.

And here are more recent examples of corporate greed triumphing over public safety: "exploding" pre-1997 airbag designs that maim or kill women, children, and seniors; anti-lock brake systems that don't brake; flimsy front seats and seatbacks; the absence of rear head restraints; and fire-prone GM pickup fuel tanks and Ford cruise-control deactivation switches. Two other examples of hazardous engineering designs that put profit ahead of safety are failure-prone Chrysler, Ford, and GM minivan sliding doors and automatic transmissions that suddenly shift into Neutral, allowing the vehicle to roll away when parked on an incline or causing it to break down in traffic.

Active safety

Advocates of active safety stress that accidents are caused by the proverbial "nut behind the wheel" and believe that safe driving can be best taught through schools or private driving courses. Active safety components are generally those mechanical systems—such as anti-lock brake systems (ABS), high-performance tires, and traction control—that may help a driver to avoid accidents if they're skillful and mature.

I am not a fan of ABS. The systems are often ineffective, failure-prone, and expensive to service. Yet they are an essential part of most systems' electronic stability control (ESC), which is a proven lifesaver. Essentially, ABS prevents a vehicle's wheels from locking when the brakes are applied in an emergency situation, thus reducing skidding and the loss of directional control. When braking on wet or dry roads, your stopping distance will be about the same as with conventional braking systems. But in gravel, slush, or snow, your stopping distance will be greater.

The theory of active safety has several drawbacks. First, a recent study of seriously injured drivers at the Shock Trauma Center in Maryland showed that 51 percent of the sample tested positive for illegal drugs while 34 percent tested positive for alcohol (*www.druggeddriving.org/ddp.html*). Drivers who are under the influence of alcohol or drugs cause about 40 percent of all fatal accidents. All the high-performance options and specialized driving courses in the world will not provide much protection from impaired drivers who draw a bead on your vehicle. And, because active safety components get a lot of use—you're likely to need anti-lock brakes 99 times more often than you'll need an airbag—they have to be well designed and well maintained to remain effective. Finally, consider that independent studies show that safe driving taught to young drivers doesn't necessarily reduce the number of driving-related deaths and injuries, as was shown in this DeKalb County, Georgia study (*Lancet*, July 2001):

The DeKalb Study compared the accident records of 9,000 teens that had taken driver education in the county's high schools with 9,000 teens that had no formal driver training. The final results showed no significant difference between the two groups. In other words, DeKalb County, Georgia, paid a large amount of money for absolutely no value.

Passive safety

Passive safety assumes that you will be involved in life-threatening situations and should be either warned in time to avoid a collision or automatically protected from rolling over, losing traction, or bearing the brunt of collision forces. Head-protecting side airbags, electronic stability control, brake override systems, daytime running lights, and a centre-mounted third brake light are four passive safety features that have paid off handsomely in lives saved and fewer injuries.

Passive safety features also assume that some accidents aren't avoidable and that, when those accidents occur, vehicles should provide as much protection as possible to drivers, passengers, and other vehicles that may be struck—without depending on the driver's reactions. Passive safety components that have consistently been proven to reduce vehicular deaths and injuries are seat belts, laminated windshields, and vehicle structures that enhance crashworthiness by absorbing or deflecting crash forces away from the vehicle's occupants.

Distracted driving

Distracted driving is a major cause of automobile accidents that can be prevented by drivers' using common sense (active safety). The danger of distracted driving is real. For example, a driver talking with other passengers in the car is said to be the cause of 81 percent of auto crashes. Auto accident statistics show that other significant causes of car accidents are listening to or changing radio stations (involved in 66 percent of all accidents) and talking on cell phones (25 percent).

Interestingly, a 2006 University of Utah study compared cell phone use to drunk driving (*www.distraction.gov/research/PDF-Files/Comparison-of-CellPhone-Driver-Drunk-Driver.pdf*). Researchers found impairments associated with using a cell phone while driving can be as profound as those associated with driving with a blood alcohol content of 0.08% (the legal limit in many countries, including Canada and the U.S.).

What about stricter law enforcement? Don't get your hopes up. A 2010 study carried out by the Highway Loss Data Institute reviewed insurance claims in New York, Connecticut, California, and the District of Columbia and compared the data to other areas without cell phone bans. Conclusion: laws banning the use of hand-held devices while driving did not reduce the rate of accidents (*www.cnn.com/2010/US/01/29/cellphone.study/index.html*).

Safety Features That Kill

In the late '60s, Washington forced automakers to include essential safety features like collapsing steering columns and safety windshields in their cars. As the years have passed, the number of mandatory safety features increased to include seat belts, airbags, and crashworthy construction. These improvements met with public approval until quite recently, when reports of deaths and injuries caused by ABS and airbag failures showed that defective components and poor engineering negated the potential life-saving benefits associated with having these devices.

For example, one out of every five ongoing NHTSA defect investigations concerns inadvertent airbag deployment, deactivation of the front passenger airbag, failure of the airbag to deploy, or injuries suffered when the bag did go off. In fact, airbags are the agency's single-largest cause of current investigations, exceeding even the full range of brake problems, which runs second.

Side Airbags—Good and Bad

Side and side curtain airbags are designed to protect drivers and passengers in rollovers and side-impact crashes, which are estimated to account for almost one-third of vehicular deaths. They have also been shown to help keep unbelted occupants from being ejected in rollovers. Head-protecting side airbags can reduce serious crash injuries by 45 percent. Side airbags without head protection reduce injuries by only 10 percent. Ideally, you want a side airbag system that protects both the torso and head.

Because side airbags aren't required by federal regulation in Canada or the States, neither government has developed any tests to measure their safety for children or small adults. Indeed, new side-protection rules went into effect in September 2009, giving automakers four years to comply with a new government-imposed "performance standard."

There's a downside to increased side airbag protection: Sit properly in your seat, or face serious injury from the deploying side airbag. Preliminary safety studies show that side airbags may be deadly to children or to any occupant sitting too close to the airbag, resting his or her head on the side pillar, or holding onto the roof-mounted assist handle. Research carried out in 1998 by safety researchers (Anil Khadikar of Biodynamics Engineering Inc. and Lonney Pauls of Springwater Micro Data Systems, *Assessment of Injury Protection Performance of Side Impact Airbags*) shows there are four hazards that pertain to most airbag systems:

1. Inadvertent airbag firing (short circuits, faulty hardware or software)
2. Unnecessary airbag firing (sometimes the opposite-side airbag will fire; the airbag may deploy when a low-speed side-swipe wouldn't have endangered occupant safety)

3. A small child, say, a three-year-old, restrained in a booster seat could be seriously injured
4. Out-of-position restrained occupants could be seriously injured

The researchers conclude with the following observation: "Even properly restrained vehicle occupants can have their upper or lower extremities in harm's way in the path of an exploding [side] airbag."

The 1998 study and dozens of other scientific papers confirm that small or tall restrained drivers face death or severe injury from frontal and side airbag deployments for the simple reason that they are outside of the norm of the 5'8", 180-pound, male test dummy.

And don't forget NHTSA's side airbag warning issued on October 14, 1999:

> Side impact airbags can provide significant supplemental safety benefits to adults in side impact crashes. However, children who are seated in close proximity to a side airbag may be at risk of serious or fatal injury, especially if the child's head, neck, or chest is in close proximity to the airbag at the time of deployment.

Protecting yourself

Because not all airbags function, or malfunction, the same way, *Lemon-Aid* has done an exhaustive analysis of U.S. and Canadian recalls, crash data, and owner complaints to determine which vehicles and which model years use airbags that may seriously injure occupants or deploy inadvertently. That data can be found in Part Three's model ratings.

 Additionally, you should take the following steps to reduce the danger from airbag deployment:

- Buy a vehicle with head-protecting side curtain airbags for front and rear passengers.
- Make sure that seat belts are buckled and all head restraints are properly adjusted (to about ear level).
- Choose vehicles with head restraints that are rated "Good" by IIHS (see Part Three).
- Insist that passengers who are frail or short or who have recently had surgery sit in the back and properly position themselves away from side airbags.
- Ensure that the driver's seat can be adjusted for height and has tracks with sufficient rearward travel to allow short drivers to remain at a safe distance (over 25 cm) away from the bag's deployment and still be able to reach the accelerator and brake.
- Consider buying pedal extensions to keep you at a safe distance away from a deploying airbag if you are short-statured.

Top 20 Safety Defects

The U.S. federal government's online safety complaints database contains well over 100,000 entries, going back to vehicles made in the late '70s. Although the database was originally intended to record only incidents of component failures that relate to safety, you will find every problem imaginable dutifully recorded by clerks working for NHTSA.

A perusal of the listed complaints shows that some safety-related failures occur more frequently than others and often affect one manufacturer more than another. Here is a summary of the most commonly reported failures:

1. Sudden, unintended acceleration
2. ABS total brake failure; wheel lock-up
3. Airbags not deploying when they should, or deploying when they shouldn't
4. Tire-tread separation
5. Electrical or fuel-system fires
6. Sudden stalling
7. Sudden electrical failures
8. Transmission failing to engage, or suddenly disengaging
9. Transmission jumping from Park to Reverse or Neutral; vehicle rolling away when parked
10. Steering or suspension failures
11. Seat belt failures
12. Collapsing seatbacks
13. Defective sliding door, door locks, and latches
14. Poor headlight illumination; glare
15. Dash reflecting onto windshield
16. Hood flying up
17. Wheel falling away
18. Steering wheel lifting off
19. Transmission lever pulling out
20. Exploding windshields

Vehicles for Older Drivers

Drivers over 80 are the fastest-growing segment of the driving population. According to Candrive, the Canadian Driving Research Initiative for Vehicular Safety in the Elderly, there are currently about 3 million senior drivers in Canada, and their numbers are expected to double by 2040. A quarter of Canadians 85 and older now have a driver's licence, and 105 licences have been issued to centenarians in Ontario and Manitoba alone. By 2030, it's estimated that there will be roughly 15,000 centenarians driving in Canada—approximately three times as many as there are today. Husbands do the bulk of family driving, which usually involves short trips (11–17 km per day, on average) for medical appointments and visits to family, friends, and shopping malls. This puts older women, who tend to outlive their husbands, in a serious bind because of their lack of driving experience—particularly in rural areas, where driving is a necessity rather than a choice.

I'm 67, so I know that older drivers, like most other drivers, want cars that are reliable, relatively inexpensive, and fuel efficient. Additionally, we require vehicles that compensate for some of the physical challenges associated with aging (I'm getting fatter, slower, and much more taciturn, I'm told) and provide protection for accidents more common with mature drivers (side impacts, for example). Furthermore, as drivers get older, they find that the very act of getting into a car (sitting down while moving sideways, without bumping their heads or twisting their necks) demands considerable acrobatic skill. And don't even ask about shoulder pain when reaching up and over for the shoulder belt!

Access and Comfort for Older Drivers

I've been told that some drivers with arthritic hands have to insert a pencil into their key ring to twist the key in the ignition. Make sure your ignition lock doesn't require that much effort. Power locks and windows are a must, especially if the vehicle will be operated with hand controls. A remote keyless entry will allow entry without having to twist a key in the door lock. A vehicle equipped with a buttonless shifter will be less difficult to activate for arthritis sufferers and drivers with limited upper-body mobility. Cruise control can be helpful for those with lower-body mobility challenges.

Get a vehicle that's easy to enter and exit. Check for door openings that are wide enough to get into and out of easily, both for you and for any wheelchairs or scooters that may need to be loaded. Make sure the door catches when opened on a slight incline so that it doesn't close as you are exiting. If necessary, your trunk or rear cargo area should have a low liftover and room to stow your wheelchair or scooter. Bench seats are preferable because they're roomier and easier to access; getting a power-adjustable driver's seat with memory is also a good idea. Make sure the seat is comfortable and has plenty of side bolstering.

Forget minivans, unless you invest in a step-up and choose one with an easily reached inside-grip handle—and don't mind bumping the left-side steering-column stalk with your knee each time you slide into the driver's seat. Incidentally, General Motors' 2009 minivans offered a Sit-N-Lift option: a motorized, rotating lift-and-lower passenger seat that's accessed through the middle door and can be taken out when not needed.

Drivers with limited mobility, or those who are recovering from hip surgery, give kudos to the Cadillac Escalade SUV and GM Venture/Montana minivans; Toyota's Echo, Yaris, Matrix, and Avalon; and small SUVs such as the Honda CR-V, Hyundai Tucson, and Toyota RAV4. Of this group, only the recently discontinued GM minivans give me cause for concern, because of their poor reliability.

Safety Features for Older Drivers

The driver's seat should be mounted high enough to give a commanding view of the road (with slower reaction times, seniors need earlier warnings). Driver's seats must offer enough rearward travel to attenuate the force of an exploding airbag, which can be particularly hazardous to older or small-statured occupants, children, or anyone recovering from surgery. Adjustable gas and brake pedals are a must for short-legged drivers.

And while we're discussing airbags, remember that they are calibrated to explode during low-speed collisions (at less than 10 km/h) and that reports of injuries caused by their deployment are commonplace. Therefore, always put at least 25 cm between your upper torso and the steering wheel.

Look for handles near the door frame that can be gripped for support when entering or leaving the vehicle, bright dashboard gauges that can be seen in sunlight, and instruments with large-sized controls.

Remote-controlled mirrors are a must, along with adjustable, unobtrusive head restraints and a non-reflective front windshield (many drivers put a cloth on the dash-top to cut the distraction). Make sure that the brake and accelerator pedals aren't mounted too close together.

As far as safety features are concerned, a superior crashworthiness rating is essential, as well as torso- and head-protecting side airbags, since most intersection collisions involving mature drivers occur when drivers are making a turn into oncoming traffic. The extra head protection can make a critical difference in side impacts. For example, with its $680 head-protecting side airbags, Toyota's 2004 RAV4 earned a "Best Pick" designation from the Insurance Institute for Highway Safety (IIHS). When tested without the head protection, it received a "Poor" rating in the side test.

Don't be overly impressed by anti-lock brakes, since their proper operation (no tapping on the brakes) runs counter to everything you have been taught, plus they aren't that reliable. Look for headlights that give you a comfortable view at night, as well as turn signal indicators that are easy to see and hear. Ensure that the vehicle's knobs and switches are large and easy to identify and that the gauges are sufficiently backlit that they don't wash out in daylight. Also, be sure to check that the dash doesn't cause windshield glare (a common problem with light-coloured dash panels). Having an easily accessed, full-sized spare tire and a user-friendly lug wrench and jack stand is also important.

Other Buying Considerations

When "New" Isn't New

Nothing will cause you to lose money faster than buying a new car that's older than advertised, has previously been sold and then taken back, has accident damage, or has had the odometer disconnected or turned back.

Even if the vehicle hasn't been used, it may have been left outdoors for a considerable length of time, causing the deterioration of rubber components, premature body and chassis rusting, or severe rusting of internal mechanical parts, which leads to brake malfunction, fuel line contamination, hard starting, and stalling.

You can check a vehicle's age by looking at the date-of-manufacture plate usually found on the driver-side door pillar. If the date of manufacture is 7/11 or earlier, your vehicle was probably one of the last 2011 models made before the September changeover to the 2012s. Redesigned vehicles or those new to the market are exceptions to this rule. They may arrive at dealerships in early spring or mid-summer and are considered to be next year's models. They also depreciate more quickly owing to their earlier launching, but this difference narrows over time. For 2011, GM plans to change the model-year of its full-sized pickups in July (two months earlier than before).

Sometimes a vehicle can be too new and cost you more in maintenance because its redesign glitches haven't been worked out yet. As Honda's North American manufacturing chief, Koki Hirashima, so ably put it, carryover models generally have fewer problems than vehicles that have been significantly reworked or just introduced to the market. Newly redesigned vehicles get quality scores that are, on average, 2 percent worse than vehicles that have been around for a while, says J.D. Power. Some surprising poor performers are the Jaguar X-Type, Nissan Altima and Quest, and Toyota Corolla and Tundra.

Because they were the first off the assembly line for that model year, most vehicles assembled between September and February are called "first-series" cars. "Second-series" vehicles, made between March and August, incorporate more assembly-line fixes and are better built than the earlier models, which may depend on ineffective "field fixes" to mask problems until the warranty expires. Second-series vehicles will sell for the same price or less, but they will be far better buys because of their assembly-line upgrades and more generous rebates. Service bulletins for Chrysler's new Caliber and Charger; GM's Solstice, Torrent, and Sky roadsters; and the Ford Fusion, Zephyr, and Milan show these vehicles all had serious quality shortcomings during their first year on the market. It usually takes a couple of years for the factory to get most of the quality glitches corrected.

There's also the very real possibility that the new vehicle you've just purchased was damaged while being shipped to the dealer and was later fixed in the service bay during the pre-delivery inspection. It's estimated that this happens to about 10 percent of all new vehicles. Although there's no specific Canadian legislation allowing buyers of vehicles damaged in transit to cancel their contracts, B.C. legislation says that dealers must disclose damages of $2,000 or more. In a more general sense, Canadian common-law jurisprudence does allow for cancellation or compensation whenever the delivered product differs markedly from what the buyer expected to receive. Ontario's revised *Consumer Protection Act* is particularly hard-nosed in prohibiting this kind of misrepresentation.

Fuel Economy Follies

Poor gas mileage is one of the top complaints among owners of new cars and minivans. Drivers say gas mileage is seldom as high as it's hyped to be; in fact, it's likely to be 10–20 percent less than advertised with most vehicles. (Gas mileage, measured in mpg, is the opposite of metric fuel consumption, measured in L/100 km. In other words, you want gas mileage to be high and consumption to be low.) *Consumer Reports* magazine once estimated that 90 percent of vehicles sold don't get the gas mileage advertised.

Why such a contradiction between promise and performance?

It's simple: Automakers cheat on their tests. They submit their own test results to the government after testing under optimum conditions. Transport Canada then publishes these self-serving "cooked" figures as its own research. One Ford service bulletin is remarkably frank in discounting the validity of these tests:

> Very few people will drive in a way that is identical to the EPA [sanctioned] tests. These [fuel economy] numbers are the result of test procedures that were originally developed to test emissions, not fuel economy.

Stephen Akehurst, a senior manager at Natural Resources Canada, which tests vehicles and publishes the annual *Fuel Consumption Guide*, admits that his lab tests vehicles under ideal conditions. He says that actual driving may burn about 25 percent more fuel than what the government tests show. Too bad we never see this fact hyped in the automakers' fuel economy ads.

Keep in mind that although good fuel economy is important, it's hardly worth a harsh ride, excessive highway noise, side-wind buffeting, anemic acceleration, and a cramped interior. You may end up with much worse gas mileage than advertised and a vehicle that's underpowered for your needs.

If you never quite got the hang of metric fuel economy measurements, click on the fuel conversion tool found at *www.euronet.nl/users/grantm/frans/fuel.html* to see how many miles to a U.S. gallon of gas your vehicle provides. A listing of the fuel consumption of all vehicles sold in Canada since 1995 written in miles per gallon and the metric equivalent can be found at *http://oee.nrcan.gc.ca/transportation/tools/fuelratings/ratings-search.cfm*.

"Miracle" Fuels

The lure of cheap, "clean" fuel has never been stronger, and the misrepresentations as to the advantages of different fuels have never been greater. Take a look at the following list of flavour-of-the-month alternate fuels that have been proposed by politicians and businesses, and consider that, except for diesel, not a single other alternate fuel is economically viable.

Ethanol and flex-fuel vehicles (FFVs)

Ethanol is the trendy "fuel of the year" for automakers, oil companies, and politicians who have their heads stuck up their tailpipes. All three groups recite the mantra that increased ethanol use will cut fuel costs, make us less dependent on foreign oil sources (goodbye, Big Oil; hello, Big Corn), and create a cleaner environment. Unfortunately, this is simply not true—it's reminiscent of the misguided embrace of the 1997 Kyoto Accord by governments who promised they would be effective in cutting emissions that lead to global warming. Ironically, research now shows signatories to the Accord produce more emissions than non-signatories.

FFVs are all the rage with the Detroit Three, and they're being promoted over hybrids and diesel engines because the switchover is less costly for automakers. They only have to modify the fuel-delivery system on their vehicles and then lobby the federal government to pay billions of dollars for new pipelines, tankers, and gas stations. Millions of their vehicles are already on the market and can run on a mixture (called E85) of 85 percent ethanol and 15 percent gasoline, but oil companies limit the supply of ethanol available because charging high gasoline prices is more profitable. Furthermore, governments won't pony up the billions of dollars needed to construct new ethanol pipelines (at an estimated cost of $1.6 million per kilometre for 322,000 km) and to convert filling stations (at an estimated cost of $240,000 per new tank and pump) just to provide real competition for gas-selling stations. At the moment, many E85 FFVs are gasoline-powered because few E85 commercial retailers can be found in Canada (only four stations existed in 2009), though there are over 1,100 stations selling E10 (only 2,414 out of 168,987 filling stations in the States sell E85 ethanol). Yet the automakers get important tax credits because they have converted much of their production to run on ethanol fuel (in theory), though most of the vehicles stay on a pure gasoline diet or drink E10.

Petro-Canada says this about the E85 shortage:

> Ethanol-blended gasoline is a fuel that typically contains up to 10% ethanol in unleaded gasoline. We use ethanol in our gasoline where legislation requires its use and where conditions warrant. The Federal Government has regulated that motor gasoline sold in Canada after Sept. 1, 2010 must contain an annual pool average of 5% ethanol. Different provincial mandates also exist, some with higher ethanol pool requirements. Because of these mandates, most grades of Petro-Canada fuel may now contain up to 10% ethanol. This represents a change from the previous state,

where premium fuel was ethanol-free at Petro-Canada. To find out if ethanol-blended gasoline is sold at a station look for the yellow labels in the pump area indicating that the fuel may contain a maximum of 10% ethanol.

Can I use this in my car?

- Fuels blended with levels of up to 10% ethanol, are safe for engine components, and do not require engine or gas-line changes in vehicles
- Since 1988, most automotive vehicles sold in Canada have been designed to use ethanol-blended gasoline, at the levels of up to 10% ethanol. If you have concerns check your owner's manual or contact the vehicle manufacturer.

Looking for E-85 ethanol for your Flex-Fuel vehicle? This blend of 85% ethanol and 15% gasoline caters to only a small percentage of vehicles. Currently we do not market this specialty-use product.

Brazil, a huge ethanol producer since the late '70s, doesn't need a pipeline because most of its sugar cane fields are located where they can distill and market the resulting ethanol, thereby forgoing expensive transportation costs. In North America, most of the corn and other ethanol-producing crops are found in the U.S. Midwest and in Central and Western Canada, far away from major population areas.

Ethanol is smokeless, burns cleaner, and (theoretically) leads to less engine maintenance. Plus, you can drink it (diluted, or with a chaser).

But will the increased use of ethanol make North America much less dependent on gasoline? No way—not if you do the math: The U.S. produces about 4 billion gallons of ethanol annually, but burnS an average of 140 billion gallons of gasoline each year.

Accepting that E85 filling stations are practically nonexistent and are expected to stay that way, here are some other jaw-dropping facts that ensure ethanol won't be the fuel of the future: The fuel costs almost as much as gasoline in some places (unless you distill it yourself); gas mileage *drops* by up to 30 percent when ethanol is used; cold-weather performance is mediocre; and the product is highly corrosive, with a particular fondness for snacking on plastic and rubber components.

Hybrids

After reading the Canadian Automobile Association's findings that a 2010 Toyota Prius hybrid will cost slightly more to run than a $15,496 2010 Chevrolet Cobalt (refer to page 24), it's hard to comprehend how the $27,800 hybrid can be called a money-saver.

As practical as the promise of ethanol fuel seemed at first, hybrids use a pie-in-the-sky alternative fuel system that requires expensive and complex electronic and mechanical components. A bare-bones Honda Civic can achieve the same fuel economy for about two-thirds the cost of the Prius without polluting the environment with exotic toxic metals leached from battery packs and powertrain components.

The Canadian Automobile Association's latest study of fuel savings of hybrids and conventional vehicles, released August 18, 2011 (*http://caa.ca/documents/CAA_Driving_Cost_English_2011_web.pdf*) says conventional vehicles have much lower operating costs. The CAA study compared a Toyota Prius with a Chevrolet Cruze and a Dodge Grand Caravan. CAA researchers found the following:

> Based on 18,000 km, a Cruze costs $8,883.85 a year to operate, which is 49.4 cents per km. A Prius on the other hand is $9,496.20 or 52.8 cents per km to operate. The gap narrows at 32,000km/year where the Cruze's total cost is $11,333.85 (35.4 cents/km) compared to $11,484.20 (35.9 cents/km) for a Prius.

Overall, the Prius costs less to drive the more it is driven, as the fixed costs (purchase price, depreciation, etc.) can be amortized over greater kilometres. The downside? Cars are driven an average 20,000 km a year in Canada. To get within striking distance of the Cruze's lower operating costs, a Prius owner would have to put an extra 12,000 kilometres on the car.

How does this help the environment or your wallet?

Other disadvantages of hybrids are their mechanical and electronic complexities, dependence on specialized dealers for basic servicing, high depreciation rates and insurance costs, overblown fuel-efficiency numbers (owners report getting 40 percent less mileage than promised), and the $3,000 cost to replace their battery packs.

Finally, consider this: Hybrid vehicles like the Toyota Prius use rare-earth minerals such as lanthanum, scandium, and yttrium mixed oxides and aluminas (which are used in almost all automotive emissions control systems). Neodymium is another rare element needed for the lightweight permanent magnets that power hybrid motors. It's a radioactive substance mined almost exclusively in China, which has threatened to restrict its sale for domestic use and slapped on heavy export duties. And there's a good reason why mining has been mostly restricted to China—the government there doesn't care if the mining and refining of these toxic minerals poisons the environment and sickens villagers—something North American "green" advocates overlook.

Western nations simply cannot afford to mine and refine neodymium within their borders due to the enormous environmental toxicity that mining it produces. In a sense, China is not cornering the neodymium market using their mineral reserves, but rather their willingness to sacrifice their environment and expose their populace to a higher cancer rate. In the end, North American motorists may trade a dependence on Middle Eastern oil for a troubling dependence on Chinese-sourced neodymium that's poisoning the Chinese people in the process.

Diesels

Diesel fuel is cleaner these days and far more fuel-efficient than ever before. Among the alternative fuels tested by independent researchers, diesel comes closest to the estimated fuel economy figures. It's also widely available and requires neither a steep learning curve in the service bay nor exotic replacement parts. Additionally, unlike hybrids, diesel-equipped vehicles are reasonably priced and hold their value quite well.

As with the changeover to unleaded gasoline two decades ago, owners of diesel-equipped Detroit-made vehicles can expect horrendously expensive maintenance costs, considerable repair downtime, and the worsening of the diesel's poor reliability trend, which was seen over the past decade with Ford's Powerstroke and General Motors' Duramax. Additionally, many of the 2011 and 2012 diesel engines now require that owners regularly fill up with urea—an unexpected extra expense and annoyance.

To pee or not to pee? Recent model diesels, like the Mercedes' Bluetec, inject a urea solution—known as AdBlue—into the exhaust to reduce nitrous oxide (NOx) emissions. Audi, BMW, VW, and the Detroit Three also use urea injection under different names.

Sheesh, it seemed like a simple solution at the time.

A yearly urea refill can be expected since the urea tank contains roughly 8 gallons (U.S.), which is good for about 19,300 kilometres (12,000 miles) of standard operation. Generally, automakers will add the urea solution at every scheduled maintenance visit.

Mercedes-Benz Blutec diesels will not run if the urea tank doesn't contain a certain amount. If the tank reaches one gallon, the car notifies the driver. It does so again with only 20 starts remaining. To reset the system, at least two gallons of AdBlue—or four half-gallon bottles, at $7.75 each—must be added. Not a lot to clean the environment, you say? Read on.

Consumer Reports was charged an outrageous $317 to put 7.5 gallons of AdBlue in its Mercedes GL320 test car at $32/gallon for the fluid, even though 7.5 gallons would cost only $116.25 in half-gallon bottles elsewhere. So, what can you do if your car or truck is urea-immobilized, there is no dealership around, or you refuse to pay through the nose for a simple fill-up?

That brings us back to our original question: "To pee or not to pee?"

Don't pee, at least not into the urea tank. Yes, human urine contains 2 to 4 percent urea, but modern diesels won't use your pee because it's too diluted and full of other substances like salts, toxins, bile pigments, hormones, and up to 95 percent water. AdBlue, TDI, and other urea products have a concentration of 32.5 percent urea mixed with deionized water. If you put anything else in the urea tank, your car or truck won't start.

Fuel economy misrepresentation

So if you can't make a gas-saving product that pours into your fuel tank or attaches to the fuel or air lines, you have to use that old standby: lie. Hell, if automakers and government fuel-efficiency advocates can do it, why not dealers?

Fuel economy misrepresentation is actionable, and there is Canadian jurisprudence that allows for a contract's cancellation if the gas-mileage figures are false (see Part Two). Most people, however, simply keep the car they bought and live with the fact that they were fooled.

There are a few choices you can make that will lower fuel consumption. First off, choose a smaller version of the vehicle style you are interested in buying. Secondly, choose a manual transmission or an automatic with a fuel-saving Fifth or Sixth gear. Thirdly, an engine with variable valve timing or a cylinder-deactivation feature will increase fuel economy by 3 and 8 percent, respectively.

Excessive Maintenance Fees

Maintenance inspections and replacement parts represent hidden costs that are usually exaggerated by dealers and automakers to increase their profits on vehicles that either rarely require fixing or are sold in insufficient numbers to support a service bay.

Alan Gelman, a well-known Toronto garage owner and co-host of "Dave's Corner Garage" on Toronto AM740, warns drivers:

There are actually two maintenance schedules handed out by car companies and dealers. The dealer inspection sheets often call for far more extensive and expensive routine maintenance checks than what's listed in the owner's manual. Most of those checks are padding; smart owners will stick with the essential checks listed in the manual and have them done by cheaper, independent garages.

Getting routine work done at independent facilities will cost about one-third to one-half the price usually charged by dealers. Just be sure to follow the automaker's suggested schedule so no warranty claim can be tied to botched servicing. Additionally, an inexpensive ALLDATA service bulletin subscription (see page 60) will keep you current as to your vehicle's factory defects, required check-ups, and recalls; tell you what's covered by little-known "goodwill" warranties; and save you valuable time and money when troubleshooting common problems.

Choosing a Reliable, Cheap Vehicle

Overall vehicle safety and body fit and finish on both domestic and imported vehicles are better today than they were three decades ago. Premature rusting is less of a problem, and reliability is improving. Repairs to electronic systems and powertrains, however, are outrageously expensive and complicated. Owners of cars and trucks made by GM, Ford, and Chrysler still report serious engine and automatic transmission deficiencies, often during the vehicle's first year in service. Other common defects include electrical system failures caused by faulty computer modules; malfunctioning ABS systems; brake rotor warpage; early pad wearout; failure-prone air conditioning and automatic transmissions; and faulty engine head gaskets, intake manifolds, fuel systems, suspensions, and steering assemblies.

Nothing shows the poor quality control of the Detroit Three automakers as much as the poor fit and finish of body panels. Next time you're stuck in traffic, look at the trunk lid or rear hatch alignment of the vehicle in front of you. Chances are, if it's a Detroit-bred model, the trunk or hatch will be so misaligned that there will be a large gap on one side. Then look at most Asian products: Usually, you will see perfectly aligned trunks and hatches without any large gaps on either side.

That, in a nutshell, is Detroit's problem, although Ford has come a long way over the past few years in improving fit and finish.

Detroit's "Good" Products

Don't get the impression that Detroit automakers can't make reasonably good vehicles, though. Ford's Mustang and its much-improved 2004–12 Focus carry little risk. GM's full-sized rear-drive vans are good buys, and its Acadia, Enclave, Equinox, Terrain, and Traverse SUVs also perform well, though long-term reliability is still unproven.

General Motors' products are quite a mixed bag: Its full-sized vans, SUVs, small cars, and joint ventures with Toyota and Suzuki have all done well, but its recent mid-sized family cars (think Malibu and Impala) are mediocre at best.

Most studies done by consumer groups and private firms show that, in spite of improvements attempted over the past two decades, vehicles made by Chrysler, GM, and (to a lesser extent) Ford still don't measure up to Japanese and some South Korean products, such as Hyundai's, in terms of drivetrain quality and technology. This is particularly evident in SUVs and minivans, where Honda and Toyota have long retained the highest reliability and dependability ratings, despite some powertrain and brake deficiencies.

Chrysler

Chrysler doesn't have much product that's popular. It will be relying mostly on its new Fiat, the Chrysler 200, and its reworked Jeep Grand Cherokee. Nevertheless, like General Motors, it does have pockets full of cash thanks to the Japanese post-earthquake sales losses and a window of almost six months before the Japanese return to full production. This will be the crunch time to see if Detroit's weakest automaker can turn itself around and make these new models a success.

Don't buy a Chrysler unless it's a well-inspected minivan. Ram pickups with a manual transmission and a diesel engine are an excellent buy from a reliability and durability standpoint, but severe steering/suspension wobble produced when passing over uneven terrain or small potholes can make the vehicle hazardous to drive.

Chrysler/Fiat: *non per la quale* ("not to be trusted"). The "Death Wobble" and "Rust Magnet" duo.

Ford

Ford sold off most of its assets and borrowed billions of dollars just before the recession hit. The fact that it didn't go bankrupt means that Ford not only has kept its own loyal customers and critical rural dealers but also is well poised to poach Chrysler, GM, Honda, Nissan, and Toyota sales.

Ford's management is less dysfunctional and more focused than what we have seen at Chrysler and GM. Moreover, the company has improved its quality control during the past several years and brought out popular new products like the Edge and Fusion. Lincoln's reliable and profitable Town Car will likely remain for a few more years as Ford's only rear-drive Lincoln, due to its popularity with seniors and fleet managers.

What models not to buy from Ford this year? The redesigned 2011 Explorer, for one.

It was glitch-prone when first launched in 1990 and will likely be troublesome during the first year as a revamped model. Early tests by *Consumer Reports* point out that its powertrain runs rough, the transmission is slow to downshift, and engine braking on hills is too abrupt. Overall handling isn't very agile, marked by slow steering response and limited road feedback, plus there's some body lean when cornering. Inside the cabin, the driver will find narrow seats with an under-sized bottom cushion, limited footroom, and the gas and brake pedals positioned too close together. Finally, Ford's much-touted Sync voice-command feature isn't user-friendly for giving simple commands.

General Motors

GM is back to making bundles of money, thanks to what's become a seller's market with the Japanese rebuilding their factories and re-jigging their supply lines. GM intends to pay off most of its bailout debt this year and invest money in new products, as well as in better quality control for existing vehicles, which trail Ford for overall reliability and durability. The company's eight divisions have been whittled down to a more manageable four (it sold Saab and Hummer, and Saturn and Pontiac have been successfully shut down). On the other hand, the company's terminated dealers are clogging the courts with hundreds of lawsuits seeking compensation for the arbitrariness of GM's actions.

Major quality deficiencies still affect most of GM's lineup, notably American-built front-drives and imported pickups. Owners cite unreliable powertrains, poor braking performance, electrical problems, and subpar fit and finish as the main offenders.

The company's increased reliance on Chinese factories to build economy cars for North America is pretty scary. Imagine: Not only are North Americans' bailout funds being used to create jobs in China, but we also will have the dubious pleasure of driving some of the worst-made automobiles in the world, imported from the country that sold us lead-laced-paint on kids' toys and poisoned pet food ingredients. Move over, Fiat! Here come Chery's economy and Brilliance's "brilliant" crashworthiness. (Don't just take my word that these are bad cars—watch the crash videos.)

According to several independent studies on Chinese manufacturing—like those done by Christensen Associates, Inc. (*www.camcinc.com/library/SoYou'reBuyingFromChina.pdf*) and by Paul Midler in *Poorly Made in China: An Insider's Account of the Tactics Behind China's Production Game* (John Wiley & Sons, 2009)—price trumps safety and quality. Your car has no brakes? No problem. We'll give you a 10 percent discount and shoot the factory foreman.

Asian Automakers

Almost all of the Asian automakers make exceptionally good cars and weathered the poor 2011 sales year better than their competitors. The only exceptions are Mitsubishi, Suzuki, and Kia; the first two automakers were crippled by an almost nonexistent dealer network (Mitsu dualed with Chrysler for some time under the Colt label), while Suzuki had little product and an equally weak dealer body. Early last year, Volkswagen bought a 20 percent interest in Suzuki to bolster its small car lineup. Since then, the two companies have found they can't work together and are expected to end their alliance.

Kia has done extremely well this past year, selling its full lineup amid accolades from independent auto reviewers for improved quality. As for Hyundai, its parent company, sales are just as good and quality is a notch better. The redesigned 2011 Accent and Elantra are a big hit and good stand-ins for Honda and Toyota small and family-sized cars, which may be in short supply this fall.

Don't buy into the myth that parts for imports are overpriced or hard to find. It's actually easier to find parts for Japanese and South Korean vehicles than for domestic ones because of the large number of units produced, the ease with which relatively simple parts can be interchanged among different models, and the large reservoir of used parts available.

Sadly, customer relations has been the Achilles' heel for Japanese automakers. Dealers are spoiled rotten by decades of easy sales and have developed a "take it or leave it" showroom attitude, which is often accompanied by a woeful ignorance of their own model lineups. This was once a frequent complaint from Honda and Toyota shoppers, though recent APA undercover surveys show a big improvement among Toyota dealers.

Poor quality has been the bugaboo for the South Korean automakers. Yet, like Honda's and Toyota's recoveries following start-up quality glitches, Hyundai (South Korea's biggest automaker) has made considerable progress in bringing quality up almost to Toyota and Honda's level.

Hyundai's 2012 Accent (left) is more powerful, better performing, and moderately higher priced. The 2012 Hyundai Elantra (right) is all new and chock full of standard features that cost extra from other automakers.

A South Korean winner: The rear-drive Hyundai Genesis comes with a 3.8L 290 hp V6 or an optional 4.6L 375 hp V8.

Up to the mid-'90s, South Korean vehicles were merely cheap, poor-quality knock-offs of their Japanese counterparts. They would start to fall apart after their third year because of subpar body construction, unreliable automatic transmission and electrical components, and parts suppliers who put low prices ahead of reliability and durability. This was particularly evident with Hyundai's Pony, Stellar, Excel, and early Sonata models. During the past decade, though, Hyundai's product lineup has been extended and refined, and quality is no longer a worry. In fact, Hyundai's 2012 upscale Genesis is a top-performing $38,999 (watch out for the $1,760 freight fee) luxury sedan that's recommended by *Consumer Reports* and *Lemon-Aid*. Also, Hyundai's comprehensive base warranty protects owners from most of the more-expensive breakdowns that may occur.

Hyundais are easily repaired by independent garages, and their rapid depreciation doesn't mean much; they cost so little initially, and entry-level buyers are known to keep their cars longer than most, thereby easily amortizing the higher depreciation rate.

Kia, a small, struggling, low-quality South Korean compact automaker bought by Hyundai in October 1998, has come a long way. At first it languished under Hyundai's "benign neglect," as Hyundai spent most of its resources on its own cars and SUVs. But during the past few years Hyundai has worked hard to improve Kia reliability and fit and finish by using more Hyundai parts in each Kia redesign and by improving quality control on the assembly line.

A good rule of thumb at this stage: stick with Kia small cars and the Sportage SUV. Give the other models time to incorporate better quality control. Kia's Forte, Optima, Rondo, Soul, and Sportage are the models with the fewest quality problems, while the Sorento and Sedona are riddled with drivetrain, electrical, brake, and fuel system defects, in addition to poor fit and finish.

European Models

Lemon-Aid doesn't recommend many European cars; there are way too many with serious and expensive quality and servicing problems. Heck, even the Germans have abandoned their own products. For example, a 2002 J.D. Power survey of 15,000 German car owners found that German drivers are happiest at the wheel of a Japanese Lexus. This survey included compact and luxury cars as well as off-roaders. Toyota won first place on quality, reliability, and owner satisfaction, while Nissan's Maxima headed the luxury class standings. BMW was the first choice among European offerings.

For those who feel the German survey was a fluke, there's also a 2003 study of 34,000 car owners with vehicles up to eight years old, published by Britain's Consumers' Association. It found that less than half of British owners would recommend a British-made Rover or Vauxhall to a friend. The most highly rated cars in the study were the Japanese Subaru, Isuzu, and Lexus: Over 85 percent of drivers would recommend them.

And there's more. In 2005, Britain's Warranty Direct, a third-party warranty provider, checked the cost of repairs and reliability of 250 of the most popular models sold in the British Isles. It found the Honda Accord to be the most reliable and the Fiat Punto to be the least reliable in its survey (are you listening, Chrysler?). Overall, Asian cars fared best in reliability and cost of repair ratings.

Honda was the brand least likely to require repairs, with Mazda, Toyota, Subaru, Nissan, Mitsubishi, and Lexus all top-ranking. Smart, Mini, and Porsche were the only European nameplates in the top 10.

Another poor performer was Land Rover. It recorded a horrendous warranty claim rate of 47 percent in an average year. This was followed up by Renault and Saab, both with a 38 percent chance of requiring a repair in an average year, while Jeep scored similarly low on the reliability index. Other reliability "bottom feeders" were Audi, Volvo, Chrysler, and Mercedes-Benz.

Mercedes not "world-class"

Here's another surprise: Although it builds some of the most expensive cars and SUVs in the world, Mercedes' quality isn't always first-class. After stumbling badly when it first launched its rushed-to-production American-made SUV for the 1998 model year, the automaker sent out many urgent service bulletins that sought to correct a surprisingly large number of production deficiencies affecting its entire lineup, including C-Class and, to a lesser extent, E-Class models.

Mercedes executives admit that the company's cars and SUVs have serious quality shortcomings, and have vowed to correct them. But such a turnaround is complicated by M-B's huge financial losses from Chrysler and Smart. The "oh, so cute" Smart division has lost billions and doesn't compare with the more-refined and safer Asian competition.

While Mercedes sorts through its woes, shoppers who can't resist having a European nameplate should buy a VW Jetta (not the cheapened base version) or an imported Ford Fiesta.

Volkswagen: On its way up?

Volkswagen's quality isn't quite as bad as Mercedes', and its sales have been on the upswing. True, VW has always been early on the scene with great concepts, but their ideas have often been accompanied by poor execution and a weak servicing network. With its failure-prone and under-serviced Eurovan and Camper, the company hasn't been a serious minivan player since the late '60s, and VW's Rabbit and Golf small cars were resounding duds. Even the company's forays into luxury cruisers have been met with underwhelming enthusiasm and general derision.

But not all the news is bad. For 2012, VW's small cars and diesel-equipped models will continue to be strong sellers. Resale values are strong, and prices will be even more competitive.

Nevertheless, with European models your service options are limited and customer-relations staffers can be particularly insensitive and arrogant. You can count on lots of aggravation and expense because of the unacceptably slow distribution of parts and their high markups. Because these companies have a quasi-monopoly on replacement parts, there are few independent suppliers you can turn to for help. And auto wreckers, the last-chance repository for inexpensive car parts, are unlikely to carry European parts for vehicles that are either more than three years old or manufactured in small numbers.

These vehicles also age badly after the five-year mark. The weakest areas remain the drivetrains, electronic control modules, electrical and fuel systems, brakes, accessories (including the sound system and AC), and body components.

Cutting Costs

Watch the Warranty

There's a big difference between warranty promise and warranty performance. Most automakers offer bumper-to-bumper warranties that are good for at least the first 3 years/60,000 km, and most models get powertrain coverage up to 5 years/100,000 km, although Mitsubishi offers a 5-year/100,000 km base warranty and a 10-year/160,000 km powertrain warranty. It's also becoming an industry standard for car companies to pay for roadside assistance, a loaner car, or hotel accommodations if your vehicle breaks down while you're away from home and it's still under warranty. This assistance may be for as long as 5 years, without any kilometre restriction. *Lemon-Aid* readers report few problems with these ancillary warranty benefits.

Don't buy a car that's warranty-dependent

If you pick a vehicle rated Recommended by *Lemon-Aid*, the manufacturer's warranty won't be that important and you won't need to spend money on additional warranty protection. On those vehicles that have a history of engine and transmission breakdowns, but the selling price is too good to turn down, budget about $1,500 for an extended powertrain warranty backed by an insurance policy. If the vehicle has a sorry overall repair history, you will likely need a $2,000 comprehensive warranty. But first ask yourself this question: "Why am I buying a vehicle that's so poorly made that I need to spend several thousand dollars to protect myself until the warranty company grows tired of seeing my face?"

Just like the weight-loss product ads you see on TV, what you see isn't always what you get. For example, bumper-to-bumper coverage usually excludes stereo components, brake pads, clutch plates, and many other expensive parts. And automakers will pull every trick in the book to make you pay for their factory screw-ups. These tricks include blaming your driving or your vehicle's poor maintenance, penalizing you for using an independent garage or the wrong fuel, or simply stating that the problem is "normal" and it's really you who is out of whack.

Part Two has all the answers to the above lame excuses. There, you will find plenty of court decisions and sample claim letters that will make automakers and their dealers think twice about rejecting your claim.

Don't pay for repairs covered by "secret" warranties

Automobile manufacturers are reluctant to publicize their secret warranty programs because they feel that such publicity would weaken consumer confidence in their products and increase their legal liability. The closest they come to an admission is to send out a "goodwill policy," "special policy," or "product update" service bulletin intended for dealers' eyes only. These bulletins admit liability and propose free repairs for defects that include faulty paint, air conditioning malfunctions, and engine and transmission failures.

If you're refused compensation, keep in mind that secret warranty extensions are, first and foremost, an admission of manufacturing negligence. You can usually find them in technical service bulletins (TSBs) that are sent daily to dealers by automakers. Your bottom-line position should be to accept a pro rata adjustment from the manufacturer, whereby you, the dealer, and the automaker each accept a third of the repair costs. If polite negotiations fail, challenge the refusal in court on the grounds that you should not be penalized for failing to make a reimbursement claim under a secret warranty that you never knew existed!

Service bulletins are written by automakers in "mechanic speak" because service managers relate better to them that way. They're great guides for warranty inspections (especially the final one), and they're useful in helping you decide when it's best to trade in your car. Manufacturers can't weasel out of their obligations by claiming that they never wrote such a bulletin.

If your vehicle is out of warranty, show these bulletins to less-expensive, independent garage mechanics so they can quickly find the trouble and order the most recent upgraded part, ensuring that you don't replace one defective component with another.

Canadian service managers and automakers may deny at first that the bulletins even exist, or they may shrug their shoulders and say that they apply only in the States. However, when they're shown a copy, they usually find the appropriate Canadian part number or bulletin in their files. The problems and solutions don't change from one side of the border to another. Imagine American and Canadian tourists' cars being towed across the border because each country's technical service bulletins were different. Mechanical fixes do differ in cases where, for example, a bulletin is for California only, or it relates to a safety or emissions component used only in the States. But these instances are rare, indeed. What is quite gratifying is to see some automakers, like Honda, candidly admit in their bulletins that "goodwill" repair refunds are available. What a shame other automakers aren't as forthcoming!

The best way to get bulletin-related repairs carried out is to visit the dealer's service bay and to attach the specific ALLDATA-supplied service bulletin covering your vehicle's problems to a work order.

Getting your vehicle's service bulletins

Free summaries of automotive recalls and technical service bulletins listed by year, make, model, and engine can be found at the ALLDATA (*www.alldata.com/TSB*) and NHTSA (*www.safercar.gov*) websites. But, like the NHTSA summaries, ALLDATA's summaries are so short and cryptic that they're of limited use. You can download the complete contents of all the bulletins applicable to your vehicle from ALLDATA at *www.alldatadiy.com* if you pay the $26.95 (U.S.) annual subscription fee. Many bulletins offering "secret warranty" coverage are reproduced in Part Three. (See the following sample bulletin summaries for the 2010 Dodge Grand Caravan minivan and the Chevrolet Silverado 1500.)

2010 DODGE TRUCK GRAND CARAVAN 3.8L V6

All Technical Service Bulletins

NUMBER	DATE	TITLE
19-002-11	01/26/2011	Steering—P/S Return Line Fluid Leak on Cold Start Up
08-001-11	01/15/2011	Audio System—Radio Software Update for Various Issues
05-001-11	01/15/2011	Brakes—Jingle/Squeak from L/H Rear of Vehicle
23-001-11	01/07/2011	Body—Grinding Noise from B-Pillar Area
08-028-10A	11/02/2010	Audio System—RBS Radio Software Updates
21-005-10A	10/23/2010	Drivetrain—A/T Transfer Gear Bearing Noises
21-006-10A	10/23/2010	Drivetrain—Auto Trans Transfer Gear Bearing Noise
21-007-10A	10/23/2010	Drivetrain—A/T Transfer Gear Bearing Noise
21-008-10	10/23/2010	A/T—Transfer Gear Bearing Noise
23-019-10	10/22/2010	Interior—Sunglass Holder Won't Stay Latched
18-028-10	10/16/2010	Engine Controls—PCM Update for Cruise Control Function
08-021-10B	09/29/2010	Body—Power Sliding Door(s) Are Inoperative
02-002-10	09/15/2010	Steering/Suspension—Steering Wheel Out of Alignment
23-014-10	08/28/2010	Body—Sliding Door Won't Latch Open
19-002-11	01/26/2011	Steering—P/S Return Line Fluid Leak on Cold Start Up
08-001-11	01/15/2011	Audio System—Radio Software Update for Various Issues
05-001-11	01/15/2011	Brakes—Jingle/Squeak from L/H Rear of Vehicle

Some things never change with Chrysler. The sliding side door continues to be unreliable and hazardous to operate, and each morning a symphony of sounds greets you.

2010 CHEVY TRUCK SILVERADO 1500 4X4 4.8L V8

All Technical Service Bulletins

NUMBER	DATE	TITLE
10-08-50-008B	01/13/2011	Seats—Driver/Passenger Heated Seats Inop./Slow to Warm
01-08-42-001H	01/05/2011	Lighting—Exterior Lamp Condensation and Replacement
09-08-66-004A	01/04/2011	Body—Soft Tonneau Cover Appears Loose/Won't Latch
09-08-66-003A	12/23/2010	Body—Tonneau Cover Fits Too Loose on Vehicle
06-08-50-009F	12/23/2010	Restraints—Passenger Presence System Information
05-08-46-004C	12/23/2010	OnStar—Number Incorrect/Incorrectly Assigned
09-06-03-004D	12/08/2010	Electrical—MIL ON/DTCs Set by Various Control Modules
09-08-64-012C	11/22/2010	Body—Side Door Body Mounted Weatherstrip Replacement
10-06-01-007B	11/17/2010	Engine—Valve Lifter Tick Noise at Start Up
07-06-05-001H	11/12/2010	Exhaust—Muffler Heat Shield Buzz During Operation
06-03-09-004C	11/11/2010	Suspension—Squeak Noise from Rear of Vehicle
07-08-42-006E	11/11/2010	Instruments—Bulb Outage Detection Restoration
10-05-23-001A	11/08/2010	Brakes—Front Brake Induced Pulsation/Vibration
10-08-58-001D	11/04/2010	Interior—Excessive Wind Noise from Interior of Vehicle
10-03-08-002A	11/03/2010	Suspension—Multiple Noises from Front of Vehicle
08-07-30-035B	11/01/2010	A/T—Water or Coolant Contamination Information
08-06-02-003A	10/27/2010	Engine—Oil Leak at Oil Cooler Hose/Pipe Assembly
10-08-44-003B	10/13/2010	Audio—Buzz Noise When Using Bluetooth
08-09-41-005A	10/13/2010	Interior—Passenger Air Bag Is Not Flush With Dash
10-08-44-006	10/11/2010	Navigation—Report Missing/Inaccurate Nav. Map Info
08-08-50-001B	10/06/2010	Interior—Front Seat Cushion Cover Becomes Detached
10-08-61-001	10/05/2010	Body—Body Mount Bolt Stripped or Will Not Loosen
02-06-04-037I	09/16/2010	Emissions—MIL ON/DTC P0446 Stored in ECM
00-08-48-005D	09/10/2010	Body—Vehicle Glass Distortion Information
04-08-50-006D	09/09/2010	Interior—Seat Cover Wrinkle/Crease/Burn Info
10-06-05-003	08/25/2010	Exhaust System—Exhaust Leak/Rattle/Rumble/Noises
08-08-52-001G	08/24/2010	Keyless Entry—Intermittent/Inoperative Remote
10-08-42-001A	08/06/2010	Lighting—Low Beam Headlamp(s) Inoperative
08-08-48-003E	07/27/2010	Body—Tapping/Clicking/Ticking Noise at Windshield Area
07-02-32-002J	07/23/2010	Steering/Suspension—Power Steering Fluid Leaking
10-08-52-003	07/21/2010	Keyless Entry—Transmitter Button Inop/Won't Program
03-00-89-008E	07/01/2010	Body—Metal Body Panel Corrosion Protection
06-08-51-005A	06/30/2010	Body—Hem Flange Sealer for Corrosion Protection
07-06-04-019D	06/28/2010	Electrical—Intermittent MIL/DTC P2138/Reduced Power
99-09-40-005F	06/23/2010	Restraints—Extender Availability for Seat Belt
06-08-61-003E	06/22/2010	Body/Frame—Underbody Pop/Clunk When Turning
02-08-42-001D	06/21/2010	Lighting—Headlamp Polycarbonate Lens Damage Prevention
07-08-44-001F	06/15/2010	Audio System—Difficult to Install Fixed Radio Antenna
09-08-47-001A	06/14/2010	Body Controls—Unable to Reprogram Body Control Module
08-09-41-002F	06/10/2010	Restraints—Air Bag Lamp ON/Multiple DTC Set
08-07-30-021E	06/07/2010	Electrical—Electrical Malfunction/Multiple DTCs

2010 CHEVY TRUCK SILVERADO 1500 4X4 4.8L V8

All Technical Service Bulletins

NUMBER	DATE	TITLE
06-08-64-035G	06/01/2010	Body—Squeak/Itching Noise in Upper Door Area
10157	05/24/2010	Campaign—Engine Harness Connection Not Latched
08-08-45-002A	05/14/2010	Body—L/H/R/H Power Mirror(s) Inoperative
10-08-42-001	05/14/2010	Lighting—Low Beam Headlamp(s) Inoperative
08-08-45-002A	05/13/2010	Body—Left/Right Power Outside Mirror Inoperative
07-03-10-012C	05/11/2010	Tires/Wheels—Rattle Noise from Wheel or Hub Cap
10-06-04-008	05/10/2010	Engine—MIL ON P0116/P1400 Set in Very Cold Temps
07-09-41-010D	05/03/2010	Restraints—Airbag Light on DTC B0071 and B0081 Set
10-08-62-001	04/29/2010	Body—New Design for Rear Bumper Bar Assembly
10-04-19-001	04/28/2010	Drivetrain—Service 4WD Light on/DTC C0379 Symptom 08
05-03-10-003F	04/27/2010	Tires/Wheels—Low Tire/Leaking Cast Aluminum Wheels
08-03-10-006C	04/27/2010	Tires/Wheels—Tire Slowly Goes Flat/Warning Light ON
05-03-10-020C	04/27/2010	Wheels/Tires—Use of Nitrogen Gas in Tires
09-08-64-011B	03/26/2010	Instruments—L/H Door Mirror Glass Distorted
06-08-44-034D	03/19/2010	Navigation Radio—Various Noises Explained
09-08-57-002B	03/17/2010	Body—General Water Leak Diagnostic Guide
00-03-10-002E	03/15/2010	Wheels—Chrome Wheel Staining/Pitting/Corrosion
06-08-64-027H	03/11/2010	Body—LH/RH Outside Rearview Mirror Glass Shake/Flutter
07-08-64-019B	03/09/2010	Body—Front Door Window Regulator Squeak Noise
10-08-50-003	03/08/2010	Restraints—Driver/Passenger Seat Head Rest Information
10-01-38-001	03/02/2010	A/C—Reduced Windshield Clearing/Defrost
08-08-64-011A	02/26/2010	Mirrors—Heated Mirrors, Defrosting Time
01-07-30-042F	02/05/2010	A/T—2-3 Upshift or 3-2 Downshift Clunk Noise
00-06-01-026C	02/03/2010	Engine—Intake Manifold Inspection/Replacement
10-08-46-001	01/27/2010	Audio—Radio Does Not Mute Enough When Using OnStar
08-04-19-004A	01/06/2010	Drivetrain—Front Axle Vent Hose Routing
99-04-20-002F	11/03/2009	Drivetrain—Clunk Noise Shifting from PARK Into Gear
08-08-67-006A	10/28/2009	Body—Headliner Wet Water Leak into Cab Past Sunroof
06-08-64-001B	10/20/2009	Body—Side Window Chipping Information
09-08-48-006	09/18/2009	Body—Stain/Film on Windshield Glass Perimeter
09-04-19-002	09/16/2009	Drivetrain—Excessive Effort When Shift 2HI to 4HI
07-03-10-008B	08/13/2009	Tires—Slight/Mild Edge Feathering Information
08-08-61-005A	07/31/2009	Body—Front/Rear Fender Liners Warped/Wavy
07-08-46-002D	07/29/2009	Audio System—Noise When Using OnStar
07-06-01-016B	07/27/2009	Engine—Noise/Damage Oil Filter Application Importance
08-06-01-008A	07/27/2009	Engine—Drive Belt Misalignment Diagnostics
05-08-51-008C	06/22/2009	Body—Bumps or Rust Colored Spots in Paint
08-08-42-005B	06/18/2009	Lighting—Headlamp Warranty Replacement Guideline
99-01-39-004C	06/12/2009	A/C—Musty Odors Emitted from (HVAC) System
09-08-110-013	06/02/2009	Interior—Sun Visor Fails to Stay in Up Position
06-08-44-015B	05/12/2009	Audio System—Noise When Using Portable Playback Unit

2010 CHEVY TRUCK SILVERADO 1500 4X4 4.8L V8

All Technical Service Bulletins

NUMBER	DATE	TITLE
09-03-09-001	05/06/2009	Suspension—Clunking Noise from Rear of Vehicle
00-05-22-002L	03/26/2009	Brakes—Disc Brake Warranty Service And Procedures
09-08-48-002A	03/19/2009	Body—Marks/Stains on Windshield When Wet
07-08-66-003B	03/18/2009	Body—Accessory Toolbox Key Cylinder Won't Unlock
09-09-40-001	02/17/2009	Restraints—Seat Belt Warning Lamp On/Buckling Issues
09-06-05-001	01/30/2009	Exhaust System—Sulfur Odor Explanation

GM's Silverado problems are far more numerous than what we see affecting Chrysler's minivans.

Trim Insurance Costs

Insurance premiums can average between $900 and $2,000 per year, depending on the type of vehicle you own, your personal statistics and driving habits, and whether you can obtain coverage under your family policy.

There are some general rules to follow when looking for insurance savings. For example, vehicles older than five years do not necessarily need collision coverage, and you may not need loss-of-use coverage or a rental car. Other factors that should be considered are as follows:

- When you phone for quotes, make sure you have your serial number in hand. Many factors—such as the make of the car, the number of doors, if there's a sports package, and the insurer's experience with the car—can affect the quote. And be honest, or you'll find your claim denied, the policy cancelled, or your premium cost boosted.
- Where you live and work also determine how much you pay. In the past, auto insurance rates have been 25–40 percent lower in London, Ontario, than in downtown Toronto because there are fewer cars in London and fewer kilometres to drive to work. Similar disparities are found in B.C. and Alberta.
- Taking a driver-training course can save you thousands of premium dollars.
- You may be able to include your home or apartment insurance as part of a premium package that's eligible for additional discounts.

InsuranceHotline.com, based in Ontario but with quotes for other provinces, says that it pays to shop around for cheap auto insurance rates. The group has found that the same insurance policy could vary in cost by a whopping 400 percent.

"Hidden" Costs

Depreciation

Depreciation is the biggest—and most often ignored—expense that you encounter when you trade in your vehicle or when an accident forces you to buy another vehicle before the depreciated loss can be amortized. Most new cars depreciate a whopping 30–45 percent during the first two years of ownership.

The best way to use depreciation rates to your advantage is to choose a vehicle listed as being both reliable and economical to own and then keep it for 10 years or more. Generally, by choosing a lower-depreciating vehicle—such as one that keeps at least half its value over four years—you are storing up equity that will give you a bigger down payment and fewer loan costs with your next purchase.

Gas Pains

 With gas prices once again headed toward the $1.30/L mark, motorists are scratching their heads trying to find easy ways to cut gas consumption. Here are three simple suggestions:

1. Buy a used compact car for half its original price. Savings on taxes, freight fees, and depreciation: about $15,000.
2. Find low-cost fuel referrals on the Internet (*www.gasbuddy.com*). You can save about 15 cents a litre.
3. Keep your vehicle properly tuned for a 10 percent savings from improved fuel economy.

More dirt on diesels

The only reasons to buy a diesel-equipped vehicle are for their potential to deliver outstanding fuel economy and for their much lower maintenance and repair costs when compared with similar-sized vehicles powered by gasoline engines. Unfortunately, independent data suggests that both claims by automakers may be false.

Let's examine the fuel-savings issue first. In theory, when compared with gasoline powerplants, diesel engines are up to 30 percent more efficient in a light vehicle and up to 70 percent cheaper to run in a heavy-duty towing and hauling truck or SUV. They become more efficient as the engine load increases, whereas gasoline engines become less so. This is the main reason diesels are best used where the driving cycle includes a lot of city driving—slow speeds, heavy loads, frequent stops, and long idling times. At full throttle, both engines are essentially equal from a fuel-efficiency standpoint. The gasoline engine, however, leaves the diesel in the dust when it comes to high-speed performance.

On the downside, fleet administrators and owners report that diesel fuel economy in real driving situations is much less than what's advertised—a complaint also voiced by owners of hybrids. Many owners say that their diesel-run rigs get about 30 percent less mileage than what the manufacturer promised.

Also undercutting fuel-savings claims is the fact that, in some regions, the increased cost of diesel fuel—because of high taxes and oil company greed, some say—makes it more expensive than regular fuel.

The diesel engine's reputation for superior reliability may have been true in the past, but no longer. This fact is easily confirmed if you cross-reference owner complaints with confidential automaker service bulletins and independent industry polling results put out by J.D. Power and others, a task done for you in Part Three's ratings section.

Many owners of diesel-equipped vehicles are frustrated by chronic breakdowns, excessive repair costs, and poor road performance. It's practically axiomatic that bad injectors have plagued Ford Power Stroke, GM Duramax engines, and (to a lesser extent) Dodge Cummins diesels.

In the past, defective injectors were often replaced at the owner's expense and at a cost of thousands of dollars. Now, GM and Ford are using "secret warranty" programs to cover replacement costs long after the base warranty has expired (11–13 years). Chrysler has been more recalcitrant in making payouts, apparently because fewer vehicles may be involved and costs can be quite high (expensive lift pumps and injectors may be faulty).

Hybrid cars

Automakers are offering hybrid vehicles like the Toyota Prius and Honda Civic and Accord Hybrids that use an engine/electric motor for maximum fuel economy and low emissions while providing the driving range of a comparable small car. Yet this latest iteration of the electric car still has serious drawbacks, which may drive away even the most green-minded buyers:

- Real-world fuel consumption may be 20 percent higher than advertised.
- Cold weather and hilly terrain can cut fuel economy by almost 10–30 percent.
- AC and other options can increase fuel consumption even more.
- Interior cabin heat may be insufficient.
- Electrical systems can deliver a life-threatening 275–500 volts if tampered with through incompetent servicing or during an emergency rescue.
- Battery packs can cost up to $3,000 (U.S.), and fuel savings almost equal the hybrid's extra costs only after about 32,000 km of use.
- Hybrids cost more to insure, and they depreciate just as quickly as non-hybrid vehicles that don't have expensive battery packs to replace.
- Hybrids make you a captive customer where travel is dependent on available service facilities.

If you find the limitations of an electric hybrid too daunting, why not simply buy a more fuel-efficient small car? Or, get a comfortable higher line of used car. Here are some environmentally friendly cars recommended by Toronto-based Environmental Defence Canada (*www.environmentaldefence.ca*):

- Ford Focus
- Honda Civic (2011) and Fit
- Hyundai Accent and Tucson
- Mazda3 and Mazda5
- Nissan Sentra and Versa (although the Versa received a two-star crash rating)
- Toyota Corolla and Yaris
- VW Golf/Jetta TDI

Test for "Real" Performance

Take the phrase "car-like handling" with a large grain of salt. A van isn't supposed to handle like a car. Since many rear-drive models are built on a modified truck chassis and use steering and suspension components from their truck divisions, they tend to handle more like trucks than cars, in spite of automakers' claims to the contrary. Also, what you see isn't necessarily what you get when you buy or lease a new sport-utility, van, or pickup, because these vehicles seldom come with enough standard features to fully exploit their versatility. Additional expensive options are usually a prerequisite to make them safe and comfortable to drive or capable of towing heavy loads. Consequently, the term "multipurpose" is a misnomer unless you are prepared to spend extra dollars to outfit your car or minivan. Even fully equipped, these vehicles don't always provide the performance touted by automakers.

Rust Protection

Most vehicles built today are much less rust-prone than they were several decades ago, thanks to more-durable body panels and better designs. When rusting occurs now, it's usually caused by excessive environmental stress (road salt, etc.), a poor paint job, or the use of new metal panels that create galvanic corrosion or promote early paint peeling—the latter two causes are excluded from most rustproofing warranties.

Invest in undercoating, and remember that the best rustproofing protection is to park the vehicle in a dry, unheated garage or under an outside carport and then wash it every few weeks. Never bring it in and out of a heated garage during the winter months, since it is most prone to rust when temperatures are just a bit above freezing; keep it especially clean and dry during that time. If you live in an area where roads are heavily salted in winter, or in a coastal region, have your vehicle's undercoating sprayed annually.

Annual undercoating, which costs around $150, will usually do as good a job as rustproofing. It will protect vital suspension and chassis components, make the vehicle ride more quietly, and allow you to ask a higher price at trade-in time. The only downside, which can be checked by asking for references, is that the undercoating may give off an unpleasant odour for months, and it may drip, soiling your driveway.

Whether you are rustproofing the entire vehicle or just undercoating key areas, make sure to include the rocker panels (make a small mark inside the door panels on the plastic hole plugs to make sure that they were removed and that the inside was actually sprayed), the rear hatch's bottom edge, the tailgate, and the wheel-wells. It's also a smart idea to stay at the garage while some of the work is being done to see that the overspray is cleaned up and all areas have been covered.

Surviving the Options Jungle

The best options for your buck are a 5- or 6-speed automatic transmission, an anti-theft immobilizer, air conditioning, a premium sound system, and higher-quality tires—features that may bring back one-third to half their value come trade-in time. Rustproofing can also make cars easier to sell in some provinces where there's lots of salt on the roads in the winter, but paint protection and seat sealants are a waste of money. Most option packages can be cut by 20 percent, while extended warranties are overpriced by about 75 percent.

Dealers make more than three times as much profit selling options as they do selling most cars (50 percent profit versus 15 percent profit). No wonder their eyes light up when you start perusing their options list. If you must have some options, compare prices with independent retailers and buy where the price is lowest and the warranty is the most comprehensive. Buy as few options as possible from the dealer, since you'll get faster service, more comprehensive guarantees, and lower prices from independent suppliers. Remember, extravagantly equipped vehicles hurt your pocketbook in three ways: They cost more to begin with but return only a fraction of what they cost when the car is resold; they drive up maintenance costs; and they often consume extra fuel.

A heavy-duty battery and suspension, and perhaps an upgraded sound system, will generally suffice for American-made vehicles; most imports already come well equipped. An engine block heater with a timer isn't a bad idea, either. It's an inexpensive investment that ensures winter starting and reduces fuel consumption by allowing you to start out with a semi-warm engine.

When ordering parts, remember that purchases from American outlets can be slapped with a small customs duty if the part isn't made in the United States. And then you'll pay the inevitable GST or HST levied on the part's cost and customs duty. Finally, your freight carrier may charge a $15–$20 brokerage fee for representing you at the border.

Smart Options

The problem with options is that you often can't refuse them. Dealers sell very few bare-bones cars and minivans, and they option-pack each vehicle with features that can't be removed. You'll be forced to dicker over the total cost of what you are offered, whether you need the extras or not. So it isn't a case of "yes" or "no," but more a decision of "at what cost?"

Adjustable Pedals and Extensions

This device moves the brake and accelerator pedals forward or backward about 10 cm (4 in.) to accommodate short-statured drivers and protect them from airbag-induced injuries.

If the manufacturer of your vehicle doesn't offer optional power-adjustable pedals, there are several companies selling inexpensive pedal extensions by mail order through the Internet; for example, go to HDS Specialty Vehicles' website at *hdsmn. stores.yahoo.net*. If you live in Toronto or London, Ontario, check out Kino Mobility (*www.kinomobility.com*).

Adjustable Steering Wheel

This option allows easier access to the driver's seat and permits a more-comfortable driving position. It's particularly useful if more than one person will drive the vehicle.

Air Conditioning

AC systems are far more reliable than they were a decade ago, and they have a lifespan of five to seven years. Sure, replacement and repair costs can hit $1,000, but that's very little when amortized over an eight- to 10-year period. AC also makes your car easier to resell.

Does AC waste or conserve fuel when a vehicle is driven at highway speeds? Edmunds, a popular automotive information website, conducted fuel-efficiency tests and concluded that there wasn't that much difference between open or closed windows, a finding confirmed by *Consumer Reports*. See *www.edmunds.com/ advice/fueleconomy/articles/106842/article.html*:

> While the A/C compressor does pull power from the engine wasting some gas, the effect appears to be fairly minimal in modern cars. And putting the windows down tends to increase drag on most cars, canceling out any measurable gain from turning the A/C off. But this depends on the model you're driving. When we opened the sunroof in our SUV, the mileage did decrease even with the A/C off. Still, in our experience, it's not worth the argument because you won't save a lot of gas either way. So just do what's comfortable.

AC provides extra comfort, reduces wind noise (from not having to roll down the windows), and improves window defogging. Factory-installed units are best, however, because you'll get a longer warranty and improve your chances that everything was installed properly.

Anti-Theft Systems

You'd be a fool not to buy an anti-theft system, including a lockable fuel cap, for your Japanese compact or sports car, which are much coveted by thieves. Auto break-ins and thefts cost Canadians more than $400 million annually. There's a one-in-130 chance that your vehicle will be stolen, but only a 60 percent chance that you'll ever get it back.

Since amateurs are responsible for stealing most vehicles, the best theft deterrent is a visible device that complicates the job while immobilizing the vehicle and sounding an alarm. For less than $150, you can install both a steering-wheel lock and a hidden remote-controlled ignition disabler. Satellite tracking systems like GM's OnStar feature are also very effective.

Battery (Heavy-Duty)

The best battery for northern climates is the optional heavy-duty type offered by many manufacturers for about $100. It's a worthwhile purchase, especially for vehicles equipped with lots of electric options. Most standard batteries last only two winters; heavy-duty batteries give you an extra year or two for about 20 percent more than the price of a standard battery.

Make sure your new vehicle comes with a fresh battery—one manufactured less than six months earlier. Batteries are stamped with a date code, either on the battery's case or on an attached label. The vital information is usually in the first two characters—a letter and a numeral. Most codes start with a letter indicating the month: A for January, B for February, and so forth. The numeral denotes the year: Say, 0 for 2000. For example, "B3" stands for February 2003.

Don't order an optional battery with cold cranking amps (CCA) below the one specified for your vehicle, or one rated 200 amps or more above the specified rating. It's a waste of money to go too high. Also, buy a battery with the longest reserve capacity you can find; a longer capacity can make the difference between driving to safety and paying for an expensive tow.

Replacement batteries are very competitively priced and easy to find. Sears' DieHard batteries usually get *Consumer Reports*' top ratings. A useful link for finding the right battery with the most CCA for your car and year is *www. autobatteries.com/basics/selecting.asp*.

Central Locking Control

Costing around $200, this option is most useful for families with small children, car-poolers, or drivers of minivans who can't easily slide across the seat to lock the other doors.

Child Safety Seat (Integrated)

Integrated safety seats are designed to accommodate any child more than one year old or weighing over 9 kg (20 lb.). Since the safety seat is permanently integrated into the seatback, the fuss of installing and removing the safety seat and finding someplace to store it vanishes. When not in use, it quickly folds out of sight, becoming part of the seatback. Two other safety benefits: You know that the seat has been properly installed, and your child gets used to having his or her "special" seat in back, where it's usually safest to sit.

Electronic Stability Control (ESC)

The latest IIHS studies conclude that as many as 10,000 fatal crashes could be prevented if all vehicles were equipped with ESC. Its June 2006 report concluded that stability control is second only to seat belts in saving lives because it reduces the risk of fatal single-vehicle rollovers by 80 percent and the chance of having other kinds of fatal collisions by 43 percent.

Electronic stability control was first used by Mercedes-Benz and BMW on the S-Class and 7 Series models in 1995 and then was featured on GM's 1997 Cadillacs and Corvettes. It helps prevent the loss of control in turns, on slippery roads, or when you must make a sudden steering correction. The system applies the brakes to individual wheels or cuts back the engine power when sensors find the vehicle is beginning to spin or skid. It's particularly useful in maintaining stability with SUVs, but it's less useful with passenger coupes and sedans.

It's worrisome that there won't be any federal standard governing the performance of these systems before 2012, considering that not all electronic stability control systems work as they should. In tests carried out by *Consumer Reports* on 2003 models, the stability control system used in the Mitsubishi Montero was rated "unacceptable," BMW's X5 3.0i system provided poor emergency handling, and Acura's MDX and Subaru's Outback VDC stability systems left much to be desired.

Engines (Cylinder Deactivation)

Choose the most powerful 6- or 8-cylinder engine available if you're going to do a lot of highway driving, if you plan on carrying a full passenger load and luggage on a regular basis, or if you intend to load up the vehicle with convenience features like air conditioning. Keep in mind that minivans, SUVs, and trucks with 6-cylinder or larger engines are easier to resell and retain their value the longest. For example, Honda's '96 Odyssey minivan was a sales dud in spite of its bulletproof reliability, mainly because buyers didn't want a minivan with an underpowered 4-cylinder powerplant. Some people buy underpowered vehicles in the mistaken belief that increased fuel economy is a good trade-off for decreased engine performance. It isn't. That's why there's so much interest in peppy 4-cylinders hooked to 5- or 6-speed transmissions and in larger engines with a "cylinder deactivation" feature.

In fact, cylinder deactivation is one feature that appears more promising than most other fuel-saving add-ons. For example, *AutoWeek* magazine found the overweight Jeep Commander equipped with a "Multiple Displacement System" still managed a respectable 13.8 L/100 km (17 mpg) on the highway in tests published in its March 2006 edition.

Honda employs a similar method, which cuts fuel consumption by 20 percent on the Odyssey. It runs on all six cylinders when accelerating, and on three cylinders when cruising. So far, there have been neither reliability nor performance complaints.

Engine and Transmission Cooling System (Heavy-Duty)

This relatively inexpensive option provides extra cooling for the transmission and engine. It can extend the life of these components by preventing overheating when heavy towing is required. It's a must-have feature for large cars made by Chrysler, Ford, or General Motors.

Extended Warranties

A smart buy if the dealer will discount the price by 50 percent and you're able to purchase the extra powertrain coverage only. However, you are throwing away $1,500–$2,000 if you buy an extended warranty for cars, vans, or trucks rated Recommended in *Lemon-Aid* or for vehicles sold by automakers that have written "goodwill" warranties covering engine and transmission failures. If you can get a great price for a vehicle rated just Average or Above Average but want protection from costly repair bills, patronize garages that offer lifetime warranties on parts listed in this guide as being failure-prone, such as powertrains, exhaust systems, and brakes.

Buy an extended warranty only as a last resort, and make sure you know what it covers and for how long. Budget $1,000 after dealer discounting for the powertrain warranty. Incidentally, auto industry insiders say the average markup on these warranties varies from 50 to 65 percent, which seems almost reasonable when you consider that appliance warranties are marked up from 40 to 80 percent.

Keyless Entry (Remote)

This safety and convenience option saves you from fiddling with your key in a dark parking lot, or taking off a glove in cold weather to unlock or lock the vehicle. Try to get a keyless entry system combined with anti-theft measures such as an ignition kill switch or some other disabler. Incidentally, some automakers no longer make vehicles with an outside key lock on the passenger's side.

 ## Paint Colour

Choosing a popular colour can make your vehicle easier to sell at a good price. DesRosiers Automotive Consultants say that blue is the preferred colour overall, but green and silver are also popular with Canadians. Manheim auctioneers say that green-coloured vehicles brought in 97.9 of the average auction price, while silver ones sold at a premium 105.5 percent. Remember that certain colours require particular care.

Black (and other dark colours): These paints are most susceptible to sun damage because of their heavy absorption of ultraviolet rays.

Pearl-toned colours: These paints are the most difficult to work with. If the paint needs to be retouched, it must be matched to look right from both the front- and side-angle views.

Red: This colour also shows sun damage, so keep your car in a garage or shady spot whenever possible.

White: Although grime looks terrible on a white car, white is the easiest colour to care for. But the colour is also very popular with car thieves, because white vehicles can be easily repainted another colour.

Power-Assisted Sliding Doors, Mirrors, Windows, and Seats

Merely a convenience feature with cars, power-assisted windows and doors are a necessity with minivans—crawling across the front seat a few times to roll up the passenger-side window or to lock the doors will quickly convince you of their value. Power mirrors are convenient on vehicles that have a number of drivers, or on minivans. Power seats with memory are particularly useful, too, if more than one person drives a vehicle. Automatic window and seat controls currently have few reliability problems, and they're fairly inexpensive to install, troubleshoot, and repair. As a safety precaution, make sure the window control has to be lifted. This will ensure no child is strangled from pressing against the switch. Power-sliding doors on minivans are even more of a danger. They are failure-prone on all makes and shouldn't be purchased by families with children.

Side Airbags

A worthwhile feature if you are the right size and properly seated, side airbags are presently overpriced and aren't very effective unless both the head and upper torso are protected. Side airbags are often featured as a $700 add-on to the sticker price, but you would be wise to bargain aggressively.

Suspension (Heavy-Duty)

Always a good idea, this inexpensive option pays for itself by providing better handling, allowing additional ride comfort (though a bit on the firm side), and extending shock life by an extra year or two.

Tires

There are three rules to remember when purchasing tires. First, neither brand name nor price is a reliable gauge of performance, quality, or durability. Second, the cheapest prices are offered by tire discounters like Tire Rack (*www.tirerack. com*), and Discount Tire Direct (*www.discounttiredirect.com*), and their Canadian equivalents like Canadian Tire and TireTrends (*www.tiretrends.com/index.php3*). Third, choosing a tire recommended by the automaker may not be in your best interest, since traction and long tread life are often sacrificed for a softer ride and maximum EPA mileage ratings.

Two types of tires are generally available: all-season and performance. "Touring" is just a fancier name for all-season tires. All-season radial tires cost from $90 to $150 per tire. They're a compromise since, according to Transport Canada, they won't get you through winter with the same margin of safety as snow tires will and they don't provide the same durability on dry surfaces as do regular summer tires. In areas with low to moderate snowfall, however, these tires are adequate as long as they're not pushed beyond their limits.

Mud or snow tires provide the best traction on snowy surfaces, but actually decrease traction on wet roads. Treadwear is also accelerated by the use of softer rubber compounds. Beware of using wide tires for winter driving; 70-series or wider give poor traction and tend to float over snow.

Remember, too, that buying slightly larger wheels and tires may improve handling—but there's a limit. For example, many cars come with 16-inch original equipment (OE) tires supplied by the carmaker. Moving up to a slightly larger size, say a 17-inch wheel, could improve your dry and wet grip handling. Going any larger could have serious downsides, though, like making the vehicle harder to control or more subject to hydroplaning ("floating" over wet surfaces), providing less steering feedback, and causing SUVs and pickups to roll over more easily.

Don't over-inflate tires to lower their rolling resistance for better fuel economy. The trade-off is a harsher ride and increased risk of a blowout when passing over uneven terrain. Excessive tire pressure may also distort the tread, reducing contact with the road and increasing wear in the centre of the tread. Under-inflation is a far more common occurrence. Experts agree that tire life decreases by 10 percent for every 10 percent the tire is under-inflated, sometimes through lack of maintenance or due to the perception that an under-inflated tire improves traction. Actually, an under-inflated tire makes for worse traction. It breaks traction more easily than a tire that is properly inflated, causing skidding, pulling to the side when braking, excessive wheelspin when accelerating, and tire failure due to overheating.

Spare tires

Be wary of space-saver spare tires. They often can't match the promised mileage, and they seriously degrade steering control. Furthermore, they are usually stored in spaces inside the trunk that won't hold a normal-sized tire. The location of the stored spare can also have safety implications. Watch out for spares stowed under the chassis or mounted on the rear hatch. Frequently, the attaching cables and bolts rust out or freeze, so the spare falls off or becomes next to impossible to use when you need it.

Self-sealing and run-flat tires

Today, there are two technologies available to help maintain vehicle mobility when a tire is punctured: self-sealing and self-supporting/run-flat tires.

Self-sealing: Ideal if you drive long distances. Punctures from nails, bolts, or screws up to 3/16 of an inch in diameter are fixed instantly and permanently with a sealant. A low air-pressure warning system isn't required. Expert testers say a punctured self-sealing tire can maintain air pressure for up to 200 km—even in freezing conditions. The Uniroyal Tiger Paw NailGard ($85–$140, depending on the size) is the overall winner in a side-by-side test conducted by Tire Rack (*www. tirerack.com*).

Self-supporting/run-flat: Priced from $175 to $350 per tire, 25 to 50 percent more than the price of comparable premium tires, Goodyear's Extended Mobility Tire (EMT) run-flat tires were first offered as an option on the 1994 Chevrolet Corvette and then became standard on the 1997 model. These tires reinforce the side wall so it can carry the weight of the car for 90 km, or about an hour's driving time, even after all air pressure has been lost. You won't feel the tire go flat; you must depend on a $250–$300 optional tire-pressure monitor to warn you before the side wall collapses and you begin riding on your rim. Also, not all vehicles can adapt to run-flat tires; you may need to upgrade your rims. Experts say run-flats will give your car a harder ride, and you'll likely notice more interior tire and road noise. The car might also track differently. The Sienna's standard Dunlop run-flat tires have a terrible reputation for premature wear. At 25,000 km, one owner complained that her Sienna needed a new set at $200 each. You can expect a backlog of over a month to get a replacement. Goodyear and Pirelli run-flat tires have been on the market for some time now, and they seem to perform adequately.

"Green" tires

No, these tires aren't coloured differently; they're simply tires with a lower rolling resistance that have been proven (through independent tests) to save fuel, which saves you money and contributes to lower greenhouse gas emissions. One recently found fuel-efficient tire that provides good traction, reasonable tread life, and low rolling resistance is the Continental Pro-Contact with EcoPlus.

Michelin's Energy Saver A/S ranks highest for fuel savings; the Cooper GFE also gives good fuel economy, but its overall performance is only average. The Department of Transportation says fuel savings can be substantial, depending on the tire, knocking down fuel consumption by 4 percent in city driving and 7 percent on the highway. *Consumer Reports* magazine pegs the annual savings at $100 per set. Lower rolling resistance tires may also produce less road noise and have a longer tread life.

Nitrogen air refills

The National Highway Traffic Safety Administration (NHTSA) has seen reduced aging of tires filled with nitrogen. Claims have also been made that nitrogen maintains inflation pressure better than air. Though the data technically does support that passenger car tires could benefit from being filled with nitrogen, tire manufacturers say that they already design tires to perform well with air inflation. And while nitrogen will do no harm, manufacturers say that they don't see the need to use nitrogen, which generally adds $5 or more per tire charge.

Consumer Reports says consumers can use nitrogen and might enjoy the slight improvement in air retention provided, but you can do just as well without paying an extra penny by performing regular inflation checks.

Which tires are best?

There is no independent Canadian agency that evaluates tire performance and durability. However, the U.S.-based NHTSA rates treadwear, traction, and resistance to sustained high temperatures; etches the ratings onto the side walls of all tires sold in the States and Canada; and regularly posts its findings on the Internet (*www.safercar.gov*). NHTSA also logs owner complaints relative to different brands. *Lemon-Aid* summarizes these complaints in the ratings of specific models in Part Three.

You can get more-recent complaint postings, service bulletins, and tire recall notices at the same government website. Check out independent owner performance ratings as compiled by Tire Rack, a large tire retailer, at *www.tirerack.com/ tires/surveyresults/index.jsp*.

Traction Control

This option limits wheelspin when accelerating. It is most useful with rear-drive vehicles and provides surer traction in wet or icy conditions.

Trailer-Towing Equipment

Just because you need a vehicle with towing capability doesn't mean that you have to spend big bucks. But you should first determine what kind of vehicle you want to do the job and whether your tires will handle the extra burden. For most towing needs (up to 900 kg/2,000 lb.), a passenger car, small pickup, or minivan equipped with a 6-cylinder engine will work just as well as a full-sized pickup or van (and will cost much less). If you're pulling a trailer that weighs more than 900 kg, most passenger cars won't handle the load unless they've been specially outfitted according to the automaker's specifications. Pulling a heavier trailer (up to 1,800 kg/4,000 lb.) will likely require a large vehicle equipped with a V8 powerplant.

Automakers reserve the right to change limits whenever they feel like it, so make any sales promise about towing an integral part of your contract. A good rule of thumb is to reduce the promised tow rating by 20 percent. In assessing towing weight, factor in the cargo, passengers, and equipment of both the trailer and the towing vehicle. Keep in mind that five people and luggage add 450 kg (almost 1,000 lb.) to the load, and that a full 227L (60 gal.) water tank adds another 225 kg (almost 500 lb.). The manufacturer's gross vehicle weight rating (GVWR) takes into account the anticipated average cargo and supplies that your vehicle is likely to carry.

Automatic transmissions are fine for trailering, although there's a slight fuel penalty. Manual transmissions tend to have greater clutch wear caused by towing than do automatic transmissions. Both transmission choices are equally acceptable. Remember, the best compromise is to shift the automatic manually for maximum performance going uphill and to maintain control while not overheating the brakes when descending mountains.

Unibody vehicles (those without a separate frame) can handle most towing chores as long as their limits aren't exceeded. Front-drives aren't the best choice for pulling heavy loads in excess of 900 kg, since they lose some steering control and traction with all the weight concentrated in the rear.

Whatever vehicle you choose, keep in mind that the trailer hitch is crucial. It must have a tongue capacity of at least 10 percent of the trailer's weight; otherwise, it may be unsafe to use. Hitches are chosen according to the type of tow vehicle and, to a lesser extent, the weight of the load.

Most hitches are factory-installed, even though independents can install them more cheaply. Expect to pay about $200 for a simple boat hitch and a minimum of $600 for a fifth-wheel version.

Equalizer bars and extra cooling systems for the radiator, transmission, engine oil, and steering are prerequisites for towing anything heavier than 900 kg. Heavy-duty springs and brakes are a big help, too. Separate brakes for the trailer may be necessary to increase your vehicle's maximum towing capacity.

Transmissions

Despite its many advantages, the manual transmission is an endangered species in North America, where manuals equip only 8–10 percent of all new vehicles (mostly econocars, sports cars, and budget trucks), and that figure is slated to fall to 6 percent this year as more vehicles adopt fuel-saving CVT transmissions, among other powertrain innovations. One theory on why the manual numbers keep falling: North American drivers are too busy with cell phones, text messaging, and cappuccinos to shift gears. Interestingly, European buyers opt for a manual transmission almost 90 percent of the time. (And they also drink cappuccinos, but usually not in 20 oz. paper takeout cups.)

Automakers are currently offering hybrid manumatic transmissions that provide the benefits of an automatic transmission while also giving the driver the NASCAR-styled fun of clutchless manual shifting. Or, if all you want is fuel savings, there are now 5- and 6-speed automatic models—and even 7- and 8-speed versions—that are fuel-sippers.

Some considerations: The brake pads on stick-shift vehicles tend to wear out less rapidly than those on automatics do; a transmission with five or more forward speeds is usually more fuel-efficient than one with three forward speeds (hardly seen anymore); and manual transmissions usually add a mile or two per gallon over automatics, although this isn't always the case, as *Consumer Reports* recently discovered. Their road tests found that the 2008 Toyota Yaris equipped with an automatic transmission got slightly better gas mileage than a Yaris powered by a manual tranny.

Unnecessary Options

All-Wheel Drive (AWD)

Mark Bilek, editorial director of *Consumer Guide*'s automotive website (*consumerguideauto.howstuffworks.com*), is a critic of AWD. He says AWD systems generally encourage drivers to go faster than they should in adverse conditions, which creates trouble stopping in emergencies. Automakers like AWD as "a marketing ploy to make more money," Bilek contends. My personal mechanic adds, "Four-wheel drive will only get you stuck deeper, farther from home."

Anti-Lock Brakes (ABS)

Like adaptive cruise control and backup warning devices, ABS is another safety feature that's fine in theory but mostly impractical under actual driving conditions. (If you want the highly recommended electronic stability control (ESC), you must use anti-lock brakes.) The system maintains directional stability by preventing the wheels from locking up. This will not reduce the stopping distance, however. In practice, ABS is said to make drivers overconfident. Many still pump the brakes and render them ineffective; total brake failure is common; and repairs are frequent, complicated, and expensive to perform.

Take the Toyota Yaris, for example. *Lemon-Aid* has learned from Canadian readers, American owners posting safety complaints on NHTSA's website, Toyota owner forms, and Toyota's own internal service bulletins that the 2007 and 2008 Yaris has serious ABS brake defects caused by faulty sensors.

Here's how T. D., a 2007 Yaris owner from Trenton, Ontario, describes the defect:

> Hi Phil. Toyota NEEDS an additional recall for ABS braking system on Yaris. Please help!
>
> Toyota appears to be ignoring a very large manufacturing problem that is directly affecting Toyota Yaris owners having to compromise their safety over the price of the repair of the housing unit/sensors/wires/harness (priced at over $1,200 per affected side). The problems appear to be within the sensor circuits, as the current housing units do not protect the circuits from the harsh Canadian winter exposure, therefore leading to corrosion of the wires and circuits and thereby leading to the replacement of the entire wheelbearing (sensor is built in the wheelbearing and cannot be replaced seperately). Thankfully, I found *www.yarisworld.com/forums/showthread.php?t=11533&highlight=rear+sensor&page=11*, and multiple other additional threads located on the *yarisworld.com* site. I have been able to have my local mechanic provide a simple, inexpensive fix ($60) for my left rear sensor, however, my right rear sensor is too far gone and needs to be replaced, for which after-market parts do not exist as of yet.
>
> I have contacted Toyota Canada, and they will provide $100 towards the repair if done by the dealership... I refuse to cooperate with the "steal-ership" any longer as they refused to admit this was a systemic/model problem and my local mechanic has gone above and beyond in researching this dilemma and repairing the flaw that has existed since I bought my car brand new.
>
> Toyota is well aware of this problem, as evident with this release, *www.etimago.com/yaris/TSB/T-SB-0120-08%20%28ABS%20M.I.L.%20ON%20DTC%20C0210%20or%20C0215%29.pdf*. However, as it states, it is only for vehicles under warranty. I bought this car for the fuel mileage... I drive A LOT and am well over the 36,000-mile [58,000-kilometre] warranty, however, I have only had this car (bought brand new off the lot) for less then three years.
>
> I have also filed a complaint with Transport Canada in regards to this safety issue, as most, according to the forum *yarisworld.com* (search "rear sensor" or "ABS brake and emergency light"), are choosing to ignore the warning lights and continue driving their vehicles without the ABS...which is fine, but there are reported cases on this site stating that the brakes are also "becoming soft" and are failing or "kicking on" at inappropriate times.

Cruise Control

Automakers provide this $250–$300 option, which is mainly a convenience feature, to motorists who use their vehicles for long periods of high-speed driving. The constant rate of speed saves some fuel and lessens driver fatigue during long trips. Still, the system is particularly failure-prone and expensive to repair, can lead to driver inattention, and can make the vehicle hard to control on icy roadways. Malfunctioning cruise-control units are also one of the major causes of sudden acceleration incidents. At other times, cruise control can be very distracting, especially to inexperienced drivers who are unaccustomed to sudden speed fluctuations.

Adaptive cruise control is the latest evolution of this feature. It senses a vehicle ahead of you and then automatically downshifts, brakes, or cuts your vehicle's speed. This commonly occurs when passing another car or when a car passes you, and it can make for a harrowing experience...especially when you are in the passing lane.

Electronic Instrument Readout

If you've ever had trouble reading a digital watch face or resetting your VCR, you'll feel right at home with this electronic gizmo. Gauges are presented in a series of moving digital patterns that are confusing, distracting, and unreadable in direct sunlight. This system is often accompanied by a trip computer and vehicle monitor that indicate average speed, signal component failures, and determine fuel use and how many kilometres you can drive until the tank is empty. Figures are frequently in error or slow to catch up.

Fog Lights

A pain in the eyes for some, a pain in the wallet for others, who have to pay the high bulb replacement costs. Fog lights aren't necessary for most drivers who have well-aimed original-equipment headlights on their vehicles.

Gas-Saving Gadgets and Fuel Additives

Ah, the search for the Holy Grail. Magic software and miracle hardware that will turn your gas-hungry Hummer into a fuel-frugal Prius when the right additive is poured into your fuel tank.

The accessory market has been flooded with hundreds of atomizers, magnets, and additives that purport to make vehicles less fuel-thirsty. However, tests on over 100 gadgets and fuel or crankcase additives carried out by the U.S. Environmental Protection Agency have found that only a handful produce an increase in fuel economy, and the increase is tiny. These gadgets include warning devices that tell the driver to ease up on the throttle or shift to a more fuel-frugal gear, hardware that reduces the engine power needed for belt-driven accessories, cylinder deactivation systems, and spoilers that channel airflow under the car. The use of any of these products is a quick way to lose warranty coverage and fail provincial emissions tests.

GPS Navigation Systems

This navigation aid links a Global Positioning System (GPS) satellite unit to the vehicle's cellular phone and electronics. Good GPS devices cost $125–$1,500 (U.S.) when bought from an independent retailer. As a dealer option, you will pay $1,000–$2,000 (U.S.). For a monthly fee, the unit connects drivers to live operators who will help them with driving directions, give repair or emergency assistance, or relay messages. If the airbag deploys or the car is stolen, satellite-transmitted signals are automatically sent from the vehicle to operators who will notify the proper authorities of the vehicle's location.

Many of the systems' functions can be performed by a cellular telephone, and the navigation screens may be obtrusive, distracting, washed out in sunlight, and hard to calibrate. A portable Garmin GPS unit is more user-friendly and much cheaper.

High-Intensity Headlights

These headlights are much brighter than standard headlights, and they cast a blue hue. Granted, they provide additional illumination of the roadway, but they are also annoying to other drivers, who will flash their lights—or give you the middle finger—thinking that your high beams are on. These lights are easily stolen and expensive to replace. Interestingly, European versions have a device to maintain the light's spread closer to the road so that other drivers aren't blinded.

ID Etching

This $150–$200 option is a scam. The government doesn't require it, and thieves and joyriders aren't deterred by the etchings. If you want to etch your windows for your own peace of mind, several private companies will sell you a $15–$30 kit that does an excellent job (try *www.autoetch.net*), or you can wait for your municipality or local police agency to conduct one of their periodic free VIN ID etching sessions in your area.

Paint and Fabric Protectors

Selling for $200–$300, these "sealants" add nothing to a vehicle's resale value. Although paint lustre may be temporarily heightened, this treatment is less effective and more costly than regular waxing, and it may also invalidate the manufacturer's guarantee at a time when the automaker will look for any pretext to deny your paint claim.

Auto fabric protection products are nothing more than variations of Scotchgard, which can be bought in aerosol cans for a few dollars—a much better deal than the $50–$75 charged by dealers.

Power-Assisted Minivan Sliding Doors

Not a good idea if you have children. These doors have a high failure rate, opening or closing for no apparent reason and injuring children caught between the door and post.

Reverse-Warning System

Selling for about $500 as part of an option package, this safety feature warns the driver of any objects in the rear when backing up. Although a sound idea in theory, in practice the device often fails to go off or sounds an alarm for no reason. Drivers eventually either disconnect or ignore it.

Rollover-Detection System

This feature makes use of sensors to determine if the vehicle has leaned beyond a safe angle. If so, the side airbags are automatically deployed and remain inflated to make sure occupants aren't injured or ejected in a rollover accident. This is a totally new system that has not yet been proven. It could have disastrous consequences if the sensor malfunctions, as has been the case with front and side airbag sensors over the past decade.

Rooftop Carrier

Although this inexpensive option provides additional baggage space and may allow you to meet all your driving needs with a smaller vehicle, a loaded roof rack can increase fuel consumption by as much as 18 percent. An empty rack can increase your gas bill by about 10 percent.

Sunroof

Unless you live in a temperate region, the advantages of having a sunroof are far outweighed by the disadvantages. You aren't going to get better ventilation than a good AC system would provide, and a sunroof may grace your environment with painful booming wind noises, rattles, water leaks, and road dust accumulation. A sunroof increases gas consumption, reduces night vision because overhead highway lights shine through the roof opening, and can lose you several centimetres of headroom.

Tinted Glass

On the one hand, tinting jeopardizes safety by reducing your night vision. On the other hand, it does keep the interior cool in hot weather, reduces glare, and hides the car's contents from prying eyes. Factory applications are worth the extra cost, since cheaper aftermarket products (costing about $150) distort visibility and peel away after a few years. Some tinting done in the United States can run afoul of provincial highway codes that require more transparency.

Cutting the Price

 ## Bidding by Fax or Email

The process is quite easy: Simply fax or email an invitation for bids to area dealerships, asking them to give their bottom-line price for a specific make and model. Be clear that all final bids must be sent within a week. When all the bids are received, the lowest bid is sent to the other dealers to give them a chance to beat that price. After a week of bidding, the lowest price gets your business. Incidentally, with the Canadian loonie headed to parity with the American dollar, try doing an Internet search for American prices and then using that lower figure to haggle with Canadian dealers.

SAMPLE FAX/EMAIL BID REQUEST

WITHOUT PREJUDICE

Date: _____

Dear Sir or Madam,

I will be purchasing a new 2012 Toyota Sienna or a new 2012 Honda Odyssey and am issuing a request for quotation to several dealerships. I am willing to travel to complete a deal.

The quoted price is to *include* my requested options as well as any applicable pre-delivery inspection, administration, documentation, freight, and delivery fees. I understand that tire tax, air conditioning tax, battery tax, and provincial and federal sales tax are extra and are not required on your quotation. The dealer may sell off the lot or order the vehicle.

Please complete the attached form and either fax or email it back to me before the deadline of *5:00 pm, April 14, 2012*. All respondents will be contacted after the deadline to confirm their bid. The winning bidder will then be contacted soon after to complete the transaction.

I will accept an alternate price quotation for a demonstration model with similar options, but this is not a mandatory requirement.

Please direct any questions via email to me at _____ and I will respond promptly. Alternately you may call me at my office at _____.

Sincerely,
Joe Buyer

Dozens of *Lemon-Aid* readers have told me how this bidding approach has cut thousands of dollars from the advertised price and saved them from the degrading song-and-dance routine between the buyer, sales agent, and sales manager ("he said, she said, the sales manager said").

A *Lemon-Aid* reader sent in the following suggestions for buying by fax or email:

> First, I'd like to thank you for writing the *Lemon-Aid* series of books, which I have used extensively in the fax-tendering purchase of my '99 Accord and '02 Elantra. I have written evidence from dealers that I saved a bare minimum of $700 on the Accord (but probably more) and a whopping $900 on the Elantra through the use of fax-tendering, over and above any deals possible through Internet-tendering and/or showroom bargaining.
>
> Based on my experience, I would suggest that in reference to the fax-tendering [or email-tendering] process, future *Lemon-Aid* editions emphasize:
>
> • Casting a wide geographical net, as long as you're willing to pick the car up there. I faxed up to 50 dealerships, which helped tremendously in increasing the number of serious bidders. One car was bought locally in Ottawa, the other in Mississauga.
> • Unless you don't care much about what car you end up with, be very specific about what you want. If you are looking at just one or two cars, which I recommend, specify trim level and all extended warranties and dealer-installed options in the fax letter. Otherwise, you'll end up with quotes comparing apples and oranges, and you won't get the best deal on options negotiated later. Also, specify that quotes should be signed. This helps out with errors in quoting.
> • Dealerships are sloppy: there is a 25–30 percent error rate in quotes. Search for errors and get corrections, and confirm any of the quotes in serious contention over the phone.
> • Phone to personally thank anyone who submits a quote for their time. Salespeople can't help themselves, they'll ask how they ranked, and often want to then beat the best quote you've got. This is much more productive than faxing back the most competitive quote (I know, I've tried that too).

Getting a Fair Price

"We Sell Below Cost"

This is no longer a bait-and-switch scam. Many dealers who are going out of business are desperate to sell their inventory, sometimes for 40 percent below the MSRP. Assuming the vehicle's cost price was 20 percent under the MSRP, astute buyers are getting up to a 20 percent discount. The chart lists the profit margins for various vehicle categories, excluding freight, PDI, and administrative fees, which you should bargain down or not pay at all. In addition to the dealer's markup, some vehicles may also have a 3 percent carryover allowance paid out in a dealer incentive program. Finance contracts may also tack on a 2 percent dealer commission.

DEALER MARKUP

DEALER MARKUP (AMERICAN VEHICLES)		DEALER MARKUP (JAPANESE VEHICLES)	
Small cars:	10%–12%	Small cars:	10%
Mid-sized cars:	13%–15%	Mid-sized cars:	11%–13%
Large cars:	16%–18%	Large cars:	15%
Sports cars:	15%–20%	Sports cars:	15%–20%
High-end sports cars:	20+%	High-end sports cars:	20+%
Luxury cars:	20+%	Luxury cars:	20+%
High-end luxury cars:	20+%	High-end luxury cars:	20+%
Minivans:	15%	Minivans:	12%–15%
High-end minivans:	16%–20%	High-end minivans:	15%–17%

Holdback

Ever wonder how dealers who advertise vehicles for "a hundred dollars over invoice" can make a profit? They are counting mostly on the manufacturer's holdback.

In addition to the MSRP, the invoice price, dealer incentives, and customer rebates (available to Canadians at *www.apa.ca*), another key element in every dealer's profit margin is the manufacturer's holdback—the quarterly payouts dealers depend on when calculating gross profit.

The holdback was set up over 45 years ago by General Motors as a guaranteed profit for dealers tempted to bargain away their entire profit to make a sale. It usually represents 1–3 percent of the sticker price (MSRP) and is seldom given out by Asian or European automakers, which use dealer incentive programs instead. There are several free Internet sources for holdback information: The most recent and comprehensive are *www.edmunds.com* and *www.kbb.com*, two websites geared toward American buyers. Although there may be a difference in the holdback percentage between American automakers and their Canadian subsidiaries, it's usually not significant.

Some GM dealers maintain that they no longer get a holdback allowance. They are being disingenuous—the holdback may have been added to special sales "incentive" programs, which won't show up on the dealer's invoice. Options are the icing on the cake, with their average 35–65 percent markup.

Can You Get a Fair Price?

Yes, but you'll have to keep your wits about you and time your purchase well into the model year—usually in late winter or spring.

New-car negotiations aren't wrestling matches where you have to pin the sales agent's shoulders to the mat to win. If you feel that the overall price is fair, don't jeopardize the deal by refusing to budge. For example, if you've brought the contract price 10 percent or more below the MSRP and the dealer sticks you with a $200 "administrative fee" at the last moment, let it pass. You've saved money and the sales agent has saved face.

Of course, someone will always be around to tell you how he or she could have bought the vehicle for much less. Let that pass, too.

To come up with a fair price, subtract two-thirds of the dealer's markup from the MSRP and then trade the carryover and holdback allowance for a reduced delivery and transportation fee. Compute the options separately, and sell your trade-in privately. Buyers can more easily knock $4,000 off a $20,000 base price if they shop early in the year, when Chrysler and GM hold their new year "fire" sales and ratchet up the competition. Remember, choose a vehicle that's in stock, and resist getting unnecessary options.

Beware of Financing and Insurance Traps

Once you and the dealer have settled on the vehicle's price, you aren't out of the woods yet. You'll be handed over to an F&I (financing and insurance) specialist, whose main goal is to convince you to buy additional financing, loan insurance, paint and seat cover protectors, rustproofing, and extended warranties. These items will be presented on a computer screen as costing only "a little bit more each month."

Compare the dealer's insurance and financing charges with those from an independent agency that may offer better rates and better service. Often, the dealer gets a kickback for selling insurance and financing. And guess who pays for it? Additionally, remember that if the financing rate looks too good to be true, you're probably paying too much for the vehicle. The F&I closer's hard-sell approach will take all your willpower and patience to resist, but when he or she gives up, your trials are over.

Add-on charges are the dealer's last chance to stick it to you before the contract is signed. Dealer pre-delivery inspection (PDI) and transportation charges, "documentation" fees, and extra handling costs are ways that the dealer gets extra profits for nothing. Dealer preparation is often a once-over-lightly affair, with a car seldom getting more than a wash job and a couple of dollars' worth of gas in the tank. It's paid for by the factory in most cases, but when it's not, it should cost no more than 2 percent of the car's selling price. Reasonable transportation charges are acceptable, although dealers who claim that the manufacturer requires the payment often inflate them.

"No Haggle" Pricing

All dealers bargain. They hang out the "No dickering; one price only" sign simply as a means to discourage customers from asking for a better deal. Like parking lots and restaurants that claim they won't be responsible for lost or stolen property, they're bluffing. Still, you'd be surprised by how many people believe that if it's posted, it's non-negotiable.

Price Guidelines

When negotiating the price of a new vehicle, remember that there are several price guidelines and dealers use the one that will make them the most profit on each transaction. Two of the more-common prices quoted are the MSRP (what the automaker advertises as a fair price) and the dealer's invoice cost (which is supposed to indicate how much the dealer paid for the vehicle). Both price indicators leave considerable room for the dealer's profit margin, along with some extra padding in the form of inflated transportation and preparation charges. If you are presented with both figures, go with the MSRP, since it can be verified by calling the manufacturer. Any dealer can print up an invoice and swear to its veracity. If you want an invoice price from an independent source, contact *www. apa.ca* or *www.carhelpcanada.com*.

Buyers who live in rural areas or in western Canada are often faced with grossly inflated auto prices compared to those charged in major metropolitan areas. A good way to get a more-competitive price without buying out of province is to check online to see what prices are being charged in different urban areas. Show the dealer printouts that list selling prices, preparation charges, and transportation fees, and then ask for his or her price to come closer to the advertised prices.

Another tactic is to take a copy of a local competitor's car ad to a competing dealer selling the same brand and ask for a better price. Chances are they've already lost a few sales due to the ad and will work a little harder to match the deal; if not, they're almost certain to reveal the tricks in the competitor's promotion to make the sale.

Dealer Incentives and Customer Rebates

Sales incentives haven't changed much in the past 30 years. When vehicles are first introduced in the fall, they're generally overpriced; early in the new year, they'll sell for about 20–30 percent less. After a year, they may sell for less through a combination of dealer sales incentives (manufacturer-to-dealer), cash rebates (manufacturer-to-customer), zero percent interest financing (manufacturer's-finance-company-to-customer), and discounted prices (dealer-to-customer).

In most cases, the manufacturer's rebate is straightforward and mailed directly to the buyer from the automaker. There are other rebate programs that require a financial investment on the dealer's part, however, and these shared programs tempt dealers to offset losses by inflating the selling price or pocketing the manufacturer's rebate. Therefore, when the dealer participates in the rebate program, demand that the rebate be deducted from the MSRP, not from some inflated invoice price concocted by the dealer.

Some rebate ads will include the phrase "from dealer inventory only." So if your dealer doesn't have the vehicle in stock, you won't get the rebate.

Sometimes automakers will suddenly decide that a rebate no longer applies to a specific model, even though their ads continue to include it. When this happens, take all brochures and advertisements showing your eligibility for the rebate plan to provincial consumer protection officials. They can use false advertising statutes to force automakers to give rebates to every purchaser who was unjustly denied one.

If you are buying a heavily discounted vehicle, be wary of "option packaging" by dealers who push unwanted protection packages (rustproofing, paint sealants, and upholstery finishes) or who levy excessive charges for preparation, filing fees, loan guarantee insurance, and credit life insurance.

Prices Go Up; Prices Go Down

This year, the best prices will come early in the first quarter of 2012 and will continue through the summer. This includes Ford's re-engineered, highly recommended 2011 and 2012 Mustang, which will likely have had its first-year factory-related deficiencies corrected on the 2012. On the other hand, if your choice has an unusually low sticker price, find out why it's so unpopular and then decide if the savings are worth it. Vehicles that don't sell because of their weird styling are no problem, but poor quality control (think Chrysler's cars and some Kias) can cost you big bucks.

Leftovers

The 2011 leftovers started to be picked clean when the 2012s arrived in September. They could be good buys, assuming you can still get one, if you can amortize the first year's depreciation by keeping the vehicle for eight years or more. But if you're the kind of driver who trades every two or three years, you're likely to come out a loser by buying an end-of-the-season vehicle. The simple reason is that, as far as trade-ins are concerned, a leftover is a "used" vehicle that has depreciated at least 20 percent in its first year. The savings the dealer gives you may not equal that first year's depreciation (a cost you'll incur without getting any of the first year's driving benefits). If the dealer's discounted price matches or exceeds the 30 percent depreciation, you're getting a pretty good deal.

 Ask the dealer for all work orders relating to the leftover vehicle, including the PDI checklist, and make sure that the odometer readings follow in sequential order. Remember as well that most demonstrators should have less than 5,000 km on the ticker and that the original warranty has been reduced from the day the vehicle was first put on the road. Also, make sure the vehicle is relatively "fresh" (about three months old) and check for warranty damage. With demos, have the dealer extend the warranty or lower the price about $100 for each month of warranty that has expired. If the vehicle's file shows that it was registered to a leasing agency or any other third party, you're definitely buying a used vehicle disguised as a demo. You should walk away from the sale—you're dealing with a crook.

Cash versus Financing

Up until recently, car dealers preferred financing car sales instead of getting cash, because of the 1–2 percent kickbacks lenders gave them. This is less the case now, because fewer companies are lending money, and those that do are giving back very little to dealers and don't want to give loans for more than two-thirds of the purchase price. Dealers are scrambling for equity and will sell their vehicles for less than what they cost if the buyer pays cash. Cash is, once again, king.

If you aren't offered much of a discount for cash, financial planners say it can be smarter to finance the purchase of a new vehicle if a portion of the interest is tax-deductible. The cash that you free up can then be used to repay debts that aren't tax-deductible (mortgages or credit card debts, for example).

Rebates versus Low or Zero Percent Financing

Low-financing programs have the following disadvantages:

- Buyers must have exceptionally good credit.
- Shorter financing periods mean higher payments.
- Cash rebates are excluded.
- Only fully equipped or slow-selling models are eligible.
- Buyers pay full retail price.

The above stipulations can add thousands of dollars to your costs. Remember, to get the best price, first negotiate the price of the vehicle without disclosing whether you are paying cash or financing the purchase (say you haven't yet decided). Once you have a fair price, you can then take advantage of the financing.

Getting a Loan

Borrowers must be at least 18 years old (the age of majority), have a steady income, prove that they have discretionary income sufficient to make the loan payments, and be willing to guarantee the loan with additional collateral or with a parent or spouse as a co-signer.

Before applying for a loan, you should have established a good credit rating via a paid-off credit card and have a small savings account with your local bank, credit union, or trust company. Prepare a budget listing your assets and obligations. This will quickly show whether or not you can afford a car. Next, prearrange your loan with a phone call. This will protect you from much of the smoke-and-mirrors showroom shenanigans.

Incidentally, if you do get in over your head and require credit counselling, contact Credit Counselling Service (CCS), a not-for-profit organization located in many of Canada's major cities (*www.creditcanada.com*).

 ## Hidden Loan Costs

The APA's undercover shoppers have found that most deceptive deals involve major banking institutions rather than automaker-owned companies.

In your quest for an auto loan, remember that the Internet offers help for people who need an auto loan and want quick approval, but don't want to face a banker. The Bank of Montreal (*www.bmo.com*), RBC (*www.rbc.com*), and other banks allow vehicle buyers to post loan applications on their websites. Loans are available to any web surfer, including those who aren't current BMO or RBC customers.

Be sure to call various financial institutions to find out the following:

- The annual percentage rate on the amount you want to borrow, and the duration of your repayment period
- The minimum down payment that the institution requires
- Whether taxes and licence fees are considered part of the overall cost and, thus, are covered by part of the loan
- Whether lower rates are available for different loan periods, or for a larger down payment
- Whether discounts are available to depositors, and if so, how long you must be a depositor before qualifying

When comparing loans, consider the annual rate and then calculate the total cost of the loan offer—that is, how much you'll pay above and beyond the total price of the vehicle.

Dealers may be able to finance your purchase at interest rates that are competitive with the banks' because of the rebates they get from the manufacturers and some lending institutions. Don't believe dealers that say they can borrow money at as much as five percentage points below the prime rate. Actually, they're jacking up the retail price to more than make up for the lower interest charges. Sometimes, instead of boosting the price, dealers reduce the amount they pay for the trade-in. In either case, the savings are illusory.

When dealing with banks, keep in mind that the traditional 36-month loan has now been stretched to 48 or 60 months. Longer payment terms make each month's payment more affordable, but over the long run, they increase the cost of the loan considerably. Therefore, take as short a term as possible.

Be wary of lending institutions that charge a "processing" or "document" fee ranging from $25 to $100. Sometimes consumers will be charged an extra 1–2 percent of the loan up front in order to cover servicing. This is similar to lending institutions adding "points" to mortgages, except that with auto loans, it's totally unjustified. In fact, dealers in the States are the object of several state lawsuits and class actions for inflating loan charges.

Some banks will cut the interest rate if you're a member of an automobile owners' association or if loan payments are automatically deducted from your chequing account. This latter proposal may be costly, however, if the chequing account charges exceed the interest-rate savings.

Loan Protection

Credit insurance guarantees that the vehicle loan will be paid if the borrower becomes disabled or dies. There are three basic types of insurance that can be written into an installment contract: credit life, accident and health, and comprehensive. Some car companies, like Hyundai, will make some of your loan payments if you become unemployed. Most bank and credit union loans are already covered by some kind of loan insurance, but dealers sell the protection separately at an extra cost to the borrower. For this service, the dealer gets a hefty 20 percent commission. The additional cost to the purchaser can be significant. The federal GST is applied to loan insurance, but RST may be exempted in some provinces.

Collecting on these types of policies isn't easy. There's no payment if your unemployment was due to your own conduct or if an illness is caused by some condition that existed prior to your taking out the insurance. Generally, credit insurance is unnecessary if you're in good health, you have no dependants, and your job is secure. Nevertheless, if you need to cancel your financial obligations, the same company that started up LeaseBusters now offers FinanceBusters (*www. financebusters.com*). They provide a similar service to a lease takeover, but for customers who have vehicle loans.

Personal loans from financial institutions (particularly credit unions) now offer lots of flexibility, like fixed or variable interest rates, a choice of loan terms, and no penalties for prepayment. Precise conditions depend on your personal credit rating.

Leasing contracts are less flexible. There's a penalty for any prepayment, and rates aren't necessarily competitive.

Financing Scam: "Your Financing Was Turned Down"

This may be true, now that credit has become more difficult to get. But watch out for the scam that begins after you have purchased a vehicle and left your trade-in with the dealer. A few days later, you are told that your loan was rejected and that you now must put down a larger down payment and accept a higher monthly payment. Of course, your trade-in has already been sold.

Protect yourself from this rip-off by getting a signed agreement that stipulates that financing has been approved and that monthly payments can't be readjusted. Tell the dealer that your trade-in cannot be sold until the deal has closed.

The Contract

How likely are you to be cheated when buying a new car or truck? APA staffers posing as buyers visited 42 dealerships in four Canadian cities in early 2002. Almost half the dealers they visited (45 percent) flunked their test, and (hold onto your cowboy hats) auto buyers in western Canada were especially vulnerable to dishonest dealers. Either dealer ads left out important information or vehicles in the ads weren't available or were selling at higher prices. Fees for paperwork and vehicle preparation were frequently excessive.

Now, 10 years later, we know dealers are much more honest. Ahem…maybe.

The Devil's in the Details

Watch what you sign, since any document that requires your signature is a contract. Don't sign anything unless all the details are clear to you and all the blanks have been filled in. Don't accept any verbal promises that you're merely putting the vehicle on hold. And when you are presented with a contract, remember it doesn't have to include all the clauses found in the dealer's pre-printed form. You and the sales representative can agree to strike some clauses and add others.

When the sales agent asks for a deposit, make sure that it's listed on the contract as a deposit, try to keep it as small as possible (a couple hundred dollars at the most), and pay for it by credit card—in case the dealer goes belly up. If you decide to back out of the deal on a vehicle taken from stock, let the seller have the deposit as an incentive to cancel the contract (believe me, it's cheaper than hiring a lawyer and probably equal to the dealer's commission).

Scrutinize all references to the exact model (there's a heck of an upgrade from base to LX or Limited), prices, and delivery dates. Make sure you specify a delivery date in the contract that protects the price.

Contract Clauses You Need

You can put things on a more-equal footing by negotiating the inclusion of as many clauses as possible from the sample additional contract clauses found on the following page. To do this, write in a "Remarks" section on your contract and then add, "See attached clauses, which form part of this agreement." Then attach a photocopy of the "Additional Contract Clauses" and persuade the sales agent to initial as many of the clauses as possible. Although some clauses may be rejected, the inclusion of just a couple of them can have important legal ramifications later on if you want a full or partial refund.

ADDITIONAL CONTRACT CLAUSES

1. **Original contract:** This is the ONLY contract; i.e., it cannot be changed, retyped, or rewritten, without the specific agreement of both parties.

2. **Financing:** This agreement is subject to the purchaser obtaining financing at _____% or less within _____ days of the date below.

3. **"In-service" date and mileage:** To be based on the closing day, not the day the contract was executed, and will be submitted to the automaker for warranty and all other purposes. The dealership will have this date corrected by the automaker if it should become necessary.

4. **Delivery:** The vehicle is to be delivered by _____, failing which the contract is cancelled and the deposit will be refunded.

5. **Cancellation:**
   (a) The purchaser retains the right to cancel this agreement without penalty at any time before delivery of the vehicle by sending a notice in writing to the vendor.
   (b) Following delivery of the vehicle, the purchaser shall have two days to return the vehicle and cancel the agreement in writing, without penalty. After two days and before thirty-one days, the purchaser shall pay the dealer $25 a day as compensation for depreciation on the returned vehicle.
   (c) Cancellation of contract can be refused where the vehicle has been subjected to abuse, negligence or unauthorized modifications after delivery.
   (d) The purchaser is responsible for accident damage and traffic violations while in possession of the said vehicle.

6. **Protected price:** The vendor agrees not to alter the price of the new vehicle, the cost of preparation, or the cost of shipping.

7. **Trade-in:** The vendor agrees that the value attributed to the vehicle offered in trade shall not be reduced, unless it has been significantly modified or has suffered from unreasonable and accelerated deterioration since the signing of the agreement.

8. **Courtesy car:**
   (a) In the event the new vehicle is not delivered on the agreed-upon date, the vendor agrees to supply the purchaser with a courtesy car at no cost. If no courtesy vehicle is available, the vendor agrees to reimburse the purchaser the cost of renting a vehicle.
   (b) If the vehicle is off the road for more than two days for warranty repairs, the purchaser is entitled to a free courtesy vehicle for the duration of the repair period. If no courtesy vehicle is available, the vendor agrees to reimburse the purchaser the cost of renting a vehicle of equivalent or lesser value.

9. **Work orders:** The purchaser will receive duly completed copies of all work orders pertaining to the vehicle, including warranty repairs and the pre-delivery inspection (PDI).

10. **Dealer stickers:** The vendor will not affix any dealer advertising, in any form, on the vehicle.

11. **Fuel:** Vehicle will be delivered with a free full tank of gas.

12. **Excess mileage:** New vehicle will not be acceptable and the contract will be void if the odometer has more than 200 km at delivery/closing.

13. **Tires:** Original equipment Firestone or Bridgestone tires are not acceptable.

_____   _____   _____
Date   Vendor's Signature   Buyer's Signature

"We Can't Do That"

Dealers and automakers facing bankruptcy can do almost anything to get your business. Don't take the dealer's word that "We're not allowed to do that"—heard most often in reference to reducing the PDI or transportation fee. Some dealers have been telling *Lemon-Aid* readers that they are "obligated" by the automaker to charge a set fee and could lose their franchise if they charge less. This is pure hogwash. No dealer has ever had their franchise licence revoked for cutting prices. Furthermore, the automakers clearly state that they don't set a bottom price, since doing so would violate Canada's *Competition Act*—that's why you always see them putting disclaimers in their ads saying the dealer can charge less.

The Pre-delivery Inspection

The best way to ensure that the PDI (written as "PDE" in some regions) will be done is to write in the sales contract that you'll be given a copy of the completed PDI sheet when the vehicle is delivered to you. Then, with the PDI sheet in hand, verify some of the items that were to be checked. If any items appear to have been missed, refuse delivery of the vehicle. If the items you check seem all in order and you accept delivery of the vehicle, once you get home, check out the vehicle more thoroughly, and send a registered letter to the dealer if you discover any incomplete items from the PDI.

Selling Your Trade-In

When to Sell

Used cars are worth more than ever because new cars are suspect (in terms of price and insecurities about warranties being honoured and dealer/automaker backup). New prices are lower than ever before, and used prices are rising. This makes it hard for most owners to figure out when is the best time to buy another vehicle. It doesn't take a genius to figure out that the longer one keeps a vehicle, the less it costs to own.

If you're happy with your vehicle's styling and convenience features and it's safe and dependable, there's no reason to get rid of it. But when the cost of repairs becomes equal to or greater than the cost of payment for a new car, you need to consider trading it in. Shortly after your vehicle's fifth birthday (or whenever you start to think about trading it in), ask a mechanic to look at it to give you some idea of what repairs, replacement parts, or maintenance work it will need in the coming year. Find out if dealer service bulletins show that it will need extensive repairs in the near future (see page 60 for how to order bulletins from ALLDATA). If it's going to require expensive repairs, you should trade the vehicle right away; if expensive work isn't predicted, you may want to keep it. Auto owners' associations provide a good yardstick. They figure that the annual cost of repairs and preventive maintenance for the average vehicle is about $800. If your vehicle is five years old and you haven't spent anywhere near $4,000 in maintenance, it would pay to invest in your old vehicle and continue using it for another few years.

Consider whether your vehicle can still be serviced easily. If it's no longer on the market, the parts supply is likely to dry up and independent mechanics will be reluctant to repair it.

Don't trade for fuel economy alone. Most fuel-efficient vehicles, such as front-drives, offset the savings through higher repair costs. Also, the more fuel-efficient vehicles may not be as comfortable to drive because of their excessive engine noise, lightweight construction, stiff suspension, and torque steer.

Reassess your needs. Has your family grown to the point that you need a new vehicle? Are you driving less? Are you taking fewer long trips? Let your car or minivan show its age, and pocket the savings if its deteriorating condition doesn't pose a safety hazard and isn't too embarrassing. If you're in sales and are constantly on the road, it makes sense to trade every few years—in that case, the vehicle's appearance and reliability become a prime consideration, particularly since the increased depreciation costs are mostly tax-deductible.

Getting the Most for Your Trade-In

Customers who are on guard against paying too much for a new vehicle often sell their trade-ins for too little. Before agreeing to any trade-in amount, read Part Three of *Lemon-Aid Used Cars and Trucks*. The guide will give your vehicle's dealer price and private selling price, and it offers a formula to figure out regional price fluctuations.

Now that you've nailed down your trade-in's approximate value, here are some tips on selling it with a minimum of stress:

- Never sign a new-vehicle sales contract unless your trade-in has been sold—you could end up with two vehicles.
- Negotiate the price from retail (dealer price) down to wholesale (private sales).

If you haven't sold your trade-in after two weekends, you might be trying to sell it at the wrong time of year or have it priced too high.

Make Money—Sell Privately

If you must sell your vehicle and want to make the most out of the deal, consider selling it yourself and putting the profits toward your next purchase. You'll likely come out hundreds of dollars ahead—buyers will pay more for your vehicle because they know cars sold by owners are more reasonably priced because there's no dealer overhead or sales commissions to pay. The most important thing to remember is that there's a large market for used vehicles in good condition in the $5,000–$7,000 range. Although most people prefer buying from individuals rather than from used-car lots, they may still be afraid that the vehicle is a lemon. By using the following suggestions, you should be able to sell your vehicle quite easily:

1. Know its value. Study dealers' newspaper ads and compare them with the prices listed in *Lemon-Aid*. Undercut the dealer's price by $300–$800, and be ready to bargain down another 10 percent for a serious buyer. Remember, prices can fluctuate wildly depending on which models are trendy, so watch the want ads carefully.
2. Enlist the aid of the salesperson who's selling you your new car. Offer him or her a few hundred dollars to find you a buyer. The fact that one sale hinges on the other, along with the prospect of making two commissions, may work wonders.

3. Post notices on bulletin boards at your office or local supermarkets, and place a "For Sale" sign in the window of the vehicle itself. Place a newspaper ad only as a last resort.
4. Don't give your address right away to a potential buyer responding to your ad. Instead, ask for the telephone number where you may call that person back.
5. Be wary of selling to friends or family members. Anything short of perfection, and you'll be eating Christmas dinner alone.
6. Don't touch the odometer. If you do, you may get a few hundred dollars more—and a criminal record.
7. Paint the vehicle. Some specialty shops charge only $300 and give a guarantee that's transferable to subsequent owners.
8. Make minor repairs. This includes a minor tune-up and patching up the exhaust. Again, if any repair warranty is transferable, use it as a selling point.
9. Clean the vehicle. Go to a reconditioning firm, or spend the weekend scrubbing the interior and exterior. First impressions are important. Clean the chrome, polish the body, and peel off old bumper stickers. Remove butts from the ashtrays and clean out the glove compartment. Make sure all tools and spare parts have been taken out of the trunk. Don't remove the radio or speakers—the gaping holes will lower the vehicle's worth much more than the cost of the sound equipment. Replace missing or broken dash knobs and window cranks.
10. Change the tires. Recaps are good buys.
11. Let the buyer examine the vehicle. Insist that it be inspected at an independent garage, and then accompany the prospective buyer to the garage. This gives you protection if the buyer claims you misrepresented the vehicle.
12. Don't mislead the buyer. If the vehicle was in an accident or some financing is still to be paid, admit it. Any misleading statements may be used later against you in court. It's also advisable to have someone witness the actual transaction in case of a future dispute.
13. Keep important documents handy. Show prospective buyers the sales contract, repair orders, owner's manual, and all other documents that show how the vehicle has been maintained. Authenticate your claims about fuel consumption.
14. Write an effective ad, if you need to use one.

Selling to Dealers

Selling to a dealer means that you're likely to get 20 percent less than if you sold your vehicle privately, unless the dealer agrees to participate in an accommodation sale based on your buying a new vehicle from them. Most owners will gladly pay some penalty to the dealer, however, for the peace of mind that comes with knowing that their eventual buyer won't lay a claim against them. This assumes that the dealer hasn't been cheated by the owner—if the vehicle is stolen, isn't paid for, has had its odometer spun back (or forward to a lower setting), or is seriously defective, the buyer or dealer can sue the original owner for fraud. Sell to a dealer who sells the same make. He or she will give you more because it's easier to sell your trade-in to customers who are interested in only that make of vehicle.

Drawing Up the Contract

The province of Alberta has prepared a useful bill of sale applicable throughout Canada that can be accessed at *www.servicealberta.gov.ab.ca/pdf/mv/ BillOfSaleReg3126.pdf*. Your bill of sale should identify the vehicle (including the serial number) and include its price, whether a warranty applies, and the nature of the examination made by the buyer.

The buyer may ask you to put in a lower price than what was actually paid in order to reduce the sales tax. If you agree to this, don't be surprised when a Revenue Canada agent comes to your door. Although the purchaser is ultimately the responsible party, you're an accomplice in defrauding the government. Furthermore, if you turn to the courts for redress, your own conduct may be put on trial.

 ## Summary

Purchasing a used vehicle and keeping it at least five years saves you the most money. It takes about eight years to realize similar depreciation savings when buying new. Giving the biggest down payment you can afford, using zero percent financing programs, and piling up as many kilometres and years as possible on your trade-in are the best ways to save money with new vehicles. Remember that safety is another consideration that depends largely on the type of vehicle you choose.

Buy Safe

Here are some safety features to look for:

1. High NHTSA and IIHS crashworthiness ratings for front, offset, and side collisions (pay particular attention to the side rating if you are a senior driver) and roof strength, plus a low rollover potential due to electronic stability control
2. Good-quality tires; be wary of "all-season" tires and Bridgestone/Firestone makes and follow *www.tirerack.com* consumer recommendations
3. Three-point seat belts with belt pretensioners and adjustable shoulder belt anchorages
4. Integrated child safety seats and seat anchors, safety door locks, and override window controls
5. Depowered dual airbags with a cut-off switch; side airbags with head protection; unobtrusive, effective head restraints that don't push your chin into your chest; and pedal extenders
6. Front driver's seat with plenty of rearward travel and a height adjuster
7. Good all-around visibility; a dash that doesn't reflect onto the windshield
8. An ergonomic interior with an efficient heating and ventilation system
9. Headlights that are adequate for night driving and don't blind oncoming traffic

10. Dash gauges that don't wash out in sunlight or produce windshield glare
11. Adjustable head restraints for all seating positions
12. Delaminated side-window glass
13. Easily accessed sound system and climate controls
14. Navigation systems that don't require a degree from MIT to calibrate
15. Manual sliding doors in vans (if children are being transported)

Buy Smart

1. Buy the vehicle you need and can afford, not the one someone else wants you to buy, or one loaded with options that you'll probably never use. Take your time. Price comparisons and test drives may take a month, but you'll get a better vehicle and price in the long run.
2. Buy in winter or later in the new year to double-dip from dealer incentives and customer rebate or low-cost financing programs.
3. Sell your trade-in privately.
4. Arrange financing before buying your vehicle.
5. Test drive your choice by renting it overnight or for several days.
6. Buy through the Internet or by fax, or use an auto broker if you're not confident in your own bargaining skills, you lack the time to haggle, or you want to avoid the "showroom shakedown."
7. Ask for at least a 25 percent discount off the MSRP, and cut PDI and freight charges by at least 50 percent. Insist on a specific delivery date written in the contract, as well as a protected price in case there's a price increase between the time the contract is signed and when the vehicle is delivered. Also ask for a free tank of gas.
8. Order a minimum of options, and seek a 30–40 percent discount on the entire option list.
9. Put the vehicle's down payment on your credit card.
10. Avoid leasing. If you must lease, choose the shortest time possible, drive down the MSRP, and refuse to pay an "acquisition" or "disposal" fee.
11. Look at Japanese vehicles made in North America, co-ventures with American automakers, and rebadged imports. They often cost less than imports and are just as reliable. However, some European imports may not be as reliable as you might imagine—Mercedes' M-Class sport-utilities, for example. Get extra warranty protection from the automaker if you're buying a model that has a poorer-than-average repair history. Use auto club references to get honest, competent repairs at a reasonable price.

Now that you know how to get a recession-proof vehicle for the least amount of money, Part Two will show you how to get your money back if that "dream car" turns into a nightmare, or if the dealer goes bankrupt.

Part Two
"I WANT MY MONEY BACK"

In *Prebushewski v. Dodge City Auto (1985) Ltd. and Chrysler Canada Ltd.*, the Supreme Court ordered Chrysler to pay $25,000 in punitive damages for denying a Saskatoon Dodge Ram owner's refund request.

Punitive Damages of $1 million!

The jury's award of punitive damages, though high, was within rational limits. The respondent insurer's conduct towards the appellant was exceptionally reprehensible. It forced her to put at risk her only remaining asset (the $345,000 insurance claim) plus $320,000 in costs that she did not have. The denial of the claim was designed to force her to make an unfair settlement for less than she was entitled to. The conduct was planned and deliberate and continued for over two years, while the financial situation of the appellant grew increasingly desperate.... Insurance contracts are sold by the insurance industry and purchased by members of the public for peace of mind. The more devastating the loss, the more the insured may be at the financial mercy of the insurer, and the more difficult it may be to challenge a wrongful refusal to pay the claim.

WHITEN V. PILOT INSURANCE CO
SUPREME COURT OF CANADA, 2002
HTTP://CA.VLEX.COM/VID/WHITEN-V-PILOT-INSURANCE-37670818

Chrysler's "Death Wobble"

When it first started happening to a buddy with a 2004 3500 Ram pickup, we... induced it by hitting some bumps at highway speed. The front tire was bouncing rapidly; a crazy sight. On his 2006 2500, he recently installed the newer, beefed-up front end from the current trucks that is supposed to prevent this from happening. I believe it has helped, but he had a failure of one of the new tie rods within a few months that put him into the ditch.... He used all OEM Dodge components, but

Dodge would not warranty anything because it was not the OEM design, even though those same components are installed on similar trucks when owners complain about the problem within the warranty period, and those trucks have also experienced tie rod failures. [See *www.cbc.ca/news/canada/british-columbia/story/2011/05/16/bc-dodgeproblem.html*]

THREAD ON THE "BOB IS THE OIL GUY" FORUM
www.bobistheoilguy.com/forums/ubbthreads.php?ubb=showflat&Number=2265118

Chrysler: "Death Wobble" Misnamed

STATEMENT TO CBC RE/RAM TRUCK CUSTOMER CONCERNS:

The name given to this condition has no basis in fact. All manufacturer vehicles equipped with a solid axle can be susceptible to this condition and, if experienced, it is routinely corrected. Indeed, this is not a safety issue, and there are no injuries involving Chrysler Group vehicles related to this allegation.

CHRYSLER CANADA
MAY 2011

Bull.

When Chrysler Canada wrote its denial, the company knew the U.S. Department of Transportation's safety investigators had already determined the following on April 4, 2011:

[We] are aware of 12 complaints of similar failures on 2008–2011 Ram 2500 & 3500 vehicles. A preliminary evaluation has been opened to assess ball joint related issues on the subject vehicles. This investigation will determine if the subject vehicles have a similar steering system design that might also present a risk of ball joint failure.

A few days after Chrysler Canada's response, CBC TV in Vancouver aired the story on May 17 on The National. The newscast, researched by Associate Producer Enza Uda and reported by Kathy Tomlinson, interviewed a Canadian Ram truck owner who said his truck had a "death wobble" after passing over small potholes or uneven stretches of road.

Six weeks after the story was broadcast, Chrysler announced the recall of 242,780 Ram pickups manufactured between 2003 and 2011. This includes the 2008 Ram 1500 and 2003–11 Ram 2500 and 3500 Heavy Duty trucks. According to NHTSA, these trucks may have a defective left tie rod ball stud that can fracture during low-speed parking manoeuvres and could result in the potential loss of directional stability in the left-hand front wheel, increasing the risk of a crash. In the end, it took a crusading CBC TV producer and determined reporter to force Chrysler to act after nine years of stonewalling Ram pickup owners.

This kind of failure isn't limited to Chrysler, and during the past 40 years *Lemon-Aid* has been published we've seen worse. From Volkswagen's self-starting "runaway Rabbits" to minivans with automatic sliding doors that open when they shouldn't or won't open when they should.

Four Roads to a Refund

If you've bought an unsafe vehicle or one that was misrepresented, or you've had to pay for repairs to correct factory-related defects, this part's for you. It's intended is to help you get your money back—without going to court or getting frazzled by a dealer's broken promises or "benign neglect." But if going to court is your only recourse, this part has the jurisprudence you'll need to cite in your complaint to get an out-of-court settlement or to win your case without spending a fortune on lawyers and research.

 Remember the "money-back guarantee"? Well, that's long gone. Automakers are reluctant to offer any warranty that requires them to take back a defective car or minivan, because they know that there are a lot of lemons out there. Fortunately, our provincial consumer protection laws have filled the gap when the base warranty expires, so now any sales contract for a new or used vehicle can be cancelled—or free repairs can be ordered—in the following situations:

1. Vehicle is unfit for the purpose for which it was purchased
2. Vehicle was misrepresented
3. Repairs are covered by a secret warranty or a "goodwill" warranty extension
4. Vehicle hasn't been reasonably durable, considering how well it was maintained, the mileage driven, and the type of driving that was done (this is particularly applicable to engine, transmission, and paint defects)

The four legal concepts enumerated above can lead to the sales contract being cancelled, the purchase price being partially refunded (*quanti minoris*), and/or damages being awarded. For example, if the seller says that a minivan can pull a 900 kg (2,000 lb.) trailer and you discover that it can barely tow half that weight or won't reach a reasonable speed while towing, you can cancel the contract for misrepresentation.

The same principle applies to a seller's exaggerated claims concerning a vehicle's fuel economy or reliability, as well as to "demonstrators" that are, in fact, used cars with false (rolled-back) odometer readings. GM's and Chrysler's secret paint warranties and Ford's engine and transmission "goodwill" programs have all been successfully challenged in small claims court. And reasonable durability is an especially powerful legal argument that allows a judge to determine what the dealer and auto manufacturer will pay to correct a premature failure long after the original warranty has expired.

Unfair Contracts

Sales contracts aren't meant to be fair. Dealers' and automakers' lawyers spend countless hours making sure their clients are well protected with one-sided contracts that they hope will discourage the filing of buyer lawsuits, inhibit class actions, or limit the amount of damages that can be claimed, or that they will get to choose the jurisdiction where the case will be heard. To this end, many businesses are using mandatory arbitration clauses that in theory are reasonable alternatives to court, but in practice are grossly unfair. Says the Quebec Union des Consommateurs:

> Consumer contracts commonly contain clauses forcing the consumer to submit to arbitration his [or her] claims against the company, while reserving to the company any recourse regarding its own claims against the consumer. Moreover, although Quebec and Ontario laws prohibit excluding exemplary damages, companies still insert such stipulations in their consumer contracts, thus again restricting consumer access to justice by getting consumers to believe that they have less rights than they actually do...If one of the main objectives of alternative dispute-resolution methods must be to facilitate access to justice, such clauses obviously counter this objective."

> [As for] class actions, [they] constitute an essential instrument for re-establishing the balance of power between merchants and consumers. This procedure notably aims to ensure access to justice for everyone whose individual recourse alone might not justify initiating legal proceedings because, for example, the dispute amounts would not be sufficient. Clauses that attempt to restrict consumer recourses, or that preclude initiating or participating in class actions, are "clearly harmful, and even opposed to public order".

> The class action proceeding is an important social tool, in enabling consumers to unite in opposition to such clauses—a powerful deterrent against reprehensible merchant practices. Prohibiting consumers from using this tool becomes abusive not only toward those who want to initiate proceedings and resolve their dispute, but also toward all consumers and society.

> As the court stated in the *Discover* case in the United States, not only do companies attempt to arm themselves against class actions, but they also try to remove any incentive to end practices that are precisely the cause of such proceedings. If only for this reason, this type of clause should be considered contrary to public order.

Called "standard form contracts," or "contracts of adhesion," these agreements are looked upon by judges with a great deal of skepticism. They know the buyer had little or no bargaining power in drawing up sales agreements, loan documents, insurance contracts, and automobile leases. Fortunately, when a dispute arises over terms or language used in a document, judges have the latitude to interpret clauses in the way most favourable to the buyer.

"Hearsay" Not Allowed

It's essential that printed evidence and/or witnesses (relatives are not excluded) are available to confirm that a false representation actually occurred, that a part is failure-prone, or that its replacement is covered by a secret warranty. Stung by an increasing number of small claims court defeats, automakers are now asking small claims court judges to disallow evidence from *Lemon-Aid*, service bulletins, or memos on the pretext that such evidence is hearsay (not proven) unless confirmed by an independent mechanic or unless the document is recognized by the automaker's or dealer's representative at trial ("Is this a common problem? Do you recognize this service bulletin? Is there a case-by-case 'goodwill' plan covering this repair?"). This is why you should bring in an independent garage mechanic or body expert to buttress your allegations. Sometimes, though, the service manager or company representative will make key admissions if questioned closely by you, a court mediator, or the trial judge. That questioning can be particularly effective if you call for the exclusion of witnesses until they're called (let them mill around outside the courtroom wondering what their colleagues have said).

Automakers often blame owners for having pushed their vehicle beyond its limits. Therefore, when you seek to set aside the contract or get a repair reimbursed, it's essential that you get the testimony of an independent mechanic and his or her co-workers in order to prove that the vehicle's poor performance isn't caused by negligent maintenance or abusive driving.

It Should Have Lasted Longer!

The reasonable durability claim is your ace in the hole. It's probably the easiest allegation to prove, since all automakers have benchmarks as to how long body components, trim and finish, and mechanical and electronic parts should last (see the "Reasonable Part Durability" chart on page 112). Vehicles are expected to be reasonably durable and merchantable. What "reasonably durable" means depends on the price paid, the kilometres driven, the purchaser's driving habits, and how well the vehicle was maintained by the owner. Judges carefully weigh all these factors in awarding compensation or cancelling a sale.

 Whatever reason you use to get your money back, don't forget to conform to the "reasonable diligence" rule that requires you to file suit within a reasonable time after the vehicle's purchase or after you've discovered the defect. If there have been no negotiations with the dealer or automaker, this period shouldn't exceed a year. If either the dealer or the automaker has been promising to correct the defects for some time, or has carried out repeated unsuccessful repairs, the delay for filing the lawsuit can be extended from the time negotiations ended.

Refunds for Other Expenses

It's a lot easier to get the automaker to pay to replace a defective part than it is to obtain compensation for a missed day of work. Manufacturers seldom pay for consequential expenses like a ruined vacation, a vehicle not living up to its advertised hype, or an owner's mental distress, because they can't control the amount of the refund. Courts, however, are more generous, having ruled that all expenses (damages) flowing from a problem covered by a warranty or service bulletin are the manufacturer's or dealer's responsibility under both common law (which covers all provinces except Quebec) and Quebec civil law. Fortunately, when legal action is threatened—usually through small claims court—automakers quickly up their ante to include most of the owner's expenses because they know the courts will probably do the same.

One precedent-setting judgment (cited in *Sharman v. Ford*, found on pages 137–138) giving generous damages to a motorist fed up with his "lemon" Cadillac was rendered in 1999 by the British Columbia Supreme Court in *Wharton v. Tom Harris Chevrolet Oldsmobile Cadillac Ltd.* ([2002] B.C.J. No. 233, 2002 BCCA 78d). In that case, Justice Leggatt threw the book at GM and the dealer in awarding the following amounts:

(a) Hotel accommodations: $ 217.17
(b) Travel to effect repairs at 30 cents per kilometre: The plaintiff claims some 26 visits from his home in Ucluelet to Nanaimo. Some credit should be granted to the defendants since routine trips would have been required in any event. Therefore, the plaintiff is entitled to be compensated for mileage for 17 trips (approximately 400 km from Ucluelet to Nanaimo return) at 30 cents per kilometre.

             $2,040.00
TOTAL: $2,257.17

[20] The plaintiffs are entitled to non-pecuniary damages for loss of enjoyment of their luxury vehicle and for inconvenience in the sum of $5,000.

Warranties

It's really not that hard to get a refund if you take it one step at a time. Vehicle defects are covered by two warranties: the *expressed* warranty, which has a fixed time limit, and the *implied* (or *legal*) warranty, which is entirely up to a judge's discretion.

Expressed Warranties

The manufacturer's or dealer's warranty is an "expressed" promise that a vehicle will perform as represented and be reasonably reliable, subject to certain conditions. Regardless of the number of subsequent owners, this promise remains in force as long as the warranty's original time/kilometre limits haven't expired. The expressed warranty given by most sellers is often full of empty promises, and it allows the dealer and manufacturer to act as judge and jury when deciding whether a vehicle was misrepresented or is afflicted with defects they'll pay to correct. Rarely does it provide a money-back guarantee.

Some of the more familiar lame excuses used in denying expressed warranty claims are "You abused the car," "It was poorly maintained," "It's normal wear and tear," "It's rusting from the outside, not the inside," and "It passed the safety inspection." Ironically, the expressed warranty sometimes says that there is no warranty at all, or that the vehicle is sold "as is." And, when the warranty's clauses (or lack thereof) don't deter claimants, some dealers simply say that a verbal warranty or representation as to the vehicle's attributes is unenforceable.

Fortunately, these attempts to weasel out of the warranty and limit the seller's liability seldom make it through judicial review. Justice Searle put it this way in the *Chams* decision (see pages 139–145):

> Ford's warranty attempts to limit its liability to what it grants in the warranty. It is ancient law that one who attempts to limit his liability by, for example, excluding common law remedies, must clearly bring that limitation to the attention of the person who might lose those remedies. The evidence in this case is clear: The buyer of even a new car does not get a warranty booklet until after purchasing the car although he "would be" told the highlights sooner.

Implied Warranties

Thankfully, car owners get another kick at the can with the implied warranty ("of fitness"). As clearly stated in the unreported Saskatchewan decision *Maureen Frank v. General Motors of Canada Limited* (found exclusively here in *Lemon-Aid* on pages 123–124)—in which the judge declared that paint discoloration and peeling shouldn't occur within 11 years of the purchase of a vehicle—the implied warranty is an important legal principle. It's solidly supported by a large body of federal and provincial laws, regulations, and jurisprudence, and it protects you primarily from hidden dealer- or factory-related defects. But the concept also includes misrepresentation and a host of other scams.

This warranty also holds dealers to a higher standard of conduct than private sellers because, unlike private sellers, dealers are presumed to be aware of the defects present in the vehicles they sell. That way, they can't just pass the ball to the automaker or to the previous owner and then walk away from the dispute. For instance, in British Columbia, a new-car dealer is required to disclose damage requiring repairs costing more than 20 percent of the price (under the *Motor Dealer Act Regulations*).

Why the implied warranty is so effective
- It establishes the concept of "reasonable durability" (see "How Long Should a Part or Repair Last?" on page 111), meaning that parts are expected to last for a reasonable period of time, as stated in jurisprudence, judged by independent mechanics, or expressed in extended warranties given by the automaker in the past (7–10 years/160,000 km for engines and transmissions).
- It covers the entire vehicle and can be applied for whatever period of time the judge decides.
- It can order that the vehicle be taken back, or that a major repair cost be refunded.
- It can help plaintiffs claim compensation for supplementary transportation, inconvenience, mental distress, missed work, screwed-up vacations, insurance paid while the vehicle was in the repair shop, repairs done by other mechanics, and exemplary (or punitive) damages in cases where the seller was a real weasel.
- It is frequently used by small claims court judges to give refunds to plaintiffs "in

equity" (out of fairness) rather than through a strict interpretation of contract law.

Fuel Economy Claims

Canadian courts are cracking down on lying dealers and deceptive sales practices, and the misrepresentation of fuel economy figures is squarely in the judiciary's sights. Ontario's *Consumer Protection Act, 2002* (*www.e-laws.gov.on.ca/html/statutes/english/elaws_statutes_02c30_e.htm*), for example, lets a vehicle buyer cancel a contract within one year of entering into an agreement if their dealer made a false, misleading, deceptive, or unconscionable representation. This includes using exaggeration, innuendo, or ambiguity as to a material fact or failing to state a material fact if such use or failure deceives or tends to deceive consumers.

This law means that new- or used-car dealers cannot make the excuse that they were fooled about the condition or performance of a vehicle, or that they were simply providing data supplied by the manufacturer. The law clearly states that both parties are jointly liable and that dealers are *presumed* to know the history, quality, and true performance of what they are selling.

Details like fuel economy *can* lead to a contract's cancellation if the dealer gives a higher-than-actual figure. In *Sidney v. 1011067 Ontario Inc. (c.o.b. Southside Motors)*, a precedent-setting case that was filed before Ontario's *Consumer Protection Act* was toughened in 2002, the buyer was awarded $11,424.51 plus prejudgment interest because of a false representation made by the defendant regarding fuel efficiency. The plaintiff claimed that the defendant advised him that the vehicle had a fuel efficiency of 800–900 km per tank of fuel when, in fact, the maximum efficiency was only 500 km per tank.

This consumer victory is particularly important as fuel prices soar and everyone from automakers to sellers of ineffective gas-saving gadgets make outlandishly false fuel economy claims. Not surprisingly, sellers try to use the expressed warranty to reject claims, while smart plaintiffs ignore the expressed warranty and argue for a refund under the implied warranty instead.

Tire Failures

Consumers have gained additional rights following Bridgestone/Firestone's massive tire recall in 2001. Because of the confusion and chaos surrounding Firestone's handling of the recall, Ford's 575 Canadian dealers stepped into the breach and replaced the tires with any equivalent tires dealers had in stock, no questions asked.

This is an important precedent that tears down the traditional liability wall separating tire manufacturers from automakers in product liability claims. In essence, whoever sells the product can now be held liable for damages. In the future, Canadian consumers will have an easier time holding the dealer, automaker, and tiremaker liable, not just for recalled products but also for any defect that affects the safety or reasonable durability of that product. This includes tire valve stem failures as well as tire pressure monitoring systems (TPMS).

The Supreme Court of Canada (*Winnipeg Condominium v. Bird Construction* [1995] 1S.C.R.85) has ruled that defendants are liable in negligence for any designs that resulted in a risk to the public for safety or health. The Supreme Court reversed a long-standing policy and provided the public with a new cause of action that had not existed before in Canada. Prior to this Supreme Court ruling, companies dodged liability for falling bridges and crashing planes by warranty exclusion and "entire-agreement" contract clauses. In the *Winnipeg Condominium* case, the Supreme Court held that repairs made to prevent serious damage or accidents could be claimed from the designer or builder for the cost of repair in tort from any subsequent purchaser. Consumers with tire or other claims relating to the safety of their vehicles would be wise to insert the above court decision (with explanation) in their claim letter and then mail or fax it to the automaker's legal affairs or product liability department. A copy should also be deposited with the clerk of the small claims court, if you have to use that recourse.

Other Warrantable Items

Safety restraints, such as airbags and seat belts, have warranty coverage extended for the lifetime of the vehicle, following an agreement made between U.S. automakers and importers. In Canada, though, some automakers try to dodge this responsibility because they are incorporated as separate Canadian companies. That distinction didn't fly with B.C.'s Court of Appeal in the 2002 *Robson* decision (*www.courts.gov.bc.ca/jdb-txt/ca/02/03/2002bcca0354.htm*). In that class action petition, the court declared that both Canadian companies *and* their American counterparts can be held liable in Canada for deceptive acts that violate the provincial *Trade Practices Act* (in this case, Chrysler and GM paint delamination):

> At this stage, the plaintiffs are only required to demonstrate that they have a "good arguable case" against the American defendants. The threshold is low. A good arguable case requires only a serious question to be tried, one with some prospect of success: see *AG Armeno Mines, supra*, at para. 25 [*AG Armeno Mines and Minerals Inc. v. PT Pukuafu Indah* (2000), 77 B.C.L.R.(3d) 1 (C.A.)].

Aftermarket products and services—such as gas-saving gadgets, rustproofing, and paint protectors—can render the manufacturer's warranty invalid, so make sure you're in the clear before purchasing any optional equipment or services from an independent supplier.

How fairly a warranty is applied is more important than how long it remains in effect. Once you know the normal wear rate for a mechanical component or body part, you can demand proportional compensation when you get less than normal durability—no matter what the original warranty said.

Some dealers tell customers that they need to have original-equipment parts installed in order to maintain their warranty. A variation on this theme requires that routine servicing—including tune-ups and oil changes (with a certain brand of oil)—be done by the selling dealer, or the warranty is invalidated.

Nothing could be further from the truth. Canadian law stipulates that whoever issues a warranty cannot make that warranty conditional on the use of any specific brand of motor oil, oil filter, or any other component, unless it's provided to the customer free of charge.

Warranty Runaround

Sometimes dealers will do all sorts of minor repairs that don't correct the problem, and then, after the warranty runs out, they'll tell you that major repairs are needed. You can prevent this nasty surprise by repeatedly bringing your vehicle into the dealership before the warranty ends. During each visit, insist that a written work order include the specific nature of the problem as *you* see it and that the work order carry the notation that this is the second, third, or fourth time the same problem has been brought to the dealer's attention. Write it down yourself, if need be. This allows you to show a pattern of nonperformance by the dealer during the warranty period and establishes that it's a serious and chronic problem. When the warranty expires, you have the legal right to demand that it be extended on those items consistently reappearing on your handful of work orders. *Lowe v. Fairview Chrysler* (see page 145) is an excellent judgment that reinforces this important principle. In another lawsuit, *François Chong v. Marine Drive Imported Cars Ltd. and Honda Canada Inc.* (see page 154), a Honda owner forced Honda to fix his engine six times—until they got it right.

A retired GM service manager gave me another effective tactic to use when you're not sure that a dealer's warranty "repairs" will actually correct the problem for a reasonable period of time after the warranty expires. Here's what he says you should do:

> When you pick up the vehicle after the warranty repair has been done, hand the service manager a note to be put in your file that says you appreciate the warranty repair; however, you intend to return and ask for further warranty coverage if the problem reappears before a reasonable amount of time has elapsed even if the original warranty has expired. A copy of the same note should be sent to the automaker.... Keep your copy of the note in the glove compartment as cheap insurance against paying for a repair that wasn't fixed correctly the first time.

Supplementary Warranties

Power Information Network data shows that 40 percent of car buyers purchase extended warranties, although only 10 percent of leased vehicles get the extra protection. Some extra warranties promise a refund of the warranty cost if no claim is made while the lease is in force. What buyers may not know, however, is that a call for roadside assistance made under the manufactuerer's warranty may be counted as a claim under the extended warranty as well. Owners are also uncomfortable with the proviso that they must keep their vehicle for the life of the contract—sometimes up to 5 years.

The manufacturer, the dealer, or an independent third party may sell supplementary warranties that provide extended coverage, and this coverage is automatically transferred when a vehicle is sold. They cost between $1,500 and $2,000 and should be purchased only if the vehicle you're buying has a reputation for being unreliable or expensive to service (see Part Three) or if you're reluctant to use the small claims courts when factory-related trouble arises. Don't let the dealer pressure you into deciding right away.

Dealers love to sell you extended warranties, whether you need them or not, because up to 60 percent of the warranty's cost represents dealer markup. Out of the remaining 40 percent comes the sponsor's administration costs and profit margin, calculated at another 15 percent. What's left to pay for repairs is a minuscule 25 percent of the original amount. The only reason that automakers and independent warranty companies haven't been busted for operating this Ponzi scheme is that only half of the vehicle buyers who purchase extended service contracts actually use them.

Those who do need help often find it difficult to collect a refund because independent companies frequently go out of business or limit the warranty's coverage through subsequent mailings. Provincial laws cover both situations. If the bankrupt warranty company's insurance policy won't cover your claim, take the dealer to small claims court and ask for the repair costs and a refund of the original warranty payment. Your argument for holding the dealer responsible is a simple one: By accepting a commission to act as an agent of the defunct company, the dealer also took on the obligations of that company. As for limiting the coverage after you have already bought the warranty policy, this practice is illegal and allows you to sue both the dealer and the warranty company for a refund of both the warranty and the repair costs.

Emissions-Control Warranties

These little-publicized warranties can save you big bucks if major engine or exhaust components fail prematurely. They come with all new vehicles and cover major components of the emissions-control system for up to 8 years/130,000 km, no matter how many times the vehicle is sold. Unfortunately, although owner's manuals vaguely mention the emissions warranty, most don't specify which parts are covered. The U.S. Environmental Protection Agency has intervened on several occasions, with hefty fines against Chrysler and Ford, and ruled that all major motor and fuel-system components are covered. These components include fuel metering, ignition spark advance, restart, evaporative emissions, positive crankcase ventilation (PCV), engine electronics (computer modules), and catalytic converter systems as well as parts like hoses, clamps, brackets, pipes, gaskets, belts, seals, and connectors. Canada, however, has no list defined by the government, so it's up to each manufacturer and the small claims courts to decide which emissions-control components are covered.

Some of the confidential technical service bulletins listed in Part Three show parts failures that are covered under the emissions warranty (stinky exhausts caused by defective catalytic converters, for example), even though motorists are routinely charged for their replacement. Ford of Canada has issued one bulletin where owners of 2002–05 Ford Taurus and Sable models will get refunds for fuel gauge repairs under the emissions warranty. Faulty fuel gauges are a common problem with all automakers, with repairs costing $300–$500.

Make sure to get your emissions system checked out thoroughly by a dealer or an independent garage before the emissions warranty expires or before having the vehicle inspected by provincial emissions inspectors. In addition to ensuring that you'll pass provincial tests, this precaution could save you up to $1,000 if your catalytic converter and other emissions components are faulty.

"Secret" Warranties

Few vehicle owners know that secret warranties exist. The closest automakers come to an admission is sending out a "goodwill policy," "product improvement program," or "special policy" technical service bulletin (TSB) to dealers or first owners of record. Consequently, the only motorists who find out about these policies are the original owners who haven't moved or haven't leased their vehicles. The other motorists who get compensated for repairs are the ones who read *Lemon-Aid* each year, wave TSBs, and yell the loudest.

Remember, second owners and repairs done by independent garages are included in these secret warranty programs. Large, costly repairs, such as blown engines, burned transmissions, and peeling paint, are often covered.

Here are a few examples of the most comprehensive secret warranties that have come across my desk during the last several years.

All Years, All Models

Automatic transmissions

Problem: Faulty automatic transmissions that self-destruct, shift erratically, gear down to "limp home mode," are slow to shift in or out of Reverse, or are noisy. **Warranty coverage:** If you have the assistance of your dealer's service manager, expect an offer of 50–75 percent (about $2,500). File the case in small claims court, and a full refund will be offered up to 7 years/160,000 km. Acura, Honda, Hyundai, Lexus, and Toyota coverage varies between seven and eight years.

Brakes

Problem: Premature wearout of brake pads, calipers, and rotors. Produces excessive vibration, noise, and pulling to one side when braking. **Warranty coverage:** *Calipers and pads:* "Goodwill" settlements confirm that brake calipers and pads that fail to last 2 years/40,000 km will be replaced for 50 percent of the repair cost; components not lasting 1 year/20,000 km will be replaced for free. *Rotors:* If they last less than 3 years/60,000 km, they'll be replaced at half the price; replacement is free up to 2 years/40,000 km. *ABS brake sensors and electrical connections:* Should last for at least 5 years/100,000 km.

Interestingly, early brake wearout, once mainly a Detroit failing, is now quite common with Asian makes as well. Apparently, brake suppliers for all automakers are using cheaper calipers, pads, and rotors that can't handle the heat generated by normal braking on heavier passenger cars, trucks, and vans. Consequently, drivers find routine braking causes rotor warpage that produces excessive vibrations, shuddering, noise, and pulling to one side when braking.

Engines

Problem: At around 60,000–100,000 km, the engine may overheat, lose power, and burn extra fuel, or possibly self-destruct. Under the best of circumstances, you may have to replace the engine's intake manifold gasket—a repair that will take a day and cost about $800–$1,000. **Warranty coverage:** If you have the assistance of your dealer's service manager, expect a full refund up to 7 years/160,000 km, although initial offers will hover at about 50 percent of the costs. If you must file a small claims court action, cite the *Chams* decision (see pages 139–145).

No matter which automaker you're dealing with, filing your claim in small claims court always sweetens the company's settlement offer. Furthermore, you likely won't have to step inside a courtroom to get your refund, since most small claims court filings are settled at the pretrial mediation stage.

Exhaust systems

Problem: A nauseating "rotten-egg" exhaust smell permeates the interior. **Warranty coverage:** At first, owners are told they need a tune-up. And then they are told to change fuels and to wait a few months for the problem to correct itself. When this fails, the catalytic converter will likely be replaced and the power control module recalibrated. The replacement and recalibration is free up to 8 years under the emissions warranty.

Chrysler, Ford, General Motors, Honda, Hyundai, and Mazda

Paint

Problem: Faulty paint jobs that cause paint to turn white, peel off of horizontal panels, or produce thin white scratches. **Warranty coverage:** Automakers will offer a free paint job or partial compensation up to six years with no mileage limitation. Thereafter, all these manufacturers offer 50–75 percent refunds on the small claims courthouse steps.

In *Frank v. GM*, the Saskatchewan small claims court set an 11-year benchmark for paint finishes. Three earlier Canadian small claims judgements extended the benchmark beyond the warranty and extended compensation to second owners and pickups.

> I wanted to let you and your readers know that the information you publish about Ford's paint failure problem is invaluable. Having read through your "how-to guide" on addressing this issue, I filed a suit against Ford for the "latent" paint defect. The day prior to our court date, I received a settlement offer by phone for 75 percent of what I was initially asking for.
>
> This settlement was for a 9-year-old car. I truly believe that Ford hedges a bet that most people won't go to the extent of filing a lawsuit because they are intimidated or simply stop progress after they receive a firm no from Ford.
>
> M.P.

How Long Should a Part or Repair Last?

How do you know when a part or service doesn't last as long as it should, and whether you should seek a full or partial refund? Sure, you have a gut feeling based on your use of the vehicle, how you maintained it, and the extent of work that was carried out on it. But you'll need more than emotion to win compensation from garages and automakers.

You can definitely get a refund if a repair or part lasts longer than its guarantee but not as long as is generally expected. But you'll have to show what the auto industry considers to be "reasonable durability." Automakers, mechanics, and the courts all have their own benchmarks as to what's a reasonable period of time or amount of mileage one should expect a part or adjustment to last. Consequently, I've prepared a chart to show what most automakers consider to be reasonable durability, as expressed by their original and "goodwill" warranties.

Many of the guidelines on the following page were extrapolated from Chrysler and Ford payouts to thousands of dissatisfied customers over the past several decades, in addition to Chrysler's original seven-year powertrain warranty (applicable from 1991–95 and reapplied from 2001–04). Other sources for this chart were the Ford and GM transmission warranties outlined in their secret warranties; Ford, GM, and Toyota engine "goodwill" programs laid out in their internal service bulletins; and court judgments where judges have given their own guidelines as to what is meant by "reasonable durability."

Safety features—with the exception of anti-lock brake systems (ABS)—generally have a lifetime warranty.

REASONABLE PART DURABILITY

ACCESSORIES

Air conditioner	7 years
Cruise control	5 years/100,000 km
Power doors, windows	5 years
Radio	5 years

BODY

Paint (peeling)	7–11 years
Rust (perforations)	7–11 years
Rust (surface)	5 years
Water/wind/air leaks	5 years

BRAKE SYSTEM

Brake drum	120,000 km
Brake drum linings	35,000 km
Brake rotor	60,000 km
Brake calipers/pads	30,000 km
Master cylinder	100,000 km
Wheel cylinder	80,000 km

ENGINE AND DRIVETRAIN

CV joint	6 years/160,000 km
Differential	7 years/160,000 km
Engine (diesel)	15 years/350,000 km
Engine (gas)	7 years/160,000 km
Radiator	4 years/80,000 km
Transfer case	7 years/160,000 km
Transmission (auto.)	7 years/160,000 km
Transmission (man.)	10 years/250,000 km
Transmission oil cooler	5 years/100,000 km

EXHAUST SYSTEM

Catalytic converter	8–10 years/100,000 km or more
Muffler	2 years/40,000 km
Tailpipe	3 years/60,000 km

IGNITION SYSTEM

Cable set	60,000 km
Electronic module	5 years/80,000 km
Retiming	20,000 km
Spark plugs	20,000 km
Tune-up	20,000 km

Airbags are a different matter. Those that are deployed in an accident—and the personal injury and interior damage their deployment will likely have caused—are covered by your accident insurance policy. However, if there is a sudden deployment for no apparent reason, the automaker and dealer should be held jointly responsible for all injuries and damages caused by the airbag. You can prove their liability by downloading data from your vehicle's data recorder. This will likely lead to a more-generous settlement from the two parties and prevent your insurance premiums from being jacked up.

Use the manufacturer's emissions warranty as your primary guideline for the expected durability of high-tech electronic and mechanical pollution-control components, such as powertrain control modules (PCM) and catalytic converters. Look first at your owner's manual for an indication of which parts on your vehicle are covered. If you come up with few specifics, ask the auto manufacturer for a list of all components covered by the emissions warranty.

Recall Repairs

Vehicles are recalled for one of two reasons: Either they are unsafe or they don't conform to federal pollution-control regulations. Whatever the reason, recalls are a great way to get free repairs and keep your car safe—if you know which ones apply to you and you have the patience of Job.

A recall doesn't mean your vehicle will become a long-term problem. Most vehicles will undergo two or three recalls during their life cycle. Indeed, recalls happen in even the best automotive neighbourhoods, with manufacturers from Acura to Rolls-Royce subject to government-mandated recalls. Even quality-snob Toyota has sustained huge recalls on all of its models in the last couple of years, affecting some 10 million vehicles.

Millions of unsafe vehicles have been recalled by automakers for the free correction of safety-related defects since American recall legislation was passed in 1966 (a weaker Canadian law was enacted in 1971). During that time, NHTSA estimates that about 28 percent of the recalled vehicles never made it back to the dealership for repairs because owners were never informed, they just didn't consider the defect to be that hazardous, or they gave up waiting for corrective parts. Yet one study that estimated the effect of recalls on safety found that a 10 percent increase in the recall rate of a particular model will reduce the number of accidents involving that model by around 2 percent (*ms.cc.sunysb.edu/~hbenitezsilv/recall.pdf*).

The automaker has three options for correcting the defect: repair, replace, or refund. This probably means a trip to the dealer. However, in the case of a tire or child seat recall, you may mail in the defective item or go to the retailer that sold the product.

If you've moved, it's smart to pay a visit to your local dealer. Give the dealer your address to get a "report card" on which recalls, free service campaigns, and warranties apply to your vehicle. Simply give the service advisor the vehicle identification number (VIN)—found on your insurance card or on the dash, just below the windshield on the driver's side—and have the number run through the automaker's computer system. Ask for a computer printout of the vehicle's history (or have it faxed to you, if you're so equipped), and make sure you're listed in the automaker's computer as the new owner. This process ensures that you'll receive notices of warranty extensions and emissions and safety recalls.

There are limitations on automotive recalls. Vehicle manufacturers are not required to perform free recalls on vehicles that are more than 10 years old. Getting repairs when the automaker says you're too late often takes a small claims court filing. But these cases are easy to win and are usually settled out of court. U.S. recalls may be voluntary or ordered by the U.S. Department of Transportation, and they can be nationwide or regional. In Canada, all recalls are considered voluntary. Transport Canada can only order automakers to notify owners that their vehicles may be unsafe; it can't force them to correct the problem. Fortunately, most U.S.-ordered recalls are carried out in Canada, and when Transport Canada makes a defect determination on its own, automakers generally comply with an owner notification letter and a recall campaign.

Voluntary recall campaigns—frequently called "Special Service" or "Safety Improvement" campaigns—are a real problem. The government does not monitor the notification of owners; dealers and automakers routinely deny there's a recall, thereby dissuading most claimants; and the company's so-called fix, not authorized by any governing body, may not correct the hazard at all. Also, the voluntary recall may leave out many of the affected models or unreasonably exclude certain owners.

Wherever you live or drive, don't expect to be welcomed with open arms when your vehicle develops a safety- or emissions-related problem that's not yet part of a recall campaign. Automakers and dealers generally take a restrictive view of what constitutes a safety or emissions defect, and they frequently charge for repairs that should be free under federal safety or emissions legislation. To counter this tendency, look at the following list of typical defects that are clearly safety-related. If you experience similar problems to these, insist that the automaker fix them at no expense to yourself, including paying for a car rental:

- Airbag malfunctions
- Corrosion affecting the safe operation of the vehicle
- Disconnected or stuck accelerators
- Electrical shorts
- Faulty windshield wipers
- Fuel leaks
- Problems with original axles, driveshafts, seats, seat recliners, or defrosters
- Seat belt problems
- Stalling, or sudden acceleration
- Sudden steering or brake loss
- Suspension failures
- Trailer coupling failures

Regional recalls

Don't let any dealer refuse you recall repairs because of where you live. In order to cut recall costs, many automakers try to limit a recall to vehicles in a certain designated region. This practice doesn't make sense, since cars are mobile and an unsafe, rust-cankered steering unit can be found anywhere—not just in certain rust-belt provinces or American states.

In 2001, Ford attempted to limit its recall of faulty Firestone tires to five American states. Public ridicule of the company's proposal led to an extension of the recall throughout North America.

Recall fatigue

Safety experts agree that the sheer number of auto recalls has resulted in "recall fatigue," where affected owners ignore urgent calls to get corrective repairs. The increasing number of recalls (for example, recalls for Toyota's sudden acceleration problem, brake failures, and rust damaged suspension/steering systems) makes drivers immune to the message, leading them to believe that nothing bad will happen to them. However, if an item is relatively expensive or the perceived threat is immediate, consumers are more likely to seek recall assistance.

Car owners are particularly responsive. In one 2009 study carried out by the NHTSA, 73 percent of recalled autos and 45 percent of child car seats were taken in for recall corrections.

Safety Defect Information

If you wish to report a safety defect or want recall info, you may access Transport Canada's website at *www.tc.gc.ca/roadsafety/safevehicles/defectinvestigations/index.htm*. You can get recall information in French or English, as well as general information relating to road safety and importing a vehicle into Canada. Web surfers can access the recall database for vehicles with model years from 1970 to the present, but unlike NHTSA's website, owner complaints aren't listed, defect investigations aren't disclosed, voluntary warranty extensions (secret warranties) aren't shown, and service bulletin summaries aren't provided. You can also call Transport Canada at 1-800-333-0510 to get additional information.

If you're not happy with Ottawa's treatment of your recall inquiry, try NHTSA's website at *www.safercar.gov*. It's more complete than Transport Canada's—NHTSA's database is updated daily and covers vehicles built since the '50s. You'll get immediate access to four essential database categories applicable to your vehicle and model year: the latest recalls, current and closed safety investigations, defects reported by other owners, and a brief summary of service bulletins that apply.

Nailing Down a Refund

Step 1: Informal Negotiations

Most vehicle owners won't take the steps outlined in the previous sections; instead, they'll try to settle things informally with a phone call. This tactic rarely works. Customer service agents (who recite policies but don't make them) will tell you the vehicle's warranty doesn't apply. This brush-off usually convinces 90 percent of complainers to drop their claims after some angry venting.

Nevertheless, don't take no for an answer. Contact someone higher up who has the authority to bend policies to satisfy your request. Speak in a calm, polite manner, and try not to polarize the issue. Talk about cooperating to solve the problem. Let a compromise emerge—don't come in with a hardline set of demands.

An independent estimate of the vehicle's defects and the cost of repairing them is essential if you want to convince the dealer that you're serious in your claim and that you stand a good chance of winning your case in court. Prepare to use your estimate to challenge the dealer who agrees to pay half the repair costs and then tries to jack up the price 100 percent so that you wind up paying the whole shot.

Don't insist on getting the settlement offer in writing, but make sure that you're accompanied by a friend or relative who can confirm the offer in court if it isn't honoured. Be prepared to act upon the offer without delay so that if the dealer or automaker withdraws it, they won't be able to blame your hesitancy.

Dealer and service manager help

Service managers have more power than you may realize. They make the first determination of what work is covered under warranty or through post-warranty "goodwill" programs, and they're directly responsible to the dealer and manufacturer for their decisions. (Dealers hate manufacturer audits that force them to pay back questionable warranty decisions.) Service managers are paid to save the dealer and automaker money while mollifying irate clients—an almost impossible balancing act. Nevertheless, when a service manager agrees to extend warranty coverage, it's because you've raised solid issues that neither the dealer nor the automaker can ignore. All the more reason to present your argument in a confident, forthright manner with your vehicle's service history and *Lemon-Aid*'s "Reasonable Part Durability" chart (see page 112) on hand.

Also bring as many technical service bulletins and owner complaint printouts as you can find from websites like NHTSA's. It's not important that they apply directly to your problem; they establish parameters for giving out after-warranty assistance, or "goodwill." Don't use your salesperson as a runner, because the sales staff are generally quite distant from the service staff and usually have less pull than you do.

If the service manager can't or won't set things right, your next step is to convene a mini-summit with the service manager, the dealer principal, and the automaker's rep. By getting the automaker involved, you run less risk of having the dealer fob you off on the manufacturer, and you can often get an agreement where the dealer and automaker pay two-thirds of the repair costs.

Step 2: Send a Registered Letter, Fax, or Email

Don't worry; no one feels comfortable writing a complaint. But if you haven't sent a written claim letter, fax, or email, you haven't really complained—or at least that's the auto industry's mindset. Send the dealer and manufacturer a polite registered letter or fax that asks for compensation for repairs that have been done or need to be done, insurance costs during the vehicle's repair, towing charges, supplementary transportation costs like taxis and rented cars, and damages for your inconvenience (see the following sample complaint letter).

NEW-VEHICLE COMPLAINT LETTER/FAX/EMAIL

WITHOUT PREJUDICE

Date: _____

Name and address of dealer: _____

Name and address of manufacturer: _____

Please be advised that I am not satisfied with my _____ [indicate year, make, model, and serial number of vehicle]. The vehicle was purchased on [indicate date] and currently indicates _____ km on the odometer. The vehicle presently exhibits the following defects:

1. Premature rusting
2. Paint peeling/discoloration

3. Water leaks
4. Other defects (explain)

[List previous attempts to repair the vehicle. Attach a copy of a report from an independent garage, showing cost of estimated repairs and confirming the manufacturer's responsibility.]

I hereby request that you correct these defects free of charge under the terms of the implied warranty provisions of provincial consumer protection statutes as applied in *Kravitz v. General Motors* (1979), I.S.C.R., and *Chabot v. Ford* (1983), 39 O.R. (2d).

If you do not correct the defects noted above to my satisfaction and within a reasonable length of time, I will be obliged to ask an independent garage to _____ [choose (a) estimate or (b) carry out] the repairs and claim the amount of $_____ [state the cost, if possible] by way of the courts without further notice or delay.

I have dealt with your company because of its competence and honesty. I close in the hope of hearing from you within five (5) days of receiving this letter, failing which I will exercise the alternatives available to me. Please govern yourself accordingly.

Sincerely,

[Signed with telephone or fax number]

Specify five days (but allow 10 days) for either party to respond. If no satisfactory offer is made or your claim is ignored, file suit in small claims court. Make the manufacturer a party to the lawsuit, especially if an emissions warranty, a secret warranty extension, a safety recall campaign, or extensive chassis rusting is involved.

Step 3: Get the Government Involved

As a former Member of Parliament, let me assure you: a complaint letter copied to your local MP brings results. Manufacturer representatives want to lobby the government with a "clean slate" and to stay "on message." The last thing they want is an MP shoving unresolved owner complaints under their nose at some committee hearing. Another advantage in getting a government official involved is that MP offices have paid staff who know who to contact in the government and industry to apply extra pressure to get your problem resolved.

Step 4: Mediation and Arbitration

If the formality of a courtroom puts you off, or you're not sure that your claim is all that solid and don't want to pay the legal costs to find out, consider using mediation or arbitration offered by these groups: the Better Business Bureau (BBB), the Automobile Protection Association (APA), the Canadian Automobile Association (CAA), small claims court (mediation is often a prerequisite to going to trial), provincial and territorial government-run consumer mediation services, and the Canadian Motor Vehicle Arbitration Plan (CAMVAP):

> I just won my case with Chrysler Canada over my 2003 Ram SLT 44 quad cab truck. I've been having PCV valves freezing up (5 PCVs in 9,000 km). After one month in the shop, I went to CAMVAP to put in my claim, went to arbitration, and won. They have agreed to buy back my truck.

CAMVAP (1-800-207-0685; *www.camvap.ca*) is the best-known organization offering free arbitration. Awards are no longer confidential (thanks to pressure exerted by the Quebec government), and the stipulation that no appeals are allowed doesn't seem enforceable, as CAMVAP says on its own website:

> If you believe that the award or result of your hearing was improper because the arbitrator erred in law or erred in his or her assessment of the facts, then you may want to consider an appeal to the courts.

The agony of arbitration

Though CAMVAP presents its arbitration program as a free, fast, and fair process, some plaintiffs who have used CAMVAP's system say that the arbitration awards aren't enforced, multiple hearings may unduly delay a final judgment, and there is an undue reliance upon successive repair attempts before a final settlement is achieved.

According to a June 2009 study done by Quebec's Union Des Consommateurs, *Consumer Arbitration and Effective Process*, the APA says this about the CAMVAP program:

> The published success rate for consumers is around 61%, but 54% of consent awards and 21% of arbitrated cases were ordered back to the dealer for yet another repair. For many consumers who have gone through the arbitration process, this is not a satisfactory resolution, but in CAMVAP's statistics they appear as a successful resolution.

According to the APA, CAMVAP falsely claims to be a program enabling a consumer who has purchased a "lemon" to obtain the vehicle's repurchase. The

APA attributes the absence of guidelines regarding "lemons" to the program's control by industry, and to the low representation of consumers and governments within the program *(www.consommateur.qc.ca/union-des-consommateurs/docu/ protec_conso/arbitrageE.pdf)*.

Getting Outside Help

Don't let poor preparation scuttle your case. Ask government or independent consumer protection agencies to evaluate how well prepared you are before going to your first hearing. Also, use the Internet and media sources to ferret out additional facts and to gather support (*www.lemonaidcars.com* is a good place to start).

Auto Industry Groups

Ontario consumers may file an online complaint with the Ontario Motor Vehicle Industry Council (OMVIC) at *www.omvic.on.ca/services/consumers/file_complaint_ info.htm*. Sure, OMVIC is the dealer's self-defence lobby—made up of around 9,000 registered dealers and 20,000 registered salespeople—but it has the following mandate:

> [T]o maintain a fair, safe and informed marketplace in Ontario by protecting the rights of consumers, enhancing industry professionalism and ensuring fair, honest and open competition for registered motor vehicle dealers.

The way your complaint is handled will test the veracity of the above-stated goals.

Alberta has a similar self-regulating auto industry group, the Alberta Motor Vehicle Industry Council (AMVIC; *www.amvic.org*). During 2004, 873 consumer files were opened with AMVIC and 844 were closed. Their investigators laid 403 charges under the *Fair Trading Act* and the Canadian *Criminal Code*. Court fines of $13,400 were levied under the *Fair Trading Act,* and the courts ordered $289,281 in restitution payments. Also, AMVIC obtained $1,687,180 by mediation in restitution for victims of unfair trade practices.

Classified Ads and Media Exposés

Put an ad in the local paper describing your plight, and ask for information from people who may have experienced a problem similar to your own. This approach alerts others to the potential problem, helps build a base for a class action or a group meeting with the automaker, and puts pressure on the local dealer and manufacturer to settle with you. Sometimes the paper's news desk will assign someone to cover your story after your ad is published, or you may gain attention by setting up a website.

Television producers and their researchers need articulate consumers with issues that are easily filmed and understood. If you want media coverage, you must summarize your complaint and have visual aids that will hold the viewer's interest (viewers should be able to understand the issues with the sound turned off). Paint delamination? Show your peeling car. Bought a "lemon" vehicle? Show your repair bills. Holding a demonstration? Make it a "lemon" parade: Target one of the largest dealers, give your group a nifty name, and then drive past the dealership in vehicles decorated with "lemon" signs.

Call a press conference in front of the agency with whom you are in disagreement. Show your vehicle and any documents that tell the story. Carry a small sign, decorate your vehicle appropriately, and be polite but firm. All you want is to meet with someone responsible to review the claim and perhaps reconsider their earlier decision.

This approach works with government functionaries just as well as it does with car dealers. It's the intensity of your story coupled with your reasonableness and some film or pictures showing your displeasure that will get the story on the afternoon radio news, the 6 p.m. TV news, and the next morning's newspaper—which will be picked up again by the open-line radio shows for another day.

An example of these tactics in action: Mario Girolami is a volunteer driver who parked his truck in downtown Calgary on May 19, 2011, to deliver aid for Slave Lake fire victims. His engine was running and he had the emergency lights lit for the few moments it took to unload bedding, etc. As he was pulling away, a Calgary Parking Authority (CPA) agent slapped him with s $315 parking ticket.

Girolami called the *Calgary Sun*, showed where he had been parked, and handed out copies of the ticket. Renato Gandia wrote the story, and the *Sun's* "Page Five" picked it up. The upshot?

The next day the ticket was cancelled and the two Parking Authority bosses responsible were fired over their actions.

Yep, complaining works, anywhere in Canada, if it's done the right way.

Federal and Provincial Consumer Affairs

Although the beefed-up *Competition Act* has some bite in regard to misleading advertising and a number of other illegal business practices, the government has been more reactive than proactive in applying the law. The *Act* also had some teeth pulled by an amendment that forces the government to prove in civil court that not only did price fixing occur, but that it also was successful in influencing prices. There is now a more passive mindset among government staffers in investigating complaints of price fixing and misleading advertising.

Nevertheless, you never know what complaint will be taken seriously and lead to government action. So it pays to at least try. Use the online Enquiry/Complaint Form found at *www.competitionbureau.gc.ca*. Five years ago, an online complaint sent by *Lemon-Aid* made Toyota cease its Access price-fixing practices and pay out almost $2 million as a settlement fee.

On the provincial side, consumer affairs staffers can still help with investigation, mediation, and some litigation. Strong and effective consumer protection legislation has been left standing in most of the provinces, and resourceful consumers can use these laws in conjunction with media coverage to prod provincial consumer affairs offices into action. Furthermore, provincial elected officials and bureaucrats aren't as well shielded from criticism as their federal counterparts. A call to your MPP or MLA, or to their executive assistants, can often get things rolling.

Invest in Protest

You can have fun and put additional pressure on a seller or garage by putting a "lemon" sign on your car and parking it in front of the dealer or garage, by creating a "lemon" website, or by forming a self-help group like the Chrysler Lemon Owners Group (CLOG) or the Ford Lemon Owners Group (FLOG). After forming your group, you can have the occasional parade of creatively decorated cars visit area dealerships as the local media are convened. Just remember to keep your remarks pithy and factual, don't interfere with traffic or customers, and remain peaceful.

One other piece of advice from this consumer advocate with more than 40 years of experience and hundreds of pickets and mass demonstrations under his belt: Keep a sense of humour, and never break off negotiations.

Finally, don't be scared off by threats that it's illegal to criticize a product or company. Unions, environmentalists, and consumer groups do it regularly (it's called "informational picketing"), and the Supreme Court of Canada in *R. v. Guinard* reaffirmed this right in February 2002. In that judgment, an insurance policyholder posted a sign on his barn claiming the Commerce Insurance Company was unfairly refusing his claim. The municipality of St-Hyacinthe, Quebec, told him to take the sign down. He refused, maintaining that he had the right to state his opinion. The Supreme Court agreed. This judgment means that consumer protests, signs, and websites that criticize the actions of corporations cannot be banned simply because they say unpleasant things.

Defamation and libel

Picketing a new car dealer or automobile manufacturer, having a "sit-in" at the local auto show, or placing an ad rounding up other "lemon" owners are all legitimate public-interest complaint tactics that get results—and lawsuits. However, the legal intimidation hanging over these actions is now a past threat thanks to a recent ruling of our Supreme Court.

In December 2009, the Canadian Supreme Court rendered two judgments that make it much harder for plaintiffs to win cases alleging defamation or libel. The first decision overturned a lower court award of $1.5 million to a forestry executive who sued the *Toronto Star*. The *Star* alleged that he had used political connections to get approval for a golf course expansion (see *Grant v. Torstar Corp.*).

The Supreme Court struck down the judgment against the newspaper because it had failed to give adequate weight to the value of freedom of expression. The court announced a new defense of "responsible communication on matters of public interest." In the court's opinion, anyone (journalists, bloggers, unions, picketers, etc.) can avoid liability if they can show that the information they communicated—whether true or false—was of public interest and they tried their best to verify it.

In another case, also involving a major Canadian newspaper, a former Ontario police officer sued the *Ottawa Citizen* after it reported that he had misrepresented his search-and-rescue work at Ground Zero in New York City after the attacks of September 11, 2001. The Supreme Court reversed the $100,000 jury award because the judges felt the article was in the public interest (see *Quan v. Cusson*).

Paint and Body Defects

The following settlement advice applies mainly to paint defects, but you can use these tips for any other vehicle defect that you believe is the automaker's or dealer's responsibility. If you aren't sure whether the problem is a factory-related deficiency or a maintenance fault, have it checked out by an independent garage or get a technical service bulletin summary for your vehicle. The summary may include specific bulletins relating to diagnosis and correction as well as information about ordering the upgraded parts needed to fix your problem.

Four good examples of favourable paint judgments are *Shields v. General Motors of Canada*; *Bentley v. Dave Wheaton Pontiac Buick GMC Ltd. and General Motors of Canada*; *Maureen Frank v. General Motors of Canada Limited*; and the most recent, *Dunlop v. Ford of Canada*.

In *Dunlop v. Ford of Canada* (No. 58475/04; Ontario Superior Court of Justice, Richmond Hill Small Claims Court; January 5, 2005; Deputy Judge M.J. Winer), the owner of a 1996 Lincoln Town Car that was purchased used in 1999 for $27,000 was awarded $4,091.64. Judge Winer cited the *Shields* decision (following) and gave these reasons for finding Ford of Canada liable:

> Evidence was given by the Plaintiff's witness, Terry Bonar, an experienced paint auto technician. He gave evidence that the [paint] delamination may be both a manufacturing defect and can be caused or [sped] up by atmospheric conditions. He also says that [the paint on] a car like this should last ten to 15 years, [or even for] the life of the vehicle.

> It is my view that the presence of ultraviolet light is an environmental condition to which the vehicle is subject. If it cannot withstand this environmental condition, it is defective.

In *Shields v. General Motors of Canada* (No. 1398/96; Ontario Court, General Division, Oshawa Small Claims Court; July 24, 1997; Robert Zochodne, Deputy Judge), the owner of a 1991 Pontiac Grand Prix had purchased the vehicle used with over 100,000 km on its odometer. Beginning in 1995, the paint began to bubble and flake, and it eventually peeled off. Deputy Judge Zochodne awarded the plaintiff $1,205.72 and struck down every one of GM's arguments that the peeling paint was caused by acid rain, UV rays, or some other environmental factor. Here are some other important aspects of this 12-page judgment that GM didn't appeal:

1. The judge admitted many of the technical service bulletins referred to in *Lemon-Aid* as proof of GM's negligence.
2. Although the vehicle had 156,000 km on its odometer when the case went to court, GM still offered to pay 50 percent of the paint repairs if the plaintiff dropped his suit.
3. The judge ruled that the failure to protect the paint from the damaging effects of UV rays is akin to engineering a car that won't start in cold weather. In essence, vehicles must be built to withstand the rigours of the environment.
4. Here's an interesting twist: The original warranty covered defects that were present at the time it was in effect. The judge, taking statements found in the GM technical service bulletins, ruled that the UV problem was factory-related, existed during the warranty period, and, therefore, represented a latent defect that appeared once the warranty expired.
5. The subsequent purchaser was not prevented from making the warranty claim, even though the warranty had long since expired, both in time and mileage, and he was the second owner.

The small claims judgment in *Bentley v. Dave Wheaton Pontiac Buick GMC Ltd. and General Motors of Canada* (Victoria Registry No. 24779; British Columbia Small Claims Court; December 1, 1998; Judge Higinbotham) builds upon Ontario's *Shields v. General Motors of Canada* decision and cites other jurisprudence as to how long paint should last on a car. If you're wondering why Ford and Chrysler haven't been hit by similar judgments, remember that they usually settle out of court.

From *Maureen Frank v. General Motors of Canada Limited* (No. SC#12 (2001); Saskatchewan Provincial Court, Saskatoon, Saskatchewan; October 17, 2001; Provincial Court Judge H.G. Dirauf):

On June 23, 1997, the Plaintiff bought a 1996 Chevrolet Corsica from a General Motors dealership. At the time, the odometer showed 33,172 km. The vehicle still had some factory warranty. The car had been a lease car and had no previous accidents.

During June of 2000, the Plaintiff noticed that some of the paint was peeling off from the car and she took it to a General Motors dealership in Saskatoon and to the General Motors dealership in North Battleford where she purchased the car. While there were some discussions with the GM dealership about the peeling paint, nothing came of it and the Plaintiff now brings this action claiming the cost of a new paint job.

During 1999, the Plaintiff was involved in a minor collision causing damage to the left rear door. This damage was repaired. During this repair some scratches to the left front door previously done by vandals were also repaired.

The Plaintiff's witness, Frank Nemeth, is a qualified auto body repairman with some 26 years of experience. He testified that the peeling paint was a factory defect and that it was necessary to completely strip the car and repaint it. He diagnosed the cause of the peeling paint as a separation of the primer surface or colour coat from the electrocoat primer. In his opinion no primer surfacer was applied at all. He testified that once the peeling starts, it will continue. He has seen this problem on General Motors vehicles. The defect is called delamination.

Mr. Nemeth stated that a paint job should last at least 10 years. In my opinion, most people in Saskatchewan grow up with cars and are familiar with cars. I think it is common knowledge that the original paint on cars normally lasts in excess of 15 years and that rust becomes a problem before the paint fails. In any event, paint peeling off, as it did on the Plaintiff's vehicle, is not common. I find that the paint on a new car put on by the factory should last at least 15 years.

It is clear from the evidence of Frank Nemeth (independent body shop manager) that the delamination is a factory defect. His evidence was not seriously challenged. I find that the factory paint should not suffer a delamination defect for at least 15 years and that this factory defect breached the warranty that the paint was of acceptable quality and was durable for a reasonable period of time.

There will be judgment for the Plaintiff in the amount of $3,412.38 plus costs of $81.29.

Some of the important aspects of the *Frank* judgment are as follows:

1. The judge accepted that the automaker was responsible, even though the car had been bought used. The subsequent purchaser wasn't prevented from making the warranty claim, even though the warranty had long since expired, both in time and mileage, and she was the second owner.
2. The judge stressed that the provincial warranty can kick in when the automaker's warranty has expired or isn't applied.
3. By awarding full compensation to the plaintiff, the judge didn't feel that there was a significant "betterment" or improvement added to the car that would warrant reducing the amount of the award.
4. The judge decided that the paint delamination was a factory defect.
5. The judge also concluded that without this factory defect, a paint job should last up to 15 years.
6. GM offered to pay $700 of the paint repairs if the plaintiff dropped the suit; the judge awarded five times that amount.

7. Maureen Frank won this case despite having to confront GM lawyer Ken Ready, who had considerable experience arguing other paint cases for GM and Chrysler.

Other Paint and Rust Cases

Martin v. Honda Canada Inc. (March 17, 1986; Ontario Small Claims Court, Scarborough; Judge Sigurdson): The original owner of a 1981 Honda Civic sought compensation for the premature "bubbling, pitting, [and] cracking of the paint and rusting of the Civic after five years of ownership." Judge Sigurdson agreed with the owner and ordered Honda to pay the owner $1,163.95.

Thauberger v. Simon Fraser Sales and Mazda Motors (3 B.C.L.R., 193): This Mazda owner sued for damages caused by the premature rusting of his 1977 Mazda GLC. The court awarded him $1,000. Thauberger had also previously sued General Motors for a prematurely rusted Blazer truck and was awarded $1,000 in the same court. Both judges ruled that the defects couldn't be excluded from the automaker's expressed warranty or from the implied warranty granted by British Columbia's *Sale of Goods Act.*

Whittaker v. Ford Motor Company (1979) (24 O.R. (2d), 344): A new Ford developed serious corrosion problems despite having been rustproofed by the dealer. The court ruled that the dealer, not Ford, was liable for the damage for having sold the rustproofing product at the time of purchase. This is an important judgment to use when a rustproofer or paint protector goes out of business or refuses to pay a claim, because the decision holds the dealer jointly responsible.

See also:

- *Danson v. Chateau Ford (1976) C.P.* (Quebec Small Claims Court; No. 32-00001898-757; Judge Lande)
- *Doyle v. Vital Automotive Systems* (May 16, 1977; Ontario Small Claims Court, Toronto; Judge Turner)
- *Lacroix v. Ford* (April 1980; Ontario Small Claims Court, Toronto; Judge Tierney)
- *Marinovich v. Riverside Chrysler* (April 1, 1987; District Court of Ontario; No. 1030/85; Judge Stortini)

Safety-Related Failures

Sudden Acceleration, Chronic Stalling, and ABS and Airbag Failures

These kinds of failures are not that difficult to win in Canada under the doctrine of *res ipsa loquitur* ("the thing speaks for itself"), meaning, in negligence cases, that liability is shown by the failure itself. In a nutshell, the exact cause doesn't have to be pinpointed, and judges are free to award damages by weighing the "balance of probabilities" as to fault.

This advantage found in Canadian law was laid out succinctly in the July 1, 1998, issue of the *Journal of Small Business Management* in its comparison of product liability laws on both sides of the border ("Effects of Product Liability Laws on Small Business" at *www.allbusiness.com/legal/laws-government-regulations/691847-1. html*):

> Although in theory the Canadian consumer must prove all of the elements of negligence (*Farro v. Nutone Electrical Ltd. 1990*; Ontario Law Reform Commission 1979; Thomas 1989), most Canadian courts allow injured consumers to use a procedural aid known as *res ipsa loquitur* to prove their cases (*Nicholson v. John Deere Ltd. 1986*; *McMorran v. Dom. Stores Ltd. 1977*). Under *res ipsa loquitur,* plaintiffs must only prove that they were injured in a way that would not ordinarily occur without the defendant's negligence. It is then the responsibility of the defendant to prove that he was not negligent. As proving the negative is extremely difficult, this Canadian reversal of the burden of proof usually results in an outcome functionally equivalent to strict product liability (*Phillips v. Ford Motor Co. of Canada Ltd. 1971*; Murray 1988). This concept is reinforced by the principal that a Canadian manufacturer does not have the right to manufacture an inherently dangerous product when a method exists to manufacture that product without risk of harm. To do so subjects the manufacturer to liability even if the safer method is more expensive (*Nicholson v. John Deere Ltd. 1986*).

In *Jarvis v. Ford* (United States Second Circuit Court of Appeal, February 7, 2002), a judgment was rendered in favour of a driver who was injured when her six-day-old Ford Aerostar minivan suddenly accelerated as it was started and put into gear. What makes this decision unique is that the jury had no specific proof of a defect. The Court of Appeal agreed with the jury award, and Justice Sotomayor (now a Supreme Court Justice) gave these reasons for the Court's verdict:

> ...a product may be found to be defective without proof of the specific malfunction:

> It may be inferred that the harm sustained by the plaintiff was caused by a product defect existing at the time of sale or distribution, without proof of a specific defect, when the incident that harmed the plaintiff:

> (a) was of a kind that ordinarily occurs as a result of product defect; and
> (b) was not, in the particular case, solely the result of causes other than product defect existing at the time of sale or distribution.

> Restatement (Third) of Torts: Product Liability § 3 (1998). In comment c to this section, the Restatement notes:

>> [There is] no requirement that plaintiff prove what aspect of the product was defective. The inference of defect may be drawn under this Section without proof of the specific defect. Furthermore, quite apart from the question of what type of defect was involved, the plaintiff need not explain specifically what constituent part of the product failed. For example, if an inference of defect

> can be appropriately drawn in connection with the catastrophic failure of an
> airplane, the plaintiff need not establish whether the failure is attributable to
> fuel-tank explosion or engine malfunction.

The jury awarded Ms. Jarvis $24,568 in past medical insurance premiums, $340,338 in lost earnings, and $200,000 in pain and suffering. For future damages, the jury awarded $22,955 in medical insurance premiums, $648,944 in lost earnings, and $300,000 for pain and suffering.

Incidents of sudden acceleration or chronic stalling are quite common. However, they are often very difficult to diagnose, and individual cases can be treated very differently by federal safety agencies. Nevertheless, getting corroborative proof may be far easier in the future, now that the U.S. Department of Transportation under NHTSA will require that automakers install "black box" accident data recorders in all vehicles and give out their access codes to accident investigators. In fact, a number of impaired drivers have already been sent to jail in Canada based on black-box-accessed data.

Sudden acceleration is considered to be a safety-related problem—stalling, only sometimes. Never mind that a vehicle's sudden loss of power on a busy highway puts everyone's lives at risk. The same problem exists with engine and transmission powertrain failures, which are only occasionally considered to be safety-related. ABS and airbag failures, however, are universally considered to be life-threatening defects. If your vehicle manifests any of these conditions, here's what you need to do:

1. Get independent witnesses to confirm that the problem exists. Your primary tools include an independent mechanic's verification, passenger accounts, downloaded data from your vehicle's data recorder, and lots of Internet browsing using *www.lemonaidcars.com* and Google's search engine. Notify the dealer or manufacturer by fax, email, or registered letter that you consider the problem to be a factory-induced, safety-related defect. Make sure you address your correspondence to the manufacturer's product liability or legal affairs department. At the dealership's service bay, make sure that every work order clearly states the problem as well as the number of previous attempts to fix it. (You should end up with a few complaint letters and a handful of work orders confirming that this is an ongoing deficiency.) If the dealer won't give you a copy of the work order because the work is a warranty claim, ask for a copy of the order number "in case your estate wishes to file a claim, pursuant to an accident." (This wording will get the service manager's attention.) Leaving a paper trail is crucial for any claim you may have later on, because it shows your concern and persistence, and it clearly indicates that the dealer and manufacturer have had ample time to correct the defect.
2. Note on the work order that you expect the problem to be diagnosed and corrected under the emissions warranty or a "goodwill" program. It also wouldn't hurt to add the phrase on the work order or in your claim letters that "any deaths, injuries, or damage caused by the defect will be the dealer's and

manufacturer's responsibility" because the work order (or letter, fax, or email) constitutes you putting them on "formal notice."

3. If the dealer does the necessary repairs at little or no cost to you, send a follow-up confirmation that you appreciate the "goodwill." Also, emphasize that you'll be back if the problem reappears—even if the warranty has expired—because the repair renews your warranty rights applicable to that defect. In other words, the warranty clock is set back to its original position. Understand that you won't likely get a copy of the repair bill, either, because dealers don't like to admit that there was a serious defect present and don't feel that they owe you a copy of the work order if the repair was done *gratis*. You can, however, subpoena the complete vehicle file from the dealer and manufacturer (this costs about $50) if the case goes to small claims or a higher court. This request has produced many out-of-court settlements when the internal documents show extensive work was carried out to correct the problem.

4. If the problem persists, send a letter, fax, or email to the dealer and manufacturer saying so, look for ALLDATA service bulletins to confirm that your vehicle's defects are factory-related, and report the failure by contacting Transport Canada or NHTSA or by logging on to NHTSA's website. Also, you may want to involve the non-profit, Montreal-based Automobile Protection Association or the Nader-founded Center for Auto Safety in Washington, D.C. (*www.autosafety.org/auto-defects*) to get a lawyer referral and an information sheet covering the problem.

5. Now come two crucial questions: Repair the defect now or later? Use the dealer or an independent? Generally, it's smart to use an independent garage if you know the dealer isn't pushing for free corrective repairs from the manufacturer, if weeks or months have passed without any resolution of your claim, if the dealer keeps repeating that it's a maintenance item, and if you know an independent mechanic who will give you a detailed work order showing the defect is factory-related and not caused by poor maintenance. Don't mention that a court case may ensue, since this will scare the dickens out of your only independent witness. An added bonus is that the repair charges will be about half of what a dealer would demand. Incidentally, if the automaker later denies warranty "goodwill" because you used an independent repairer, use the argument that the defect's safety implications required emergency repairs, carried out by whoever could see you first.

6. Dashboard-mounted warning lights usually come on prior to airbags suddenly deploying, ABS brakes failing, or engine glitches causing the vehicle to stall out. (Sudden acceleration usually occurs without warning.) Automakers consider these lights to be critical safety warnings and generally advise drivers to immediately have their vehicle serviced to correct the problem when any of the warning lights come on (advice that can be found in the owner's manual). This fact bolsters the argument that your life was threatened, emergency repairs were required, and your request for another vehicle or a complete refund isn't out of line.

7. Sudden acceleration can have multiple causes, isn't easy to duplicate, and

is often blamed on the driver mistaking the accelerator for the brakes or failing to perform proper maintenance. Yet NHTSA data shows that with the 1992–2000 Explorer, for example, a faulty cruise-control or PCV valve and poorly mounted pedals are the most likely causes of the Explorer's sudden acceleration. So how do you satisfy the burden of proof showing that the problem exists and it's the automaker's responsibility? Use the legal doctrine called "the balance of probabilities" by eliminating all of the possible dodges the dealer or manufacturer may employ. Show that proper maintenance has been carried out, you're a safe driver, and the incident occurs frequently and without warning.

8. If any of the above defects causes an accident, or if the airbag fails to deploy or you're injured by its deployment, ask your insurance company to have the vehicle towed to a neutral location and clearly state that neither the dealer nor the automaker should touch the vehicle until your insurance company and Transport Canada have completed their investigation. Also, get as many witnesses as possible and immediately go to the hospital for a check-up, even if you're feeling okay. You may be injured and not know it because the adrenalin coursing through your veins is masking your injuries. A hospital exam will easily confirm that your injuries are accident-related, which is essential evidence for court or for future settlement negotiations.

9. Peruse NHTSA's online accident and service bulletin database to find reports of other accidents caused by the same failure, bulletins that indicate part upgrades, current defect investigations, and reported failures that have resulted in recalls or closed investigations.

10. Don't let your insurance company bully you. Refuse to let them settle the case if you're sure the accident was caused by a mechanical failure. Even if an engineering analysis fails to directly implicate the manufacturer or dealer, you can always plead the aforementioned balance of probabilities. If the insurance company settles, your insurance premiums will soar and the manufacturer will get away with the perfect crime.

Toyota's "Lag and Lurch"

Toyota's sudden acceleration problems have been joined by another safety defect that delays acceleration from a stop and then suddenly shoots the car forward as the electronic sensors finally pick up the throttle command. This results in near rear-enders as the car appears to stall and then darts forward. Toyota has known about this "lag and lurch" safety hazard for well over a decade, and apparently it afflicts almost its entire fleet of vehicles.

Using the Courts

It is well known that disputes that go before the courts can last a very long time. The plaintiff may face interminable delays setting and postponing hearing dates; long, drawn-out hearings, procedural roadblocks, and appeals; and long-awaited judgments. For example, in the judicial district of Montreal, the period between filing a legal claim and the hearing date is 14 to 15 months. British Columbia's small claims division registered in 2006 a median period of 296 days from filing a legal claim to the hearing date.

 ## Top 10 Legal Phrases You Should Know

When using Canadian courts it's a good idea to be trilingual, with a good knowledge of English, French, and Legalese. The following phrases are ones that you are mostly likely to encounter when filing or pleading a lawsuit:

Audi alteram partem: "Hear the other side." It is most often used to refer to the principle that no person should be judged without a fair hearing in which each party is given the opportunity to respond to the evidence against him or her.

Caveat emptor: "Let the buyer beware." Purchasers are responsible for checking whether goods suit their needs. This concept ruled the consumer protection movement until the publication of Ralph Nader's *Unsafe at Any Speed* in the '60s. That book, which exposed the Corvair's design deficiencies, argued that more effective legislation was needed to force a "seller beware" mindset. British Columbia, Saskatchewan, and Quebec were the first provinces to apply this doctrine in legislation relative to automobile warranties and the interpretation of what is reasonable durability.

Ex post facto law: "From after the action." A law that retroactively changes the legal consequences (or status) of actions committed or relationships that existed prior to the enactment of the law.

Ignorantia juris non excusat: "Ignorance of the law excuses no one." A legal principle holding that a person who is unaware of a law may not escape responsibility for violating that law.

Pro bono publico: "For the public good." The term is generally used to describe professional work undertaken voluntarily and without payment as a public service.

Mens rea: "A guilty mind." Considered one of the necessary elements of a crime. This goes to the defendant's intent.

Quanti minoris: "A reduced amount," or "diminished value." A partial refund may be claimed based upon the reduced value of a product due to the manufacturer's or seller's negligence or misrepresentation. This principle was used successfully against Nissan and Ford of Canada by the Automobile Protection Association in hundreds of small claims court cases during the '70s. Refunds up to $300 were awarded as compensation to buyers who were sold "redated" new vehicles that were the previous year's model. Nissan appealed the awards to the Supreme Court of Canada, claiming small claims courts were unconstitutional because lawyers were barred from pleading. A second argument was that the small claims courts lacked jurisdiction because the proper remedy was a cancellation of the sale. This would have taken the cases out of the courts $300 maximum jurisdiction. The Supreme Court rejected both arguments (See *Nissan v. Pelletier*).

Ratio decidendi: "The point in a case which determines the judgment," or "the principle which the case establishes."

Res ipsa loquitur: "The thing speaks for itself." The elements of duty of care and breach can be sometimes inferred from the very nature of an accident or other outcome, even without direct evidence of how any defendant behaved.

Restitutio in integrum: "Restoration to the original condition." This is one of the primary guiding principles behind the awarding of damages in common law negligence claims. The general rule, as the principle implies, is that the amount of compensation awarded should put the successful plaintiff in the position he or she would have been in had the wrongful action not been committed. Thus, the plaintiff should clearly be awarded damages for direct expenses, such as medical bills and property repairs, and the loss of future earnings attributable to the injury (which often involves difficult speculation about future career and promotion prospects). This is also a term used to describe how far insurance companies must go in repairing accident damage.

When to Sue?

If the dealer you've been negotiating with agrees to make things right, give him or her a deadline for completing the repairs and then have an independent garage check them over. If no offer is made within 10 working days, file suit in court. Make the manufacturer a party to the lawsuit only if the original, unexpired warranty is still in place; if your claim falls under the emissions warranty, a TSB, a secret warranty extension, or a safety recall campaign; or if there is extensive chassis rusting caused by poor engineering.

Which Court?

Most claims can be handled without a lawyer in small claims court, especially now that courts' jurisdictions vary from $5,000 to $25,000. Still, it's up to you to decide what remedy to pursue—that is, whether you want a partial refund or a cancellation of the sale. To determine the refund amount, add the estimated cost of repairing the existing mechanical defects to the cost of prior repairs. Don't exaggerate your losses or claim for repairs that are considered to be routine maintenance. A suit for the cancellation of a sale involves practical problems. The court requires that the vehicle be "tendered," or taken back, to the seller at the time the lawsuit is filed. This leaves you without transportation for as long as the case continues, unless you purchase another vehicle in the interim. If you lose the case, you must then take back the old vehicle and pay the accumulated storage fees. You could go from having no vehicle to having two—one of which is a clunker!

Generally, if the cost of repairs or the sales contract amount falls within the small claims court limit (discussed later), file the case there to keep your costs to a minimum and to get a speedy hearing. Small claims court judgments aren't easily appealed, lawyers aren't necessary, filing fees are minimal (about $125), and cases are usually heard within a few months. In fact, your suit is almost always best argued in the provincial small claims court to keep costs and frustrations down and to get a quick resolution within a few months.

> Mr. Edmonston, I emailed you earlier in the year seeking help on my small claims case against Ford. I'm happy to report that I won my case and received a $1,900 settlement cheque from Ford in the mail yesterday! As you may recall I have a 1991 Explorer that has a significant paint peel problem.
>
> MARK G.

Here's another reason not to be greedy: If you claim more than the small claims court limit, you'll have to go to a higher court—where costs quickly add up, lawyers routinely demand 30 percent of your winnings or settlement, and delays of a few years or more are commonplace.

Small Claims Courts

Crooked automakers scurry away from small claims courts like cockroaches from bug spray, not because the courts can issue million-dollar judgments or force litigants to spend a fortune in legal fees (they can't), but because dealers and manufacturers don't want the bad publicity arising from the filings and eventual judgments. Other disincentives are that small claims courts can award sizeable sums to plaintiffs not represented by lawyers, and they make jurisprudence that other judges on the same bench are likely to follow.

For example, in *Dawe v. Courtesy Chrysler* (Dartmouth Nova Scotia Small Claims Court; SCCH #206825; July 30, 2004), Judge Patrick L Casey, Q.C., rendered an impressive 21-page decision citing key automobile product liability cases from the past 80 years, including *Donoghue, Kravitz,* and *Davis.* The court awarded $5,037 to the owner of a new 2001 Cummins engine–equipped Ram pickup with the following problems: It wandered all over the road; lost power, or jerked and bucked; shifted erratically; lost braking ability; bottomed out when passing over bumps; allowed water to leak into the cab; produced a burnt-wire and oil smell in the interior as the lights would dim; and produced a rear-end whine and wind noise around the doors and under the dash. Dawe had sold the vehicle and reduced his claim to meet the small claims threshold. Anyone with water leaking into the interior or problems with the engine, transmission, or suspension will find this judgment particularly useful.

Interestingly, "small claims" court is quickly becoming a misnomer, now that Alberta, Nova Scotia, British Columbia, Yukon, and Ontario allow claims of up to $25,000, and other provinces permit $5,000–$20,000 filings. The fees in Canada for a claim before a small claims division are $15 in the Northwest Territories for any claim of $500 or less, and $39 for a claim exceeding $500. The highest fees for a claim filed by a consumer are $200, in Alberta, for a claim of $7,501 to $25,000, and only $100 for any claim of $7,500 or less. Claims before small claims divisions don't generally incur other fees.

See the following table, and check your provincial or territorial court's website for specific rules and restrictions.

SMALL CLAIMS COURT LIMITS

PROVINCE/TERRITORY	CLAIM LIMIT	COURT WEBSITE
Alberta	$25,000	www.albertacourts.ab.ca
British Columbia	$25,000	www.courts.gov.bc.ca
Manitoba	$10,000	www.manitobacourts.mb.ca
New Brunswick	$ 6,000	www.gnb.ca/cour
Newfoundland and Labrador	$ 5,000	www.court.nl.ca
Northwest Territories	$10,000	www.nwtcourts.ca
Nova Scotia	$25,000	www.courts.ns.ca
Nunavut	$20,000	www.nucj.ca
Ontario	$25,000	www.ontariocourts.on.ca
Prince Edward Island	$ 8,000	www.gov.pe.ca/courts
Quebec	$ 7,000	www.justice.gouv.qc.ca
Saskatchewan	$20,000	www.sasklawcourts.ca
Yukon	$25,000	www.yukoncourts.ca

There are small claims courts in most counties of every province, and you can make a claim in the county where the problem happened or where the defendant lives and conducts business. Simply go to the small claims court office and ask for a claim form. Remember, you must identify the defendant correctly, which may require some help from the court clerk (look for other recent lawsuits naming the same party). Crooks often change their company's name to escape liability; for example, it would be impossible to sue Joe's Garage (1999) if your contract is with Joe's Garage, Inc. (1984).

At this point, it wouldn't hurt to hire a lawyer or a paralegal for a brief walk-through of small claims procedures to ensure that you've prepared your case properly and that you know what objections will likely be raised by the other side. If, instead, you'd like a lawyer to do all the work for you, there are a number of law firms around the country that specialize in small claims litigation. "Small claims" doesn't mean "small legal fees," though. In Toronto, some law offices charge a flat fee of $1,000 for a basic small claims lawsuit and trial.

Remember that you're entitled to bring to court any evidence relevant to your case, including written documents, such as a contract, letter, or bill of sale or receipt. If your car has developed severe rust problems, bring a photograph (signed and dated by the photographer) to court. You may also have witnesses testify in court. It's important to discuss a witness's testimony prior to the court date. If a witness can't attend the court date, he or she can write a report and sign it for representation in court. This situation usually applies to an expert witness, such as an independent mechanic who has evaluated your car's problems.

If you lose your case in spite of all your preparation and research, some small claims court statutes allow cases to be retried in exceptional circumstances, at a nominal cost. If a new witness has come forward, additional evidence has been discovered, or key documents (that were previously not available) have become accessible, apply for a retrial.

Alan MacDonald, a *Lemon-Aid* reader who won his case in small claims court, gives the following tips on beating Ford over a faulty automatic transmission:

> I want to thank you for the advice you provided in my dealings with the Ford Motor Company of Canada Limited and Highbury Ford Sales Limited regarding my 1994 Ford Taurus wagon and the problems with the automatic transmission (Taurus and Windstar transmissions are identical). I also wish to apologize for not sending you a copy of this judgment earlier...(*MacDonald v. Highbury Ford Sales Limited*, Ontario Superior Court of Justice in the Small Claims Court London, June 6, 2000, Court File #0001/00, Judge J.D. Searle).
>
> In 1999, after only 105,000 km, the automatic transmission went. I took the car to Highbury Ford to have it repaired. We paid $2,070 to have the transmission fixed, but protested and felt the transmission failed prematurely. We contacted Ford, but to no avail: Their reply was we were out of warranty, period. The transmission was so poorly repaired (and we went back to Highbury Ford several times) that we had to go to Mr. Transmission to have the transmission fixed again nine months later at a further $1,906.02.
>
> It is at that point that I contacted you, and I was surprised, and somewhat speechless (which you noticed) when you personally called me to provide advice and encouragement. I am very grateful for your call. My observations with going through small claims court involved the following: I filed in January of 2000, the trial took place on June 1 and the judgment was issued June 6.
>
> At pretrial, a representative of Ford (Ann Sroda) and a representative from Highbury Ford were present. I came with one binder for each of the defendants, the court and one for myself (each binder was about 3 inches thick, containing your reports on Ford Taurus automatic transmissions, ALLDATA Service Bulletins, Taurus Transmissions Victims (Bradley website), Center for Auto Safety (website), Read This Before Buying a Taurus (website), and the Ford Vent Page (website)).
>
> The representative from Ford asked a lot of questions (I think she was trying to find out if I had read the contents of the information I was relying on). The Ford representative

then offered a 50 percent settlement based on the initial transmission work done at Highbury Ford. The release allowed me to still sue Highbury Ford with regards to the necessity of going to Mr. Transmission because of the faulty repair done by the dealer. Highbury Ford displayed no interest in settling the case, and so I had to go to court.

For court, I prepared by issuing a summons to the manager at Mr. Transmission, who did the second transmission repair, as an expert witness. I was advised that unless you produce an expert witness you won't win in a car repair case in small claims court. Next, I went to the law school library in London and received a great deal of assistance in researching cases pertinent to car repairs. I was told that judgments in your home province (in my case Ontario) were binding on the court; that cases outside of the home province could be considered, but not binding, by the judge.

The cases I used for trial involved *Pelleray v. Heritage Ford Sales Ltd.*, Ontario Small Claims Court (Scarborough) SC7688/91 March 22, 1993; *Phillips et al. v. Ford Motor Co. of Canada Ltd. et al,* Ontario Reports 1970, 15th January 1970; *Gregorio v. Intrans-Corp.*, Ontario Court of Appeal, May 19, 1994; *Collier v. McMaster's Auto Sales*, New Brunswick Court of Queen's Bench, April 26, 1991; *Sigurdson v. Hillcrest Service & Acklands (1977)*, Saskatchewan Queen's Bench; *White v. Sweetland*, Newfoundland District Court, Judicial Centre of Gander, November 8, 1978; *Raiches Steel Works v. J. Clark & Son*, New Brunswick Supreme Court, March 7, 1977; *Mudge v. Corner Brook Garage Ltd.*, Newfoundland Supreme Court, July 17, 1975; *Sylvain v. Carroseries d'Automobiles Guy Inc. (1981)*, C.P. 333, Judge Page; [and] *Gagnon v. Ford Motor Company of Canada, Limited et Marineau Automobile Co. Ltée. (1974)*, C.S. 422–423.

In court, I had prepared the case, as indicated above, [and] had my expert witness and two other witnesses who had driven the vehicle (my wife and my 18-year-old son). As you can see by the judgment, we won our case and I was awarded $1,756.52, including pre-judgment interest and costs.

Key Court Decisions

The following Canadian and U.S. lawsuits and judgments cover typical problems that are likely to arise. Use them as leverage when negotiating a settlement or as a reference should your claim go to trial. Legal principles applying to Canadian and American law are similar; however, Quebec court decisions may be based on legal principles that don't apply outside that province. You can find a comprehensive listing of Canadian decisions from small claims courts all the way to the Supreme Court of Canada at *www.canlii.org* (Canadian Legal Information Institute).

Additional court judgments can be found in the legal reference section of your city's main public library or at a nearby university law library. Ask the librarian for help in choosing the legal phrases that best describe your claim.

LexisNexis (*global.lexisnexis.com/ca*) and FindLaw (*www.findlaw.com*) are two useful Internet sites for legal research. Their main drawback, though, is that you may need to subscribe or use a lawyer's subscription to access jurisprudence and other areas of the sites. However, there *is* a free online summary of class actions filed in Canada at *classactionsincanada.blogspot.com*. It's run by Ward Branch, one of the legal counsels in the Canada-wide, $1.2 billion class action settled several years ago by General Motors for defective engine intake manifold gaskets.

 An excellent reference book that will give you plenty of tips on filing, pleading, and collecting your judgment is Justice Marvin A. Zuker's *Ontario Small Claims Court Practice 2012* (Carswell, 2011). Judge Zuker's annual publication is easily understood by non-lawyers and uses court decisions from across Canada to help you plead your case successfully in almost any Canadian court.

Product Liability

Almost three decades ago, before *Robson*, the Supreme Court of Canada clearly affirmed in *Kravitz v. GM* that automakers and their dealers are jointly liable for the replacement or repair of a vehicle if independent testimony shows that it is afflicted with factory-related defects that compromise its safety or performance. The existence of secret warranty extensions or technical service bulletins also help prove that the vehicle's problems are the automaker's responsibility. For example, in *Lowe v. Fairview Chrysler* (see page 145), technical service bulletins were instrumental in showing in 1989 that Chrysler had a history of automatic transmission failures similar to what we see in Ford and GM vehicles today.

In addition to replacing or repairing the vehicle, an automaker can also be held responsible for any damages arising from the defect (refer to *Wharton*, page 103). This means that loss of wages, supplementary transportation costs, and damages for personal inconvenience can be awarded. However, in the States, product liability damage awards often exceed millions of dollars, while Canadian courts are far less generous.

When a warranty claim is rejected on the pretext that you "altered" the vehicle, failed to carry out preventive maintenance, or drove abusively, manufacturers *must* prove to the court that there's a link between their allegation and the failure (see *Julien v. General Motors of Canada Ltd.* (1991), 116 N.B.R. (2d) 80).

Before settling any claim with GM or any other automaker, search the Internet to read the latest information from dissatisfied customers who've banded together and set up their own self-help websites.

Implied Warranty (Reasonable Durability)

This is that powerful "other" warranty that they never tell you about. It applies during and after the expiration of the manufacturer's or dealer's expressed or written warranty and requires that a part or repair will last a "reasonable" period of time. Look at the "Reasonable Part Durability" chart on page 112 for some guidelines on what you should expect.

Judges usually apply the implied or legal warranty when the manufacturer's expressed warranty has expired and the vehicle's manufacturing defects remain uncorrected. The landmark Canadian decisions upholding implied warranties in auto claims have been *Donoghue v. Stevenson*, [1932] A.C. 562 (H.L.), and *General Motors Products of Canada Ltd. v. Kravitz*, [1979] 1 S.C.R. 790.

In *Donoghue*, the court had to determine if the manufacturer of a bottle of ginger beer owed a duty to a consumer who suffered injury as a result of finding a decomposed snail in the bottle after consuming part of the bottle's contents. Lord Atkin, in finding liability against the manufacturer, established the principle of negligence. His reasons have been followed and adopted in all the common-law countries:

> The rule that you are to love your neighbour becomes in law, you must not injure your neighbour; and the lawyer's question, who is my neighbour? receives a restricted reply. You must take reasonable care to avoid acts or omissions which you can reasonably foresee would be likely to injure your neighbour. Who, then, is my neighbour?

> The answer seems to be persons who are so closely and directly affected by my act that I ought reasonably to have them in contemplation as being so affected when I am directing my mind to the acts or omissions which are called in question.

Over 45 years later, in Quebec, *Kravitz* said essentially the same thing. In that case, the court said the seller's warranty of quality was an accessory to the property and was transferred with it on successive sales. Accordingly, subsequent buyers could invoke the contractual warranty of quality against the manufacturer, even though they did not contract directly with it. This precedent is now codified in articles 1434, 1442, and 1730 of Quebec's *Civil Code* (see *Tardif v. Hyundai Motor America* at *www.canlii.org/fr/qc/qccs/doc/2004/2004canlii7992/2004canlii7992.html* for a full analysis of warranties, hidden defects, and misrepresentation relating to Hyundai's inability to be truthful about its horsepower ratings).

Minivan Doors (Windstar "Mental Distress")

In *Sharman v. Formula Ford Sales Limited, Ford Credit Limited, and Ford Motor Company of Canada Limited* (Ontario Superior Court of Justice; Oakville, Ontario; No. 17419/02SR; 2003/10/07), Justice Shepard awarded $7,500 to the owner of a 2000 Windstar for mental distress resulting from the breach of the implied warranty of fitness, plus $7,207 for breach of contract and breach of warranty. The problem with the Windstar was that its sliding door wasn't secure and leaked air and water after many attempts to repair it. The judge cited the *Wharton* decision as support for his award for mental distress:

> The plaintiff and his family have had three years of aggravation, inconvenience, worry, and concern about their safety and that of their children. Generally speaking, our contract law did not allow for compensation for what may be mental distress, but that may be changing. I am indebted to counsel for providing me with the decision of

the British Columbia Court of Appeal in *Wharton v. Tom Harris Chevrolet Oldsmobile Cadillac Ltd.*, [2002] B.C.J. No. 233, 2002 BCCA 78. This decision was recently followed in *Tiavra v. Victoria Ford Alliance Ltd.*, [2003] B.C.J. No. 1957.

In *Wharton*, the purchaser of a Cadillac Eldorado claimed damages against the dealer because the car's sound system emitted an annoying buzzing noise and the purchaser had to return the car to the dealer for repair numerous times over two-and-a-half years. The trial court awarded damages of $2,257.17 for breach of warranty with respect to the sound system, and $5,000 in non-pecuniary damages for loss of enjoyment of their luxury vehicle and for inconvenience, for a total award of $7,257.17....

In the *Wharton* case, the respondent contracted for a "luxury" vehicle for pleasure use. It included a sound system that the appellant's service manager described as "high end." The respondent's husband described the purchase of the car in this way: "[W]e bought a luxury car that was supposed to give us a luxury ride and be a quiet vehicle, and we had nothing but difficulty with it from the very day it was delivered with this problem that nobody seemed to be able to fix. So basically we had a luxury product that gave us no luxury for the whole time that we had it."

It is clear that an important object of the contract was to obtain a vehicle that was luxurious and a pleasure to operate. Furthermore, the buzzing noise was the cause of physical, in the sense of sensory, discomfort to the respondent and her husband. The trial judge found it inhibited listening to the sound system and was irritating in normal conversation. The respondent and her husband also bore the physical inconvenience of taking the vehicle to the appellant on numerous occasions for repairs.

In my view, a defect in manufacture that goes to the safety of the vehicle deserves a modest increase. I would assess the plaintiff's damage for mental distress resulting from the breach of the implied warranty of fitness at $7,500.

Free Engine Repairs

In the following judgments, Ford was forced to reimburse the cost of engine head gasket repairs carried out under the implied warranty—long after the expressed warranty had expired.

Dufour v. Ford Canada Ltd. (April 10, 2001; Quebec Small Claims Court, Hull; No. 550-32-008335-009; Justice P. Chevalier): Ford was forced to reimburse the cost of engine head gasket repairs carried out on a 1996 Windstar 3.8L engine.

Schaffler v. Ford Motor Company Limited and Embrun Ford Sales Ltd. (Ontario Superior Court of Justice, L'Orignal Small Claims Court; Court File No. 59-2003; July 22, 2003; Justice Gerald Langlois): The plaintiff bought a used 1995 Windstar in 1998. The engine head gasket was repaired for free three years later under Ford's seven-year extended warranty. In 2002, at 109,600 km, the head gasket failed again, seriously damaging the engine. Ford refused a second repair.

Justice Langlois ruled that Ford's warranty extension bulletin listed signs and symptoms of the covered defect that were identical to the problems written on the second work order ("persistent and/or chronic engine overheating; heavy white smoke evident from the exhaust tailpipe; flashing 'low coolant' instrument-panel light even after coolant refill; and constant loss of engine coolant"). The judge concluded that the dealer knew of the problem well within the warranty period and was therefore negligent. The plaintiff was awarded $4,941 plus 5 percent interest. This award included $1,070 for two months' car rental.

John R. Reid and Laurie M. McCall v. Ford Motor Company of Canada (Superior Court of Justice, Ottawa Small Claims Court; Claim No. 02-SC-077344; July 11, 2003; Justice Tiernay): A 1996 Windstar bought used in 1997 experienced engine head gasket failure in October 2001 at 159,000 km. Judge Tiernay awarded the plaintiffs $4,145 for the following reasons:

> A Technical Service Bulletin dated June 28, 1999, was circulated to Ford dealers. It dealt specifically with "undetermined loss of coolant" and "engine oil contaminated with coolant" in the 1996–98 Windstar and five other models of Ford vehicles. I conclude that Ford owed a duty of care to the Plaintiff to equip this vehicle with a cylinder head gasket of sufficient sturdiness and durability that would function trouble-free for at least seven years, given normal driving and proper maintenance conditions. I find that Ford is answerable in damages for the consequences of its negligence.

Chams v. Ford Motor Company of Canada, Limited, and Courtesy Ford Lincoln Sales, Limited (Ontario Superior Court of Justice, Small Claims Court; London, Ontario; Claim No. 5868, Court File No. 103/04; November 22, 2004; Deputy Justice J.D. Searle):

Reasons for Judgment

1. J.D. SEARLE DEPUTY J.: The defendant Ford Motor Company of Canada, Limited, hereinafter referred to as "Ford" is a corporation based in Oakville, Ontario and is a manufacturer of motor vehicles. The defendant Courtesy Ford Lincoln Sales Limited, hereinafter referred to as "Courtesy" is a corporation which carries on the business of a Ford dealer in the city of London in the county of Middlesex.

2. Samir Chams resides in the city of London. In 1997 he purchased from Courtesy a low kilometerage 1995 Ford Windstar van with a 3.8 liter engine. By 1998 at the latest Ford was aware the head gaskets of such engines had a defect which could destroy the engine. In 2000 it offered to the plaintiff and other owners an "additional warranty" for this defect but limited the warranty to seven years from the date the vehicle first went into service or 160,000 kilometers, whichever came first. Upon receiving notice of the additional warranty in 2000 the plaintiff took his van to Courtesy but no problems were manifest. For the plaintiff the original warranty had expired by passage of time. The additional warranty expired on March 08, 2002 by passage of time.

3. On January 11, 2004, some 22 months after the additional warranty expired, the plaintiff's engine overheated and was destroyed within a matter of minutes.

The van had only 80,000 kilometers on the odometer. In due course the engine was replaced at a cost of over $4,000.00 paid by the plaintiff. As the court understands the plaintiff's case he is suing outside the expired warranty. Against Ford he alleges manufacturing defect. Against Courtesy he alleges negligence in 2000 in not replacing the defective head gasket to avoid possible engine destruction or at least telling him that was an option at his own expense. He also invokes manufacturer's warranty.

4. Ford contends it has no responsibility beyond its warranty and the destruction of the engine was from a cause or causes other than the head gasket. The court finds the highly probable cause of destruction of the engine was failure of the head gasket. The allegation of alternate causes is speculation not supported by the evidence. Pure economic loss does not apply because there was damage to property. See also *Winnipeg Condominium Corporation No. 36 v. Bird Construction Co. Ltd.* [1995] 1 S.C.R. 85.

5. Courtesy contends it was not negligent: the additional warranty issued by Ford only applied to cases with manifest problems and to merely replace a head gasket at a cost to the customer of $1,200.00 to $1,400.00 in the absence of manifest problems did not make economic sense.

6. In the Nova Scotia case of *Ford v. Kenney* (2003, unreported) Boudreau J. of the Nova Scotia Supreme Court was hearing an appeal from a decision of the Small Claims Court Adjudicator. At page 5 of the oral reasons His Lordship said:

> Ford Motor Company has the right to decide which vehicles they are going to provide repairs to and which vehicles they are not. That doesn't mean that they couldn't be successfully challenged by that on negligent proper negligent manufacturing evidence, but there was not that evidence in this case.

7. *Campbell v. Ford* is a judgment of the Nova Scotia Small Claims Court rendered on January 31, 2002 and not reported. The plaintiff's 1995 Ford Windstar van was showing signs of head gasket problems and the head gasket was replaced at 168,000 [km] at the $1,600.00 expense of the plaintiff. At 207,000 kilometers the engine was destroyed. The engine was rebuilt or replaced at a much greater cost. In both instances the vehicle was beyond the kilometerage caps of both the original and additional warranties.

8. The Adjudicator dismissed the replacement of the head gasket as pure economic loss but said of the engine rebuilding or replacement:

> It is certainly arguable that if the head gasket failed and it was due to negligence of the designer/manufacturer and that failure in turn caused physical damage to the property of the Claimant, consequential damage to the engine itself, that may well be a recoverable head of damage and the basis for an action in negligence.

> The Adjudicator found there was insufficient admissible and reliable evidence to establish a causal connection between the gasket failure sought to be corrected at 168,000 kilometers and the destruction of the engine at 207,000 kilometers. The important point is that the Adjudicator was

discussing the potential liability of Ford quite apart from its original or additional warranties.

9. *Beshara v. Barry* is an Ontario Small Claims Court judgment of Tierney J. with reasons released a few days before trial in the case at bar and not yet reported. The unrepresented plaintiff sued the president of Ford for the estimated cost of replacing an engine similar to the one in the case at bar. The action was dismissed because the failure occurred after the expiry of Ford's original and additional warranties and the negligence alleged was that of the repairer and not Ford. The repairer was not a party.

10. The foregoing cases were furnished to the court by the agent for Ford. In each case involving Ford that company was successful. The court did additional research.

11. In *Kozoriz v. Chrysler Canada Ltd.* [1992] O.J. No. 3937 the problem was a transaxle seal which failed at 16,000 kilometers. Thereafter there was frequent leaking and repair work. As the van neared the 80,000 kilometer warranty expiry the 80,000 kilometer inspection was done at a Chrysler dealership and no problem was found with the trans-axle seal or the transmission. A few days later in Iowa there was an expensive failure of these apparently related parts. Tierney J. of the Ontario Small Claims Court found both parts failed due to a nearly continuous leak of the seal since 16,000 kilometers.

12. Chrysler pleaded the failure occurred after the expiry of the 80,000 kilometer warranty. In part the warranty described itself as "[a] guarantee of the quality and engineering excellence." Judge Tierney found that to be equivalent to a warranty that the product was free of defect. He found the axle seal was defective almost immediately and failed after only 16,000 kilometers and the defect led to the transmission damage after the expiry of the warranty. At page 3:

> Those damages occurred as a direct result of the manufacturer's breach of warranty. For that reason, it is my view that the amounts are recoverable as damages for breach of contract, even though the actual breakdown occurred after the warranty period had expired.

13. A similar case is *Shields v. General Motors of Canada Ltd.* [1997] O.J. No. 5434 (Ont. Sm. C.C.). A 1991 Pontiac with a three year warranty began losing an extensive amount of its paint in 1995. Zochodne, D.J. found the problem was a failure to ensure proper bonding when the vehicle was being painted originally. At page 6:

> The defect, which I have found, that is the lack of primer surfacer, occurred at the time the vehicle was manufactured. At that point, however, the defect was latent. The defect became patent when the paint began to bubble, flake and then peel off the vehicle.

That being the case His Honour found the warranty must respond to the loss. Judgment was in favour of the plaintiff.

14. *Schaffler v. Ford Motor Co. of Canada and Embrum Ford Sales Ltd.* [2003] O.J. No. 3165 (Ont. Sm. C.C.) is yet another Ford Windstar case involving an engine identical to the one involved in the case at bar. On March 02 of 2000, August 06 of 2001 and October 16 of 2001 the plaintiff took the van to Embrum with problems involving coolant levels, one of the indicia of head gasket failure. On those dates the respective kilometerages were 59,850, 84,000 and 89,000. The additional warranty expired by passage of time on August 07, 2002. Two months later there was serious damage to the engine as a result of head gasket failure.

15. Deputy Judge Langlois found the dealer liable for failure to diagnose the head gasket problem and Ford liable on its additional warranty which had been invoked by the plaintiff within the additional warranty period although the major damage occurred after expiry of the warranty.

16. It is distressing to note that although Barry Holmes was able in the case at bar to produce cases from both Ontario and Nova Scotia when Ford was successful he produced none where Ford was not successful. That includes the Schaffler case of one year ago and in which he was Ford's representative. In the case at bar he was Ford's agent and only witness.

17. In the case at bar the plaintiff received notice in 2000 from Ford of a potential problem with the head gasket in his van. His response was to take the van to Courtesy and enquire what should he done about it. Although they are only estimates the van was 5.5 years from the original warranty start date and had traveled 49,000 kilometers. Courtesy took in the van and gave the plaintiff and his family a ride home. About one half hour later Courtesy called and said the van was ready to be picked up. There was no paperwork introduced at trial evidencing this occurrence and it is probable none exists. William Taylor was the service manager and a helpful and credible witness at trial. He was not surprised at the absence of paperwork and said by way of summary that "[w]e do not charge for conversation."

18. It is probable that what happened is this: the plaintiff took his van to Courtesy, did not have the Ford notice with him, told Courtesy he had received a notice about head gaskets, asked what should [be] done and got a ride home. Courtesy was readily able to identify the van by its vehicle identification number and pull up its file on the vehicle, including at least references to technical service bulletins and notices affecting the plaintiff's vehicle and others in its class.

19. Having received no report from the plaintiff nor made any observations themselves the Courtesy service people would not be aware of any of the mostly gross symptoms Ford said could trigger warranty work on the head gasket. According to Mr. Taylor Courtesy had done "a lot" of gasket-related work under the warranty program in 1999 and 2000. In the absence of reports or observations of at least one of the gross symptoms Courtesy would inspect the head gasket only if the customer paid. The court finds the absence of paperwork on this visit by the plaintiff makes it a near certainty there was no gasket inspection.

20. One of the four symptoms listed in the Ford notice received by the plaintiff in 2000 was "constant loss of coolant" and another was flashing of the "low coolant" sensor light. Neither the plaintiff nor his wife testified to the existence

of either of these symptoms and Courtesy does not note, except perhaps informally on the back of a work order, whether coolant has been "topped up." The plaintiff's vehicle was well maintained and in otherwise good condition throughout with much of the servicing done at Courtesy and some oil changes at a large department store if Mrs. Chams was shopping there.

21. Based on what Courtesy knew at the time of this visit Mr. Taylor would not recommend changing the head gasket for two reasons: the cost would be $1,200.00 to $1,400.00 to head off a problem which was only potential and there is a risk of non-payment and alienation if the work is done and the customer starts contending it is warranty work. The mechanic who owns and operates the independent vehicle repair shop which eventually replaced the plaintiff's engine said that due to the problems which can arise from it he will not permit his shop to change a head gasket for the sole purpose of changing the head gasket.

22. Nothing more relevant to an engine problem happened until Sunday, January 11, 2004. The Chams family fueled the van and moved it a short distance to a car wash. While entering the wash the plaintiff noticed the engine temperature digital readout was climbing. It maximized after the wash when they were back on the street. Mr. Chams pulled into the next "Petro" or "petrol" station and looked under the hood but saw nothing awry. He drove about two blocks to his house where the engine would not restart.

23. He asked a friend knowledgeable about motor vehicles to come over. That person observed coolant coming from the exhaust and coolant mixed with oil under the hood. The van was towed to Courtesy that day or early the next.

24. The diagnosis was "coolant in cylinders, no start, no heat, intermittent hydraulic lock. No start due to coolant leak inside engine. Suspect head cracked." The recommendation was replacement of the engine with a rebuilt engine. The kilometerage was noted to be 80,671. The charge for the inspection was $79.00 plus tax, later voluntarily waived by Mr. Taylor in recognition of several members of the Chams family being good customers and, no doubt, because of the arising of a warranty issue. Further, according to Mr. Chams he had urged a friend with a similar vehicle to his to go to the dealer in 2000 and the result was the replacement of the head gasket.

25. Courtesy advised Mr. and Mrs. Chams the problem was not covered by warranty. The occurrence was 22 months after the expiry of the additional warranty. Mr. and Mrs. Chams spent time unsuccessfully trying to get Ford and Courtesy to take responsibility for the problem. Either directly or indirectly the Chams had the van towed to Automotive Solutions. That is a London vehicle repair shop owned and operated by Mohamed Omar who employs two class "A" automotive mechanics in the shop and who himself is in the final stage of his apprenticeship. Mr. Omar testified.

26. The van was stored at Automotive Solutions for about three months until a rebuilt engine and ancillary equipment was purchased by Mr. Chams and installed by Automotive Solutions on and about May 01.

27. When he studied the engine of the Chams van, seemingly in the company of one of his licensed mechanics, Mr. Omar observed the engine appeared not to have been apart before. The head gasket was found to [be] "blown." Coolant was

mixed with oil. The coolant had leaked into the inner part of the engine through the No. 1 cylinder where it could mix with the oil. Oil mixing with coolant can cause the head gasket to "blow." One purpose of the head gasket is to prevent coolant getting into the interior of the engine.

28. In the opinion of Mr. Omar if the head gasket failed in 2000 the vehicle could not be driven until 2004. Head gaskets in most cars do not fail by 80,000 kilometers. He was aware the 3.8 liter Ford engine had a head gasket problem and he has worked on "a few" with such a problem. He is not "100% sure" of the reason for the failure of the Chams engine.

29. William Taylor is the Courtesy service manager. Courtesy did "a lot" of head gasket related repairs to 3.8 liter engines in 1999 and 2000. He understands the problem is a head gasket wrongly configured or "too weak." He has not seen the Chams engine but testified that theoretically the damage could be caused by a defective head gasket, a cracked head or the timing cover.

30. Barry Holmes was Ford's agent and only witness. He is a licensed mechanic and is employed by Ford in its product liability department. His direct evidence was largely on the Ford warranty and there was little or no evidence by him on defect or otherwise the cause of the major engine damage. On cross examination he said he did not know the failure rate of the head gaskets in the affected 3.8 liter engines. On further examination he acknowledged it was possibly 85% but he was not sure and had not brought that information to court with him. The court does not accept that denial of knowledge. The court notes its comments above with respect to cherry picking of cases. Mr. Holmes is a Ford product liability employee. The figure of 85% figured in another case involving a Ford 3.8 liter engine. The case at bar is at least the third nearly identical case in which Mr. Holmes has been noted in the reasons for judgment as Ford's agent or witness or both. The court finds that Ford knows it has had a failure rate of at least 85% in this head gasket which is a component which can quickly destroy an engine if it fails. That makes it nearly a certainty that unless the offending gasket is replaced in time the engine will be destroyed by its failure.

31. As to warranty this court finds, as was found in the *Shields* case, (*supra*), the defect was in existence and known to the giver of the warranty not only during the period of the additional warranty but also during the period of the original warranty. Ford is therefore liable on its warranty.

32. As to negligence there can be no doubt the gasket has had a design or manufacturing defect which has existed since the time of design or manufacture. It is that defect which caused the destruction of the plaintiff's engine and made its replacement necessary.

33. Ford's warranty attempts to limit its liability to what it grants in the warranty. It is ancient law that one who attempts to limit his liability by, for example, excluding common law remedies, must clearly bring that limitation to the attention of the person who might lose those remedies. The evidence in this case is clear the buyer of even a new car does not get a warranty booklet until after purchasing the car although he "would be" told the highlights sooner.

34. Courtesy was not negligent nor in breach of any other obligation to the plaintiff. Ford would not entertain repairs under either of its warranties unless certain "symptoms" had become manifest before the work was done. The court has no

doubt Mr. Chams would have declined if Courtesy had asked if he would pay $1,200.00 to $1,400.00 to replace the head gasket in 2000 when his vehicle was manifesting no problem. The action is therefore dismissed against Courtesy with costs of $375.00 payable by Ford. This court will leave the fancy dancing of Bullock orders and the like to the higher courts.

35. At trial the focus was understandably on liability with damages consigned to the periphery. The rebuilt engine and ancillary parts were obtained from a NAPA dealer. The net NAPA bill is $2,375.67 but to that must be added a down payment of $250.00 and from it must be deducted a core deposit of $300.00. The old core is still available for credit. The radiator and water pump are valid expenses in that they are essential to obtaining a NAPA warranty on the rebuilt engine.

36. One legitimate Automotive Solutions bill is for $776.25 for towing and storage. The other is for $1,383.45 for labour, fluids, minor parts and an alternator. Storage is acceptable, particularly when one notes the absence of a substitute vehicle claim or loss of use. The alternator could not be proved as related to the engine failure and so $126.50 will be deducted.

37. Damages are assessed at $4,358.87 and there will be judgment in that amount against Ford. That sum will attract interest pursuant to the provisions of the *Courts of Justice Act* from January 12, 2004. The Clerk is requested to make that calculation.

38. As to costs a sealed document has now been opened and found to be an October 18, 2004 offer by Ford to settle by waiving allowable costs which stood at $25.00 or $75.00 at the time of the offer.

39. The trial was scheduled for two days but was completed in one. Mr. Ferguson was helpful to the court, particularly by creating document briefs for all parties, thus collecting dozens of potential exhibits into a handful. The court agrees with Mr. Ferguson's contention that many of the [I]nternet printouts collected by or on behalf of the plaintiff and included in one of the briefs were nevertheless inadmissible. Mr. Dupuis as agent for the plaintiff put in his client's case in a way that was economical in terms of trial time but nevertheless thorough and it underscores the need for reform of the law which does not currently permit the court to award a counsel fee with respect to agents even in substantial cases. The plaintiff shall have costs fixed at $200.00 against Ford.

General Motors Intake Manifold Gasket Class Action

A Canadian class action lawsuit was launched on April 24, 2006—with *Lemon-Aid's* help—and sought $1.2 billion in damages to compensate owners of 1995–2004 GM vehicles with defective engine intake manifold gaskets. A year later, GM Canada settled out of court for an estimated $40 million.

Automatic Transmission Failures

Lowe v. Fairview Chrysler-Dodge Limited and Chrysler Canada Limited (May 14, 1996; Ontario Court (General Division), Burlington Small Claims Court; No. 1224/95):

This judgment, in the plaintiff's favour, raises important legal principles relative to Chrysler:

- Internal dealer service bulletins are admissible in court to prove that a problem exists and certain parts should be checked out.
- If a problem is reported prior to a warranty's expiration, warranty coverage for the problematic component(s) is automatically carried over after the warranty ends.
- It's not up to the car owner to tell the dealer or automaker what the specific problem is.
- Repairs carried out by an independent garage can be refunded if the dealer or automaker unfairly refuses to apply the warranty.
- The dealer or automaker cannot dispute the cost of the independent repair if it fails to cross-examine the independent repairer.
- Auto owners can ask for and win compensation for their inconvenience, which in this judgment amounted to $150.
- Court awards add up: Although the plaintiff was given $1,985.94, with the addition of court costs and prejudgment interest, plus costs of inconvenience fixed at $150, the final award amounted to $2,266.04.

New-Vehicle Defects

Bagnell's Cleaners v. Eastern Automobile Ltd. (1991) (111 N.S.R. (2nd), No. 51, 303 A.P.R., No. 51 (T.D.)): This Nova Scotia company found that the new van it purchased had serious engine, transmission, and radiator defects. The dealer pleaded unsuccessfully that the sales contract excluded all other warranties except for those contained in the contract. The court held that there was a fundamental breach of the implied warranty and that the van's performance differed substantially from what the purchaser had been led to expect. An exclusionary clause could not protect the seller, who failed to live up to a fundamental term of the contract.

Burridge v. City Motor (10 Nfld. & P.E.I.R.; No. 451): This Newfoundland resident complained repeatedly of his new car's defects during the warranty period, and he stated that he hadn't used his car for 204 days after spending almost $1,500 for repairs. The judge awarded all repair costs and cancelled the sale.

Davis v. Chrysler Canada Ltd. (1977) (26 N.S.R. (2nd), No. 410 (T.D.)): The owner of a new $28,000 diesel truck found that a faulty steering assembly prevented him from carrying on his business. The court ordered that the sale be cancelled and that $10,000 in monthly payments be reimbursed. There was insufficient evidence to award compensation for business losses.

Fox v. Wilson Motors and GM (February 9, 1989; Court of Queen's Bench, New Brunswick; No. F/C/308/87): A trucker's new tractor-trailer had repeated engine malfunctions. He was awarded damages for loss of income, excessive fuel consumption, and telephone charges under the provincial *Sale of Goods Act*.

Gibbons v. Trapp Motors Ltd. (1970) (9 D.L.R. (3rd), No. 742 (B.C.S.C.)): The court ordered the dealer to take back a new car that had numerous defects and required 32 hours of repairs. The refund was reduced by mileage driven.

Johnson v. Northway Chevrolet Oldsmobile (1993) (108 Sask. R., No. 138 (Q.B.)): The court ordered the dealer to take back a new car that had been brought in for repairs on 14 different occasions. Two years after the car's purchase, the buyer initiated a lawsuit for the purchase price and general damages. General damages were awarded.

Julien v. GM of Canada (1991) (116 N.B.R. (2nd), No. 80): The plaintiff's new diesel truck produced excessive engine noise. The dealer claimed that the problem was caused by the owner's engine alterations. The plaintiff was awarded the $5,000 cost of repairing the engine through an independent dealer.

Magna Management Ltd. v. Volkswagen Canada Inc. (May 27, 1988; Vancouver (B.C.C.A.); No. CA006037): This precedent-setting case allowed the plaintiff to keep his new $48,325 VW while awarding him $37,101—three years after the car was purchased. The problems were centred on poor engine performance. The jury accepted the plaintiff's view that the car was practically worthless with its inherent defects.

Maughan v. Silver's Garage Ltd. (Nova Scotia Supreme Court; 6 B.L.R., No. 303, N.S.C. (2nd), No. 278): The plaintiff leased a defective backhoe. The manufacturer had to reimburse the plaintiff's losses because the warranty wasn't honoured. The court rejected the manufacturer's contention that the contract's exclusion clause protected the company from lawsuits for damages resulting from a latent defect.

Murphy v. Penney Motors Ltd. (1979) (23 Nfld. & P.E.I.R.; No. 152, 61 A.P.R., No. 152 (Nfld. T.D.)): This Newfoundland trucker found that his vehicle's engine problems took his new trailer off the road for 129 days during a seven-month period. The judge awarded all repair costs, as well as compensation for business losses, and cancelled the sale.

Murray v. Sperry Rand Corp. (Ontario Supreme Court; 5 B.L.R., No. 284): The seller, dealer, and manufacturer were all held liable for breach of warranty when a forage harvester did not perform as advertised in the sales brochure or as promised by the sales agent. The plaintiff was given his money back and reimbursed for his economic loss, based on the amount his harvesting usually earned. The court held that the advertising was a warranty.

Oliver v. Courtesy Chrysler (1983) Ltd. (1992) (11 B.C.A.C., No. 169): This new car had numerous defects over a three-year period, which the dealer attempted to fix to no avail. The plaintiff put the car in storage and sued the dealer for the purchase price. The court ruled that the car wasn't roadworthy and that the plaintiff couldn't be blamed for putting it in storage rather than selling it and purchasing another vehicle. The purchase price was refunded, minus $1,500 for each year the plaintiff used the car.

Olshaski Farms Ltd. v. Skene Farm Equipment Ltd. (January 9, 1987; Alberta Court of Queen's Bench; 49 Alta. L.R. (2nd), No. 249): The plaintiff's Massey-Ferguson combine caught fire after the manufacturer had sent two notices to dealers informing them of a defect that could cause a fire. The judge ruled under the *Sale of Goods Act* that the balance of probabilities indicated that the manufacturing defect caused the fire, even though there wasn't any direct evidence proving that the defect existed.

Western Pacific Tank Lines Ltd. v. Brentwood Dodge (June 2, 1975; B.C.S.C., No. 30945-74; Judge Meredith): The court awarded the plaintiff $8,600 and cancelled the sale of a new Chrysler New Yorker that suffered from badly adjusted doors, water leaks into the interior, and electrical short circuits.

Leasing

Ford Motor Credit v. Bothwell (December 3, 1979; Ontario County Court (Middlesex); No. 9226-T; Judge Macnab): The defendant leased a 1977 Ford truck that had frequent engine problems, characterized by stalling and hard starting. After complaining for one year and driving 35,000 km (21,750 mi.), the defendant cancelled the lease. Ford Credit sued for the money owing on the lease. Judge Macnab cancelled the lease and ordered Ford Credit to repay 70 percent of the amount paid during the leasing period. Ford Credit was also ordered to refund repair costs, even though the corporation claimed that it should not be held responsible for Ford's failure to honour its warranty.

Schryvers v. Richport Ford Sales (May 18, 1993; B.C.S.C., No. C917060; Justice Tysoe): The court awarded $17,578.47, plus damages, to a couple who paid thousands of dollars more in unfair and hidden leasing charges than if they had simply purchased their Ford Explorer and Escort. The court found that this price difference constituted a deceptive, unconscionable act or practice, in contravention of the *Trade Practices Act*, R.S.B.C. 1979, c. 406.

Judge Tysoe concluded that the total of the general damages awarded to the Schryvers for both vehicles would be $11,578.47. He then proceeded to give the following reasons for awarding an additional $6,000 in punitive damages:

> Little wonder Richport Ford had a contest for the salesperson who could persuade the most customers to acquire their vehicles by way of a lease transaction. I consider the actions of Richport Ford to be sufficiently flagrant and high-handed to warrant an award of punitive damages.
>
> There must be a disincentive to suppliers in respect of intentionally deceptive trade practices. If no punitive damages are awarded for intentional violations of the legislation, suppliers will continue to conduct their businesses in a manner that involves deceptive trade practices because they will have nothing to lose. In this case I believe that the appropriate amount of punitive damages is the extra profit Richport Ford

endeavoured to make as a result of its deceptive acts. I therefore award punitive damages against Richport Ford in the amount of $6,000.

Salvador v. Setay Motors/Queenstown Chev-Olds (Hamilton Small Claims Court; Case No. 1621/95): Robert Salvador was awarded $2,000 plus costs from Queenstown Leasing. The court found that the company should have tried harder to sell the leased vehicle, and at a higher price, when the "open lease" expired.

Incidentally, about 3,700 dealers in 39 American states paid between $3,500 and $8,000 each in 2004 to settle an investigation of allegations that they and Ford Motor Credit Co. overcharged customers who terminated their leases early.

See also:

- *Barber v. Inland Truck Sales* (11 D.L.R. (3rd), No. 469)
- *Canadian-Dominion Leasing v. Suburban Super Drug Ltd. (1966)* (56 D.L.R. (2nd), No. 43)
- *Neilson v. Atlantic Rentals Ltd. (1974)* (8 N.B.R. (2nd), No. 594)
- *Volvo Canada v. Fox* (December 13, 1979; New Brunswick Court of Queen's Bench; No. 1698/77/C; Judge Stevenson)
- *Western Tractor v. Dyck* (7 D.L.R. (3rd), No. 535)

Return of security deposit

Dealers routinely keep much of their lease customers' security deposits when their leases expire. However, that action can always be challenged in court. In the following claim, settled out of court, Ontario lawyer Harvey Goldstein forced GMAC and a GM dealer to refund his $525 security deposit:

1. The Plaintiff Claims:
   (A) Return of his security deposit of $525.00; and a finding that no amount is owing to the Defendants;
   (B) Alternatively, damages in the above amount;
   (C) Prejudgment interest on $525.00 at the rate of 2% per month (24% per annum) from June 22, 2005, to the date of this Claim, and thereafter on the date of payment or Judgment at the rate of 4% per annum, pursuant to Section 128 of the *Courts of Justice Act*, R.S.O. (1990) as amended;
   (D) Post-judgment interest at the post-judgment rate of interest, pursuant to Section 129 of the *Courts of Justice Act*, R. S. O. (1990) as amended;
   (E) His costs of this action;
   (F) Punitive damages in an amount to be determined; and
   (G) Such further and other relief as this Honorable Court deems just and proper.

• • •

4. On or about June 10, 2005, the Plaintiff advised the Defendant North York Chevrolet Oldsmobile Ltd. that he wanted it to inspect the said vehicle for chargeable damage prior to its return or that he be present when it was inspected after its return to the said Defendant.

5. The said Defendant advised that it had no control over the inspection process and that the Defendant GMAC Leaseco Limited would inspect the vehicle only after the lease expired, the vehicle was returned to the dealer and the Plaintiff was not present.

6. The Plaintiff sent an email on June 10, 2005 to the Defendant GMAC Leaseco Limited asking it for an inspection prior to the vehicle being returned.

7. The said Defendant did not respond to the request.

8. The Plaintiff called and spoke with a representative of the said Defendant on June 17, and wrote her a letter sent by fax the same day, again asking that an inspection be scheduled in his presence. The said Defendant did not respond to the letter.

9. On June 23, 2005, the Plaintiff again called the said Defendant. He was told that it had no record of the vehicle being returned to the dealership.

10. Shortly thereafter, the Plaintiff called the Defendant North York Chevrolet Oldsmobile Ltd. to enquire as to the status of his security deposit. The said Defendant advised that it had no record of the vehicle being returned to it.

11. Not having heard from either Defendant, the Plaintiff called the Defendant GMAC Leaseco Limited on July 15, 2005. He was advised that he owed the said Defendant $550.00, less the amount of the security deposit held by it. He was further advised that details of its claim to that amount could be found on the said Defendant's website. He was told that it did not inspect the said vehicle until July 7, 2005, 15 days after it was left in the dealership's service bay. He was told that the vehicle was at an auction and that he could not inspect the alleged damages for which the Defendants claimed compensation. He was advised that no adjustment would be made to their claim even though the vehicle was returned with 20,000.00 kilometers less than allowed by the lease agreement. Further, he was told that the alleged damages to the vehicle were not repaired prior to sending it to auction.

12. The Plaintiff denies that the vehicle required repairs claimed by the Defendants and puts them to the strict proof thereof.

13. The Plaintiff further claims that the process by which the Defendants seek to claim compensation from him is unfair, open to abuse and contrary to the principles of natural justice. The Defendants pay the fee of the alleged independent inspectors and deny the Plaintiff the opportunity to dispute the charges in any meaningful fashion. Further, its delay in inspecting the vehicle for 15 days, leaves open the question of when, if ever, the damages occurred.

Repairs: Faulty Diagnosis

Davies v. Alberta Motor Association (August 13, 1991; Alberta Provincial Court, Civil Division; No. P9090106097; Judge Moore): The plaintiff had a used 1985 Nissan Pulsar NX checked out by the AMA's Vehicle Inspection Service prior to buying it. The car passed with flying colours. A month later, the clutch was replaced, and then numerous electrical problems ensued. At that time, another garage discovered that the car had been involved in a major accident, had a bent frame and a leaking radiator, and was unsafe to drive. The court awarded the plaintiff $1,578.40 plus three years of interest. The judge held that the AMA set itself out as an expert and should have spotted the car's defects. The AMA's defence—that it was not responsible for errors—was thrown out. The court held that a disclaimer clause could not protect the association from a fundamental breach of contract.

False Advertising: Vehicle Not as Ordered

When you're buying a new vehicle, the seller can't misrepresent the vehicle through a lie or a failure to disclose important information. Anything that varies from what one would commonly expect or from the seller's representation must be disclosed prior to signing the contract. Typical scenarios are odometer turn-backs, accident damage, used or leased cars sold as new, new vehicles that are the wrong colour or the wrong model year, or vehicles that lack promised options or standard features.

Goldie v. Golden Ears Motors (1980) Ltd. (Port Coquitlam; June 27, 2000; British Columbia Small Claims Court; Case No. CO8287; Justice Warren): In a well-written eight-page judgment, the court awarded plaintiff Goldie $5,000 for engine repairs on a 1990 Ford F-150 pickup in addition to $236 court costs. The dealer was found to have misrepresented the mileage and sold a used vehicle that didn't meet Section 8.01 of the provincial motor vehicle regulations (unsafe tires, defective exhaust and headlights).

In rejecting the seller's defence that he disclosed all information "to the best of his knowledge and belief," as stipulated in the sales contract, Justice Warren stated the following:

> The words "to the best of your knowledge and belief" do not allow someone to be willfully blind to defects or to provide incorrect information. I find as a fact that the business made no effort to fulfill its duty to comply with the requirements of this form. The defendant has been reckless in its actions. More likely, it has actively deceived the claimant into entering into this contract. I find the conduct of the defendant has been reprehensible throughout the dealings with the claimant.

This judgment closes a loophole that sellers have used to justify their misrepresentation, and it allows for the cancellation of the sale and damages if the vehicle doesn't meet highway safety regulations.

Lister v. Scheilding (c.o.b. Kar-Lon Motors) [1983] (O.J. No. 907 (Co. Ct.)): Here, the plaintiff was entitled to rescind the contract because of the defendant's false representation. The defendant failed to state that the motor had been changed and was not the original motor.

MacDonald v. Equilease Co. Ltd. (January 18, 1979; Ontario Supreme Court; Judge O'Driscoll): The plaintiff leased a truck that was misrepresented as having an axle stronger than it really was. The court awarded the plaintiff damages for repairs and set aside the lease.

Seich v. Festival Ford Sales Ltd. (1978) (6 Alta. L.R. (2nd), No. 262): The plaintiff bought a used truck from the defendant after being assured that it had a new motor and transmission. It didn't, and the court awarded the plaintiff $6,400.

Bilodeau v. Sud Auto (Quebec Court of Appeal; No. 09-000751-73; Judge Tremblay): This appeals court cancelled the contract and held that a car can't be sold as new or as a demonstrator if it has ever been rented, leased, sold, or titled to anyone other than the dealer.

Chenel v. Bel Automobile (1981) Inc. (August 27, 1976; Quebec Superior Court (Quebec); Judge Desmeules): The plaintiff didn't receive Jacob brakes, essential to transporting sand in hilly regions, with his new Ford truck. The court awarded the plaintiff $27,000, representing the purchase price of the vehicle less the money he earned while using the truck.

Lasky v. Royal City Chrysler Plymouth (February 18, 1987; Ontario High Court of Justice; 59 O.R. (2nd), No. 323): The plaintiff bought a 4-cylinder 1983 Dodge 600 that had been represented by the salesman as being a 6-cylinder model. After putting 40,000 km on the vehicle over a 22-month period, the buyer was given her money back, without interest, under the provincial *Business Practices Act*.

Rourke v. Gilmore (January 16, 1928; *Ontario Weekly Notes*, Vol. XXXIII, p. 292): Before discovering that his new car was really used, the plaintiff drove it for over a year. For this reason, the contract couldn't be cancelled. However, the appeals court instead awarded damages for $500, which was quite a sum in 1928!

Insurance Liability

If you believe your insurance policy will protect you from liability when driving, like in an at-fault collision, you may be wrong. In "Deconstructing Automobile Insurance" (*papers.ssrn.com/sol3/papers.cfm?abstract_id=1262084*), Queen's University law professor Erik Knutson cited recent decisions by Canada's Supreme Court that he believes "significantly narrowed the scope of automobile coverage by restricting the once-expansive interpretive exercise to a more nuanced and categorical application":

> The Supreme Court's present approach to automobile insurance coverage fails to honour long-standing insurance law interpretation concepts and represents a results-driven process which puts principle by the wayside. The implications are serious and potentially far-reaching. In the end, the result may be less efficient, and ultimately less just, than the previous state of the law.

> The driving public cannot reliably predict when an accident is covered or not covered by automobile insurance. Neither can lawyers assisting accident victims or auto insurers. For example, if a driver operating a vehicle drops a child off to play and the child is seriously hurt crossing the street, is the child covered by first party no-fault automobile benefits from the driver's policy? Is the driver protected for his negligence

by his third party liability automobile insurance policy, in the event the child sues the driver? Is any underinsured or uninsured automobile coverage available in the event of a shortfall in available compensation? Or is the child's loss not covered at all? The answer, according to the Supreme Court of Canada: it depends.

The Court effectively created two interpretive tests for two types of insurance: a broad test for first party no-fault benefits and a narrower test for third party liability insurance. Despite the broadly worded coverage clause, the Court held that auto insurance coverage can only be triggered in the third party liability situation if the at-fault tortfeasor is at fault as a motorist. The Court's aim surely must have been to simplify the coverage question by restricting automobile coverage to standard two-vehicle auto collision situations and their corollaries. The shift to this default rule, from the previous default rule of pro-coverage as long as a vehicle is essentially in the factual matrix, surprisingly does not do anything to ameliorate the efficiency of the system. In fact, it makes the system more unpredictable.

Secret Warranty Claims

It's common practice for manufacturers to secretly extend their warranties to cover components with a high failure rate. Customers who complain vigorously get extended warranty compensation in the form of "goodwill" adjustments.

Tepei v. Uniroyal: Canadians injured by an American-manufactured tire can file their claim in American courts where jury awards tend to be more generous (*www.crossborderlaw.com*). In this 2004 case, a Washington jury awarded $9.1 million (U.S.) in damages to the six Canadian plaintiffs (*www.crossborderlaw.com/PDF/CBL-Tepei-Verdict-040429.pdf*).

The jury found that the driver's negligence was the sole cause of the plaintiffs' injuries; nevertheless, the *Tepei v. Uniroyal* case shows that Canadian plaintiffs need a thorough knowledge of the laws on both sides of the border to maximize their recovery whenever United States law is implicated in litigation.

The pre-trial legal maneuvering between the parties and Michelin over *forum non conveniens* and choice-of-law issues suggests that while U.S. corporate defendants will aggressively contest the efforts of Canadian plaintiffs to seek redress for injuries caused by defective American products, the American courts are generally open to such claims for relief.

In Washington, as well as in the majority of states around the U.S. which have abandoned the *lex loci delecti* approach to choice-of-law issues, it is likely that a Canadian plaintiff who chooses to sue an American manufacturer in a state with some connection to the product in question would find the courts willing to entertain both jurisdiction over the case and the application of the American forum's products liability law—irrespective of where the injury to the plaintiff actually took place.

Indeed, many of the cases relied upon by Michelin in its attempt to suggest the place of the Tepei accident was "fortuitous" could be turned against a corporate defendant, supporting the argument that an injury occurring in Canada "could have occurred anywhere."

François Chong v. Marine Drive Imported Cars Ltd. and Honda Canada Inc. (May 17, 1994; British Columbia Provincial Small Claims Court; No. 92-06760; Judge C.L. Bagnall): Mr. Chong was the first owner of a 1983 Honda Accord with 134,000 km on the odometer. He had six engine camshafts replaced—four under Honda "goodwill" programs, one where he paid part of the repairs, and one via a small claims court judgment. (Please note that Honda's earlier engine problems and its arrogant attitude have since moderated a bit.)

In his ruling, Judge Bagnall agreed with Chong and ordered Honda and the dealer to each pay half of the $835.81 repair bill for the following reasons:

> The defendants assert that the warranty which was part of the contract for purchase of the car encompassed the entirety of their obligation to the claimant, and that it expired in February 1985. The replacements of the camshaft after that date were paid for wholly or in part by Honda as a "goodwill gesture." The time has come for these gestures to cease, according to the witness for Honda. As well, he pointed out to me that the most recent replacement of the camshaft was paid for by Honda and that, therefore, the work would not be covered by Honda's usual warranty of 12 months from date of repair. Mr. Wall, who testified for Honda, told me there was no question that this situation with Mr. Chong's engine was an unusual state of affairs. He said that a camshaft properly maintained can last anywhere from 24,000 to 500,000 km. He could not offer any suggestion as to why the car keeps having this problem.
>
> The claimant has convinced me that the problems he is having with rapid breakdown of camshafts in his car [are] due to a defect, which was present in the engine at the time that he purchased the car. The problem first arose during the warranty period and in my view has never been properly identified nor repaired.

Punitive Damages

Punitive damages (also known as "exemplary damages") allow the plaintiff to get compensation that exceeds his or her losses as a deterrent to those who carry out dishonest or negligent practices. These kinds of judgments, common in the U.S., sometimes reach hundreds of millions of dollars. Canadian courts, however, seldom award substantial punitive damages.

Nevertheless, there have been a few relatively recent cases where the Supreme Court of Canada has shocked the business establishment by levying huge exemplary damage awards. One such case was the *Whiten v. Pilot Insurance Co.* decision rendered in 2002. In this case, the plaintiff's home caught fire and burned to the ground, destroying all of the home's contents and killing three pet cats. Pilot Insurance made a single $5,000 payment for living expenses and covered the family's rent for a couple of months, and then cut off the rent payments without forewarning the family. The insurance claim went to trial, based on the respondent's allegation that the family had torched their own home, even though the local fire chief, the respondent's own expert investigator, and its initial expert all said there was no evidence whatsoever of arson. The original trial jury awarded the plaintiff compensatory damages and $1 million in punitive damages. Pilot Insurance fought this decision at the Court of Appeal, where the punitive damages award was reduced to $100,000. The case was then taken all the way to the Supreme Court, where the trial jury's unprecedented award of $1 million was restored:

> The jury's award of punitive damages, though high, was within rational limits. The respondent insurer's conduct towards the appellant was exceptionally reprehensible. It forced her to put at risk her only remaining asset (the $345,000 insurance claim) plus $320,000 in costs that she did not have. The denial of the claim was designed to force her to make an unfair settlement for less than she was entitled to. The conduct was planned and deliberate and continued for over two years, while the financial situation of the appellant grew increasingly desperate. The jury evidently believed that the respondent knew from the outset that its arson defence was contrived and unsustainable. Insurance contracts are sold by the insurance industry and purchased by members of the public for peace of mind. The more devastating the loss, the more the insured may be at the financial mercy of the insurer, and the more difficult it may be to challenge a wrongful refusal to pay the claim.

Punitive damages are rarely awarded in Canadian courts against automakers. When they are given out, it's usually for sums less than $100,000. In *Prebushewski v. Dodge City Auto (1985) Ltd. and Chrysler Canada Ltd.*, the plaintiff got $25,000 in a judgment handed down in 2001 and confirmed by the Supreme Court in 2005. The plaintiff's 1996 Ram's running lights had shorted and caused her truck to burn to the ground, and Chrysler had refused her claim. The court basically said that aggrieved car owners may sue for much more than the depreciated value of what they bought under provincial consumer protection statutes. The Supreme Court reaffirmed the power of the lower courts to assess an additional financial penalty to punish automakers that treat their customers unfairly and ensure they don't repeat the offence.

Vlchek v. Koshel (1988; 44 C.C.L.T. 314, B.C.S.C., No. B842974): The plaintiff was seriously injured when she was thrown from a Honda all-terrain cycle on which she had been riding as a passenger. The court allowed for punitive damages because the manufacturer was well aware of the injuries likely to be caused by the cycle. Specifically, the court ruled that there is no firm and inflexible principle of law stipulating that punitive or exemplary damages must be denied unless the defendant's acts are specifically directed against the plaintiff. The court may apply punitive damages "where the defendant's conduct has been indiscriminate of focus, but reckless or malicious in its character. Intent to injure the plaintiff need not be present, so long as intent to do the injurious act can be shown."

See also:

- *Granek v. Reiter* (Ontario Court, General Division; No. 35/741)
- *Morrison v. Sharp* (Ontario Court, General Division; No. 43/548)
- *Schryvers v. Richport Ford Sales* (May 18, 1993; B.C.S.C., No. C917060; Judge Tysoe)
- *Varleg v. Angeloni* (B.C.S.C., No. 41/301)

Provincial business practices acts cover false, misleading, or deceptive representations and allow for punitive damages should the unfair practice toward the consumer amount to an unconscionable representation (see *Canadian Encyclopedic Digest (C.E.D.)*, Third Edition, s. 76, pages 140–145). Here are some specific cases to keep in mind:

- Exemplary damages are justified where compensatory damages are insufficient to deter and punish. See *Walker et al. v. CFTO Ltd. et al.* (1978; 59 O.R. (2nd), No. 104; Ontario C.A.).
- Exemplary damages can be awarded in cases where the defendant's conduct was "cavalier." See *Ronald Elwyn Lister Ltd. et al. v. Dayton Tire Canada Ltd.* (1985; 52 O.R. (2nd), No. 89; Ontario C.A.).
- The primary purpose of exemplary damages is to prevent the defendant and all others from doing similar wrongs. See *Fleming v. Spracklin* (1921).
- Disregard of the public's interest, lack of preventive measures, and a callous attitude all merit exemplary damages. See *Coughlin v. Kuntz* (1989; 2 C.C.L.T. (2nd); B.C.C.A.).
- Punitive damages can be awarded for mental distress. See *Ribeiro v. Canadian Imperial Bank of Commerce* (1992; Ontario Reports 13 (3rd)) and *Brown v. Waterloo Regional Board of Commissioners of Police* (1992; 37 O.R. (2nd)).

Now that you know how to get the best deal for less money while protecting your rights, take a look at Part Three to see which cars and trucks to pick and which ones to avoid.

Part Three
THE BEST FOR LESS

Given the stronger than expected performance in Canada, we are maintaining our full-year sales forecast unchanged even as volumes are expected to weaken over the summer due to a shortage of vehicles from Japanese automakers.... The sales gains have been strongest in the resource-rich provinces of Western Canada, with purchases west of the Ontario-Manitoba border jumping 14 percent year over year in March 2011.

SCOTIA ECONOMICS
GLOBAL AUTO REPORT, MAY 11, 2011

This Vancouver, B.C., ad shows that large truck and SUV prices have been especially competitive recently due to higher fuel costs and the need to sell off remaining 2011 inventory before the 2012s arrived in September. In all new car or truck deals, ask for an automaker "loyalty" rebate and that the "freight" fee be dropped. If you are eligible, ask for the $1,000 Costco discount, or a recent graduate $500 incentive.

All automakers build bad cars and trucks—some more often than others. Ask Honda, Nissan, and Toyota. Or perhaps, Jaguar and Volkswagen will share their stories with you.

The trick is to know which models and years have the most problems. Like wine, vintage is important. For example, four decades ago, most Japanese small cars were underpowered rustbuckets; British cars were electrical system nightmares (joke: "Lucas is the Prince of Darkness and inadvertently invented the intermittent windshield washer"); the Italians used fuel systems that seldom held their "tune" and came packaged in biodegradable bodies; and the Germans made bizarre-behaving, hard-to-diagnose, and parts-challenged models that included VW's self-starting, fire-prone Rabbits (garage owner and Toronto 740AM radio broadcaster Alan Gelman knows the stories: he had to jury-rig VW "fix-it" kits so rainwater wouldn't run down the antenna mount and into the wiring, closing the circuit and starting the car). Since then, some automakers, like Ford, Honda, Hyundai, and Mazda, have gotten much better at building reliable, fuel-efficient vehicles. Others, like Audi, Cadillac, Chrysler, Jaguar, Jeep, Kia, Mercedes, Nissan, Saab, and Volvo, have gotten worse.

Honda, for example, introduced the CVCC engine in 1975; it was fuel-efficient, produced low emissions, and didn't require a catalytic converter or unleaded fuel to meet emissions standards. Problem was it was prone to self-destruction and cost up to $5,000 to repair or replace. Quebec mechanics jokingly referred to the CVCC as the "*ça va couter cher*" ("it will be expensive") engine. Honda heard the guffaws and dropped the CVCC in the early '80s. Today, its entire lineup is above reproach.

Toyota quality, on the other hand, has gone in the opposite direction. After coasting for over a decade on its high-quality reputation, Toyota's problems with brakes and sudden, unintended acceleration have made buyers wary of its cars and trucks. *Lemon-Aid*, for instance, doesn't recommend any new Toyota unless it is equipped with a brake override system.

"Hot" Cars: One Chance in 100

Car buyers have a new menace to consider: Radiation.

In the three months following the March 11 meltdown of four nuclear power plants at the Fukushima-Daiichi facility situated on Japan's east coast, four shipping ports (one in Chile; three in Russia) have quarantined or sent back 84 radiation-contaminated new and used vehicles. The Japan Automobile Manufacturers Association says it has begun radiation testing on all vehicle shipments for the domestic and export markets.

Gammawatch.com sells a combo watch and Geiger counter called the Gamma Watch Basic for $250. They have been back-ordered for months.

Radiation-contaminated cars are still getting through. In fact, The Associated Press estimates that about 1 percent of new Japanese cars shipped into South America are radioactive. Radiation levels outside the Japanese reactors are eight times the normal level. This is the minimal amount of radiaion some cars could be trailing back to the States. Although this is not considered a public health danger, if some cars were exposed to iodine-131, this could trigger thyroid cancer.

- In early April, Russian Customs officials in Vladivostok seized a cargo of 50 radioactive cars from Japan. Their level of radiation was two times higher than normal.
- On April 19, Russian customs officials in the far eastern port of Nakhodka said seven cars imported from Japan showed an increased level of radiation. A spokeswoman said that the radiation level in close proximity to the cars was up to seven times higher than the permitted maximum.

- Last May, Russian police turned back six used cars arriving from Japan because the vehicles were contaminated with radioactive isotopes emitting radiation at rates between two and three times higher than acceptable levels. Laboratory tests of the six autos showed them to be polluted with caesium-134 and caesium-137, elements that have a half-life of 30 years.
- That same May, according to the Mainichi *Daily News*, customs agents in Chile detected various levels of radiation on 21 vehicles shipped from Japan. A few vehicles proved so contaminated they had to be returned to Japan.

No one wants to buy a car, truck, or SUV that has a 1 percent chance emitting residual radiation. Yet, there's little that can be done, except for scanning every vehicle imported into our country. Even that isn't enough, though. If you look at the map at right, you will see auto suppliers on Fukushima's doorstep. These companies make parts for automakers around the world, including the Detroit Three. Those parts will also have to be scanned.

Prediction: Soon some Detroit Three auto dealer or enterprising TV station will show a new Japanese import setting off a Geiger counter.

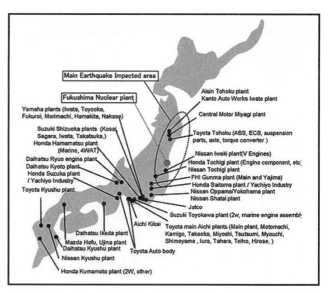

What Makes a Good Car or Truck?

The vehicle should first live up to the promises made by the manufacturer and dealer. It must be reasonably priced, provide safe highway performance, protect occupants in a crash, be fuel-efficient, and be capable of lasting 15 years without a series of major repairs; it should cost no more than about $800 a year to maintain; and it should provide you with a fair resale value a few years down the road. Parts should be affordable and easily available, and competent servicing shouldn't be hard to find.

And don't believe for one moment that the more you spend, the better the vehicle. For example, most Hondas are as good as more-expensive Acuras. The same is true of Toyota and Lexus. Even more surprising is that some luxury makes offer you merely a dressed-up entry model with a luxury-car price. The extra money buys you more features of dubious value and newer, unproven technology like rear-mounted video cameras and failure-prone electronic gadgetry.

J. D. Power and Associates has noted in its 2011 Dependability Study that these high-tech improvements increase the chance something will go wrong. Says David Sargent, vice president of global vehicle research at J.D. Power and Associates:

> Automakers, as a whole, have made significant improvements in reducing traditional problems, particularly with vehicle interiors; engines and transmissions; and steering and braking during the past several years. However, as manufacturers add new features and technologies to satisfy customer demand and new legislation, they face the potential for introducing new problems.

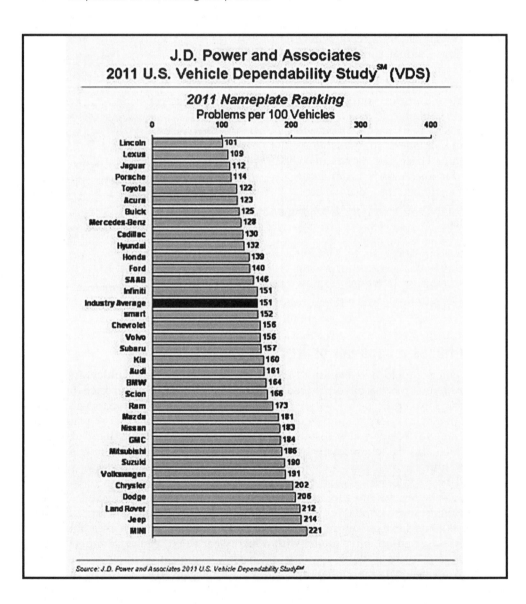

Source: J.D. Power and Associates 2011 U.S. Vehicle Dependability Study℠

In terms of road performance, at the very minimum, every vehicle must be able to merge safely onto a highway and have adequate passing power for two-lane roads. Steering feel and handling should inspire confidence. The suspension ought to provide a reasonably well-controlled ride on most road surfaces. Ideally, the passenger compartment will be roomy enough to accommodate passengers comfortably on extended trips. The noise level should not become tiresome or annoying. As a rule, handling and ride comfort are inversely proportional—good handling requires a stiff suspension, which pounds the kidneys, while a softer suspension that cushions those kidneys leaves you lacking in the handling department.

Lemon-Aid follows these five simple rules when rating new vehicles:

1. We believe the best rating approach is to combine a driving test with an owners' survey of past models (only *Consumer Reports* and *Lemon-Aid* do this).
2. Owner responses must come from a large owner pool (over a million responses from *CR* subscribers, for example). Anecdotal responses should then be cross-referenced, updated, and given depth and specificity through NHTSA's safety complaint prism. Responses must again be cross-referenced through automaker internal service bulletins to determine the extent of a defect over a specific model and model-year range and to alert owners to problems that are likely to occur.
3. Rankings should be predicated upon important characteristics measured over a significant period of time, unlike "Car of the Year" contests or polls of owners who have just bought their car.
4. Data must come from unimpeachable sources like *Consumer Reports, Which?,* ALLDATA, and NHTSA (crash and safety reports). There should be no conflicts of interest, such as advertising, consultant ties, or self-serving tests done under ideal conditions for an extra fee.
5. Tested cars must be bought or rented, and serviced—not borrowed from the car company and pampered as part of a journalists' fleet lent out for ranking purposes.

Responsible auto raters shouldn't hit up dealers or manufacturers for free test vehicles under any circumstances, but most auto columnists and some consumer groups compromise their integrity by doing so. Test vehicles should be rented or borrowed from an owner. I've adopted this practice from my early experience as a consumer reporter. Nissan asked me to test drive its new 1974 240Z—no strings attached. I took the car for a week, had it examined by an independent garage, spoke with satisfied and dissatisfied owners, and accessed internal service bulletins and government-logged owner safety complaints. The car's poor brake design apparently made it unsafe to drive, and I said so in my report. Nissan sued me for $2 million, fixed the brakes through a "product improvement campaign," and then dropped the lawsuit two years later. I was never offered another car.

Definitions of Terms

Key Facts

This year, we rate many more cars, trucks, and SUVs than ever before, and include previews of some 2013 models for readers planning to buy a new vehicle in mid-2012. We also include "miles per gallon" (mpg) in addition to our usual "litres per 100 kilometres" (L/km) in deference to our metric-challenged readers. American prices are given as benchmarks for haggling successfully with Canadian dealers or when negotiating cross-border deals.

Prices: We list the manufacturer's suggested retail price (MSRP) range, in effect at press time and applicable to standard models. That price will likely fluctuate considerably during the year as customer rebates and manufacturer-to-dealer sales incentives kick in. Check the latest MSRP figure periodically on both sides of the border by accessing each manufacturer's website (like *www.honda.com* and *www.honda.ca*). Vehicles that aren't selling well usually carry the heftiest discounts and/or rebates; check the "Cost Analysis" section for a vehicle's predicted price negotiability.

Destination charges and the pre-delivery inspection (PDI) fee are quasi-fraudulent "back doors" into your wallet. Offer half of the indicated amount. Also, don't fall for the $99–$475 "administration fee" scam, unless the bottom-line price is so tempting that it won't make much difference. Sticking to your principles is one thing; losing an attractive deal is another.

Tow limit: Note that towing capacities differ depending on the kind of powertrain/suspension package or towing package you buy. And remember that there's a difference between how a vehicle is rated for cargo capacity or payload and how heavy a boat or trailer it can pull. Do not purchase any new vehicle without receiving very clear information from the dealer, in writing, about a vehicle's towing capacity and the kind of special equipment you'll need to meet your requirements. Ask the manufacturer of whatever it is you plan to tow (trailer, boat, etc.) what model and year would best meet your requirements to be certain you'll have what you need. Whichever model you choose, make sure to have the towing capacity and necessary equipment written into the contract.

Load capacity: This is defined as the safe combined weight of occupants and cargo (such as luggage). It is taken from the manufacturer's rating or from *Consumer Reports'* calculated safe load. Exceeding this maximum weight can adversely affect a vehicle's handling or make it unstable.

Ratings

We rate vehicles on a scale of one to five stars, with five stars as our top ranking. We use owner complaints, confidential technical service bulletins (TSBs), and test drives to ferret out serious factory-related defects, design deficiencies, and servicing glitches.

This guide emphasizes important new features that add to a vehicle's safety, reliability, road performance, and comfort, and points out those changes that are merely gadgets and styling revisions. Also noted are important improvements to be made in the future, or the dropping of a model line. In addition to its overall rating, each vehicle's strong and weak points are summarized.

Interestingly, some vehicles that are identical but marketed and serviced by different automakers may have different ratings. This variation occurs because servicing and after-warranty assistance may be better within one dealer network than another.

It takes about six months to acquire enough information for a fair-minded evaluation of a car's or truck's first year on the market, unless the vehicle has been available elsewhere under another name. Most new cars and trucks hit the market before all of the bugs have been worked out, so it would be irresponsible to recommend them before owner reports and internal service bulletins give them an "okay." Sadly, as we have seen with Toyota's acceleration problems and GM's poorly shifting transmission, it may take several years to correct some factory powertrain glitches.

Recommended: This rating indicates a "Best Buy," and it applies to many Asian models. Recommended vehicles usually combine a high level of crashworthiness with good road performance, few safety-related complaints, decent reliability, and a better-than-average resale value. Servicing is readily available, and parts are inexpensive and easy to find.

Above Average: Vehicles in this class are pretty good choices. They aren't perfect, but they're often more reasonably priced than their competition. Most vehicles in this category have quality construction, good durability, and plenty of safety features as standard equipment. On the downside, they may have expensive parts and servicing, too many safety-related complaints, or only satisfactory warranty performance—one or all of which may have disqualified them from the Recommended category.

Average: Some deficiencies or flaws make these good second choices. In many cases, certain components are prone to premature wear or breakdown or don't perform as well as the competition. An Average rating can also be attributed to such factors as substandard assembly quality, lack of a solid long-term reliability record, a substantial number of safety-related complaints, or a deficient parts and service network.

Below Average: This rating category denotes an unreliable or poorly performing vehicle that may also have a poor safety record. Getting an extended warranty is advised.

Not Recommended: Chances of having major breakdowns or safety-related failures are omnipresent. Inadequate road performance and poor dealer service, among other factors, can make owning one of these vehicles a traumatic and expensive experience, no matter how cheaply it's sold.

Vehicles that have not been on the road long enough to assess, or that are sold in such small numbers that owner feedback is insufficient, are either given a Not Recommended rating or left unrated.

Quality and reliability

Lemon-Aid bases its quality and reliability evaluations in the "Rating" and "Overview" sections on owner comments, confidential manufacturer service bulletins, and government reports from NHTSA safety complaint files. We also draw on the knowledge and expertise of professionals working in the automotive marketplace, including mechanics and fleet owners. The aim is to have a wide range of unbiased (and irrefutable) data on quality, reliability, durability, and ownership costs. Allowances are made for the number of vehicles sold versus the number of complaints, as well as for the seriousness of problems reported and the average number of problems reported by each owner.

Technical Service Bulletins (TSBs) give the most probable cause of factory-related defects on previous model years that will likely be carried over to the 2012 versions. TSBs are reliable sources of information because manufacturers depend on the dealer corrections outlined in their bulletins until a permanent, cost-effective engineering solution is found at the factory, which often takes several model years and lots of experimentation.

As you read through the ratings and manufacturers' confidential service bulletins, you'll quickly discover that most Japanese and South Korean manufacturers are far ahead of Chrysler and GM in terms of maintaining a high level of quality control in their vehicles. European makes are even worse performers, especially with VW/Audi's failure-prone DGS 6-speed transmissions.

Safety features and crashworthiness

Some of the main features weighed are a model's crashworthiness scores and the availability of front and side airbags, effective head restraints, assisted stability and traction control, and front and rearward visibility.

Frontal and side crash protection figures are taken from the National Highway Traffic Safety Administration's (NHTSA) New Car Assessment Program. For the front crash test, vehicles are crashed into a fixed barrier, head-on, at 57 km/h (35 mph). NHTSA uses star rankings to show the likelihood, expressed as a percentage, of belted occupants being seriously injured. The more stars, the greater the protection.

NHTSA's side crash test represents an intersection-type collision with a 1,368 kg (3,015 lb.) barrier moving at 62 km/h (38.5 mph) into a standing vehicle. The moving barrier is covered with material that has "give" to replicate the front of a car.

A vehicle's rollover resistance rating is an estimate of its risk of rolling over in a single-vehicle crash, not a prediction of the likelihood of a crash. The lowest-rated vehicles (one star) are at least four times more likely to roll over than the highest-rated vehicles (five stars) when involved in a single-vehicle crash.

In 2009, NHTSA upgraded the government safety standard governing roof crush resistance, a major factor in rollover accidents. The new rule requires that vehicles weighing 6,000 lb. or less must be able to withstand a force equal to three times their weight applied alternately to the left and right sides of the roof. However, vehicles weighing between 6,000 lb. and 10,000 lb. need only withstand 1.5 times their own weight on the roof.

The Insurance Institute for Highway Safety (IIHS) rates head-restraint and frontal, offset, roof, and side crash protection as "Good," "Acceptable," "Marginal," or "Poor." In the Institute's 64 km/h (40 mph) offset test, 40 percent of the total width of each vehicle strikes a barrier on the driver's side. The barrier's deformable face is made of an aluminum honeycomb, which makes the forces in the test similar to those involved in a frontal offset crash between two vehicles of the same weight, each going just less than 64 km/h.

Though IIHS's 50 km/h (31 mph) side-impact test is carried out at a slower speed than NHTSA's side test, the barrier uses a front end shaped to simulate the typical front end of a pickup or SUV. The Institute also includes the degree of head injury in its ratings.

Cost Analysis and Best Alternatives

Winter prices for the 2011 and 2012 models are much lower than last year's prices on some vehicles, such as full-sized trucks, SUVs, and vans. As long as fuel costs stay high, this trend is likely to continue. As the cost of oil dips below $80 (U.S.) a barrel, large vehicles become more in demand and carry higher prices. Small cars and hybrids, in this case, would be less popular and discounted accordingly. Leasing deals are also expected to pick up now that the American automakers have renewed their links with major lending agencies.

In our selection of alternative buys, we consider whether a vehicle's 2011 or 2012 redesign measurably improves that vehicle's performance over the previous model. If it doesn't, we suggest you choose the earlier model or consider a different vehicle. Redesigns of the 2011 BMW X3, Honda Odyssey, Mercedes-Benz E350, Toyota 4Runner and Sienna, and VW Jetta, for example, have lowered the models' ratings in certain performance areas. On the other hand, some auto manufacturers have hit the bull's eye this year with redesigns that markedly improve overall performance. Among these are the Hyundai Elantra and Kia Sorento and Sportage.

2011 and 2012 Winners and Losers

New models entering the market for the first time also met with mixed owner reactions. The Chevrolet Cruze, Ford Fiesta, and Mazda2 are big successes, with dealers reporting only a few weeks' supply. The Cruze's success is all the more surprising considering that the first-year 2011s weren't well built. For example, sometimes the steering wheel would separate from the steering column. Honda's Accord Crosstour (a raised hatchback with optional AWD, mediocre handling, limited cargo space, and reduced rear visibility) and the CR-Z (a small hybrid with unrealized sport-car performance pretensions and unimpressive fuel economy) have both been greeted with a yawn.

2011 AND 2012 HIGHLIGHTS

NEW MODELS	NEW DESIGNS	NEW "GREEN" CARS
Audi A7	Acura RL	BMW 1 Series (EV)
Buick Verano	Audi A6	Chevroler Volt (plug-in hybrid)
Cadillac XTS	Honda Civic	Ford Focus (EV)
Chevrolet Sonic	Hyundai/Kia Accent/Rio	Infiniti M35 (hybrid)
Chevrolet Spark	Hyundai Azera	Lexus CT 299h (hybrid)
Fiat 500	Lexus GS	Nissan Leaf (EV)
Ford C-Max	Mercedes CLS	Toyota Prius V (hybrid)
Hyundai Veloster	Mercedes ML-Class	Volvo V70 (plug-in hybrid)
Range Rover Evoque	Nissan Quest	
Saab 9-4X	VW New Beetle	
Scion iQ	VW Passat	

GM's Sonic will show if an American-built, South Korean–designed small car can win over Honda Fit and Nissan Versa shoppers.

Honda's CR-Z promises more than it delivers. It's proof that Honda sometimes gets things wrong.

2011 and 2012 Disappointments

BMW 5 Series GT—Launched just a few years ago, this BMW has misjudged its market that wants conservatively styled sedans that don't have an ungainly liftback or a high load floor. Mercedes laughs all the way to the bank.

BMW X6—A "sports activity coupe" (SAC?) that answers a question no one asked. This $100,000 turbocharged trans-something is outsold almost eight to one by the more traditional and cheaper X5. An endangered species.

Ford Flex and Lincoln MKT—Two other mashed minivans that are losing out to the GM Traverse, Hyundai Santa Fe, and Toyota Highlander. Ford predicted sales of 100,000 in 2011, but has sold only about 2,000 a month so far.

Honda Insight—One of the least expensive hybrids available in North America. The first hybrid had such a checkered reliability and performance history that Honda took it off the market for a few years. Now that it has returned, Honda marketing gurus are learning to their dismay that car buyers have long memories. Toyota sells seven Prius hybrids for every Insight that makes it out of the showroom.

Mercedes-Benz R-Class—Mercedes first called this low-riding minivan a "sports cruiser" and when that was met with underwhelming enthusiasm, changed the name to "family cruiser" (anything to avoid the dreaded "minivan" moniker). Somber styling, awkward long rear doors, poor reliability, and a 7-speed transmission that "hunts" for the right gear.

Smart Fortwo—Buyers want more than a cute, toy-like mini-compact. American megadealer Roger Penske has dumped the brand, which seals Smart's fate in North America. Canadian dealers are desperately looking for a "Smart" move from Mercedes that will reduce the car's price and add more safety and convenience features.

Toyota Tundra—Who says Toyota can't make bad vehicles? The Tundra is one. A history of powertrain, suspension, and steering problems combined with Toyota's tsunami of safety recalls has most GM and Ford truck owners staying with the brand they know. Predicted 2010 sales: 200,000. Actual sales: a bit over 93,000 units.

Nissan Quest—Another Japanese reject, the Quest continues its sales spiral with its latest fourth-generation makeover. What happened? Abysmally poor quality, poor fit and finish, and an interior that is much smaller than the outside configuration promises. This will be the next minivan to be dumped.

Subaru Tribeca—A Subaru version of the ugly and unpopular Pontiac Aztek, the Tribeca's odd rounded styling and triangular grille has turned off buyers since the car was first launched in 2005. Now the car has a new look, but it, too, is failing to catch on with an unimpressed public.

Warranties

A manufacturer's warranty is a legal commitment. It promises that the vehicle will perform in the normal and customary manner for which it is designed. If a part malfunctions or fails (unless it's because of owner negligence or poor maintenance), the dealer must fix or replace the defective part or parts and then bill the automaker or warranty company for all the part and labour costs. Warranties are an important factor in *Lemon-Aid*'s ratings. Unfortunately, it has been our experience that most automakers inflate the costs of scheduled maintenance work and then whine that independent garages are taking away their customers.

Most new-vehicle warranties fall into two categories: bumper-to-bumper, for a period of three to five years, and powertrain, for up to 5 years/100,000 km. Automakers sometimes charge an additional $50–$100 fee for repairs requested by purchasers of used vehicles with unexpired base warranties. For snowbirds, the federal and provincial governments can charge GST and sales tax on warranty and non-warranty repairs done south of the border—so beware. Also, keep in mind that some automakers, like Honda, may not honour your warranty if a vehicle is purchased in the States and registered in Canada.

Cross-Border Warranty Restrictions

Cross-border sales still remain a viable alternative for buyers who want to save thousands of dollars on new and used top-end, fully equipped models. A couple years ago, many automakers refused to honour warranties in Canada on vehicles bought in the U.S. and brought to Canada. That tactic didn't cut it with consumers, so this year buyers will find fewer warranty restrictions from a chastened auto industry. (See Appendix III for a simple step-by-step guide to getting thousands of dollars off your next car or truck when shopping in the States).

Canada's non-profit Automobile Protection Association has drawn up a list of companies and identified whether they have warranty restrictions on vehicles bought in the United States (check *www.apa.ca* for changes).

AMERICAN VEHICLES

High-Tech Glitches

The slowdown in improvement is largely attributable to increased rates of problems with electronic features in vehicles, including audio, entertainment and navigation systems and new safety features, such as tire pressure monitoring systems.

DAVID SARGENT

J. D. POWER AND ASSOCIATES, MARCH 17, 2011

Chevrolet Volt: An Electric Edsel?

The Chevrolet Volt electric car is a marvel in many ways, but so were automatic seat belts, the Ford Edsel and yes, the Sony Betamax. None of those lasted long, and now people are beginning to wonder about the Volt's long-term prospects and those of current electric cars in general.

A few recent driving impressions, including one in the well-read magazine *Consumer Reports*, have pointed to the limited range, high cost and potentially annoying traits that are likely to make the Volt and its main competitor, the Nissan Leaf, unappealing to the majority of drivers. After months of buildup and often gushing reviews, it seems now as if the automotive consumer sector is exhaling and rediscovering skepticism.

JONATHAN WELSH

WALL STREET JOURNAL, MARCH 6, 2011

The 2009 shakeout of the American auto industry left Ford as the only clear winner. Despite having just scrapped its Mercury division in the States, Ford has the best brand mix, a relatively satisfied dealer body, and great relations with its suppliers. All this contributed to the company's 2011 best first-quarter earnings since 1998, with smaller, option-laden, fuel-efficient cars generating much of the revenue.

Ford earned $2.55 billion, a 22 percent increase from a year ago, as it shifted away from huge trucks and concentrated upon a more balanced and profitable array of downsized SUVs, family cars, and compacts. Averaged out, Ford squeezed a profit of $1,519 per vehicle during the first quarter, which was a 59 percent increase over earnings from the same period in 2010. Through March 2011, Ford has posted an operating profit for seven consecutive quarters and almost tripled its pretax profit in Europe.

For 2012 Ford brings back a redesigned Focus, with an all-electric plug-in, and introduces a new seven-passenger, European-designed microvan, called the C-Max (not available in Canada).

Chrysler and General Motors: Bankruptcy and Bailouts

Chrysler and General Motors got bailout loans of $80 billion to ease their passage through bankruptcy in 2009. GM came out of bankruptcy with $17 billion in remaining debt and with four model divisions less.

The Obama administration is putting the best possible spin on the bailouts, now that Chrysler and GM are paying back much of the borrowed money.

"Since GM and Chrysler emerged from bankruptcy, the auto industry has created 115,000 jobs, its strongest period of job growth since the late 1990s," one White House study explained. "GM, Ford and Chrysler have all returned to profitability, and in 2010, the Detroit Three gained market share for the first time since 1995."

Sounds good, but the Devil's in the details:

- President Obama says, "Chrysler has repaid every dime and more of what it owes American taxpayers for their support during my presidency—and it repaid that money six years ahead of schedule." True, but this counts only the money given to Chrysler since Obama took office. Bush's Chrysler's TARP bailout, supported by President-elect Obama, has not been repaid. The company has paid back only $11.2 billion of the $12.5 billion it received. When will we get the remaining $1.3 billion? Never, says the U.S. Treasury Department.
- The White House tells us "once Chrysler is sold to Fiat, the automaker will be in private hands." Mama Mia! Chrysler will become an Italian car company, and likely more of its auto manufacturing will be shipped overseas to Europe and China. Private hands? Of those hands, 46 percent will be stocks held by the United Auto Workers.
- The government promises "96,000 workers laid off in the 4th quarter of 2008 will be rehired." But who really knows? Some reports show 331,000 auto industry jobs were lost during the recession; only 76,000 have returned.
- More than 650,000 retired automakers and their family members lost their health insurance.
- Investors in $27 billion worth of GM bonds, including mutual funds and thousands of individual investors, ended up with stock that was practically worthless.
- Wall Street has little faith in Detroit automakers. GM's stock had an initial public offering at $33 a share in November 2010. That stock fell to $22.71 a share by October 13, 2011. Ford's shares have fallen from $18.97 to $11.39 over the same period.
- Uncounted thousands of suppliers were shut down after being stiffed by Chrysler and GM.

- Auto dealers lost their franchises inexplicably and then were welcomed back when they threatened to sue. This created a sullen, litigious dealer body.
- Victims of defective GM and Chrysler vehicles waiting to be paid damages won't be so fortunate and may not have the right to lodge a future claim.
- The industry mini-revival may be due as much to bungling by the Japanese (read: Toyota safety recalls); several earthquakes in Japan last March, a devastating tsunami, and the meltdown of four nuclear reactors at Fukushima; and a sales surge in China and Europe. One thing is certain: the major Japanese players are "off the ice" through the rest of 2011, giving American, European, and South Korean automakers a clear field to rack up impressive sales gains.

University of Pennsylvania law professor David Skeel points out in a June 6, 2011, *Wall Street Journal* op-ed piece that both GM and Chrysler could have survived the bankruptcy process without bailouts. Of course, some jobs would have gone, and the companies may have changed owners, but that's already happened with Fiat's takeover of Chrysler; Hummer, Saab, and Volvo's recent ownership by the Chinese; and Tata Motors' buyout of Jaguar and Land Rover. Skeel argues that "this should have happened without Washington risking billions of taxpayers' dollars — $14 billion of which is likely never to be repaid."

We leave the last word to *The Truth About Cars* editor Edward Niedermeyer (*www. thetruthaboutcars.com/2011/04/industry-bailout-what-bailout*):

> So, what did the bailout do right? Cutting capacity, or in less politically-palatable terms, firing people. Ironic, isn't it, that a policy that's being defended as a jobs-saving measure did its best work (at least according to the OEMs [original equipment manufacturers]) when it put people out of work? Meanwhile, feel free to draw your own conclusions about the fact that the industry liked the "capacity rationalization" aspects of the bailout, while feeling like the bailout didn't do enough. Saving jobs, as we've pointed out for some time, is not the same as saving companies...in fact, the two goals often clash significantly.
>
> In any case, both OEMs and suppliers picked the government's rescue of Chrysler as the least-positive impact of the auto industry rescue. Some 42% of OEMs feel rescuing Chrysler was negative for the industry, while 20% of suppliers sign on to the same sentiments, despite being largely positive about the GM bailout.

GM, on the other hand, is more of a mixed bag. First and foremost, the company has become profitable and has paid back most of its bailout debt to the American and Canadian governments. Its model lineup has been relegated to four Detroit-based divisions instead of eight. And, although GM's products are fewer, the company has a number of popular 2011 models like the Cruze, Equinox, Terrain, and Traverse.

On the other hand, the automaker's dealer body is not nearly as lean as GM said it must be after many dealers forced their way back into the network as a result of arbitration settlements.

Finally, General Motors' quality control still has a long way to go to catch up with Ford and Asian automakers. Most common failures involve the transmission, brakes, suspension, and the electrical/fuel system. Fit and finish is abysmal.

New Products

GM's New Vehicles

GM will be adding three small cars for 2012: The Chevrolet Spark (the smallest); the Chevrolet Sonic; and the Buick Verano, a luxurious compact sedan spun off of the Chevrolet Cruze platform. Cadillac will introduce the 2012 XTS, a front-drive replacement for the departing DTS and STS.

The Buick Verano.

Spark

The South Korean–built Spark five-door hatchback is an ideal city car that sips fuel and fits into tight spaces, thanks to its short length. Interior appointments are adequate, and there's plenty of headroom and legroom for tall occupants both in the front and rear. Three adults in the rear? Only if they are on leave from Barnum & Bailey.

Selling for an estimated $12,500, the Chevrolet Spark's base engine is a 1.0L 4-cylinder that puts out 67 hp. A more powerful 1.2L version harnesses 80 horses. Forget about speed. This is one of the slowest cars you will find. Don't leave the city.

Sonic

Chevrolet's Aveo will be replaced in 2012 with the Chevrolet Sonic (another Aveo), a small compact that needs to poach customers who would be tempted by Honda's Fit, Ford's Fiesta, the all-new Mazda2 or recently reworked Mazda3, and the revamped Hyundai Accent or Kia Rio. Priced at $14,495, the base Sonic carries a 1.8L 4-cylinder engine. An optional 1.4L turbocharged powerplant is available. Both engines are borrowed from the Chevrolet Cruze, produce 138 hp (18 hp more than the Fiesta) and come with either a 6-speed manumatic or a 5- or 6-speed manual (also used by the Cruze).

Chrysler's Lineup

Chrysler is also making money. Its 2011 first-quarter earnings were $116 million versus a loss of $197 million a year ago, representing the company's first profit since 2006. This turnaround was possible due to Chrysler's post-bankruptcy clean balance sheet, fewer dealers and employees, a lean model lineup, and less Japanese competition due to the earthquake in Japan. The redesigned Jeep Grand Cherokee and Dodge Ram pickup are both selling reasonably well, and minivan sales have picked up, too. Nevertheless, the company's old model lineup will be at a serious disadvantage going into 2012, when Ford's full 2012 lineup of popular cars, crossovers, SUVs, and trucks and GM's popular SUVs and trucks will cut into Chrysler sales.

The Ohio-built Sonic is a five-passenger compact that's available as a four-door sedan or a five-door wagon. Psst... It's really a redesigned, renamed Aveo. Here's what GM says: "The new small car will carry the Sonic name in Canada, Mexico, and the United States. The vehicle will continue to be called Aveo in 50 other countries."

Fiat price gouging?

Will high fuel prices and a limited warranty for 3 years/60,000 km entice buyers to purchase a 2012 Fiat 500? Doubtful. Too many owners remember Fiat turning tail in 1984 and leaving hapless North American Fiat car owners with worthless warranties and rust-cankered junk.

Canadians also feel they are being gouged by unfair pricing when compared with prices and features available in the States. Says one blogger at *http://fiat-500-usa-forum-archives. 965414.n3.nabble.com/why-so-much-more-expensive-in-canada-td2808046.html*:

Why is the 500 much more expensive in Canada? I think we are really screwed in Canada...

- To make it comparable, you have to add $350 for the Bose system that is optional in Canada while included in USA
- The PDI is $1400 in Canada vs $500 in USA
- The full warranty for Canada is for 3 years vs. 4 years in the US (but the drivetrain in Canada is 5 years, instead of 4)
- The 3 years of service is not there in Canada (that's worth at least $1000)
- The interest rate on a loan in the USA seems about 3% while Fiat Canada is at 6%. That difference could add at least $1500 to the price so all in all, even if the Canadian dollar is worth more than the US dollar ($1.03 US for $1 Cdn.)

we still end up [about] $3000...for the same car. For a car around $20 000 that's almost 20%...more. Can you believe this?

And another at *http://clubsmartcar.com/index.php?showtopic=23056&st=20&start=20*:

Out of curiosity I went to the US site to compare standard features and price. The US Pop comes with $2000+ more in standard features and the US has a better warranty. Makes the Fiat less interesting for myself, knowing that the Canadians are being taken for about $3000 on every car.

And another at *http://www.fiatvidz.com/fiat/fiat-500-at-the-2011-toronto-auto-show.html*:

I really like the new 500, I just can't bring myself to pay the extra 30% to buy one here in Canada (with our dollar above par) as compared to the equivalent US car. On top of that, the US also gets a better warranty (one extra year) and free service for 3 years. Hopefully Fiat Canada will correct this pricing and service discrepancy in the future.

This Year in Detroit

So what does the future hold for Chrysler, Ford, and General Motors?

Lots of short-term profits for the Detroit Two and Fiat/Chrysler through the winter of 2012, while Japanese auto manufacturers restructure their assembly plants and rebuild the supplier and distribution chain. China's love for American vehicles will continue, and Japanese and Chinese automakers will participate for the first time in co-ventures where they share manufacturing facilities. We will see many more fuel-efficient vehicles in the $13,000–$19,000 range in 2012—mostly coproductions with South Korean and European automakers. The Asian link is a plus for reliability because many of the Asian platforms and components, like the Mazda6 parts found in Ford's Fusion, have been used and improved over many years and are much more dependable than their Detroit counterparts. In fact, *Consumer Reports* has given the Fusion high marks for safety and overall performance. But be careful: this isn't always the case. Chrysler's Mercedes hookup and a number of other co-ventures with other countries' products didn't do very well. The jury is still out on the European-derived Ford Fiesta, which may have its own reliability and parts supply problems.

Another trend that will be obvious this year is the ever-increasing number of models that employ hybrid and all-electric powertrains. These two fuel-saving innovations have been used for years, but the cost of production generally wipes out any fuel savings and makes these "green" vehicles unobtainable without hefty government subsidies that can reach $8,500 (CDN) per vehicle.

GM is loaded with unsold trucks and SUVs. Its 15–25 percent discounts are a good deal. Dropping freight charges and adding a $1,000 Costco bonus would be nice, too.

The 2012 Ford Focus is redesigned this year, which adds about $2,000 to its base price. Plus, there's an extra $1,400 freight charge. Some dealers will drop the price by $1,000 for Costco members.

So, with the auto industry rebounding and so many products to choose from, what should the prospective buyer of a Chrysler, Ford, or GM model do this year?

Take advantage of 2011 clearance sales now, or wait until early 2012, when manufacturers' sales incentives to dealers and customer rebates both kick in on the 2012 models. Remember, the larger, more fully loaded trucks and SUVs offer the steepest discounts. This Calgary dealer also gives a $1,000 Costco rebate.

In early 2012 there will be a larger choice of fuel-efficient models and large cars and trucks will cost less as oil prices stay in the $90–100 (U.S.) per barrel range. Japanese manufacturers will offer sweeter rebates and sales incentives as the winter flows into spring. Car shoppers can then get some good buys at ridiculously low prices while the industry turmoil transforms a seller's market into a buyer's market.

The SE model mentioned in this ad sells for $16,099, so the price listed is a real bargain. On the other hand, if the lower price applies only to the $12,999 entry-level S model, you may do well only if the 0 percent financing applies and no freight charges are added.

Chrysler/Fiat

One Last Chance

Chrysler invented the minivan and still does very well there, and the company should do better as both Toyota and Honda, its main competitors, struggle to overcome the effects of the earthquake disaster. Other segments look, well, rougher. The sedans are stylish, but they're going up against superior cars from Chevy, Ford, and even the upstart Koreans. There's always hope in pickups, but the Ram brand is a perennial number three to Ford's F-150 and Chevy's Silverado.

MATTHEW DEBORD
BNET, MAY 2, 2011

Chrysler 200 Review

If this is the best vehicle Detroit exports, then Glenn Beck is right....

[N]o number of LEDs can hide a profile that looks like a loggerhead turtle. If this car came in tortoise shell, the EPA would have to put it on the endangered sedan list to prevent trappers and automotive enthusiasts from rightfully shooting it into extinction.

SCOTT BURGESS
THE DETROIT NEWS, MARCH 10, 2011

Chrysler has crawled back from the grave, thanks to an arranged marriage, with a questionable dowry, with Italy's Fiat. Aside from the fast-tracked Fiat 500, most fruits of this union won't reach dealer showrooms until 2012. There's not a lot of time left for co-owner Fiat to turn the company around. Chrysler will be officially "owned" by Fiat by the end of this year when Fiat buys a majority of Chrysler's shares and renames the company Fiat/Chrysler, making the Detroit Three into the Detroit Two and one dual national.

Of the Detroit-based automakers, Chrysler has had the furthest to go in improving performance, quality, and reliability. Granted, the company has beautifully styled cars, like the 300, and high-performance models, like the Viper, Challenger, and Charger; plus, its latest full-sized Ram 1500 pickup is noted for its impressive power and ride comfort. Still, this is of little comfort when tire valve stems self-destruct, transmission control modules short-circuit, engines constantly stall out in traffic, or the automatic transmission suddenly downshifts as the car is cruising on the highway:

The contact owns a 2011 Dodge Grand Caravan and stated that while driving 65 mph [105 km/h], the vehicle began to downshift and lunge forward. The contact had to quickly react because of the traffic behind the vehicle and drove onto the emergency lane and shut off the vehicle. The contact restarted the vehicle and took it to the dealer who was unable to diagnose the failure. Immediately after the contact drove away from the dealer, the failure re-occurred. The contact drove onto the emergency lane over to the side of the road and the Check Engine light came on. The minivan was towed to a dealer who ran another diagnostic test. A faulty transmission control module was causing the vehicle to suddenly downshift and jerk. The failure mileage was 200 miles [322 km].

Type in "automatic transmission failures," and Google throws up a picture of a Chrysler minivan (well, almost). All kidding aside, Chrysler has gone from a company noted for engineering innovation and strong, high-performance muscle cars to being known for ABS, AC, electrical system, and minivan automatic sliding door failures and automatic transmissions that need replacing after only a few years. Poor fuel economy and subpar fit and finish, with the associate clunks, squeaks, rattles, and exhaust drone (see bulletin below), combined with a mediocre ride and handling, are other Chrysler traits you won't see mentioned in the company's brochures. To be fair, Chrysler did come out last year with a new Pentastar V6 engine and transmission that so far appear to be reliable, good performers.

EXHAUST DRONE/VIBRATION

BULLETIN NO.: 11-001-11   DATE: JANUARY 26, 2011

EXHAUST DRONE OR VIBRATION AT 2200–2500 RPM
2011 200/Avenger/200 Convertible
OVERVIEW: This bulletin involves installing a revised exhaust isolator and repositioning the exhaust system.

More about Chrysler quality (or lack thereof): *Consumer Reports'* October 2009 edition says that two-thirds of Chrysler's models were below average and that the Chrysler Sebring convertible was the worst-rated car, with 2.8 times more problems than average. Other bottom-feeders: the Sebring/Avenger and Charger sedans, the Caliber hatchback, and the Liberty, Nitro, and Wrangler SUVs. *Consumer Reports* doesn't recommend any 2012 Chrysler model. Neither does *Lemon-Aid.*

The most apparent problem with Chrysler is its almost total dependence on trucks, SUVs, and minivans, aside from the few passenger cars it offers. And even the cars it does sell are huge, like the large, fuel-wasting Magnum, 300, and Charger. When gasoline was relatively cheap, big was profitable, but now cheaply made small cars are more in demand and turn a profit through greater volume.

Having said this, if fuel costs stay in the range of $80 bucks (U.S.), the Japanese don't quickly return to the market, and Chrysler's new powertrains and Fiat connection endure, the automaker could be riding high this time next year.

Chrysler's 2011 and 2012 models are mostly a bad idea, except for the minivans. The 2012s are warmed-over versions of the 2011s with new powertrains and more Fiat models and components. For instance, the Jeep Wrangler will get Chrysler's Pentastar V6 engine and a small sedan based on Fiat's platform and will go on sale in early 2012, replacing the Dodge Caliber. Work has started on a 2013 Fiat-based

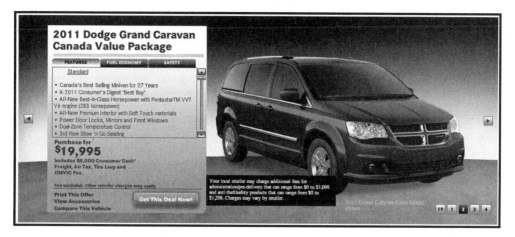

2011 Dodge Grand Caravan Canada Value Package

FEATURES | FUEL ECONOMY | SAFETY

Standard

• Canada's Best Selling Minivan for 27 Years
• A 2011 Consumer's Digest 'Best Buy'
• All-New Best-in-Class Horsepower with PentastarTM VVT V6 engine (283 horsepower)
• All-New Premium Interior with Soft Touch materials
• Power Door Locks, Mirrors and Front Windows
• Dual-Zone Temperature Control
• 3rd Row Stow 'n Go Seating

Purchase for
$19,995
Includes $8,000 Consumer Cash*
Freight, Air Tax, Tire Levy and
OMVIC Fee.

Tax excluded. Other retailer charges may apply.

Print This Offer
View Accessories
Compare This Vehicle

Get This Deal Now!

Your local retailer may charge additional fees for administration/pre-delivery that can range from $0 to $1,098 and anti-theft/safety products that can range from $0 to $1,298. Charges may vary by retailer.

2011 Grand Caravan Crew Model shown

Chrysler/Fiat is clearing out its 2011 minivan inventory through exceptionally low prices that include freight fees. Online ads usually offer the lowest prices possible. But take a close look at the details. Here we have Chrysler's $19,995 MSRP for a 2011 Grand Caravan that normally sells for $28,995. A real savings. But be careful when you visit the dealer. The ad says the dealer can jack up the sales price two ways: through an "administrative charge" and "delivery," or "destination" fee up to $1,098. Plus, the addition of unspecified "anti-theft and safety products" sold by the dealer could add as much as $1,298 more to the price. Tell the dealer to take a hike with these added charges.

replacement for the mid-sized Dodge Avenger and Chrysler 200 sedans, while a slew of other Chrysler models are heading for the last roundup, as Sergio Leone plays a mournful harmonica.

The carried-over Jeep Grand Cherokee and Fiat 500 Mexican import are two redesigns of vehicles that were never rated highly. Until Chrysler/Fiat can show some stability and quality improvement, smart buyers should steer clear of the company's products this year. The only exceptions are the minivan lineup—but only if you get an extended transmission warranty and can take advantage of some bargain prices.

PURCHASE FOR
$19,998
2011 DODGE JOURNEY SE CANADA VALUE PACKAGE
CANADA'S #1 SELLING CROSSOVER^

Chrysler Canada has cut the 2012 Journey's price to $18,995, but you still may spend more than $2,000 for delivery and dealer "administrative" fees.

200/AVENGER

bad buy

The Chrysler 200.

RATING: Not Recommended. As Scott Burgess, auto critic for the *Detroit Pree Press* puts it: "The 200 shows how Band-Aids on sheet metal never really stick." The next step down from the Chrysler 300, the 200 is a reworked Sebring in disguise, and is available in a sedan or convertible format. Highway performance has been considerably improved with stiffened body mounts, a smoother suspension, a raised roll centre, an upgraded rear sway bar and tires, improved noise reduction, and a softened ride. **Strong points:** A more stylish appearance; a gentler, more comfortable ride; better handling; and a classier, quieter interior. V6 engine gives plenty of power. Easy access to the interior. Standard side curtain airbags and electronic stability control. IIHS gives the 200 sedan its top rating for good performance in front, side, rollover, roof strength, and rear crashworthiness tests. The convertible version scored similarly, except there was no roof rating. **Weak points:** The base 4-cylinder engine coupled to the Jurassic 4-speed tranny is a puny performer and lacks reserve power for passing and merging. The optional 6-speed transmission helps the acceleration, but shifts are harsh and too frequent. Only average fuel economy. Uncomfortable front seats have insufficient thigh room. Interior feels small, closed in. Smallish trunk. Because the 200 was rushed into production and is based on the mediocre Sebring and Avenger twins, there is a high likelihood the car will be dropped by Fiat before the 200's first-year defects are corrected. NHTSA hasn't crash-tested the 200 model. Three-quarter rear visibility is seriously compromised by the C-pillars. **New for 2012:** The 2012 Dodge Avenger R/T arrives with a stiffer, sportier suspension, a performance-tuned exhaust for the standard V6, and different interior and exterior styling that includes a rear spoiler.

OVERVIEW: Like its Dodge Avenger twin, the 200 carries a base 2.4L 4-cylinder or an optional 3.6L Pentastar V6 engine. Entry-level models use a 4-speed automatic transmission while the 6-speed automatic is optional. A 6-speed dual-clutch automatic (an automatically shifted manual transmission) will be optional on the much-awaited 4-cylinder Limited model.

The Chrysler Sebring *cum* 200 and the Dodge Avenger are two sides of the same coin. What you save from a low selling price you will lose through frequent repairs, excessive depreciation, and time spent waiting for a tow, a taxi, or a mechanic. *Consumer Reports* put out this warning to readers on March 18, 2011:

> Introduced in 2007, the Sebring and its platform-mate Dodge Avenger were poster children for automotive under-achievement. Reliability out of the box was lousy, and both cars have hovered at the bottom of our family sedan Ratings. Further dampening our impressions, we had a *Consumer Reports*–owned Sebring that almost stranded our staff members on several occasions.

COST ANALYSIS: This is a "work in progress" car that is outclassed by Ford and the Asian competition. **Best alternatives:** The Ford Fusion, Honda Civic (2011) or Accord, and Hyundai Sonata. **Options:** As the 4-banger is a sad joke, hobbled by its 4-speed gearbox, get the better-performing—make that "only performing"—V6 powerplant. **Rebates:** $250–$500 rebates and discounts plus low-cost financing on all models should kick in early in the new year. **Depreciation:** Very fast. For example, a 2011 200 LX that originally sold for $19,995 (plus $1,400 freight) is now worth about $14,000. The same model-year Avenger SE that also sells for $19,995 is now worth about $13,000. Leftover 2011 models are selling for $1,500 less. **Insurance cost:** Average. **Parts supply/cost:** Parts are mostly taken from the Sebring and Avenger bin, so they are reasonably priced and easily found. **Annual maintenance cost:** Average. **Warranty:** Bumper-to-bumper 3 years/60,000 km; powertrain 5 years/100,000 km; rust perforation 5 years/160,000 km. **Supplementary warranty:** Getting an extended powertrain warranty is a smart idea. **Highway/city fuel economy:** *2.4L 4-speed auto.:* 6.7/9.9 L/100 km, 42/29 mpg. *2.4L 6-speed auto.:* 6.4/10.5L/100 km, 44/27 mpg. *3.6L 6-speed auto.:* 6.8/11.0 L/100 km, 42/26 mpg. *Convertibles: 2.4L 4-speed auto.:* 6.9/10.3 L/100 km, 41/27 mpg. *2.4L 6-speed auto.:* 6.8/11.5 L/100 km, 42/25 mpg. *3.6L 6-speed auto.:* 6.8/11.0 L/100 km, 42/26 mpg.

KEY FACTS

CANADIAN PRICE (NEGOTIABLE): *LX:* $19,995, *Touring:* $22,995, *Limited:* $26,995, *Convertible LX:* $29,995, *Convertible Touring:* $36,495, *Convertible Limited:* $38,495, *Avenger SE Value Package:* $17,995, *Avenger SXT:* $22,995, *Avenger SXT Plus:* $26,495
U.S. PRICE: *LX:* $19,245, *Touring:* $21,540, *Limited:* $23,945, *S:* $26,240, *Convertible Touring:* $26,445, *Convertible Limited:* $31,440, *Convertible S:* $31,940, *Avenger Express:* $19,245, *Avenger Mainstreet:* $21,340, *Avenger LUX:* $23,745, *Avenger Heat:* $23,840, *Avenger R/T:* $23,545, *Avenger R/T AWD:* $25,545 **CANADIAN FREIGHT:** $1,400
U.S. FREIGHT: $750
POWERTRAIN (FRONT-DRIVE)
Engines: 2.4L 4-cyl. (173 hp) • 3.6L V6 (283 hp); Transmissions: 4-speed auto. • 6-speed manumatic.
DIMENSIONS/CAPACITY (SEDAN)
Passengers: 2/3; Wheelbase: 108.9 in.; H: 58.4/L: 191.7/W: 72.5 in.; Legroom F/R: 42.4/36.2 in.; Cargo volume: 13.6 cu. ft.; Fuel tank: 62L/regular; Tow limit: 1,000 lb.; Load capacity: 865 lb.; Turning circle: 36.5 ft.; Ground clearance: 6.1 in.; Weight: 3,389 lb.

OWNER-REPORTED PROBLEMS: Brake, transmission, suspension, and fuel, electrical, and audio system failures, electrical malfunctions, paint peeling, and poorly assembled body panels:

> Just bought a 2011 200 S series a week ago and already having paint peeling problems. Took it back to the dealer and they are looking at repainting back bumper and trunk...the paint color is BlackBerry. My 200 has a lot of little defects in the paint. Dust particles and such. Not a good finish. Not to mention that it had some type of overspray on it when I picked it up.... I did get Chrysler to repaint my back bumper... looks great...now having electrical problems...MIL (Check Engine) Light turns on... ESP Lights turns on for no apparent reason...loud noise in engine compartment... car stops after 3 minutes using remote start.... "WHAT A PIECE OF ****"... The car is less then two months old.... Buyer beware!

CHALLENGER, CHARGER ★ ★

The Dodge Charger.

RATING: Below Average. These gas-guzzlers aren't very reliable, and you get more high-performance thrills with fewer maintenance bills from dozens of other entries; among them, the Chevrolet Camaro, Ford Mustang V6, and Hyundai Genesis. **Strong points:** Its undeniable these "muscle" cars have exceptional retro styling, horsepower to burn (as in, "What do you mean the fuel tank is on EMPTY, again?"), and cachet. *Happy Days* reruns are here, again. The 3.6L V6 has proven to be much more reliable than either of the two V8s, and it burns less fuel, but powertrain dependability has come under fire from owners of 2009–11 models. The Challenger was given five stars by NHTSA for front and side crashworthiness, and four stars for rollover resistance. The Challenger has had fewer quality issues than the Charger, but it hasn't been on the market as long. *Charger:* Various interior improvements, tighter suspension and steering; and an all-new adaptive suspension system for the SRT8. This system automatically tunes the suspension system and also has manual controls the driver can set to "Auto" or "Sport" mode to tune the suspension to his or her preference. Outward visibility has also been improved by an enlarged windshield area. The Charger earned five stars for frontal protection and four stars for rollover resistance. No testing was done for side-impact protection. IIHS rated the Charger "Good" for frontal offset protection. **Weak points:** *Challenger:* Despite recent upgrades to improve performance and comfort, you will still find a stiff, jarring ride; handling that's not particularly agile; overly assisted steering that requires constant correction; and marginal rear headroom. The Challenger is in dire need of an interior facelift similar to the Charger's. *Charger:* The Charger was rated "Poor" by IIHS for side-impact crashworthiness; head-restraint protection was rated "Marginal." There are many quality issues that mostly concern the automatic transmission, brakes, suspension, climate system, and fit and finish. **New for 2012:** Most features will be carried over unchanged from the 2012 model year. An 8-speed automatic will be on V6 Chargers—eventually. The Charger R/T and SRT8 and all Challengers stick with the 5-speed Mercedes automatic for another year; they are not expected to get 8-speeds until 2014.

OVERVIEW: Using the same platform and engines as the Chrysler 300, the Charger and Challenger combine a potent mixture of Hemi V8 power, rear drive, and an independent suspension supplied by Mercedes. Combined with the company's Multi-Displacement System (MDS), which shuts down half the cylinders under light load, the 5.7L Hemi engine produces more horsepower and slightly better fuel economy than previous engines. The downside is finding suitable Hemi engine repairs from a trimmed dealership network with limited parts inventories.

KEY FACTS

CANADIAN PRICE (VERY NEGOTIABLE):
Challenger SXT: $26,995, *Challenger SXT Plus:* $28,995, *Challenger R/T:* $36,395, *Challenger R/T Classic:* $38,390, *Challenger SRT8:* $47,995, *Charger SE:* $29,995, *Charger SXT:* $29,995, *Charger SXT Plus:* $33,995, *Charger R/T:* $37,995 **U.S. PRICE:** *Challenger SE:* $24,895, *Challenger Rallye:* $26,895, *Challenger R/T:* $29,895, *Challenger R/T Plus:* $31,895, *Challenger R/T Classic:* $33,195, *Challenger SRT8:* $43,780, *Charger SE:* $25,395, *Charger Rallye:* $27,645, *Charger Rallye Plus:* $29,395, *Charger RT:* $30,395, *Charger RT Plus:* $32,395, *Charger RT Road and Track Package* $33,395, *Charger RT Max:* $35,$30, **CANADIAN FREIGHT:** $1,400 **U.S. FREIGHT:** $750
POWERTRAIN (REAR-DRIVE/AWD)
Engines: 3.6L V6 (292 hp) • 3.6L V6 (305 hp) • 5.7L V8 (370–372 hp) • 6.4L V8 (470 hp); Transmissions: 5-speed auto.; *Challenger:* 6-speed man. • 6-speed auto.
DIMENSIONS/CAPACITY
Passengers: 2/3; Wheelbase: 116 / 120 in.; *Challenger:* H: 57/L: 198/W: 76 in., *Charger:* H: 58/L: 200/W: 75 in.; Headroom F/R: *Charger:* 2.5/ 2.0 in.; Legroom F/R: *Charger:* 41.5/ 28.0 in.; Cargo volume: 16 cu. ft.; Fuel tank: 68–72L/regular; Tow limit: *Challenger:* Not recommended, *Charger:* 1,000–2,000 lb.; Load capacity: 865 lb. est.; Turning circle: 41 ft.; Ground clearance: 4.5 in.; Weight: *Challenger:* 3,720–4,140 lb., *Charger:* 3,728–4,268 lb.

Although these cars are fun to drive and buy you entry into the high-performance "winner's circle," in the end, you will be the loser. High fuel, insurance, and depreciation costs will quickly thin out your wallet. Plus, the absence of a comprehensive seven-year or lifetime powertrain warranty is like performing a high-wire act without a net. Both of these cars will likely have a short shelf life, judging by Fiat's stated goal of doing more with less (horsepower). Chrysler revived the Hemi name in 2002 with a 5.7L Hemi V8 engine used in its pickups and then extended it to the 300 Ram Wagon sedan—a winning combination that revived lagging pickup, sedan, and wagon sales. But that was when fuel was relatively cheap. For 2012, bigger is definitely not better.

COST ANALYSIS: Look for discounts and rebates to drop list prices by about 20 percent, thus putting pressure on leftover 2011 model year prices and sweetening 2012 model discounts early next year. The Challenger will continue with V6 and Hemi V8 engines to better compete with the Chevrolet Camaro and horsepower-boosted Ford Mustang V6. It's also the largest, roomiest, and heaviest entrant among these classic American sport coupes. But its lack of agility makes it more of a Clydesdale than a "pony car." **Best alternatives:** The Ford Mustang V6 or Hyundai Genesis Coupe. **Options:** You'll want the 3.6L V6 engine for better all-around performance with less of a fuel penalty. Servicing will be easier and less expensive than with either of the Hemi powerplants. **Rebates:** $3,500–$7,000 rebates and discounts, plus zero percent financing by the spring of next year. **Depreciation:** Talk about fast depreciation: a 2011 Challenger SE that originally sold for $27,000 is now worth about $21,000. Depreciation is even faster with the Charger: A 2011 Charger SE that once sold for $30,000 is now worth $10,000 less—the SXT takes a $9,000 hit. **Insurance cost:** What the market can bear. You want high performance, you get high insurance rates. **Parts supply/cost:** Parts are not a problem due to the many different models using the same Chrysler 300 parts. Engine and body components are expensive and complex to troubleshoot, especially now that Chrysler has fewer dealers, parts suppliers, and skilled mechanics. **Annual maintenance cost:** Average; higher than average once the warranty expires. **Warranty:** Bumper-to-bumper 3 years/60,000 km; powertrain 5 years/100,000 km; rust perforation 5 years/160,000 km. **Supplementary warranty:** An extended powertrain warranty is a wise choice, since Chrysler is too cheap to provide Canadians with a lifetime powertrain warranty like the one offered in the States. **Highway/city fuel economy:** *Challenger 3.6L:* 7.3/11.7 L/100 km, 39/24 mpg. *Challenger 5.7L, man.:* 8.2/13.8 L/100 km, 34/20 mpg. *Challenger 6.4L, SRT8:* 8.8/15.1 L/100 km, 32/19 mpg. *Challenger 6.4L, SRT8 auto. with fuel saver:* 9.2/15.6 L/100 km, 31/18 mpg. *Charger 3.6L:* 7.3/11.7 L/100 km, 39/24 mpg. *Charger 5.7L with fuel saver:* 8.0/13.5 L/100 km, 35/21 mpg. *Charger 5.7L AWD with fuel saver:* 8.5/14.4 L/100 km, 33/20 mpg.

OWNER-REPORTED PROBLEMS: *Challenger:* Not an inordinate number of problems reported. Those that have surfaced concern mostly the engine and transmission, brakes, fuel system, and fit and finish. *Charger:* Owners report many more problems with the transmission, brakes, suspension, and body construction.

The Chrysler 300.

RATING: Average. These cars were modestly refined and restyled for the 2011 model year. They carry the new Pentastar 3.6L V6 hooked to a 6-speed automatic transmission. Popular 2012 8-speeds are back ordered to such an extent that Chrysler has put a hold on the model until late August 2012. **Strong points:** There's plenty of power with the latest V6 hooked to the 6-speed automatic gearbox. You will also enjoy acceptable handling, a remarkably quiet and spacious interior, and a large trunk. The touring model gives a smoother, more-comfortable ride than does the 300C, which is the performance-oriented variant. Chrysler has also enlarged the window area for better visibility and reworked the interior so that it feels less claustrophobic, is more user-friendly, and looks classier. **Weak points:** Hemi-equipped models are way overpriced, and the 300's resale values have fallen considerably. Standard towing capability is less than one would expect from a rear-drive. Some of the electronics derived from Mercedes' luxury models have had serious reliability problems. **New for 2012:** The V6-equipped Chrysler 300C will feature an 8-speed automatic later in the 2012 model year, and then that gearbox will be phased in for the V8 models. In its second year of production, the relatively new 292 hp 3.6L V6 will be standard; a 363 hp 5.7L V8 is optional. SRT8s will use a production version of the 6.4L Hemi with 465 hp and MDS for better gas mileage (expected in late 2012). Restyled doors with thinner pillars improve outward visibility by 15 percent; a new dual-pane panoramic sunroof gives twice the outward visibility of a standard sunroof. New entertainment systems and driver comfort features.

KEY FACTS

CANADIAN PRICE (VERY NEGOTIABLE):
Touring: $32,995, *Limited:* $34,995, *C:* $39,995, *AWD:* $41,995 **U.S. PRICE:** *300:* $27,170, *Limited:* $31,170, *C:* $38,170 **CANADIAN FREIGHT:** $1,400 **U.S. FREIGHT:** $935
POWERTRAIN (REAR-DRIVE/AWD)
Engines: 3.6L V6 (292 hp) • 5.7L V8 (363 hp); Transmissions: 5-speed auto. • 8-speed auto.
DIMENSIONS/CAPACITY (BASE)
Passengers: 2/3; Wheelbase: 120 in.; H: 58.4/L: 199/W: 75 in.; Headroom F/R: 4.5/2.5 in.; Legroom F/R: 41.8/40.1 in.; Cargo volume: 16.3 cu. ft.; Fuel tank: 68L/regular; Tow limit: 2,000 lb.; Load capacity: 865 lb.; Turning circle: 41 ft.; Ground clearance: 4.7–5.0 in.; Weight: *300:* 3,961–4,513 lb.

OVERVIEW: Front-drives are out and rear-drives are in, again, along with all-wheel drive and complicated Hemi V8 engines—all the ingredients for endless repair waits and extra expenses as these elegantly styled, complicated-to-service sedans start putting on the miles and come closer to their warranty expiry date. The V8 is rather exceptional, in that it features Chrysler's Multi-Displacement System, which uses eight cylinders under load and then switches to 4-cylinder mode when cruising. So far, this feature has worked reliably well.

COST ANALYSIS: Excess weight and large engines drive up fuel costs; consequently, resale values are dropping because buyers are shifting to smaller, more-economical sedans. **Best alternatives:** Ford's Fusion comes with optional all-wheel drive and a 230 hp 3.0L V6 that offers smooth power for about $32,000. There's also the Honda Accord Crosstour, Subaru Forester or Legacy, Suzuki SX4 Hatchback, and Toyota Sienna. **Options:** You may want to order the $2,000 SafetyTec Package. True, these options add complexity to the car's innards and increase the risk of electronic failures, but some of the safety features are worthwhile. They include blind-spot alert, cross-path detection, forward collision warning, a front- and rear-obstacle-detection system, adaptive cruise control, driver-side automatic day/night mirror, mirror-mounted turn signals, universal garage door opener, rain-sensing wipers, rear fog lights, and steering-linked adaptive and self-dimming bi-xenon headlights. The $3,300 Limited Luxury Package is not so useful; it gives the dealer a $4,000 profit and adds little to your driving experience or safety, except for the power-adjustable pedals. A "premium" paint job is not worth its $1,000 premium, either; even the $300 "special" paint application is of doubtful value. **Rebates:** Expect $4,000–$5,000 discounts or rebates and low-interest financing programs by late winter. **Depreciation:** Higher than average. For example, a 2009 Chrysler 300C SRT8 equipped with a Hemi V8 sold new for $53,695; today its resale value is barely $24,000. No, that's not a misprint: $24,000. You would have done much better with a 2011 base 300 version that sold new for $32,000. It is now worth about $21,500, only $2,500 shy of the two-year-older SRT8's resale value. **Parts supply/cost:** Expect long delays and high costs. **Annual maintenance cost:** Higher than average. **Warranty:** Bumper-to-bumper 3 years/60,000 km; powertrain 5 years/100,000 km; rust perforation 5 years/160,000 km. **Supplementary warranty:** Get an extended powertrain warranty thrown into the deal. **Highway/city fuel economy:** *3.6L: 7.3/11.7 L/100 km, 39/14 mpg. 5.7L 300C (cylinder deactivation): 8.0/13.5 L/100 km, 35/30 mpg. 5.7L AWD: 8.7/13.4 L/100 km, 32/21 mpg.* Owners report, however, that real-world fuel consumption for both engines is far more than these estimates.

OWNER-REPORTED PROBLEMS: One car caught on fire while parked and then exploded:

> My 2008 300 Touring was parked in a parking lot. The alarm started going off by itself. A fire started out of nowhere from under the hood. Then my car exploded from the front to the back through the exhaust pipe. I only had 6,100 or so miles [9,800 km] on my car.

Chronic electrical shorts and stalling; vehicle rolls backward when stopped on an incline; automatic transmission clicking and banging into gear; transmission will suddenly slip into a lower gear; electronic stability control is ineffective on ice:

> I rented a Chrysler 300 over this past weekend. I want you to know that it was the scariest ride I've had in a while. Have you ever tested the electronic stability program on ice? It not only does not work, it is extremely dangerous. I had to drive about 600 miles [965 km] on icy and windy Wyoming roads which proved to be quite scary in the 300 with ESP.

CD player won't play a complete disc, and parts aren't available to repair the problem; steering knocks when turning; brakes drag and pulsate when stopping; horn won't sound if the car is not running or if it isn't hit in the right spot:

> In a panic, a driver will likely not meet these location/force requirements and the horn will not sound, resulting in other drivers and pedestrians not receiving a warning.

Defective rack and pinion steering; poorly performing Goodyear Integrity tires:

> Goodyear Integrity tires hydroplane every time it rains. I have already had one accident because I couldn't stop. I've run a red traffic light and I have experimented in a parking lot and hydroplaned at 15 mph [24 km/h].

GRAND CARAVAN, TOWN & COUNTRY ★★★

The Dodge Grand Caravan.

RATING: Average. Last year's refinements corrected many of these minivans' past deficiencies, giving both minivans an upgraded rating from Below Average to Average. It will take several years to find out if the use of the new Pentastar V6 and

KEY FACTS

CANADIAN PRICE (VERY NEGOTIABLE):
Grand Caravan SE Value Package:
$20,995, *SXT:* $24,995, *Crew:* $27,995,
R/T: $32,495, *Town & Country Touring:*
$33,995, *with leather:* $35,995, *Limited:*
$39,995 **U.S. PRICE:** *Grand Caravan
Cargo:* $21,800, *Express:* $23,995,
Mainstreet: $25,845, *Crew:* $28,795,
R/T: $30,695, *Town & Country Touring:*
$30,260, *Touring-L:* $32,660, *Limited:*
$39,825 **CANADIAN FREIGHT:** $1,400 **U.S.
FREIGHT:** $835

POWERTRAIN (FRONT-DRIVE)
Engines: 3.6L V6 (283 hp); Transmission:
6-speed auto.

DIMENSIONS/CAPACITY
Passengers: 2/2/3; Wheelbase: 121 in.;
H: 69/W: 77/L: 203 in.; Headroom F/R1/
R2: *Grand Caravan:* 6/5/0 in., *Town &
Country:* 3.5/4.5/0.0 in.; Legroom F/
R1/R2: *Grand Caravan:* 41.0/30.5/
27.0 in., *Town & Country:* 41/31/25 in.;
Cargo volume: 61.5 cu. ft.; Fuel tank:
76L/regular; Tow limit: 3,800 lb.; Load
capacity: 1,150 lb.; Turning circle: 41 ft.;
Ground clearance: 5.0 in.; Weight: *Grand
Caravan:* 4,600 lb., *Town & Country:*
4,755 lb.

an upgraded automatic transmission (introduced on the 2011s) cures Chrysler's decades-old powertrain maladies, but owner feedback is positive—so far. As for long-term servicing, it seems repairs and parts shouldn't be a problem. If Chrysler's Fiat gamble doesn't pay off and Chrysler goes belly up for a third time, it's quite likely that the minivan and Jeep divisions will be sold separately and will keep producing products and parts. **Strong points:** Very reasonably priced and subject to deep discounting. Early reliability reports on the Pentastar V6 and reworked automatic transmission are positive. The tight chassis and responsive steering provide a comfortable, no-surprise ride. Stiffer springs have greatly improved handling and comfort. Manoeuvring around town is easy. Lots of innovative convenience features, user-friendly instruments and controls, two side-sliding doors, easy entry and exit, and plenty of interior room. Dual airbags include knee bolsters to prevent front occupants from sliding under the seat belts. Remote-controlled power door locks can be programmed to lock when the vehicle is put in gear. Chrysler has developed a mechanism that releases the power door locks and turns on the interior lights when the airbag is deployed. Both vehicles were given NHTSA's top, five-star rating for frontal and side crashworthiness; rollover resistance earned four stars. **Weak points:** Power steering is vague and over-assisted as speed increases. Downshifting from the electronic gearbox provides practically no braking effect. Brake pedal feels mushy, and the brakes tend to heat up after repeated applications, causing considerable loss of effectiveness (fade) and warping of the front discs. The ABS system has proved to be unreliable on older vans, and repair costs are astronomical. A sad history of chronic powertrain, AC, ABS, and body defects that are exacerbated by the automaker's hard-nosed attitude in interpreting its after-warranty assistance obligations. Rear-view camera screen image isn't bright enough. Get used to a cacophony of rattles, squeals, moans, and groans caused by the vehicle's poor construction and subpar components. Chrome ring around the passenger-side heater deck causes a distracting reflection in the side-view mirror in the Town & Country. Fuel consumption is worse than advertised. **New for 2012:** An upgraded suspension. Fed up with jokes about its minivans being only for soccer moms, Chrysler now sells a lower-sitting R/T high-performance model described as a "man van." Redesigned minivans will appear in 2014.

OVERVIEW: These versatile minivans return with a wide array of standard and optional features that include anti-lock brakes, child safety seats integrated into the seatbacks, flush-design door handles, and front windshield wiper and washer controls located on the steering-column lever for easier use. Childproof locks are standard. Chrysler mated the Pentastar V6 to a 6-speed automatic transmission, which is just as fuel-thrifty as the much less powerful outgoing model. Beginning with the 2011 models, there was an important improvement in emergency handling and stopping power, and a new fuel economizer switch that changes the transmission shift schedule for better mileage. There's a new spoiler, LED tail lamps, a lower ride height, lower rolling resistance tires, reduced brake and rear bearing drag (this increases gas mileage), and a retuned suspension with different spring rates. No more Swivel 'n Go seats, but the new seats are more comfortable, and captain's chairs in the middle row have returned.

COST ANALYSIS: Go for the more-refined 2011 model's second series leftovers, made in the middle of 2011, or buy a 2012 early in the year. This will allow the factory to work out any bugs found with the new V6 and automatic transmission. **Best alternatives:** Honda's Odyssey should be your first choice, with the Toyota Sienna placing second. Full-sized GM rear-drive vans are also worth considering. They are more affordable and practical buys if you intend to haul a full passenger load, do regular heavy hauling, are physically challenged, use lots of accessories, or take frequent motoring excursions. Don't splurge on a new luxury Chrysler minivan: Chrysler's upscale Town & Country may cost up to $10,000 more than a Grand Caravan, yet be worth only a few thousand dollars more after five years on the market. **Options:** Town & Country's $2,000 leather interior isn't worth the extra cost. Sliding side doors make it easy to load and unload children, but they are failure-prone. You may wish to pass on the tinted windshields: they seriously reduce visibility. Ditch the failure-prone Goodyear original-equipment tires, and remember that a night drive is a prerequisite to check out headlight illumination, which many have called inadequate. **Rebates:** The 2012 models will likely get $3,000–$6,000 discounts on the Grand Caravan and Town & Country or zero percent financing throughout the year. **Depreciation:** Faster than average. Check this out: A $39,995 2011 Town & Country is now worth $28,500; a 2011 Grand Caravan SE that sold for $27,995 now has a $21,500 resale value. **Insurance cost:** About average for a minivan. **Parts supply/cost:** Higher than average, especially for AC, transmission, and ABS components, which are covered under a number of "goodwill" warranty programs. **Annual maintenance cost:** Repair costs are average during the warranty period. **Warranty:** The base warranty is inadequate if you plan to keep your minivan for more than five years. Bumper-to-bumper 3 years/60,000 km; powertrain 5 years/100,000 km; rust perforation 5 years/160,000 km. **Supplementary warranty:** An extended powertrain warranty is a must-have. If buying the warranty separately, bargain it down to about one-third of the $2,000 asking price. Chrysler minivans can be expected to have some brake, suspension, AC, body, and electrical system deficiencies similar to previous versions. Quality control has been below average since these vehicles were first launched more than 20 years ago and, surprisingly, got much worse after the 1990 model year introduced limp-prone transmissions. **Highway/city fuel economy:** *3.6L:* 7.9/12.2 L/100 km, 36/23 mpg.

OWNER-REPORTED PROBLEMS: Town & Country front passenger-side seat belt alert may be disabled due to a software glitch:

> Service manager informed me that Chrysler found in manufacturing that this passenger seat belt alert did not work correctly, so they disabled it in software. He further said that if or when a software update becomes available to fix the problem, I would be informed of the fix.

Frequent tire valve stem failures:

> Tire valve stem broke, resulting in an immediate flat tire. This is the second failure of this vehicle. I have had this happen on more than one of the same make and model of vehicles.

Owners say sliding-door failures make them afraid to drive these minivans. Their complaints also focus on electrical glitches, erratic AC performance, and early brake wear (see *forum.chryslerminivan.net*). In one NHTSA-logged complaint, the minivan, used as a hearse, was deemed unsafe to transport...dead bodies?

> All electrical equipment stopped working on the way home from the dealership. No gauges, no power windows or doors, no turn signals, no brake lights, no A/C, no radio. The only thing[s] working were the windshield wipers, which came on by themselves and I could not shut them off. All the warning lights on the dash lit up. Made it home and called the dealership. Van has less than 100 miles [160 km] on it and already in for service. Called dealership Monday afternoon, they can't find any problems, must be the TIPM (Totally Integrated Power Module). They have ordered the part, but it is on backorder until who knows when. Van has been deemed unsafe to drive until repaired. Dealership provided me with a small sedan to drive until fixed, but this van was purchased by my funeral home to use for body transportation, stretchers, caskets, etc. Sedan is totally useless for my business.

The speed control feature automatically shifts transmission into low gear with a thud, and high engine revs whenever the vehicle goes down an incline. At other times, the vehicle will lose all power until the ignition key is reinserted. Also, vehicle may shut down whenever both wheels pass over a pothole or speed bump. Other owners note the premature wearout of the cooling system, clutch, front suspension components, wheel bearings, air conditioning, and body parts (trim, weather stripping becomes loose and falls off; plastic pieces rattle and break easily). The front brakes need constant attention, if not to replace the pads or warped rotors after two years or 30,000 km, then to silence the excessive squeaks when braking. And don't expect engine compression to help with braking:

> As we have experienced to our horror on numerous occasions driving on the west coast (Vancouver Island), while trying to maintain vehicle control on a downhill stretch of

paved road, this 4-speed electronic transmission system is incapable of providing any engine braking assistance whatsoever. The only alternative is to ride the brakes to maintain vehicle control.

SERVICE BULLETIN-REPORTED PROBLEMS: AC condenser road debris damage can be avoided by installing a condenser guard supplied by Chrysler (under warranty, of course). TSB #23-047-06 is very useful for determining when a cracked windshield should be replaced under warranty. Power liftgate failures can be easily corrected by recalibrating the power control module, says TSB #08-045-06. NHTSA has recorded numerous complaints of airbags deploying unexpectedly—when passing over a bump in the road or simply when turning the vehicle on—or failing to deploy in an accident. Owners who find the sliding door obstruction detection feature too sensitive need to reflash the electronic module. Also, 2011 models built before December 13, 2010, need to reflash the powertrain control module (PCM) to extinguish a lit MIL warning light.

RAM 1500, 2500, 3500 PICKUP ★★★

The Dodge Ram 1500.

RATING: Average. **Strong points:** The crew cab model comes with a cargo bed that's longer than that of most of the competition but not as huge as the Mega Cab; a Mega Cab/long bed configuration is also available on the Ram Heavy Duty models. The best engine choice, until the Pentastar V6 proves itself, is the 4.7L V8, with 310 horsepower and 330 pound-feet of torque; it's a good match for medium-duty work. Compare the stability and ride with Toyota trucks, and you will be impressed by Chrysler's better handling and more-comfortable ride. 2012 Ram 1500s will return with standard safety features that include head-protecting side curtain airbags for both front and rear seating and an anti-skid system that includes trailer-sway control. *2010 1500 four-door Regular Cab, 1500 four-door Crew*

KEY FACTS

CANADIAN PRICE (VERY NEGOTIABLE): *1500 ST V6 4×2:* $20,495, *4×4:* $24,845, *1500 SXT:* $21,495, *4×4:* $25,845, *1500 SLT:* $23,495, *4×4:* $26,945, *1500 Outdoorsman:* $24,290, *4×4:* $28,040, *1500 Big Horn:* $30,245, *4×4:* $33,890, *1500 Sport:* $32,145, *4×4:* $32,495, *1500 Laramie:* $34,970, *4×4:* $38,420, *1500 Laramie Longhorn:* $47,965, *4×4:* $51,415, *2500 ST:* $27,345, *4×4:* $32,945, *2500 SXT:* $28,345, *4×4:* $33,945, *2500 SLT:* $29,445, *4×4:* $35,045, *2500 Outdoorsman:* $35,595, *4×4:* $40,090, *2500 Laramie:* $42,245, *4×4:* $45,695, *2500 Powerwagon:* $44,040, *2500 Laramie Longhorn:* $47,245, *4×4:* $50,695, *3500 ST:* $42,395, *4×4:* $45,845, *3500 SXT:* $43,395, *4×4:* $46,845, *3500 SLT:* $44,495, *4×4:* $47,945, *3500 Laramie:* $54,195, *4×4:* $57,595, *3500 Laramie Longhorn:* $62,490, *4×4:* $65,940 **U.S. PRICE:** *1500 ST:* $20,810, *4×4:* $25,265, *1500 Tradesman:* $21,805, *4×4:* $26,260, *1500 Express:* $22,855, *4×4:* $27,310, *1500 SLT:* $25,430, *4×4:* $29,000, *1500 Outdoorsman:* $28,025, *4×4:* $31,595, *1500 Sport R/T:* $31,115, *1500 Lone Star:* $31,660, *4×4:* $34,480, *1500 Big Horn:* $31,660, *4×4:* $34,880, *1500 Sport:* $34,035, *4×4:* $34,475, *1500 Laramie:* $38,055, *4×4:* $40,805, *1500 Laramie Longhorn:* $43,065, *4×4:* $46,210, *2500 ST:* $27,975, *4×4:* $30,950, *2500 SLT:* $30,755, *4×4:* $33,970, *2500 Outdoorsman:* $33,450, *4×4:* $36,665, *2500 Laramie:* $42,245, *4×4:* $44,495, *2500 Lone Star:* $37,410, *4×4:* $40,855, *2500 Big Horn:* $37,410, *4×4:* $40,855, *2500 Laramie:* $41,050, *4×4:* $44,495, *2500 Laramie Longhorn:* $44,975, *4×4:* $48,420, *2500 Powerwagon:* $45,110, *3500 ST:* $35,995, *4×4:* $39,095, *3500 SLT:* $39,170, *4×4:* $42,340, *3500 Lone Star:* $45,685, *4×4:* $48,620, *3500 Big Horn:* $45,685, *4×4:* $48,620, *3500 Outdoorsman:* $46,215, *4×4:* $49,150, *3500 Laramie:* $49,405, *4×4:* $52,340, *3500 Laramie Longhorn:* $53,780, *4×4:* $56,715 **CANADIAN FREIGHT:** $1,400 **U.S. FREIGHT:** $975

POWERTRAIN (REAR-DRIVE/PART-TIME/FULL-TIME AWD)
Engines: 3.7L V6 (215 hp) • 4.7L V8 (310 hp) • 5.7L V8 (390 hp) • 6.7L Diesel (Cummins); Transmissions: 4-speed auto. • 5-speed auto. • 6-speed man.

DIMENSIONS/CAPACITY (BASE)
Passengers: 3/2; Wheelbase: 141 in.; H: *1500:* 77, *2500:* 79/W: 80/L: 228 in.; Headroom F/R: 6/4 in.; Legroom F/R: *1500:* 40.5/25.0 in., *2500:* 40/26 in.; Fuel tank: 132L/ regular; Tow limit: 5,655 lb.; Load capacity: *1500:* 1,120 lb., *2500:* 1,945 lb.; Turning circle: *1500:* 50 ft., *2500:* 51 ft.; Ground clearance: *1500:* 10.5 in., *2500:* 8.0 in.; Weight: *1500:* 5,655 lb., *2500:* 7,130 lb.

Cab, and 1500 four-door Quad Cab: NHTSA awarded five stars for frontal crashworthiness and four stars for rollover resistance. *2010 2500 Extended Cab 4×2 and 4×4:* These models earned four and three stars, respectively, for rollover resistance. *All 2010 1500 models:* IIHS gave frontal crash protection and head restraints a "Good" rating. **Weak points:** The 3.7L V6 is a mediocre performer when compared with the Pentastar V6's potential, especially when hooked to a more-efficient 5-speed automatic. The fuel-thirsty Hemi V8 isn't a wise choice either. Its cylinder-deactivation feature is helpful, but not very. The Hemis are also complicated to service, and parts are often back ordered. Full-time AWD and electronic stability control (ESC) are optional. IIHS gave side crash protection a "Marginal" rating. Mediocre braking. If you are a short driver, you may not be able to see over the raised hood. **New for 2012:** Rams get the new 6-speed truck transmission with their V8-equipped models. *Ram 1500:* The Ram 1500 was an all-new truck for the 2009 model year. New features that are carried on the 2011 and 2012 models include an iPod connector, active head restraints, and an improved tire pressure monitoring system. *Ram 2500/3500:* The heavy-duty Ram gets a thorough going-over, including the addition of a crew cab. The styling follows that of the Ram 1500, but with a bigger, more-masculine look, while the interior is upgraded with new materials and amenities. A retuned suspension provides a more-comfortable ride. Engines are carryovers: the 5.7L Hemi V8 and the 6.7L Cummins turbodiesel. Fleet customers will be able to purchase a biodiesel-capable version of the Cummins engine that runs on B20 (20 percent biodiesel/80 percent petroleum diesel). Maximum GVWR is up to 25,400 lb., while the Ram 2500 gained 2,000 lb. of trailer towing capacity with the 4.1 rear axle.

OVERVIEW: These trucks are considerably improved, and so many have been sold over the years that their maintenance can be carried out by most independent garages—with the exception of the Hemi engine, which requires more specialized dealership support. The only reason these trucks have not been given a higher rating is their poor on-road performance ("death wobble," etc. and powertrain failures).

Ram 2500 and 3500 models feature either the Hemi gas engine or the highly desirable Cummins diesel. As for power, Ford's new diesel has higher peak torque, but the Cummins is still the best choice for providing low-end torque. *2011 Ram 2500/3500/4500/5500 Chassis cab:* The Ram 2500's tow rating increased on 2011 models from 20,000 to 22,000 lb. with the diesel and 4.1 axle ratio thanks to a beefier rear suspension and axle. Both the 2500 and 3500 have a standard EVIC (Electronic Vehicle Information Center), standard tire pressure monitoring, and standard trailer brake control on all but ST models.

COST ANALYSIS: Go for the 2012 or second-series 2011 Ram 1500 if you want to see whether the new V6 engine lives up to its hype. If you're inclined to stick with the V8s—including the problematic Hemi—then go for a discounted, carried-over 2011. The ideal combination is the diesel engine coupled to a manual transmission to dodge (pun intended) Chrysler's automatic transmission breakdowns. **Best alternatives:** Honda Ridgeline and the Nissan Frontier. Ford's F-Series is the best Detroit alternative to the Ram. It was also redesigned at the same time as the Ram with a more-solid-feeling structure and larger cabs and cargo beds, as well as additional compartments and dividers. Ford F-Series trucks took a big step forward on the powertrain front last year with its introduction of the twin-turbocharged EcoBoost V6 and a strong new base V8 engine. Leftover 2011 base Silverado and Sierra models aren't a smart buy, despite what may be a bargain price. On the other hand, the redesigned 2011 Heavy Duty (HD) versions are much more refined than previous model years, though they have a less accommodating, less comfortable crew cab. **Rebates:** These trucks will likely get $5,000 rebates or discounting plus zero percent financing throughout the year as higher fuel prices cut into the sales of the bigger rigs. **Depreciation:** Average, but much faster than average for the V8-equipped models. Diesels with manual transmissions hold their value best. **Insurance cost:** Average. **Parts supply/cost:** Parts prices are higher than average, especially for Hemi engine, AC, transmission, and ABS components; parts are often back ordered. **Annual maintenance cost:** Repair costs are average during the warranty period;

however, this doesn't include lost wages or lost use of the truck due to long waits for back-ordered parts, which is a frequent complaint. **Warranty:** The base warranty is inadequate if you plan to keep your pickup for more than five years. Bumper-to-bumper 3 years/60,000 km; powertrain 5 years/100,000 km; rust perforation 5 years/160,000 km. **Supplementary warranty:** Consider buying an extended powertrain warranty. If buying the warranty separately, bargain it down to about one-third of the $2,000 asking price. **Highway/city fuel economy:** *3.7L V6:* 10.0/14.8 L/100 km, 28/19 mpg. *4.7L V8:* 10.0/15.6 L/100 km, 26/18 mpg. *5.7L V8 MDS:* 10.2/15.4 L/100 km, 28/18 mpg. *5.7L V8 4×4 MDS:* 10.8/16.2 L/100 km, 26/17 mpg.

OWNER-REPORTED PROBLEMS: Recall repairs to the rear axle spindle delayed until September 2012:

> The problem is...the rear axle pinion bearing on my truck may not receive adequate lubrication under certain driving conditions. This lack of lubrication condition could cause the pinion bearing to seize and cause a loss of vehicle control and/or a crash without warning. I have contacted three different servicing dealers, and have been told three different stories. The one common factor they have is that parts are not available, and backorders weren't being processed. I feel like I'm getting the run-around.... The manufacturer left me a message, after my numerous complaints, stating that parts were being expedited for me, but they are not returning my phone calls now. They don't seem to be concerned over this "safety recall" since I can't get my truck fixed. My truck's axles has not failed as of yet. I can't seem to get the recall done though to prevent a failure. If Dodge is going to drag this out, they need to cover the cost of rental vehicles for affected customers until they can get the recall done. I'm concerned for the safety of my family while in this truck.

Owners report Chrysler is also delaying the carrying out of a steering and door latch recall. Sudden, unintended acceleration; gas pedal stuck to the floor; vehicle suddenly downshifts:

> The problem is when traveling, uphill-downhill or on level, if you are above 45 mph [72 km/h] and you stop applying gas pedal to coast. The vehicle will coast until you reach approximately 40 mph [64 km/h] at which time the transmission will downshift into 3rd gear. This causes an abrupt slowing without alerting vehicle behind you. This could in effect cause a rear collision because the brake lights are not activated, and the gearing is low in rear axle which causes the vehicle to slow at a faster rate than normal.

The airbag warning light comes on for no reason; two dealers could not get the airbag sensor replacement parts; the chrome trim ring around the console-mounted shifter reflects the sun into the driver's eyes; at 70 km/h, the truck shakes violently and veers out of lane when passing over small bumps, or when driving with the rear windows rolled down:

The contact owns a 2011 Dodge Ram 1500 quad. While driving above 50 mph [80 km/h], the contact noticed that when he would roll the rear windows down, the vehicle would shake excessively almost causing the contact to lose control of the vehicle. The dealer was aware of the issue, informed the contact that there were not related recalls and offered no additional assistance.

Frequent front shock failures; excessive vibration:

City of Ottawa has four (4) Dodge Ram 5500 units, bought in March 2010 with VIN numbers listed below, all have been plagued with steering problems which [cause them to drift] at speeds over 70 km/h and [are] difficult to control when facing consecutive small bumps—so much that in my test ride I was afraid I could end up in the opposite lane of traffic and cause a head-on collision. My personal concern is that if new or inexperienced drivers face such steering, it could cause accident, damage or even fatality if it goes unchecked. Unfortunately the dealerships (Southbank and Capital Dodge) seem to have very little knowledge of the root cause and no capacity to do real analysis and testing on these units. Chrysler Corporate has been contacted via 1-800 phone calls and fleet emails and files were opened on all our units but that has been the extent of their co-operation, and even the local service managers have not heard from Chrysler's engineering or the district service manager who usually tends to such calls.

Another Ram owner calls the steering vibration and shimmy a "Death Wobble":

My truck has been to the dealer numerous times to correct a shimmy or as the service writer called it a "death wobble". The dealer has felt the issue and on numerous occasions tried to fix it. Including aligning the vehicle out of factory specs on the advice from the Ram engineers. They have also swapped the steering stabilizers with a heavier duty one from the 1 ton Ram 3500. Neither fix has worked to correct the shimmy or the slight pull to the right. The truck is flat-out dangerous to drive and I did not realize how bad until I was towing a 5200 lb boat at 65 mph [105 km/h]. Neither the weight or the speed should have been a problem for this ¾ ton truck but after driving over an expansion joint the truck started to shimmy and that combined with the trailer sway almost killed someone. The only reason someone did not die in that instant is I was the only person within a mile. If someone would have been in the left lane I would have taken them out with a truck and trailer that was nearly uncontrollable.

Exhaust fumes invade the cabin:

The contact owns a 2011 Dodge Ram 2500. The contact stated that while stopped at a traffic light, the exhaust began leaking into the cabin of the vehicle on the passenger side. The contact stated that the odor was overpowering when the vehicle was stopped. The vehicle was taken to the dealer who was unable to diagnose the failure. The vehicle was not repaired and the manufacturer was not made aware of the failure. The failure mileage was 1,000 [1,609 km].

Gas spews out of filler tube when filling up; wheel lug nuts sheared and wheel flew off truck; defective suspension front struts; sudden steering lockup; windshield wipers fall off because they no longer have a retention bolt.

SERVICE BULLETIN-REPORTED PROBLEMS: *2003–11 Rams:* Dangerous vibration at highway speeds (did someone say "death wobble?") fixed by a recent recall.

HIGHWAY STEERING WHEEL VIBRATION	
BULLETIN NO.: 22-001-11	DATE: JANUARY 22, 2011

2010–11 RAM 1500 Pickup, 2500, 3500, 2011 Cab Chassis, and 2011 4500/5500 Cab Chassis.
OVERVIEW: This bulletin involves test driving the vehicle for vibration felt at the steering wheel during highway speeds and if necessary performing road force variation to the tires and/or replacing the steering wheel.
SYMPTOM: The customer may experience excessive steering wheel vibration when driving at highway speeds.

WRANGLER ★ ★

RATING: Below Average. Wrangler is one of the most off-road-capable Jeeps ever made, but it falls far short when driven on-road. What this fun-to-drive, competent off-roader gives in impressive "bush" performance is taken away by its overall poor reliability and dangerous on-road performance highlighted by the powertrain suddenly jumping out of gear when the outside temperature drops, and the steering and suspension going into a "death wobble" after passing over potholes or speep bumps. Plus, its short wheelbase, loud and porous cabin, and mediocre highway performance makes this modern, entry-level Jeep CJ annoying at best as a daily commuter and outright uncomfortable as a road trip vehicle. But the Jeep cachet is fun if off-road thrills are your forte and you exercise common sense in how you drive. **Strong points:** The Pentastar V6 and an upgraded transmission will hopefully smooth out the 2012 powertrain's performance. The Wrangler comes with a roomy, plush cabin and a more-rigid frame that enhances handling; on the downside, it makes for a stiff ride. The front seat has plenty of headroom; the Unlimited models with four doors have 1.6 inches more legroom in the back. The Unlimited also has very generous cargo space. Safety features include stability control with rollover sensing, hill start assist, and anti-lock brakes. **Weak points:** These little SUVs are selling at their full list price and are not likely to be discounted by much as the year progresses. There is only a small amount of cargo room in the back of the two-door model; the previous V6 engine is coarse and underpowered; and the 6-speed manual transmission is anything but smooth. Handling is compromised by vague steering, a stiff ride, and low cornering limits (standard stability control is a plus), and violent shaking makes the vehicle practically uncontrollable ("death wobble") when passing over small bumps at cruising speeds:

> While driving my Jeep Wrangler at about 35–40 mph [56–64 km/h] over a rough spot on the road, I experienced horrible front end shake that I could not control until I pulled the car over. I'm very lucky there was nobody else in front or in back of me because I had no control of my vehicle. I looked into this online and have learned it's called the "Death Wobble" and it's happened to many other Jeep owners.

Another dangerous characteristic of the Wrangler is the transmission's tendency to jump out of gear whenever the weather turns cold or the vehicle passes over uneven terrain. Owners also report that the Wrangler's off-road prowess is compromised by poor original-equipment tires and thin body panels. Although there's not much you can do about the body panels, *www.tirerack.com* can give you invaluable, unbiased tips on the best and cheapest tires for the kind of driving you intend to do. Front seat side airbags are offered as an option; without them, crashworthiness is unimpressive. Taller people may find that the legroom is limited in both the front and rear seats. Fuel economy? It isn't as good as advertised. **New for 2012:** A more fuel-efficient 3.6L Pentastar V6 hooked to a 5-speed automatic transmission, new interior and exterior, and Quadra Coil suspension with regular, heavy-duty, or off-road tuning (depending on trim).

OVERVIEW: The Wrangler is the smallest and least expensive (we're talking bare bones here) Jeep you can find. It's an iconic SUV that can easily handle open-air off-road driving anywhere you choose and still be presentable for Saturday night cruising downtown. How's this for versatility: The standard soft top can be folded

KEY FACTS

CANADIAN PRICE (FIRM): *2-door Sport:* $19,345, *4-door Unlimited:* $24,445, *2-door Sahara:* $26,245, *2-door Rubicon:* $29,245, *4-door Unlimited Rubicon:* $34,495 **U.S. PRICE:** *2-door Sport:* $22,045, *Sport S:* $24,245, *Sahara:* $27,745, *Sahara 70th:* $29,055, *Mojave:* $29,975, *Rubicon:* $29,820
CANADIAN FREIGHT: $1,400
U.S. FREIGHT: $800
POWERTRAIN (REAR-DRIVE/PART-TIME/FULL-TIME AWD)
Engine: 3.6L V6 (290 hp); Transmissions: 6-speed man. • 5-speed auto.
DIMENSIONS/CAPACITY (BASE)
Passengers: 2/3; Wheelbase: 116 in.; H: 71/W: 74/L: 173 in.; Headroom F/R: 5.5/5.0 in.; Legroom F/R: 41/28 in.; Cargo volume: 34.5 cu. ft.; Fuel tank: 70L/regular; Tow limit: 3,500 lb.; Load capacity: 850 lb.; Turning circle: 43 ft.; Ground clearance: 8 in.; Weight: *Sport:* 3,849 lb., *Rubicon:* 4,165 lb.

down or the available hard top can be taken off. Then, if you want more adventure, the doors can be removed and the windshield folded down—in effect, creating many different vehicles out of one.

The two-door Wrangler is offered in Sport, Sahara, and Rubicon trim with standard four-wheel drive powered by a 290 hp 3.6L V6 engine, hooked to a standard 6-speed manual with Overdrive or an optional 5-speed automatic with Overdrive. Also standard is electronic stability control with roll control, traction control, brake assist, and hill hold control. The Rubicon offers equipment that off-road enthusiasts usually pick up from independent suppliers, like heavy-duty axles, front and rear electronic locking differentials, 32-inch BF Goodrich mud tires, a sway bar disconnect system, rock rails, and a heavy-duty transfer case with a 4:1 low-gear ratio. The available Freedom Top three-piece modular hardtop allows panels to be removed above the driver or passenger. Other options include Dual Top Group, half doors, remote start system, front seat-mounted side airbags, and a multimedia infotainment system with 30-gigabyte hard drive and navigation system. The Unlimited is the first four-door Wrangler that carries five people and their luggage. It's the only four-door convertible available that offers rear-drive or four-wheel drive, making it equally at home on the trail or in the wilds of your local shopping mall's parking lot.

COST ANALYSIS: The 2012 model has a substantially improved powertrain and is a better buy than any 2011 leftover. **Best alternatives:** Honda CR-V or Element, Hyundai Tucson, Kia Borrego, Nissan Xterra, Subaru Forester, and Toyota RAV4. But remember, none of these other models can follow the Wrangler off-road. In fact, with its new engine and transmission, the 2012 Jeep Wrangler could outperform them on-road as well. **Options:** The three-piece Freedom Top and the Sunrider Soft Top are nice touches, but beware of water and wind leaks. Keep an eye out for the optional suspension system, which includes larger shock absorbers and heavy-duty springs. An aftermarket anti-theft system is also a plus. Ditch the Firestone tires. **Rebates:** The 2011 models are practically sold out, and they are expected to stay in short supply. Therefore, expect to buy a 2012 with a small discount of no more than 5 percent on the higher-end models, if you are lucky. Four-door models are even harder to find, and they are selling at a premium with little haggling allowed. **Depreciation:** Faster than average, despite their overall popularity. A 2009 two-door X model that sold for $19,995 is worth barely $11,500 today. Even the much-in-demand 2009 four-door, entry-level Unlimited Sport version that originally retailed for $25,695 is now fetching only about $15,000—a $10,695 loss after barely two years. This is why you should hold onto your Wrangler until the depreciation losses have levelled off after five to eight years. **Insurance cost:** Higher than average. **Parts supply/cost:** Higher than average, especially for AC, transmission, and ABS components. **Annual maintenance cost:** Repair costs are average during the warranty period, but if Chrysler goes down for the count, these expenses become your responsibility. **Warranty:** Bumper-to-bumper 3 years/60,000 km; powertrain 5 years/100,000 km; rust perforation 5 years/160,000 km. **Supplementary warranty:** Get an extended powertrain warranty. Also, brake, powertrain, and exhaust system repairs should be carried out by agencies that provide extensive warranties on their work (lifetime). **Highway/city fuel economy:** *3.8L V6 man.: 10.6/13.9 L/100 km, 27/20 mpg. 2010 3.8L V6 auto.: 10.5/14.4 L/100 km, 27/29 mpg.* No data yet on the 2012 3.6L and 5-speed automatic transmission.

OWNER-REPORTED PROBLEMS: Owners report frequent airbag failures, fuel-tank leaks, fuel-pump failures, malfunctioning fuel gauges, chronic engine stalling (accompanied by a lit Electronic Throttle Control warning light) when accelerating or decelerating, front-end torsion bar failures and fluid leaks, and clutch master and slave cylinder leaks and premature replacement. The 6-speed manual transmission sometimes pops out of gear; the automatic transmission slips erratically in and out of Second gear and leaks fluid:

> 2011 Jeep Wrangler Rubicon Unlimited. 6-spd transmission pops out of 2nd and 4th gear when weather is cold. 2nd gear "crunches" when going into gear. It's been in for service on the transmission 3 times now in 3,500 miles [5,630 km]. Problem seems to be getting worse. In cold temperatures, the vehicle is very difficult and dangerous to drive.

The power steering locks up; and there's excessive and premature brake wear, leading to brake failures. Other brake complaints concern the vehicle pulling to the left when braking; the rear brakes suddenly locking up while driving in the rain and approaching a stop sign; and the vehicle going into open throttle position when the brakes are applied. There have also been many instances where drivers mistook the accelerator for the brake because the pedals are so close together. Body welds and seams are susceptible to premature rusting, and there have been frequent complaints about peeling paint and water leaks:

> Soft top leaks on both sides in the front. Seats getting stained and the carpet is starting to smell. Water stains on the doors, steering column, and down the dash.

The worst leaks occur at the bottom of the windshield frame. An easy way to check for this is to examine the underside of the frame to see if there's excessive rust. This has consistently been a problem area for Jeeps, hence all of the ads for after-market windshield frames. Watch for corroded windshield bracket bolts. The good news is that you can replace the windshield frame and all of the seals relatively cheaply. One failure that *can't* be repaired cheaply is a cracked windshield, another common Wrangler owner complaint.

SERVICE BULLETIN-REPORTED PROBLEMS: *2009–10 models:* Free installation of a chime device to warn when the transmission fluid is overheating (Customer Satisfaction Campaign #J31, June, 2010); *2007–10 models:* Manual transmission pops out of gear (March 2, 2010, TSB #21-001-10).

GRAND CHEROKEE ★★

KEY FACTS

CANADIAN PRICE (NEGOTIABLE): *Laredo:* $37,995, *Laredo X:* $42,995, *Limited:* $46,995, *Overland:* $49,995 **U.S. PRICE:** *Laredo:* $30,215, *Laredo X:* $34,215, *Limited:* $36,715, *Overland:* $39,260, *SRT8:* $49,000 **CANADIAN FREIGHT:** $1,400 **U.S. FREIGHT:** $750 **POWERTRAIN (REAR-DRIVE/PART-TIME/ FULL-TIME AWD)**
Engines: 3.6L V6 (290 hp) • 5.7L V8 (360 hp) • 6.4L V8 (470 hp) Transmissions: 5-speed auto. • 6-speed auto. • 8-speed auto.

DIMENSIONS/CAPACITY (BASE)
Passengers: 2/3; Wheelbase: 114.8 in.; H: 69.4/W: 84.8/L: 189.8 in.; Cargo volume: 36.3 cu. ft.; Fuel tank: 80L/ regular; Tow limit: 3,500–7,200 lb. (the higher towing capacity applies to the 4×2 model); Load capacity: 850 lb.; Turning circle: 37.1 ft.; Ground clearance: 11.1 in.; Weight: *Sport:* 3,849 lb., *Rubicon:* 4,165, lb.

RATING: Below Average for two important reasons: Firstly, during the past decade the Grand Cherokee has been beset with chronic automatic transmission, brake system, and electrical system defects in addition to abysmally bad fit and finish. Take, for example, the fact that Jeep placed 27th out of 33 brands in J.D. Power and Associates' ranking of initial quality released in June 2010. Secondly, this year's extensively reworked model is beginning to show some of the same powertrain deficiencies decried in the past. *Lemon-Aid* has learned from 40 years of rating Chrysler cars and trucks that revamped Chrysler models can be more problematic than previous models. **Strong points:** The 290 hp Pentastar V6 boosts power with 80 horses more than the previous 3.8L V6 engine. It features Variable Valve Timing, showing an increase of 33 percent in horsepower and 11 percent in torque over its predecessor, while also supposedly improving fuel economy up to 11 percent. Features on the base Cherokee include active front head restraints, 17-inch alloy wheels, dual-zone AC, passive keyless entry with push-button start, eight-way power driver's seat, 60/40 flat-folding rear seats, a front passenger seat that folds flat, fog lamps, CD/MP3 stereo, Sirius satellite radio, heated mirrors, tilt and telescopic steering column, automatic headlamps, a tire pressure monitor, and hill start assist. **Weak points:** Judging by initial orders, the new Grand Cherokee will likely sell at a premium during its first year on the market, but cooler heads will eventually prevail and the cost will go down by the summer of 2012. Another reason to wait until mid-2012 to buy the new Grand Cherokee: The automatic transmission and electrical system have shown some quality glitches in the first series production. Give Jeep time to work things out...if it can. Things that probably won't get fixed this model year: The V6 engine is a bit harsh at high rpms, there's excessive body roll with hard cornering, and the front seat cushions lack bolstering. **New for 2012:** Not much, except for the expected early 2012 introduction of a high-performance SRT8 version. It will be equipped with the 470 hp 6.4L Hemi V8 that comes with the 2011 Dodge Challenger and powers the SRT versions of the Charger and 300 as well. An 8-speed automatic is expected to arrive later in the year. At launch, though, the SRT8 will carry the existing 5-speed automatic. The Grand Cherokee's major redesign in 2011 produced a restyled, roomier interior and a more-sculpted exterior. It now comes with a larger fuel tank and a base fuel-efficient 3.6L V6 or an optional 5.7L Hemi V8. Both engines are coupled to a 5-speed automatic transmission on the 2011 versions. Newly available is an upgraded 6-speed transmission used with V8-equipped models. A Selec-Terrain system can be preset for auto, sport, sand/mud, snow, and rock settings. An optional Quadra-Lift air suspension raises or lowers the ride height. The UConnect electronic feature on all models offers automatic crash notification, emergency calls, roadside assistance calls, remote door unlock, and stolen vehicle location assistance.

OVERVIEW: 18 years ago, Jeep created the premium SUV segment with the introduction of its upscale Grand Cherokee, then quickly lost sales momentum by falling behind in highway performance and quality control. Jeep sold about 300,000 Grand Cherokees in 1999 and roughly 50,300 in 2009. This year's upgrades seek to recapture the lost ground in a competitive field that Asian automakers, GM, and Ford dominate. In fact, Jeep has repowered its base model and used fuel-saving technology to provide more V6 and V8 power without sacrificing fuel economy.

The 2012 Grand Cherokee is built on a proven rear-drive unibody platform that the Mercedes-Benz ML has used for years; when combined with new front and rear independent suspension systems, the result is enhanced on-road handling and comfort. Also, the stiffer body reduces noise, vibration, and harshness.

The reworked Grand Cherokee is also loaded with safety and security features that include standard electronic stability control, electronic roll mitigation, trailer-sway control, hill-start assist, and hill-descent control; full-length side curtain airbags to protect front and rear outboard passengers; seat-mounted side thorax airbags to enhance collision protection of the driver and front passenger; active head restraints that deploy in the event of a rear collision; an optional park assist system that detects stationary objects; a blind spot/rear cross-path detection system; adaptive cruise control that decreases a vehicle's preset cruise-control speed when closing in on another vehicle or when another vehicle pulls into the same lane (this has been a failure-prone feature in the past); a forward collision warning system that detects when the vehicle may be approaching another vehicle too rapidly; and a remote starting feature.

COST ANALYSIS: Okay. By now you know the 2011 model was substantially improved, so don't waste your money on the more expensive 2012 version; however, don't buy until prices come down early in 2012. This will give the factory more time to get the 2011 redesign "bugs" fixed (see "Owner-Reported Problems"). **Best alternatives:** Honda CR-V or Element, Hyundai Tucson, Subaru Forester, and Toyota RAV4. Remember, none of these other models can follow the Grand Cherokee off-road, but better than that, they won't be following it to the repair bay, either. **Options:** The $1,250 sunroof option will only add more rattles and noise while giving you less headroom. Ditch the Firestone and Bridgestone tires. **Rebates:** The 2012 models are seriously back-ordered, so wait until production picks up and rebates are sweetened during late winter or early spring. Also, it's axiomatic that redesigned models produced during the second half of the model year have fewer factory-related glitches. **Depreciation:** Traditionally, the Grand Cherokee loses its value faster than the Wrangler, but not as rapidly as the Commander, which is essentially a stretched Grand Cherokee with cramped second- and third-row seating. A 2007 Laredo 4×4 Grand Cherokee that sold for $40,285 is now worth about $13,000. In comparison, a 2007 upscale Commander that sold for $51,815 is now worth only $1,500 more ($14,500) than the same year's Grand Cherokee. **Insurance cost:** Higher than average. **Parts supply/cost:** Higher than average, especially for AC, transmission, and ABS components. **Annual maintenance cost:** Repair costs are average during the warranty period, but if Chrysler goes down for the count, these expenses become your responsibility. **Warranty:** Bumper-to-bumper 3 years/60,000 km; powertrain 5 years/100,000 km; rust perforation 5 years/160,000 km. **Supplementary warranty:** Get an extended powertrain warranty. Also, brake, powertrain, and exhaust system repairs should be carried out by agencies that provide extensive warranties on their work (lifetime). **Highway/city fuel economy:** 3.6L: 8.9/13.0 L/100 km, 32/22 mpg. 5.7L: 10.6/15.7 L/100 km, 27/18 mpg (thanks to the Multi-Displacement System (MDS) feature on the V8).

OWNER-REPORTED PROBLEMS: Most complaints centre on the automatic transmission, electrical system (especially vehicle stalling, or not starting), and fit and finish problems.

The 6-speed manual transmission sometimes pops out of gear; the automatic transmission slips erratically in and out of Second gear, suddenly downshifts, and leaks fluid:

> Transmission shifted into 4 wheel drive (4WD) low, suddenly, accompanied by a clunk and change in vehicle speed from downshifting. Lights came on in the dash indicating loss of traction control and 4WD service needed. This event continued to happen sporadically while driving until we made it back to the dealership. Since downshifting into 4WD occurred while driving at normal roadway operating speeds (approximately 20–40 mph) it certainly felt like a safety issue, compounded by the fact that traction

control was lost as a result. Once back at the dealership, the service department found that the transfer case had an internal failure. The vehicle was in the shop for about 3 weeks and while the transfer case was replaced under warranty. Due to this negative experience with the vehicle we no longer felt safe driving it, and ended up trading it in for another vehicle just a few weeks after getting it back from the shop.

•

There is a strong smell of transmission fluid and a large pool of fluid discharged under the vehicle. The car was towed and returned to the dealership. The dealer's technician reported, "technician performed visual inspections and clean off of fluid, found the transmission cooler lines at the radiator had disconnected due to not be improper connection."

Yes, there are reports of sudden, unintended acceleration, too:

The contact owns a 2011 Jeep Grand Cherokee 4×4. While stopped at the light, the Check Engine light illuminated and the vehicle suddenly accelerated while the brake was depressed. There was an abnormal increase in RPMs to 3,000. The contact placed the gear in park, turned the vehicle off and the engine returned to normal for a moment before continuing to accelerate abnormally. The vehicle was taken to the dealer who performed a diagnostic and located the failure at the throttle body. The dealer replaced the accelerator pedal and the throttle body but to no avail as the failure continued to recur. The manufacturer was contacted and they advised the contact to take the vehicle back to the dealer. The vehicle was not repaired. The failure mileage was 4,000 [6,440 km] and the current mileage was 4,300 miles [6,920 km].

•

On March 24th, 2011 it was beginning to snow, I was stopped at the corner stop sign waiting to make a right turn and the car surged forward into the intersection, skidding onto the sidewalk, just missing a pedestrian and a utility pole. If it was my daughter driving, who is a new driver, I don't think she would have been so lucky as to miss the pedestrian or the pole. This time I called the dealer and told them I almost died in the car, due to the same problem, sudden acceleration, Engine and Throttle light on. They actually had the nerve to tell me to drive the car to the dealer for service.... There were 3 electrical failures leading up to the complete electrical and engine system shutting down while driving.

Frequent airbag failures, fuel-tank leaks, fuel-pump failures, malfunctioning fuel gauges, front end torsion bar failures and fluid leaks, and clutch failures. The power steering locks up, and there's excessive and premature brake wear, leading to brake failures. Other brake complaints concern the vehicle pulling to the left when braking, the rear brakes suddenly locking up while driving in the rain and approaching a stop sign, and the vehicle going into open throttle position when the brakes are applied. There have also been many instances where drivers mistook the accelerator for the brake because the pedals are so close together. The tire pressure monitoring system is malfunction-prone. Body welds and seams are susceptible to premature rusting; there have been frequent complaints about peeling paint and water leaks. Doors fail to latch due to faulty hinges; tailgate back glass exploded when the tailgate was opened, and Chrysler denied the warranty claim.

SERVICE BULLETIN-REPORTED PROBLEMS: *2011 Grand Cherokees:* Engine power sag, hesitation may be fixed by changing the power control module. On the other hand, a shudder felt when accelerating, decelerating, or when coasting may only require the reflashing or replacement of the drivetrain control module. Power liftgate won't open or close. Rear shock absorber buzz, squeak, or rattle may signal the need to replace both rear upper shock mounts. Excessive exhaust noise can be corrected by replacing the exhaust pipe/catalytic converter assembly. Steering fluid leak, noise:

STEERING—LOW SPEED MOAN/FLUID LEAK AT STEERING RACK

BULLETIN NO.: 19-006-10   DATE: DECEMBER 16, 2010

MOAN LIKE SOUND DURING PARKING LOT MANEUVERS AND/OR FLUID WEEPING AT RACK AND PINION

2011 Grand Cherokee

OVERVIEW: This bulletin involves test driving the vehicle and/or inspecting the rack and pinion and if necessary replace.

SYMPTOM/CONDITION: The customer may experience a moan like sound during parking lot maneuvers and/or fluid weeping at the rack and pinion.

BODY—WATER LEAKS FROM OVERHEAD CONSOLE AREA

BULLETIN NO.: 23-031-10   DATE: DECEMBER 15, 2010

WATER DRIPPING OUT OF THE OVERHEAD CONSOLE SUNGLASS HOLDER BIN

2011 Grand Cherokee

OVERVIEW: This bulletin involves inspecting the overhead console sunglass holder bin and if necessary replacing the windshield.

SYMPTOM/CONDITION: Water dripping out of the overhead console sunglass holder bin.

Ford

Horrible, horrible, horrible!!!

Automatic transmission? Horrible horrible horrible!!! I have taken my 2011 Ford Fiesta in at least 6 times to fix the transmission, which is completely shot, and every time I get it back they state that "they all do that" or "it's perfectly fine." That is complete rubbish! On the freeway my car will shift up and down randomly to the point that it sounds like the engine will explode. The car shifts really really hard and

I smell burning clutch every time I drive the car. The most the dealership has done is reflashed the transmission computer (which would not accept the flash), and to make matters worse the service manager even told me to get lost and take it somewhere else because he was done wasting his time on the car.

2011 FIESTA OWNER
SAFERCAR.GOV COMPLAINTS
HTTP://WWW-ODI.NHTSA.DOT.GOV/COMPLAINTS/RESULTS.CFM

The Emperor's New Clothes

In rating Ford's new products this year, I am reminded of the Hans Christian Andersen tale "The Emperor's New Clothes." You know how it goes. Two weavers promise an emperor a new suit of clothes invisible to those who are stupid, incompetent, or unfit for their positions. When the Emperor parades before his subjects in his new clothes, a child cries out, "But he isn't wearing anything at all!"

We are seeing a renaissance of failure-prone and erratically performing transmissions (manuals on the Mustang, automatics on the Explorer, Fiesta, and Fusion).

Quality and Performance

Ford is like the Emperor's tailors: Some of its latest model offerings fall far short of the company's carefully orchestrated hype. Highway performance is much less than promised, head restraints are poorly designed, interior instruments and controls are far from user-friendly, high-tech communication and navigation gizmos are needlessly complicated, and quality control is woefully inadequate (see the reports on "lag and lurch" self-destructing manual transmissions in the Mustang section and failure-prone automatics in the Fusion section). Yet, Ford's products represent the best of what was formerly called the Detroit Big Three—shows how far the benchmark has been lowered.

After former USA CEO Jac Nasser's firing in 2001, it took Ford five years to begin its slow road to better quality control and financial stability, through selling many of the businesses and auto companies Nasser had purchased earlier. Ironically, his ineptitude saved Ford from bankruptcy because it forced Ford to trim costs and borrow money when loan rates were low, several years before GM and Chrysler went bankrupt.

In the past decade, powertrain defects, faulty suspensions and steering components, and premature brake wear and brake failures were the primary concerns of Ford owners. The company's engine and automatic transmission deficiencies affected most of its products and these deficiencies have existed since the early '80s, judging by *Lemon-Aid* reader reports, NHTSA complaints, confidential Ford internal documents, and technical service bulletins. The quality of body components has traditionally remained far below Japanese and South Korean standards.

Ford's Fiesta fled North America after its short 1978–1980 model run. It was an unreliable car then and may be just as problem-prone with the return of the 2012 model.

Ford's 2012 Explorer "doesn't compete with the best in this class," says *Consumer Reports*.

In fact, two 2012 models, the Fiesta and Explorer, have already proven to be major disappointments say owners, *Motor Trend*, *Consumer Reports*, and Ford's own confidential service bulletins.

To be fair, although most of Ford's models can't match their Asian competition in terms of performance and reliability, they are better built than what else is coming out of Detroit/Turin. Nevertheless, the Fiesta should not have these defects. When Ford discovered similar problems with its European-derived 2000 Focus, the automaker took five years to turn that lemon into a Recommended car. With today's unforgiving auto market, Ford doesn't have five years. While it's "debugging" the Fiesta, Ford must extend the car's base warranty to cover powertrain defects for at least seven years. Additionally, the carmaker should be generous in giving out free "goodwill" repairs to correct other factory-related problems.

Ford's much ballyhooed, redesigned 2011 Explorer handles less like a truck and provides better fuel economy now that Ford has replaced its body-on-frame platform with a car-like unibody chassis. Unfortunately, the reworked Explorer also brings with it serious performance and quality control deficiencies decried by both *Consumer Reports* and *Motor Trend*. Surprisingly, *Consumer Reports* gave the Explorer an easier time than *Motor Trend* did in this May 2011 article:

> We didn't like driving the Explorer very much.... Massive, freaky, comical torque steer (the vehicle pulls to one side when accelerating). The big Ford also rode worse than much of the competition.... We also had issues with the seating position...the chassis needs some refinement.... Car feels wobbly at speed—not confidence inspiring.... The My Ford Touch system shut down for about 60 seconds, taking away all climate, stereo, phone, and navigation controls.

Consumer Reports' June 2011 edition confirms many of *MT*'s findings: *CR* points out that the 6-speed automatic transmission shifts slowly at times, the engine is noisy, handling is mediocre with excessive body roll when cornering, and the slow steering transmits little road feedback. Interior ergonomics and comfort apparently wasn't Ford's "Job 1" with the reworked Explorer, either: The driving position is described as "flawed" with limited foot room, a poorly placed footrest, and pedals that are mounted too close together. Front seat cushions felt narrow and too short; rear cushions too hard, too low, or too short. *CR* rated fit and finish as average, and the MyFord Touch system was judged to be overly complicated with the Sync-voice-command system often misunderstanding simple commands.

The frustration of working with Ford's electronic systems was said to be the main reason why the company tumbled from a fifth-place ranking to 23rd in J.D. Power's 2011 Initial Quality Index. Lincoln dropped from eighth place in the 2010 survey to 17th this year. *Consumer Reports* magazine has declined to recommend several new Ford SUVs over concerns that the system is too confusing and doesn't work well.

David Sargent, vice president of global vehicle research at J.D. Power confirms *CR*'s findings. He believes much of Ford's owner dissatisfaction has to do with the latest version of its Sync entertainment and phone system, which is incorporated into the new MyFord Touch interface.

"People were finding several problems with the system in that it would crash, freeze, black out," said Sargent. "Beyond that, people complained that it was more complex to use than they would like."

The J.D. Power study said the most problematic areas in all new vehicles were the engine and transmission and the audio, entertainment, and navigation components. There were also more frequent customer-reported problems of vehicles shaking or hesitating while shifting gears or accelerating, and vehicle electronic systems malfunctioning or not working properly. Among all auto companies studied, the J.D. Power report found that only a quarter of redesigned models performed better than the 2010 models they replaced.

Lexus brand vehicles scored best with an average of 73 problems per 100 vehicles. Honda, Acura, Mercedes-Benz, and Mazda rounded out the top five. The bottom five were Dodge, Suzuki, Mitsubishi, Volkswagen, and Mini.

Ford is shifting its product mix to smaller vehicles that use more-reliable Japanese components and are assembled more cheaply in Mexico or offshore. Like most major automakers, Ford is copying European designs, importing some models directly from Europe, then transferring their production to North America. The 2012 Focus, for example, is modelled after the highly rated European variant and will include a plug-in electric version. The small 2012 Fiesta four-door sedan/hatchback that was first imported from Europe during the 2010 model year is now settling in the States. By selling and building worldwide models that are virtually identical, Ford can keep production costs down and quickly get to market more agile, fuel-efficient, and highway-proven vehicles that follow the marketplace's shifting trends.

Better Crashworthiness, Inflatable Seat Belts

Ford has been a leader this year in developing more crashworthy cars and trucks and in offering innovative inflatable rear seat belts. In fact we can balance out some of our negative 2012 Explorer comments by stressing that the 2011 Explorer was the first vehicle to offer the industry-first rear inflatable seat belts, and is a Top Safety Pick from the Insurance Institute for Highway Safety (IIHS). In total, Ford has 12 vehicles named as 2011 Top Safety Picks.

More "Green" Machines

Get used to the term EcoBoost. It is used by Ford to describe its new family of turbocharged and direct-injected 4-cylinder and 6-cylinder gasoline engines that deliver power and torque consistent with larger displacement powerplants. Engines using the EcoBoost design are touted to be to be 20 percent more fuel-efficient than naturally aspirated engines. Ford says the EcoBoost's power output and fuel efficiency rival hybrid and diesel engine technology and the company intends on using it extensively in future vehicle applications. The F-150 trucks' 3.5L EcoBoost engine, utilizing turbo and direct injection, is going to give other competitors a run for their money. It easily out performs the Chevrolet and Dodge 1500.

Ford's compact gasoline-powered C-Max minivan won't be coming to Canada. Ford is worried the minivan will cannibalize sales of its other three-row, seven-passenger vehicles like the Explorer, Flex, and Lincoln MKT. Instead, Ford will import two "green" minivans: the two-row C-Max Hybrid and the Energi plug-in hybrid. Ford is obviously trying to pirate sales from the Toyota Prius Hybrid and Nissan's Leaf electric vehicle.

Ford's Turnaround

How did it happen that a kid from Boeing could call the shots and make Ford turn itself around in the short five-year period from 2006 to 2010? And, without going bankrupt or getting much of a government handout?

Ford's "non-auto" CEO, Alan Mulally, simply went back to the basics of quality car-building, seeking the biggest bang for the corporate buck while treating suppliers and customers with respect. Something the automaker's former CEO, Jac Nasser, never could get right.

Since Mulally came on board, the Escape SUV, Focus, Fusion, and F-Series pickups have picked up steam in new-vehicle sales and have won *Consumer Reports*, J.D. Power, and *Lemon-Aid* praises for their improved quality control. In fact, it is amazing to see how the Focus, once Ford's poster child for bad design and lousy quality, only had two owner safety-related complaints with the NHTSA this year, while most car companies post 50 or more (Fiesta's half-year total was 29).

Ford has come the farthest of the Detroit Three in returning to its core business with very little government funding. Many of its models have become more competitive from performance and reliability standpoints. In fact, most of its vehicles have scored Average or higher in *Consumer Reports*' reliability surveys. For example, Ford made considerable improvements to its F-Series pickups, the Ford Flex crossover (which looks ready to challenge the imports), and the freshened Fusion. As far as hybrids go, the Fusion looks good, but the Escape Hybrid has proven itself since 2004 to be as good as or better than the Toyota Prius Hybrid.

The Escape Hybrid is reasonably priced, fuel-frugal, and fairly reliable.

FIESTA ★★

RATING: Below Average. Powertrain problems are maybe just a first-year glitch, but Ford's history says otherwise. **Strong points:** The car accelerates well with the manual gearbox and has good steering, handling, and fuel economy. There is also just adequate space in the front of this five-seater for the driver and passenger (Honda's Fit provides more room for passengers and cargo). A manual 5-speed transmission is standard, and a 6-speed automated manual is optional. Little noise intrudes into the well-appointed cabin. Most gauges and instruments are easy to see and access. Available safety features include ABS, traction control, an anti-skid system, side curtain airbags, front side airbags, and a driver knee airbag. A tilt and telescopic steering wheel, height-adjustable driver seat, and capless fuel filler also

2011 Fiestas have had serious automatic transmission failures. Pass up the 2012 until we see if Ford can build a better-performing and more reliable powertrain.

KEY FACTS

CANADIAN PRICE (NEGOTIABLE): *Sedan S:* $14,449, *Sedan SE:* $17,699, Hatchback *SE:* $18,349, *Sedan SEL:* $19,749 **U.S. PRICE:** *Sedan S:* $13,200, *Hatchback:* $15,500 **CANADIAN FREIGHT:** $1,450 **U.S. FREIGHT:** $795
POWERTRAIN (FRONT-DRIVE)
Engines: 1.6L DOHC 4 (120 hp); Transmissions: 5-speed man. • 6-speed manumatic.
DIMENSIONS/CAPACITY
Passengers: 2/3; Wheelbase: 98 in.; H: 58 /L: 173.6/W: 66.8 in.; Legroom F/R: 42.2/31.2 in.; Cargo volume: 12.8 cu. ft.; Fuel tank: 45L/regular; Tow limit: Not recommended; Turning circle: 34.4 ft.; Ground clearance: 6.7 in.; Weight: 2,578 lb.

come with the car. Despite its small size, the 2011 Ford Fiesta earned four stars for overall crashworthiness from NHTSA. IIHS gave it top marks in frontal offset, side, and rear impact occupant protection, as well as protection from excessive roof intrusion into the cabin. A relatively high ground clearance reduces "belly drag" in the snow (an inch higher than the Toyota Yaris and VW Jetta); the cabin is welcoming; and luxury features are available. **Weak points:** Owners report that the automatic transmission cuts gas mileage by almost 15 percent. Rear passenger space is cramped; even Honda's Fit has more storage space than the Fiesta five-door hatchback. Drivers find the head restraints force a chin-to-chest driving position that's so uncomfortable they're removing the head restraints altogether. Seats could use a bit more lumbar and thigh bolstering. Armrest is too far forward on the Fiesta door. Rear seatbacks may not lock into position, allowing any cargo to fly forward, as a deadly projectile, in a sudden stop. Limited cargo and rear seat space. **New for 2012:** Nothing significant.

OVERVIEW: Available as a five-door hatchback or sedan, this 120 hp 1.6L 4-cylinder minicar is a front-drive subcompact manufactured and marketed throughout the world since 1976. Its return to Canada and the U.S. in the fall of 2010 makes it the first Fiesta model to be sold in North America since 1980. Essentially, Ford plans to import the little car from Europe until it can transfer production to Canada and the United States. Without a doubt, the Fiesta has what it takes to be a fine small car, in theory. The only caveat is that Ford has never imported a European-derived vehicle that went on to become a success in North America. Poor quality, performance, and servicing have afflicted most of these imports and sent them packing back to Europe. Will the Fiesta repeat history? Don't be the first to find out.

COST ANALYSIS: The 2011 and 2012 Fiesta models aren't very different from each other; go for the 2012 since prices aren't expected to increase by much and the extra year will give Ford time to fix the car's first-year factory-related bugs, like those affecting the automatic transmission:

> This vehicle, bought new in September, 2010, had loud sounds coming from the engine area. Ford has put 2 new transmissions in it. The 3rd repair attempt was diagnosed as a problem that "engineering has to come up with a solution". Ford, on two of the 3 repair attempts, sent out a field engineer to inspect the vehicle. The first engineer (on the 2nd repair attempt) said to put another new transmission in the vehicle, (the 2nd new transmission to be put on the vehicle). This still did not solve the problem. The problem, according to the service manager (on the 3rd repair attempt—2 at the dealer, and this 1st attempt at another dealer, third overall) said "It's the clutch. We took other cars out, and with the laptop we were able to duplicate it on every one of them." The duplication he was speaking of involves the transmission and its clutch system, just introduced this model year of 2011 by Ford. It is the 6 speed automatic transmission, with a dual clutch. The situation is that when you come to a sudden stop, the transmission does not downshift to a lower gear fast enough. When you try to accelerate, after a sudden stop, the vehicle seems stuck in a higher gear. The car momentarily stalls before taking off. This is very dangerous when trying to cross lanes of a highway at busy times. We do not feel safe in it. We were told, in an email, by a Ford customer service manager, "As I explained to you on the phone the Ford engineers are aware and are researching a solution for your vehicle's concern. Your vehicle is safe to drive so you may continue to enjoy it while waiting to be contacted by [name withheld] service manager at the dealer and myself".

Another sudden, unintended acceleration experience may be related to the cruise control feature:

> While driving with the cruise control set at 40 mph [64 km/h], the vehicle suddenly accelerated up to 60 mph [97 km/h] and the rpms increased to over 500 rpms. The contact shut the cruise control off and the speed resumed its normal state. The vehicle was taken to an authorized dealer where the computer was reprogrammed. The failure occurred again and the vehicle was taken back to the dealer. The manufacturer had not been notified. The failure mileage was 8,000 miles [12,870 km].

And if the cruise control is okay, watch out for the ventilation duct falling:

> Ventilation duct falls onto driver's right foot during vehicle operation, inhibiting the driver's ability to control the accelerator.

Interestingly, Fiesta models take a huge price jump with the bundled optional AC included. **Best alternatives:** Honda Civic (2011) or Fit, Hyundai Accent or Elantra, Kia Rio, Mazda2 or Mazda3, and Nissan Versa. The Ford Focus is the better buy, if you must buy a Ford. Its fuel economy is similar, and you get a more comfortable ride with more room. **Options:** Be wary of original-equipment Firestone or Bridgestone tires. **Rebates:** $500 to $1,000 in early 2012; probably more once word gets out about the poor quality. **Depreciation:** Below average. **Insurance cost:** Below average. **Parts supply/cost:** Average. **Annual maintenance cost:** Estimated to be average. **Warranty:** Bumper-to-bumper 3 years/60,000 km; powertrain 5 years/100,000 km; rust perforation 5 years/unlimited km. **Supplementary warranty:** A good idea for the powertrain, judging by owner complaints and internal service bulletins covering the first-year 2011 models. **Highway/city fuel economy:** *Man.:* 5.3/7.1 L/100 km, 53/40 mpg. *SFE auto:* 4.9/6.8 L/100 km, 58/42 mpg. *Auto.:* 5.1/6.9 L/100 km, 55/41 mpg.

OWNER-REPORTED PROBLEMS: Engine stalling and surging along with poor transmission performance partly due to a defective transmission control module. Electrical shorts and a few fit and finish deficiencies.

One car had so many electrical problems, it was bought back by Ford; another Fiesta caught fire:

> Attorney writes on behalf of clients in regards to vehicle catching fire while driving: The driver of the vehicle stated he was driving with the cruise control activated, when suddenly the vehicle began to lose power and the heater stopped working. The driver stopped the vehicle, after seeing a glare at the driver's side window. He turned the vehicle off and removed the key. The fire started in the front of the vehicle under the dashboard. According to the fire report, the fire was due to an electrical problem.

Sudden power steering failure. Driver's seat belt latch may not "catch." A rust-prone muffler is a common issue. One owner says passing other cars is a death-defying experience and the fuel economy rating and odometer readings are not believable:

> While passing a car, vehicle's engine revved up to high and car was not responding. While passing a car, I almost had a head-on collision. Odometer has a false reading while driving. It should have been a 500 mile [800 km] round trip. The car registered 1,200 miles [1,930 km]. This is a ploy to make the warranty expire faster. Also, I am not getting the mileage the Ford people promise.

SERVICE BULLETIN-REPORTED PROBLEMS: *2011 Ford Fiesta:* Engine stalling and surging along with poor transmission performance may be due to a malfunctioning transmission control module. Automatic transmission fluid leak from the clutch housing will require a major repair covered by the base warranty (TSB #11-6-8). Poor or no engine start, or transmission engagement:

AUTOMATIC TRANSMISSION-ENGINE START, TRANSMISSION ENGAGEMENT, AND/OR MIL ON WITH DTCs—BUILT ON OR BEFORE 9/11/2010

BULLETIN NO.: 11-5-24   DATE: MAY 26, 2011

ISSUE: Some 2011 Fiesta vehicles equipped with an automatic transmission and built on or before 9/11/2010 may exhibit transmission engagement concerns in Drive or Reverse when shifting from Park to Drive or Reverse, no engagement, delayed engagement, intermittent engagement, noise during engagement, and/or a malfunction indicator lamp (MIL) with powertrain diagnostic trouble codes (DTCs). One or more of the following DTCs may typically be set: P0116, P06B8, P0805, P0809, P087A, P087E, P0884, P2831, P283A, P2832, P2835, P2836 and/or P2837. Some vehicles may exhibit DTC P0700 without any accompanying fault codes. Some vehicles may exhibit an engine no crank or intermittent start with DTC P0850. Some vehicles may exhibit concerns with or without DTCs.

Engine block heater coolant leakage and spillover into the spark plug well:

COOLING SYSTEM—COOLANT LEAK INTO SPARK PLUG WELLS

BULLETIN NO.: 10-19-5   DATE: NOVEMBER 10, 2010

COOLANT LEAK IN SPARK PLUG WELL—ENGINE MISFIRE

2011 Fiesta

ISSUE: Some 2011 Fiesta vehicles may experience a coolant leak from the cup plug in the spark plug well area. The vehicle may exhibit coolant leak from the valve cover breather orifice located on the back center of the valve cover behind spark plug boot number 4 with or without symptoms and may also experience an engine misfire with diagnostic trouble codes (DTCs) stored in PCM memory due to the coolant leak in the spark plug well area.

A/T CONTROLS—HARD START/VARIOUS A/T ENGAGEMENT ISSUES

BULLETIN NO.: 10-19-6   DATE: NOVEMBER 10, 2010

ENGINE START CONCERNS, AUTO TRANS ENGAGEMENT CONCERNS LEAVING PARK AND/OR CHECK ENGINE LIGHT WITH DTC P06B8, P0884

2011 Fiesta

ISSUE: Some 2011 Fiesta vehicles may exhibit a hard start, no start, intermittent start, noise from bell housing during start and/or various automatic transmission engagement concerns such as no engagement or intermittent no engagement in Drive or Reverse when shifting from Park to Drive or Reverse, grinding noise during engagement and/or a check engine light with transmission control module (TCM) diagnostic trouble code (DTC) P06B8 or P0884.

FOCUS   ★★★★

RATING: Above Average. **Strong points:** Stylish, excellent handling and road-holding; a commanding view of the highway; plenty of interior space for occupants and cargo; well-appointed interior offers plenty of high-tech options; a user-friendly control layout; improved quality control; and impressive fuel economy. Very reliable during the last five years, which is all the more surprising because

KEY FACTS

CANADIAN PRICE (NEGOTIABLE): *Sedan S:* $14,499, *Sedan SE:* $17,699, *SES:* $20,399 **U.S. PRICE:** *Sedan S: $16,500, Sedan SE: $17,400, Five-door: $18,200, SEL: $20,300, Titanium: $23,200*
CANADIAN FREIGHT: $1,450 **U.S. FREIGHT:** $795
POWERTRAIN (FRONT-DRIVE)
Engine: 2.0L DOHC 4 (160 hp); Transmissions: 5-speed man. • 6-speed auto.
DIMENSIONS/CAPACITY
Passengers: 2/3; Wheelbase: 104.3 in.; H: 57.8/L: 178.5/W: 71.8 in.; Headroom N/A; Legroom F/R: 43.7/33.2 in.; Cargo volume: 13.2 cu. ft.; Fuel tank: 47L/ regular; Tow limit: Not recommended; Turning circle: 36 ft.; Weight: 29,07 lb.

the 2000–04 models were quintessential lemons. Standard ABS, stability and traction control, and side-curtain airbags. NHTSA gave the two-door 2010 Focus five stars for frontal crashworthiness, three stars for side protection, and four stars for rollover resistance. The four-door model was rated a bit differently: It got four stars for frontal crash-worthiness, five stars for side protection, and three stars for rollover resistance. IIHS gave its top rating ("Good") for frontal offset and side crash protection. **Weak points:** Mediocre acceleration, excessive engine and road noise, infotainment controls can be finicky, backseat is a little short on legroom and IIHS gave head-restraint/rear crash protection only an "Average" rating. Head restraints also receive criticism for being angled downward too sharply, forcing the head to bend forward. **New for 2012:** Redesigned, with an accent on a restyled interior and exterior, along with more torsional rigidity to hush creaks and rattles and keep rain and noise out of the cabin. Another plus is the Focus's standard torque vectoring control—a first for a car in this class. This feature increases vehicle stability by adding brake force to wheels on one side during turns, which helps keep the vehicle under control. The 2012 also gets two new electronic features called MyKey and MyFord. MyFord integrates entertainment, navigation and communication into a touchscreen console, while MyKey is a safety feature that restricts vehicle speed and stereo volume when someone else takes the car out on Friday night (guess who?) and forgets your admonishments.

The Focus Electric

A new electric-powered Focus will arrive in late 2011. Ford says it will beat the Chevrolet Volt and NissanLeaf fuel-economy numbers. Charge time on the Focus Electric is predicted to be three to four hours using a 240-volt system—half the time needed by the Leaf, thanks to an on-board charger that is twice as powerful as the Nissan's. A charge on regular 120-volt household current, though, will take almost 20 hours, or about the same as a Leaf. Ford will include a 120-volt cord with the Focus. A Ford-made 240-volt home charger will be sold through Best Buy for

Unlike other electric cars, the Focus Electric won't look much different than the gasoline-powered Focus models.

approximately $1500 U.S., including installation. The Electric employs a 123 hp electric motor that has less horsepower but more torque than the 155 hp, 2.0L 4-cylinder engine in the conventional 2012 Focus. A single-speed transmission will get you to a top speed of 135 km/h (84 mph). Aside from the quieter operation, lack of shifting, and additional weight (Ford quotes a curb weight of 3,691 pounds, or about 700 pounds heavier than a gas-powered five-door). Obviously, that much weight will degrade both ride and handling, but what the heck, the energy is *free* (not).

OVERVIEW: This year's Focus has been completely redesigned without much of a price increase. It provides better fuel economy, gives a more supple ride, and stands tall up against the Chevrolet Cruze, Honda Fit, Hyundai Elantra, and Mazda3. The sedan comes with basics like an audio system with an AM/FM radio, single-disc CD player and MP3 capability, an auxiliary input jack, and a tilt and telescopic steering wheel. Hatchbacks include a few more standard features like MyKey. All models use a 2.0L 4-cylinder engine, torque vectoring control, and airbags with adaptive venting technology that reduce pressure for smaller occupants.

COST ANALYSIS: The reworked 2012 Focus, available as a sedan or hatchback, is much more refined than the previous year's model, which makes it well worth a few extra loonies. **Best alternatives:** Take a good look at the Honda Fit—one of the roomiest and most practical hatchbacks around. The Fit is almost $3,000 cheaper than the Focus hatch and $1,200 cheaper than the Focus sedan. Don't overlook the Chevrolet Cruze Hyundai Elantra, and Mazda3 trio, either. They also will appeal to budget-minded shoppers who value performance, cabin space to comfortably seat five, high fuel economy, and a reasonable sales price. **Options:** Ditch the original-equipment Firestones. **Rebates:** $1,500 to $2,500. **Depreciation:** Average. **Insurance cost:** Average. **Parts supply/cost:** Average. **Annual maintenance cost:** Average. **Warranty:** Bumper-to-bumper 3 years/60,000 km; powertrain 5 years/100,000 km; rust perforation 5 years/unlimited km. **Supplementary warranty:** A good idea for the powertrain. **Highway/**

city fuel economy: *Man.:* 5.6/8.0 L/100 km, 50/35 mpg. *Auto.:* 5.8/8.2 L/100 km, 49/34 mpg.

OWNER-REPORTED PROBLEMS: Not many problems reported. Compared with the Fiesta's 29 safety-related complaints for 2011, Focus owners posted only two. Previous postings related a few incidents of engine stalling and surging, premature brake caliper and rotor replacements, electrical shorts, and minor fit and finish deficiencies.

SERVICE BULLETIN-REPORTED PROBLEMS: *2011:* Ford says excessive road wander, steering drift, or uneven rear tire wear may require the installation of a new right rear lower control arm (January 25, 2011, TSB #11-1-1). *2008–11:* An underbody squeak or creaking noise may be silenced by replacing the parking brake cables and routing eyelets (December 16, 2011, TSB #10-24-06). Paint damage? Here is Ford's "secret warranty" that will pay for a new paint job. Shh!

LOWER BODY PAINT ABRASION/DAMAGE

BULLETIN NO.: 10-15-6   **DATE: AUGUST 16, 2010**

PAINT DEGRADATION/ROAD ABRASION

2008–11 Focus

ISSUE: Some 2008–11 Focus vehicles may experience paint damage or road abrasion on the rocker panel and on the side of the vehicle located slightly ahead of the rear tires on both 2 door and 4 door models. Rocker Panel, 1/4 panel, dog leg and/or rear door, dependent on model. This has been reported in geographical areas that commonly experience snow and ice conditions and use various forms of traction enhancers.

ACTION: Follow the Service Procedure steps to correct the condition.

NOTE: Per the warranty and policy manual paint damage caused by conditions such as chips, scratches, dents, dings, road salt, stone chips or other acts of nature are not covered under the new vehicle limited warranty. However, paint abrasion at the dog leg area due to the above circumstances is a unique condition on the focus and, as a result, repairs are eligible for basic warranty coverage.

FUSION, MKZ   ★★/★★★

RATING: *Fusion:* Below Average. *MKZ:* Average. **Strong points:** Stylish, but no "Car of the Year." Overall reliability (except for the automatic transmission) is impressive with the Lincoln MKZ. Good acceleration and fair handling; steering is tight, precise, and vibration-free; and Mazda's 4-cylinder and V6 engines are competent, thrifty, and dependable. Added rigidity and additional chassis tweaking have resulted in a car that will seat five passengers (four in comfort) and corner reasonably well. The Fusion/MKZ Hybrid uses an Atkinson-cycle version of the 2.5L engine, and its fuel economy estimates are better than most of the competition. It can run on one or both of its power sources (to balance acceleration and fuel economy) and requires no plug-in charging. NHTSA gives the Fusion/MKZ and the Fusion/MKZ Hybrid five stars for front and side

The Ford Fusion.

crashworthiness and four stars for rollover resistance; the AWD model earned five stars for rollover resistance. **Weak points:** A noisy 4-cylinder engine; dangerously flawed transmission performance during the past several years; unreliable brake performance; and cramped rear seating. Vehicle wanders all over the road, and head restraints are pure torture. Poor visibility through the rear windshield. Super-fast depreciation: A 2007 Fusion SE V6 that sold for $26,899 is now worth only $9,000. A base 2007 Lincoln MKZ that first sold for $37,499? Its resale value is about $12,500. **New for 2012:** The 2012 Fusion and Lincoln MKZ are mostly carryovers of the 2011 models. Prices for the 2012 models are unreasonably high.

OVERVIEW: These practically identical mid-sized sedans are set on a lengthened Mazda6 platform and offer four engines: two 4-cylinders, one of which is a hybrid, and two V6s. The smaller engines can be coupled to either a 6-speed manual or a 6-speed automatic transmission; there's no choice with the V6, which comes with a 6-speed automatic. The 4-cylinder comes solely in front-drive; the 3.0L is available in front-drive or all-wheel drive, while the 3.5L is uniquely AWD. The hybrid variant is a spinoff of the Mazda6 and the Ford Escape Hybrid—two vehicles that have been recommended for years by *Lemon-Aid* for both their quality and performance.

KEY FACTS

CANADIAN PRICE (NEGOTIABLE): *Fusion S:* $21,549, *SE:* $24,749, *SEL:* $27,749, *SEL V6:* $30,749, *SEL V6 AWD:* $32,749, *Sport AWD:* $36,849, *Hybrid:* $35,749, *MKZ Front-drive:* $40,050, *AWD:* $42,550, *Hybrid:* $43,850, **U.S. PRICE:** *Fusion S:* $19,850, *Hybrid:* $28,600, *MKZ Front-drive:* $34,645, *Hybrid:* $34,645 **CANADIAN FREIGHT:** $1,400 **U.S. FREIGHT:** $850
POWERTRAIN (FRONT-DRIVE)
Engines: 2.5L 4-cyl. (175 hp) • 2.5L 4-cyl. hybrid (191 hp) • 3.0L V6 (240 hp) • 3.5L V6 (263 hp); Transmissions: 6-speed man. • 6-speed auto. • CVT
DIMENSIONS/CAPACITY (FUSION)
Passengers: 2/3; Wheelbase: 107 in.; H: 56.9/L: 190.6/W: 72.0 in.; Headroom F/R: 2.5/2.5 in., Legroom F/R: 40.5/28.0 in.; Cargo volume: 16 cu. ft.; Fuel tank: 45L/regular; Tow limit: No towing; Load capacity: 850 lb.; Turning circle: 39 ft.; Ground clearance: 5.0 in.; Weight: 3,285 lb.

So why are these cars so bad if they come from such good stock? The answer is that Ford hasn't had much time to fully assess and correct factory-related defects that generally show up during the second and third year of ownership. For example, NHTSA has only recorded a couple of dozen safety-related complaints on the 2011 Fusion—yet the 2010 model has generated almost 200 complaints, or almost four times the benchmark of 50 complaints per model year used by *Lemon-Aid*. Only four complaints have been posted relative to the 2010 Lincoln.

Why does *Consumer Reports* rate the Fusion and MKZ as Recommended while *Lemon-Aid* rates them as Below Average and Average? Mostly because we count the many transmission and brake complaints reported by owners. *Lemon-Aid* gets tipped off early to the presence of safety- and performance-related defects by studying thousands of consumer complaints logged by NHTSA and then comparing these complaints to factory-generated confidential service bulletins sent weekly to auto dealerships. *Consumer Reports* drives the vehicle and publishes its member comments. No service bulletins or NHTSA-logged complaints are studied, nor are non-members polled.

COST ANALYSIS: Fusion models have taken an average $2,500 price jump over the past year, and the Hybrid model almost twice that. Obviously, Ford is taking advantage of the Japanese hybrid shortage caused by that country's March earthquake/tsunami. Since 2011 and 2012 models are essentially identical, your best buy would normally be a 15-percent-discounted 2011 version bought early in the new year. For example, a 2011 Lincoln sells for $34,878 after a $5,000 manufacturer's rebate is deducted. If you are looking for a Fusion Hybrid, or a Lincoln, consider shopping in the States, where you can buy these cars for much less. **Best alternatives:** Honda Accord, Hyundai Elantra or Tucson, Mazda6, Nissan Altima, and Toyota Camry. **Options:** Pass on the leaky sunroof and original-equipment Firestone/Bridgestone tires. **Rebates:** Don't expect much on the 2012s until the spring of next year. At present, Ford is offering a $5,000 rebate on the 2011 MKZ. **Depreciation:** Much faster than average. **Insurance cost:** Average; the hybrid premium costs more than average. **Parts supply/cost:** Average availability and cost, except for hybrid components, which may be hard to get due to limited supplies in Japan. Hybrid part costs are moderately expensive, although most parts are taken from the Mazda or Escape Hybrid bins. **Annual maintenance cost:** Repair costs have been average during the three-year warranty period. **Warranty:** Bumper-to-bumper 3 years/60,000 km; powertrain 5 years/100,000 km; rust perforation 5 years/160,000 km. **Supplementary warranty:** A good idea. Their first three years on the market have shown the Fusion and its brothers to be prone to serious automatic transmission failures, making an extended powertrain warranty worthwhile. **Highway/city fuel economy:** *2.5L:* 6.9/9.4 L/100 km, 41/30 mpg. *Auto.:* 6.9/9.4 L/100 km, 44/30 mpg. *3.0L:* 7.3/11.1 L/100 km, 29/35 mpg. *3.0L AWD:* 7.8/11.8 L/100 km, 36/24 mpg. *3.5L AWD:* 8.3/12.7 L/100 km, 34/22 mpg. *Hybrid:* 5.4/4.6 L/100 km, 52/61 mpg.

OWNER-REPORTED PROBLEMS: Lincoln airbags failed to deploy in an accident, and both front seatbacks collapsed in a rear-ender. Fusion owners say the knee airbag restricts brake pedal access and the brakes are too weak:

> Ever since I got the car (new) I noticed that even when the brake is fully depressed to the floor while driving on a smooth surface, not enough friction was being applied to rotors to cause the ABS system to engage. There should be enough friction to lock the wheels, forcing the ABS to pump. The only time I can get the ABS to engage is on uneven roads, and on snow and ice where the tires have less traction.... It feels as though I'm applying only 90% pressure when in fact I'm flooring the pedal. This occurs when pads are cold, warm or hot. I took it to the dealer. The tech drove it with me and agreed that it doesn't seem right. We then took a new Fusion off the lot (was not a Sport, but I'm not sure what version) and it had the same problem. Emergency stops are downright scary. I almost hit someone.

Chronic automatic transmission failures and erratic shifting:

> The transmission seized while travelling at 100 kilometers per hour, causing rapid deceleration while on highway. Shortly after coming to a stop on the side of the road, the transmission failed to engage, despite engine running.

> •

> Automatic transmission shifting is unpredictable. 1–2 and 2–3 gear shift will rev at high rpm and slam into gear. Merging into traffic or at any intersection where cross traffic does not stop is very dangerous as acceleration is non-existent until it slams hard into gear. The car has done this from 1st week of ownership. Besides safety issue, the transmission at this rate will not last long. This issue is mainly present when 1) cold or 2) after the car has sat for a couple days making it difficult for the dealer to act on anything. This is a very well known problem with 2010 Ford Fusions and now many people are complaining of this issue with the 2011 Fusion (not the Sport model as it uses different transmission).

> •

> I bought a 2011 Ford Fusion on Nov. 26, 2010. The day I brought it home, the problems started. It bangs so hard into reverse that it feels like someone ran into the car with a bulldozer. It has dead spots in the acceleration, and often goes above 5000 rpm when shifting just going down a normal flat highway. The problems have gotten worse and more frequent and are completely random. It happens with a warm engine, cold engine, in rain, snow, sun, and even after being driven for 4 hours straight. I now have over 6000 miles [9,660 km] on the car and the dealership has done nothing because Ford won't authorize anything because the car is not "putting out any codes." They say they have never heard of such problems, but online forums have hundreds of the same complaints with 2010 Fusions. My fear is that the acceleration will fail when I am on the expressway or in heavy traffic or that my transmission will just fall out completely. This is my first new car, and I can't afford to get another one or a long court battle. Help! It's not just an inconvenience, it's unsafe.

Sudden stalling when the car is underway; Hybrid brake pedal is mounted too close to the accelerator pedal; head restraints force driver's head forward and downward (chin-to-chest).

MUSTANG ★ ★ ★ ★ ★ / ★

best buy

RATING: *Automatic transmission–equipped models:* Recommended. *Manual transmission–equipped versions:* Not Recommended. Mustang has gone back to its muscle car roots while keeping prices in check. **Strong points:** Base models come equipped with a host of safety, luxury, and convenience features. Fast acceleration, and impressive handling, braking, and resale value. Better-than-average past crashworthiness, standard major safety features, and good overall reliability. **Weak points:** A poorly performing manual transmission that can get you killed; all bets are off on the GT500 powertrain's long-term durability; and rear-seat room is limited. There is a huge markup on higher-end Mustangs in Canada versus the States; well worth a trip south. **New for 2012:** No significant changes.

OVERVIEW: The perfect "back to the future" retro sports car, the Mustang's body panel creases reign supreme. And more than four decades after its debut, the original pony car still stands strong, both stylistically and in its highway performance. The Mustang offers a V6 or a V8 in the GT engines. Keep in mind, though, that the V6 is an entirely different, more-powerful powerplant than the 2010 version. Body assembly has also improved considerably.

There was a huge horsepower boost on the base 2011 Mustang that turned a wimpish 210 hp V6 into a sizzling 305 hp. Incidentally, the 2011–12 GT500 ratcheted up performance by a few notches, too, with an all-new aluminum-block engine that produces 550 hp. Other goodies on the 2011–12 Mustangs: a new limited-clip differential, larger brakes (taken from the 2010 GT), electronic power steering, a retuned suspension, stiffer rear anti-roll bars, and convertibles get less body flexing through the use of shock-tower braces. Another big change is fold-down rear head restraints to improve rear visibility. For parents, there's the MyKey system, which allows owners to limit the car's maximum speed and audio volume. The 2012 Mustang will hopefully have its manual transmission problems fixed. If you plan to buy a manual-equipped model, rent one for a few days to ensure the tranny performs as it should.

Shelby: The Shelby GT500 got a power boost and other refinements during the past couple of years to improve engine cooling and performance. Ford says its revamped transmission and final-drive gearing give better acceleration off the starting line with improved highway fuel economy. The GT500 comes in both coupe and convertible versions.

COST ANALYSIS: Get a 2012 model that will likely have corrected the redesign glitches seen with the 2011 version. Anyhow, there are few unsold 2011s available, and those that are on dealer lots aren't discounted by much. Finally, this may be the ideal car to buy in the States if you live close to a large American city; the price difference may be at least $3,000 to $8,000 and availability shouldn't be a problem. **Best alternatives:** Not the resurrected Camaro. Consider this: The Mustang beats Camaro in horsepower and fuel economy. Furthermore, confidential internal reports show that Mustangs have far fewer factory-related problems than the Camaro (manual transmissions being the only exception).

KEY FACTS

CANADIAN PRICE (FIRM): *Coupe V6: $22,999, V6 Premium: $26,999, V6 Premium Convertible: $31,399, Coupe GT: $38,699, Convertible GT: $42,999, Boss Coupe: $48,199, Shelby GT500: $60,549, Shelby GT500 Convertible: $65,249* **U.S. PRICE:** *Coupe V6: $22,310, V6 Premium: 26,310, GT: $29,310, GT Premium: $33,310, Boss 302: $40,310, V6 Convertible: $27,310, Premium V6 Convertible: $33,695, GT Premium Convertible: $38,695, Shelby GT500: $48,810, Shelby GT500 Convertible: $53,810,* **CANADIAN FREIGHT:** $1,350 **U.S. FREIGHT:** $850 **POWERTRAIN (REAR-DRIVE)** Engines: 3.7L V6 (305 hp) • 5.0L V8 (402 hp) • 5.0L V8 (412 hp) • 5.4L V8 (540 hp); Transmissions: 6-speed man. • 6-speed auto. **DIMENSIONS/CAPACITY** Passengers: 2/2; Wheelbase: 107.1 in.; H: 55.6/L: 188.1/W: 73.9 in.; Headroom F/R: 5.0/1.0 in.; Legroom F/R: 40.5/23.5 in.; Cargo volume: 13.4 cu. ft.; Fuel tank: 60.1L/regular; Tow limit: 1,001 lb.; Load capacity: 720 lb.; Turning circle: 33.4 ft.; Ground clearance: 5.7 in.; Weight: 3,585 lb.

Forget about the Dodge Challenger. Its 250 hp engine and heavy body take it out of the running. Plus, rumour has it that the model is likely to be dropped as fuel prices go higher. Three fun and reliable competitors would be the Hyundai Genesis, Infiniti G25 or G27, or the Mazda Miata. **Options:** An anti-theft system (one that includes an engine immobilizer) and good tires recommended by *www.tirerack.com.* Stay away from the notchy, erratic-shifting 6-speed Getrag manual transmission (see *http://www.webstatschecker.com/stats/keyword/2011_mustang_manual*). **Rebates:** $1,000 rebates, plus low-interest financing. **Depreciation:** Average. For example, a new $24,800 2009 base Mustang now costs almost $16,000 used. The convertibles fare even better: An entry-level 2010 that sold for $29,700 has a resale value of $23,500. Expect the boosted horsepower on the entry-level V6 engine (which rivals that of the 2010 GT V8) to send the older GT's resale value plummeting. **Insurance cost:** Way higher than average. **Parts**

supply/cost: Inexpensive and easily found among independent suppliers; some delays getting engine and body components. **Annual maintenance cost:** Lower than average. Most independent mechanics will be able to fix a Mustang. **Warranty:** Bumper-to-bumper 3 years/60,000 km; powertrain 5 years/100,000 km; rust perforation 5 years/unlimited km. **Supplementary warranty:** Not necessary. Put your money into handling options and theft protection. **Highway/city fuel economy:** Fuel consumption is cut in the new 3.7L V6 (manual) to a frugal 6.9/11.2 L/100 km, 41/25 mpg. *3.7L V6 auto.:* 6.4/10.7 L/100 km, 44/26 mpg. *3.7L V6 convertible auto:* 7.8/11.9 L/100 km, 36/24 mpg. *5.0L V8 man.:* 7.7/12.2 L/100 km, 37/23 mpg. *5.0L V8 auto.:* 7.9/11.8 L/100 km, 36/24 mpg. *5.4L V8 man.:* 8.8/14.5 L/100 km, 32/19 mpg.

OWNER-REPORTED PROBLEMS: When the redesigned 2011 Mustang came out, factory-related safety defect reports posted at NHTSA doubled to 56 incidents. This figure is slightly higher than average, but it is not unusual for a vehicle that has undergone so many changes. The MT82 manual transmission is designed by Ford's JFT joint venture with Getrag in Germany and built in a four-way joint venture plant in China. It represents the majority of NHTSA-logged safety complaints. Here is how the Japlonik Forum (*http://jalopnik.com/5792482/faulty-chinese+built-transmissions-plague-new-ford-mustang*) describes the problem, followed by some typical NHTSA-registered owner complaints:

> The MT82 transmission in question is built by Ford and supplier Getrag at a joint venture in Nanchang, China—a point that has only added to the ire of some customers. And it's not the first time owners of that transmission have reported trouble shifting; the same problems were reported by owners of Land Rover Defenders.

> Since the first complaints surfaced last year, Ford has attempted to soothe angry owners and quietly offered several possible fixes, from replacing bolts in the flywheel to new clutches to even swapping out the transmission fluid. While some of those repairs have satisfied customers, several report that the problems returned—especially the balky 1st–2nd shift.

> •

> Since vehicle was new, MT82 transmission is very difficult to shift in cold weather. Frequent synchro grinding in 1–2, 2–3, and 3–4 shifts, now getting worse in summer conditions. Starting to grind during the 1–2 and 2–3 shift. Especially when transmission is cold, when turning left (1–2), and when shifting on rough pavement. Vehicle has been into the shop for a fluid change (TSB), which did not help. Ford refuses to acknowledge the issue or implement further corrective action. I am concerned the condition will continue to develop into the dangerous failure mode other owners are beginning to see (failure to engage gear). A recall should be issued on the MT82 transmission immediately.

> •

The manual transmission on my 2011 Ford Mustang has erratic shifting which has caused me to nearly be rear-ended twice now and hit by oncoming traffic as it fails to go into gear, even with the clutch fully engaged.

•

The shudder/vibration closely resembles going over rumble strips. It can be unnerving as it feels like something is going wrong with the car! I have read forums and it seems like I am not the only person that has been experiencing this problem with the 2011 Mustang. This problem can be distracting as you drive and the vibration cannot be good for the drivetrain. Some or all of these 2011 Mustang manual cars have a problem and Ford must address this issue now!

Automatic transmissions may suddenly downshift:

While traveling between 70 and 75 mph [113 and 121 km/h] when I let off the throttle my car will downshift (automatic transmission) to lower gear causing a dangerous condition. It is like hitting the brakes without the brake light going on. Also when coming to stop sign it abruptly downshifts, I have not been hit in the rear yet but I am concerned. Brought to dealer three times. Dealer denies condition because he cannot duplicate it. This is an intermittent condition. I am starting to see it documented on forums.

Head restraints force drivers to adopt a chin-to-chest posture (a common design defect on many Ford models):

The head restraint design on the 2011 Ford Mustang is defective for taller drivers. I am 6'1" but my 5'8" wife also complains. Even at its tallest adjustment, I must hold my head forward in an unnatural and fatiguing position. I'm not the only one with this complaint, as the Mustang forums are filled with similar complaints from other drivers—many of whom report simply removing the head restraint altogether. According to the forums, Ford says to increase the angle of the seatback, but then the steering wheel is too far away—and I do not have short arms (35" sleeve length). My current solution is to raise the head restraint about 2" higher than the highest detent provided by Ford. Even though the unit is still in place, and seems secure when I push on it, I'm concerned about how it will perform in a crash because it is not latched into place and there's less of the rods down in the seatback for support. The other alternative is to remove the unit altogether, as some other Mustang owners have reported doing. Ford's design forces taller drivers into one of three unsafe modes: 1. Drive the car with one's head tilted forward in a position that is both tiring and distracting. 2. Remove the head restraint entirely. 3. Raise the head restraint above the highest detent leaving it free to move and also with questionable amount of rod in the seatback.

Front passenger-side airbag is disabled when a normal-sized adult is seated.

SERVICE BULLETIN-REPORTED PROBLEMS: Fuel gauge reading drops from half to "E" and manual transmission clutch pedal remains on floor on high RPM shifts.

ESCAPE, TRIBUTE ★ / ★ ★ ★ ★

The Ford Escape.

RATING: *2012 model:* Not Recommended; totally redesigned by Ford and dropped by Mazda. *2011 model:* Above Average; nevertheless, some points were taken away for the Escape's mediocre braking and reliability concerns. The Tribute is Mazda's version of the Escape, but without a hybrid variant. **Strong points:** *2011 model:* Peppy V6 performance and a roomy interior that includes a large rear bench seat, lots of cargo space, improved braking, standard stability control, and a convenient Sync voice-control system. NHTSA gave the Escape and Escape Hybrid top marks (five stars) for front and side crashworthiness; three stars were awarded for rollover resistance. IIHS also gave its top rating ("Good") to the Escape for frontal offset, side, and rear crash protection (head-restraint effectiveness). **Weak points:** *2011 model:* There is a huge price difference between the Canadian and American high-end models. The 4-cylinder engine lacks grunt in the upper gear ranges; both the 4-banger and V6 are unusually noisy engines; handling is not precise and the ride is somewhat jarring and busy; a noisy interior; the folding second seat isn't very user-friendly; and fit and finish doesn't impress. **New for 2012:** Everything. The 2012 Escape shares its platform with the 2012 Focus and C-Max minivan; it will be slightly smaller than the 2011 (about the size of a Mazda5) but should be roomier, be less of a gas-burner, and have a smoother ride thanks to a far more sophisticated suspension system. Mazda's Tribute will be replaced in 2012 by a new compact SUV, called the CX-5.

OVERVIEW: The decade-old Escape and Tribute are good buys with many standard features and reasonably good overall reliability, but they were in dire need of the 2012 redesign to create a roomier interior and improve ride and handling. The hybrid still uses a 4-cylinder powerplant, but a new engine processor first installed on the 2010s allows the Escape to switch from electric to gasoline mode almost imperceptibly.

COST ANALYSIS: The 2012s are radically different from last year's model and will likely enjoy "no haggle" pricing until more Asian competition hits the marketplace in early 2012. The redesign is bound to cause headaches for first-year buyers hit by factory-related quality glitches and mechanics who aren't used to troubleshooting this new model. Actually, if you can afford to wait, don't buy a 2012 until next summer; if you can't wait, get a discounted 2011 version. **Best alternatives:** Honda CR-V, Kia Rondo, Mazda5, Subaru Forester, and Toyota Matrix. **Options:** Nothing that is essential. **Depreciation:** Average. **Insurance cost:** Average. **Parts supply/cost:** Reasonably priced parts for gasoline-powered models, but parts are frequently back ordered. Hybrid parts are expensive and hard to get; the short supply is expected to get worse as suppliers recover from the March earthquake in Japan. **Annual maintenance cost:** Average. **Warranty:** Bumper-to-bumper 3 years/60,000 km; powertrain 5 years/100,000 km; rust perforation 5 years/unlimited km. **Supplementary warranty:** Getting an extended powertrain warranty is a good idea. **Highway/city fuel economy:** *2011 models: 2.5L: 7.2/9.2 L/100 km, 39/21 mpg. Auto.: 7.0/9.4 L/100 km, 40/30 mpg. 2.5L AWD: 7.7/10.4 L/100 km, 37/27 mpg. 3.0L V6: 8.0/10.9 L/100 km, 35/26 mpg. 3.0L AWD: 8.8/11.6 L/100 km, 32/24 mpg. Hybrid: 6.5/5.8 L/100 km, 43/49 mpg. Hybrid AWD: 7.4/7.0 L/100 km, 39/43 mpg.*

OWNER-REPORTED PROBLEMS: Airbags fail to deploy, driver's seat collapses, or seatbelt latch pops open:

The contact rented a 2011 Ford Escape. While the contact was driving less than 20 mph [32 km/h] approaching an intersection, an opposing vehicle suddenly crashed into the front end of the contact's vehicle, causing a head-on collision. The contact sustained injuries to the shoulder, chest, and to the left arm and leg. The airbags failed to deploy. The seat belt unlatched from the buckle mechanism during the crash.... The approximate failure mileage was 75 miles [120 km].

•

Ford Escape 2011 had a car accident on May 17th 2011. I was hit from behind and with the impact I hit the car in front of me. When I was hit the air bags did not deploy, also the driver's seat broke in half.

KEY FACTS

CANADIAN PRICE (NEGOTIABLE):
XLT 2.5L man.: $21,549, 2.5L auto.: $27,149, 2.5L 4×4 man.: $29,549, 3.0L FWD man.: $31,149, 4×4: $27,999, LTD 2.5 4×4: $35,099, LTD 3.0L 4×4: $36,699, Hybrid 4×2: $39,949, Hybrid 4×4: $42,349, Limited Hybrid 4×2: $44,949, Limited Hybrid 4×4: $47,349
U.S. PRICE: *XLS 4×2 man.: $21,240, 4×2 auto.: $22,470, 4×4: $24,220, XLT FWD: $24,670, 4×4: $26,420, 3.0L FWD: $25,865, 4×4: $27,615, LTD FWD: $26,277, 4×4: $28,027, 3.0L 4×4: $29,222, Hybrid 4×2: $30,570, 4×4: $32,320, Limited: $33,080, 4×4: $34,830* **CANADIAN FREIGHT:** $1,350
U.S. FREIGHT: $850
POWERTRAIN (FRONT-DRIVE)
2011 version: Engines: 2.5L 4-cyl. (171 hp) • 2.5L 4-cyl. hybrid (177 hp) • 3.0L V6 (240 hp); Transmissions: 5-speed man. • CVT • 6-speed auto.
DIMENSIONS/CAPACITY
2011 version: Passengers: 2/3; Wheelbase: 103 in.; H: 70/L: 175/W: 70 in.; Headroom F/R: 3.0/4.0 in.; Legroom F/R: 40.5/28.0 in.; Cargo volume: 37.5 cu. ft.; Fuel tank: 61L/regular; Tow limit: 3,500 lb.; Load capacity: 1,000 lb.; Turning circle: 42 ft.; Ground clearance: 7.0 in.; Weight: 3,605 lb.

Spontaneous windshield cracks and sunroof/side window shattering; distorted windshields; liftgate glass exploded; Ford denied warranty claim despite putting out the service bulletin below that confirms it is a Ford manufacturing defect:

> I was closing the back hatch on my 5 week old 2011 Ford Escape when the back glass shattered everywhere. I contacted Ford Motor Company and they related to me that the back glass was not covered. So, of course I had to replace my back glass for approx $400. Exactly 2 days after the new glass was installed, it happened again. When closing the liftgate the back glass shattered. This time the glass company replaced it for free, but when contacting the Ford company and dealership they were very rude and disrespectful. After contacting the better business bureau, still nothing was done. It has not happened since, but now I try not to put anything into the back of my car so I don't have to lift the hatch.

Transmission fluid leakage (possible causes: a faulty AC condenser hose or condenser; cost to replace: $750–$1,025 U.S.). Oil filler tube is located directly above the exhaust manifold, creating a fire risk; cable lines fail, causing pedal to become inoperable; vehicle will not hold when stopped on an incline; sudden loss of braking ability or power steering; excessive steering noise may require the replacement of the entire steering assembly; one vehicle's parking brake failed, and the vehicle rolled backwards down a hill; excessive glare from the instrument panel blinds driver; LED readout is washed out by sunlight; tire jack won't raise the vehicle high enough to change the tire. *Hybrid:* Surprisingly for a vehicle that has such a complicated electrical system, there aren't any complaints concerning the hybrid components. One would normally expect to see, on average, 50 or so reports per model year. With the current model, owners report some brake failures.

SERVICE BULLETIN-REPORTED PROBLEMS: Broken liftgate window glass on 2010–11 models:

LIFTGATE WINDOW GLASS BROKEN

BULLETIN NO.: 10-22-10   DATE: NOVEMBER 22, 2010

FORD: 2010–11 Escape; MERCURY: 2010–11 Mariner

ISSUE: Some 2010–11 Escape and Mariner vehicles built on or before 10/15/2010 may experience the liftgate window glass breaking, typically when colder ambient temperatures are present.

ACTION: Follow the service procedure steps below to correct the condition.

1. The liftgate should be closely inspected for any signs of impact or external damage.
   a. If evidence of damage is present, do not continue with procedure.
   b. If no evidence of damage is found, proceed to Step 2.
2. Replace the liftgate window glass. The new glass includes a revised through-bolt striker design.

WARRANTY STATUS: Eligible Under Provisions Of New Vehicle Limited Warranty Coverage

OPERATION	DESCRIPTION	TIME
102210A	2010–11 Escape, Mariner	0.8 Hr.
	Front, rear squeak, creak noises on	
	2001 to 2011 models.	

Various sunroof operating issues on 2011 models:

VARIOUS SUNROOF OPERATING ISSUES

BULLETIN NO.: 10-24-3 **DATE: DECEMBER 18, 2010**

ROOF OPENING PANEL WILL NOT COMPLETELY CLOSE, FULLY VENT, OR SIT FLUSH WHEN CLOSED, AND/OR ERRATIC OPERATION

2011 Escape, Mariner.

ISSUE: Some 2011 Escape and Mariner vehicles equipped with a roof opening panel may exhibit one or more of the following roof opening panel symptoms: not completely closing when auto-commanded closed from a fully opened position, rear of roof opening panel glass not seated properly when closed—not completely opening to full vent position, closing from vent position results in glass dropping below roof opening, sliding rearward/forward un-commanded with glass remaining slightly open.

ACTION: Follow the Service Procedure steps below to correct the condition.

1. Replace roof opening panel motor assembly. Refer to Workshop Manual (WSM), Section 501-17.
2. Perform roof opening panel motor initialization. Refer to WSM, Section 501-17.

PART NUMBER	PART NAME
9L8Z-15790-B	Motor Assembly

WARRANTY STATUS: Eligible Under Provisions of New Vehicle Limited Warranty Coverage.

IMPORTANT: Warranty coverage limits/policies are not altered by a TSB. Warranty coverage limits are determined by the identified causal part.

OPERATION	DESCRIPTION	TIME
102403A	2011 Escape, Mariner: Replace The Roof Opening Panel Motor Assembly Includes Time To Perform Roof Opening Panel Initialization (Do Not Use With Any Other Labor Operations)	2.9 Hrs.

EXPLORER ★★

RATING: Below Average. First-year production flaws and poor highway performance hobble what should have been Ford's best SUV. **Strong points:** Standard stability control and average reliability with the V6 engine; NHTSA gave the Explorer five stars for frontal and side crashworthiness and three stars for rollover resistance, while IIHS scored frontal offset protection as "Good" and side protection and head-restraint effectiveness as "Acceptable." **Weak points:** Prices are set too high, but they can easily be haggled downward as sales figures start to decline in the new year; the longer you delay your purchase, the better quality you'll likely find as Ford tackles early production defects that usually pop up with its redesigned models. The most likely problem areas for the next several years: costly powertrain failures in addition to faulty brake, electrical system, and suspension components, and subpar body construction. Downshifts are slow and abrupt, braking can be hard to modulate on hills, steering is vague, and cornering produces lots of body

KEY FACTS

CANADIAN PRICE (VERY NEGOTIABLE):
V6 FWD: $31,549, *4×4:* $34,549, *XLT V6 FWD:* $37,449, *4×4:* $40,449, *Limited FWD:* $42,749, *4×4:* $45,749 **U.S. PRICE:** *V6 FWD:* $28,360, *4×4:* $30,360, *XLT V6 FWD:* $31,520, *4×4:* $33,520, *LTD FWD:* $37,535, *4×4:* $39,535 **CANADIAN FREIGHT:** $1,350 **U.S. FREIGHT:** $815

POWERTRAIN (REAR-DRIVE/4×4/AWD)
Engines: 4.0L V6 (210 hp) • 4.6L V8 (292 hp); Transmissions: 5-speed auto. • 6-speed auto.

DIMENSIONS/CAPACITY
Passengers: 2/3/2; Wheelbase: 114 in.; H: 73/L: 193/W: 74 in.; Headroom F/R1/R2: 2.5/4.0/0.5 in.; Legroom F/R1/R2: 40.5/28.0/27.0 in.; Cargo volume: 48 cu. ft.; Fuel tank: 85L/regular; Tow limit: 5,210 lb.; Load capacity: 1,275 lb.; Turning circle: 38 ft.; Ground clearance: 7.0 ft.; Weight: 4,905 lb.

lean. Drivers have to contend with limited footroom; brake and accelerator pedals mounted too close to each other; narrow, poorly-cushioned seats that lack sufficient thigh support; telematics that are distracting and failure-prone; a dash offering a confusing array of small buttons, crowded displays, and redundant controls; and head restraints that are literally a pain in the neck. The cabin is an adequate size, but it's not quite as roomy as what is offered by the Dodge Durango, Ford Flex, or Chevy Traverse. Cargo space is the smallest of the group and the third row is somewhat cramped. **New for 2012:** Carried over relatively unchanged. 2012 models will likely return with a naturally aspirated 3.5L V6, much like the Mustang's V6 2.0L EcoBoost, which should deliver at least 9.4L/100 km (25 mpg) on the highway. Still smarting from the Explorer's "rollover" reputation, Ford introduced a Curve Control feature on its 2011 models to enhance directional stability. It will return with the 2012s along with Terrain Management, a feature that instantly adapts to a variety of road and driving conditions.

OVERVIEW: The 2011–12 Explorer's new unibody construction cuts weight, which saves fuel, and gives more car-like road manners to the SUV. It offers front-drive, all-wheel drive, or four-wheel drive that can be left engaged on dry pavement and has a low-range gear for off-roading. Available safety features include ABS, traction control, an anti-skid system, side curtain airbags, and front side airbags. A third-row seat increases carrying capacity to seven passengers. Explorer's capless fuelling system allows owners to fill their fuel tanks without having to remove a gas cap, and the optional Sync voice-activated cell phone and MP3 player control system is particularly useful.

The Sport Trac was discontinued in October 2010, even though Ford said in earlier press releases that production would end in 2011. Essentially an Explorer with a pickup bed, the Sport Trac debuted in 2001 as one of the first pickups with four full-sized doors, a comfortable four-passenger cabin, and a short cargo bed. Set on the Explorer's wheelbase, stretched by about 17 inches, it was offered with either a V6 or V8 engine and boasts a top towing capacity of 7,160 lb. Its performance pluses and minuses mirror those of its brother, and defects affecting the one usually also affect the other.

COST ANALYSIS: Many competitive car-based crossover SUVs that are more refined and better-performing can be found in this price range; most of them are just as family-friendly, too, while offering a wide array of safety features, better fuel economy, and a less troublesome powertrain setup. Remember, Ford's past redesigns have always been afflicted by numerous factory-related powertrain defects and inflated prices for the first couple of years. **Best alternatives:** Honda CR-V or Ridgeline, Hyundai Tucson or Santa Fe, and Toyota RAV4. **Options:** Be wary of the $1,700 Ironman Package. You are essentially getting larger tires, heated seats, a roof rack, and floor mats. **Rebates:** On the 2011s, look for $3,000 rebates, $2,000 discounts, and zero percent financing. 2012 Explorers will likely get 10 percent discounts and zero-interest financing by the summer of 2012. **Depreciation:** Much faster than average. A 2009 base Explorer 4×4 that sold for $36,000 is now worth about $21,000. **Insurance cost:** Above average. **Parts supply/cost:** Parts are easy to find and are reasonably priced. **Annual maintenance cost:** Average while under warranty; higher than average thereafter, primarily because of powertrain breakdowns. **Warranty:** Bumper-to-bumper 3 years/60,000 km; powertrain 5 years/100,000 km; rust perforation 5 years/unlimited km. **Supplementary warranty:** Getting an extended powertrain warranty would be wise. **Highway/city fuel economy:** 3.5L V6: 8.0/11.9 L/100 km, 35/24 mpg; 4×4: 8.8/12.5 L/100 km, 32/23 mpg.

OWNER-REPORTED PROBLEMS: Owners continue to complain that the head restraints are literally a pain in the neck and can be dangerous if the airbags deploy:

> The head rest pushes the driver's head towards the windshield due to its perpendicular design.... If the air bag were to deploy, the driver could become seriously injured. The contact called the manufacturer and was informed that the vehicle was designed in that manner and no compensation would be provided.

Mediocre automatic transmission performance and fit and finish deficiencies; sun visors are poorly designed; driver's foot presses on the foot rest bar when attempting to apply the brakes:

> The contact stated that when he tried to apply the brakes, his foot pressed on a bar that's next to the brake pedal, instead of the pedal. The vehicle was taken to the dealer who stated that was the way the vehicle was designed and they could not alter it.

SERVICE BULLETIN-REPORTED PROBLEMS: Ford continues to have problems with the MyFord Touch and MyLincoln Touch telematics systems in the 2011 Edge, Explorer, and Lincoln MKX. In TSB 11-4-18 issued on April 27, Ford said the problems include blank screens, missing presets, lack of voice recognition, the incorrect dialing of phone numbers and display problems with the backup camera. Various functionality concerns with MyFord Touch and MyLincoln Touch built on or before March 30, 2011 (TSB #11-4-18). Inability to unlock door (TSB #11-4-14). Inaccurate fuel economy and temperature displays (TSB #11-4-12). Noise from front bolster at highway speeds (TSB #11-4-6). False DTC P188D (TSB #11-4-1). Lower valance comes loose (TSB #11-3-26). Blind Spot Information System or Cross Traffic Alert false blockages or trouble codes (TSB #11-3-19). Noise through front speakers (TSB #1-3-12).

F-150, F-250, F-350, F-450 PICKUP ★★★★

The Ford F-150.

RATING: Above Average. The F-150 has seen the best of times and the worst of times and is now coming out of a multi-year sales slump that almost forced Ford into bankruptcy. **Strong points:** Easily negotiated prices as fuel prices rise and truck prices fall. Handling is a breeze, although the ride is a bit stiff; a roomy cab with lots of convenient storage bins; a power-opening centre rear window; and a spring-assisted tailgate. NHTSA gave the 2010 F-150 five stars for front and side crashworthiness and four stars for rollover resistance. The F-250 wasn't tested.

IIHS also gave the F-150 top marks ("Good") for frontal offset, side, and rear crashworthiness. **Weak points:** The powertrain is a bit rough and loud, and braking is just acceptable. Long-term reliability has yet to be determined. This is especially important because these trucks have disappointed owners after each redesign since the mid-'80s. Poorly-designed head restraints force your chin to your chest. **New for 2012:** A bit more power and a slightly restyled interior and exterior. Pickups using a medium-duty chassis cab, scheduled for a market launch in the fourth quarter of 2011, will be available with the 6.8L V10 engine. Ford says gross vehicle weight ratings for Class 6 and Class 7 medium-duty trucks equipped with the V10 will range from 20,500 to 30,000 pounds.

OVERVIEW: The Ford F-Series ruled the roost for 30-odd years as the bestselling pickup in North America. Then Ford's house of cards came tumbling down. Abetted by lousy diesel engines; failure-prone powertrains, suspensions, and steering assemblies; and body construction that would make the Marquis de Sade cry, Ford began to lose market share a decade ago, and has only recently bounced back. Its 2009–11 models give hope that some of the worst design deficiencies have been corrected and that Ford is finally on the road to better truck quality. So far, NHTSA-logged complaints and *Consumer Reports* member surveys feedback gives the impression these are much better-made pickups. The 2012 models are carryovers of the 2011 models, which were much improved: by getting more power and a slight exterior restyling. Look for a new twin-turbo V6, the new EcoBoost engine, and a new Coyote V8 on most of the F-Series. The SVT Raptor gets a 6.2L 411 hp V8. The larger trucks will be led by the all-new Ford-engineered 6.7L Power Stroke V8 turbodiesel. The 2011 Ford F-150 SVT Raptor with an available all-new 6.2L V8 will produce 411 hp, making it the most powerful half-ton truck on the market today. The Raptor is 7 inches wider than the standard F-150 and is also styled differently.

COST ANALYSIS: Unless you're looking for a high-performance Raptor or are in dire need of an engine boost, look for a cheaper, leftover 2011 version (discount should be in the 10–15 percent realm).

KEY FACTS

CANADIAN PRICE: *F-150 Regular:* $21,549, *F-150 Super Cab:* $23,947, *Super Crew Cab:* $31,129, *F-250 XL 4x2 Super Duty Regular Cab:* $35,499, *Super Cab:* $38,599, *4x4:* $38,899 *Crew Cab long bed:* $40,599, *XLT 4x2 Crew Cab long bed:* $46,849, *Lariat 4x2 Crew Cab long bed:* $55,049, *Crew Cab:* $28,781, *F-350 Regular:* $26,230, *Super Cab:* $28,466, *Crew Cab:* $29,928, *F-450 4x2:* $41,968, *F-450 4x4:* $45,064 **U.S. PRICE:** *F-150 XL:* $22,790; *STX:* $25,880; *XLT:* $26,500, *FX2:* $33,460, *Lariat:* $34,495, *FX4:* $37,010, *SVT Raptor:* $41,935, *King Ranch:* $42,175, *Platinum:* $43,985, *Lariat LTD:* $47,580, *Harley Davidson:* $48,380; *F-250:* $28,505, *F-350:* $29,225, *F-450:* $48,835 **CANADIAN FREIGHT:** $1,350 **U.S. FREIGHT:** $975

POWERTRAIN (REAR-DRIVE/PART-TIME 4×4/AWD)

Engines: 4.6L V8 (248 hp) • 4.6L V8 (292 hp) • 5.4L V8 (310 hp) 6.2L V8 (385 hp) • 6.4L V8 diesel (350 hp) • 6.7L V8 diesel (385 hp) • 6.8L V10 (362 hp) • 3.5L V6 (365 hp) • 3.7L V6 (302 hp) • 5.0L V8 (360 hp) • 6.2L V8 (411 hp); Transmissions: 4-speed auto. • 5-speed auto. • 6-speed auto. • 6-speed man.

DIMENSIONS/CAPACITY

Passengers: 2/1 up to 3/3; Wheelbase: 121 in.; H: 69/L: 201/W: 77 in.; Headroom F/R: 4.5/3.5 in.; Legroom F/R: 40.0/29.5 in.; Fuel tank: 98.4L/regular, *Raptor:* 94L/regular, *Harley-Davidson:* 136L/regular; Tow limit: *F-150:* 5,400lb.; *F-250:* 12,500 lb.; Load capacity: 1,480–5,100 lb.; Turning circle: 48 ft.; Ground clearance: 8.5 in.; Weight: 5,620 lb.

Check lower American prices on the Internet by Googling "Ford USA," and compare the prices to "Ford Canada." With high-end pickups, $10,000 or more can be saved. **Best alternatives:** GM's Silverado and Sierra base models and HD series, Honda's Ridgeline, Nissan's Titan, and dead-last Chrysler's "Jurassic" Ram equipped with a Cummins diesel and a more-reliable manual transmission. Some trucks that are ideal for lighter duties, like the Ford Ranger (2011) and Mazda B-Series (2010), have been taken off the market. Nissan's Frontier or King Cab are also worth considering. **Options:** Take a pass on the Firestone/Bridgestone tires, heated seats, and Lariat Chrome package. **Rebates:** $3,000–$5,000 rebates and low-cost financing on the larger trucks. **Depreciation:** Much faster than average during the first three years of ownership. For example, a 2009 entry-level F-150 that sold new for $24,199, is now worth about $9,000 less. **Insurance cost:** Above average. **Parts supply/cost:** Reasonably priced parts are easy to find, mainly because many independent suppliers specialize in new and used F-Series parts. **Annual maintenance cost:** Average. **Warranty:** Bumper-to-bumper 3 years/60,000 km; powertrain 5 years/100,000 km; rust perforation 5 years/unlimited km. **Supplementary warranty:** Getting an extended bumper-to-bumper warranty is a good idea. **Highway/city fuel economy:** *3.5L V6:* 9.0/12.9 L/100 km, 31/22 mpg; *6.2L V8:* 11.4/16.9 L/100 km, 25/17 mpg; *3.5L V6 4×4:* 9.0/12.9 L/100 km, 30/20 mpg; *6.2L V8 4×4:* 12.7/18.3 L/100 km, 22/15 mpg; *3.7L V6:* 8.9/12.9 L/100 km, 32/22 mpg; *3.7L 4×4:* 9.8/13.4 L/100 km, 21/15 mpg; *5.0L V8:* 9.7/13.9 L/100 km, 29/20 mpg; *5.0L V8 4×4:* 10.5/15.0 L/100 km, 27/19 mpg; *Raptor 6.2L V8 4×4:* 14.2/19.1 L/100 km, 20/15 mpg.

OWNER-REPORTED PROBLEMS: One fire started under the driver's door, another ignited via the exhaust system, a third broke out near the brake master cylinder on an F-250; another F-250 suddenly accelerated; a familiar litany of transmission and steering failures:

> Transmission fluid pours out of overflow when under load (pulling a trailer). This fluid dumps on exhaust system and starts a fire. This [occurred] at 2,500 miles [4,000 km] on June 25, 2011. Truck is still at dealer, no resolution.

> •

> The vehicle caught fire while parked. The fire originated within the engine compartment at or around the master cylinder and wiring harness area as it enters the firewall. The vehicle was completely destroyed in the fire.

> •

> The contact owns a 2011 Ford F-250. While attempting to merge onto the interstate the vehicle hesitated and the gear would not shift into second or third gear causing the transmission to shift with greater force, and the rear wheels to lock. The vehicle was taken to the dealer numerous times for the failure. The dealer's diagnostic test indicated that the transmission was sending incorrect signals. The transmission computer was reprogrammed several times. The failure was not corrected and the

vehicle continued to hesitate while attempting to shift gears. The manufacturer filed a report. The vehicle was not repaired. The failure mileage was 200 miles [320 km].

●

F-150 Platinum Extended Cab. Steering is extremely stiff/spongy/hard to turn off-center. Must constantly fight side winds and road crowns. As if only 10% power-assisted. Dangerous as required constant attention to steering. Others who have driven it comment the same and will not drive truck again.

●

2011 Ford F-250. Consumer states six incidents of sudden unexpected, unexplained high acceleration. The consumer stated two of the six incidents were at a very high RPM and so forceful, that it nearly propelled the vehicle into other vehicles.

Head restraints are uncomfortable and dangerous:

Headrest forces driver's chin into the chest. Dealer stated that this is the new safety design. Headrests are non-adjustable. Also, they are very wide and, in conjunction with the frame post at the rear of the doors, create a blind spot on both sides of the pickup.

●

The truck owner stated that the driver's and passenger side headrests were not adjustable and constantly struck him in the back of the neck. The manufacturer stated that this was a new design for safety. He was concerned that his neck could be seriously injured due to the air bags in the event of a crash.

SERVICE BULLETIN-REPORTED PROBLEMS: Take note that Ford has a secret warranty extension covering fuel injector replacements on 2008 and 2009 F-250 through F-550 trucks equipped with a 6.4L diesel engine (Customer Satisfaction Program #09B08). Until March 31, 2010, Ford replaced, free of charge, injectors that had prematurely worn O-rings. After that date, only "emergency" repairs were covered. This free repair also applied to subsequent owners. Although expired, this "goodwill" warranty is useful as a benchmark to owners of other models/years with expired warranties.

2011 F-Super Duty vehicles equipped with a 6.7L engine may have an exhaust leak or odour coming from the exhaust pressure sensor tube-to-exhaust pipe connection. 2011 F-250, F-350, F-450 and F-550 may run rough, not start (TSB #11-6-10). 2011 F-250, F-350 with 6.2L engine may exhibit 2–3 shift flare or delayed Reverse engagement; repair may require the replacement of solenoid band Number 3 (TSB #11-5-19). 2008-11 F-Super Duty may produce a pop or clunk noise heard/felt under floor pan when turning, and may be more noticeable when cold (TSB #10-7-3). 2011 F-250, F-350, and F-450 may have severe steering wheel oscillation after passing over rough pavement (TSB #11-6-14). 2011 F-Super Duty vehicles equipped with a 6.7L engine may have an exhaust leak or odour coming from the exhaust pressure sensor tube-to-exhaust pipe connection. 2011 Raptors may have a defective rear driveshaft yoke. It will be replaced for free up to June 14, 2012.

General Motors

What, No Volt?

You know what I'd rather have them do—this will make my Republican friends puke— as gas is going to go down here now, we ought to just slap a 50-cent or a dollar tax on a gallon of gas…. People will start buying more Chevrolet Cruzes than Suburbans.

GM CEO DAN AKERSON
THE DETROIT NEWS. JUNE 7, 2011

No, a higher fuel tax won't drive people to GM showrooms. Not until the automaker makes vehicles that are reasonably priced and reliable. It is ironic, though, that the automaker that killed its own electric car over a decade ago now wants Ottawa and Washington to slap a tax on fuel so the company's "green" vehicles will sell. Evidently, government corporate bailouts, and provincial consumer rebates of $8,500 to $10,000, aren't enough of a stimulus to help the company put the pedal to the metal.

Now GM says we should buy gasoline at $1.50 a litre, so we will feel so much pain in our wallet, that we will be numb when forking over $46,000 for a Chevy Volt electric car, or when buying a relatively untested Chevrolet Cruze.

New Models

A new Chevy Spark and Captiva, Buick Verano and Regal, electric Volt, and Cadillac XTS round out the lineup of GM's 2012 models. Most of the equipment changes have to do with new engines, a wider availability of 6-speed transmissions, better fuel economy, and "decontenting" through option package deletions.

This year, GM's model lineup will have lots of overlap and brand dilution as GM sells thinly disguised Chevrolets and Daewoos (Aveo/Sonic) through Chevrolet-Buick-GMC dealers. This shoring up of Buick dealers has hurt Cadillac, whose products look more and more like upscale Buicks with little Cadillac cachet. In China, where Buicks were once the car driven by top government officials, the brand is now enjoying a strong resurgence as the epitome of American auto luxury.

Don't believe GM hype that the company has learned its lesson from over-dealering, overlapping models, rebadging (selling the same model under a different name), and keeping "dog" models around long after they've been rejected by the market. Product differentiation is still left half-finished with the company's remaining models.

Nevertheless, car sales have been on the upswing for GM throughout 2011 and it looks like they will stay positive well into 2012. Fleet sales have rebounded this year, representing 25 percent of total North American sales, and residual values remain strong. Historically, low resale values have long plagued the industry, driving down the value of both new and used products. But that has turned around this year. New and redesigned models and a lack of new Japanese product have given GM brands a healthy residual value and the declining supply of used cars means that two- and three-year-old vehicles are worth a lot more than original projections.

"Sticker Shock" Returns

Greed has returned to the truck and SUV market as automakers take advantage of pent-up consumer demand and a lessening of Japanese competition to announce huge price increases for 2011–12 and tack on a slew of unjustified extra charges in the process. Fortunately, prices will fall after the December holidays, as they always do. In effect, prices usually go down by at least 20 percent and will probably get cut by much more this year, depending on how much Asian automakers want to spend on discounts and sales incentives to recapture lost market share during the past disaster-ridden year.

Smart buyers will wait out the auto show hooplah and pick up discounted bargains. Just remember to carefully scrutinize ads and offers that include bogus delivery and dealers' fees.

Phony Prices

GM Canada's website (*www.gm.ca/gm/english/divisional-showroom/SVV,6/dealer-view/d2c3/95306/335Q724BL*) lists the manufacturer's suggested retail prices for its lineup of this year's vehicles and includes a $2,045 charge for freight costs, "dealer fees," and a $100 AC tax payment. The freight charge and dealer fees are nothing more than profit padding allowing the company to then offer a $2,660 "Price Adjustment" deducted from the MSRP, freight, dealer fees, and AC tax.

This sleight of hand gives the shopper the illusion of a savings or reduction of the MSRP, when actually there is none (see how this is done with a new Impala, for example, at *http://configurator.autodata.gm.ca/GMCanada/buildYourVehicle.html?lang=en*).

What is particularly offensive and likely illegal in this pricing scheme is that it is not up to GM to set the amount of the dealer's fees and to do so certainly opens the company up to a charge of price-fixing. This practice also contradicts GM's assertion on its website:

> Price includes freight, air conditioning tax and dealer fees. Retail sales taxes, other applicable taxes, or license fees are not included. Dealers are free to set individual prices.

How can the dealers set their own prices when GM's price chart has already itemized the freight and AC tax charge? Obviously the rest of the amount is dealer fees, which GM is setting. Most automakers stay away from including dealer fees in any cost charts so as not to run afoul of Ottawa's *Competition Act*. GM obviously feels it can get away with the practice.

Don't you just feel just peachy over the millions of dollars in bailout money given to GM by the feds and provinces in 2009?

Increased Fuel Economy

For 2012, GM will introduce its eAssist, or "light electrification" fuel-saving technology. This feature uses a small lithium-ion battery and a 15 kw motor-generator that gives electric boost during sustained acceleration, cuts off fuel during deceleration, regenerates during braking, and switches to electric power when stopped.

This technology is expected to cut fuel consumption by 25 percent, which rivals the mileage claims of hybrids, without the extra hybrid cost. Look for eAssist as a standard feature in the 2012 Buick LaCrosse and as an optional item in the 2012 Buick Regal and the 2013 Chevy Malibu.

Other fuel-saving measures will come from a shift to 4-cylinder engines: last year, 46 percent of GM's sales were 4-cylinder vehicles, up from only 25 percent five years ago. The engines are changing too: variable-valve timing, active fuel management, direct injection, and new liquid petroleum gas (LPG) alternative-fuel vehicles are on the way.

Trucks and SUVs

General Motors' truck and SUV division is halfway through its own restructuring as GM confronts stricter fuel-economy standards, stricter diesel-fuel NOx emissions rules that require regular urea fill-ups, gas price spikes that drive product planners batty, and a buying public that wants car-like handling and performance in their truck or SUV. Although the Tahoe, Yukon, Suburban, and Yukon XL will likely soldier on until at least 2013, the smaller, last-in-class Colorado and Canyon pickups will be discontinued in 2012.

GM's base 2011 pickups (1500 series) return unchanged; however, the 2500 and 3500 HD lineup will offer many new powertrain, suspension, and interior upgrades. These are major improvements that make these models more competitive with Ford's Super Duty lineup. Dodge trucks, on the other hand, are not as technologically sophisticated as GM's or Ford's. Ford's trucks will continue to have the high-tech edge since the improvements were made earlier and Ford has fixed many of the first-year production glitches, while GM's HD changes may open the door to major production glitches this year.

As buyers downsize from Detroit SUVs to CR-Vs, RAV4s, Foresters, and Tucsons, GM comes to the party a bit late; nevertheless, its SUVs and pickups are credible competitors that are gaining market share from the downsized boom and limited Asian production.

Quality Control

Not good. As much as Ford's lineup has shown tangible quality improvements in the past two years, Chrysler has been mostly smoke and mirrors with its future riding on a new V6 powertrain and Fiat mini-compact fuel-sippers, and GM is stuck somewhere in the middle with small improvements that don't seem to make much difference to its overall poor quality reputation. Granted there are some vehicles that are exceptionally well-made, like the small Equinox SUV, but the overall impression is that the company lets problems carry over year after year.

GM's quality control needs serious improvement. Buyers are suspicious and its engines and automatic transmissions still aren't as reliable or as durable as those of the Asian competition. Furthermore, GM brake and electronic components often fail prematurely and cost owners big bucks to diagnose and repair. The quality and assembly of body components remains far below Asian standards.

Chinese Competition

It is unlikely, for a variety of reasons, that exports from Chinese auto factories will pose much of a threat to GM or other North American automakers in the short run. Firstly, the Asian market prefers American cars. Additionally, most of the Chinese automakers are small and have to work overtime just to supply their domestic market with cars and parts. Furthermore, manufacturing costs are rising in China following unprecedented labour union victories that have raised the minimum autoworker wage by 30 percent. Finally, North American consumers aren't likely to buy cars made in China. They are rightfully distrustful of a country that exports poisoned pet food, sells lead-laced toys, and tries to rip off American automakers by selling their new car as a Chevy (changed to Chery after a flurry of lawyers' letters from GM).

The General Motors Aveo.

RATING: *Aveo:* Mediocre quality and poor road performance make the Aveo a Below Average buy; *Sonic:* The car has potential, but it is Not Recommended during its first year on the market. **Strong points:** *Aveo:* Soft pricing and easily repaired. *Sonic:* More fun to drive than the Aveo; a refined powertrain, a nice array of standard features, and much better handling with a more comfortable ride than the Aveo. **Weak points:** *Aveo:* Unimpressive fuel economy; mediocre handling degraded by vague steering and excessive body lean when cornering or braking; uncomfortable seats; and mediocre fit and finish. Depreciation is so rapid that a 2008 base model that sold for $13,000 is now worth only $6,500. Worse still is the car's poor reliability; almost every component has come up short. *Sonic:* Firm pricing; and many first-year factory-related defects. **New for 2012:** Goodbye, Aveo, hello, Aveo/Sonic.

OVERVIEW: The base price for both cars is quite reasonable; however, the Aveo is more deeply discounted, while the Sonic price will be harder to bargain down during its first year on the market.

COST ANALYSIS: *Aveo:* End of run models will be cheaper by $1,500, but they will lose double that amount as soon as they leave the showroom; what you save in the showroom, will likely be lost in the service bay. *Sonic:* Not a good idea to invest in this first-year model. Sure, it's simply constructed and supported by GM, but servicing, parts, and overall performance have yet to be rated with feedback from actual owners. **Best alternatives:** Honda Fit, Hyundai Accent, and Nissan Versa. **Rebates:** GM will offer $1,500 discounts and rebates on 2011 Aveos to make room for a new Aveo, er, Sonic. **Options:** *Aveo:* Anti-lock brakes with the engine immobilizer system. **Depreciation:** *Aveo:* Faster than average. **Insurance cost:**

KEY FACTS

CANADIAN PRICE (SOFT): *Aveo LS:* $14,150; *LT:* $:16,850; *Aveo5:* $13,950; *Aveo5 LT:* $16,650 **CANADIAN PRICE (FIRM):** *Sonic:* TBA. Use the U.S. price as your bargaining benchmark. **U.S. PRICE:** *Sonic LS Sedan:* $14,495, *Hatch:* $15,395; *LT:* $15,695; *Hatch:* $16,495; *LTZ Sedan:* $17,295; *Hatch:* $17,995 **CANADIAN FREIGHT, DEALER FEES, AND AC TAX:** $2,045 (Pay half of the freight charge, nothing for "dealer fees," and $100 AC tax) **U.S. FREIGHT:** $975 **POWERTRAIN (FRONT-DRIVE)** Engines: 1.6L 4-cyl. (108 hp) • *Sonic:* 1.8L 4-cyl. (138 hp) • 1.4L 4-cyl. turbo (138 hp); Transmissions: 4-speed auto. • *Sonic:* 5-speed man. • 6-speed auto. **DIMENSIONS/CAPACITY** Passengers: 2/3; Wheelbase: 97.6 in.; H: 53.9/L: 169.7/W: 67.3 in., Headroom F/R: 5.0/2.0 in.; Legroom F/R: 41/26 in.; Maximum load: 860 lb.; Cargo volume: 12.4 cu. ft. Fuel tank: 45L/regular; Tow limit: Not recommended; Turning circle: 35 ft.; Ground clearance: 5 in.; Weight: 2,557–2,579 lb.; *Sonic:* Passengers: 2/3; Wheelbase: 99.4 in.; H: 59.7/L: 159/W: 68.3 in.; Cargo volume: 19.0 cu. ft.; Fuel tank: 45L/regular; Tow limit: Not recommended; Turning circle: 34.5 ft.; Ground clearance: 4.9 in.; Weight: 2,800 lb.

Average. **Parts supply/cost:** *Aveo:* Parts aren't hard to find and are relatively inexpensive. **Annual maintenance cost:** *Aveo:* Average. **Warranty:** Bumper-to-bumper 3 years/60,000 km; powertrain 5 years/160,000 km; rust perforation 6 years/160,000 km. **Supplementary warranty:** A good idea to get an extended powertrain warranty for both vehicles. **Highway/city fuel economy:** *Aveo:* Man.: 5.7/7.6 L/100 km, 49/37 mpg. Auto.: 5.8/8.2 L/100 km, 49/34 mpg.

OWNER-REPORTED PROBLEMS: *Aveo:* Engine and transmission malfunctions; early failures of the fuel system, suspension, electrical system, and climate control. Windshield wipers cannot clean the window—they are useless at highway speeds and the washer fluid sprays too low when the car is stopped.

SERVICE BULLETIN-REPORTED PROBLEMS: Tires leak air or suddenly go flat; poor radio reception; radio does not mute when using OnStar.

CRUZE ★★★

RATING: An Average buy that's still relatively untested. Remember, the Daewoo-engineered Cruze is brought to you by the same quality-challenged company that made the unimpressive Aveo (with Chevrolet), the Reno and Forenza (with Suzuki), and the gone-but-not-lamented Pontiac LeMans (all on its own). **Strong points:** A peppy, smooth, and efficient turbocharged engine; good steering and handling; upscale interior; a large trunk; quiet cabin; and comfortable front seats. Eco gives impressive fuel economy. Received NHTSA's top crashworthiness award of five stars for frontal and side protection; rollover resistance scored four stars. IIHS rates frontal, side, head restraint, and roof crash protection as "Good." **Weak points:** Expect lots of first-year factory-related defects associated with the powertrain with the 2012s; fuel economy is not extraordinary with base models; firm suspension makes you feel every bump in the road; Bluetooth feature often

KEY FACTS

CANADIAN PRICE (VERY NEGOTIABLE):
LS: $16,940, *LS+:* $18,695, *LT Turbo:* $21,540, *LT Turbo+:* $22,915, *ECO:* $26,825 **U.S. PRICE:** *LS:* $16,525, *ECO:* $18,425, *1LT:* $18,425, *2LT:* $20,925, *LTZ:* $22,225 **CANADIAN FREIGHT, DEALER FEES, AND AC TAX:** $2,045 (This is padded profit. Pay half of the freight charge, nothing for "dealer fees," and $100 for AC tax.) **U.S. FREIGHT:** $720
POWERTRAIN (FRONT-DRIVE)
Engines: 1.8L 4-cyl. (136 hp) •
1.4 turbocharged four (138 hp);
Transmissions: 6-speed man. • 6-speed auto.
DIMENSIONS/CAPACITY
Passengers: 2/3; Wheelbase: 105.7 in.; H: 58.1/L: 181/W: 70.7 in.; Legroom F/R: 42.3/35.4 in.; Cargo volume: 15.0 cu. ft.; Fuel tank: 59L/regular; Tow limit: 1,000 lb. No towing for ECO model.; Turning circle: 35.7 ft.; Ground clearance: 6.5 in.; Weight: 3,056 lb.

disconnects during phone calls; cramped rear seating with seat cushions set too low; rear-view mirror blocks the view through the front windshield; limited storage area; a boring exterior; and unproven long-term reliability. **New for 2012:** Some powertrain upgrades—namely, a more widely available 6-speed manual transmission and a 2 mpg highway increase for some automatic transmission models. Sometime in 2013, GM will sell in Canada a diesel-engine-equipped 2.0L Cruze.

OVERVIEW: The Chevrolet Cruze is built in Lordstown, Ohio, and replaced last year the poor-selling Chevrolet Cobalt and its Pontiac G5 twin as the leading homegrown compact car from GM. This wasn't hard to do, since the Cobalt ranked a disappointing 24th out of 30 "affordable small cars" rated by *U.S. News and World Report*.

Cruze comes as a four-door sedan equipped with a fuel-frugal 136 hp 1.8L 4-cylinder engine. The Eco version uses a 138 hp turbocharged 1.4L 4-cylinder engine. A 6-speed manual transmission is standard on the LS and Eco; a 6-speed automatic is optional on those models, but comes standard on the LT and LTZ. Buyers get a wide choice of standard safety features that include ABS, traction control, an antiskid system, side curtain airbags, front and rear side airbags, and front knee airbags. The Eco models come with tires that have ultra-low rolling resistance (meaning they are better at gripping the road) and other aerodynamic improvements designed to enhance fuel economy.

European and Australian car columnists who have tested earlier, local versions of the Cruze have mixed opinions. They praise the Cruze for its interior quality/space and modern styling, while criticizing the car's weight, wimpy engines, and mediocre handling. Drivers don't want just style or fuel economy; they want performance, too, which may stop the Cruze dead in its tracks if fuel costs stay reasonable enough for drivers to stick with less-fuel-efficient, but better-performing, vehicles.

Best alternatives: Some good alternative models are the Ford Focus, Honda Civic (2011) or Fit, Hyundai Accent, Mazda2 (after it has been on the market a while), or a VW Jetta (with a more reliable manual transmission). **Options:** The turbocharged 4-banger and premium tires. **Rebates:** $500 rebates at year's end. **Depreciation:** Average. **Insurance cost:** Average. **Parts supply/cost:** Average supply and cost. **Annual maintenance cost:** Average. **Warranty:** 60-day money-back guarantee as long as you don't drive more than 4,000 km. Bumper-to-bumper 3 years/60,000 km; powertrain 5 years/160,000 km; rust perforation 6 years/160,000 km. **Supplementary warranty:** An extended powertrain warranty would be a wise investment. **Highway/city fuel economy:** *Eco 1.4L man.:* 4.6/7.2 L/100 km, 55/36 mpg. *Auto.:* 5.1/7.8 L/100 km, 51/33 mpg. *1.8L man.:* 5.4/7.8L/100 km, 52/36 mpg. *1.8L auto.:* 5.6/9.2 L/100 km, 50/31 mpg. Despite the above figures put out by the federal government (*http://oee.nrcan.gc.ca/ transportation/tools/fuelratings/ratings-results.cfm*), Cruze owners say real gas mileage is much less than what is advertised.

COST ANALYSIS: Stay away from the first-year 2011s; factory problems are far too common. 2012 models will be a more reliable buy even with their expected $500 increase. You may wish to wait for a diesel-equipped Cruze next year. It will likely be patterned after the Australian 2.0L 4-cylinder version and could boost gas mileage to around 4.7 L/100 km (50 mpg). This almost ties with Toyota's Prius gas/ electric hybrid ($27,800), which gets 4.6L/100 km (51 mpg) in the city and 4.9L/100 km (48 mpg) on the highway, according to tests run by the Washington-based Environmental Protection Agency. Cars with diesel engines generally cost more than those with gasoline engines. Volkswagen, for example, sells its diesel—a TDI (turbo diesel injected) four-door—for $2,400 more than its gasoline counterpart. The base version of the Cruze is $16,940; a diesel version would add about $2,000 to that figure. When these costs are added up, the Cruze diesel purchase price would be about $9,000 less than the Prius.

OWNER-REPORTED PROBLEMS: Steering wheel may separate from the steering assembly (2011 models recalled). Sudden, unintended acceleration, and the car sometimes lags when cruising. Owners say they have experienced chronic automatic transmission failures and malfunctions:

My 2011 Cruze was delivered Dec 1, 2010, in the middle of winter. Initially, I thought it was just the breaking-in period. After 3 months, I took it to a GM dealer and software for engine and transmissions were reloaded.

1 to 2 and 2 to 3 and sometimes 3 to 4 gears hesitate when engine is cold. Dealer rechecked and replaced transmission servo on my Cruze. Noticeable improvement. No more hesitation in shifting 1 to 2; hesitation in 2 to 3 and sometimes 3 to 4 remained.

Dealer rechecked. No code shows. I requested to test another Cruze on the dealer's lot after engine and transmission were re-calibrated. Their Cruze behaved the same way and no code showing. Dealer wrote a report to GM and refused to do any further work on my car, claiming it is GM's design.

I contacted GM Canada who suggested [I] try [to] have another dealer look into my issue. Even after Customer Care in Oshawa, Canada spoke to the dealers, two other dealers in my area also refused to even look at my car. Both claim other Cruzes on their lot behave the same. I have escalated my issue to next level at the GM Customer Care Center.

Besides complaints found on Internet Cruze forums, Washington safety officials at NHTSA have been alerted to serious manual and automatic transmission problems:

My new 2011 Chevy Cruze has a major hesitation when trying to accelerate the car. This problem occurs consistently all the time from Day 1. Brought the car in for service for this problem to the Chevy dealer where I purchased the car from and they said there is nothing they can do to correct this hesitation problem. This is dangerous when you need the speed to pass on the highway and you don't have it when the accelerator is pushed. I was told at the Chevy dealer that this car has six gears for a 4-cylinder engine. It needs a 6-cylinder engine to change these six gears properly. Why would GM Chevrolet design a car like this with this problem?

•

I am very disappointed with my new 2011 Chevy Cruze Eco (1.4L 6-speed manual transmission). The car loses power especially when I try to accelerate up hills, total loss of power and lack of response. This keeps happening out on the freeway. I have my foot pressed all the way down on the accelerator, but no response from the car. Car has slowed down to 30 mph [48 km/h] going up the hills on freeway putting me in an unsafe position. It happens on level surfaces too. Trying to get the car going when at a stop light is hard too. I give the car gas and get very slow response. When it does respond, the car is very jerky going thru the gears. Afraid this may cause an accident for failure to move out and with the traffic.

•

I bought a brand new 2011 Chevy Cruze LS. After about two weeks of driving the vehicle I notice that when driving it in manual and coming to a stop the car would violently shift into first gear. I took the car back to the dealership and they contacted GM. They also test drove every Chevy Cruze LS model and non-turbo engine Cruze they had in stock and found the same problem. They contacted GM again and GM informed them that they were aware of the problem with the LS and non-turbo engine models and that they do not have a solution to fix the problem. I then contacted GM and asked them about their 30-day guarantee on their vehicles. They then informed me that they do have that policy but unfortunately would not honor it because of my case. When I asked them what they planned to do about the problem they informed me that they will continue to sell the vehicle and recall them later when they are able to find a solution to fix the problem.

Other safety-related incidents reported to NHTSA include airbags that failed to deploy when they were needed, "spongy" brakes accompanied by a delayed response; power steering failures, and in one incident, the steering wheel came off in the driver's hand:

While driving my new 2011 Chevy Cruze on Highway 10 in Minnesota, without any warning or any other indications the steering wheel fell off in the hands of the driver. We crossed several lanes of traffic and finally got the car stopped just inches from hitting the guardrail.

SERVICE BULLETIN-REPORTED PROBLEMS: Free service campaign to lubricate the front strut assemblies (Service Bulletin No. 10381, issued November 19, 2010); water leak at right tail light (a free service campaign); and another free service campaign to replace the brake sensor; lack of power and engine rattling:

LACK OF POWER WITH DTCs OR RATTLE	
BULLETIN NO.: 10-06-04-016	DATE: DECEMBER 20, 2010

ENGINE LACK OF POWER WITH DTCs P0011, P0014, P000A, P000B, P0012, P0015 OR ENGINE RATTLE NOISE (REMOVE OIL FILTERS FROM INTAKE AND EXHAUST CAMSHAFT POSITION ACTUATOR SOLENOID VALVES)

2008–11 Chevrolet Aveo; 2011 Chevrolet Cruze (US and Canada); 2009–11 Chevrolet Cruze (Export Only); 2008–09 Pontiac G3, Wave; 2008–09 Saturn Astra

CONDITION: Some customers may comment on lack of power with DTCs or an engine rattle noise from the sprockets.

Another reason cause for the Cruze's loss of power may be electrical in nature, a problem affecting most of GM's car and truck lineup since 2005 (see bulletin on the following page). Drivetrain noise when shifting between Reverse and Drive is a common Cruze problem shared with a number of other GM models. The fix takes about an hour and is a warranty item (see bulletin on the following page).

INTERMITTENT MIL/DTC P2138/REDUCED POWER

BULLETIN NO.: 7-06-04-019D

DATE: JUNE 28, 2010

INTERMITTENT MALFUNCTION INDICATOR LAMP (MIL) ILLUMINATED, DTC P2138 WITH REDUCED ENGINE POWER (REPAIR INSTRUMENT PANEL (IP) TO BODY HARNESS CONNECTOR)

2005–11 GM Passenger Cars and Light Duty Trucks (Including Saturn); 2005–09 HUMMER H2; 2006–10 HUMMER H3; and the 2005–09 Saab 9-7X.

CAUSE: This condition may be caused by water intrusion into the instrument panel (IP) to body harness connector, which carries the APP sensor signals to the ECM/PCM. This water intrusion results in a voltage difference between APP Sensor 1 and APP Sensor 2 that exceeds a predetermined value for more than a calibrated period of time, setting P2138

DRIVETRAIN—NOISE SHIFTING BETWEEN REVERSE & DRIVE

BULLETIN NO.: 09-04-95-001C

DATE: OCTOBER 18, 2010

CLICKING TYPE NOISE FROM FRONT OR REAR OF VEHICLE WHEN SHIFTING BETWEEN REVERSE AND DRIVE OR ON HARD ACCELERATION (ADD WASHER TO WHEEL DRIVE SHAFT)

2010–11 Buick LaCrosse; 2011 Buick Regal; 2008–11; Cadillac CTS, CTS Wagon, Coupe (Includes V Series); 2010–11 Cadillac SRX; 2010 Chevrolet Camaro Built Prior to June 1, 2009; (V8 Engine (All) and V6 Engine (Manual)) or February 17, 2010 (V6 Engine (Automatic); 2010–11 Chevrolet Equinox; 2011 Chevrolet; Cruze; and 2010-2011 GMC Terrain.

MALIBU ★ ★ ★

RATING: Average. The Malibu's performance strengths are compromised by the car's so-so reliability. **Strong points:** Good V6 powertrain set-up. Well-appointed; provides a comfortable though firm ride; better-than-average handling thanks to an independent suspension. Plenty of passenger and luggage space, and few squeaks and rattles. NHTSA gives the Malibu a five-star crashworthiness score for side protection and four stars for frontal crash protection and rollover resistance. IIHS says frontal offset, side, rear, and roof crash protection is "Good," as is standard stability control. **Weak points:** Expect lots of powertrain and brake problems. The base 4-cylinder engine with the automatic transmission is barely adequate for highway driving and a full load. The car, despite its restyling, still seems to be more plastic than metal. Rear head restraints block visibility and there is a serious blind spot when looking out the passenger rearview mirror. IIHS gives the Malibu a "Marginal" rating for head-restraint effectiveness. **New for 2012:** Restyled and set on GM's new Epsilon II platform, shared with the Buick Regal and LaCrosse. The platform change makes the Malibu slightly wider and a little taller, thereby creating a roomier interior. The interior will also be restyled with better access to instruments and controls and will use higher-grade materials.

OVERVIEW: The Malibu is a popular front-drive, mid-sized sedan distinguished by its nice array of standard features. The base Malibu is "powered" (if you can call it that) by GM's wimpy 169 hp 2.4L 4-cylinder powerplant, found on many of its compact cars. Most buyers will be tempted to pay extra for the torquier and smoother 252 hp 3.6L V6.

KEY FACTS

CANADIAN PRICE (VERY NEGOTIABLE): *LS:* $26,040, *LT:* $28,390, *Platinum:* $30,040, *LTZ:* $35,040 **U.S. PRICE:** *LS:* $21,975, *1LT:* $22,975, *2LT:* $25,385, *LTZ:* $27,165 **CANADIAN FREIGHT, DEALER FEES, AND AC TAX:** $2,045 (This is price gouging. Pay half of the freight charge, nothing for "dealer fees," and $100 for the AC tax.) **U.S. FREIGHT:** $720 **POWERTRAIN (FRONT-DRIVE)** Engines: 2.4L 4-cyl. (169 hp) • 3.6L V6 (252 hp); Transmissions: 4-speed auto. • 6-speed auto. **DIMENSIONS/CAPACITY** Passengers: 2/3; Wheelbase: 112.3 in.; H: 57/L: 191.8/W: 70.3 in.; Headroom F/R: 4.0/2.0 in., 5.0/4.5 in.; Legroom F/R: 41.5/30.0 in.; Cargo volume: 15.1 cu. ft.; Fuel tank: 61L/regular; Tow limit: 1,000 lb.; Load capacity: 915 lb.; Turning circle: 42 ft.; Ground clearance: 5.0 ft.; Weight: 3,460 lb.

The Malibu's styling is quite conservative and uncluttered. A fold-flat passenger seat and a 60/40-split rear folding bench seat maximize the interior room. Other useful standard amenities include a driver-seat power height adjuster; a telescoping steering column that also tilts; power windows, door locks, and outside mirrors; and power-adjustable brake and accelerator pedals (LS and LT).

COST ANALYSIS: The 6-speed automatic is worth the extra cost and the 2012 model has enough improvements over the 2011 version to merit its slightly higher price.

Best alternatives: The Honda Accord has more usable interior space, is super reliable, and has quicker and more-accurate steering; Hyundai's Elantra is cheaper and just as well put together and the costlier Sonata is still worth considering; and Toyota's Camry is plusher, though not as driver-oriented. Other cars worth considering are the Mazda3 and Mazda6, and Nissan Sentra. **Options:** The V6 and premium tires. **Rebates:** $1,000 rebates should kick in sometime during the new year. **Depreciation:** Average. **Insurance cost:** Higher than average. **Parts supply/cost:** Malibu uses generic GM parts that are usually easy to find and reasonably priced. However, since the company came out of bankruptcy, parts are often back-ordered for weeks at a time. **Annual maintenance cost:** Average.

Warranty: 60-day money-back guarantee as long as you don't drive more than 4,000 km. Bumper-to-bumper 3 years/60,000 km; powertrain 5 years/160,000 km; rust perforation 6 years/160,000 km. **Supplementary warranty:** An extended powertrain warranty would be a wise investment. **Highway/city fuel economy:** *2.4L:* 6.5/9.5 L/100 km, 43/30 mpg. *2.4L 6-speed:* 5.9/9.4 L/100 km, 48/30 mpg. *V6:* 7.8/12.2 L/100 km, 36/23 mpg.

OWNER-REPORTED PROBLEMS: At the top of the list are engine and transmission failures resulting in the sudden loss of power and the automatic transmission going into "limp" mode:

> I was accelerating from the entry lane of a mostly empty (thankfully) rural highway when suddenly a warning message Service Traction Engine Power Reduced Service ESC appeared on the dash monitor. I lost power and could not get above 45 mph [72 km/h]. The transmission appeared to be locked into a gear level. I contacted Chevy and they told me it is a safety feature. Here's the problem: if I had been doing a high speed merge on a major highway the power loss could have caused an accident not to mention getting me killed. I think the feature is engineered into the software that controls the engine/transmission. A detected fault triggers the action. Incidentally, there was no prior notice, warning lights, etc., that would have indicated a problem. The lack of notice exacerbates the danger.

Electrical system glitches (door locks that open and close randomly, for example); frequent replacement of brake and suspension components; AC malfunctions; very poor fit and finish; poorly designed head restraints that produce a painful chin-to-chest driving position. Safety-related complaints include an engine compartment fire while the car was parked; airbags that deploy inadvertently or fail to deploy; and faulty airbag modules. Park gear won't hold the vehicle parked on a hill; the 6-speed transmission hesitates before shifting; the vehicle has a tendency to wander to the left side of the road into oncoming traffic; door locks cannot be disabled to extricate an accident victim; sudden brake loss; premature warpage of the brake rotors; very loose steering; steering loss; sudden steering lock-up; chronic steering shimmy; frequent stalling for unexplained reasons; cruise control doesn't hold the set speed and may cause the car to suddenly accelerate with a wide-open throttle; original-equipment tires don't have gripping power and fail prematurely; severe glare from the dash onto the windshield; and inaccurate fuel gauges.

SERVICE BULLETIN-REPORTED PROBLEMS: Intermittent reduced power; brake rotor noise and pulsation; a guide to various electrical malfunctions; inoperative low-beam headlights; and water leaks onto front and rear passenger floor.

IMPALA, LACROSSE ★★

The Chevrolet Impala.

RATING: Below Average. **Strong points:** *Impala:* Comes with an array of standard features, provides a comfortable ride, and has an easily accessed interior, highlighted by a convenient flip-down centre console in the middle of the bench seats and rear seatbacks that fold flat, opening up cargo storage space. NHTSA gave the Impala a five-star crashworthiness rating for front and side protection and four stars for rollover resistance. IIHS scored front, side, and rear crashworthiness as "Good," while roof strength and rear crash protection (head restraints) was judged to be "Acceptable." *LaCrosse:* The 3.0L V6 provides smooth acceleration and works well with the 6-speed automatic transmission, though it could use more high-speed torque. Handling and ride are better than average, owing to recent suspension and steering refinements. For extended highway use, you'll find the 3.6L powerplant is better suited to your needs. Adequate rear legroom and a front bench seat. A much better reliability record than the Impala. Like the Impala, the LaCrosse got five stars for front and side crashes, and four stars for rollover resistance. IIHS scored front, side, roof, and rear crashworthiness as "Good." Stability control is a standard LTZ feature. **Weak points:** *Impala:* The automatic 4-speed transmission is sometimes slow to downshift, and the Overdrive is clunky; this is a car that cries out for a 6-speed automatic

KEY FACTS

CANADIAN PRICE (VERY NEGOTIABLE): *Impala LS:* $29,370, *LT:* $30,350, *LTZ:* $32,700, *LaCrosse CX:* $31,645, *CX V6:* $32,795, *CXL:* $34,795, *AWD:* $38,245, *CXS:* $40,795 **U.S. PRICE:** *Impala LS:* $24,495, *LT:* $25,710, *LTZ:* $30,035, *LaCrosse CX:* $26,490, *CXL:* $29,050, *CXS:* $33,260 **CANADIAN FREIGHT, DEALER FEES, AND AC TAX:** $2,045 (Pay half of the freight charge, nothing for "dealer fees," and $100 for the AC tax.) **U.S. FREIGHT:** $750

POWERTRAIN (FRONT-DRIVE/AWD)
Engines: *Impala:* 3.5L V6 (207 hp) • 3.6L V6 (302 hp) • 3.9L V6 (230 hp) • 5.3L V8 (303 hp), *LaCrosse:* 2.4L 4-cyl. (182 hp) • 3.0L V6 (255 hp) • 3.6L V6 (280 hp); Transmissions: *Impala:* 4-speed auto., *LaCrosse:* 6-speed auto.

DIMENSIONS/CAPACITY
Passengers: 2/3; Wheelbase: *Impala:* 110.5 in., *LaCrosse:* 111.7 in.; *Impala:* H: 58.7/L: 200.4/W: 72.9 in.; *LaCrosse:* H: 58.9/L: 197.0/W: 73.1 in.; Headroom F/R: 4.0/1.5 in.; Legroom F/R: *Impala:* 40.5/26 in.; Fuel tank: 64L/regular/premium; Cargo volume: 16 cu. ft.; Tow limit: 1,000 lb.; Load capacity: *Impala:* 945 lb., *LaCrosse:* 915 lb.; Turning circle: *Impala:* 41.0 ft., *LaCrosse:* 38.8 ft.; Ground clearance: *Impala:* 6.0 in.; Weight: *Impala LS, LT:* 3,555 lb., *LTZ:* 3,649 lb., *LaCrosse CX:* 3,948 lb.

gearbox. Rear seating is uncomfortable for three, and obstructs rear visibility due to the tall, wide rear-seat head restraints:

> I cannot see when using the rear view mirror due to the reduced visibility caused by the head rests on the rear seats. The view when using the rear view mirror is obstructed significantly with only 4 inches of visibility between the ceiling of the car and the top of the head rests. Also, the side mirrors are small increasing the poor visibility in this vehicle. The head rests problem would have been noticed if the car salesman had not sat in backseat in the middle. The car dealership suggested that the car be taken to a local seat cover company to have the headrests rebuilt. This is a new car and should not have problems such as this.

Engine and transmission deficiencies have been commonplace. Bland styling; subpar body construction is evidenced by poorly aligned doors and a constant chorus of squeaks, rattles, and clunks when cruising. **New for 2012:** The 2012 Impala and LaCrosse will offer GM's revised 3.6L V6 and a 6-speed automatic as standard fare. According to GM's 2012 order guide the new engine will produce 302 horsepower. The new ratings make the 2012 Impala almost as powerful as the discontinued Impala SS model.

OVERVIEW: Impala is one of GM's least-competitive products and should have been culled from the herd years ago. Keeping the Impala without major upgrades (no, a 302 hp V6 and 6-speed tranny aren't enough) weakens the Chevrolet brand and gives Ford's Fusion and Chrysler's 200 a boost. With the V8 option gone, the car is overwhelmed by its unimpressive highway performance and overall lack of quality. It will soldier on until 2014 without any significant changes. Everyone agrees that GM has given up on large front-drive sedans as a competitive volume product, and is relying instead on crossovers and downsized SUVs to take up the slack.

This year's better-performing powertrain with cylinder deactivation is an important upgrade, but it should have been offered a decade ago; it may have arrived too late to save the nameplate.

Anyone who wants a remotely competitive full-sized GM sedan will have to look at one of GM's luxury brands and dig much deeper into their wallet. Specifically, they will have to look at Buick or Cadillac's flagships, the LaCrosse or the XTS.

Two years ago, the mid-sized LaCrosse was completely restyled, and its four-wheel independent suspension was retuned to improve the ride and handling. The available all-wheel-drive system employs a limited-slip differential to send torque to whichever wheel has more traction for better control on slippery roads.

COST ANALYSIS: 2011 Impala and LaCrosse models are discounted about 10 percent and are practically identical to the 2012s. **Best alternatives:** The more-reliable, better-performing Honda Accord, Mazda6, Hyundai Elantra, and Toyota Camry or Avalon. Those wanting a bit more performance should consider the BMW 3 Series. More room and better performance can be had by purchasing a Hyundai Tucson or a Honda CR-V. **Options:** Pass on the Impala's rear spoiler, which obstructs rear visibility and is of doubtful utility. **Rebates:** *Impala:* The Impala is in a marketing segment that's steadily losing ground to Japanese entries. The longer you wait, the cheaper these cars will become. Look for the return of $2,000 rebates on Impalas throughout 2012. *LaCrosse:* Its recent redesign has created some buying buzz and this has kept the price higher than it should be; GM will reinstate $500 rabates throughout the year. **Depreciation:** *Impala:* Incredibly fast; a 2007 Impala LS that sold new for $25,230 is now worth only $9,500. *LaCrosse:* Again, depreciation is a big minus. A 2007 LaCrosse (which was called the Allure from 2005–09) CX that sold for $26,395 is now worth $10,500. **Insurance cost:** Higher than average. **Parts supply/cost:** Moderately priced parts that aren't hard to find. **Annual maintenance cost:** Higher than average. Independent garages can perform most non-emissions servicing; however, cylinder deactivation makes you a prisoner of GM dealer servicing. **Warranty:** 60-day money-back guarantee as long as you don't drive more than 4,000 km. Bumper-to-bumper 4 years/80,000 km; powertrain 5 years/160,000 km; rust perforation 6 years/160,000 km. **Supplementary warranty:** Essential, especially after the third year of ownership. Get an extended powertrain warranty to protect you from the usual GM engine and transmission problems. **Highway/city fuel economy:** *Impala* 3.5L: 6.7/10.8 L/100 km, 42/26 mpg. 3.9L: 7.4/12.0 L/100 km, 38/24 mpg. *LaCrosse* 2.4L: 6.5/10.8 L/100 km, 43/26 mpg. 3.6L: 7.3/12.2 L/100 km, 39/23 mpg. *AWD 3.6L:* 7.7/12.7 L/100 km, 37/22 mpg.

OWNER-REPORTED PROBLEMS: Electrical system failures. The airbag is disabled when an average-sized occupant sits in the passenger seat. Front and rear brakes rust easily and wear out early, and the discs warp far too often. Shock absorbers and MacPherson struts wear out or leak prematurely. The power rack-and-pinion steering system degenerates quickly after three years and is characterized by chronic leaking. Poor body fit, particularly around the doors, leads to excessive wind noise and water leaking into the interior. *Impala:* Airbag failures; chronic stalling; engine sputters, hesitates; driver-side wheel falls off; vehicle jerks when passing over rough pavement; car rolls back at a stop; excessive front-end vibration; brake rotors on one vehicle had to be replaced at 7,500 km; popping sound on stopping, starting, and turning; left and right control-arm, lower control-arm, ball joint, and steering failures; and a poorly designed Reverse lighting feature. *LaCrosse:* Driver-side airbag deployed inadvertently, causing an accident; chronic stalling; intermittent brake failure; broken rear tie-rod bolt:

> I was driving our Buick LaCrosse with 3036 miles on it, at 58 mph [93 km/h], when the wheel began to jerk back & forth violently. I was skidding down the road unable to steer. I was able to get to the side of the road and eventually have the car towed in. The right rear tie rod bolt had broken. When this happened the suspension control arm was bent. Both parts have been replaced.

A similar suspension steering failure was reported by this LaCrosse owner:

We bought a new 2011 Buick LaCrosse CXS 11-15-10, drive it 200 miles [320 km] and the front suspension failed in Costco parking lot at 10 mph [16 km/h] and no impact. The rim popped open at the center seam creating a big oval opening that locked up on the brake caliper, stopping the wheel, which snapped the tie rod end, letting the tire wedge into the inner fender then the A-arm bent and caused some damage to the engine cradle. My wife cracked her head on the side window it went down so fast. The General Motors engineer came to investigate the incident, found no impact damage, but refused to discuss the structural failure of the left front suspension. The tire shows no impact bruises and the rim has no damage except for a small chunk on the inside of the rim where the steering ram popped the rim when it locked into the inter fender. My point: if this happened at highway speed it would have caused a major accident. The rim started this chain reaction, but at such a minor speed the suspension should not have failed. I was told that this is a new suspension for the 2011 CXS Sport model. Please look into this. I do not want to risk my family's safety when I feel uncomfortable with the structural integrity of this new suspension and have asked for a refund.

Glass moonroof suddenly exploded:

Moonroof front glass of my 2011 Buick LaCrosse exploded outward while traveling 60 mph [97 km/h] on interstate. Sounded like a gun going off. Climate control was on "Auto".

Vehicle wanders all over the road; automatic transmission suddenly pops out of gear:

The car "dropped" from Drive into Neutral every time I accelerated from a turn into traffic. This problem was demonstrated to the dealer; dealer said park it now. Question is how many Buicks were manufactured with this very dangerous defect. The 2 times this happened, prior to knowledge of the/a problem, if I had not been able to return to "Drive" and proceed with maximum acceleration, we would have been unquestionably hit by approaching cars.

Brake pad, caliper, and rotor failures; distracting mirror reflection where the speedometer and tachometer are reflected through the driver-side window out onto the side mirror when driving at night; memory seat recall malfunctions; incorrect driver's manual instructions:

The manual described the method to move the transmission lever from Park to Neutral without starting the engine, for the purpose of towing the vehicle or moving it without starting the engine if the battery was dead or the engine will not start for any other reason. The manual stated to set the parking brake, which cannot be done if the battery is dead because the parking brake is electrically operated.

SERVICE BULLETIN-REPORTED PROBLEMS: Intermittent reduced power; clicking, ticking noises on cold startup are part of the fuel pump's normal operation; noisy shifting between Reverse and Drive; loose driver/passenger windshield pillar moulding; and increased rpms when shifting.

RATING: Below Average. The rating has been lowered this year because the Lucerne has been dropped by GM. The car hasn't sold in large volume, and its mechanicals are relatively complex. Owners therefore can expect to pay multiple visits to the service bay to see if back-ordered parts have arrived and if the problem was finally fixed. **Strong points:** A nice array of useful standard equipment at an affordable base price, but costs go up quickly as the options grow. Good V8 powertrain performance. The electronic 4-speed transmission works imperceptibly, but it exacts a high fuel penalty. Cruise control is much smoother without all those annoying downshifts we've learned to hate in GM cars. Handling is acceptably predictable, though a bit slow with variable-assist power steering. A comfortable ride and a plush interior; quiet-running; plenty of passenger and cargo room. NHTSA gave the Lucerne its top, five-star rating for front crash protection and rollover resistance; IIHS says the car's frontal offset crash protection is "Good" and side protection is "Acceptable." **Weak points:** GM isn't serious with this model: Giving the "Super" version a powerful Cadillac Northstar–derived V8 and then hooking it to a rudimentary 4-speed automatic is worse than taking a shower in a raincoat. Acceleration isn't breathtaking with the base V6 either; at higher revs, torque falls off quickly. The V8 tends to fishtail when at full throttle. Power steering is a bit vague at highway speeds; ponderous handling caused partly by a mediocre suspension and over-assisted steering; and panic braking causes

KEY FACTS

CANADIAN PRICE (VERY NEGOTIABLE):
CX: $36,035 *CXL:* $38,775, *Premium:* $43,800, *Super:* $57,315 **U.S. PRICE:** *CX:* $27,995, *CXL:* $31,395, *Premium:* $33,940, *Super:* $43,720 **CANADIAN FREIGHT, DEALER FEES, AND AC TAX:** $2,045 (Pay half of the freight charge, nothing for "dealer fees," and $100 for the AC tax.) **U.S. FREIGHT:** $750 **POWERTRAIN (FRONT-DRIVE)** Engines: 3.9L V6 (227 hp) • 4.6L V8 (292 hp); Transmission: 4-speed auto.

DIMENSIONS/CAPACITY
Passengers: 2/3; Wheelbase: 114.8 in.; H: 58/L: 203/W: 74 in.; Headroom F/R: 3.0/2.5 in.; Legroom F/R: 42.5/31.5 in.; Cargo volume: 17 cu. ft.; Fuel tank: 70L/ regular; Load capacity: 925 lb.; Tow limit: 1,000 lb.; Turning circle: 47 ft.; Ground clearance: 5.0 in.; Weight: 4,095 lb.

considerable nose-diving, which also compromises handling. Fuel-thirsty; poor-quality mechanical and body components; obstructed front and rear visibility. Following NHTSA tests, side crashworthiness scored a disappointing two stars out of five and IIHS gives a "Marginal" rating for head-restraint effectiveness. **New for 2012:** Nothing significant.

OVERVIEW: Buick's Lucerne was a good idea discarded early when sales waned; 2011 was its last model year. It is a competent front-drive family car that replaced the LeSabre and Park Avenue in 2006. Though not a very fuel-efficient four-door sedan, its generous discounting will give you plenty of change in your pockets to buy the extra gas. Clean body lines and a large platform make for an aerodynamic, pleasing appearance and a roomy interior with more rear seatroom than the LaCrosse. The standard 3.9L V6 is rough-running and noisy when pushed. CXS models are powered by a high-performance V8, which offers much better low- and mid-range throttle response.

COST ANALYSIS: Get a 25 percent discount on the end-of-run 2011 model. **Best alternatives:** Ford Taurus, Hyundai Genesis Coupe, and Lexus ES series. **Options:** Go for the more-powerful V8. **Rebates:** Look for big rebates and discounts of $4,000–$5,000+ as this car ends its days. **Depreciation:** Faster than average. **Insurance cost:** Higher than average. **Parts supply/cost:** Parts aren't hard to find, but they can be pricey. **Annual maintenance cost:** Average. **Warranty:** 60-day money-back guarantee as long as you don't drive more than 4,000 km. Bumper-to-bumper 4 years/80,000 km; powertrain 5 years/160,000 km; rust perforation 6 years/160,000 km. **Supplementary warranty:** An extended powertrain warranty will come in handy. **Highway/city fuel economy:** 3.9L V6: 7.4/12.0 L/100 km, 38/24 mpg. 4.6L V8: 8.7/13.8 L/100 km, 32/20 mpg.

OWNER-REPORTED PROBLEMS: Below-average quality. Owners single out the brakes, suspension, and fit and finish as the most troublesome areas. No airbag deployment; cruise control causes the vehicle to surge; steering linkage bolts detach, causing steering failure; speedometer and fuel gauges can't be read in daylight; the driver-side mirror doesn't give a clear view to the rear; side mirrors fog up; front pillars create a blind spot; and the fuel gauge gives inaccurate readings. Safety-related complaints logged by NHTSA include sudden, unintended acceleration while parking; low-beam headlights that switch to high-beams and won't return to low; door stoppers that don't hold the door open on a moderate incline; and a navigation system that can't be seen when the gear shift is in Drive:

> You have to take your eyes off the road and turn your body towards center of car to see the directions for navigation and also to see dials on radio. Wrote a letter to CEO of GM in Jan. 2010. At first, they said it was [because of] my stature that I could not see navigation nor radio (am 4'9") and that if I wanted to rectify this situation, I would have to pay $800 for a different radio. Since then, I went to the dealer and had the car test driven by the service manager. I have a work order confirming this. Results: no one can see the navigation system in the drive position. Called GM—was angry, as they lied to me. They now admit that this is a problem.

SERVICE BULLETIN-REPORTED PROBLEMS: Drivetrain clunk noise; brake pulsations/noise; poor radio reception; shock absorber strut leakage; tires slowly go flat; and side window chipping.

CAMARO ★★★★

RATING: Above Average going into its third year on the market. **Strong points:** Impressive V6 and V8 acceleration with reasonable fuel economy and nice steering/handling. Interior trim looks and feels to be of better quality and the seats provide good lateral support and are easy to adjust. Very few serious reliability complaints since the 2010 factory glitches were fixed. NHTSA awarded the Camaro four stars for frontal and side crashworthiness and five stars for rollover resistance. **Weak points:** No headroom; if you are 6'2" or taller, your head will be constantly brushing up against the headliner; rear seating is a "knees-to-chin" affair; not much cargo room; small trunk and trunk opening. Owners report that fit and finish glitches are everywhere; exterior styling seems to have been slapped together by a committee; the rear, especially, is ugly and obstructs rear visibility; plus, the car is set too high to look "sporty." IIHS hasn't yet crash-tested the Camaro. **New for 2012:** A more powerful, better-performing, and restyled ZL1 arrives this year. It will carry an estimated 550 hp 6.2L supercharged V8 hooked to a Tremec TR-6060 6-speed manual transmission. GM includes a stronger driveshaft, rear axles, rear differential housing, and limited-slip differential. GM has added a new suspension system (called Magnetic Ride Control) and aluminum wheels, electric power steering, upgraded rear stabilizer bars, and more-effective Brembo brakes.

OVERVIEW: The 2011–12 Chevrolet Camaro continues to breathe life into General Motors' iconic high-performance two-door coupe and convertible pony car. This year we see the return of the, LS, 1LT, 2LT, 1SS, and 2SS models offered with either

KEY FACTS

CANADIAN PRICE (VERY NEGOTIABLE): *LS man.:* $26,995, *1LT man.:* $28,065, *2LT man.:* $32,505, *1LT Conv.:* $29,275, *2LT Conv.:* $32,775, *1SS man.:* $37,065, *2SS auto.:* $41,905, *1SS Conv.:* $36,775, *2SS Conv.:* $39,775 **U.S. PRICE:** *LS man.:* $23,200, *2LS man.:* $24,400, *1LT man.:* $25,200, *2LT man.:* $28,350, *1SS:* $31,850, *2SS:* $35,450, *1LT Conv.:* $30,150, *2LT Conv.:* $34,100, *1SS Conv.:* $37,900, *2SS Conv.:* $40,600, *ZL1:* $47,000 (est.) **CANADIAN FREIGHT, DEALER FEES, AND AC TAX:** $2,045 (Cut the freight charge in half, pay nothing for "dealer fees," and hand over $100 for the AC tax.) **U.S. FREIGHT:** $900 **POWERTRAIN (REAR-DRIVE)** Engines: 3.6L V6 (312 hp) • 6.2L V8 (400–426 hp) • 6.2L supercharged V8 (550 hp); Transmissions: 6-speed man. • 6-speed auto. **DIMENSIONS/CAPACITY** Passengers: 2/2; Wheelbase: 112.3 in.; H: 54.2/L: 190.4/W: 75.5 in.; Cargo volume: 11.3 cu. ft.; Fuel tank: 71.9L/ regular; Tow limit: No towing; Turning circle: 37.7 ft.; Weight: 3,769–3,849 lb.

a base 304 hp 3.6L V6 or an optional V8. The 1SS and 2SS come with a manual transmission hooked to a 426 hp 6.2L V8; automatic-equipped versions get the same V8, but harness "only" 400 hp and GM's Active Fuel Management cylinder deactivation. Available safety features include ABS, traction control, an anti-skid system, front side airbags, and side curtain airbags.

COST ANALYSIS: Camaros are "hot," and this year's sales have beaten the equally popular Ford Mustang by a small margin. This means there will be no bargains; dealers can ask for (and get) the full suggested retail price. Smart buyers will wait on the more reasonably priced, second-series model due out in the spring of 2012. **Best alternatives:** The Ford Mustang and Hyundai Genesis Coupe. Ford's Mustang Shelby GT500 competes against the Camaro ZL1. The base Camaro is no longer in the running against the 305 hp V6-equipped Mustang. When you compare V8s, the Mustang GT is the clear winner where price is concerned; at over $50,000 the high-performance Camaro variants are way overpriced. Normally, the Dodge Challenger would also be a "challenger," but it doesn't have the power to compete. **Options:** Buying the GPS navigation aids, special wheels, and Xenon headlights from independent retailers can save you thousands, but don't waste your money on the power sunroof, leather upholstery, or heated seats. And don't let the dealer sell you poorly performing original-equipment summer tires. **Rebates:** Rebates and discounts of only $1,000–$2,000 because the Camaro is still seen as a "hot" American-built sports car. **Depreciation:** Very slow. A 2010 base model that sold for $26,995 is now worth $21,500. Not much lost for a year's use. **Insurance cost:** Much higher than average. **Parts supply/ cost:** Not easily found and quite costly. At present, dealers have a monopoly on parts and service. **Annual maintenance cost:** Higher than average; there's no competition. **Warranty:** 60-day money-back guarantee as long as you don't drive more than 4,000 km. Bumper-to-bumper 4 years/80,000 km; powertrain 5 years/160,000 km; rust perforation 6 years/unlimited km. **Supplementary warranty:** An extended powertrain warranty is a good idea, considering that the Camaro is going into only its third year on the market. **Highway/city fuel economy:** *3.6L V6:* 7.1/12.4 L/100 km, 40/23 mpg. *Auto.:* 6.6/11.2 L/100 km, 43/25 mpg. *SS man. and 6.2L V8:* 8.2/13.2 L/100 km, 34/21 mpg. *Auto.:* 8.0/13.3 L/100 km, 35/21 mpg.

OWNER-REPORTED PROBLEMS: Very few complaints have been reported, and GM's internal service bulletins are relatively clean of references to major component failures, except for engine oil leaks, on almost its entire 2003–2011 vehicle lineup. GM also offers a free transmission fix on V8-equipped models. Says GM:

> This free service procedure will replace the three torque converter bolts and modify a transmission dust cover on **some** 2011 model year vehicles equipped with the 6.2L V8 SFI engine and automatic transmission (RPO MYC). A small number of these vehicles were produced with torque converter bolts that do not provide adequate thread engagement with the new two piece flywheel. If a bolt loosened, a clanking noise may be noticeable.

Valve lifter ticking has also been a problem affecting V8-equipped Camaros and a host of GM's other vehicles:

ENGINE—VALVE LIFTER TICK NOISE AT START UP

BULLETIN NO.: 10-06-01-007B   DATE: NOVEMBER 17, 2010

ACTIVE FUEL MANAGEMENT (AFM) ENGINE, VALVE LIFTER TICK NOISE AT START UP WHEN ENGINE HAS BEEN OFF FOR 2 HOURS OR MORE (EVALUATE NOISE AND/OR REPLACE VALVE LIFTERS)

2007 Buick Rainier

2009 Buick LaCrosse Super, Allure Super (Canada Only)

2007 Cadillac Escalade
    Built Prior to April 1, 2006 with 6.2L Engine RPO L92 (These engines were built with AFM Hardware but the AFM system was disabled)

2010–11 Cadillac Escalade

2007 Chevrolet Monte Carlo

2007–09 Chevrolet Impala

2007–11 Chevrolet Avalanche, Silverado, Suburban, Tahoe, TrailBlazer

2010–11 Chevrolet Camaro SS

2007–11 GMC Envoy, Sierra, Yukon

2007–08 Pontiac Grand Prix

2008–09 Pontiac G8

2007–09 Saab 9-7X
    Equipped with AFM (Active Fuel Management) and V8 Engine RPO L76, L94, L99, LC9, LFA, LH6, LMG, LS4, LY5 or LZ1

A few owner reports have surfaced relative to the convertible top not working due to an electrical short-circuit; the passenger-side airbag may be disabled due to a faulty sensor whenever an average-sized adult is seated; there may be excessive steering vibration when cruising; and many cars were sold with inadequate summer tires:

> The tires on my 2011 Chevy Camaro (and other models) are Perelli P-Zero tires which are "summer" tires as indicated by the manufacturers. These tires are not recommended for near freezing temps. The auto manufacturer failed to inform me the tires (which are stock) are only recommended for warm weather. I believe the manufacturer has not informed most customers of the situation. My research indicates these tires these tires exhibit more problems with handling in cold temps as tire wear increases. The manufacturer of the auto has indicated to me that their engineers are confident these tires are safe, but the tire manufacturer continues to recommend against using these tires in near freezing temps. As most of the continental USA is

exposed to near freezing and below freezing temps, I am concerned these tires will result in crashes which could be avoided if the auto manufacturer provided proper tires for our climate. This is a problem which may go unnoticed as most accidents go un-investigated or an investigator will not consider the temps were near or below freezing at the time of the accident.

•

2011 Camaro tires do not grip the road properly & low temperatures like here in N.Y. during the winter months. I just purchased this vehicle & at no point was I told that the tires are for summer use only. This is my only vehicle & has to be used all year round. I did not think spending top dollar for a performance vehicle was going to mean that I could only operate it safely 8 months out of the year? This vehicle was shipped to NY, to be sold in NY! Why would this happen? The tires cannot be trusted & I fear it will cause someone their life.

Although the Camaro hasn't been on the road long enough to get reliable failure rates on its various components, one group of owners and Camaro enthusiasts at *www.camaro5.com/forums/index.php* prepared a table of defects seen with the first-year 2010 models.

SERVICE BULLETIN-REPORTED PROBLEMS: Engine oil leaks from the rear engine cover; intermittent power loss; engine moan/growl/groan/whine; drivetrain clunk noise or rear clicking sound; power front seat noise when moving the seat forward; GM says fuel system clicking or ticking is normal; trunk lid binds; tires go flat; and rear bumper paint peeling.

CORVETTE ★★★

RATING: Average; a brawny, bulky sport coupe that's slowly evolving into a more-refined machine. But quality control continues to be subpar, and safety-related transmission and body deficiencies are common. The Corvette does deliver high-performance thrills—along with suspension kickback, numb steering, and seats that need extra bolstering. Overall, get the quieter and less temperamental base Corvette; it delivers the same cachet for a lot less money. **Strong points:** Powerful and smooth powertrain that responds quickly to the throttle; the 6-speed gearbox performs well in all gear ranges and makes shifting smooth, with short throws and easy entry into all gears. Easy handling; enhanced side-slip angle control helps to prevent skidding and provides better traction control. No oversteer, wheel spinning, breakaway rear ends, or nasty surprises, thanks partly to standard electronic stability control. Better-than-average braking; the ABS-vented disc brakes are easy to modulate, and they're fade-free. The car has a relatively roomy interior, user-friendly instruments and controls, and lots of convenience features. There's a key-controlled lockout feature that discourages joy riding by cutting engine power in half. All Corvettes are also equipped with an impressively effective PassKey theft-deterrent system that uses a resistor pellet in the ignition to disable the starter and fuel system when the key code doesn't match the ignition lock. All models come with standard side airbags and revised interiors. Convertibles get a trunk spoiler, and cars equipped with manual transmissions get a Performance Traction Management system that modulates the engine's torque output for fast starts. This feature also manages engine power when the driver floors the accelerator when coming out of a corner. **Weak points:** Vague steering; limited rear visibility; inadequate storage space; poor-quality powertrain; mediocre fit and finish; cabin amenities and materials that are not up to the competition's standards; and no crashworthiness or rollover data available from NHTSA or IIHS. The Corvette's sophisticated electronic and powertrain components have low tolerance for real-world conditions. The car is so low that its front air dam scrapes over the smallest rise in the road. Expect lots of visits to the body shop. **New for 2012:** Nothing to take to the races.

OVERVIEW: Standard models come with a 430 hp 6.0L V8 mated to a 6-speed manual or optional automatic transmission; keyless access with push-button start; large tires and wheels (18-inch front, 19-inch rear); HID xenon lighting; power hatch pull-down; heated seats; and an AM/FM/CD/MP3 player with seven speakers and in-dash six-CD changer.

KEY FACTS

CANADIAN PRICE (VERY NEGOTIABLE): *Base Coupe:* $67,135, *Grand Sport:* $74,960, *Convertible:* $77,040, *Grand Sport Convertible:* $83,740, *Z06:* $95,705, *ZR1:* $128,600 **U.S. PRICE:** *Base Coupe 1LT:* $49,045, *2LT:* $50,240, *3LT:* $53,250, *4LT:* $56,750, *Grand Sport 1LT:* $55,045, *2LT:* $56,240, *3LT:* $59,250, *4LT:* $62,750, *Z06 1LZ:* $74,375, *2LZ:* $77,040, *3LZ:* $81,545, *Convertible 1LT:* $54,045, *2LT:* $57,235, *3LT:* $60,245, *4LT:* $63,745, *ZR1 1ZR:* $111,600, *3ZR:* $111,600 **CANADIAN FREIGHT, DEALER FEES, AND AC TAX:** $2,145 (Pay half of the freight charge, nothing for "dealer fees," and $100 for the AC tax.) **U.S. FREIGHT:** $950 **POWERTRAIN (REAR-DRIVE)** Engines: 6.2L V8 (430 hp) • 7.0L V8 (505 hp) • 6.2L V8 Supercharged (638 hp); Transmissions: 6-speed man. • 6-speed auto.

DIMENSIONS/CAPACITY
Passengers: 2; Wheelbase: 106 in.; H: 49/L: 175/W: 73 in.; Headroom: 4 in.; Legroom: 41 in.; Cargo volume: 11 cu. ft.; Fuel tank: 68.1L/premium; Tow limit: Not recommended; Load capacity: 390 lb.; Turning circle: 42 ft.; Ground clearance: 4.5 in.; Weight: 3,280 lb.

Z06

Although not quite as fast as the Dodge Viper, this is the fastest model found in the Corvette lineup (0–100 km/h in 3.6–4.2 seconds). It's also the lightest Z06 yet, thanks to the magic of Detroit re-engineering. Instead of just adding iron and components to carry extra weight, GM has reinforced the rear axle and 6-speed clutch; installed coolers everywhere; adopted a dry-sump oil system to keep the engine well oiled when cornering; and added wider wheels and larger, heat-dissipating brakes. These improvements added about 50 kg of weight, which was trimmed by using cast-magnesium in the chassis structure and installing lighter carbon-fibre floorboards and front fenders. Net result: a monster Vette that is rated for 300+ km/h and weighs less than the base model.

To be honest, the Z06 chassis isn't very communicative to the driver, so the car doesn't inspire as much driving confidence as does the European competition, although it does feature standard stability control for when you get too frisky.

COST ANALYSIS: Go for a base model; simply use common sense instead of the Performance Traction Management system and forego jackrabbit starts and high-speed cornering. Keep in mind that premium fuel and astronomical insurance rates will further drive up your operating costs. A word about the ZR1: It's like investing in Cisco or Dell—don't! A 2010 model that sold new for $128,515 is now worth $100,000. **Best alternatives:** Other sporty models worth considering are the Ford GT or Shelby GT500 Mustang and the Porsche 911 or Boxster. The Nissan 370Z looks good on paper, but its quality problems carried over year after year make it a risky buy, much like Nissan's attractively styled Quest. **Options:** Remember, performance options rarely increase performance to the degree promised by the seller; the more performance options you buy, the less comfort you'll have, the more things can go wrong, and the more simple repairs can increase in complexity. Run-flat tires are not a good investment, either. They are hard to find and expensive. Forget about the head-up instrument display that projects speed and other data onto the windshield; it's annoyingly distracting and you'll end up turning it off. **Rebates:** The Corvette is so popular that GM normally doesn't have to offer rebates to boost sales, but there will be some small discounts starting late in 2011 as fuel costs moderate. If gasoline prices spike, Camaro sales will fall and rebates will be substantially higher. **Depreciation:** Much faster than you would imagine and nowhere near the resale prices promised by salespeople. For example, an entry-level 2005 Corvette that sold for almost $67,395 new is now worth about $21,000. **Insurance cost:** Astronomical. **Parts supply/cost:** Parts are pricey and often back-ordered. **Annual maintenance cost:** Higher than average. **Warranty:** 60-day money-back guarantee as long as you don't drive more than 4,000 km. Bumper-to-bumper 3 years/60,000 km; powertrain 5 years/160,000 km; rust perforation 6 years/160,000 km. **Supplementary warranty:** A smart idea to protect you from frequent drivetrain failures. **Highway/city fuel economy:** *6.2L man.:* 7.7/12.9 L/100 km, 37/22 mpg. *Auto.:* 8.1/14.3 L/100 km, 35/20 mpg. *7.0L man.:* 8.2/14.2 L/100 km, 34/20 mpg. *Auto.:* 8.2/14.2 L/100 km, 34/20 mpg. *ZR1 man.:* 10.2/15.5 L/100 km, 28/18 mpg.

OWNER-REPORTED PROBLEMS: Harsh, delayed transmission shifts; active handling system and traction control constantly malfunction; car can only be driven in "reduced power mode":

> The service department has investigated the problem with the active handling system and the traction control system at least three times already. I have driven the car less than 1,350 miles [2,170 km]. From the time I purchased the vehicle it has been out of service for more than 18 days and has been in the shop for service 13 days.

Harsh squeaks and rattles caused by the car's structural deficiencies. The car was built as a convertible and, therefore, has too much body flex. Servicing the sophisticated fuel injection systems isn't easy, even (especially) for GM mechanics. The headliner sags and blocks the rear-view mirror view; the right rear axle suddenly snaps in half; chronic stalling and excessive steering vibration; and the fuel tank will take only half a tank of gasoline:

> My Corvette will only take a half-tank of gas before auto-shutoff is activated. To fill tank I have to turn nozzle upside down. This method causes fuel overflow and spillage on the ground.

SERVICE BULLETIN-REPORTED PROBLEMS: Persistent oil leaks over a period of eight years that affect most of GM's model lineup; intermittent reduced power; various noises from the lift-off roof while driving; and cracks in the transparent removable roof panel.

CTS ★ ★ ★

RATING: Average. As Cadillac reinvents itself in a futile attempt to lure younger buyers, its cars are becoming more complex and less distinctive. **Strong points:** Roomier cabin than other cars in this class (the Sport Wagon's generous cargo

KEY FACTS

CANADIAN PRICE (VERY NEGOTIABLE):
3.6 Coupe: $47,450, *AWD:* $50,080,
3.0L Sedan: $40,455, *AWD:* $44,780,
3.0L Wagon: $44,130, *AWD:* $46,755,
3.6L Performance Wagon: $50,760,
Performance AWD Wagon: $53,795,
CTS-V Coupe: $71,250, *Sedan:* $72,565
U.S. PRICE: *Sport Sedan:* $33,345,
Coupe: $38,365, *Wagon:* $38,465,
CTS-V Sedan, Coupe, or Wagon:
$63,660 **CANADIAN FREIGHT, DEALER
FEES, AND AC TAX:** $2,145 (Pay half of
the freight charge, no "dealer fees", and
$100 for the AC tax.) **U.S. FREIGHT:** $950
POWERTRAIN (REAR-DRIVE/AWD)
Engines: 3.0L V6 (270 hp) • 3.6L
V6 (304 hp) • 6.2L V8 (556 hp);
Transmissions: 6-speed man. • 6-speed
auto.
DIMENSIONS/CAPACITY (BASE CTS)
Passengers: 2/3; Wheelbase: 113 in.;
H: 58/L: 192/W: 73 in.; Headroom F/R:
3.0/1.5 in.; Legroom F/R: 44.0/28.5 in.;
Cargo volume: 14 cu. ft.; Fuel tank: 70L/
premium; Tow limit: 1,000 lb.; Load
capacity: 890 lb.; Turning circle: 38 ft.;
Ground clearance: 5.0 in.; Weight:
3,940 lb.

space is especially noteworthy); a tasteful, well-appointed interior loaded with high-tech gadgetry; competent and secure handling; and available all-wheel drive. NHTSA has given five stars for side crashworthiness and four stars for front crash protection and rollover resistance. IIHS awarded its top rating of "Good" for frontal offset, side, roof, and rear (head restraint) crashworthiness. **Weak points:** Not as agile as its rivals; sport suspensions may be hard on the kidneys; poor rear visibility; and an awkward driving position caused by uneven pedal depth and limited knee room due to the intrusion of the centre stack. Owners also complain of fit and finish deficiencies and frequent electronic malfunctions. Rear-seat access requires some acrobatics due to the low rear roofline, and the rear seatback could use additional bolstering. Also, the trunk's narrow opening adds to the difficulty of loading bulky items. **New for 2012:** A CTS coupe came out in July 2011.

OVERVIEW: *CTS Sedan and Coupe:* A 270 hp 3.0L V6 is the standard engine; the 304 hp 3.6L is optional. *CTS Sport Wagon:* Slightly shorter than the CTS sedan, the CTS Sport Wagon provides 7.6 metres (25 feet) of cargo space accessible via a power-assisted liftgate. The Sport Wagon also carries a base 3.0L and optional 3.6L V6 and employs either a rear-drive or all-wheel-drive system, plus a suspension that can be adjusted from cushy to sporty (firm). *CTS-V Sedan and Coupe:* This 556 hp "muscle" Cadillac returns with no significant changes. The Coupe version uses a smaller 3.6L V6. Standard safety features include anti-lock disc brakes, traction control, stability control, front-seat side airbags, full-length side curtain airbags, and GM's OnStar emergency communications system.

COST ANALYSIS: Go now for the cheaper, 2011 version, or wait to get a 2012 in late winter, when Japanese and South Korean competition will heat up, force prices down, and lead to more generous customer rebates and dealer sales incentives. Think carefully about whether you want all-wheel drive: that option will cost you about $4,500 more with the base 3.0L engine or $2,600 when coupled to the 3.6L engine. **Best alternative:** Acura TL SH-AWD, BMW 3 Series, Hyundai Genesis, Infiniti G37, and Lincoln MKS or Town Car. **Options:** Neither the adaptive cruise control nor the advanced DVD navigation system is worth the extra money. **Rebates:** $4,000–$6,000 in sales incentives. **Depreciation:** Unbelievably fast. A 2005 base CTS that sold new for $37,800 is now worth a little over $9,000; a 2005 CTS-V that went for $70,000 new now sells for no more than $12,000.

Insurance cost: Higher than average. **Parts supply/cost:** Parts are often back-ordered and electronic components are quite pricey. **Annual maintenance cost:** Higher than average. **Warranty:** 60-day money-back guarantee as long as you don't drive more than 4,000 km. Bumper-to-bumper 4 years/80,000 km; powertrain 5 years/160,000 km; rust perforation 6 years/160,000 km. **Supplementary warranty:** A good thing to have. **Highway/city fuel economy:** *3.0L:* 7.2/11.23 L/100 km, 39/25 mpg. *3.6L:* 6.9/11.4 L/100 km, 41/25 mpg. *3.6L AWD:* 7.9/13 L/100 km, 36/22 mpg. *CTS-V man.:* 10.5/14.9 L/100 km, 27/19 mpg. *CTS-V auto.:* 11/17.5 L/100 km, 28/16 mpg.

OWNER-REPORTED PROBLEMS: Sudden acceleration caused driver death because there was no brake override feature; engine and transmission failures, noisy automatic transmission:

> I purchased a new 2011 Cadillac CTS Coupe. It continuously makes a groaning sound which appears to be coming from the rear part of the drive train. The dealer changed the differential fluid to correct the problem. However, the problem remains. I believe this sound is produced by a defective component in the drive train (differential, bearings, etc.), which will ultimately lead to a component failure that can cause a serious accident.

Electrical system glitches; fit and finish defects; excessive vibration and powertrain drone/boom when the car is underway at 64–121 km/h; inoperative low-beam headlights; sunroof may implode; windshield pillar moulding may come loose; and the speedometer may display a speed 6 km/h (4 mph) less than the actual speed.

SERVICE BULLETIN-REPORTED PROBLEMS: Tires leak air or suddenly go flat; inoperative power liftgate; GM says noisy fuel system on cold start is normal; faulty propshaft bolts; powertrain noise or vibration when cruising; noise when shifting between Reverse and Drive can likely be silenced by adding a washer to the wheel driveshaft.

EQUINOX, TERRAIN ★★★★

RATING: Above Average. **Strong points:** Most of the important safety devices are standard (traction control, an anti-skid system, front side airbags, and side curtain airbags). Other handy features include remote engine start, a navigation system, a wireless cell phone link, DVD entertainment, a hard drive for storing digital audio files, a rear-view camera, and a power liftgate. GMC's MultiFlex rear seat can be moved 20 cm (8 in.) fore and aft to better accommodate people and cargo. The Terrain shares its basic design and powertrain with the Chevrolet Equinox. Besides a plethora of airbags, the Terrain also comes with ABS, traction control, and an anti-skid system. A rear-view camera is standard on all Terrain models. Thrilling acceleration with the V6 and manual transmission; the 4-cylinder engine and automatic gearbox are acceptable and fairly quiet; acceptable handling and

The General Motors Terrain.

KEY FACTS

CANADIAN PRICE (FIRM): *LS:* $23,995, *2LT:* $25,795, *LTZ:* $32,750 **U.S. PRICE:** *LS:* $22,995, *4x4:* $24,745, *ECO:* $18,425, *1LT:* $24,160, *4x4:* 25,910, *2LT:* $26,220, *4x4:* $27,970, *LTZ:* $28,570, *4x4:* $30,320 **CANADIAN FREIGHT, DEALER FEES, AND AC TAX:** $2,045 (Cut the freight charge In half, pay nothing for "dealer fees," and give $100 for the AC tax.) **U.S. FREIGHT:** $950 **POWERTRAIN (AWD)** Engines: 2.4L 4-cyl. (182 hp) • 3.0L V6 (264 hp); Transmission: 6-speed auto.

DIMENSIONS/CAPACITY

Passengers: 2/3; Wheelbase: 112.5 in.; H: 66.3/L: 187.8/W: 72.5 in.; Legroom F/R: 41.2/39.9 in.; Cargo volume: 63.7 cu. ft.; Fuel tank: 59L/regular; Tow limit: 1,500 lb. (LS), 1,500 to 3,000 lb. (all others); Turning circle: 40 ft.; Ground clearance: 7.8 in.; Weight: 3,786 lb.

braking combined with a comfortable ride. Plenty of passenger room; a quiet interior; most controls are well laid out; very comfortable seating; and a smooth-performing, fuel-sipping manual drivetrain. NHTSA gives the Equinox and its Terrain twin five stars for rollover resistance, and frontal and side occupant protection. After testing both vehicles, IIHS gave a "Good" designation for frontal, side, roof, and rear (head restraint) crash protection. **Weak points:** V6 fuel economy is below average, but is a fair trade-off for the extra power; the 4-cylinder engine comes up short when passing other vehicles or merging into traffic; some delayed downshifting with the V6, and handling is better with the Honda competition; uncommunicative, numb steering; tall head restraints cut rear visibility; the dash buttons all look the same; cheap-looking, easily scratched, and hard-to-keep-clean door panels and dash materials. Overall reliability has only been average: the transmission, suspension, electrical, and fuel systems have been problematic, and fit and finish continues to get low marks. Not quite as much cargo space as seen in some rival makes; and some dash controls are difficult to reach. **New for 2012:** Carried over without any important changes.

OVERVIEW: With seating for five, this four-door cross-over SUV offers a choice of two engines: a base 182 hp

2.4L 4-cylinder and an optional 264 hp 3.0L V6. Both variants are teamed with a smooth-performing 6-speed automatic transmission, and front-drive and all-wheel drive are available with all models. Stay away from 2009 or earlier models; they perform poorly and tend to fall apart after three years.

COST ANALYSIS: Try to get a similar, discounted 2011 model. The redesigned 2010 Equinox was restyled and given more-powerful engines in addition to some other new features. Consider it your used car alternative. **Best alternatives:** Some good alternative models are the Honda CR-V, Hyundai Tucson, and Subaru Forester. **Options:** The turbocharged 4-banger and premium tires. **Rebates:** $500 rebates at year's end. **Depreciation:** Average. **Insurance cost:** Average. **Parts supply/cost:** Average supply and cost. **Annual maintenance cost:** Average. **Warranty:** 60-day money-back guarantee as long as you don't drive more than 4,000 km. Bumper-to-bumper 3 years/60,000 km; powertrain 5 years/160,000 km; rust perforation 6 years/160,000 km. **Supplementary warranty:** Not needed. **Highway/city fuel economy:** *2.4L auto.:* 6.1/9.2 L/100 km, 46/31 mpg. *AWD:* 6.9/10.1 L/100 km, 41/28 mpg. *3.0L auto.:* 8.1/12.4 L/100 km, 35/23 mpg. *AWD:* 8.6/12.9 L/100 km, 33/22 mpg. Despite the above figures put out by the federal government (*http://oee.nrcan.gc.ca/transportation/tools/fuelratings/ratings-results.cfm*), Equinox owners say real gas mileage is much less than what is advertised:

> Sales agent assured my wife the 2011 Equinox would get better than 30 mpg [7.8 L/100 km]. And if it didn't get the mileage it could be fixed. Well, after multiple trips to three dealerships it is very obvious that we were lied to. After 5000 miles [8,000 km] we still only get around 22 mpg [10.7 L/100 km] highway. I called the Chevrolet complaint line just to be told that that mpg was under best driving conditions. In other words they were going to do nothing to fix the problem even though the sales person lied to my wife right in front of my sister. I will tell you this: I have bought my last Chevrolet.

OWNER-REPORTED PROBLEMS: An unusually low number of safety-related owner complaints have been reported to NHTSA, while *Consumer Reports'* 2011 member survey says the vehicle has shown major reliability problems through the 2009 model year. Those owner reports relate to problems with the powertrain, fuel, climate, and electrical systems, brakes, and fit and finish. Interestingly, there aren't any service bulletins that show major failures. NHTSA: Airbags failed to deploy; rear glass exploded as door was shut:

> Vehicle was parked under a carport in full shade. I opened the driver's side door, got in, shut the door as I always do, and the rear glass exploded outward. There was no chip or crack in the glass. We took many pictures of the glass where it is obvious that the glass burst outward, glass spewed all down my driveway. The glass broke all around the edges of the frame and a large hole in the middle. Prior to this, we took the vehicle to the dealership to fix a rattle in the liftgate. I know that the liftgate had to be taken apart and reassembled for this fix. The dealership says the glass fell

inward (and after being hauled halfway across town on a wrecker, it sure looks like it did) and that in any case, glass is not covered under the warranty. I called GM and the rep said it should be covered.

Engine loses power, stalls, and warning light comes on; fuel pump on the 4-cylinder model leaks and contaminates the engine oil; hesitation before going into gear; harsh transmission engagement; transmission "kicks" when shifting into third and foot is taken off the gas pedal; electronic power steering system causes the steering to "stick" during high-speed cruising when there's normally not that many steering corrections; battery is often dead (see "Service Bulletin-Reported Problems"); driver cannot access the radio controls while driving with seat belt fastened; when the driver's door is opened, door bottom trim may cut one's leg or ankle:

> My spouse was opening the driver's door and the trip at the bottom of the door (which is fiberglass material) cut her leg about six to eight inches above the left ankle. The trim sticks when the driver's door is opened. It took 16 stitches to close the wound. The trim needs to re-finished or tapered to prevent others from getting hurt. This is a really bad cut and she was in a lot of pain.

Sudden, unintended acceleration and the car sometimes lags when cruising. Owners say they have experienced chronic automatic transmission failures and malfunctions; other safety-related incidents reported to NHTSA include airbags that failed to deploy when they were needed; "spongy" brakes accompanied by a delayed response; power steering failures; and in one incident, the steering wheel came off in one driver's hand.

SERVICE BULLETIN-REPORTED PROBLEMS: Reduced engine power (see Cruze section); GM says it is normal to hear your fuel pump clicking/ticking, especially at higher operating temperatures; drivetrain noise when shifting from Drive to Reverse (add washer to wheel driveshaft, as outlined in another Cruze bulletin); inoperative low-beam headlights is a common failing. Battery drain: No, your Equinox hasn't been taken over by aliens; this is just one of GM's electronic module glitches that also affects the Terrain. GM's free service campaign means you can get the module recalibrated and a free battery charge until 2013.

ENCLAVE, TRAVERSE, ACADIA ★★★★

RATING: Above Average. These are practically identical seven- and eight-passenger crossover SUVs with the Traverse being the most recent addition. **Strong points:** All three vehicles have five-star front and side NHTSA crashworthiness scores, while rollover resistance earned them each four stars. IIHS awarded these models a "Good" rating for front, side, roof, and rear collision crash protection. Sales have been hit hard by high fuel costs and tighter credit, making 20 percent discounts not unusual with these models. Although they are fuel-thirsty SUVs, maintenance costs and mechanical/body failures aren't excessive. Saturn's discontinued Outlook

The General Motors Acadia.

has the same characteristics as this trio and sells used at a 50 percent discount. **Weak points:** Side airbags sometimes fail to deploy; head restraints force your chin into your chest; transmission oil leaks and malfunctions; fuel pump flow module fails, making the engine run rough or stall; inaccurate fuel gauges; a noisy suspension; and headlight failures. **New for 2012:** Revised powertrain configurations and additional colours.

OVERVIEW: These large SUVs are an endangered species, and GM is likely to pull the plug at any time. Still, they are tough and versatile; prices are easily bargained down.

KEY FACTS

CANADIAN PRICE (VERY NEGOTIABLE): *Enclave 2x4 CX:* $45,730, *4x4:* $53,700, *Traverse1LS 2x4:* $37,890, *AWD:* 40,890; *Acadia SLE 2x4:* $40,135, *4x4:* $43,135 **U.S. PRICE:** *Enclave CX:* $34,675, *CXL-1:* $37,790, *CXL-2:* $41,155; *Traverse:* $29,370–$40,250; *Acadia:* $31,740–$42,175 **CANADIAN FREIGHT, DEALER FEES, AND AC TAX:** $2,045 (Pay half of the freight charge, ignore the "dealer fees," and give $100 for the AC tax.) **U.S. FREIGHT:** $975 **POWERTRAIN (FRONT-DRIVE/AWD)** Engine: 3.6L V6 (288 hp); Transmission: 6-speed auto. **DIMENSIONS/CAPACITY (ENCLAVE)** Passengers: 7/8; Wheelbase: 119 in.; H: 72.5/L: 201.5/W: 79 in., Cargo volume: 115.3 in. (behind 1st row); 67.5 in (behind 2nd row); 23.2 in (behind 3rd row); Fuel tank: 83L/regular; Tow limit: 4,500 lb.; Turning circle: 40.4 ft.; Ground clearance: 8.4 in.; Weight: 4,780–4,985 lb.

COST ANALYSIS: Prices continue to drift downward as new arrivals start appearing on dealers' lots. Buy a discounted 2011 for the best price/quality advantage now that higher fuel prices are pushing SUV and truck base prices way down; $10,000 discounts are commonplace, particularly in Alberta and British Columbia. **Best alternatives:** The Ford Flex, Honda Pilot, Hyundai Veracruz, and Mazda CX-9. If you don't mind downsizing a notch, consider the Ford Edge, Hyundai Santa Fe, and Nissan XTerra. **Options:** Stay away from Firestone and Bridgestone original-equipment tires; *tirerack.com* is your best contact for dependable and well-performing tires. **Rebates:** $1,000 rebates throughout 2012. **Depreciation:** Faster than average. **Insurance cost:** Much higher than average. **Parts supply/cost:** Parts aren't hard to find and are competitively priced. **Annual maintenance cost:** Average. **Warranty:** Bumper-to-bumper 4 years/80,000 km; powertrain 5 years/160,000 km; rust perforation 6 years/160,000 km. **Supplementary warranty:** Not needed. **Highway/city fuel economy:** *2WD:* 8.4/12.7 L/100 km, 34/22 mpg. *AWD:* 9.0/13.4 L/100 km, 31/21 mpg.

OWNER-REPORTED PROBLEMS: A Traverse caught fire while cruising on the highway:

> Occupants smelt fuel and pulled over. Witnesses advised that immediately pulling over the vehicle was on fire in the engine compartment and within 60 seconds the fire was observed in the front driver passenger seat area. The driver and passenger had moved to the back seat area to try and free a 4-year-old child from the car seat. The female passenger then exited the rear driver window suffering critical burns in the fire. The male driver expired in the back seat of the vehicle. Bystanders removed the child.

Airbag failed to deploy; sudden, unintended acceleration; car continued accelerating after accelerator was released (brakes were inoperative); brake failures:

> The brand new vehicle has been serviced five times for braking failure. While waiting at a traffic light the ABS kicked in and the brake went to the floor. The sensors have been changed/debris cleaned/frayed wires replaced. The vehicle is still not repaired.

Driver's shoe can become stuck to the carpeting, thereby engaging the accelerator; vehicle will not "hold" when stopped on an incline:

> The vehicle rolls back on any incline, there is no hand brake in the center console, and according to DOT safety this is not legal. Most crossovers and/or SUVs of this size roll back a few inches before the transmission pins engage and stop the roll back. I was told from GMC that the component was removed so that the transmission doesn't have to be serviced for 100,000 miles [160,900 km]. GMC told us the only thing they are willing to do is install an after-market hand control and will pay a percentage toward the cost. To me this sounds like a band-aid fix to a bigger problem.

It is impossible to read the speed due to faint backlighting and small numbers. Rear window began slowly cracking while car was parked in the garage; Poorly designed, chin-to-chest head restraints in the front, middle, and rear seats:

The middle and rear seats in the vehicle have head restraints that tilt forward and are not adjustable or removable and make it extremely difficult (impossible) to install car seats or high-back boosters correctly and safely. The seat belts are also very difficult to reach/buckle for a passenger in a booster seat. They are very low in the seat.

SERVICE BULLETIN-REPORTED PROBLEMS: GM has a free fix for increased rpms during certain shifts (see also the LaCrosse section); the automaker also says fuel pump clicking or ticking on cold startup is normal; intermittent reduced power; tires leak air or suddenly go flat; delayed shifting; gear oil smell in the cabin; squawk, creak noise from the front of the vehicle; and an inoperative driver's power seat.

ESCALADE, TAHOE, YUKON ★★★

The Cadillac Escalade.

RATING: Average, but hurry: Dealers are dumping these SUVs as GM winds down their production in favour of smaller, more-car-like crossover SUVs. All three vehicles are practically identical, though the Escalade comes with a 6.2L V8 and a plusher interior and is also more gadget-laden. **Strengths:** Strong acceleration; many powertrain configurations; standard stability control; a quiet interior and comfortable ride; good towing capability; parts aren't hard to find and are reasonably priced; and repairs can be done by independent garages. A hybrid version is available. NHTSA gave these SUVs five stars for frontal and side passenger protection and three stars for rollover resistance. **Weaknesses:** Extremely poor fuel economy; rapid depreciation; small third-row seat sits too low and doesn't fold into the floor; ponderous handling; long braking distances; and below-average reliability. Specific problem areas include loss of brakes; faulty

KEY FACTS

CANADIAN PRICE (VERY NEGOTIABLE):
Escalade EXT Base: $82,055, *Escalade 1SA Package:* $87,080, *ESV:* $90,795, *EXT:* $90,975, *Escalade Hybrid:* $97,225, *Tahoe LS 2×4:* $51,600, *4×4:* $56,060; *Tahoe Hybrid 2×4:* $70,860, *4×4:* $73,845, *Yukon SLE 2×4:* $51,600, *4×4:* $56,060, *Denali AWD:* $74,845, *Hybrid 2×4:* $70,860, *4×4:* $73,845, *4×4 Denali:* $82,535 **U.S. PRICE:** *Escalade AWD:* $63,455, *Escalade Hybrid:* $74,135; *ESV:* $66,080, *EXT:* $62,160; *Tahoe LS 2×4:* $37,980, *4×4:* $42,040, *LTZ 2×4:* $51,465, *4×4:* $54,570, *Hybrid 2×4:* $51,145, *4×4:* $53,950, *Yukon SLE 4×2:* $39,780; *SLT:* $45,265; *SLE 4×4:* $43,790; *SLT 4×4:* $48,120

CANADIAN FREIGHT, DEALER FEES, AND AC TAX: $2,145 (Pay half of the freight charge, refuse to pay anything for "dealer fees," and give $100 for the AC tax.) **U.S. FREIGHT:** $975

POWERTRAIN (FRONT-DRIVE/AWD)
Engines: 5.3L V8 (320 hp) • 6.2L V8 (403 hp) • 6.0L V8 (332 hp); Transmissions: 6-speed auto. • CVT

DIMENSIONS/CAPACITY
Passengers: *Escalade:* 3/3/2; *Tahoe:* 3/33; Wheelbase: *Escalade:* 116 in.; *Hybrid:* 202.5 in.; H: 74.3/L: 202.5/W: 79 in., Cargo volume: 16.9 cu. ft. (behind 3rd row); Fuel tank: 98L/regular; Tow limit: *Escalade:* 8,100 lb; *Hybrid:* 5,600 lb.; Payload: *Escalade:* 1,609 lb.; *Hybrid:* 1,484; Turning circle: 40.4 ft.; Ground clearance: 9.0 in.; Weight: *Escalade:* 5,691–5,943 lb.; *Hybrid:* 6,116 lb.

powertrain, suspension, and climate controls; and various body glitches. IIHS hasn't yet tested these vehicles for crashworthiness. **New for 2012:** Nothing significant, except for new powertrain configurations and more optional features.

OVERVIEW: These three trucks are only masquerading as car-like SUVs and will likely not last another two years if fuel prices continue their upward ride.

COST ANALYSIS: In the new year prices will fall and you will get these large SUVs for almost a third off the original price. **Best alternatives:** The Buick Enclave, Chevrolet Equinox and Terrain, Ford Flex, GMC Acadia and Traverse, Honda Pilot, Hyundai Veracruz, Mazda CX-9, and Toyota Highlander. **Options:** Don't accept factory Bridgestone or Firestone tires. Independent suppliers will sell you better tires for less money. Also, stay away from the $2,065 glitch-prone power-sliding sunroof. **Rebates:** Escalade buyers get $2,000 throughout the year; Hybrid is excluded until 2012. **Depreciation:** Incredibly fast. Good for used buyers, a kick in the pants for owners selling after two to five years. Let's look at how much we lose with the top-of-the-line model of each brand: A 2007 Escalade ESV that sold new for $79,030 is now worth $30,000; the same model-year $61,075 Tahoe LTZ AWD sells for $18,500; and a 2007 GMC Yukon XL that sold new for $66,170 won't fetch more than $23,000. **Insurance cost:** Much higher than average. **Parts supply/cost:** Parts are easy to find and competitively priced. **Annual maintenance cost:** Average. **Warranty:** Bumper-to-bumper 4 years/80,000 km; powertrain 5 years/160,000 km; rust perforation 6 years/160,000 km. **Supplementary warranty:** Not needed. **Highway/city fuel economy:** *Escalade AWD:* 10.8/17.7 L/100 km, 26/16 mpg. Other models should produce similar figures. Hybrid figures are not available.

OWNER-REPORTED PROBLEMS: Barely a half dozen owner complaints when 150 would be the norm. *Consumer Reports* subscribers confirm the vehicles' powertrain and electrical system shortcomings in addition to major complaints relative to subpar body construction and low-quality materials. Chrome-plated door handles peel and cut fingers; as the rear window was closing, one passenger's finger was trapped in the weather stripping and was amputated. Escalade power rear cargo door may be hazardous says one father, who is thankful his son wasn't killed when the door failed:

> 2011 Cadillac Escalade ESV 26771 power rear cargo door is a serious safety hazard. Son was seriously hurt at airport luggage claims when a power rear cargo door was closing, came down on his head and face without warning of any kind that this door was closing. The door is so large and heavy as it comes down, it's fast and does not retract back up when it hits something. The driver had no warning that a person was behind him as he closed the door. This is a very serious problem that could kill someone and should be corrected. This door should be changed so that it cannot open from overhead. This door is too large and heavy to have something coming down from that distance that's above the top of the Escalade. This is a very serious safety problem someone will be killed or lose body parts if this design is not changed. This is a very poor design.

Owners also report serious electrical shorts and drive system malfunctions. Hard automatic transmission shifts also noted. For over a decade owners have decried the slap-dash fit and finish of these top-of-the-line vehicles.

SERVICE BULLETIN-REPORTED PROBLEMS: Oil leaks from the rear engine cover or at the oil cooler hose pipe assembly; intermittent reduced engine power; leaking power steering fluid; valve lifter tick noise at start-up; muffler heat shield buzz during operation; inoperative low beam headlights; tires leak air or suddenly go flat; airbag warning light comes on for no reason; tapping/clicking/ticking noise at the windshield area; multiple noises from the front of the vehicle; passenger airbag may not be flush with the dash; and a remedy for hard third-row seat removal and installation. GM has a free fix for AC water leaks.

SILVERADO 1500, 2500, SIERRA, HD ★★★

The Chevrolet Silverado 1500.

CANADIAN PRICE (VERY NEGOTIABLE): *1500 WT Regular Cab 4×2:* $28,440, *Regular Long Cab 4×2:* $28,740, *Regular Long Cab 4×4:* $32,340, *Extended Standard Cab 4×2:* $31,665, *Extended Standard Cab 4×4:* $36,190, *Extended Long Cab 4×2:* $34,340, *Extended Long Cab 4×4:* $37,875, *Crew Cab 4×2:* $34,025, *Crew Cab 4×4:* $37,785, *LS:* $40,220, *LT:* $41,755, *LTZ:* $50,205, *Hybrid 1SH Package:* $49,685, *Hybrid 1SJ Package:* $57,370, *2500HD WT Regular Cab 4×2:* $37,780, *Regular Cab 4×4:* $41,380, *Extended Cab 4×2:* $41,095, *Extended Cab 4×4:* $44,695, *Crew Cab 4×2:* $43,010, *Crew Cab 4×4:* $46,835, *3500 HD WT Extended Cab 4×2:* $39,430, *Extended Cab 4×4:* $46,650, *Crew Cab 4×2:* $44,965, *Crew Cab 4×4:* $48,565 **U.S. PRICE:** *1500HD WT 4×2:* $21,235 *4×4:* $24,475, *LS 4×2:* $30,745, *LS 4×4:* $33,895, *LT 4×2:* $26,810, *LT 4×4:* $30,170, *XFE:* $33,610, *4×2 LTZ:* $39,010, *4×4 LTZ:* $42,160, *Hybrid 1HY 2×4:* $38,725, *4×4:* $41,875, *Hybrid 2HY 2×4:* $45,055, *4×4:* $48,205, *2500HD WT 4×2:* $28,415, *4×4:* $31,370, *LT 4×2:* $31,260, *LT 4×4:* $34,410, *LTZ 4×2:* $42,040, *LTZ 4×4:* $45,190, *3500HD WT 4×2:* $34,160, *4×4:* $37,115, *LT 4×2:* $37,415, *LT 4×4:* $40,565,

LTZ 4×2: $42,735, *LTZ 4×4:* $45,885, *Big Dooley WT 4×2:* $34,365, *4×4:* $41,790, *LTZ 4×2:* $43,080, *4×4:* $46,230 **CANADIAN FREIGHT, DEALER FEES, AND AC TAX:** $2,045 (Pay half of the freight charge, nothing for "dealer fees," and $100 for the AC tax.) **U.S. FREIGHT:** $950

POWERTRAIN (FRONT-DRIVE)

Engines: 4.3L V6 (195 hp) • 4.8L V8 (302 hp) • 5.3L V8 (315 hp), *Hybrid:* 6.0L V8 (332 hp) • 6.2L V8 (403 hp) • 6.6L V8 TD (397 hp); Transmissions: 4-speed auto. • 6-speed auto., *Hybrid:* CVT

DIMENSIONS/CAPACITY

Passengers: *1500:* 2/1, *2500:* 3/3; Wheelbase: *1500:* 144 in., *2500:* 133.6–167 in.; *1500:* H: 74/L: 230/W: 80 in., *2500:* H: 77/L: 240/W: 80 in.; Headroom F/R: *1500:* 6.5/6.0 in., *2500:* 6.0/5.0 in.; Legroom F/R: 41.5/29 in., *2500:* 40.5/27 in.; Fuel tank: 129L/regular; Tow limit: *Hybrid:* 6,100 lb., *1500:* 7,500 lb., *2500:* 13,600 lb., *HD Turbo Diesel:* 15,600 lb; Load capacity: *1500:* 1,570 lb., *2500:* 2,260 lb.; Turning circle: *1500:* 50 ft., *2500:* 55 ft.; Ground clearance: 9.5 in.; Weight: *1500:* 5,435 lb., *2500:* 6,920 lb.

RATING: Average. Although *Lemon-Aid* rates Ford 1500 and Super Duty models as Above Average, GM's HD series is catching up quickly. Unfortunately, the Dodge Ram (with its I6 Cummins) comes in a distant third—even with unbelievably steep discounts. True, GM's 1500 pickups are slowly improving, but they are still held back by a platform dating to model-year 2007. All the more reason why GM should eliminate the duplication of its divisions and merge GMC with Chevrolet. Money saved should go into a major redesign of the 1500 series to match the improvements now seen with GM's Heavy Duty (HD) series. *Quo vadis*, Chrysler? Without R&D cash to build a competitive truck, Chrysler will never regain the truck market share it has lost to Ford, GM, and the Asian automakers. **Strong points:** *1500:* Good choice of engines and transmissions; standard electronic stability control; comfortable seating; lots of storage capability; good fuel economy. Since its 2008 redesign, the Silverado handles much better, offers a steadier, more-controllable ride (no more "Shakerado"), and has a more-refined, comfortable cabin. NHTSA gave the Silverado 1500 and 1500 Hybrid five stars for side crash protection and four stars for frontal crashworthiness and rollover resistance; the 2500 has scored between three and four stars for rollover resistance; and the Silverado 3500 series hasn't yet been rated. IIHS has given the Silverado 1500 a "Good" rating for frontal offset protection and an "Acceptable" score for side-impact crashworthiness and head-restraint effectiveness. *2500:*

These heavy-duty work trucks are built primarily to be load-carrying vehicles capable of working off-road, although this year's independent front end should improve handling and smooth out the ride. The standard engine is a powerful 360 hp 6.0L V8 backed up by a 397 hp 6.6L turbodiesel. This year's improvements on the HD models help GM catch up to Ford in handling and ride comfort. For example, the ability to control 10,000-pound-plus loads when descending with the Exhaust Brake system gives GM a feature that Ford Super Duty trucks have used for some time. Hopefully, this new system will be glitch-free during its first few years on the market. The same wish should be made for GM's relatively new Duramax engine. GM's 2010 3500 HDs were outclassed when compared with Ford's 2010 Super Duty powerplant hooked to a new 6-speed transmission. Finally, while the GM Allison transmission has been around since the late '40s, it hasn't performed as well as Ford's all-new TorqShift 6-speed found in the Super Duty models. Again, maybe GM's revised Allison tranny will enhance durability, make for smoother shifting, and remove the annoying downshift clunks GM truck owners have lived with for decades. **Weak points:** 1500: Powertrain smoothness and reliability doesn't measure up to what the Dodge Ram, Ford-150 Series, Honda Ridgeline, and Nissan Titan can provide. The steering is over-assisted; there's excess body lean when cornering; climate controls aren't very user-friendly; and the servicing network is rather limited. GM Duramax-equipped pickups need diesel exhaust fluid (urea) refills every 8,000 kilometres (5,000 miles). This is more frequent than the oil change one usually does every 12,000 kilometres (7,500 miles). Furthermore, the urea-filling process can be costly and complicated, as this diesel owner found out and posted to NHTSA:

> The contact owns a 2011 Chevrolet Silverado 3500HD(NA). The contact stated that the computer was programmed to limit the speed of the vehicle when the diesel exhaust fluid was too low. He noticed that when he filled the fuel tank, the computer did not recognize that the tank was full and the diesel warning light continued to illuminate on the instrumental panel. The vehicle had not been inspected by a dealer but was contacted; they informed him that the only remedy was for them to drop the diesel tank and empty the fluid for the computer to reprogram itself. The vehicle had not been repaired. The failure mileage was approximately 6,500 miles [10,400 km].

IIHS says the 1500's roof crashworthiness merits a "Marginal" rating. Seat pelvic/thorax and head curtain side airbags are available but aren't standard on the 2500 HD; Ford Super Duty trucks have them as a standard safety feature. **New for 2012:** Chevrolet's 2012 Silverado and the practically identical GMC Sierra will return relatively unchanged, Although the HD models were only slightly restyled last year, they got oodles of mechanical improvements that are carried over to this year's models. A new 6.6L Duramax turbo diesel delivers 397 horsepower and is touted as being more fuel efficient than before; towing capability is cranked up to 20,000 lb.; on the 3500s, there's a higher payload capacity up to 6,000 lb.; the 2500 payload limit is 3,100 lb.; a larger fuel tank allows 1,090 km (680 miles) between fill-ups with the 6.6L diesel; a new exhaust brake feature provides greater control on grades and reduces brake pad wear; and the standard four-wheel disc system has been revamped to deliver a smoother and quicker response. Snow plow capability is available for all 4×4 cab configurations and the frame has five times more torsional stiffness and better vibration control than the 2010 versions. 2012s will also return with a stronger independent front suspension; improved upper and lower control arms; a revised front suspension to eliminate squeaks and clunks and improve the ride; a revised rear suspension to support greater loads while minimizing axle "hop"; and an improved power steering gear. And, to further enhance a quiet ride, noise from the engine, steering pump, and chassis has been reduced. Standard safety features for 2012 include StabiliTrak electronic stability control systems on all single-rear-wheel models; larger, four-wheel disc brakes with standard four-wheel ABS; a new high-strength steel tubular frame cross member that enhances safety and improves crashworthiness; trailer sway control on all single-rear-wheel models; and hill start assist also standard on single-rear-wheel models.

OVERVIEW: All V8s are flex-fuel capable, and the 4.8L and 5.3L engines have variable valve timing. Trucks with the 5.3L engine were also given a 6-speed automatic transmission and a revised rear axle ratio. All 1500 models have standard electronic stability control, seat-mounted side airbags, and side curtain airbags. All stereos also get a USB port. The Chevrolet Silverado 1500 didn't get a new turbodiesel V8 engine because GM is putting most of its money on changes to the HD lineup. Basically, this large pickup is a twin of the GMC Sierra and is offered in regular-, extended-, and crew-cab body styles. Regular cabs seat up to three passengers; extendeds and crews can carry six. There are three bed lengths: 5.8, 6.6, and 8.0 feet. Silverados offer two interiors: "pure pickup" and "luxury inspired." The 5.3 V8 saves fuel through Active Fuel Management cylinder deactivation. V6 and 4.8L V8 Silverados are coupled to a 4-speed automatic transmission. A 6-speed automatic is used with the 5.3L and 6.2L V8s. Rear-drive is standard and two four-wheel drive systems are optional: a part-time setup that shouldn't be left engaged on dry pavement, and GM's AutoTrac, which can go anywhere. Both have a low-range gear for off-roading.

The Silverado 1500 Hybrid has a 6.0L V8 that pairs with an electric motor, producing 332 hp. It can run on one or both of its power sources depending on driving demands, and doesn't need to be plugged in. The hybrid has a continuously variable automatic transmission and a maximum towing capacity of 6,100 lb.

COST ANALYSIS: Buy the almost identical, but cheaper, 2011 base 1500 series. Get a redesigned 2011 HD if you need the additional power. Remember, safety and performance ratings and owner complaints will probably apply to the Sierra and Hybrid models as well, with just a few exceptions. **Best alternatives:** The Ford F-Series and Honda Ridgeline. **Options:** Consider the $600 Exterior Plus package, which includes a remote starter, fog lights, a garage door opener, and a locking tailgate with the EZ Lift feature. Also, consider getting adjustable gas and brake pedals if you need to put extra space between you and the steering-wheel-mounted airbag. **Rebates:** $4,000 in sales incentives on the 2011 and 2012 HD models; about half as much on the 1500 series. As summer approaches, the rebates may almost double. **Depreciation:** Faster than average. **Insurance cost:** Much higher than average. **Parts supply/cost:** Parts aren't hard to find and are competitively priced by independent suppliers. **Annual maintenance cost:** Higher than average. **Warranty:** 60-day money-back guarantee as long as you don't drive more than 4,000 km. Bumper-to-bumper 4 years/80,000 km; powertrain 5 years/160,000 km; rust perforation 6 years/160,000 km. **Supplementary warranty:** Recommended. **Highway/city fuel economy:** *4.3L 2WD:* 10.0/14.1 L/100 km, 28/20 mpg. *4.3L 4WD:* 11.3/14.9 L/100 km, 24/19 mpg. *4.8L 2WD:* 10.6/14.7 L/100 km, 27/19 mpg. *4.8L 4WD:* 11.1/15.4 L/100 km, 25/18 mpg. *5.3L 2WD:* 10.1/14.5 L/100 km, 28/19 mpg. *5.3L 4WD:* 10.3/14.7 L/100 km, 27/19 mpg. *6.2L AWD:* 10.8/17.7 L/100 km, 26/16 mpg. *Hybrid 2WD:* 9.2/9.8 L/100 km, 31/29 mpg. *Hybrid 4WD:* 9.8/10.5 L/100 km, 29/27 mpg.

OWNER-REPORTED PROBLEMS: Powertrain, fuel system, suspension, and fit and finish deficiencies. Safety-related complaints include airbags that suddenly deploy for no reason; Sudden, unintended acceleration:

> Second report—sudden acceleration, 2011 GMC Sierra PU truck. On December 20, 2010 I was traveling to visit friends. While on highway I set the cruise control for 70 mph. I exited the freeway and traveled approximately 5 miles on city streets. Upon entering a bedroom township known for speed traps I attempted to engage the cruise control for 30 mph [48 km/h]. When pressing the cruise control to set the speed I was traveling (30 mph) the truck down shifted and accelerated rapidly (to 4000 rpm). I immediately tapped the brake and the cruise control disengaged. This is the second time for this truck to down shift and accelerate rapidly. A previous report was made in November 2010.

Engine surging when the brakes are applied; ABS brakes activate on their own and cause the truck to suddenly decelerate; a sticky brake pedal will activate the ABS system, causing the truck to sway and shake violently; brakes failed and airbags did not deploy during collision; steering wheel suddenly locked up:

> Accelerating up on ramp with wheel turned. While merging with traffic at speed, wheel locked in turned position. Forced wheel back straight with much force and a loud pop sound from steering due to the amount of force required, many people would not be able to unlock wheel and may crash. This has happened two times in last 30 days. Dealer refuses to make repairs, claims cannot make happen when in their possession.

Excessive transmission noise (clunk) and hesitation, then bangs into gear; rear axle has too much play and could cause the differential and wheel to fail:

> When I first drove my new truck I noticed a subtle knocking noise coming from the rear when driving slowly over a bump. The dealer's mechanic agreed there was something wrong and called GM tech assistance (71-910-553230) and found the rear axle had too much play. The groove on the axle that retains the C retaining clip was machined too close to the end of the shaft. They replaced the axle. Only a person with mechanical experience could have detected the subtle noise. Had it gone undetected, eventually the C clip would likely fail and the axle and wheel would have slid out of the differential housing. I doubt this machining fault on the axle is unique to my truck.

Waterleaks into the cabin; while making a left turn, passenger-side door opened; windshield wipers and washer suddenly come on by themselves, obscuring vision; sun visors don't block the sun's rays sufficiently; beware of original-equipment (OEM) tires that perform badly on wet roads:

> OEM tires have extremely poor wet pavement traction. First incident occurred less than 30 days after purchasing the vehicle. It had rained heavily for an extended time that day and continuing moderately into the evening. Approaching the intersection where I intended to make a turn onto a side street, I began slowing to what I considered a safe and prudent speed given the road conditions. Upon applying the brakes the vehicle could not be stopped resulting in sliding completely straight through the intersection, luckily on a green signal light, and with no other traffic in my path.... Second incident, again on wet pavement, was after making a complete stop at a traffic light controlled intersection. When the signal light changed to green, I started negotiating a left turn. Approximately halfway through the intersection, at a speed of less than 10 mph [16 km/h], rear tires lost traction and the rear of the the vehicle tried to swap ends.

Goodyear tires may hydroplane on wet roads.

SERVICE BULLETIN-REPORTED PROBLEMS: Intermittent reduced power (see bulletin in the Cruze section); engine valve lifter ticking at startup; won't shift into overdrive:

WON'T SHIFT INTO OVERDRIVE

BULLETIN NO.:10-07-30-008B   DATE: NOVEMBER 10, 2010

WOT 4-5 SHIFT FLARE OR TIE UP WITH DTC P0733, P0777, P0735 OR P2723 STORED, INTERMITTENT SLIP IN REVERSE (INSPECT SEALS, REPLACE PISTON/CLUTCH PLATES IF DAMAGED)

2006–11 Chevrolet Silverado and GMC Sierra equipped with Allison(R) 1000 Automatic Transmission (RPO MW7)

CONDITION: Some customers may comment that the transmission won't shift into overdrive, WOT 4-5 shift perceived as either tie-up or flare, intermittent slipping in Reverse or shift inhibited when selecting Reverse. DTC P0777 Pressure Control Solenoid "B" Stuck On or P0735 Incorrect 5th Gear Ratio may be stored. These conditions may not appear until after some mileage and operation, sometimes in the 32,000 to 64,000 km (20,000 to 40,000 mi) range.

CAUSE: This condition may be caused by a torn or cut 3rd, 5th and reverse clutch piston bonded seal. Correction: Inspect the 3rd, 5th and Reverse clutch piston seals for tears or damage on the ID and OD lips and clutch plates for signs of excessive heat and slipping. Replace the piston and clutch plates if damaged. Refer to 1-2-3-4 and 4-5-6 Clutch Assembly and 3-5 Reverse Clutch Assembly Installation in SI. Refer to the GM Electronic Parts Catalog (EPC) for part numbers. Following the piston replacement, reset the transmission adaptive parameters and run "Fast Learn."

Muffler heat shield buzz when driving; squeak noise from rear of vehicle; various noises heard from the front of the vehicle; front brake pulsation/vibration; oil leak at oil cooler hose/pipe assembly; another oil leak from the rear cover; power steering fluid leaking; passenger airbag is not flush with dash; front seat cushion cover detaches; body mount bolt stripped or will not loosen; exhaust leak, rattle, or rumble noise; inoperative low-beam headlights; tapping, clicking, ticking noise at the windshield area; tires leak air or suddenly go flat; excessive interior wind noise; underbody clunk or pop noise while turning or driving on uneven road surfaces (install body mount insulators on all affected 2004–10 large SUVs and trucks); faulty propshaft bolts; poor diesel engine performance:

DIESEL—POOR ENGINE PERFORMANCE/LOW POWER

BULLETIN NO.: 11-06-04-001   DATE: JANUARY 11, 2011

MALFUNCTION INDICATOR LAMP (MIL) ILLUMINATED, POOR ENGINE PERFORMANCE WITH LOW POWER, DTC P0299, P0513, P0606, P0622, P2202 AND/OR P22A0 SET (REPROGRAM ENGINE CONTROL MODULE (ECM))

2010 Chevrolet Express; 2011 Chevrolet Express, Silverado; 2010 GMC Savana; and 2011 GMC Savana, Sierra equipped with 6.6L Duramax(TM) Diesel Engine RPO LML or LGH.

CONDITION: Some customers may comment that the malfunction indicator lamp (MIL) is illuminated and the engine performance is poor with low power. The technician may observe on a scan tool one or more of the following DTC(s) P0299, P0513, P0606, P0622 (Express and Savana only), P2202 and/or P22A0 set as Current or in History.

CAUSE: This condition may be caused by an anomaly in the engine control module (ECM) software.

ASIAN VEHICLES

Minivans Win, Nissan 350Z Loses

The rollover risk in SUVs used to outweigh their size/weight advantage, but that's no longer the case, [thanks to electronic stability control].... Pound for pound, SUVs have lower death rates.

ANNE MCCARTT, SENIOR VICE PRESIDENT FOR RESEARCH
INSURANCE INSTITUTE FOR HIGHWAY SAFETY, JUNE 2011

We Were Hijacked by Pirates

Toyota doesn't want me to speak out, but I can't stand it anymore and somebody has to tell it like it is. The root cause of their problems is that the company was hijacked, some years ago, by anti-family, financially oriented pirates.

JIM PRESS, FORMER PRESIDENT OF TOYOTA USA
THE DETROIT NEWS, FEBRUARY 24, 2010

Deception and Disaster

2011 was the year Toyota suffered one blow after another, including a takeover by company "pirates," two earthquakes, a tsunami, and four nuclear reactor meltdowns.

After losing billions of dollars in sales, paying millions in fines for ignoring owner safety complaints, and losing its reputation as a maker of safe, reliable, and high-quality vehicles, disaster struck the heart of Toyota's business.

On March 11, 2011, a massive earthquake, 9.0 on the Richter scale, struck Fukushima, the region where Toyota builds many of its vehicles (especially hybrids and hybrid components) and also the location of hundreds of key Toyota parts suppliers.

Then came a devastating tsunami that leveled that which hadn't been destroyed earlier. Following that, four nuclear plants melted down, spewing deadly radioactive particles into the air and water.

All that was missing was an invasion of frogs and locusts.

Almost all major automakers have been hurt by the Japanese disasters because the manufacturers buy components from local suppliers. From powertrains to computer modules, the supply chain has been disrupted and the parts contaminated.

Car company publicists have reassured dealers and customers alike: Manufacturing will return to "normal" by year's end. That said, three Russian and one Chilean seaport have turned back contaminated new and used cars hailing from the region; tea sales from the area (said to be the equivalent of France's "champagne" province) are banned; and dangerous levels of radiation have found their way into the Japan's meat and produce chain.

Don't expect a return to "business as usual." When the first Toyota, Honda, or Nissan arrives in our ports and sets off the familiar clicking of a Geiger counter, Japanese car sales will take another nosedive, perhaps permanently.

Stonewalling Safety

Buttressing Toyota USA president Jim Press's allegations, cited on the preceding page, Toyota owner complaints in the late '90s began to show more brake, powertrain, fuel-delivery, and suspension deficiencies than ever before. Toyota insiders told *Lemon-Aid* that Toyota's non-family executives wanted to quickly boost market share and profit, even if it meant quality and safety would suffer. The family tradition of quality, etc., was sidelined while members of the Toyoda family took a backseat in the overall administration of the company. This was confirmed by many Toyota documents subpoenaed by U.S. Congress in early 2010—and later confirmed by Jim Press.

Following Toyota's testimony before Congress in 2010, the U.S. Department of Transportation fined the company $48 million for dragging its feet in recalling its vehicles after sudden, unintended acceleration and brake failures were confirmed by the company's in-house analyses. This year, following one of the worst worldwide recessions in living memory and a series of cataclysmic natural disasters, the Japanese auto industry is struggling to get back on its feet even while, now more than ever, Japanese manufacturers are plagued by questions concerning the quality of their vehicles. Independent reports show that the "decontenting" of new vehicles over the past 15 years has brought down both quality and reliability. Taking on new suppliers and building new plants, as the manufacturers have, will inevitably create more quality problems, especially if the Japanese auto execs keep their "do more with less" mantra.

Rarely does "more for less" succeed in the auto industry, unless you are dealing with bloated, inefficient, and poorly administered automakers, which is not the profile of most Japanese companies. The math doesn't add up. Usually you get "less for less," especially when it comes to quality and dependability: cars are decontented, owner complaints are shrugged off, and supplier payouts are cut. Examples are everywhere: Toyota since 1997, Honda since the 2008 Accord and

2012 Civic redesigns, Nissan's failure-plagued, constant-work-in-progress Quest minivan, and most recently, Hyundai's poor-quality 2011 Elantra and Sonata.

Import Winners and Losers

Through July, sales rose 10 percent from a year earlier for Hyundai and 28 percent for Kia, while deliveries fell 28 percent for Honda and 23 percent for Toyota, the largest Asia-based automaker.

South Korean vehicles—once the laughing stock of car columnists and consumer advocates—have caught up to within a hair's breadth of the Japanese competition in terms of quality and sales. Hyundai is finally putting better-quality parts in its Kia subsidiary's cars, SUVs, and minivans, although it seems to be too little, too late for some Kia models like the Sedona, Sorento, and Spectra.

The emerging BRIC (Brazil, Russia, India, and China) economies are also major players in both the production and the sale of new vehicles for Asian, European, and North American manufacturers. For example:

- Brazil is a big producer of ethanol and ethanol-fuelled vehicles, which it sells to its own burgeoning market and throughout the world. The country is also a major builder of conventional cars and car parts. Quality control on Brazilian vehicles has been average to above average.
- Russia's car industry is booming from both a production and a sales standpoint. Unfortunately, Russian cars are almost as badly built as what China spews out.
- Although struggling, India's Tata Motors is ramping up production at both the high and low ends of the auto market. Its March 2008 purchase of Jaguar and Land Rover from Ford (Ford took a $3 billion bath) reinforces the truism that cash and cachet will always trump common sense (right, Mr. Trump?). Since the purchase, Tata has gone to the Indian government and asked for money. Tata's low-end $2,500 Nano car is remarkably cheap and practical, though basic to the extreme. It's scheduled to arrive in North America in late 2012 and sell for $7,000. The jury is still out as to the overall quality of the Nano and recently produced Jaguar and Land Rover models.
- Chinese car quality is non-existent; Chinese manufacturers make some of the least-crashworthy and poorest-quality vehicles one can find. Yet the Chinese market is larger and hotter than the flagging U.S. market by about a million more units annually. No wonder Ford, GM, and Chrysler spent some of their government loans in China to build joint factories. Their merged sales are presently soaring and that more than compensates for the earlier U.S. downturn.

Everybody knows the Japanese and South Koreans know how to build reliable, fuel-sipping vehicles. Whether they're cars, minivans, sport-utilities, or pickups, and whether they're built in Japan, Canada, Mexico, or the United States, Asian cars give you much more performance and fuel economy for your money than if you were to buy the equivalent vehicle made by Chrysler, Ford, or General Motors—or by most European automakers, for that matter. Most of all, you can count on most Asian vehicles to be easy to repair and relatively slow to depreciate—both admirable qualities in a volatile auto market where models quickly disappear and hapless owners may be left with irreparable, worthless pieces of junk in their driveways (hello, Jaguar, Land Rover, Saab, and Volvo). Undoubtedly, Asian automakers have a more-realistic mix of models that can withstand the vagaries of the marketplace as fuel prices rise and fall. They also know how to squeeze the most profit out of the cars they sell.

It's simple, really. Sell vehicles with less quality content at a higher price. No matter if this practice makes the cars unsafe and unreliable. This is the crisis we are facing thanks to the penny-pinching bean-counters at Honda, Hyundai, Kia, and Toyota. No, automakers don't always learn from their past mistakes.

Cost-cutting is apparent throughout the Civic's interior, from the cheap headliner and ubiquitous hard plastics to the unlined trunk lid. The Civic was once one of our highest-rated small sedans and was our Top Pick in that category as recently as 2007, but it now scores too low to be recommended says Consumers Union, publisher of *Consumer Reports*.

Honda's 2012 Civic: Wake up and smell the citrus.

Honda's Civic, once renowned for cutting-edge performance, bulletproof reliability, and top-quality craftsmanship, has just been relegated to near the bottom of the quality heap by *Consumer Reports*, which explained its decision in the following press release published July 8, 2011:

> We have seen a number of redesigned models do worse in our overall road-test score than the ones they replaced. But the 2012 Honda Civic sets a new mark. That highly anticipated redesign dropped a whopping 17 points—from a very good 78 to a mediocre 61.... Compared with its predecessor, the 2012 Civic is less agile and has lower interior quality. It also suffers from a choppy ride, long stopping distances, and pronounced road noise.... While other models, including the class-leading Hyundai Elantra, have gotten better after being redesigned, the Civic now ranks near the bottom of its category. It's ahead of only the Volkswagen Jetta, which plunged 16 points after its own recent redesign.

The sharp July sales decline for Toyota and Honda has cut sales for Asia-based carmakers by 10.3 percent, while U.S.-based brands increased 9.9 percent. Sales rose 7.6 percent for General Motors, 5.9 percent for Ford Motor Co., and 20 percent for Chrysler Group LLC, which is majority owned by Fiat SpA.

No matter how you cut it, the global auto market has changed dramatically during the past two years. Asian and European automakers will be playing catch-up to the Detroit/Turin Three for at least the next decade through mergers and joint projects, essentially giving truth to the age-old dictum "If you can't beat 'em, join 'em."

Acura

Acura, a division of Honda, sells seven different models in Canada. They are the (Canadian-only) CSX compact sedan, RL luxury performance sedan, the TL performance luxury sedan, the TSX sport sedan, the (living on borrowed time) turbocharged RDX luxury crossover SUV, the MDX luxury SUV, and ZDX four-door sport coupe.

Acuras are good buys, but let's not kid ourselves—most Acura products are basically fully loaded Hondas with a few additional features and unjustifiably high prices. Despite the fact that Acura and Honda dealers have abhorred real price competition for years, poor sales during the past year have forced them to give sizeable rebates and other sales incentives to customers. In their own right, maintenance costs are low, depreciation is generally slower than average, though there are some exceptions, and reliability and quality are much better than average. What few defects Acuras have are usually related to squeaks, rattles, minor trim glitches, and accessories such as the navigation, climate control, and sound systems.

But here's a major worry: With an apparent decline in Honda quality and performance confirmed by owners, consumer groups, and some car critics, how much of this contagion will spread over into Acura's production, which uses the same suppliers and failure-prone components?

CSX ★★★★

RATING: Above Average. Strictly for Canadian buyers desperate to pay extra cash for an Acura nameplate. **Strong points:** The CSX *is* a gussied-up Civic; the differences are in the styling treatment, the equipment, and the trim levels; it's also a well-balanced car that is both practical and fun to drive. In terms of equipment, the Acura CSX falls somewhere in between the loaded Civic EX-L and the high-performance Civic Si. It has more than enough power; handling is better than average; interior room is adequate, with lots of thoughtful storage areas; controls are a breeze to decipher and access; visibility is fairly good; outstanding workmanship and top-quality materials are evident everywhere (all automakers' Ontario plants are renowned for high quality control); its resale value is extraordinarily high; and low-cost leases are available. All CSX models use the same energy-absorbing frame structure that's found on the Civic, so crashworthiness ratings should match the Civic's NHTSA scores of four stars for both front crash protection and rollover resistance. **Weak points:** You are paying excess cash for a bit more cachet. Prices are firm, and freight charges are excessive. The 5-year/unlimited km corrosion perforation warranty is rather chintzy when compared with what is offered by less-prestigious automakers. The redesigned 2012 model has yet to be crash-tested, but all CSX models use the Civic's frame structure, which received only two stars for side crashworthiness from NHTSA. **New for 2012:** See the Honda Civic section. The 2012 CSX has been redesigned and restyled similarly to the 2012 Civic. Arrival in Canada may be delayed until late 2011.

OVERVIEW: The CSX came on the scene as the 2006 model replacement for the discontinued entry-level EL, a successful Honda spin-off that was made in Canada for Canadians. Today's CSX I-TECH is essentially a restyled, more-powerful luxury version of the Honda Civic sedan.

Base models offer many useful features, like electronic stability control, anti-lock brakes, side airbags, side curtain airbags, heated mirrors with integrated turn signals, steering-wheel audio controls, a CD/MP3 player, automatic climate control, cruise control, power windows, and a 60/40 split-folding rear seat.

COST ANALYSIS: Go for the much-improved 2012 version. Better yet, try to buy a second-series CSX (built in March or later), which will have fewer factory-related goofs than the initial run. **Best alternatives:** Consider the cheaper Honda Civic Si, or Hyundai Elantra (redesigned this year), Mazda3 Touring (manual transmission), Nissan Sentra, and Subaru Impreza. **Options:** Ditch the Bridgestone and Firestone tires for Michelin, Yokohama, or Pirelli. **Rebates:**

KEY FACTS (2011 MODELS; SEE THE 2012 HONDA CIVIC FOR 2012 CSX CHANGES)

CANADIAN PRICE (VERY NEGOTIABLE): *I-TECH man.:* $24,290, *I-TECH auto.:* $25,790 **CANADIAN FREIGHT:** $1,395 **POWERTRAIN (FRONT-DRIVE)** Engines: 2.0L 4-cyl. (155 hp) • 2.0L 4-cyl. (197 hp); Transmissions: 5-speed man. • 5-speed auto. • 6-speed man. **DIMENSIONS/CAPACITY** Passengers: 2/3; Wheelbase: 106.2 in.; H: 56.4/L: 178.8/W: 68.9 in.; Legroom F/R: 41.8/36.3 in.; Cargo volume: 12 cu. ft.; Fuel tank: *I-TECH:* 50L/regular; Tow limit: 1,000 lb.; Load capacity: 850 lb.; Turning circle: 39 ft.; Ground clearance: 5.9 in.; Weight: *I-TECH:* 2,894 lb.

Rebates are not likely; look for limited discounting. **Depreciation:** Average. A 2007 CSX sold new for $25,990; today, the car is worth almost half its original value, or $12,000. Detroit-made cars usually lose half their value between their second and third year of use. **Insurance cost:** Higher than average. **Parts supply/cost:** Average. **Annual maintenance cost:** Less than average. **Warranty:** Bumper-to-bumper 5 years/100,000 km; rust perforation 5 years/unlimited km. **Supplementary warranty:** A waste of money. **Highway/city fuel economy:** *I-TECH:* 6.4/8.7 L/100 km, 44/32 mpg.

OWNER-REPORTED PROBLEMS: Most complaints are about premature front brake caliper and rotor wear causing the car to shudder or pull sharply to one side when braking. Other niggling glitches concern body panel gaps, too many squeaks and rattles, paint fading and peeling, and problematic climate control and electrical systems.

SERVICE BULLETIN-REPORTED PROBLEMS: Similar to problems outlined in the Honda Civic section.

TL ★★★★

Acura's 2012 TL looks and handles better. Plus, it burns less fuel.

RATING: Above Average. **Strong points:** Comes in front-drive and all-wheel drive. Much better fuel economy, thanks to the addition of the 6-speed transmission: 2012s are rated 6.8/10.4 L/100 km (TL & TL Tech 6AT), 7.6/11.4 L/100 km (SH-AWD 6AT models), and 8.0/11.9 L/100 km (SH-AWD Tech 6MT model). Plenty of power; comfortable ride; well constructed, with quality mechanical and body components; and awarded NHTSA's maximum five-star occupant protection rating in all categories. Head restraints are given a "Good" rating by IIHS. **Weak points:** Some harsh shifts in Drive, excessive road noise that are unacceptable for a luxury car of this caliber and expense; not as agile as the competition; suspension may be too firm for some; tight rear seating and some acrobatics required for tall passengers entering the rear seat area; buttons, buttons, everywhere. Also, the side mirrors are a bit narrow, reducing rear visibility. **New for 2012:** A new Sequential SportShift 6-speed automatic transmission delivers improved performance and fuel economy; a new Elite model is added to the TL SH-AWD lineup; all models are slightly restyled.

OVERVIEW: The TL combines luxury and performance in a nicely styled, front-drive, five-passenger sedan that uses the same chassis as the Accord and CL coupe. Two engines are offered and are mated to either a 6-speed manual or a 6-speed automatic Sequential SportShift automatic transmission. A limited-slip differential provides impressive acceleration in a smooth and quiet manner. Handling is much improved, with a firm suspension and relatively responsive steering. Bumps can be a bit jarring, but this is a small price to pay for the car's high-speed stability.

Interior accommodations are better than average all around; the cockpit layout is very user-friendly, although learning which buttons perform what tasks takes some practice. Visibility fore and aft is unobstructed.

Standard safety features include ABS, stability and traction control, front seat belt pretensioners, childproof door locks, three-point seat belts, head-protecting airbags, and a transmission/brake interlock.

COST ANALYSIS: Get the 2012 upgraded model for the fuel savings and better overall performance. **Best alternatives:** Consider the Hyundai Genesis or the cheaper Azera, Lexus ES, Nissan Maxima, and Toyota Avalon. **Options:** Don't waste your money on the satellite navigation system; it's confusing to calibrate and hard to see; the Elite trim option isn't worth the extra dough; and ditch the Bridgestone and Firestone tires. **Rebates:** $1,500 rebates; some discounting. **Depreciation:** Slower than average. **Insurance cost:** Higher than average. **Parts supply/cost:** Easily found and moderately priced, especially most mechanical and electronic components, with the exception of some body parts. **Annual maintenance cost:** Less than average. **Warranty:** Bumper-to-bumper 5 years/100,000 km; rust perforation 5 years/unlimited km. **Supplementary warranty:** Not needed. **Highway/city fuel economy (2011):** *3.5L:* 7.5/11.6 L/100 km, 38/24 mpg. *3.7L AWD man.:* 8.0/11.9 L/100 km, 35/24 mpg. *3.7L AWD auto.:* 8.1/12.3 L/100 km, 35/23 mpg.

OWNER-REPORTED PROBLEMS: Very few complaints, except for electrical shorts, minor body fit and finish deficiencies, including sash and door squeaks, misaligned dash, and paint delamination/spotting. Navigation feature can sometimes be annoying to use.

KEY FACTS

CANADIAN PRICE (NEGOTIABLE): *Base:* $39,490, *TECH:* $42,990, *SH-AWD:* $43,490, *TECH:* $46,990, *Elite:* $48,990 **U.S. PRICE:** *Base:* $35,605, *SH-AWD:* $39,155 **CANADIAN FREIGHT:** $1,895 **U.S. FREIGHT:** $885 **POWERTRAIN (FRONT-DRIVE/AWD)** Engines: 3.5L V6 (280 hp) • 3.7L V6 (305 hp); Transmissions: 6-speed man. • 6-speed auto.

DIMENSIONS/CAPACITY
Passengers: 2/3; Wheelbase: 109.3 in.; H: 57.2/L: 194/W: 74 in.; Headroom F/R: 3.5/3.5 in.; Legroom F/R: 42.5/36.2 in.; Cargo volume: 13.1 cu. ft.; Fuel tank: 70L/premium; Tow limit: 1,000 lb.; Load capacity: 850 lb.; Turning circle: 38.4 ft.; Ground clearance: 5.9 in.; Weight: 3,726–3,948 lb.

TSX ★★★

KEY FACTS

CANADIAN PRICE (NEGOTIABLE): *Base:*
$31,890, *Sport Wagon:* est. $30,000,
Premium: $33,690, *TECH package:*
$37,990, *V6 TECH package:* $41,890
U.S. PRICE: *Base:* $29,610, *Sport Wagon:*
$30,960 **CANADIAN FREIGHT:** $1,895
U.S. FREIGHT: $885
POWERTRAIN (FRONT-DRIVE/AWD)
Engines: 2.4L 4-cyl. (201 hp) • 3.5L V6
(280 hp); Transmissions: 5-speed auto. •
6-speed man.
DIMENSIONS/CAPACITY
Passengers: 2/3; Wheelbase: 107 in.;
H: 57/L: 186/W: 73 in.; Headroom F/R:
3.0/2.5 in.; Legroom F/R: 41/27.0 in.;
Cargo volume: 13 cu. ft.; Fuel tank:
70L/premium; Tow limit: 1,000 lb.; Load
capacity: 850 lb.; Turning circle: 36.7
ft.; Ground clearance: 5.9 in.; Weight:
3,440 lb.

RATING: Average. This car is essentially the modified Accord sold in Europe. Buyers comparing the TSX with the Accord or TL will quickly discover that the TSX has less head and shoulder room up front and a more-cramped rear-seat area. **Strong points:** Great steering and handling; generously appointed; instruments and controls are well laid-out; improved navigation system controls; good fit and finish; and reasonable fuel economy. NHTSA crash tests give five stars for driver and passenger crash protection in frontal collisions and side impacts and for rollover resistance. Occupant protection in offset, side, and rear crashes is "Good" according to IIHS. A 5-year/100,000 km bumper-to-bumper warranty. **Weak points:** The 4-cylinder is underpowered, and the V6 is overpriced. Premium fuel negates the small engine's fuel-sipping savings; the interior is a bit snug, especially in the rear; the low roofline hampers rear access; overly sensitive seat sensors may disable the airbag, even when an average-sized adult is seated; and the rear seats have insufficient thigh support. **New for 2012:** The 2011 TSX got a few styling and mechanical upgrades last year, as well as a new wagon variant; the 2012 models are carried over with only minor changes.

OVERVIEW: TSX is an entry-level sports car/wagon equipped with a base 201 hp 2.4L 4-cylinder engine and an optional 280 hp 3.5L V6 that competes in a luxury-sedan niche where V6 power is commonplace. It gets excellent gas mileage but runs on premium fuel only. The car is sportier than the TL, yet it isn't as harsh as the discontinued high-performance RSX. Nevertheless, brake fade is still present after successive stops, manual shifts aren't as quick as with other cars in this class, and the V6 option doesn't give you sportier handling than the 4-banger.

COST ANALYSIS: Get a cheaper, almost-identical 2011 model. Acura has thrown in a cornucopia of standard safety, performance, and convenience features—like standard stability and traction control, and head-protecting side airbags—to make the luxury sedan and sport wagon attractive to shoppers who feel size and V6 power aren't everything. Yet, when you consider the TSX's price is about $8,000 more than a 4-cylinder Honda Accord, you have to wonder whether the vehicle has a lot of cachet—or if its manufacturer has a lot of nerve. **Best alternatives:** Other cars worth considering, although they aren't as well made as the TSX, are the Audi A4, BMW 328i, Buick Regal, Infiniti G37, Lexus IS 250 and 350, and the Lincoln MKZ. The BMW 3 Series and Mercedes C-Class look good but aren't as reliable as the TSX and will likely cost a bundle to maintain. The TSX's size and good looks outclass the TL by far, and the V6 puts it about where the former TL was in size and power. **Options:** Ditch the Bridgestone and Firestone original equipment tires for better-performing Michelin, Yokohama, or Pirelli. **Rebates:** $2,000 rebates, some discounting, and low finance rates. **Depreciation:** A bit slower than average; a $36,100 2007 TSX is worth about $16,000. **Insurance cost:** Higher than average. **Parts supply/cost:** Easily found and moderately priced, especially most mechanical and electronic components. **Annual maintenance cost:** Less than average. **Warranty:** Bumper-to-bumper 5 years/100,000 km; rust perforation 5 years/unlimited km. **Supplementary warranty:** Not needed. **Highway/city fuel economy:** *4-cylinder man.:* 6.8/9.9 L/100 km, 42/29 mpg. *4-cylinder auto.:* 6.2/9.3 L/100 km, 46/30 mpg. *6-cylinder auto.:* 7.0/10.7 L/100 km, 40/26 mpg.

OWNER-REPORTED PROBLEMS: Brakes (noisy brake pads and premature brake caliper and rotor wear); paint peeling and spotting; malfunctioning power accessories and entertainment systems; vehicle suddenly stalled while exiting a freeway. In a crash, seat belt did not restrain driver. Troublesome original equipment Michelin tires.

SERVICE BULLETIN-REPORTED PROBLEMS: Navigation screen may go blank after start-up.

RL

RATING: Average. Known as the Honda Legend to the rest of the world. **Strong points:** Acceptable acceleration that's smooth and quiet in all gear ranges; fuel-efficient 6-speed automatic transmission; average steering and handling; loaded with goodies; above-average reliability; top-quality body and mechanical components; all seats are well cushioned and give plenty of thigh support; good all-around visibility; impressive five-star ratings for front and side occupant

KEY FACTS

CANADIAN PRICE (NEGOTIABLE): *Base:* $64,690 **U.S. PRICE:** *Base:* $46,830
CANADIAN FREIGHT: $1,895
U.S. FREIGHT: $860
POWERTRAIN (AWD)
Engines: 3.7L V6 (300 hp); Transmission: 6-speed auto.
DIMENSIONS/CAPACITY
Passengers: 2/3; Wheelbase: 110.2 in.; H: 57.2/L: 195.8/W: 72.7 in.; Headroom F/R: N/A.; Legroom F/R: 42.4/36.3 in.; Cargo volume: 13.1 cu. ft.; Fuel tank: 70L/premium; Tow limit: 1,000 lb.; Load capacity: 850 lb.; Turning circle: 36.7 ft.; Ground clearance: 6.1 in.; Weight: 4,083 lb.

protection and rollover resistance; IIHS rates rear, offset, and side occupant protection "Good"; a comprehensive 5-year/100,000 km bumper-to-bumper warranty. **Weak points:** Way overpriced and overweight; suspension may be too firm for some; slow steering response; mediocre handling; interior feels cramped (the less-expensive TL offers you AWD with the same engine and is almost as roomy); dash console looks and feels disorganized; audio and navigation systems aren't easy to use; high fuel consumption; problematic navigation system controls. **New for 2012:** Re-engineered and restyled; arrival of the 2012s has been delayed until late fall.

OVERVIEW: Acura's flagship luxury sedan uses the MDX's V6 hooked to a standard 6-speed automatic gearbox and all-wheel drive (stick shift isn't available). The RL is loaded with innovative high-tech safety and convenience features, like heated front seats, front and rear climate controls, a rear-seat trunk pass-through, xenon headlights (get used to oncoming drivers flashing their headlights at you), "smart" side airbags, front seat belt pretensioners, ABS, traction control, and an anti-skid system.

COST ANALYSIS: A prime candidate for cross-border shopping when you consider the RL's $18,000+ markup in Canada. Don't try to save money buying a discounted 2011; the 2012 is much improved. As with all redesigned models, buy an RL built during the second half of 2012. **Best alternatives:** BMW 535xi, Infiniti M35/M35x, and Mercedes-Benz E350. You may want to take a look at the TL sedan, as well. **Options:** Nothing. These cars come stuffed to the gills. **Rebates:** At least

$10,000 of rebates and discounts to bring the MSRP down to a more-rational level. **Depreciation:** Quicker than average, which is surprising for an Acura: a 2007 RL, bought for $63,900, now sells for $24,000...ouch! **Insurance cost:** Higher than average. **Parts supply/cost:** Most mechanical and electronic components are easily found and moderately priced. Body parts may be hard to come by, and they can be expensive. **Annual maintenance cost:** Less than average. **Warranty:** Bumper-to-bumper 5 years/100,000 km; rust perforation 5 years/unlimited km. **Supplementary warranty:** Not needed; the base warranty is fairly applied. **Highway/city fuel economy:** 8.2/12.2 L/100 km, 34/23 mpg.

OWNER-REPORTED PROBLEMS: Electrical, climate control, and audio system failures, accessories that malfunction, and fit and finish glitches.

SERVICE BULLETIN-REPORTED PROBLEMS: Nothing applicable to the 2011–12 models.

MDX ★★★

RATING: Average. **Strong points:** Power is supplied smoothly, with minimal engine noise in all gear ranges; average steering, and handling is helped by the Super Handling All-Wheel Drive (SH-AWD) and Active Damper System (the latter is available in the Elite edition); loaded with goodies; above average reliability; top-quality body and mechanical components; a five-star crashworthiness rating for side occupant protection and a four-star rating for frontal protection and rollover resistance; IIHS rates rear, offset, and side occupant protection "Good"; a comprehensive 5-year/100,000 km bumper-to-bumper warranty. **Weak points:** Overpriced and overweight; acceleration and handling are acceptable but don't inspire confidence; the default suspension setting degrades emergency handling; the rear third seat is a tight fit; the dash console isn't user-friendly; audio and navigation systems are needlessly complicated; high fuel consumption. **New for 2012:** Nothing important.

KEY FACTS

CANADIAN PRICE (NEGOTIABLE): *Base:* $51,190, *TECH package:* $57,290, *Elite package:* $61,990 **U.S. PRICE:** *Base:* $42,230, *TECH package:* $45,905
CANADIAN FREIGHT: $1,895 **U.S. FREIGHT:** $860
POWERTRAIN (AWD)
Engine: 3.7L V6 (300 hp); Transmission: 6-speed auto.
DIMENSIONS/CAPACITY
Passengers: 2/3/2; Wheelbase: 108.3 in.; H: 68.2/L: 191.6/W: 78.5 in.; Headroom F/R: 4.0/4.0 in.; Legroom F/R: 41.2/38.7 in.; Cargo volume: 42 cu. ft.; Fuel tank: 72.7L/premium; Tow limit: 5,000 lb.; Load capacity: 1,160 lb.; GVWR: 5,732 lb.; Turning circle: 37.6 ft.; Ground clearance: 8.2 in.; Weight: 4,550 lb.

OVERVIEW: Introduced as a 2001 model, the MDX got its first complete redesign for the 2007 model year, making this mid-sized sport-utility more competitive. Acura's revamping has smoothed out the powertrain's functions, made the vehicle a bit more agile, and softened the suspension. On the other hand, the car loses its grip during avoidance manoeuvres, has a cramped interior when carrying a full passenger load, and the busy dashboard has tiny buttons everywhere.

COST ANALYSIS: Get a discounted, practically identical 2011 version. **Best alternatives:** The BMW X5, Buick Enclave, Chevrolet Traverse, Infiniti FX35, and Lexus RX series, or one of the models from the GMC Acadia trio. Would you like comparable Asian performance and reliability for about $11,000 less? Try a Honda Pilot (the MDX's cheaper cousin) for its additional passenger- and cargo-hauling capability, a Nissan Xterra, or a Toyota Highlander. The Volvo XC90 and Mercedes ML320, ML350, or ML550 have adequate cargo room with all the rows down, but they have neither comparable cargo room behind the second row nor comparable quality control and dealer servicing. Furthermore, Ford's announcement that Volvo has been sold to Chinese interests compromises the future of Volvo sales and servicing in North America. **Options:** Forget the satellite navigation system. **Rebates:** Look for $2,000 rebates on the 2011 models, and a similar amount in the late winter applicable to the early 2012 models. **Depreciation:** Much faster than average; a 2007 base MDX is barely worth $23,000 (quite a comedown for a vehicle that sold originally for $52,300). **Insurance cost:** Higher than average. **Parts supply/cost:** Most mechanical and electronic components are easily found and moderately priced. Body parts may be hard to come by, and they can be expensive. **Annual maintenance cost:** Average. **Warranty:** Bumper-to-bumper 5 years/100,000 km; rust perforation 5 years/unlimited km. **Supplementary warranty:** Not needed; the base warranty is fairly applied. **Highway/city fuel economy:** 9.6/13.2 L/100 km, 29/21 mpg.

OWNER-REPORTED PROBLEMS: Noisy brake pads and premature brake wear; malfunctioning power accessories and entertainment systems. No complaints on the 2011s have been reported to NHTSA.

RATING: Average. **Strong points:** Adequate power, though turbo lag (a delay between throttle application and acceleration) is a big minus. Handles like a tall sports car: tight and responsive, with excellent braking. Seating and driving positions work for occupants of all sizes. The nicely appointed interior is well laid-out, with plenty of small storage areas; the seats have good thigh and back support; above average reliability; top-quality mechanical components; a five-star crashworthiness rating for front and side occupant protection, and a four-star rating for rollover resistance; IIHS rates rear, offset, and side occupant protection "Good"; a comprehensive 5-year/100,000 km bumper-to-bumper warranty. **Weak points:** The buzzy, fuel-thirsty 4-cylinder engine competes in a class where 6- and 8-cylinders are the norm; turbo lag; stiff-riding, with some jostling when passing over uneven terrain; more pavement noise than one would expect in a luxury car; the interior pillars look very unrefined, with some misaligned plastics; difficult to learn the computerized audio, climate, and navigation systems; no engine temperature gauge, and the turbo boost gauge is superfluous; the small space-saver spare tire has no place in a car this expensive. The front-drive version is sold in the States only. **New for 2012:** Returns relatively unchanged.

KEY FACTS

CANADIAN PRICE (NEGOTIABLE): *Base:* $39,990, *TECH package:* $42,990
U.S. PRICE: *Base:* $32,620, *TECH package:* $35,720 **CANADIAN FREIGHT:** $1,895 **U.S. FREIGHT:** $860
POWERTRAIN (AWD)
Engine: 2.3L 4 Turbo (240 hp); Transmission: 5-speed auto.
DIMENSIONS/CAPACITY
Passengers: 2/3; Wheelbase: 104.3 in.; H: 65.1/L: 182.4/W: 73.6 in.; Headroom F/R: 4.0/3.5 in.; Legroom F/R: 40.5/27.5 in.; Cargo volume: 27.8 cu. ft.; Fuel tank: 72.7L/premium; Tow limit: 1,500 lb.; Load capacity: 870 lb.; GVWR: 5,732 lb.; Turning circle: 41 ft.; Ground clearance: 6.2 in.; Weight: 3,941 lb.

OVERVIEW: Essentially a Honda CR-V clone, the RDX carries Honda's first turbocharged 4-cylinder engine, which makes it a pleasure to drive but a pain to fuel. The RDX takes over from the MDX as Acura's entry-level crossover SUV. Although its dimensions are similar to that of the Honda CR-V, the RDX uses a unique platform developed to handle the vehicle's advanced all-wheel-drive system and peppy turbocharged engine.

COST ANALYSIS: Get the practically identical 2011 model and compare prices in the States; there are sizeable reductions south of the border. The premium for the RDX can be whittled down to about half as much through smart haggling. The extra dough gets you a more-powerful drivetrain, a more-refined interior, more tech gadgets, and different front-end styling. If these attributes don't turn you on, then save yourself the $4,000–$8,000 and get a CR-V. **Best alternatives:** Subaru Forester, Toyota RAV4 (only with brake override), BMW X3, Honda CR-V, Infiniti EX, and Mazda CX-7. **Rebates:** Look for $3,000 rebates on the 2011s, and a similar amount applicable to the early 2012 models in the summer of 2012. **Options:** The Bluetooth satellite navigation system should be compared with the less-expensive Garmin devices. The $4,000+ technology package—the 10-speaker audio system with satellite radio and the full computerized navigation package with backup camera—is a money-waster. **Rebates:** With a top price of $40,490, there are at least $5,000 worth of rebates and discounts that you can use to bring the suggested list price down to an acceptable level. **Depreciation:** Much faster than average: A first-year 2007 base model that sold for $41,000 now fetches $17,500. **Insurance cost:** Higher than average. **Parts supply/cost:** Except for turbo components, most mechanical and electronic components are easily found and moderately priced. Body parts may be hard to come by, and they can be expensive. **Annual maintenance cost:** Average. **Warranty:** Bumper-to-bumper 5 years/100,000 km; rust perforation 5 years/unlimited km. **Supplementary warranty:** Not needed. **Highway/city fuel economy:** 8.7/11.7 L/100 km, 32/24 mpg.

OWNER-REPORTED PROBLEMS: Poor audio reception. Most of the problems reported by owners concern accessories, like the gauges, instruments, AC, and entertainment system; electrical short circuits; and noisy brakes that wear out prematurely.

SERVICE BULLETIN-REPORTED PROBLEMS: Oil leaks from the engine cylinder head cover:

ENGINE OIL LEAKS FROM THE CYLINDER HEAD COVER

BULLETIN NO.: 10-049   DATE: NOVEMBER 24, 2010

2007–10 RDX–ALL; 2011 RDX 2WD–From VIN 5J8TB2...BA000001 thru 5J8TB2...BA001016; 2011 RDX 4WD– From VIN 5J8TB1...BA000001 thru 5J8TB1...BA000980

SYMPTOM: The cylinder head cover is leaking engine oil.

PROBABLE CAUSE: There is paint overspray in the gasket groove in the cylinder head cover.

CORRECTIVE ACTION: Remove the cylinder head cover, and sand away the paint overspray.

RATING: Below Average for a luxury car that could have been made by Acura's Tonka division. **Strong points:** The V6 and 6-speed automatic combine to provide smooth and sufficient power for all driving situations; a firm ride; handles reasonably well; plenty of safety, performance, and convenience features that are luxurious and high-tech; a well-appointed interior. Reliability has always been first class. NHTSA gives five stars for side crash protection; four stars for frontal protection and rollover resistance. **Weak points:** Location, location, location. Where to put your passengers? Where to put your cargo? Where do you put your head to see out the side and back windows? This is a claustrophobia-inducing small SUV that is a poster child for poor design. It has a cramped backseat, Cirque du Soleil rear seat access, limited cargo space, a low roof, and a tall beltline. **New for 2012:** Returns without any significant changes.

KEY FACTS

CANADIAN PRICE (NEGOTIABLE): *Base:* $54,990

U.S. PRICE: *Base:* $46,020 **CANADIAN FREIGHT:** $1,895 **U.S. FREIGHT:** $860

POWERTRAIN (AWD)
Engine: 3.7L (300 hp); Transmission: 6-speed auto.

DIMENSIONS/CAPACITY
Passengers: 2/3; Wheelbase: 108.3 in.; H: 62.8/L: 192.4/W: 78.5 in.; Legroom F/R: 42.2/35.7 in.; Cargo volume: 26.2 cu. ft.; Fuel tank: 79.5L/premium; Tow limit: 1,500 lb.; Load capacity: 870 lb.; Turning circle: 38.5 ft.; Ground clearance: 7.9 in.; Weight: 4,410 lb.

OVERVIEW: An MDX-based coupe-like luxury SUV, the ZDX carries a hefty 300 hp 3.7L V6 that is coupled to a 6-speed automatic transmission. If you're looking for a utilitarian family-hauler with towing capability and comfortable back seats, the ZDX is the wrong car for you.

COST ANALYSIS: Get the practically identical 2011 model, and seriously consider saving $10,000 by getting your ZDX in the States, where both the base price and freight charges are much less. Be prepared for a big depreciation hit: a year-old 2010 Tech Package version that first sold for $59,590 is now worth only $47,000.

Best alternatives: The Acura MDX has more rear passenger and cargo space, with the same interior quality and technology, all for about $4,000 less than the ZDX, and only slightly worse fuel economy. The BMW X6 is also worth considering. **Rebates:** Look for $2,000 rebates on the 2011s, and a similar amount in the summer of 2012 applicable to the early 2012 models. **Options:** Nothing more is needed. **Depreciation:** Fairly rapid. **Insurance cost:** Higher than average. **Parts supply/cost:** Most mechanical and electronic components are used on other Acura models, so they are easily found and moderately priced. Body parts are unique and not easily found due to low-volume ZDX sales; this can add to collision repair time and cost. **Annual maintenance cost:** Average. **Warranty:** Bumper-to-bumper 5 years/100,000 km; rust perforation 5 years/unlimited km. **Supplementary warranty:** Not needed. **Highway/city fuel economy:** 8.8/12.7 L/100 km, 32/22 mpg.

OWNER-REPORTED PROBLEMS: Electrical short circuits and brake calipers/rotors that quickly wear out.

SERVICE BULLETIN-REPORTED PROBLEMS: Acuras don't generate many service bulletins or NHTSA-logged owner complaints—one of the main reasons Acuras and Hondas are so popular.

Honda

Starting Over

Honda, Nissan, and Toyota were the auto manufacturers hit hardest by natural disasters in Japan earlier this year, though Honda is having the worst time re-starting production. Consequently, these automakers are suffering from extremely tight car inventories, which have caused Honda and Toyota sales to fall by double digits, posting their worst June results since 1997, says *Edmunds*:

> Honda's plants have taken longer to resume full production both in Japan and the U.S. than those of Toyota Motor Corp. and Nissan Motor Corp. Honda said its net profit for the 2012 fiscal year will decline by 63%, mainly because of the impact of the quake. Honda expects lingering issues to slow production of its popular Civic due to parts shortages. For the Canadian market, the Civic is built in Allison, Ontario and its production lines have been hobbled by insufficient parts coming from Japan.

Honda will ramp up production in the fall of 2011; however, industry insiders don't see supply being anywhere near normal before 2012. Additionally, many parts suppliers will need much more time to rebuild their factories and re-establish new working relationships with other factories to ensure they can provide quality parts at reasonable prices. Yes, Humpty Dumpty can be fixed, but it will take more time than the automakers are letting on and the pieces might not fit together very well at first. Which would be another blow to Honda's and Toyota's reputations for building quality car and trucks.

But why would Asian automakers warn of long delays, especially for hybrid cars and parts, if that would cause them to lose sales? The objective of keeping market share is to sign up as many customers as possible, as soon as possible, to keep the cash flowing and the dealers content—even if you have to promise early delivery with your fingers crossed behind your back.

Of course production delays will become more frequent throughout the year and Honda will offer buyers more generous rebates, low-cost financing, and cheap leases to make room for next year's models. Over this past summer we have seen the three largest Japanese automakers (Honda, Nissan, and Toyota) drop prices and hike sales incentives to poach buyers from competitors. Now they are pushing prices higher to sell their reduced inventory for what the market will bear.

Take advantage of any sweetened deals you find, as long as you also remember to add a clause to the sales contract specifying a firm delivery date and a penalty the dealer must pay if that date is missed.

Honda is not bringing much new product to the table this year. Except for a disappointingly redesigned Civic compact and CR-V SUV, Honda's 2012 lineup is carried over without any significant changes. For the most part, Honda engineers have slightly tweaked the 2012 models to enhance fuel economy, safety, comfort, and convenience. In this way, the automaker hopes to turn its sales slump around, despite more small-car competition from recent arrivals like the Chevrolet Cruze, Ford Fiesta and Focus, Hyundai Elantra and Sonata, and the Mazda2.

In June, Civic sales in Canada totalled 4,682 units—a respectable figure beaten by the Hyundai Elantra, which found 4,975 new owners that month.

Here are the top 10 bestselling cars in Canada during the first six months of 2011:

1. Honda Civic: 26,371
2. Hyundai Elantra: 24,283
3. Toyota Corolla: 18,853
4. Chevrolet Cruze: 18,769
5. Mazda3: 18,446
6. Volkswagen Jetta: 14,068
7. Ford Focus: 12,659
8. Hyundai Accent: 11,304
9. Ford Fusion: 10,154
10. Hyundai Sonata: 9,269

One tweak that Honda hasn't admitted to doing, but which has caused an apparent decline in quality over the past several years, is the "decontenting" of its product lineup. Examining Honda owner complaints against confidential Honda service bulletins and NHTSA ODI owner safety complaints, it's obvious that quality content has been reduced to make the most profit from each sale. This is the same strategy that Toyota Canada adopted in 1997, which led to a $2 million settlement with the Ottawa Competition Bureau price-fixing probers (acting on a *Lemon-Aid* petition) and resulted in a $48 million fine levied by Washington's NHTSA for delaying recalls in 2010.

Can Honda close Pandora's box and return to performance and quality trumping quick profits and greater market share? After all, Ford exorcized many of its own devils. However, with the arrival of a seriously decontented 2012 on which many Acuras are based (principally, the CSX), quality and performance will likely take a back seat to fuel economy and comfort.

One fear among owners is that reduced quality could cut the resale value of both Honda and Acura models. So far this hasn't been the case. The *Canadian Black Book* concludes that Hondas have the fourth-best 48-month residual values in Canada. It is estimated that four years from now a typical Honda car will be worth 47.7 percent of its original price, while the four-year residual value for a Honda truck or SUV would be 48.8 percent.

Of course, this isn't counting the expected lowered residual value of Hondas and Acuras following the company's massive discounting and increased sales incentives as Honda struggles to increase its cash flow, as it's besieged by owner complaints and buyer skepticism.

FIT ★★★★★

RATING: Recommended. This four-door, five-passenger mini hatchback is surprisingly roomy and reasonably fuel-efficient, thanks to its small, 1.5L 4-cylinder engine mated to a 5-speed manual transmission. Slotted below the Civic, the Fit is one of the better choices among the 2012 small cars. **Strong points:** Plenty of smooth, quiet power with either the manual or automatic transmission; handles and brakes like a sports car; good interior ergonomics;

standard power accessories, ABS, and side curtain airbags; versatile interior; above average crashworthiness ratings; quality craftsmanship; and good resale value. **Weak points:** A busy ride. If you thought the Ford Fusion head restraints were a "pain in the neck," read on:

> The head rest pushes my head forward and strains my neck to the point that I either have to sit upright away from the seat or stretch my neck far out in pain. Either way it is not safe, whether in case of accident or generally for my health. With no cool-off period on new cars in California, I cannot return the car, which at this point has 12 miles [19 km] on it, so I am forced to drive unsafely. I ran Google search for Honda head rest complaints and found out that customers have been complaining about Honda's new head rests for the same very reason since 2007 for most of their models—from Accord and Odyssey to Fit.

> What makes the matter worse is that you cannot reverse the headrest as there are grooves only on one of the two support poles. By making head restraint extremely uncomfortable to use, Honda is forcing its customers to drive unsafely, specifically without head restraint. I spoke to [the] service manager at my dealer and he told me that Honda does not have adjustable or reversible head restraints.

> He is also aware of the complaints from the customers. Solution should be easy to implement by making the head rest reversible for those like me with neck or back problems. I drove Hondas for 18 years and cannot believe that Honda has not responded to 3 years of continuous complaints.

Traction control and an anti-skid system are available, but only for the more-expensive models. Owner complaints include the following: The airbag failed to deploy; rear view is a bit narrow; some transmission seal leaks; weak AC; small gas tank; fuel sloshing noise heard under the front seats; no floormats; touchy, squeaky brakes; vehicle sways and wanders when encountering moderate side winds; jerky acceleration when driving in traffic; excess gear shifting over hilly terrain; some interior engine and road noise; bland exterior and interior styling; paint peeling and delamination; no centre armrest; dealers won't budge on prices; and owners say fuel economy is overstated by about 30 percent. There are reports that manual-transmission-equipped Fits are rare and seldom sell for their suggested retail price. **New for 2012:** Nothing significant.

OVERVIEW: The 2012 Honda Fit is small on the outside, but big on the inside. It sips fuel and still performs well. Sure, its 1.5L engine isn't in the big leagues, but you will seldom realize you're driving a mini-compact. Hey, nine seconds to 100 km/h using a manual gearbox? That's outstanding, considering the competition (Toyota's Prius, seniors on walkers, and the Canadian Senate). The Fit beats most of its competitors and is no slouch with an automatic, either. Handling is easy and predictable, but the ride is somewhat choppy due to the car's small size. Innovative seats allow you to lift the rear seat's base up against the backrest to make room for bulky items, or the seat can be folded flat, which doubles the cargo space. You can even configure the seats to make a small bed.

NHTSA gives the Fit its top rating of five stars for occupant protection in a frontal collision; five stars for driver protection in a side impact; and four stars for side passenger protection and rollover prevention. Reliability has been above average, judging by NHTSA and *Consumer Reports* postings, as well as European owner reviews of the Jazz/Fit.

COST ANALYSIS: Save money by buying a practically identical 2011 version. **Best alternatives:** Other good econocars this year are the Honda Civic (2011), Hyundai Accent, Mazda3, and the Nissan Versa. Toyota's Yaris? It's a bit scary with its history of brake sensor failures. The Chevy Aveo, Dodge Avenger, and Mercedes Smart Car bring up the rear of the pack; they're cheap, but problematic. The Smart is especially weak, with sales that have tumbled from 24,622 units in 2008 to a tad over 5,000 cars sold in 2010. **Options:** Nothing worth the extra money. **Rebates:** Look for $1,000 rebates on the 2011 models and a similar amount in the new year, applicable to the early 2012s. Remember, sales have fallen below expectations, making dealers happy to haggle. **Depreciation:** A little slower than average. For example, a 2008 Fit that sold for $15,000 is still worth about $9,000. **Insurance cost:** Average. **Parts supply/cost:** No trouble finding parts at a fair price. **Annual maintenance cost:** Less than average. **Warranty:** Bumper-to-bumper 5 years/100,000 km; rust perforation 5 years/unlimited km. **Supplementary warranty:** Basic warranty is sufficient. **Highway/city fuel economy:** *Man.:* 5.7/7.2 L/100 km, 50/39 mpg. *Auto.:* 5.5/7.1 L/100 km, 51/40/ mpg. Interestingly, tests prove the automatic gearbox is more fuel-efficient than the manual transmission.

OWNER-REPORTED PROBLEMS: Incredibly well made. Only 30 complaints logged by NHTSA during the past two years when 100 would be the norm. Owners of 2010 models report sudden acceleration and airbag failures; windshield stress fractures; painful head restraints; seat belts that break and a tire jack that may bend sideways when lifting the car; periodic brake failures; paint chipping and premature cosmetic rusting; insufficient legroom that causes drivers to apply the brakes and accelerator at the same time; and the dashboard's elevated design obstructs forward visibility. Road debris easily destroys the AC condenser on earlier models—an expensive repair not covered under warranty—but discounts are given under a "goodwill" warranty.

CIVIC ★★★

RATING: Average. Civic's redesign isn't a big deal, and it certainly is no reason to go out and buy a 2012 thinking you are getting a better car. You're not. It has completely new sheet metal but looks the same as last year's model; the interior has more space, but few passengers will notice. The base 1.8L engine is a carryover, and despite some tweaking, power is only slightly changed. Fuel economy is improved a bit with the manual transmission and more so with the 5-speed automatic. This said, many buyers will find the Chevrolet Cruze and Hyundai Elantra cheaper, more stylish, and better-equipped. As Canada's most popular small car for the past 13 years (although Hyundai's Elantra is closing the gap), the Honda Civic is one of the best-performing small cars around. It's a comfortable, refined,

KEY FACTS

CANADIAN PRICE (NEGOTIABLE): *DX:* $14,990, *LX Coupe:* $17,990, *EX:* $21,190, *EX-L:* $24,890, *Si:* $25,990, *Hybrid Sedan:* $27,350 **U.S. PRICE:** *DX 2 d. manual Sedan:* $15,605, *Auto.:* $16,405, *4d. manual Sedan:* $15,805, *Auto.:* $16,605, *LX 2d manual Sedan:* $17,655, *4d. manual Sedan:* $17,855, *2d. auto. Sedan:* $18,455, *4d. auto. Sedan:* $18,655, *Si 2d manual:* $22,205, *Si 4d manual:* $22,405 *Base Hybrid:* $24,050 **CANADIAN FREIGHT:** $1,395 **U.S. FREIGHT:** $770 **POWERTRAIN (FRONT-DRIVE)**
Engines: (Hybrid)1.5L 4-cyl. (110 hp) plus electric motor (23 hp) • 1.8L 4-cyl. (140 hp) • 2.04L 4-cyl. (201 hp); Transmissions: 5-speed man. • 5-speed auto. • 6-speed man. • CVT auto.

DIMENSIONS/CAPACITY (SEDAN)
Passengers: 2/3; Wheelbase: 105.1 in.; H: 56.5/L: 177.3/W: 69 in.; Headroom F/R: 3.0/2.0 in.; Legroom F/R: 42.0/36.2 in.; Cargo volume: 12.5 cu. ft.; Fuel tank: 50L/regular; Load capacity: 850 lb.; Turning circle: 35.4 ft.; Weight: 2,672 lb.

DIMENSIONS/CAPACITY (HYBRID)
Passengers: 2/3; Wheelbase: 105.1 in.; H: 56.5/L: 177.3/W: 69 in.; Headroom F/R: 3.0/2.0 in.; Legroom F/R: 42.0/36.2 in.; Cargo volume: 10.7 cu. ft.; Fuel tank: 47L/regular; Tow limit: N/A; Load capacity: 850 lb.; Turning circle: 35.4 ft.; Weight: 2,853 lb.

and time-tested vehicle that is also Canadian-built. Be wary of buying from first-series production, however. Honda redesigns embody lots of factory- and supplier-related mistakes that can take at least a year to correct, as was painfully true with the Accord's 2008 redesign. **Strong points:** Honda's "death grip" on no-haggle pricing has been broken. Poor sales have forced the company to offer sizeable rebates and sales incentives. This means you should politely tell your Honda dealer that the list price isn't acceptable and that you want at least a 5 percent discount. The sales agent will hem and haw, but you will get that discount as the new year approaches and the Civic's performance and quality control problems come to light. These cars are noted for good acceleration; a smooth-shifting automatic transmission; great handling and good cornering control; responsive, direct steering; and a comfortable, firm ride. A quieter cabin houses the two-tier instrument panel and instruments and controls are easily accessed. A tilt/telescoping steering wheel is standard, and interior space is more than adequate for most adults. Best of all, these cars generally have a strong resale value. **Weak points:** Not as reliable as previous models; plus, performance and comfort is subpar. Something as simple as painful, poorly designed head restraints are a case in point. They must have been designed by the Marquis de Sade working under the tutelage of Toyota CEO Akio "I didn't know our cars would suddenly accelerate, with no brakes, Senator…sniff, sniff" Toyoda. Malfunctioning indicator lights:

> I purchased a brand new 2012 Civic EX, and a week later the indicator lights start flicking on and off. I take it in to have it serviced (at this point I am really disappointed having to take in a week-old car to have it serviced), and after 5 DAYS! at the service center, they call me and tell me that the problem has been solved. I go down and pick it up, but 4 days later, the indicator lights start flicking on again. So I take it in and here I am waiting for the reply from the dealership.

A bland interior and exterior; the coupe's steeply raked front windshield cuts forward visibility; the expansive dash shelf and sloping nose make it tough to judge distance when parking, and rear visibility isn't impressive, either; the suspension may be too firm for some; the coupe's interior noise is less isolated than in the sedan; the coupe's rear access takes some effort, and seating is a bit cramped; trunk hinges intrude into the cargo area; and there are some fit and finish problems. **New for 2012:** A complete redesign.

OVERVIEW: The reworked Civic went on sale last May and is the first of three Hondas to be redesigned within the year; the other two are the CR-V crossover primed for November 2011 and the revamped Accord, due out in September 2012.

Honda has been beaten up by the competition, which has many new or refreshed models such as the Chevrolet Cruze, Ford Focus and Fiesta, Hyundai Elantra, Kia Forte, and Toyota Corolla. Hyundai and Kia in particular are keeping ahead by using better-quality materials and skilled craftsmanship backed up by low prices and comprehensive warranties.

Honda's newer models have failed to find much traction in the market. For instance, sales of the CR-Z sporty hybrid and Accord Crosstour crossover have been major disappointments to say the least.

Now it's the Civic's turn.

Neither changing the Civic's superb "driver in charge" driving dynamics nor adding to its girth (yes, it has grown to about the size of a 1994 Accord), the 2012 revision targets greater fuel economy on its entry-level Civic and adds a paltry four more horses to the Si model's output. Engines are hooked to either a 5-speed manual or automatic transmission (competitors use six speeds), while the costlier Si makes do with a 6-speed manual. There's also a revised, cheap-looking plastic two-tier instrument panel, and the car is about 40 pounds lighter. The wheelbase is shorter by an inch and a half, and the Si gets stiffer suspension settings and a limited-slip differential. 2012 Civic hybrids now carry a 1.5L engine, instead of the previous model's 1.3L; the electric motor has slightly more horsepower and uses a stop-start fuel-saving mode; and a new lithium ion battery has been added. HF hybrids are styled more aerodynamically and roll on low-resistance tires. Honda has dropped the stop-start feature on the HF to keep down cost and complexity.

Standard features are 15-inch wheels, stability control, side-curtain airbags, ABS brakes, power windows, and auto-off headlights. Unlike much of the competition, entry-level Civics lack AC, radio refinements, and power mirrors and door locks.

COST ANALYSIS: A year-long slump in Honda sales has led to some price discounting as well as more-affordable leases and financing charges. Civics also retain higher resale values than most cars, taking the sting out of the excess loonies you may have originally paid. **Best alternatives:** Civic faces some formidable competitors this year, like Chevrolet's new fuel-efficient Cruze, Ford's brand new high-tech and restyled Focus, the fuel-efficient and more aggressively styled Hyundai Elantra, a peppy and stylish Mazda3, the "pocket rocket" Kia Forte, and a larger and less expensive VW Jetta. **Options:** If you go with fewer, less expensive options, such as on interior/exterior trim, wheel packages etc., you can get a Civic for around $3,000 less than advertised. Try to get a free extra set of ignition keys written into the contract; Honda's anti-start, theft-protection keys may cost as much as $150 per set. Steer clear of the standard-issue radio and problematic Firestone or Bridgestone tires. **Rebates:** Mostly related to leasing and low-cost financing. **Depreciation:** Slower than average. A 2008 Civic Coupe that once sold for $17,000 is still worth almost $11,000. **Insurance cost:** Average. **Parts supply/cost:** Reasonably priced and easily found at dealers and independent suppliers. Hybrid parts may be back ordered due to production cutbacks in Japan. **Annual maintenance cost:** Much less than average. **Warranty:** Bumper-to-bumper 3 years/60,000 km; powertrain 5 years/100,000 km; rust perforation 6 years/unlimited km. **Supplementary warranty:** Not needed. **Highway/city fuel economy:** *1.8L (140 hp) man.:* 5.4/7.4 L/100 km, 52/38 mpg. *Auto.:* 5.7/8.2 L/100 km, 50/34 mpg. *2.0L man.:* 6.8/10.2 L/100 km, 42/28 mpg. *Hybrid:* 5.3 L/100 km (combined highway/city), 44 mpg.

OWNER-REPORTED PROBLEMS: Let's start with faulty seat belts and airbags: A fire ignited in the seat belt wiring under the passenger seat; seat belts tighten progressively when connected; a child was injured when he became entangled in an unfastened rear centre shoulder belt, which retracted, cutting off his air; seat belts don't always retract into the harness; airbag warning light stays lit even though an adult passenger occupies the seat; seat belts fail to lock up in a sudden panic stop; and there have been a multitude of complaints of inadvertent side airbag deployment, or failing to deploy in collisions.

Mechanical failures are legion. Most common failings are fractured front tie rod, causing complete steering loss; sudden acceleration or surging when AC or heater is engaged, or when the steering wheel is turned sharply; car veers sharply to the right when braking; brake and accelerator pedal are mounted too close together. Surging when brakes are applied; sudden acceleration:

> The contact owns a 2012 Honda Civic. The contact was reversing into a residential garage when the vehicle abnormally accelerated forward as the brake was disengaged. On a different occasion, while driving uphill and releasing the brakes, the vehicle accelerated in reverse instead. In order to prevent the vehicle from rolling backward, the contact would continuously depress the accelerator pedal. The vehicle was taken to the dealer who stated that the failure was normal. The manufacturer was made aware of the failure who did not offer any assistance. The vehicle was not repaired.

•

> Sudden acceleration surge, to the point of having to completely hold the brake with both feet. At one point, after putting car into Neutral, the engine revved to 7000 rpm before owner could turn car off.

Cruise control doesn't stay at its set speed; chronic stalling accompanied by steering-wheel lock-up. Engine momentarily maintains high rpm when decelerating. Fuel leakage into the engine compartment while vehicle is underway; car has to warm up a few minutes before brakes will work properly; vehicle rolls back when stopped on an incline with automatic transmission engaged; transmission surges forward when put in Reverse (blamed on transmission solenoid); automatic transmission will suddenly downshift in traffic; when accelerator pedal is tapped at less than 5 km/h, vehicle suddenly passes from Drive to Neutral to Reverse; transmission won't easily go into First gear; steering wheel wouldn't lock when parked; steering wheel shakes when turned sharply to the left or right; sunlight reflection from the dashboard to the windshield reduces visibility; taller drivers' vision blocked by nonadjustable, windshield-mounted rear-view mirror; driver's sun visor keeps falling down, obstructing vision; loose driver's seat; head restraint pushes head too far forward:

> I have tilted the seat back as far as I safely can and still be able to drive. I am [a] 53 year old female, 5'3" tall, and wear bifocals. I am having difficulty focusing from tachometer to speedometer to road because I cannot [move] my head to use the right

part of my glasses to see. I cannot tilt my head back at all because of the headrest. I also experienced a headache that evening as well due to eye strain. The NHSTA changed their headrest regulations in 2008. Test dummies for large males were used and then standards were put in place. After spending thousands of dollars on a new car, I am unable to safely drive it. I have to either remove, turn around, or jerry-rig a remedy for the headrest in order to drive and not suffer neck, back, shoulder, and visual pain. The cost is my safety in an accident. Or, I can leave the headrest and drive with my posture in a horrid position. I cannot sit up straight, my head is forced downward so I cannot use my bifocals properly, and I cannot tilt the seat back any further and still see over the dashboard.

Windshield cracked suddenly; difficult to see through bottom of windshield; with AC engaged at night, a film covers rear windshield (said to be caused by either an engine head gasket failure or "outgassing" from the interior's plastic trim); AC blamed for emitting toxic fumes:

> The HVAC (air conditioning/heating system/defroster) immediately started spewing toxic mold/mildew spores on a new vehicle test-driven at the dealer's. It occurs while driving, after running the air conditioning for a few minutes, turning the air conditioning off (while leaving the fan running) and waiting a few minutes. It then stinks for a few minutes and then disappears.

Other factory-related annoyances that may mostly injure your wallet, or fry your nerves: Hard starts, engine won't crank, or suddenly stalls; engine oil leaks; car won't move in Drive; early automatic transmission replacement, transmission fluid leaks, and noisy engagement; stalling in Reverse or Drive; manual transmission grinds when shifting into Third gear; heater blower motor overheats or blows a fuse; malfunctioning alternator; noise from the wheel bearing, brake pedal booster, clutch pedal, or master cylinder; oil leaks from the lower engine block crack; motor mounts failure; faulty main rear crankshaft seal; sluggish performance when it rains or when passing through a large puddle; transmission periodically won't shift into Third or Fourth gear (torque converter replaced); premature wheel bearing replacement; excessive steering shimmy; and front strut leakage causes noise and difficult handling; tire rims easily collect snow, ice, and dirt; and Dunlop and Firestone tires have tread separation and the premature wearout of brake pads and discs:

> My 2011 Honda Civic LX-S has only 13,000 miles [21,000 km] on it and my break pads have already worn down to nothing and had to be replaced yesterday. The repair guy told me there is absolutely no way that at such low miles that this should have happened. There must have been a problem with the original breaks on my car and $378 later, I already had to replace them.

Body fit and finish and accessories are also problematic: A-pillar, dash, or sunroof rattles; windows bind or come out of run channels; doors and trunk lid hard to close; inoperable fuel-door handle; body and bumper paint peeling and cracking; poorly mounted driver's seat; inoperable door locks and power windows; trunk cannot be opened from the cabin area; a driver-side window that won't roll back up; sun visors that fall apart; an erratic fuel gauge, speedometer, and tachometer; an interior light that hums as it dims; lousy radio speakers; water leaks through the door bottoms, from the tail light into the trunk, and onto the driver-side footwell carpet; windows that often come off their tracks; Trunk springs fail; exterior and interior lights dim to an unsafe level; rear running lights fail due to a faulty fuse box; heated side mirrors gradually lose their reflective ability; an AC condenser that is easily destroyed by road debris and doesn't cool properly, and condensate that drips from under the glove compartment (heating core needs to be replaced to fix the problem); dashboard buzzing; front and rear windshield creaking. And loose, rattling seat belt adjusters, door panels, and door latches.

INSIGHT

bad buy ★

RATING: Not Recommended. The Insight is not long for this world (in Canada). As much as Canadian sales reps say they have a long-term commitment, Honda insiders say the Insight's days are numbered. **Strong points:** The Insight hybrid will save you a bit on fuel, and it costs less than the more-refined Toyota Prius. It also has a versatile hatchback design. **Weak points:** For the small savings over a Prius, you'll have to contend with lethargic acceleration; Insight crawls up hills:

> Car has small engine that needs assistance from electric motor. Electric motor helps the car during acceleration and climbing. The car should not charge the battery on climbs. As a result of this, extra load is added on the engine during climbs. With a 1300CC engine going up a grade, this could be very dangerous as you don't have enough power to climb at a certain rate other cars are capable of. If you visit *insight-central.net* there are a lot of complaints about this. Honda needs to re-program the cars not to force charge during climbs. I understand that if the battery was very low or drained that force charging on climbs are a necessary evil. But my battery was 75% full!

The occasional brake failure (just like the Prius); a jumpy, jerky ride; a hard-to-access interior; cheap-looking plastics and carpeting; and cramped, poorly supported, knees-to-your-chin rear seats that are real head-bangers every time the car passes over uneven terrain. Get used to a raspy exhaust and moaning CVT gearbox when accelerating. Long-term reliability is unproven. **New for 2012:** Nothing noteworthy.

OVERVIEW: The Insight sells for less than the Accord, and the car comes with multiple airbags, automatic climate control, power windows and locks, heated mirrors, CD audio with auxiliary jack, and anti-lock brakes. The EX gives you Bluetooth connectivity, a USB interface, paddle shifters, stability control, and a navigation system of doubtful utility.

COST ANALYSIS: This car has very little to offer except for some fuel savings and the cachet of buying a "green" car. But be wary of the hype: Your "green" machine" uses toxic rare earth elements that kill workers in developing countries, and its electrical energy comes from coal-burning utilities. And the cost for a new battery pack is best left unsaid. **Best alternatives:** The Ford Escape Hybrid, Hyundai Accent, Mazda3, Nissan Sentra, and Suzuki SX4. **Options:** Steer clear of the standard-issue radio and problematic Firestone or Bridgestone tires. **Rebates:** $2,500 early in the new year; if the car stays around that long. **Depreciation:** Average—a 2010 second-generation version that sold originally for $24,000 is now worth about $18,000. **Insurance cost:** Higher than average. **Parts supply/ cost:** Electronic parts are expensive and hard to find. **Annual maintenance cost:** Average so far, but long-term costs are likely to be high. **Warranty:** Bumper-to-bumper 3 years/60,000 km; powertrain 5 years/100,000 km; rust perforation 6 years/unlimited km. **Supplementary warranty:** Not needed. **Highway/city fuel economy:** LX: 4.5/4.8 L/100 km, 63/59 mpg. EX: 4.6/ 5.0L/100 km, 61/56 mpg.

OWNER-REPORTED PROBLEMS: Airbags failed to deploy in a frontal collision. Sudden brake failures in Drive and Reverse (hybrids from all automakers have a history of sudden brake failures):

> My husband and I were pulling into the garage of our home when our 2010 Honda Insight going about 2 miles per hour [3 km/h] would not stop when my husband put on the brake. The car crashed into the inside wall of our garage causing damage to the front end of the car, garage wall, and destroyed a sitting bench that was in front of the garage wall. As a passenger in the car, I saw my husband who was driving the car put the brake pedal all the way to the floor and the car would not stop! We had no control of the vehicle, and absolutely no brakes. After we crashed into the garage

---

KEY FACTS

CANADIAN PRICE (NEGOTIABLE): *LX:* $23,900, *EX:* $27,500 **U.S. PRICE:** *LX:* $19,800, *EX:* $21,300 **CANADIAN FREIGHT:** $1,395 **U.S. FREIGHT:** $770 **POWERTRAIN (FRONT-DRIVE)** Engine: 1.3L 4-cyl. (98 hp); Transmission: CVT **DIMENSIONS/CAPACITY** Passengers: 2/3; Wheelbase: 100.3 in.; H: 56.1/L: 172.2/W: 66.6 in.; Headroom F/R: 5.0/1.5 in.; Legroom F/R: 40.5/26.5 in.; Cargo volume: 15.8 cu. ft.; Fuel tank: 50L/regular; Tow limit: Not recommended; Load capacity: 850 lb.; Turning circle: 36 ft.; Weight: 2,755 lb.

wall, he placed the car in Reverse and once again the brakes would not stop the car and we ended up in the road.

When coasting to a stop the car will suddenly accelerate; low beams don't adequately light up the road; there is no way to restrict access to the fuel-filler nozzle; weather stripping constantly peels off:

> The contact was driving approximately 55 mph [89 km/h] when he began to hear an unusual slapping noise from the roof and could see something slapping against the rear window. The vehicle was pulled over and the contact found that half of the weather stripping from the roof had fractured from the vehicle. He removed the entire weather stripping and the vehicle was taken to an authorized dealer where it was repaired. The failure recurred one year later.

Tire pressure monitor will indicate a low tire pressure when tire pressure is within normal limits; painful head restraints:

> Severe neck and upper back pain caused by the headrest angle of a 2010 Honda Insight which I am told is mandated by your standards. I am a 5'6" female. The head rests forces my head forward to the point where my chin is almost resting on my chest. And I'm forced to look over the top of my eye glasses which I am required to wear to drive. I have tried the headrests in all positions.

CR-V ★★★★★

RATING: Recommended only as a mid-2012 buy to allow for redesign glitches to be corrected. **Strong points:** A slightly more-powerful, smoother-running 4-banger. Still, owners could use a bit more grunt for merging. Fuel economy and handling are fairly good—especially with standard electronic stability control (though Honda's ESC system does have some drawbacks). The ride is firm but comfortable, with communicative steering, progressive brake pedal feel, and a 5-speed automatic transmission that performs flawlessly. The lift-up tailgate is much more convenient than the swing-out version used in previous years. More legroom than ever before, thanks to the roomy rear seats that recline and slide independently and fold down to create a flat cargo floor. **Weak points:** Production has been halved, despite strong CR-V sales, so many shoppers will be bidding on fewer vehicles, driving up prices until early 2012. 2012 styling is confused with rear quarter visions that are more stylish than functional (think Pontiac Aztek). No V6, and ABS is a standard feature only as part of the high-trim CR-V EX package. High-speed cornering is not recommended, due to excessive body lean and the cost of replacement tires. The CR-V's stopping distance is not the best in its class; earlier restyling reduced cargo space and visibility; and Honda still needs to tweak the powertrain controls to correct a serious hesitation-before-acceleration problem that crops up from time to time in owner reports. Steering continues to be a bit stiff; the ride is bumpy at times; and annoying highway noises are omnipresent when at cruising speeds. **New for 2012:** Redesigned with new interior and exterior styling (similar to the KIA Sportage), a more fuel-efficient engine, and more room. Finally, a 6-speed automatic is expected to replace the 2011's 5-speed.

OVERVIEW: One of Honda's few bestsellers during these hard economic times, the CR-V has distanced itself from the Toyota Sienna and enhanced the driving experience by making a driver-communicative SUV that is as reliable as it is cheap to service. This is a driver's car, with a peppy, fuel-saving 4-cylinder engine that has sufficient power for most occasions (okay, going uphill fully loaded isn't the 4-banger's forte) and sips gas. You always feel in control, contrary to the experience in many of the larger SUVs where the vehicle cocoons the driver into a quasi-somnolent state.

CR-Vs are equally manoeuvrable in tight quarters as they are on winding roads, and they don't get blown about as much when cruising in stiff crosswinds. The Real Time 4WD system works well on slippery roads, where the feature automatically engages the wheels for maximum traction. Another interesting high-tech improvement is the Grade Logic Control, which automatically downshifts or upshifts when driving up or down a hill. Also, Honda has reduced engine idle vibration and noise.

KEY FACTS

CANADIAN PRICE (NEGOTIABLE): *LX:* $27,300, *LX 4WD:* $29,300, *EX:* $31,500, *EX 4WD:* $33,000, *EX-L 4WD:* $34,500, *EX-L Navi. 4WD:* $35,500 **U.S. PRICE:** *LX:* $22,545, *LX 4WD:* $23,795, *EX:* $24,845, *EX 4WD:* $25,595, *EX-L:* $27,795, *EX-L 4WD:* $29,745 **CANADIAN FREIGHT:** $1,395 **U.S. FREIGHT:** $810 **POWERTRAIN (FRONT-DRIVE/AWD)** Engine: 2.4L 4-cyl. (180 hp); Transmission: 5-speed auto. **DIMENSIONS/CAPACITY** Passengers: 2/3; Wheelbase: 103.1 in.; H: 66.1/L: 177.8/W: 71.6 in.; Headroom F/R: 4.0/4.0 in.; Legroom F/R: 40.1/29.0 in.; Cargo volume: 25.5 cu. ft.; Fuel tank: 50L/regular; Tow limit: 1,500 lb.; Load capacity: 850 lb.; Turning circle: 39 ft.; Ground clearance: 7.2 in.; Weight: 3,404 lb.

COST ANALYSIS: Sales were up 28 percent through June 2011, so buying a cheaper 2011 model is not very realistic; likely they will have all been sold and you will miss out on the 2012's improvements. Delay your purchase until mid-2012 when quality will be better and prices more negotiable. **Best alternatives:** The CR-V's biggest competitor is the Toyota RAV4. If you don't mind going downscale a bit, consider a Hyundai Tucson. **Options:** Steer clear of the standard-issue radio and the Continental, Firestone, or Bridgestone tires. **Rebates:** Not likely. **Depreciation:** Much slower than average. **Insurance cost:** Average. **Parts supply/cost:** Reasonably priced and easily found at dealers and independent suppliers. **Annual maintenance cost:** Much less than average. **Warranty:** Bumper-to-bumper 3 years/60,000 km; powertrain 5 years/100,000 km; rust perforation 6 years/unlimited km. **Supplementary warranty:** Not needed. **Highway/city fuel economy:** *Front-drive:* 7.1/9.8 L/100 km, 40/29 mpg. *AWD:* 7.5/10.1 L/100 km, 38/28 mpg. If the 6-speed automatic does arrive this year, expect a tad more fuel economy.

OWNER-REPORTED PROBLEMS: Sudden, unintended acceleration:

> I bought a new 2011 Honda CR-V and have a serious safety issue. The engine maintained its speed or accelerated on four separate occasions when I applied the brake and tried to stop. The worst incident occurred when I tried to come to a stop at a red light with cars in front of me. I applied brake and car stopped but engine raced. I had to apply very strong pressure to brake to hold car in place. Engine was racing and car was pulling forward. I shifted to neutral, engine continued to race and then I heard a loud knocking sound come from engine like a washing machine makes when it is out of balance. I was very scared. I turned engine off and then at green light turned engine on and it was OK. This happened four separate times when the car had just over 200 miles [320 km] on it, just over 400 miles [640 km], 723 miles [1,160 km], and 819 miles [1,320 km].

> I did not have a foot on both gas and brake, the mats are the Honda mats that come with car and are fastened to the floor and were not on the gas. This really happened, very scary. Reported to Honda and took car in twice. Honda said there were no codes and the brakes looked OK. They said to call American Honda which I did. I reported it as a serious safety issue. Honda said someone would get in touch with me the next day. It's been a week and no one has contacted me. I have owned the car for 40 days and driven it less than 850 miles [1,370 km] and this has happened four times and been in the shop twice.

Some owners would like a little "intended" acceleration: There are reports that when the accelerator is pressed hard, there is a loss of power and downshifting is delayed, just when extra power is needed (see "Service Bulletin-Reported Problems"); painful head restraints:

> The front seat head restraints in the 2011 Honda CR-V are tilted too far forward, resulting in severe neck strain followed by headaches. While Honda suggests positioning the seat tilted back, this does not alleviate the problem and results in a safety issue since my wife then has difficulty seeing over the hood and grasping the steering wheel.

Electrical system shorts, premature brake wear, airbags fail to deploy, AC condenser is destroyed by road debris (a chronic failure on most of Honda's lineup), bent wheel studs can easily snap, brake rotors wear out prematurely, windshield washer nozzles freeze up in cold weather, the engine oil pan leaks, and a serious right rear blind spot may be worsened by the 2012's redesigned rear-quarter windows

Traction control has also been a problem with earlier models:

> Traction control doesn't work well during winter. It doesn't work well too when the vehicle is parked on a parking that slopes up with about 6 inches [15 cm] of snow. I was in a hurry to go to work but I got towed the first time when my 2008 CRV was only 5 months old because it could not go forward when it was in the parking that slopes up even if I already plowed the snow. It could only reverse but didn't want to go forward.

Poor stability and rapid tread wear experienced with Continental original-equipment tires:

> Continental OEM tire on Honda CRV causes vehicle to slide out of control on snow covered roads and constantly lose traction in rear. We have had numerous near-accidents because of the poorly designed low rated tires. My wife is afraid of driving the CRV now. Two Honda dealers inspected vehicle for possible vehicle stability assist problem and both dealers confirmed that VSA was functioning properly. Dealer #2 stated that he had similar issues with other CRV owners because of the tires. Looking at tire reviews on line the Continental Contact 4×4 is rated as a very poor tire that wears out very quickly and with similar issues as I have stated. Even the authorized Continental dealer in my area says the tires are poor quality and has rarely seen them make 20,000 miles [32,187 km].

Omnipresent vibrations, rattles, noisy seatbelt retractors, and a "popping" sound:

> I unfortunately discovered a very annoying problem with the front passenger's seat belt retractor. Similar to the problem discussed in the Honda service bulletin 05-073, "A squeak or rattle is heard from the seat belt retractors while driving over bumps or rough roads." My problem comes from the front passenger seat and not the rear seats. I contacted the dealer I purchased the vehicle from, and they said the problem cannot be repaired. However, the service bulletin 05-073 states the issue was remedied by installing a rubber floor boot to insulate the retractors from the body.

SERVICE BULLETIN-REPORTED PROBLEMS: An engine oil leak at the rear of the cylinder head cover may be caused by a defective No. 5 rocker shaft holder. The left rear wheelwell doesn't have enough seam sealer. This may allow water to leak into the interior under the rear seat on the 2011s. Honda has set up a free repair campaign to apply sealer. A loss of power when accelerating may be caused by faulty PGM-FI software.

ACCORD, CROSSTOUR ★★★★/★★★

RATING: *Accord:* Above Average. *Crosstour:* Average. The Accord is no longer the benchmark for dependability and performance in the family-sedan niche and it doesn't handle redesigns very well. In 1997, *Lemon-Aid* concluded that Toyota was "decontenting" its vehicles: keeping its prices down by giving owners less quality. We subsequently lowered our rating for Toyota. In its 2009 redesign of the Accord, Honda adopted the same practice. Result: Accord safety-related complaints increased five-fold, reaching 800+ incidents for that model year alone. Consequently, we have lowered Honda's rating, as well. Interestingly, the Accord Crosstour has registered less than a dozen safety complaints over the past two years. **Strong points:** Like most Hondas, this is a driver's car, while its primary

KEY FACTS

CANADIAN PRICIE (NEGOTIABLE): *Accord Sedan SE:* $25,990, *EX:* $27,490, *EX-L:* $29,790, *EX-L Navi.:* $31,790, *EX V6:* $30,190, *EX-L:* $29,790, *EX-L Navi:* $31,790, *EX-L V6:* $33,390, *EX-L V6 Navi.:* $35,390; *Accord Crosstour EX-L:* $34,900, *EX-L 4WD:* $36,900, *EX-L 4WD Navi.:* $38,900 **U.S. PRICE:** *Accord Coupe LX-S:* $22,555, *EX:* $23,880, *EX-L:* $26,880, *EX-L Navi.:* $28,880, *EX-L V6:* $29,305, *EX-L V6 Navi.:* $31,305; *Accord Crosstour EX:* $29,670, *EX-L:* $32,570, *EX-L 4WD Navi.:* $34,770 **CANADIAN FREIGHT:** $1,395 **U.S. FREIGHT:** $770; (Crosstour) $810

POWERTRAIN (ACCORD FRONT-DRIVE)
Engines: 2.4L 4-cyl. (177 hp) • 2.4L 4-cyl. (190 hp) • 3.5L V6 (271 hp); Transmissions: 5-speed man. • 5-speed auto. • 6-speed man.

DIMENSIONS/CAPACITY (ACCORD SEDAN)
Passengers: 2/3; Wheelbase: 110.2 in.; H: 58.1/L: 194.0/W: 72.6 in.; Headroom F/R: 6.5/3.5 in.; Legroom F/R: 41.5/30 in.; Cargo volume: 14 cu. ft.; Fuel tank: 65L/regular; Tow limit: 1,500 lb.; Load capacity: 850 lb.; Turning circle: 37.7 ft.; Weight: 3,236–3,298 lb.

POWERTRAIN (CROSSTOUR FRONT-DRIVE/4WD)
Engine: V6 (271 hp); Transmission: 5-speed auto.

DIMENSIONS/CAPACITY (CROSSTOUR SEDAN)
Passengers: 2/3; Wheelbase: 110.1 in.; H: 58.1/L: 196.8/W: 74.7 in.; Headroom F/R: 6.5/3.5 in.; Legroom F/R: 41.5/30 in.; Cargo volume: 25.7 cu. ft.; Fuel tank: 65L/regular; Tow limit: 1,500 lb.; Load capacity: 850 lb.; Turning circle: 40.2 ft.; Ground clearance: 8.1 in.; Weight: 3,852–4,070 lb.

competitor, the Toyota Camry, is basically the Japanese version of your dad's Oldsmobile. It's one of the largest mid-sized cars on the market and provides excellent acceleration with all engines. It's roomy and well-equipped with user-friendly instruments and controls as well as a telescoping steering column. The car handles and rides well, thanks to large tires, a sturdy chassis, and standard stability control. It has earned the top, five-star crashworthiness scores from NHTSA for front, side, and rollover protection. The Accord was also given a "Good" rating by IIHS for head-restraint effectiveness, frontal offset, and side-impact protection. Roof crashworthiness was rated "Average." *Crosstour:* Responsive handling, a comfortable ride, and a car-like driving position. NHTSA scores: five stars for frontal and side occupant crash protection and four-star rollover resistance. IIHS scores tracked the Accord scores, except for roof crashworthiness (see below). **Weak points:** Mediocre fuel economy with the V6, and some road noise intrusion into the cabin area. An astoundingly high number of performance and reliability defects on the 2008–09 models, with apparently biodegradable brakes topping the list. Annoying windshield dash reflection; distorted windshields; and creaks and rattles. Many owner reports of airbags that explode for no reason or fail to deploy, brake failures, and sudden, unintended acceleration. *Crosstour:* Limited rear visibility, strut towers intrude into storage space, and the sloping rear-end styling compromises the Crosstour's utility. A more-practical rear-end design could raise those numbers considerably. IIHS rated roof crash protection as "Mediocre." **New for 2012:** Nothing significant; 2012 will herald the next revamping.

OVERVIEW: A well-designed family car, the Accord was last redesigned for the 2008 model year and jumped leagues ahead of the competition by giving owners superior road performance and a roomy interior with loads of safety and convenience features thrown in. Too bad build quality and reliability deteriorated so much following that last redesign. Three model years later, Honda has recovered its quality edge to where it is as good as the South Koreans and on par with some Ford and GM models. This quality improvement can be seen in the 2010–11 Crosstour, which has a negligible number of owner complaints despite its new design.

Last year, fuel economy was improved slightly on the 4-cylinder engine; the SE model replaced the base LX model; alloy wheels, eight-way power driver's seat, Bluetooth connectivity, automatic headlamps, and a security system became standard on all models. Six-CD stereo and USB audio interface are standard features on all EX models and above.

If you want good fuel economy and performance with a conventional powertrain, choose one of the two 4-cylinder engines. The V6 is a bit of a gas hog and is needed for highway travel with a full load only. Ride comfort and responsive handling are assured by a suspension and steering set-up that enhances driver control. And what about space? Accord sedans are roomier than ever before, with interior dimensions and capacity that provide more interior space than you'll likely need.

Fast and nimble without a V6, this is the mid-sized sedan of choice for drivers who want maximum fuel economy and comfort along with lots of space for grocery hauling and occasional highway cruising. With the optional V6, the Accord is one of the most versatile mid-sized cars you can find. It offers something for everyone, and its high resale value means there's no way you can lose money buying one.

Accord Crosstour

The two-year-old Crosstour is billed as a "crossover utility vehicle," which is Honda-speak for a high-riding hatchback family station wagon equipped with four-wheel-drive capability. This five-seater Accord spin-off is equipped similarly to the Acura 2010 ZDX four-door sport coupe. There is a disappointing 25.7 cubic feet of cargo space and 51.3 cubic feet with the rear seatbacks folded; this is less than the Toyota Venza, Nissan Murano, and Subaru Outback, which each have more than 60 cubic feet of cargo space. It is 300–500 pounds heavier than the Accord, depending on whether you choose the base or AWD model.

COST ANALYSIS: Buy a cheaper, practically identical 2011 model. Furthermore, since the MSRP is quite soft, this year's price increase can likely be whittled down considerably—*with* an extended warranty thrown in. Crosstour prices have plummeted due to poor sales, its controversial rear-end styling, and limited cargo space. **Best alternatives:** BMW 3 Series, Hyundai Elantra and Sonata, Mazda6, and Toyota Camry. *Crosstour:* Nissan Murano, Subaru Outback, and Toyota Venza. **Options:** The V6 gives a smoother ride and has lots of reserve power for passing and merging, though the 4-banger will do for most driving needs. The DVD navigation with voice control found on the EX and V6 coupe is a bit gimmicky, but it's easier to use and understand than most of the competition's systems (especially what Ford has adopted). **Rebates:** Not likely until early 2012, except for some attractive leasing and financing deals. *Crosstour:* Look for $3,000–$5,000 sales incentives as Honda tries to boost sales. **Depreciation:** Slightly slower than average for all models. For example, both the 2010 Accord and Crosstour are now worth about $29,000. **Insurance cost:** Higher than average. **Parts supply/cost:** Good availability, and moderately priced. **Annual maintenance cost:** Less than average. **Warranty:** Bumper-to-bumper 3 years/60,000 km; powertrain 5 years/100,000 km; rust perforation 5 years/unlimited km. **Supplementary warranty:** Not needed. **Highway/city fuel economy:** *2.4L 4-cylinder auto.:* 5.8/8.8 L/100 km, 42/39 mpg (with fuel-saving feature). *3.5L V6 6-speed man.:* 7.8/12.6L/100 km, 22/36 mpg (with fuel-saving feature). *Auto.:* 6.7/11L/100 km, 26/42 mpg (with fuel-saving feature). *Crosstour auto. 2WD:* 7.2/11.5 L/100 km, 39/25 mpg (with fuel-saving feature). *Auto. 4WD:* 8.0/12.3L/100 km, 35/23 mpg (with fuel-saving feature).

OWNER-REPORTED PROBLEMS: Until the 2008 revamping, each Accord model year would usually have a few dozen reliability problems reported by owners to various government agencies and to *Lemon-Aid*; however, this is no longer the case. Honda's 2008 Accord has an incredible 855 consumer complaints logged by NHTSA alone, a number which is over five times the complaint average for most vehicles. The safety-related incidents mostly concern powertrain, brake, and body defects. Yet the 2010 models show barely a couple dozen complaints, leading one to conclude that either Honda fixed many of the factory-related glitches or the problems are still ticking away, waiting to fail when the two-year mark is reached.

Here are some of the most-dangerous and most-frequent problems reported. Sudden, unintended acceleration:

> Vehicle suffers from an un-commanded acceleration/throttle problem which is completely reproducible. It affects the low-speed behavior of the vehicle particularly during turns where there is potential for loss of control.

Spontaneous shattering of the sunroof; steering wheel locks up when making a left-hand turn; allegedly dangerous steering design that does return the steering wheel to the centre to pull the car out of a turn; painful head restraints:

> I want to make you aware of how new NHTSA regulations for the design of head restraints have injured me physically and financially. I traded in a 2000 Toyota for a 2011 Honda, only to find that the head restraint gave me severe neck muscle spasms. The dealer explained that since 2008, all new cars must follow updated NHTSA regulations in head restraints. I went to many dealerships to find a head restraint that I could tolerate. All of them had the same pain-producing, federally mandated style. Finally, after much searching, I found a Ford SUV that had a more tolerable head restraint. I was very relieved because I was afraid that I would have to buy an old used car in order to continue driving. I have mild neck arthritis, and your new style of head restraints caused me such discomfort that I was willing to sell my 5-day-old Honda Accord (with 225 miles [360 km]) and lose thousands of dollars (due to depreciation)! In addition, I worry that the head restraints are hurting other people. I am a physician, and I know that chronic repetitive stress can sometimes lead to severe injury.

Oil leak from the engine's rear main seal area required a new short block; Transmission and suspension noise when the car is put into Reverse:

> The noise is coming from the transmission and left side suspension when the car is put in reverse. I contact Honda of North America and inquire about the loud noise. They told me that there is no recall on my car. I then contact the dealership that I bought the car from to check it out. I meet with the service manager and I let him listen to the noise. He then stated that it was normal, which I find very strange. About a few days later the loud noise from the transmission also came a new problem: a loud clonking noise from the left side front suspension.

Chronic premature wearout of the front and rear brake pads (especially the rear pads). Loud and constant brake squealing (not a brake rotor/pad failure):

Dealer has checked to be sure there has not been a re-design of pads—and there has not been. A check on *Consumer Reports* web site under the forum for Honda shows this is a widespread problem. Although most got at least 12 to 15 thousand miles [19,000–24,000 km], I live in hills, which may explain part of the difference. Having to replace rear brake pads every 9,000 or 10,000 miles [14,500 or 16,000 km] is a safety problem.

A popping/knocking front suspension or steering rack noise; seatback digs into driver's back or causes legs to go numb:

Just purchased a 2011 Honda Accord. The driver's seat in this car causes your legs to go numb after about 30 miles [48 km] (a definite safety issue). Since experiencing the problem I have found countless forums online with people experiencing the same thing. This problem has been going on since 2008 apparently and Honda has not addressed this issue. This seat should be recalled immediately. If having your feet fall asleep while driving isn't a safety issue I don't know what is.

•

Seats in 2001 Accord are extremely uncomfortable resulting in me being diagnosed with sciatica. I have had severe leg and back pain since purchasing this car in March and am otherwise healthy. Honda denies issue despite hundreds of similar complaints online.

Leaking fuel pump; engine cylinders shut down at the wrong time/speed:

Car was also shutting the cylinders down at 30 mph [50 km/h], not the 55 mph [90 km/h] it was designed to do to save fuel. It was returned to us and 3 days later started doing it again. Returned to dealer and was told it had the wrong plugs in it. They changed the plugs and returned the Accord to us. We drove the car about 90 miles [145 km], and it started, again.

Hole in AC condenser likely caused by road debris; metal creaking sound around the rear shelf deck likely due to broken spot welds in the rear shelf of the car; when the AC is activated, the headlights and interior lighting dim or flicker; and remote door locking and unlocking failures. Crosstour rear visibility obstructed:

Honda Accord Crosstour design defect impedes proper rear-view vision. The rear window of the vehicle has a heavy bar running horizontally in the middle of the window. The bar may have been required for the structure of the rear door, but it substantially blocked the rear vision for the driver.

ODYSSEY

RATING: Above Average. The Odyssey outclasses Toyota's Sienna in driving pleasure and is just a bit more reliable. In a Sienna, the driver is "driven"; in an Odyssey, the driver does the driving by being more actively involved in the overall performance of the vehicle. There have, however, been frequent reports of safety- and performance-related failures, notably involving the electrical system, and this is likely to occur more frequently with future redesigns. Of particular concern are airbag malfunctions, brake defects leading to sudden brake loss, and the frequent replacement of the brake calipers and rotors. **Strong points:** Plenty of power for high-speed merging; a spacious, versatile, and quiet interior; and numerous safety and convenience features. Lots of mid-range torque means less shifting when the engine is under load. Car-like ride and handling; a spacious interior; comfortable seats; second-row middle seats can be folded down as an armrest or removed completely, much like the middle-row captain's chairs, which can slide fore or aft, in unison or separately; second-row power windows; floor-stowable, 60/40-split third-row seats; easy back seat entry and exit; a convenient second driver-side door and a power tailgate; an extensive list of standard equipment; and most controls and displays are easy to reach and read. Safety is enhanced with standard vehicle stability assist and traction control to prevent rollovers and improve handling; side curtain airbags with rollover sensors for all rows; and adjustable

KEY FACTS

CANADIAN PRICE (NEGOTIABLE): *LX:* $29,990, *EX:* $33,990, *EX RES:* $35,490, *EX-L RES:* $40,990, *Touring:* $46,990 **U.S. PRICE:** *LX:* $28,075, *EX:* $31,225, *EX-L:* $34,725, *EX-L Navi.:* $36,725, *Touring:* $41,030, *Touring Elite:* $43,525 **CANADIAN FREIGHT:** $1,395 **U.S. FREIGHT:** $810

POWERTRAIN (FRONT-DRIVE)
Engine: 3.5L V6 (244 hp); Transmission: 5-speed auto.

DIMENSIONS/CAPACITY
Passengers: 2/3/3; Wheelbase: 118.1 in.; H: 68.8/L: 202.1/W: 77.1 in.; Headroom F/R1/R2: 4.5/5.5/2.0 in.; Legroom F/R1/R2: 41.5/31/28 in.; Cargo volume: 38.4 cu. ft.; Fuel tank: 80L/regular; Tow limit: 3,500 lb.; Load capacity: 1,320 lb.; Turning circle: 36.7 ft.; Ground clearance: 5 in.; Weight: 4,387 lb.

brake and accelerator pedals. NHTSA gives the 2012 Odyssey five stars for front and side crashworthiness and four stars for rollover protection. IIHS says head restraints and roof strength offer "Good" protection to occupants, and also gives a "Good" frontal and side protection rating. **Weak points:** Fuel consumption isn't as low as Honda promises, despite its innovative cylinder deactivation system. Unlike with the Sienna, all-wheel drive isn't available; middle-row seats don't fold flat like in other minivans, so they need to be stowed somewhere else; second-row head restraints block visibility; front-passenger legroom is marginal, owing to the restricted seat travel; it's difficult to calibrate the radio without taking your eyes off the road; some tire rumble, rattles, and body drumming at highway speeds; and rear-seat head restraints impede side and rear visibility. The storage well won't take any tire larger than a "space saver," meaning you'll carry your flat in the back. **New for 2012:** Nothing important; the 2011 was extensively redesigned.

OVERVIEW: The Odyssey has a lean look, but the interior is wide and long enough to accommodate most large objects. Sliding doors are offered as standard equipment, and if you buy the EX version, they will both be power-assisted. Sufficient power is supplied by a competent V6, which includes variable cylinder deactivation to increase fuel economy. Gas consumption may be cut up to 10 percent by the engine's ability to automatically switch between 6-cylinder and 3-cylinder activation, depending on engine load.

Last year's 2011s were redesigned to incorporate the following changes: a restyled interior and wider/lower exterior, with the reworked front end taking its cue from the Accord Crosstour (frog-eye headlights were dropped); more user-friendly instruments and controls; and a wider interior that permitted Honda to install a multi-configurable second-row bench seat that spreads the seats out and uses a total of five latch positions for child seats, as well as more-ample third-row seats. If you need extra cargo space, you can easily fold the third row seats, add the cargo, and bring the kids up into the second row. Additional comfort and infotainment features include an HDMI port; a wide screen to play one movie for all or play two separate video feeds simultaneously (copying Toyota's Sienna); a removable console with a hidden bin; and a small cooler in the central stack of the dash. Honda also boasts that not only has its 4-cylinder engine fuel economy improved on the 2011 model, but its 3.5L V6 will be more fuel-frugal than the Sienna's 4-banger, giving Odyssey owners 12.4L/100 km (19 mpg) in the city and a hard-to-believe 8.4L/100 km (28 mpg) on the highway. The brakes were made larger, and independent rear suspension was added.

COST ANALYSIS: Stagnant sales over the past year have forced Honda dealers to discount their upgraded 2011s by as much as 10 percent through lower transaction prices and attractive lease/loan programs. That's the better buy if you can find some leftovers on dealers' lots. If a 2012 is your choice, make sure you have a specific delivery date spelled out in the contract, along with a protected price, in case there's a price increase while you're waiting for delivery. **Best alternatives:** For better handling and reliability, the closest competitor to the Odyssey is Toyota's Sienna minivan. One major difference between the two models is the seating. Toyota's are like La-Z-Boy armchairs and are a chore to remove. Honda seats are more basic and are easier to install or remove. The Mazda5 and Chrysler's Caravan are acceptable choices for different reasons: This year's redesigned Mazda5 has less room but burns less fuel (without a high-tech engine add-on), and Chrysler's minivans aren't as reliable as the Odyssey or Mazda but offer better prices, lots of room for people and things, and plenty of convenience and safety features. The Kia Sedona minivan is also a decent choice. If you're looking for lots of towing "grunt" and plenty of usable space, rear-drive GM full-sized vans are fairly reliable vehicles that often carry sizeable discounts that will get larger as Toyota and Nissan ramp up production in 2012. Try to resist the gimmicky video entertainment, DVD navigation system, and expensive leather seats. See if you can trade the original-equipment Firestone or Bridgestone tires for something better (check with *www.tirerack.com*). **Rebates:** Any patient haggler will get a few thousand dollars cut from the base price; your goal should be to get at least 10 percent taken off of the MSRP. Low-cost financing and leasing programs will also help bring down the transaction price. **Depreciation:** Average. Expect half the resale value to be lost after four years. For example, a 2008 Odyssey LX that originally sold for $33,600 ($400 more than the 2006 version) is now worth about $18,500; a 2006 LX can be picked up for $12,000. **Insurance cost:** Higher than average. **Annual maintenance cost:** Average. **Parts supply/cost:** Moderately priced parts; availability is better than average because the Odyssey uses many generic Accord parts. CVT transmission and cylinder deactivation parts may be costly and could be hard to find outside the Honda dealer network. **Warranty:** Bumper-to-bumper 3 years/60,000 km; powertrain 5 years/100,000 km; rust perforation 5 years/unlimited km. **Supplementary warranty:** Not needed. **Highway/city fuel economy:** 8.5/13.3 L/100 km, 33/21 mpg. *EX-L & Touring:* 7.8/2.3 L/100 km, 36/23 mpg.

OWNER-REPORTED PROBLEMS: The 58 owner safety-related complaints registered by NHTSA for the 2011s is about average. Among them: The middle seat belt that hangs from the top of the car can act as a hangman's noose where children are involved:

> 10-year-old daughter wrapped it around her neck. The seat belt locked and you could not release it except to cut it off. Police were called to cut the belt. She had bruises on her neck but nothing more serious. Thank God I did not brake hard or she could have been strangled. They should have an emergency release button or a better location for the seat belt. Out of reach of a curious toddler.

Airbags didn't deploy after a severe rear-ender; airbag cover warps; early engine failure; electrical malfunction causes a partial shutdown (see *www.odyclub.com/ forums/54-2011-Odyssey/137322-battery-charge-low.html*):

> Since taking delivery of my 2011 Honda Odyssey it has had a faulty battery sensor. This is a known issue that is not being addressed. The sensor falsely reports that the battery is low and disables some of the onboard equipment including interior lights and pathway lights leaving car in the dark.

•

I am getting the "Battery Charge Low" Warning. Have taken the car to the dealership and spoke to them. They state it's not a problem and I need to drive the car more. It is concerning that the car shuts the dome lights, even the dash lights, off automatically. This is a supposed safety item of the car that I am to ignore? I am deeply concerned regarding this issue. First, Honda is not acknowledging the seriousness of this—"Ignore it. It's not a problem." Second, this issue, I feel, is potentially placing my family in danger if the battery cannot stay charged. Finally, this is not an infrequent issue as evidenced by the number of posts/complaints on the NHTSA website and other forums on the web (www.odyclub.com) yet Honda continues not to put out a TSB regarding this problem.

•

The wife is worried that if it is real and ignored she may be left stranded, which could be a danger to her in these times. Honda has sent a "service news article" to their dealers about this problem but again, their comment to fix the problem is to charge the battery and momentarily disconnect the battery sensor for 10 sec, and again this was done to our vehicle and was only a short-term fix. Within days it was doing it again. Honda needs to step up to the plate and get this generic problem fixed.

Engine surges to 6000 rpms in Neutral with both feet on the brakes; automatic transmission breakdowns; transmission slams into gear or suddenly locks in low gear while the vehicle is underway; erratic downshifts; steering pulls continually to the right; premature replacement of the front strut assemblies; poor handling in snow, despite traction control; many complaints of road debris destroying the AC condenser; tire pressure monitoring system is disabled by a cell phone:

I purchased a brand new 2011 Honda Odyssey Touring Elite 4 weeks ago. As I drove home from the lot my TPMS (tire pressure monitoring system) light came on and stayed on. I immediately drove back to the dealer service center. Initially they thought it was just tire pressure but quickly realized it was an actual error of the TPMS system. One of the techs said he has seen this on one other 2011 Odyssey and that it is triggered by smart cellular phone interference. He told me it would probably happen again if I used my cell phone in the van. So they reset the TPMS error and I turned off my cell and drove for 30 minutes with no issues. So then I turned my cell phone on, and still no issues for another 5 minutes. Then my wife called and at the exact moment my cell phone rang the TPMS went into error again. So the service center tells me this is something they can't fix. They are waiting for a fix from Honda. When I submitted the case to Honda Corp Customer Care they say that this is not a "known issue" and that they are not actively working on a resolution for it. When TPMS error occurs the TPMS system is completely disabled automatically by the vehicle computer. Therefore, my van currently does not have TPMS protection. I just spoke with my dealer service center again and they tell me they now have 5 reports of this same problem on 2011 Odyssey Elites.

Windshield shattered on its own; excessive wind noise from the passenger and driver pillar area; ambient footwell lighting is too dim; third-row folding seat collapsed and broke a child's fingers; side sliding door frequently malfunctions by closing unexpectedly, opening when the vehicle is underway, and failing to retract when closing on an object. The EXL's running board is dangerously slippery when wet; some near-falls, many bruised shins. Brakes are another major problem area highlighted by sudden brake loss after the VSA light comes on (some dealers suggest unplugging the VSA); brake loss when backing out of a parking lot; brake pedal sometimes sinks to the floor; premature front brake wear and excessive noise; and a history of mushy braking:

> We noticed the brakes appeared to be soft and spongy. When I finally took it in for service, I was told it needed a new master cylinder (at 2,800 miles [4,500 km]), which they replaced. After I picked it up, I drove it a few miles and the brakes still felt soft and spongy, so I drove back to the dealership. The service manager then drove the car and told me, "That's the way the Odyssey brakes are."

SERVICE BULLETIN-REPORTED PROBLEMS: Driver's-side sliding door won't unlock or open; dash centre panel may be loose; paint peels off the front bumper where it meets the front fender.

ELEMENT ★★★★

RATING: Above Average; a bargain that will disappear at the end of 2011. **Strong points:** Easy handling; standard electronic stability control and side curtain airbags; wide doorways make loading and unloading cargo a breeze; a spacious interior and washable floor; good fit and finish; all seats fold back to make a small bed; and versatile rear seats can fold to the side or be removed completely. NHTSA-tested crashworthiness is rated five stars for front and side occupant protection and three stars for rollover protection. IIHS says frontal offset

KEY FACTS

CANADIAN PRICE (NEGOTIABLE): *LX:* $26,990, *SC:* $31,690, *EX 4WD:* $32,090 **U.S. PRICE:** *LX:* $20,825, *Auto.:* $22,825, *EX:* $22,935, *EX AWD:* $22,075
CANADIAN FREIGHT: $1,395
U.S. FREIGHT: $810
POWERTRAIN (FRONT-DRIVE/AWD)
Engine: 2.4L 4-cyl. (166 hp);
Transmission: 5-speed auto.
DIMENSIONS/CAPACITY
Passengers: 2/2; Wheelbase: 101.3 in.; H: 70.3/L: 169.9/W: 77.1 in.; Headroom F/R: 7.5/2.0 in.; Legroom F/R: 41/31 in.; Cargo volume: 74.5 cu. ft.; Fuel tank: 80L/regular; Tow limit: 1,500 lb.; Load capacity: 675 lb.; Turning circle: 36 ft.; Ground clearance: 7.0 in.; Weight: 3,527 lb.

protection, side-impact protection, and head restraint effectiveness are "Good." **Weak points:** The automatic transmission hobbles the 4-cylinder engine; a stiff, jerky ride; large roof pillars obstruct outward visibility; driving position is uncomfortable for some; the rear-hinged rear side doors don't open independently of the front doors; and excessive road noise. With both the Element and the Pilot, Honda maintains a death grip on dated styling that screams "We're dying over here!" **New for 2012:** No noteworthy changes.

OVERVIEW: Based on the Honda Civic platform, the Element is a small, boxy SUV that is more of a cargo-hauler than a passenger-carrier. This doesn't take away the fact that the vehicle comes well-appointed and is powerful enough with its 4-banger and automatic transmission to accomplish most driving chores. Last year's 2011s were given an improved suspension, upgraded shock absorbers, and better brakes.

COST ANALYSIS: The Element will be dropped by year's end, and hungry dealers will offer discounted prices to make room for the car's 2012 replacement. Expect a 10 percent reduction of the MSRP. Buy an upgraded 2011 version to snare the most sales incentives and get a better-quality second-series model. **Best alternatives:** Try to get your mind around a less-quirky-looking and more-versatile wagon or hatchback, like the Chevrolet Cruze, Honda Fit, Hyundai Elantra, Kia Rondo or Soul, Mazda5, Nissan Versa, Suzuki SX4, or Toyota Matrix. **Options:** Be wary of poorly performing Bridgestone and Firestone original-equipment tires. **Rebates:** Good leasing and low-finance deals; discounts of about 5 percent. **Depreciation:** Slower than average; a 2008 LX front-drive that went for $25,290 new now sells for $14,500. **Insurance cost:** Average. **Annual maintenance cost:** Average. **Parts supply/cost:** Parts are easy to find and relatively inexpensive. **Warranty:** Bumper-to-bumper 3 years/60,000 km; powertrain 5 years/100,000 km; rust perforation 5 years/unlimited km. **Supplementary warranty:** Not necessary. **Highway/city fuel economy:** *Front-drive:* 8.1/10.5 L/100 km, 35/27 mpg. *AWD:* 8.3/11.0 L/100 km, 34/26 mpg.

OWNER-REPORTED PROBLEMS: Very few safety-related complaints recorded by NHTSA during the past two model years. In fact, overall reliability has proven to be exceptionally good, judging by the few service bulletins published. Nevertheless, you can expect problems with the premature wearout of key brake components (preceded by mushy braking), mysterious windshield cracks, and malfunctioning tire-pressure sensors. Other complaints: the windshield shatters too easily and its loose mounting may cause rattling at the dash juncture.

PILOT ★★★★

RATING: Above Average. The second-generation Pilot has grown into a large-sized people-carrier that offers a comfortable ride, first-class handling, and plenty of passenger space. **Strong points:** Adequate power for highway cruising; superb handling; a versatile interior; seating for up to eight; the third-row seat folds flat into sections to free up storage space; and there's a small storage area in the floor. Chock full of safety and convenience features and earning good crashworthiness scores (a four-star overall rating, four stars for frontal and rollover protection, five stars for side protection, and "Good" head-restraint protection). Overall reliability has been better than average. The Pilot also has standard vehicle stability assist and traction control to prevent rollovers and enhance handling, side curtain airbags with rollover sensors for all rows, and adjustable brake and accelerator pedals. The GPS and voice operation feature are easy to use—with a little practice. **Weak points:** Mediocre acceleration accompanied by some torque steer; so-so braking; and a boxy exterior. Unimpressive fuel economy—the much-heralded cylinder deactivation system doesn't save as much fuel as Honda fantasizes, and it makes the vehicle seriously underpowered. Suspension ineffectively absorb bumps or shocks. Interior plastic materials and overall fit and finish aren't up to Honda's reputation for quality, and road noise is omnipresent.

KEY FACTS

CANADIAN PRICE (NEGOTIABLE): *LX:* $34,820, *LX 4WD:* $37,820, *EX 4WD:* $40,720, *EX-L 4WD:* $43,020, *EX-L res 4WD:* $44,620, *Touring 4WD:* $48,420 **U.S. PRICE:** *LX:* $28,320, *LX 4WD:* $29,920, *EX:* $31,170, *EX 4WD:* $32,770, *EX-L:* $34,270, *EX-L 4WD:* $35,870, *Touring 2WD:* $39,070, *Touring 4WD:* $40,670 **CANADIAN FREIGHT:** $1,395 **U.S. FREIGHT:** $810

POWERTRAIN (FRONT-DRIVE/AWD)
Engine: 3.5L V6 (250 hp); Transmission: 5-speed auto.

DIMENSIONS/CAPACITY
Passengers: 2/3/3; Wheelbase: 109.2 in.; H: 71.0/L: 190.9/W: 78.5 in.; Headroom: F/R1/R2: 40/39.8/38.2 in.; Legroom: F/R1/R2: 41.4/38.5/32.1 in.; Cargo volume: 18 cu. ft.; Fuel tank: 79.5L/regular; Tow limit: 3,500–4,500 lb.; Load capacity: 1,320 lb.; Turning circle: 36.7 ft.; Ground clearance: 8.0 in.; Weight: 4,319 lb.

The centre console can be confusing to operate until you've studied it. Honda needs to make the radio and AC operation more user-friendly, with fewer buttons. Reliability is above average, but not as good as what you get with the Element. **New for 2012:** Carried over practically unchanged.

OVERVIEW: It's the mouse that roars and squeaks at times. The Pilot is truck-like on the outside, but it's a much tamer vehicle when you look closely. It combines car-like comfort and handling in a crossover package where ride comfort, utility, and passenger accommodations are foremost.

COST ANALYSIS: Pilot sales have rebounded this year, but dealers are willing to dicker a bit over prices, while Honda sweetens its leasing and financing deals. Unsold 2011 Pilots are eligible for all kinds of automaker incentives that will drive down the 2012 model prices, as well, but not before the first quarter of 2012. Be prepared to delay your purchase until then, if salespeople won't haggle. **Best alternatives:** GM's heavily discounted Tahoe and Yukon SUVs are selling at bargain prices. A GM Terrain or Traverse would also be worth considering. **Options:** Nothing essential. **Rebates:** Look for $2,000–$4,000 discounts, attractive low financing rates, and special leasing prices. **Depreciation:** Slower than average. **Insurance cost:** Higher than average. **Annual maintenance cost:** Below average. **Parts supply/cost:** Average availability. Most parts are moderately priced, except for cylinder deactivation components, which may be costly because only Honda dealers sell them. **Warranty:** Bumper-to-bumper 3 years/60,000 km; powertrain 5 years/100,000 km; rust perforation 5 years/ unlimited km. **Supplementary warranty:** A waste of money. **Highway/city fuel economy:** *Front-drive:* 8.7/12.7 L/100 km, 32/22 mpg. *AWD:* 9.1/13.1 L/100 km, 31/22 mpg.

OWNER-REPORTED PROBLEMS: More owner complaints than with the Element: Airbags failed to deploy; sudden, unintended acceleration and brake failure; mushy brakes; electrical failures may cause car to shut down; front wheel came off:

> My wife and I were driving home on the night of June 2nd, 2010 and were turning on the street we live on when the right front wheel just laid over. We had it towed to the dealership and they informed us that they thought that either the bolts were not properly torque at the factory or possibly they just broke. These were the bolts that hold the spindle on.

Several owners also say unprotected wiring in the undercarriage area could be life-threatening if damaged:

> Wheel sensor wires on 2011 Honda Pilot are exposed and unprotected under the vehicle which when damaged, disable anti-lock braking system (ABS), vehicle stability assist (VSA), and the variable torque management (VTM-4) systems. Exposed wires are prone to be cut or damaged by road debris and hazards. Due to the wire being exposed, it was damaged and caused an out-of-pocket expense of approx. $266.00 to repair on a brand new vehicle with only 2,600 miles [4,180 km] on it. This could

have been easily avoided if the wire had been protected by a braided covering or metal tube. Wires should not be exposed within the undercarriage of a vehicle, especially ones that are responsible for safety features.

Automatic transmission fluid leaks; secondary hood latch has failed when passing over rough roads; rear tailgate window exploded while vehicle was parked in a garage (window was replaced under warranty, which shows Honda realizes this is a quality issue and not a routine insurance claim for damage caused from an outside source). Original-equipment Goodyear tire sidewall failures; the rear AC system will not shut off from the front control panel; and the driver's seat height adjustment lowers on its own while the Pilot is underway.

Pilot dealer servicing has also been found wanting:

> Spontaneous star crack in lower center windshield, spontaneous rear hatch and passenger door opening while driving with my young child in the rear passenger seat (with "locked" doors), transmission rattle upon slow acceleration or coast at second and third gears…Honda dealer said call insurance about windshield, something must have "hit" windshield without me knowing it, said "found no abnormal noises" and "cannot duplicate" rattle noise because different people have different driving patterns, said "cannot duplicate" doors opening while driving, dealer did not "fix" any of these safety issues, just told us to pick up the car…. After research on Internet, I believe these to be manufacturer defects.

SERVICE BULLETIN-REPORTED PROBLEMS: Moonroof malfunctions; loose/broken third-row seatback cover; inoperative keyless remote; sun visor falls down; auxiliary power socket comes out of console; front suspension clicking on acceleration/braking; and a fix for tailgate rust spots and stains.

RIDGELINE ★★★★★

best buy

KEY FACTS

CANADIAN PRICE (NEGOTIABLE): *DX:* $34,990, *VP:* $36,690, *EX-L:* $41,490, *EX-L Navi.:* $43,690 **U.S. PRICE:** *RT:* $29,150, *RTS:* $31,855, *RTL:* $34,730, *RTL Navi.:* $37,080 **CANADIAN FREIGHT:** $1,395 **U.S. FREIGHT:** $810

POWERTRAIN (FRONT-DRIVE/4WD)

Engines: 3.5L V6 (250 hp); Transmission: 5-speed auto.

DIMENSIONS/CAPACITY

Passengers: 2/3; Wheelbase: 122 in.; H: 70.3/L: 207/W: 69 in.; Headroom F/R: 6.5/4.5 in.; Legroom F/R: 42/28 in.; Fuel tank: 83.3L/regular; Tow limit: 5,000 lb.; Load capacity: 1,554 lb.; Turning circle: 42.6 ft.; Ground clearance: 7.5 in.; Weight: 4,504 lb.; GVWR: 6,051 lb.

RATING: Recommended. A top performer. **Strong points:** Some room for price haggling, mostly on financing and leasing deals. Good, quiet acceleration; a smooth-shifting automatic transmission; secure handling and good cornering control; communicative, direct steering; comfortable, supple ride; friendly cabin environment where everything is easily accessed and storage spaces abound; tailgate opens either vertically or horizontally; all-weather, lockable trunk beneath the cargo bed; and no intrusive wheel arch in the five-foot-long bed. Reliability and overall dependability are legendary, and crashworthiness is exemplary. **Weak points:** High sales price; excessive road noise; bed is too small for some needs; not well-suited for off-roading. **New for 2012:** Carried over without any major changes.

OVERVIEW: The Ridgeline mixes performance with convenience. It's an ideal truck for most jobs, as long as you keep it on the highway. Off-road, this unibody pickup offers only medium performance relative to its nearest body-on-frame competitors, the Toyota Tacoma and the Nissan Frontier. Its long wheelbase and independent rear suspension give the Ridgeline an impressive in-bed trunk and excellent road manners, but make it difficult for the truck to traverse anything that's rougher than a stone road or has a breakover angle greater than 21 degrees. NHTSA crashworthiness ratings are outstanding: Front and side occupant protection is rated five stars, and rollover protection is given four stars. IIHS gives its top score ("Good") for frontal and side occupation protection and qualifies head-restraint protection also as "Good" for all 2009–11 models.

COST ANALYSIS: Go for the upgraded 2011 models and bypass the identical, costlier 2012s. Weak sales have built up dealer inventories, and the general car-buying population hasn't discovered these trucks yet. Remember, small and mid-sized pickups retain a higher resale value than most cars. So, even if you pay more than expected, you will probably recoup the difference come trade-in time. **Best alternatives:** Other pickups worth considering are the Ford F-Series, the GM Silverado and Sierra duo, Nissan Frontier, and Toyota Tacoma. **Options:** Firestone and Bridgestone original-equipment tires will not give you the best performance or durability; try to trade them for something better. **Rebates:** Look for $2,000– $4,000 rebates in the winter of 2012. **Depreciation:** Slower than average; a 2008 model that sold new for $35,000 now costs about $20,000. **Insurance cost:** Higher than average. **Parts supply/cost:** Mostly reasonably priced and easily found at dealers and independent suppliers. Body parts are a bit costly and harder to find. **Annual maintenance cost:** Laughably low. **Warranty:** Bumper-to-bumper 3 years/60,000 km; powertrain 5 years/100,000 km; rust perforation

6 years/unlimited km. **Supplementary warranty:** A waste of money. Very few safety-related incidents have been reported to NHTSA federal investigators or by *Consumer Reports* members within the last four model years. Also, internal manufacturer service bulletins show no major failure trends. **Highway/city fuel economy:** 9.8 L/14.1 100 km, 29/20 mpg.

OWNER-REPORTED PROBLEMS: No NHTSA complaints posted for the 2011 model; only 10 recorded for the 2010. Rear passenger window exploded while the truck was parked. Engine surges when coming to a stop; premature failure of the automatic transmission; brake and accelerator pedals are mounted too close together; many AC heater failures due to defective wiring or fan motor switch (one fire reported); centre sliding portion of the rear window exploded for no reason. Snow collects under the wipers while driving and freezes them to the cowl:

> The wipers shut off under the increased momentary load. The only way to get them to reset is to stop, turn the vehicle off and restart it. This is very difficult to do when you are completely blinded with slush looking forward.

Snow collects in the wheel rims causing dangerous wheel/steering shake. Loose tailgate cables cause the tailgate to malfunction; door latches springs are too weak; side wall tread suddenly flew off the original-equipment Michelin LTX tires; the heated seats heat up even when the switch is turned off; and the XM satellite radio loses its setting unless rebooted after restarting in CD mode.

SERVICE BULLETIN-REPORTED PROBLEMS: Rear seat leg doesn't fold flat; tailgate wont open in Swing Mode/handle is stiff.

Hyundai

Hyundai and its Kia lineup are racking up impressive sales across Canada for three reasons: Their vehicles are relatively cheap when compared with the competition, their quality is almost equal to the best that comes from Japan, and owners can count on getting a comprehensive base warranty that other companies don't offer. The company is on a much surer footing than it was in the late '70s, when Hyundai Canada was run by a ragtag gang of Toronto-based auto newbies who had their collective head up their collective exhaust pipe. They made money by dumping cheap but poor-quality Pony, Stellar, and Excel compacts into the market to compete against equally poor-quality American small cars. At that time, Hyundai got an important toehold in the North American market because Detroit iron was too expensive and not very fuel-efficient and fuel prices were going through the roof. However, when fuel became relatively cheap again, you couldn't give a Hyundai away.

Korean Quality?

No kidding. Hyundai quality control has gone from pitiful to exceptional except for some redesigned models like the glitch-ridden 2011 Sonata. This general quality turnaround has been accomplished through the use of better-made components and corporate espionage. In fact, Hyundai hired away a bevy of Toyota's top quality-control engineers in 2003—and got a satchel-full of Toyota's secret documents in the bargain. Following a cease-and-desist letter from Toyota in 2006, Hyundai returned the pilfered papers and assured Toyota that they never looked at the secret reports stolen from the company (wink, wink; nudge, nudge). Industry insiders say the privileged information was a major factor in Hyundai's leapfrogging over the competition with better quality-control systems.

It's ironic that Hyundai and Kia are copying the marketing strategy employed by Japanese automakers over the past four decades: Secure a solid beachhead in one car segment, and then branch out from there with redesigns every three years. Models that don't sell get dumped, like the Entourage minivan, Tiburon, and Azera. Hyundai is also sharing components with its Kia subsidiary to keep production costs down while raising Kia quality (yes, *Consumer Reports* now recommends the Kia Forte, Soul, and Sorento).

Unfortunately, all is not rosy for Hyundai from a quality perspective. Its latest redesign, the 2011 Sonata, is a mess—a potentially lethal mess. Owners of these cars report steering malfunctions that drive the Sonata to one side of the road or the other, sudden, unintended acceleration, malfunctioning powertrains, and headlights that give inadequate lighting.

Normally, these kinds of complaints would be quickly addressed by Hyundai, but that doesn't seem to be the case here, judging by owner reports registered by the U.S. federal government.

The Elantra has been affected by similar safety problems, notably steering malfunctions. Could it be that Hyundai is following Toyota and Honda production practices a little too closely and is giving owners less content for more money?

For 2012, the South Koreans are continuing to invest heavily in North America as they troll for dealers recently dumped by bankrupt Chrysler and General Motors. They are bringing out an extensive lineup of fuel-efficient new cars, minivans, and SUVs, and are targeting increasingly upscale customers without forgetting their entry-level base. For example, Hyundai has enhanced its luxury lineup with the Genesis luxury sedan and the Genesis Coupe, a Camaro/Mustang stalker. The 2011 Equus is a $62,999, V8-powered rear-drive luxury sedan aimed squarely at the BMW 5 Series and the Mercedes-Benz E-Class. Equus was developed on the rear-drive Genesis sedan platform, but the wheelbase was stretched by 10.9 cm (4.3 in.). It's 29 cm (11.4 in.) longer than the 2010 Mercedes E-Class.

At the other end of the fuel economy spectrum, both Hyundai and Kia intend to launch several new fuel-frugal small cars in the near future and offer drivers fuel-saving options that include a hybrid Sonata, smaller engines, direct-injection gasoline engines, plug-in hybrids, and fuel cell technology. Hyundai calls the fuel economy initiative "Blue Drive"—a fancy name for cheaper models with less content, less weight, and more miles per gallon. For example, Blue Edition models have a lower gear ratio and tires with less rolling resistance. Power windows and door locks, as well as other formerly standard amenities, will become optional, thereby trading convenience for cash savings.

Hyundai is also giving each 2012 Sonata a Blue Link communications system that provides a direct connection to emergency services in the event of an accident. The feature also gives traffic and weather updates and allows owners easy access to roadside assistance. Smartphones can be connected with Blue Link to help owners locate their vehicle in large shopping malls or to follow "Junior" when he takes the car out on the weekend. The system can keep track of where the vehicle is being driven and how fast it's going.

ACCENT ★★★

RATING: Average; the car is way overpriced. **Strong points:** Well-appointed; good fuel economy; adequate engine and automatic transmission performance in most situations; easy handling; comfortable and quiet ride; fair amount of interior room; comfortable driving position with good visibility and height-adjustable, form-fitting bucket seats that provide plenty of support; an incredibly good reliability record, with few complaints relative to safety or quality control; and it's cheap on gas. A 5-year/100,000 km bumper-to-bumper warranty. Some impressive but conflicting crashworthiness scores (see the "Weak points"): NHTSA crash tests give the Accent five stars for frontal collision crashworthiness and four stars for side impact protection and rollover resistance. Frontal offset crash protection, roof strength and head restraints rated "Acceptable" by IIHS. **Weak points:**

KEY FACTS

CANADIAN PRICE (NEGOTIABLE):
Hatchback L: $13,599; *Auto:* $14,599; *Sedan L:* $13,199; *Auto:* $14,399; *GL:* $14,999; *Auto:* $16,199; *GLS:* $17,999 **U.S. PRICE:** *GLS:* $14,195 (plus $1,200 for an automatic transmission), *GS:* $14,595 ($1,000 more for an automatic tranny), *SE:* $15,795 (again, $1,000 more for an automatic gearbox)
CANADIAN FREIGHT: $1,495
U.S. FREIGHT: $760
POWERTRAIN (FRONT-DRIVE)
Engine: 1.6L 4-cyl. (138 hp); Transmissions: 6-speed man. • 6-speed auto.
DIMENSIONS/CAPACITY (SEDAN)
Passengers: 2/3; Wheelbase: 101.2 in.; H: 57.1/L: 172/W: 66.9 in.; Headroom F/R: 4.5/2.0 in.; Legroom F/R: 41.833.3 34.3 in.; Cargo volume: 13.7 cu. ft.; Fuel tank: 43L/regular; Tow limit: N/A; Load capacity: 850 lb.; Turning circle: 34.1 ft.; Ground clearance: 5.5 in.; Weight (L): 2,396; (auto.) 2,462 lb.

Price-gouging while the Japanese are out of play dealing with the earthquake's aftermath. Automatic transmission hobbles horsepower; engine could use a bit more torque and noise-vibration dampening; ride is on the firm side; numb steering feel; and acrobatic rear-seat entry/exit with the hatchback. Head restraints and side crash protection were rated "Poor." **New for 2012:** A fourth-generation redesign. The two-door hatchback has been discontinued, the four-door is larger, the same engine now bridles 28 more horses, and new standard safety features have been added.

OVERVIEW: Remember how we said Hyundai is unabashedly copying Asian automakers in its 2012 lineup of cars and SUVs? This year we see Hyundai transforming its entry-level Accent into a larger, upscale compact the same way the Civic was incrementally improved and enlarged to now join the Accord in the family car class. All of these improvements have added thousand to the Accent's base price, however, making this front-drive, entry-level sedan no longer one of the cheapest feature-laden small cars sold in North America. Carrying a homegrown direct-injection 1.6L 4-cylinder engine coupled to a standard 6-speed manual transmission (the 6-speed automatic is optional), the Accent offers bare-bones motoring, but includes standard features such as a height-adjustable driver's seat, four-wheel disc brakes, active front head restraints, a tilt steering wheel, power locks, CD/MP3 stereo with USB and iPod interface, and floor mats. Air conditioning is optional.

COST ANALYSIS: Will success spoil Hyundai? If they keep their prices at present levels, absolutely: Chevrolet's and Ford will be laughing all the way to the bank. Stay away from the Accent until 2012, when prices will come down and quality will improve. **Best alternatives:** Chevrolet Cruze, Ford Focus, Honda Fit or Civic (2011), Mazda3, Nissan Versa or Sentra, Suzuki SX4, and Toyota Yaris. **Options:** Not needed. **Rebates:** $1,000–$2,000 through low-cost financing, leasing deals, and discounting. **Depreciation:** Slower than average. **Insurance cost:** Average. **Parts supply/cost:** Parts aren't hard to find, and they're reasonably priced. **Annual maintenance cost:** Average. **Warranty:** Bumper-to-bumper 5 years/100,000 km; rust perforation 5 years/unlimited km. **Supplementary warranty:** No longer needed, such is the improvement in quality control. **Highway/city fuel economy:** *Man.:* 4.9/6.7 L/100 km, 58/42 mpg. *Auto.:* 4.8/7.8L/100 km, 59/36 mpg.

OWNER-REPORTED PROBLEMS: Airbags failed to deploy; on the freeway, accelerator, brakes, and steering wheel locked up; sudden brake loss after passing over a bump; brakes are weak, noisy, and tend to pull the car to one side:

> Brakes repeatedly grind with a crunching noise in snowy conditions to point where I have difficulty stopping vehicle. Pulls to right and steering wheel shakes to point where you can see it moving from a distance. Feels like pedal is locking and brakes are not working properly making vehicle very unsafe. I've been driving for over 35 years and owned many different vehicles and have never experienced anything like this in a braking system. Hyundai dealership claims *normal* for a Hyundai however I test drove another new Accent this morning to compare under the exact same road conditions and it did not shake, grind, pull to the right like mine does and it stopped when I applied the brakes. I drove all over the lot to try and get it make noise or fail to stop but it felt perfect. I again got back into my car and my car again shook, grinded and did not stop near as quickly as the other Accent.

Car suddenly lost power and misfired when cruising on the highway; engine surging when stopped; delayed automatic transmission engagement; power-steering pump whine; turn signal malfunctions; key sticks in the ignition; and Kumho tire premature wear and blistering. One owner reports that groundhogs love to snack the car's undercarriage cables on them, thereby disabling the tranny and key dash gauges:

> I put down moth balls and fox scent to ward the hogs off, but they love Accent wires; losing the transmission and speedometer can make driving a little dangerous.

SERVICE BULLETIN-REPORTED PROBLEMS: Harsh delayed shift diagnosis on the 6-speed automatic transmission.

ELANTRA, TOURING ★★★★★/★★★

KEY FACTS

CANADIAN PRICE (NEGOTIABLE): *L:* $14,999, *L auto.:* $16,199, *L Touring:* $14,999, *GL:* $17,399, *GL auto.:* $18,599, *GLS man.:* $19,799, *GLS auto.:* $20,999, *GLS Sport:* $22,049, *GLS Sport auto.:* $23,249 **U.S. PRICE:** *GLS auto.:* $17,445, *Touring:* $15,995 (add $1,200 for a CVVT automatic tranny), *Limited:* $20,445 **CANADIAN FREIGHT:** $1,495 **U.S. FREIGHT:** $760

POWERTRAIN (FRONT-DRIVE)
Engine: 1.8L 4-cyl. (148 hp) • 2.0L 4-cyl. (138 hp); Transmissions: 5-speed man. • 6-speed man. • 4-speed auto. • 6-speed auto.

DIMENSIONS/CAPACITY (TOURING)
Passengers: 2/3; Wheelbase: 106.3 in.; H: 56.5/L: 178.3/W: 69.9 in.; Headroom F/R: 2.5/2.0 in.; Legroom F/R: 43.6/33.1 in.; Cargo volume: 14.8 cu. ft.; Fuel tank: 48L/regular; Tow limit: 2,000 lb.; Load capacity: 850 lb.; Turning circle: 34.8 ft.; Ground clearance: 5.5 in., Weight: 2,661 lb.

RATING: *Elantra*: Recommended; *Touring*: Average. **Strong points:** New 4-cylinder has plenty of pep for daily chores and comes with a smooth-shifting 6-speed automatic transmission; good handling and a quiet, comfortable ride; electronic stability control comes with the SE trim; 2011 revamping gave the car a more fluid, stylish exterior and a well-appointed and spacious interior; comfortable seats; the seatback slides far enough back to easily accommodate drivers over six feet tall; classy, quiet interior; and impressive crashworthiness scores. NHTSA gives the car five stars for frontal crash protection and four stars for side and rollover protection. IIHS gives Elantra its top, "Good" rating for frontal, side, rear, and roof, crashworthiness. A good base warranty is standard. *Touring*: A compact wagon with a spacious, versatile interior; handles well and has excellent braking. **Weak points:** Engine feels sluggish when in Active Eco mode; noisy brakes are sometimes a bit grabby and take some skill to modulate; excessive engine noise when accelerating; some wind and road noise; and the dash vents should be mounted higher. *Touring*: Not as good a performer as the Elantra. The ride is quite firm, there's little steering feedback, engine noise invades the cabin, fuel economy isn't as good as the Elantra, and first and second gear are too far apart. **New for 2012:** Not much new after the car's redesign last year. This year Hyundai has added an Active Eco System, which modifies engine and transmission control for improved fuel economy of about 7 percent. Other changes: fog lights to the GLS Preferred Package and improved horn sound.

OVERVIEW: Elantra's sharp new styling is hard to miss and its roomy interior pushes the car into the mid-size category. A wagon version, called the Touring, arrived in early 2009. A 148 hp 1.8L and 138 hp 2.0L 4-cylinder power the base Elantra and Touring, respectively. The 1.8L is coupled to a 6-speed manual or automatic transmission, while the Touring uses a more rudimentary 5-speed manual or 4-speed automatic.

COST ANALYSIS: Get a discounted, upgraded 2011 model or wait until 2012 when this year's prices will fall to a reasonable level. **Best alternatives:** The Chevrolet Cruze, Ford Focus, Honda Civic (2011) or Accord, Mazda3, Suzuki SX4, and Toyota Corolla. **Options:** Go for the automatic transmission: It's quieter and has smoother shifting than the manual, and fuel economy isn't much affected. Also, check to see if your Elantra has a spare tire and jack. Most don't. **Rebates:** $1,000 rebates and low-cost financing. **Depreciation:** Slower than average, which is surprising because it's not often that you see a 2008 South Korean vehicle (Elantra L) worth more than half its $16,000 original price. **Insurance cost:** Average. **Parts supply/ cost:** Parts are easy to find and reasonably priced, with heavy discounting by independents. **Annual maintenance cost:** Average. **Warranty:** Bumper-to-bumper 5 years/100,000 km; rust perforation 5 years/unlimited km. **Supplementary warranty:** Not needed. **Highway/city fuel economy:** *1.8L man.:* 4.9/6.8 L/100 km, 58/42 mpg. *Auto.:* 4.9/69 L/100 km, 58/41 mpg. *Touring 2.0L man.:* 6.4/8.9 L/100 km, 44/32 mpg. *Touring auto.:* 6.5/8.7 L/100 km, 43/32 mpg.

OWNER-REPORTED PROBLEMS: Airbags failed to deploy:

> My wife and I were involved in an accident. Another car ran the red light and hit us. My wife and I were injured and our car was totaled. None of the airbags went off on our brand new Hyundai Elantra. We were later told by Hyundai that passenger airbags don't always go off because of weight variations in some adults. My wife is 5'4" and her weight is normal for her height.

In another incident, both airbags deployed for no reason; airbag warning light and tire-pressure monitoring system alert come on for no reason; two electrical fires reported with the 2010 Touring; chronic stalling, believed to be a fuel-pump-related problem; sudden, unintended acceleration accompanied by loss of braking capability; cruise control suddenly resets itself to a higher speed; throttle sensor sticks when cruising; automatic transmission jumps out of gear:

> 2011 Hyundai Elantra with 800 miles on it. Transmission violently bucks at highway speeds and then shifts to Neutral. There is suddenly no throttle response at speeds exceeding 60 mph, requiring the car to be coasted to safety if possible. After turning off the key and restarting, the problem appears to be gone.

Defective solenoids blamed for early transmission failures; car may roll away even with emergency brake applied; faulty electronic stability control:

> Dry day, normal acceleration, traction control killed power upon entering highway traffic, leaving us sitting in 50–55 mph [80–89 km/h] traffic, then cleared up, twice within 3 hours. Also on same day, 60 mph [97 km/h] on a two-lane road, the skid control light came on and applied the left front brake pulling me into oncoming traffic, I reacted quickly and brought auto back to my lane and turned off skid control. This happened once before. Fortunately there was no traffic. The Skid Control light came on then went back out both times. One failure seemed to be the traction control, the other was the skid control. I suspect a bad wheel speed sending unit. So far the dealer has found nothing.

Lower ball joint failure:

> The contact owns a 2011 Hyundai Elantra. The contact stated that while driving approximately 20 mph [32 km/h], the front end of the vehicle collapsed. The vehicle was towed to an authorized dealer where the contact was informed that the front passenger side lower ball joint fractured. The vehicle was not repaired. The

manufacturer was made aware of the failure, but offered no assistance. The failure mileage was 4,000 [6,400 km].

Sudden steering lock-up; the car continually pulls to the right when cruising or when coming to a stop:

Hyundai Elantra Touring pulls to the right while accelerating and traveling at 50 mph [80 km/h]. It hurts your wrist to keep it straight on the road. Alignment and tire rotation don't solve the problem.

Brakes freeze up when vehicle is driven through snow; Continental and Kumho Solus original equipment tires are noted for sidewall failures ("bubbling"). Elantra owners consider the lack of a spare tire and canned air in the trunk to be unsafe practices:

Car dealers are allowed to sell new cars with no spare tire or jack. Their policy is to only include a can of air which may or may not work when needed. They are also not keeping replacement tires in stock. This can of air is a hazard to keep in a car in Arizona when the temperatures in the summer reach 115 degrees [46°C]. And with the dealership not stocking the tires, my car was not drivable and strands the motorist.

SERVICE BULLETIN-REPORTED PROBLEMS: Troubleshooting an automatic transmission that stays in Third gear, goes into "failsafe mode," or has an illuminated MIL alert.

SONATA ★★

RATING: Below Average. Like Honda, Hyundai cars don't tolerate redesigns very well (see "Owner-Reported Problems"). **Strong points:** A credible alternative to most Detroit-bred family cars. Sizzling V6 power, and it burns only a bit more than the 4-banger does; good handling; and comfortable ride. Well equipped and stylish; user-friendly controls and gauges; spacious trunk, and a conveniently low lift-in height; and the fairly quiet cabin comfortably seats three in the back. The standard Blue Link communications feature is part "Big Brother" and part emergency caller. NHTSA awarded the 2011 Sonata five stars for front and side crashworthiness and five stars for rollover resistance. IIHS gave the Sonata a "Good" rating for front offset protection, head-restraint effectiveness, roof crush-resistance, and side-impact protection. Owners also get a comprehensive base warranty. **Weak points:** Quality, judging from last year's model and a few similar complaints on the 2012. *Lemon-Aid* has lowered the car's rating this year until we see to which side the quality pendulum is swinging. Prices have been boosted thousands of dollars during the past few years; fuel economy could be better; the suspension is somewhat bouncy and noisy; lots of body lean under hard cornering; and the steering lacks feedback. **New for 2012:** Blue Link communication device is standard.

OVERVIEW: This mid-sized sedan is a top-rated pick by *Consumer Reports* and its sales, particularly since last year's 2011 redesign, have been spectacular. Unfortunately, the car is not that good, judging from owner experiences with the 2011 version.

Until the car was redesigned that year, only a few dozen owner complaints would appear on NHTSA safety database. For example, the 2010 model has 31 incidents reported where the two-year norm would be a hundred reports. Contrast that with the redesigned 2011 model's profile: up through July 2011, that model year alone has elicited 348 safety-related reports posted on NHTSA's website at *www-odi.nhtsa.dot.gov/complaints/results.cfm*. In the past, incremental powertrain, performance, safety, convenience, and styling changes were absorbed without provoking such large-scale owner dissatisfaction.

Not this time.

Styled similarly to the Honda Accord, the redesigned Sonata meets or exceeds the engine performance standards of its competitors, although its fuel economy isn't as good. The Sonata rides on a double-wishbone front suspension and a multi-link rear suspension that is more softly sprung than usual, making the car a bit "bouncier" than its competitors.

While making the 2011 Sonata unsafe through poor design and factory deficiencies, Hyundai has added standard safety features that have proven their worth. For example, this year's model includes four-wheel ABS; stability and traction control; front and side curtain airbags; front and rear seat belt pretensioners; an integrated rear child safety seat; and a "smart" passenger-side airbag that won't deploy if the passenger weighs less than 30 kg (66 lb.). Well, at

KEY FACTS

CANADIAN PRICE (NEGOTIABLE): *GL:* $22,649, *GL auto.:* $24,249, *GLS auto.:* $26,249, *Limited:* $28,999, *2.0T:* $28,999, *2.0T Limited:* $31,749 *Hybrid:* $29,999 **U.S. PRICE:** *GLS auto.:* $19,695, *SE:* $23,095, *SE 2.0T:* $24,645, *Limited:* $26,345, *2.0T Limited:* $28,095, *Hybrid:* $25,795 **CANADIAN FREIGHT:** $1,565 **U.S. FREIGHT:** $760
POWERTRAIN (FRONT-DRIVE)
Engines: 2.4L 4-cyl. (198 hp) • 2.0L 4-cyl. turbo (274 hp); Transmissions: 6-speed man. • 6-speed auto.
DIMENSIONS/CAPACITY
Passengers: 2/3; Wheelbase: 110 in.; H: 57.9/L: 189; 8/W: 72.2 in.; Headroom F/R: 3.0/3.0 in.; Legroom F/R: 45.5/34.6 in.; Cargo volume: 16.4 cu. ft.; Fuel tank: 70L/regular; Tow limit: N/A; Load capacity: 860 lb.; Turning circle: 35.8 ft.; Weight: 3,161–3,316 lb.

least that's the theory—in practice, owners report the airbag is often disabled no matter what the passenger's weight.

COST ANALYSIS: Stay away from the 2011 model, no matter how cheap a leftover may be. You will end of spending your savings in the service bay, or in an emergency room. Instead, wait a year or so for the car's problems to be fixed. Remember, it took Honda two model years to get the Accord back on track and we are still keeping our fingers crossed. **Best alternatives:** The Chevrolet Cruze, Ford Focus and Fusion, Honda Accord, Hyundai Elantra, Nissan Sentra, Mazda5 or Mazda6, and Toyota Camry. **Options:** Choose the V6 engine for better performance and handling; you will lose only a bit of fuel economy. If you get the 4-banger, keep in mind that good fuel economy means putting up with more engine noise. Be wary of the sunroof; it eats up a lot of headroom and has a history of leaking. **Rebates:** As you get into the new year, expect $2,000 rebates and zero percent financing or attractive leasing deals on all models. **Depreciation:** Average; similar to the Elantra: a $22,300 2008 base Sonata is now worth slightly more than half that amount. **Insurance cost:** Average. **Parts supply cost:** Easy to find and relatively inexpensive. **Annual maintenance cost:** Average. **Warranty:** Bumper-to-bumper 5 years/100,000 km; rust perforation 5 years/ unlimited km. **Supplementary warranty:** Not needed. **Highway/city fuel economy:** *Auto. 2.0L:* 6.0/9.3 L/100 km, 47/30 mpg. *Man. 2.4L:* 5.7/8.7 L/100 km, 50/32 mpg. *Auto. 2.4L:* 5.7/9.4 L/100 km, 50/30 mpg. *Hybrid:* 4.6/5.5 L/100 km, 61/51 mpg.

OWNER-REPORTED PROBLEMS: Sudden, unintended acceleration when passing other cars; same thing happens when shifting to Reverse; cruise control resets itself to a higher speed; sudden hybrid engine failure due to water intrusion in rainy weather:

Engine can easily become hydro-locked in heavy rain and road splash-back from other vehicles due to the design of the direct air intake of the Sonata Hybrid. With its design, it does not have any water baffles to prevent water from entering the air filter and once it enters the air filter box, there are no drain holes for it to drain out. This forces the water through the engine as that is the only way for it to get out of the filter box.

When the engine stalled, no electronic control warning lights were illuminated and the car remained in the "ready" state. This could lead to damage of the HEV system and battery pack. Per the technician servicing the car, they stated that the HEV warning light only illuminated when the HEV battery reaches 15% charge (the point at which they have to replace it).

This contradicts with the owner's manual as well as counteracts the purpose of a warning lamp. Due to the nature of the design where the computer controls when the engine starts/stops, the engine can damage itself before preventative action can be taken. For example, when the engine stalls due to water ingestion through the air filter and the oxygen sensor determines it cannot compensate, the engine will stall, but before the situation can be rectified, the computer attempted to restart the engine causing it to become hydro-locked.

With my experience, I am convinced that the design of the car is flawed and unreliable to drive in a heavy rain scenario which leaves it unusable several times a year. I have owned several hybrids in the past (2002 and 2005 Toyota Prius) that I operated through the same conditions as your vehicle and I did not experience any problems with them. Additionally, with the Toyota, when the engine stalls against the computer's control (e.g.: running out of fuel), the HEV and Engine warning light both illuminated and the "ready" light was de-illuminated.

Passenger side airbag disabled when normal-sized adult occupies the seat; airbags fail to deploy in a high-speed collision; parked vehicle rolled downhill, even though transmission was left in Drive; manual transmission lunges forward when shifting from first to second gear; poorly-located cruise control Resume button inadvertently activates the feature:

> While using the cruise control the car leaped ahead several times after I had applied the brake (because I was getting too close to the car in front of me) and was temporarily handling speed without the cruise control. Nearly had an accident on two such occasions. Then I figured out what was happening. The "resume" button is so close to the rim of the wheel, and so exposed that the heel of my right hand was touching it inadvertently and the cruise control reengaged when I didn't want it to and didn't know it was happening. [In my opinion,] your button needs to be relocated or protected by a ridge.

Vehicle pulls sharply to the left or right when accelerating, requiring constant correction (see *www.youtube.com/watch?v=kolqvbpp3_A&Feature=Channel_video_title*).

Relative of a driver who died when her 2011 Sonata inexplicably ran into the left-side guardrail believes the car may have been at fault:

> There are numerous complaints about the power steering of 2011 Sonatas on various websites. One of them is the website of auto recalls for consumers (*www.argc.org/complaints/2011/Hyundai/Sonata/steering/problem.aspx*). 117 out of 266 complaints (67%) on 6/12/2011 are related to the steering column. This is a safety concern, because it pulls the vehicle to the left stronger and stronger as the speed accelerates above 25 mph [40 km/h].

•

> I purchased a 2012 Sonata in late June. Technically this is the second one I purchased. I can explain it this way. The first one I bought had a horrible pulling issue. It pulled right aggressively. Before I took delivery I test drove it and had the salesman drive with me. Even he said this is dangerous and not right. The dealership put it in the shop and they said they fixed it with an alignment. I test drove it again and it was

even worse. I refused to buy that car. They found me another one. At first it seemed to drive fine on the test drive. I should have driven it more than a couple blocks. Same issue as the first one after I took delivery. The car pulled and still pulls right, especially at highway speeds. Borderline dangerous on the highway. So, the dealership took it in again and worked the camber. Unpredictable....There are people all over the country having the same problem with the 2012 Sonata steering. Some Sonata techs say it's the same problem they had in 2011 when the recall was announced.

Premature wearout of the rear brakes; noisy shocks/struts; low-beam headlights give inadequate illumination:

There is a sharp boundary between headlight illumination on the lower area and darkness above. On all but level roadway, this hazardous defect is apparent. Many roads where I live in Pennsylvania are twisting and hilly. Traversing those roads with this Sonata using the low-beam headlights unnerving and dangerous. When the front of the car dips into even a slight downgrade, the road ahead is illuminated to about 40 feet [12 m] in front of car. Line of sight through windshield has at least half the view unlit.

Left tail light fell out of its mounting inside the trunk due to the plastic mount crumbling; rear windshield exploded after door was closed; sun visors are not long enough (vertically) to keep sun from blinding the driver; the horn is weak, makes a short sound, and sometimes won't sound at all:

Wife activated the horn to get my attention. It sounded one short beep and went dead. Has not worked since. Horn can hardly be heard standing next to the car let alone trying to get someone's attention inside a vehicle with the windows rolled up and the radio on....There are hundreds of complaints about the sound or failure of these horns on the Internet forums.

Hard starts, no starts:

The only reliable solution for starting the car is to depress the brake pedal and depress the Engine Start button for a minimum of 10 seconds. I've placed the key fob in several locations in the car (dashboard, cup holder, smart key holder) with no repeatable success. After a visit to the dealership, they cannot find a problem. However, a search on the Internet shows other owners experiencing the same problem.

SERVICE BULLETIN-REPORTED PROBLEMS: Automatic transmission malfunctions; transmission shifts harshly and drops into "safe" default mode; delayed shift diagnosis. Malfunctioning oil temperature sensor (see following page). Squeaking noise when turning steering wheel; water leaks onto the front-seat passenger floor; alarm system self-activates; remedy for glovebox rattle, creak. Hyundai has issued nine free service campaigns (included in the table on the following page) to address the many faults found with the 2011 Sonata. This means you will know the service manager on a first name basis and likely read all the *Service Bay Reports* magazines in the waiting room (see following page).

A/T—MIL ON/FAIL-SAFE MODE/DTCs P0711/P0712/P0713

BULLETIN NO.: 10-AT-004

DATE: FEBRUARY, 2010

AUTOMATIC TRANSMISSION OIL TEMPERATURE SENSOR DTC P0711, P0712 & P0713;

2010 TUCSON, 2010 SANTA FE, 2011 SONATA

DESCRIPTION: Incorrect operation of the oil temperature sensor may result in the following symptoms:

1. Check Engine Light illuminated
2. Transaxle held in 3rd gear Fail-Safe
3. Diagnostic Trouble Codes P0711, P0712 or P0713

ALL TECHNICAL SERVICE BULLETINS

NUMBER	DATE	TITLE
11-01-013	04/20/2011	Campaign TF3—Fuel Door Sticking
11-AT-009	04/15/2011	A/T—Failsafe Mode/MIL ON/Multiple A/T Solenoid DTCs
11-AT-008	04/11/2011	A/T—TCM/ECM Adaptive Value Rest/Relearn Procedure
11-FL-003-1	03/18/2011	Cooling System—MIL ON/DTC P0128 Stored in Memory
11-01-005	02/08/2011	Campaign TE7—Satellite Radio Buttons Sticking
11-AT-002	01/18/2011	A/T—MIL ON/DTCs P0717/P0721/P0722/Stays in 3rd gear
11-BD-001	01/06/2011	Body—Fuel Door Intermittently Inoperative
10-FL-018	12/08/2010	Engine Controls—ETC Adaptive Value Reset/Relearn Proc.
10-01-050	12/08/2010	Campaign TE1—Fuel Door Latch Actuator Inspection
10-01-049	12/06/2010	Campaign TE0—Overhead Console Lamp Replacement
10-01-047	11/23/2010	Campaign TD9—Rattles from Glove Box Area
10-01-046	11/19/2010	Campaign TD8—Overhead Console Replacement
10-01-037-1	11/16/2010	Campaign TD0—TCM Software Updates
10-01-045	11/16/2010	Campaign TD7—Overhead Console Replacement
10-01-041	11/02/2010	Campaign TD4—Navigation Map Data Update
10-BD-007	10/22/2010	Body/Fuel System—Rattles upon Acceleration
NHTSA10V426000	09/23/2010	Recall 10V426000—Steering Shaft Connector
10-BD-005	07/23/2010	Interior—Glove Box Rattle/Creak Noise
10-AT-006	03/18/2010	A/T—Harsh/Delayed Shift Diagnostics

GENESIS COUPE, SEDAN ★★★★

RATING: Above Average. The Genesis coupe and sedan are impressive upscale rear drive vehicles with different performance characteristics and widely varying retail prices. **Strong points:** The 3.8L engine gives breathtaking power to the coupe and quick acceleration when used with the sedan, although the sedan's 5.0L V8 is a real tire burner. Well-appointed, first-class interior fit and finish; a quiet, vibration-free, and spacious cabin; and clear and easy-to-read gauges. The sedan has plenty of room fore and aft and has posted impressive crashworthiness

rankings. NHTSA gave the sedan its top, five-star rating for front, side, and rollover occupant protection with the coupe (second-generation 2010 version) and sedan; IIHS frontal offset, side-impact, roof, and head-restraint protection were rated "Good." Average fuel economy for both vehicles. **Weak points:** The 2011 coupe's 4-cylinder turbo is both noisy and hooked to an imprecise 6-speed manual transmission; the optional 4.6L V8 is like having a sixth finger: it's there, but not all that useful. Expect the coupe to have a choppy, stiff ride, while the sedan has some body roll in hard cornering due to its more supple, "floaty" suspension (Infiniti and BMW models have stiffer suspensions that produce a more-secure feeling). Cramped rear seating with the coupe; Navigation and audio system controls are cumbersome. Hyundai recommends premium fuel for extra horsepower from the 4.6L V8, but it's not worth the higher fuel cost for just a few more horses. V6 reliability is above average; V8s are average. **New for 2012:** The Coupe will likely receive the same 333 hp 3.8L V6 that is destined for the Genesis

KEY FACTS

CANADIAN PRICE (NEGOTIABLE): *Coupe 2.0T:* $24,899, *Auto.:* $26,399, *2.0T GT Man.:* $31,149, *3.8 Man.:* $32,999, *3.8 GT Man.:* $36,499, *Auto.:* $38,299, *Sedan:* $38,999 **U.S. PRICE:** *Coupe 2.0T:* $22,250, *R-SPEC:* $24,500, *2.0T Premium:* $26,750, *3.8 R-SPEC:* $26,750, *3.8 Grand Touring:* $29,750, *3.8 Track:* $30,750, *Sedan:* $34,200 **CANADIAN FREIGHT:** *Coupe:* $1,565, *Sedan:* $1,760 **U.S. FREIGHT:** $850

POWERTRAIN (REAR-DRIVE)

Engines: 3.3 V6 (268 hp) • 3.8L V6 (290 hp) • 4.6L V8 (368 hp) • 5.0L V8 (429 hp); Transmissions: 6-speed man. • 5-speed manumatic • 6-speed manumatic

DIMENSIONS/CAPACITY (SEDAN)

Passengers: 2/3; Wheelbase: 115.6 in.; H: 58.1/L: 196.3/W: 74.4 in.; Headroom F/R: N/A; Legroom F/R: 44.3/38.6 in.; Cargo volume: 15.9 cu. ft.; Fuel tank: 65L–73L/regular/premium; Tow limit: 5,000 lb.; Ground clearance: 5.2 in.; Turning circle: 36 ft.; Weight: 3,824–3,971 lb.

DIMENSIONS/CAPACITY (COUPE)

Passengers: 2/3; Wheelbase: 115.6 in.; H: 58.3/L: 195.6/W: 73.4 in.; Cargo volume: 15.9 cu. ft.; Fuel tank: 65L–73L/regular/premium; Tow limit: 5,000 lb.; Ground clearance: 5.2 in.; Turning circle: 36 ft.; Weight: 3,748 lb.

sedan. It features direct injection and provides more horsepower than the outgoing V6 (306 hp) and power-slaps its 6-cylinder pony-car rivals, the Chevy Camaro (312 hp) and Ford Mustang/Dodge Challenger (305 hp).

OVERVIEW: Hyundai's Genesis targets BMW and Mercedes-Benz big spenders with its own luxury rear-drive until the Equus gets its footing. The smaller Genesis Coupe was launched in 2010, a year after the sedan, and targets the Chevrolet Camaro, Dodge Challenger, Ford Mustang, and Nissan 370Z.

These luxury cars are loaded with high-tech safety gear that includes ABS, traction control, an anti-skid system, side curtain airbags, front side airbags, and rear side airbags. There's also a heated and cooled driver's seat, wireless cell phone link, a navigation system with a hard drive for storing digital music files, a rear-view camera, and front and rear obstacle detection. A knob in the centre console governs audio, navigation, and other functions.

COST ANALYSIS: Coupe or sedan? The 2012 Genesis coupe is the better buy only if it gets a revised V6 and an improved manual transmission. Any 2011 leftovers are not worth the 2012 upgrades you will miss. **Best alternatives:** *Sedan:* The BMW 3 Series, Ford Taurus, Lincoln MKS, Mercedes-Benz E-Class, and Toyota Avalon. *Coupe:* The Chevrolet Camaro, Ford Mustang, and—for sheer sportster thrills without the bills—Mazda MX-5. **Options:** Stay away from last year's noisy 2.0L 4-cylinder engine and the overly complicated navigation system. Rubber floor mats ($90 and $65) and a trunk cargo net ($70) are worth buying from an independent retailer for about half the Hyundai prices listed above. **Rebates:** These cars are hot and are likely to stay that way. A $1,000–$1,500 rebate may be offered if Ford and GM cut their pony-car prices, which is doubtful. **Depreciation:** Varies from average to slower than average, depending on whether you buy the coupe or the sedan. For example, a 2010 base Genesis sedan that originally sold for $39,000 is now—barely a year later—worth about $29,500. The coupe from the same year does better: original selling price was $24,500, value today is $19,500. **Insurance cost:** Higher than average. **Parts supply/cost:** Parts are likely to be expensive and in short supply; due to the low volume and warranty, independent suppliers generally don't carry Genesis parts. **Annual maintenance cost:** Should be average. **Warranty:** Bumper-to-bumper 5 years/100,000 km; rust perforation 5 years/unlimited km. **Supplementary warranty:** Not needed. **Highway/city fuel economy:** *Coupe 2.0L man.:* 6.6/10.1 L/100 km, 43/28 mpg. *Coupe 2.0L auto.:* 6.6/10.4 L/100 km, 43/27 mpg. *Coupe 3.8L man.:* 7.6/12.0 L/100 km, 37/24 mpg. *Coupe 3.8L auto.:* 7.3/11.9 L/100 km, 39/24 mpg. *Sedan 3.8L:* 7.2/11.4 L/100 km, 39/25 mpg. *Sedan 4.6L:* 8.1/12.6 L/100 km, 35/22 mpg. Owners complain that their gas mileage is about 20 percent less than what Hyundai advertises:

This vehicle is rated at 20 mpg city, 30 mpg highway. The mileage has consistently been poor. It now has 4,200 miles on it and highway mileage with the cruise control on, in warm weather, with no load other than the driver is around 24 mpg. I had it checked by Hyundai and they replaced the O2 sensor. This improved the highway mileage slightly from 23 to 24 mpg. It has never approached 25 mpg let alone 30 mpg. I have read about others complaining about the poor mileage on 4-cylinder genesis coupes. If the mileage ratings had been more accurate I would not have even considered buying this car.

OWNER-REPORTED PROBLEMS: Electronic stability control (ESC) locked driver's brakes when he was turning the vehicle; more ESC and Bluetooth malfunctions; early replacement of the automatic transmission; Small pebble damaged the AC condenser ($800). *Coupe:* Stalling upon acceleration:

While trying to normally accelerate, the car virtually died. Acceleration flat spot. Somewhat similar to the old carbureted cars. Very infrequent, however, the other day losing acceleration almost caused a major accident.

Sedan: Sudden, unintended acceleration:

While attempting to park, the vehicle suddenly accelerated causing the Genesis to crash twice into a parked vehicle and then into a pole.

SERVICE BULLETIN-REPORTED PROBLEMS: A faulty transmission solenoid may activate the Check Engine alert and send the transaxle into "Fail-Safe" limp mode. *Coupe:* Engine rpms slowly drop to idle; front bumper gaps; quarter panel creak, tick when passing over rough roads; sunroof sun shade slides open when car accelerates; and the anti-theft alarm self-activates. *Sedan:* No start in Park, Neutral; self-activating anti-theft alarm; and brake lights flash for no reason. Troubleshooting tips to eliminate sunroof creaking, ticking.

TUCSON ★★★★★

RATING: Recommended. **Strong points:** Reasonably priced and well equipped; V6 engine provides smooth, sustained acceleration; sure-footed (thanks to the standard stability control) and smooth-riding; improved front-drive braking; a roomy and easily accessed cabin; and above average reliability. NHTSA gave the 2010 Tucson a five-star crashworthiness rating for front- and side-impact occupant protection and a four-star rating for rollover protection. IIHS rated frontal, side, rear, and roof crashworthiness as "Good." **Weak points:** The 4-cylinder engine struggles with a full load, and the expected fuel economy doesn't materialize. Vehicle isn't as agile as others in its class. Electric steering feels vague; lacks feedback at highway speeds. **New for 2012:** A few changes to improve fuel economy and distance via a new Active ECO System that improves throttle response, low rolling resistance tires, high-efficiency air conditioning and a larger fuel tank. 2012s also come with larger front disc brakes on the front-wheel drive models for improved brake performance; larger rear suspension bushings for better ride quality; premium shocks for the Tucson GLS; and upgraded side mirrors for the GLS.

OVERVIEW: The Tucson is Hyundai's compact crossover that was first introduced for the 2005 model year. It is smaller than the Santa Fe and built on the same Elantra-based platform as the Kia Sportage. The standard powerplant in all Tucsons is a 2.0L DOHC 4-cylinder engine. The optional all-wheel-drive system can send 99 percent of the power to the front wheels or split the traction between the front and rear wheels. Last year Hyundai restyled the Tucson and put in a better powertrain setup. The hybrid launch has been delayed until 2012.

COST ANALYSIS: Buy the 2012 for a handful of important fuel economy and safety upgrades. **Best alternatives:** The Honda CR-V and Toyota RAV4. **Options:** Nothing important. **Rebates:** Expect $2,000 discounts, zero percent financing, and attractive leasing deals on all models, except the new hybrid, in early 2012. **Depreciation:** Less than average. A 2009 base Tucson originally sold for $21,195; today, it is worth $15,000. **Insurance cost:** Average. **Parts supply/cost:** Easy to find and relatively inexpensive. **Annual maintenance cost:** Less than average. **Warranty:** Bumper-to-bumper 5 years/100,000 km; rust perforation 5 years/unlimited km. **Supplementary warranty:** Not needed. **Highway/city fuel economy (2011):** 2.0L man.: 7.4/10.1 L/100 km, 38/28 mpg. Auto.: 6.5/9.1 L/100 km, 43/31 mpg. 2.4L man.: 6.9/10 L/100 km, 41/28 mpg. Auto: 6.3/9.5 L/100 km, 45/30 mpg. 4WD man.: 7.4/10.6 L/100 km, 38/27 mpg. 4WD auto.: 7.1/10.1 L/100 km, 40/28 mpg.

KEY FACTS

CANADIAN PRICE (NEGOTIABLE): L man.: $19,999, Auto.: $22,899, GL auto.: $24,599, GL AWD: $26,599, GLS: $26,599, GLS AWD: $28,899, Limited AWD: $32,349, Limited AWD Navi.: $34,349 **U.S. PRICE:** GL: $19,045, GLS: $22,195, Limited AWD Navi.: $28,555
CANADIAN FREIGHT: $1,595
U.S. FREIGHT: $810
POWERTRAIN (FRONT-DRIVE/AWD)
Engines: 2.0L 4-cyl. (165 hp) • 2.4L 4-cyl. (176 hp); Transmissions: 5-speed man. • 6-speed manumatic
DIMENSIONS/CAPACITY
Passengers: 2/3; Wheelbase: 103.9 in.; H: 65.2/L: 173.2/W: 71.7 in.; Headroom F/R: 5.0/4.0 in.; Legroom F/R: 41.2/38.7 in.; Cargo volume: 25.7 cu. ft.; Fuel tank: 58L/regular; Tow limit: 1,000–2,000 lb.; Load capacity: 860 lb.; Turning circle: 34.7 ft.; Ground clearance: 6.7 in.; Weight: 3,139/3,175 lb.

OWNER-REPORTED PROBLEMS: Firewall insulation caught fire; rear window shattered spontaneously; automatic transmission jerks and slams into gear:

> Sudden downshifting with loud clunk and lurching of vehicle at 35 mph [55 km/h]. Felt as if I had been hit from behind by another vehicle. Instinctively hit the brakes and pulled over to check for exterior damage, and found none. Continued down the road and experienced unusual increases in rpms. When I arrived at my destination, the vehicle would not go in Reverse. Owned vehicle only 11 days. Incident occurred at 500 miles [800 km].

Loss of brakes for a couple of seconds after passing over speed bumps or small pothole; when accelerating to merge with traffic, the vehicle hesitates and then decelerates while the gas pedal is fully depressed. Vehicle sways left and right while cruising; rear of the vehicle slides as if it were on ice; rear-tire lock-up; speed sensor wires are vulnerable to road debris:

> Wires are located behind the tires and are fully exposed to road debris. They can be easily severed, thereby affecting ABS and traction control. The wire sticks out 3 inches in open air of the undercarriage and are located close enough to the tires that if they kick up any debris, it is in the direct path of the wire.

SERVICE BULLETIN-REPORTED PROBLEMS: Harsh, delayed shift diagnosis. A faulty oil temperature sensor could lead to the automatic transmission sticking in Third gear and a lit Check Engine light.

SANTA FE ★★★★★

best buy

RATING: Recommended. This SUV does almost everything right. **Strong points:** A long list of standard equipment; acceptable acceleration with the base 2.4L 4-cylinder, but the 3.5L V6 gives you more power and good fuel economy as well.

It delivers more than 100 horsepower more than the 4-cylinder engine, yet EPA fuel economy ratings are not that far apart. A smooth-shifting automatic transmission; good steering response; fairly agile; a comfortable, controlled ride enhanced by comfortable seats (Hyundai dropped third-row seating two years ago); standard stability/traction control and full-body side curtain airbags; a roomy interior that easily accommodates both passengers and cargo; simple, user-friendly controls; and better than average quality control. NHTSA gave the Santa Fe a five-star rating for front- and side-impact protection and four stars for rollover resistance. IIHS rated frontal, side, rear, and roof crashworthiness as "Good." **Weak points:** The 2.4L four could use more low-end power; vague steering; ride quality on the SE and Limited may be too stiff for some; seats have short cushions; and you will have to get used to some annoying suspension and road noise. **New for 2012:** Not much, except for a redesigned front grille and low rolling-resistance tires (GLS).

OVERVIEW: The Santa Fe is a competitively priced family SUV that is at the small end of the mid-size sport-utility lineup. It offers impressive room, good build quality, and many standard safety and performance features that cost a lot more when bought with competing models. Revamped last year, the Santa Fe now has better-performing, fuel-thrifty powertrains and additional cabin space.

KEY FACTS

CANADIAN PRICE (NEGOTIABLE): *2.4 GL: $23,999, 2.4 GL auto.: $26,499, 3.5 GL auto.: $28,999, 3.5 GL AWD: $29,699, 3.5 GL FWD Sport: $31,299, 3.5 GL AWD Sport: $33,299, Limited: $35,799, Limited Navi.: $37,599* **U.S. PRICE:** *GLS: $21,845, SE: $26,145, Limited: $27,195* **CANADIAN FREIGHT:** $1,595 **U.S. FREIGHT:** $810

POWERTRAIN (FRONT-DRIVE/AWD)
Engines: 2.4L 4-cyl. (175 hp) • 3.5L V6 (276 hp); Transmissions: 6-speed man. • 6-speed auto.

DIMENSIONS/CAPACITY
Passengers: 2/3; Wheelbase: 106.3 in.; H: 67.9/L: 184.1: W: 74.4 in.; Headroom N/A; Legroom F/R: 42.6/36.8 in.; Cargo volume: 78.2 cu. ft.; Fuel tank: 75L/regular; Tow limit: 3,500 lb.; Load capacity: 1,120 lb.; Turning circle: 35.4 ft.; Ground clearance: 8.1 in.; Weight: 3,725-3,875 lb.

COST ANALYSIS: Don't waste your money on a 2012; instead, buy an almost identical, discounted 2011 model for thousands less. **Best alternatives:** GM Terrain, Traverse, Acadia, or Enclave; Nissan Xterra; Toyota RAV4 or Highlander. **Rebates:** Expect $3,000 rebates, zero percent financing, and cheap leases on all models, starting in the late fall. **Depreciation:** Average. **Insurance cost:** Average. **Parts supply/cost:** Easy to find, and relatively inexpensive. **Annual maintenance cost:** Average. **Warranty:** Bumper-to-bumper 5 years/100,000 km; rust perforation 5 years/unlimited km. **Supplementary warranty:** Not needed. **Highway/city fuel economy:** *2.4L man.: 7.7/11 L/100 km, 37/26 mpg. Auto: 7.2/10.4 L/100 km, 39/27 mpg. 2.4L 4WD: 8.0/10.6 L/100 km, 35/27 mpg. 3.5L: 7.6/10.2 L/100 km, 37/28 mpg. 3.5L 4WD: 7.7/10.6 L/100 km, 37/27 mpg.*

OWNER-REPORTED PROBLEMS: Sudden acceleration accompanied by loss of braking; when accelerating, vehicle pulls sharply to the left:

My 2011 Santa Fe pulled hard to the left (the side I wanted to pass on) when passing gear was used. I came very close to hitting the car to my left. The dealer's service manager claims this is normal due to torque knuckle steering. (It happened when he drove my SUV and he told me that I would have to get used to it!!!) We also tried another SUV and experienced the same problem.

Raw gas smell both inside and outside the vehicle; Santa Fe frequently shuts down when underway; a loud knock and transmission jerk occurs whenever the vehicle is first started; when shifting, the jerkiness of the transmission feels like someone is hitting the rear end.

SERVICE BULLETIN-REPORTED PROBLEMS: Automatic transmission malfunctions; defaults to the "failsafe" mode; harsh transmission engagement; no start in Park or Neutral; sunroof creaking, ticking; turn signals don't cancel. Service Campaign #098 provides for the replacement of the rear brake calipers, free of charge:

CAMPAIGN 098–REAR BRAKE CALIPER INSPECTION/REPLACEMENT

BULLETIN NO.: 10-01-048   DATE: DECEMBER 2010

2011 SANTA FE
IMPORTANT: DEALERS MUST PERFORM THIS CAMPAIGN ON ALL AFFECTED VEHICLES PRIOR TO CUSTOMER RETAIL DELIVERY AND WHENEVER AN AFFECTED VEHICLE IS IN THE SHOP FOR ANY MAINTENANCE OR REPAIR.
DESCRIPTION: This bulletin provides information on 2011 Santa Fe (CM) vehicles manufactured between September 28th and November 25, 2010. Improperly machined rear brake calipers may cause fluid leakage past the brake caliper piston seal resulting in low brake fluid level warning lamp illumination.

VERACRUZ ★★★★

RATING: Above Average. **Strong points:** The powerful V6 and 6-speed automatic transmission perform flawlessly to deliver smooth acceleration and a comfortable ride. NHTSA and IIHS gave the Veracruz their top ratings for offset and front- and side-impact protection. Rollover resistance got four stars, and head-restraint effectiveness was rated "Acceptable." Backed by a comprehensive base warranty.

Weak points: Some suspension noise, and not as agile as the competition. **New for 2012:** Carried over unchanged, except for new 18-inch wheels and a revised grille that looks almost exactly like the 2010–11 grille.

OVERVIEW: The seven-passenger Veracruz uses a stretched Santa Fe platform and offers all the safety, performance, and convenience features you'll find on SUVs that cost $10,000 more.

COST ANALYSIS: Buy a discounted 2011; the 2012s are practically identical. **Best alternatives:** Competes mostly with other higher-end mid-sized crossovers, like the Honda Pilot, Lexus RX series, and Nissan Murano. **Options:** Stay away from original-equipment Bridgestone or Dunlop tires; Michelins are much better performers and are more durable. **Rebates:** Expect $3,000 rebates, low-interest financing, and sweet leasing deals. **Depreciation:** Faster than average. A 2008 Limited that originally sold for $46,595 is now worth barely $22,500. **Insurance cost:** Above average. **Parts supply/cost:** Not easy to find; moderately expensive powertrain components. **Annual maintenance cost:** Higher than average. **Warranty:** Bumper-to-bumper 5 years/100,000 km; rust perforation 5 years/unlimited km. **Supplementary warranty:** Not needed. **Highway/city fuel economy:** 4WD: 8.5/12.7 L/100 km, 33/22 mpg. AWD: 8.9/13.2 L/100 km, 32/21 mpg.

OWNER-REPORTED PROBLEMS: Airbag warning light comes on for no reason; sudden, unintended acceleration while vehicle is in Reverse. Premature wearout of brake calipers and out-of-round rotors:

> Hyundai has brake and rotor issues and won't do anything about it....The vehicle off the lot had rotor problems. Had them shaved, then replaced and they were worn out within a year... If you search Internet you will find brake issue with all vehicles from Hyundai!

Rear hatch opens on its own; opened rear hatch may suddenly fall down; high- and low-beam headlights can't be adjusted separately, causing the high beams to shoot up way too high, and low beams are too low:

> High and low beam headlights are not adjustable individually. Choice #1=low beam at proper angle and high beam aimed at the top of trees ahead. Choice #2=high beam straight ahead and low beam 20 feet ahead of vehicle. Either way is unsafe. Hyundai knows of this problem but do not want to do anything about it even though there is a remedy published on the Internet.

KEY FACTS

CANADIAN PRICE (NEGOTIABLE): *GL:* $32,499, *Premium:* $34,999, *Premium AWD:* $36,999, *GLS:* $39,999, *Limited:* $44,999 **U.S. PRICE:** *GLS:* $28,345, *Limited:* $34,395 **CANADIAN FREIGHT:** $1,595 **U.S. FREIGHT:** $810 **POWERTRAIN (FRONT-DRIVE/AWD)** Engine: 3.8L V6 (260 hp); Transmission: 6-speed auto.

DIMENSIONS/CAPACITY
Passengers: 2/3/2; Wheelbase: 110.4 in.; H: 68.9/L: 190.6/W: 76.6 in.; Headroom F/R1/R2: 3.0/4.0/1.0 in.; Legroom F/R1/R2: 42.6/38.4/31.5 in.; Cargo volume: 40 cu. ft.; Fuel tank: 78L/regular; Tow limit: 3,500 lb.; Load capacity: 1,160 lb.; Turning circle: 36.7 ft.; Ground clearance: 8.1 in.; Weight: 3,253 lb.

Infiniti

Unlike Toyota's Lexus division, which started out with softly sprung vehicles akin to your dad's fully loaded Oldsmobile, Nissan's number one alter ego has historically stressed performance over comfort and opulence, and has offered buyers lots of high-performance features at what were initially very reasonable prices. But the company got greedy during the mid-'90s. Its Infiniti lineup became more mainstream and lost its price and performance edge, particularly after the company stripped out or downgraded the Q45's features, resurrected its embarrassingly incompetent G20, and dropped the J30 and J30t.

But Infiniti is fighting to get that performance edge back. There are now greater differences between Nissan and Infiniti vehicles, even though most models share the same platform. Infinitis usually add more-powerful engines, more gears, more-luxurious interior appointments, and steering and suspensions tweaked for sportier driving. These improvements have produced a new roster of sporty luxury vehicles: the Infiniti G, EX, FX, M, and QX.

The 2012 Infiniti lineup is carried over with practically no significant changes, since most of the upgrades and launching of new modelss was donewere launched last year. In fact, the 2011 model year was one of the busiest years in Infiniti's now 22-year history. For example, there was the introduction of the all-new M luxury sedan and QX and significant model- line extensions in the form of the entry-level G25 sedan and Infiniti M hybrid.

Although Infinitis are sold and serviced by a small dealer network across Canada, this limited support base compromises neither availability nor quality of servicing. Furthermore, these cars are reasonably dependable, so there is less need for service. The only two drawbacks are that powertrain and body parts are sometimes in short supply and that adding on complicated high-tech features drives up servicing costs and practically guarantees a higher failure rate for electronic components.

G25, G37	★★★/★★★★

RATING: *G25:* Average. *G37:* Above Average. **Strong points:** *G25:* This entry-level sedan is fitted with a 218 hp 2.5L V6 whichthat skimps on acceleration but burns about fifteen15 percent less fuel. Only a handful of owner complaints posted on the NHTSA (safercar.gov) website and top marks were given by the same agency for rollover resistance. *G37:* A powerful, smooth, and responsive powertrain; predictable, sporty handling; and a firm but comfortable ride. The car is fairly agile, quiet, and comfortable. The convertible has five horses less than the coupe (325 hp) but lots more than you'll find with the equivalent BMW or Mercedes. Crashworthiness is impressive: NHTSA gives the G37 a five-star ranking for frontal, side, and rollover occupant protection. IIHS gives it a "Good" rating for

The Infiniti G25.

frontal offset and side crashworthiness and an "Acceptable" grade for roof strength. Few owner complaints. **Weak points:** The $1,950 freight and predelivery inspection fee is highway robbery. G25: You get less power and less equipment than the G37; there is no manual transmission or sports package option; the V6 is noisy when pushed. G37: There's a small rear seat and cargo area; towing is not advised; and IIHS rated head-restraint effectiveness as "Marginal." The convertible model has even less room and has yet to be crash tested. **New for 2012:** No major changes for the new model year, except that the convertible gets a standard spare tire (replacing the previous repair kit).

OVERVIEW: The G37 is a premium mid-sized car with SUV pretensions. It is sold as a two-door coupe, a four-door sedan, and a two-door convertible with a power-retractable hardtop. The G37 targets shoppers who would normally buy the Acura

KEY FACTS

CANADIAN PRICE (NEGOTIABLE): *G25 Sedan:* $36,390, *G25x AWD Sedan:* $40,450, *G25x AWD Sedan Sport:* $45,540, *G37x AWD Sedan:* $43,450, *G37x AWD Sedan Sport:* $48,540, *G37x AWD Sedan M6 Sport:* $46,540, *G37 Coupe:* $46,700, *G37x AWD Coupe:* $49,200, *G37x AWD Sport Coupe:* $51,700, *G37x AWD M6 Sport Coupe:* $49,200, *G37 IPL G Coupe:* $57,200, *G37 Convertible Sport:* $58,300, *G37 Convertible Sport M6:* $58,300, *G37 Convertible Premier Edition:* $61,600 **U.S. PRICE:** *G25 Sedan:* $32,000, *G25 Journey:* $33,400, *G25x AWD:* $35,000, *G37 Journey:* $35,800, *G37x AWD:* $37,400, *G37 Sport 6MT:* $40,200, *G37 Coupe:* $37,150, *G37 Coupe Journey:* $38,600, *G37x Coupe AWD:* $40,250, *G37x Coupe Sport MT:* $43,350, *G37 IPL G Coupe:*

$48,900, *G37 Convertible:* $45,700, *G37 Convertible Sport 6MT:* $50,200 **CANADIAN FREIGHT:** $1,950 **U.S. FREIGHT:** $895

POWERTRAIN (REAR-DRIVE/AWD)

Engines: 3.7L V6 (328 hp sedan; 330 hp coupe; 325 hp convertible) • 2.5L V6 (218 hp); Transmissions: 6-speed man. • 7-speed auto.

DIMENSIONS/CAPACITY

Passengers: 2/2; 2/3; Wheelbase: 112.2 in.; H: 54.7–55.3/L: 183.1/W: 71.8 in.; Headroom F/R: 2.5/1.5 in.; Legroom F/R: 41/27.5 in.; Cargo volume: 7.4–13.5 cu. ft.; Fuel tank: 76L/premium; Tow limit: 1,000 lb.; Load capacity: 900 lb.; Turning circle: 35.4 ft.; Ground clearance: 5.1 in.; Weight: 3,642–3,847 lb.

RDX or the BMW 328i, or X3. The convertible model is priced right within striking range of BMW's 328i/335i Cabriolet and the Lexus IS 250 or IS 350 C convertible. The Mercedes-Benz CLK350 AMG Edition Cabriolet has priced itself out of that market.

COST ANALYSIS: The G25's greatest advantage compared with the competition is its price—the base model starts at $36,390— thousands of dollars less than most competitors, like the $41,300 BMW 328i. This advantage may be purely illusory when the exorbitant $1,950 freight costs and some trim upgrades are taken into account. Nevertheless, Infiniti predicts the G25 will account for 30 to 50 percent of G sedan sales. Smart buyers will shop around for cheaper 2011 versions built after April 2011 to give time for factory fixes time to correct the inevitable first-year production snafus. The same advice holds true for the G37. Look for a discounted 2011 version because it's practically identical to the costlier 2012. You can also save big bucks by shopping in the States for some of the pricier G37 models (just look at the preceding price differences). **Best alternatives:** The BMW 328i Series or X3. **Options:** The limited-slip differential in the Sport package. **Rebates:** $3,000+ discounts, low-cost financing, and attractive leases; discounts will be sweetened in early 2012. **Depreciation:** Average. **Insurance cost:** Higher than average. **Parts supply/cost:** Expensive parts that can be easily found in the Maxima parts bin. **Annual maintenance cost:** Lower than average. **Warranty:** Bumper-to-bumper 4 years/100,000 km; powertrain 6 years/110,000 km; rust perforation 7 years/unlimited km. **Supplementary warranty:** Not needed. **Highway/city fuel economy:** *Man.: 7.9/12.4 L/100 km, 36/23 mpg. Auto.: 7.5/11.2 L/100 km, 38/25 mpg. AWD: 7.8/11.7 L/100 km, 36/24 mpg. Convertible man.: 8.4/12.9 L/100 km, 34/22 mpg. Auto.: 7.8/11.9 L/100 km, 36/24 mpg. Coupe man.: 7.9/12.4 L/100 km, 36/23 mpg; Manumatic 7-speed: 7.8/11.7 L/100 km, 38/25 mpg.*

OWNER-REPORTED PROBLEMS: *G25:* iPhone/iPod malfunctions:

> When an iPhone is connected to the iPod interface in the vehicle the playback sips and is intermittent. It occurs every time the iPhone is connected and is continuously intermittent throughout the play time. This problem causes undue attention to be paid to the problem cited and not the task of driving safely.

G37: Gas station automatic fuelling nozzles shut off after a few seconds; vehicle suddenly accelerated while in Park with the engine running:

> I purchased a new 2011 Infiniti G37X. About 1 month into ownership of the car I had the car parked in my driveway running while I walked to the end of the driveway to pick up my garbage cans. I heard a crash, I found the car crashed into my garage doing damage to the car, my garage wall and my son's bike. The car was still in Park when I found it. I feel there is something wrong with the car. My driveway is flat.

Engine surges when braking (confirmed by TSB #ITB07-048), or is slow to brake:

I own a two-month old Infiniti G37X. When braking at highway speed, the engine does not seem to slow down as fast as it should. I brought this to my Infiniti dealer this week. They conducted tests on it and found that it "performs as designed." However, they acknowledged that the transmission does not slow down when the brake is applied—that the engine is designed to "click down" from gear to gear. But when braking hard at a highway speed, the car does not slow down immediately because of this design.

•

Made a fairly hard brake for a red light—car slid a little to a stop, but continued accelerating at 2500 to 3500 rpms while I held both feet on the brake to keep it in place. It was like holding back a revved up jet—rpms would not come down even when I shifted car to Neutral.

The convertible has some body shake. Engine tapping, clicking sound at start-up requires the use of a costlier "factory" oil; transmission suddenly downshifted to 15 km/h from 100km/h:

A chip was changed. However, the failure occurred three more times. The dealer then stated that the fluid in the vehicle was too full and was the cause of the failure.

The manual transmission gears grind when shifting, causing a delayed shift, especially in Sixth gear; transmission was replaced under warranty. The anti-traction feature activated on its own and caused the wheels to lock on a rainy day; defective Bridgestone Pole Position tires; Tire Pressure light did not come on when tire went flat; premature brake replacement; the area between the gas pedal and centre console gets quite hot; audio system malfunctions; and poor fit and finish. Incidentally, this car is not as much a "chick magnet" as it is a rodent attractant:

Infiniti G37 has electrical wiring insulation made of soy-based polymer. Soy-based polymer is apparently biodegradable. The problem is that it is also attractive to rodents, who eat the wiring, creating electrical safety hazards. It also creates an economic stress on consumers and insurers who have to pay for repairs done to these automobiles, which Infiniti claims are not covered under any existing warranty.

SERVICE BULLETIN-REPORTED PROBLEMS: *G25/37:* Troubleshooting multiple transmission problems (see bulletin on page 348); Steering pull/drift or steering wheel is off-centre; automatic transmission shifter boot may come loose; drivebelt noise; and the warranty is extended under Campaign PO308 in relation to the radio seek function and Campaign PO385 relative to reprogramming the G25's engine control module (ECM). *G37:* Bluetooth voice recognition issues; convertible top water leak at windshield header; AC blows warm air at idle; and door accent garnish replacements.

2009–11 G37 Sedan, Coupe, and Convertible; 2011 G25 Sedan.

NOTE: 2011 G37 Coupe IPL (Infiniti Performance Line) is not included in this TSB.

IF YOU CONFIRM:

- Any of these incorrect gear ratio DTCs stored: P0732, P0733, P0734, P0735, P0729 and/or P1734
- A slight vehicle vibration/shutter with light acceleration at low speeds, and/or
- At times, the engine rpm goes up (about 200 to 250 rpm) during the 3rd to 4th upshift, or the 4th to 5th upshift and/or
- Engine braking feel is more than expected with deceleration, and/or
- The 2nd to 1st down shift is harsher than expected.

EX35 ★★★

RATING: Average. The EX and G series are entry-level Infinitis with the most to offer from a price and quality perspective—as long as you have short legs or never ride in the rear seat. **Strong points:** Drives like a car with power to spare, and the smooth, responsive automatic/manual transmission works flawlessly with the well-calibrated V6; overall, the car is much more agile, quiet, and comfortable than the G series. A classy, though small, interior. NHTSA gives the EX35 a five-star rating for side-impact occupant protection and four stars for frontal and rollover safety. IIHS rates the EX35 "Good" for frontal, side, rear, and roof crash-worthiness. **Weak points:** Not as sporty as Infiniti's sport sedans or some of BMW's crossovers; really a four-seater; limited cargo space; back seat occupants must keep a knee-to-chin posture when the front seats are pushed all the way back; taller drivers will want more headroom (especially with the sunroof-equipped Journey model); right-rear visibility is compromised by right-rear head restraint and side pillar; no towing; and fuel economy is unimpressive. **New for 2012:** The addition of HomeLink Universal Transceiver as standard equipment on the Journey.

OVERVIEW: Offering the room of a small station wagon, the EX35 is a small, upscale SUV wannabe that targets shoppers who would normally buy the Acura RDX or the BMW X3. Smaller than the Infiniti FX, it is priced in the same range as the Infiniti G series and is essentially a G35 wagon. Not for off-road, but definitely a comfortable, well-equipped, and versatile vehicle for most driving needs. Last year, the 2011 models were given a 7-speed automatic transmission; better instrument panel illumination; and revised 18- and 19-inch wheels.

COST ANALYSIS: Buying a 2011 or a 2012 is an easy decision to make. With the 2012 models not offering anything to justify their higher price, a discounted second-series 2011 is the better deal. EX sales have been sluggish, so if you opt for an improved 2011 and wait until the winter or spring of 2012 for prices to fall, you could do well. By then, the higher prices will have likely been cut through extra rebates and other sales incentives, making the upgraded 2011 models far cheaper than the 2012 versions. The new 7-speed automatic may give a slight boost to fuel economy, but keep in mind that any new powertrain is a risky buy during its first year on the market. Also, the larger 18-inch wheels may make for a bumpier ride and cut your gas mileage. **Best alternatives:** Acura RDX, BMW 3 Series or X3, and Lincoln MKX. **Options:** The Navigation Package is overpriced and mostly fluff. **Rebates:** $4,000+ discounts, low-cost financing, and cheaper leases; discounts will become even more generous in early 2012 as the temperature drops and the competition heats up. Nissan and Infiniti have had a series of delays in rebuilding from the damage caused by the Fukushima quakes, so rumour has it that they will be offering the most enticing rebates and other sales incentives. **Depreciation:** Average. **Insurance cost:** Higher than average. **Parts supply/cost:** Expensive parts that can be easily found in the Maxima parts bin. **Annual maintenance cost:** Lower than average. **Warranty:** Bumper-to-bumper 4 years/100,000 km; powertrain 6 years/110,000 km; rust perforation 7 years/unlimited km. **Supplementary warranty:** Not needed. **Highway/city fuel economy:** EX 3.5L AWD and 7-speed auto.: 8.5/12.4 L/100 km, 33/23 mpg.

OWNER-REPORTED PROBLEMS: Passenger-side front airbag may be disabled when a normal-sized adult is seated. The Adaptive Cruise Control feature no longer uses an audible warning system following recall repairs. Poor-quality body hardware; for example, the hitch will break if you tow anything at all. Says one owner:

KEY FACTS

CANADIAN PRICE (NEGOTIABLE): *EX35 AWD:* $42,200 **U.S. PRICE:** *Base:* $35,200, *AWD:* $36,600, *Journey:* $37,400, *Journey AWD:* $38,800 **CANADIAN FREIGHT:** $1,950 **U.S. FREIGHT:** $895 **POWERTRAIN (REAR-DRIVE/AWD)** Engine: 3.5L V6 (297 hp); Transmission: 7-speed auto. **DIMENSIONS/CAPACITY** Passengers: 2/3; Wheelbase: 110.2 in.; H: 61.9/L: 182.3/W: 71 in.; Headroom F/R: 3.0/3.0 in.; Legroom F/R: 42/26 in.; Cargo volume: 18.6 cu. ft.; Fuel tank: 76L/premium; Tow limit: N/A; Load capacity: 860 lb.; Turning circle: 36 ft.; Ground clearance: 5.5 in.; Weight: 3,757–3,979 lb.

It will probably do damage even if you only use it for a bike rack. It is a very nicely built part which fits exactly as advertised, however, it mounts to the bumper supports, which are made of a very flimsy sheet metal. As a result, continued up and down motion such as a bouncy bike rack or the routine undulations of a trailer captured by the ball mount will fatigue and break the metal that holds the bumper mounting supports to the car.

SERVICE BULLETIN-REPORTED PROBLEMS: Steering pull/drift or steering wheel is off-centre; Bluetooth voice recognition issues; and door accent garnish replacements.

FX35, FX50 ★★★★

The Infiniti FX35.

KEY FACTS

CANADIAN PRICE (NEGOTIABLE): *FX35:* $53,250, *FX50:* $66,250 **U.S. PRICE:** *FX35:* $42,600, *AWD:* $44,050, *FX50:* $57,600 **CANADIAN FREIGHT:** $1,950 **U.S. FREIGHT:** $895 **POWERTRAIN (REAR-DRIVE/AWD)** Engine: 3.5L V6 (303 hp) • 5.0L V8 (390 hp); Transmission: 7-speed auto. **DIMENSIONS/CAPACITY** Passengers: 2/3; Wheelbase: 113.5 in.; H: 66.1/L: 191.2/W: 75.9 in.; Cargo volume: 24.7 cu. ft.; Fuel tank: 90L/ premium; Tow limit: 3,500 lb.; Turning circle: 36.7 ft.; Ground clearance: 7.3 in.; Weight: 4,299 lb., 4,575 lb.

RATING: Above Average. **Strong points:** Both engines have power to spare, delivered by a smooth and quiet drivetrain. Handling is precise and secure. Decent towing capacity and torque. The roomy interior uses high-quality materials and simple controls. Body hardware and fit and finish get top marks. **Weak points:** A stiff ride; limited rear visibility, not much cargo room, and engine noise invades the cabin. **New for 2012:** A revised front grille and fascia.

OVERVIEW: These are well-appointed, luxury crossover SUVs that drive and ride like heavy sports sedans—not agile, but acceptably responsive. The primary difference between the two vehicles is their engines, plus a few additional features.

COST ANALYSIS: It will be hard to haggle before the new year, due to the popularity of the FX series and their short supply. The huge difference in price between Canada and the States make these vehicles prime candidates for cross-border shopping. South of the border, the price may be cut by $10,000 and the freight fee reduced by $1,000. **Best alternatives:** BMW X6 xDrive. **Options:** Nothing is needed; the lane-departure warning system may sound false alerts. **Rebates:** Look for discounts of about 10 percent as well as some very attractive leasing deals in the first quarter of 2012. **Depreciation:** Average. **Insurance cost:** Higher than average. **Parts supply/cost:** Expensive powertrain and body parts that aren't easily available. **Annual maintenance cost:** Higher than average. **Warranty:** Bumper-to-bumper 4 years/100,000 km; powertrain 6 years/110,000 km; rust perforation 7 years/unlimited km. **Supplementary warranty:** Not needed. **Highway/city fuel economy:** *FX35:* 9.3/13.3 L/100 km, 30/21 mpg. *FX50:* 10.1/14.6 L/100 km, 28/19 mpg.

OWNER-REPORTED PROBLEMS: Early replacement of brake calipers and rotors; car lurches forward when started; electronic malfunctions stall the car; and sound system malfunctions.

SERVICE BULLETIN-REPORTED PROBLEMS: FX35/50: Steering pull/drift or steering wheel is off-centre; Bluetooth voice recognition issues; improper seat climate control operation; and door accent garnish replacements.

M37, M56 ★★★★

The Infiniti M37.

RATING: Above Average. These vehicles are the high-performance successors to the discontinued Q45. The major difference between the M37 and M56 is engine size, plus additional performance and convenience gadgets. **Strong points:** Well appointed; superior acceleration and respectable fuel economy with the V6 coupled to the 7-speed automatic transmission. Good handling; easy entry and exit;

KEY FACTS

CANADIAN PRICE (NEGOTIABLE): *M37:* $52,400, *M37x AWD:* $54,900, *M37 Sport:* $63,400, *M56:* $66.200, *M56x AWD:* $68,700, *M56 Sport:* $73,400, *M Hybrid:* $67,300 **U.S. PRICE:** *M37:* $47,700, *M37x AWD:* $49,850, *M56:* $59,100, *M56x AWD:* $61,600, *M Hybrid:* $53,700 **CANADIAN FREIGHT:** $1,950 **U.S. FREIGHT:** $895

POWERTRAIN (REAR-DRIVE/AWD)

Engines: (Hybrid) 3.5L V6 (360 net hp) • 3.7L V6 (330 hp) • 5.6L V8 (420 hp); Transmission: 7-speed auto.

DIMENSIONS/CAPACITY

Passengers: 2/3; Wheelbase: 114.2 in.; H: 59.1/L: 194.7/W: 72.6 in.; Headroom F/R: 4.0/3.0 in.; Legroom F/R: 41/30 in.; Cargo volume: 14.9 cu. ft.; Fuel tank: 90L/premium; Load capacity: 860 lb.; Turning circle: 36.7 ft.; Weight: 3,858 lb., 4,012 lb.

and head restraints lower into the seatback; NHTSA gives both vehicles a four-star rollover resistance rating and five stars for side protection. **Weak points:** Some road noise, and premium fuel is required. **New for 2012:** An all-new, 360-horse-power M Hybrid.

OVERVIEW: The M37 and M56 rear-drive/AWD luxury sedans ride on a four-wheel independent suspension and carry either a V6 or V8 engine. They share the QX's drivetrain but are set on a shorter wheelbase. Because of their lighter curb weight and their potent engines, these cars can do 0–100 km/h in less than six seconds. Forget about fuel economy, though.

New technologies include Infiniti Drive Mode Selector, a driver-selectable four-mode control of throttle and transmission mapping; Active Noise Control, which reduces engine noise, providing a quieter cabin; a blind spot warning and intervention feature that helps the driver return the vehicle back toward the center of the lane of travel in the event of unintended drift; and Active Trace Control, which adjusts engine torque and the control of braking at each of the four wheels to help enhance cornering performance.

As Infiniti's first-ever hybrid, the 2012 Infiniti Hybrid delivers V8 performance with 4-cylinder fuel efficiency. Powered by the Infiniti Direct Response Hybrid™ System, the Infiniti M Hybrid is the first V6 true luxury performance "driver's" hybrid—and the only such vehicle to offer more than 350 horsepower (360 net horsepower) and Infiniti-estimated 32 mpg (7.4 L/100 km) fuel economy.

2011 improvements were:include nNew M37 and M56 model designations, with rear-wheel drive or Infiniti's Intelligent All-Wheel Drive system. The M37 features a 330 hp 3.7L V6 engine with 27 more horses than the previous generation M35's 3.5L V6, while the M56 offers 95 additional horses with its all-new 420 hp 5.6L V8. Both engines feature Infiniti's advanced VVEL (Variable Valve Event &and Lift) system, and all models are equipped with a standard 7-speed automatic transmission. A special Sport Touring Package, offered on rear-drive models, includes 4-Wheel Active Steer (4WAS), sport-tuned suspension, sport brakes, and 20-inch wheels and tires.

Techno-gadgets abound in the 2012 models and they include an upgraded navigation system, a Bose studio surround premium audio system, Intelligent Cruise Control (full-speed range), Lane Departure Warning and Lane Departure

Prevention systems, Distance Control Assist, Intelligent Brake Assist with Forward Collision Warning, and Front Pre-Crash Seat Belts.

COST ANALYSIS: The M37 is Infinti's entry-level M model, while the M56 piles on the safety, performance, and convenience options to give shoppers more high-performance thrills and luxury. It comes packed with all the techno-goodies car companies stuff into their vehicles to impress shoppers who have money to burn. **Best alternatives:** The Acura RL V6, Audi A6, Cadillac DTS, and BMW 5 Series. **Options:** The limited-slip differential in the Sport Touring Package. **Rebates:** $4,000+ discounts, low-cost financing, and attractive leases; discounts will be sweetened in early 2012. **Depreciation:** Average. **Insurance cost:** Higher than average. **Parts supply/cost:** Expensive parts that aren't that hard to find. **Annual maintenance cost:** Lower than average. **Warranty:** Bumper-to-bumper 4 years/100,000 km; powertrain 6 years/110,000 km; rust perforation 7 years/ unlimited km. **Supplementary warranty:** Not needed. **Highway/city fuel economy:** *M37 rear-drive:* 7.6/11.4 L/100 km, 37/25 mpg. *AWD:* 8.3/12 L/100 km, 34/24 mpg. *Sport:* 7.6/11.4 L/100 km, 37/25 mpg. *M56:* 8.0/12.9 L/100 km, 35/22 mpg. *AWD:* 8.5/13.4 L/100 km, 33/21 mpg. *Sport:* 7.6/11.4/L/100 km, 35/22 mpg.

OWNER-REPORTED PROBLEMS: Poorly designed sun visors on the 2011 models:

> Sun visor does not fold back far enough blocking tall driver's view of road. Left edge of sun visor trim preventing proper adjustment. Note that 2012 visors have been slightly redesigned and work properly.

Difficulty in steering the 2011 M37S; and a variety of sound system malfunctions on all models.

SERVICE BULLETIN-REPORTED PROBLEMS: *M37:* Harsh shifts, multiple diagnostic trouble codes set, and vibration; steering pull/drift or steering wheel is off-centre; low battery voltage or no start; driver's power seat won't adjust; and Bluetooth voice recognition issues. The warranty is extended under Campaign PO336 and PO328 relative to navigation and four-wheel steering software updates. *M56:* All of the above, plus rough cold idle; steering wheel finish peeling; and Campaign PO353 (ECM update).

QX (QX56) ★★★

RATING: Average. Now called the QX, this is a large SUV that trades fuel economy and handling for power and comfort. **Strong points:** Comfortable and powerful, the QX uses a smooth-shifting automatic transmission that delivers more than enough power in all gear ranges; and provides more towing capacity and torque than your average Brontosaurus. The car has a plush interior and standard navigation system, plus more gadgets and convenience features than you will ever need (nine cup holders and four bottle holders). You'll also find plenty of interior room and predictable, responsive handling (thanks to the independent rear suspension).

The Infiniti QX.

KEY FACTS

CANADIAN PRICE (NEGOTIABLE): *Base:* $73,000 **U.S. PRICE:** *Base:* $58,700, *4WD:* $61,800 **CANADIAN FREIGHT:** $1,950 **U.S. FREIGHT:** $895
POWERTRAIN (AWD)
Engine: 5.6L V8 (400 hp); Transmission: 7-speed auto.
DIMENSIONS/CAPACITY
Passengers: 2/3/2; 2/3/3; Wheelbase: 121.1 in.; H: 62.6/L: 208.3/W: 79.9 in.; Cargo volume: 16.6 cu. ft.; Fuel tank: 98L/premium; Tow limit: 8,500 lb.; Load capacity: N/A; Turning circle: 41.6 ft.; Ground clearance: 9.2 in.; Weight: 5,850 lb.

NHTSA gives the 2010 QX56 a five-star ranking for front-impact occupant protection and three stars fore rollover resistance. **Weak points:** Way overpriced— a poster child for cross-border shopping. Fuel economy is brutal, although not as bad as with previous models because of the 7-speed transmission. You also get a stiff, jarring ride and road handling is mediocre. The high step into the interior isn't for shy ladies. Steering-wheel-mounted controls are needlessly complex. The jury's still out over the car's long-term reliability. **New for 2012:** Nothing important.

OVERVIEW: This is Infiniti's SUV luxury flagship, loaded with every conceivable safety, performance, and convenience feature one could ever imagine. Yet, someone forgot to design a decent-sized third-row rear seat that's large enough for most people.

Although the QX has been on the market in Canada since 2004 and has a loyal following, the car almost got axed this year due to rising fuel prices and the trend of downsized vehicles in each market niche. But, when Infiniti realized the average QX owner was estimated at 45 years old—seven years younger than the average age for luxury car owners in North America—the automaker had a change of heart. Instead of dumping the QX, Infiniti will use it as a "halo" car to draw in new buyers to the company's other luxury offerings…at least for a year or two longer.

The 2011s got a number of improvements, including: a V8 with 80 more horses; a 7-speed automatic transmission with Adaptive Shift Control; a stiffer platform that reduces body roll; and a revised four-wheel-drive system. Styling is more curvaceous, less Armada; the car lost 161 pounds; fuel economy was increased by 14 percent; and the second-row seating got additional legroom that now bests seating found in the Mercedes-Benz GL450, the QX's closest rival. Third-row seats became power-adjustable to get out of the way of boarding passengers, and they added a power-reclining feature for added comfort.

COST ANALYSIS: It will be hard to haggle, due to the popularity of the QX series. Thus, you have two recourses: Wait until spring of 2012 for prices to moderate by about $5,000, or buy the car in the States and save up to $14,000 U.S. (if you include the reduced freight fees). **Best alternatives:** Nissan's Armada, or GM's Tahoe, Yukon, Denali, or Escalade. The GM vehicles are deeply discounted, ride better, have greater curb appeal, and are quieter. The Mercedes GX and Audi Q7 are much better looking alternatives, but they aren't as reliable. **Options:** Nothing is needed. **Rebates:** Look for discounts of about 10 percent as well as some very attractive leasing deals in the second quarter of 2011. **Depreciation:** Faster than average. A new 2009 that sold for $70,000 now sells for $43,000. **Insurance cost:** Higher than average. **Parts supply/cost:** Expensive parts that aren't easily found with independent suppliers. **Annual maintenance cost:** Higher than average. **Warranty:** Bumper-to-bumper 4 years/100,000 km; powertrain 6 years/110,000 km; rust perforation 7 years/unlimited km. **Supplementary warranty:** A good idea for the powertrain. **Highway/city fuel economy:** 10.3/15.7 L/100 km, 27/18 mpg.

OWNER-REPORTED PROBLEMS: Hazardous suspension/steering wobble when passing over uneven terrain:

> Our 2011 Infinity QX56 cannot be properly controlled at speed when any rough pavement, pothole, bridge connection joints, or similar is run over. The vehicle shakes violently with little if any control by the driver. On numerous occasions the vehicle drifts out of the lane. No accidents have ever occurred but at least three near misses on interstate driving have occurred. At highway speeds it is scary and quite dangerous.

Windshield crack appeared under the wiper while the vehicle was parked in a garage overnighte; some brake failures and frequent brake repairs; malfunctioning rear air-levelling suspension makes the rear bottom-out without any alert sent to the driver and makes trailer-towing a white-knuckle experience. Excessive steering shake and shimmy when passing over small bumps in the road; power accessories often malfunction; and the sound system is glitch-prone.

SERVICE BULLETIN-REPORTED PROBLEMS: Harsh shifts, multiple DTCsdiagnostic trouble codes set, hesitation, vibration, and other automatic transmission issues; steering pull/drift or steering wheel is off-centre.

Kia

Good Car, Bad Car

I like Kia. Especially now that it doesn't make every model a failure-prone "Jack-in-the-Box" full of costly repair surprises as it did a few years back. Buyers now have more confidence in Kia cars, SUVs, and minivans that have become more functional, fuel-efficient, and stylish than ever before. Unlike most automakers, who have had poor sales during the past two years, Hyundai and its Kia subsidiary are breaking sales records with a much improved lineup. The company has done this during an economic recession by covering practically all the market niches, except trucks.

While Hyundai goes upscale with high-tech and fuel-frugal models placed throughout its model lineup, Kia is putting its money into an expanded lineup of less-expensive fuel-efficient vehicles that carry more standard features, are freshly styled, and have fewer reliability problems. Positive reports from buyers of Kia's recently redesigned cars, minivans, and SUVs have led industry analysts to conclude that Hyundai's product improvement efforts have paid off with the Borrego, Rio, Rondo, Sportage, and Soul.

On the other hand, models like the Sorento and Optima continue to anchor Kia's quality ratings with sudden acceleration heading the list along with otherof serious defects that includealong automatic transmission, steering, and brake failures. Nevertheless, *Consumer Reports* says Kia has improved quality and performance sufficiently that it can now give the Sorento its "Recommended" rating.

Not so, *Lemon-Aid*. We will maintain the Sorento's and Optima's (formerly Magentis) Below Average designations for another year in view of the large number of life-threatening transmission and steering failures we have discovered. We are also hopeful Kia and its dealers will stop saying these failures are "normal" and will correct these and other safety hazards before lives are lost.

RIO, RIO5

RATING: Average. The Rio sedan and Rio5 hatchback combine good fuel economy and interior room with useful standard features. **Strong points:** The 1.6L engine is usually adequate for most chores, and handling is acceptable, with plenty of steering feedback and good brakes; the ride is also comfortable, though sometimes busy; and passenger and cargo room are better than average. Crash protection seems to be Kia's "forte" (yes, pun intended). NHTSA gave the Rio four stars for frontal, side, and rollover crash protection and IIHS rates the Rio's frontal offset, rear, and roof protection as "Acceptable." **Weak points:** Slow acceleration with the automatic transmission; insufficient highway passing power; excessive engine

The Kia Rio.

noise at higher speeds; harsh ride when passing over small bumps; trunk lid hinges intrude into the trunk area; actual fuel consumption is much higher than what is promised; poor rear-corner visibility with the Rio5; and below-average crashworthiness scores for side collisions. **New for 2012:** Carried over relatively unchanged, except for the inclusion of Idle Stop and Go. This gas-saving feature shuts down the engine when the car is idling and restarts it when the brake pedal is released.

OVERVIEW: The base Rio sedan won't spoil you with electronic gadgets and la-di-da comfort and convenience features, but it's an adequately equipped, solid econocar. Available as a four-door sedan or as the five-door hatchback Rio5, it comes with a manual transmission, an optional 4-speed automatic, wind-up windows, and manual door locks. On the other hand, safety features that are extra-cost items on more-expensive cars—like front seat belt pretensioners, disc brakes on all four wheels, and six airbags (dual frontal, front-seat side-impact, and full-coverage side curtain)—are standard features.

KEY FACTS

CANADIAN PRICE (NEGOTIABLE): *Rio EX:* $13,695, *EX Convenience:* $14,900, *Rio5 EX:* $14,095, *Rio5 EX Convenience:* $16,495, *Rio5 Sport:* $18,795 **U.S. PRICE:** *Rio base, man.:* $12,295, *LX:* $14,995, *SX:* $16,095, *Rio5 LX auto.:* $15,095, *SX auto.:* $16,395 **CANADIAN FREIGHT:** $1,455 **U.S. FREIGHT:** $695 **POWERTRAIN (FRONT-DRIVE)** Engine: 1.6L 4-cyl. (138 hp); Transmissions: 6-speed man. • 6-speed auto. **DIMENSIONS/CAPACITY (RIO)** Passengers: 2/3; Wheelbase: 98.5 in.; H: 57.9/L: 167/W: 66.8 in.; Headroom F/R: 4.5/2.0 in.; Legroom F/R: 40/25 in.; Cargo volume: *Rio:* 9.0 cu. ft., *Rio5:* 15.8 cu. ft.; Fuel tank: 45L/regular; Tow limit: Not recommended; Load capacity: 850 lb.; Turning circle: 32.3 ft.; Weight: 2,435–2,505 lb.

COST ANALYSIS: The discounted 2011s are cheaper buys than the almost identical 2012 version, but the price difference isn't that much. **Best alternatives:** The Ford Focus, Honda Fit, Hyundai Accent, Mazda3, and Nissan Versa, are more-refined small cars that offer better performance while also conserving fuel. **Options:** Nothing important. **Rebates:** Look for $1,500 rebates or discounts and low financing rates in late 2011. **Depreciation:** Slower than average. **Insurance**

cost: Average. **Parts supply/cost:** Average costs; parts aren't hard to find. **Annual maintenance cost:** Less than average. **Warranty:** Bumper-to-bumper 5 years/100,000 km; powertrain 5 years/100,000 km; rust perforation 5 years/ unlimited km. **Supplementary warranty:** A wise buy for the engine/tranny considering Kia's previous powertrain troubles. **Highway/city fuel economy:** *Man.:* 5.8/7.1 L/100 km, 49/40 mpg. *Auto.:* 5.6 /7.7 L/100 km, 50/38 mpg.

OWNER-REPORTED PROBLEMS: Sharing the Accent platform and using more Hyundai components has undoubtedly improved Kia's quality, judging by J.D. Power survey results and the lower number of owner complaints. The Rio and Rio5 have registered fewer owner complaints than the newer Kia Soul. Nevertheless, the following problems have been reported: automatic transmission malfunctions; tie-rod and ball joints broke away from the chassis while vehicle was turning; poor fit and finish; premature brake repairs; electrical shorts; airbags failed to deploy in a frontal collision; passenger-side airbag was disabled, even though an average-sized occupant was seated; sudden acceleration in Reverse, with loss of brakes; brakes locked up when applied; and the rear window shattered when the driver's door was closed.

SERVICE BULLETIN-REPORTED PROBLEMS: Campaign SA042 allows for a free ECM update to improve automatic transmission shifting; reducing power steering and brake noise.

SOUL ★★★★

RATING: Above Average; poor-quality materials and craftsmanship bring down the car's rating. **Strong points:** Inexpensive and well equipped with safety devices like ABS, stability control, six airbags, and active head restraints—features that are rare on entry-level small cars. More- powerful engines and better-performing, fuel-sipping powertrains. User-friendly, simple controls; plenty of interior room, especially when it comes to headroom; excellent front and side visibility; comfortable seats; a competent engine (the 2.0L is a better choice for reserve power); a compliant suspension, without undue body roll or front-end plow; and fairly agile cornering, with good steering feedback. Again, Soul does well in crashworthiness tests: NHTSA awards the car four stars for front, side, and rollover crash protection and IIHS rates the 2011 Soul as "Good" in frontal offset, side, roof strength, and head restraint occupant crash protection. **Weak points:** Base engine could use more grunt at low engine rpm. Omnipresent rattles; excessive wind and road noise; and many body and fit and finish glitches. Limited cargo room when compared to its rivals; poor-quality, easily broken, or prematurely worn interior items. A busy highway ride; fuel economy is seriously overstated; poor rearward visibility through the small rear windshield and thick rear pillars. Many fit and finish glitches. **New for 2012:** Lots of goodies: a 6-speed manual and automatic tranny; the base engine now puts out 135 hp (up from 122 hp); fuel economy jumps from 26 mpg city/31 highway to 28/34; LED tail light clusters for higher-spec trims and LED projector headlights; redesigned hood and front and rear bumpers; and a quieter cabin.

KEY FACTS

CANADIAN PRICE (NEGOTIABLE): *1.6:* $15,995, *2.0 2U:* $18,595, *2.0 4U:* $20,595, *Retro:* $21,295, *Auto.:* $22,195, *Burner:* $21,595, *SX:* $22,395, *4U Luxury:* $23,995 **U.S. PRICE:** *1.6L man.:* $13,300, *2.0L man:* $15,495, *Auto.:* $16,495, *2.0 Sport auto.:* $18,495 **CANADIAN FREIGHT:** $1,650 **U.S. FREIGHT:** $695

POWERTRAIN (FRONT-DRIVE)

Engines: 1.6L 4-cyl. (135 hp) • 2.0L 4-cyl. (160 hp); Transmissions: 6-speed man. • 6-speed auto.

DIMENSIONS/CAPACITY

Passengers: 2/3; Wheelbase: 100.4 in.; H: 63.4/L: 161.6/W: 70.3 in.; Headroom F/R: 5.0/5.5 in.; Legroom F/R: 40/27 in.; Cargo volume: 19.3 cu. ft.; Fuel tank: 48L/regular; Load capacity: 850 lb.; Turning circle: 34.4 ft.; Weight: 2,624–2,855 lb.

OVERVIEW: Fairly well equipped, the Soul is a cheap little four-door hatchback/wagon that combines safety with acceptable urban performance while keeping your fuel bills low. The best combination is the 2.0L engine hooked to a 6-speed manual transmission. Invest in the ABS and stability control by moving upscale.

COST ANALYSIS: Forget the cheaper, leftover 2011s; you will miss out on important 2012 upgrades. **Best Alternatives:** Other contenders are the Hyundai Elantra, Nissan Cube or Versa, and Toyota Corolla. **Options:** Larger 18-inch wheels and the driver's seat height adjuster. Forget the space-robbing sunroof. **Rebates:** Look for $1,000 rebates and low financing rates in late 2011. **Depreciation:** Slightly faster than average. A base 2010 Soul that retailed for $15,500 is now worth $10,500. **Insurance cost:** Average. **Parts supply/cost:** Average costs; some parts delayed. **Annual maintenance cost:** Average. **Warranty:** Bumper-to-bumper 5 years/100,000 km; powertrain 5 years/100,000 km; rust perforation 5 years/unlimited km. **Supplementary warranty:** A wise buy for the engine/tranny, considering Kia's previous powertrain troubles. **Highway/city fuel economy:** *1.6L:* 6.3/7.7 L/100 km, 45/37 mpg.

OWNER-REPORTED PROBLEMS: Airbags failed to deploy when vehicle hit a deer; brake pedal is too small; rear brake failure caused a rear-ender; automatic transmission slips and often sticks in gear or grinds when going into Second gear; fuel spews out when refueling; driver door fails to latch; steering column came off while car was underway; accident report questions the Soul's high crashworthiness score:

> We rear-ended a 2004 Expedition in our 2010 Kia Soul at 20 mph [32 km/h]. My wife sustained a "traumatic brain injury" as a result of the air bag wiring harness being cut in half (both sides) before the sensors were activated. I have photos of the wiring hardness cut in the accident and the car. My 29-year-old wife will now spend the rest of her life disabled. This is a dangerous car. Kia states the airbags will not activate at 20 mph [32 km/h]. This is not a 5 star frontal impact design. The fuel shut off did not activate, "all safety features failed." [Ed. Note: NHTSA cut the rating to four stars on the subsequent 2011 model.]

A plethora of fit and finish deficiencies, including chips in the glass and paint, and door panels that scratch with the slightest touch:

> My 2010 Kia Soul has such severe interior damage from the sub-standard material they used that the market value has depreciated far beyond the norm. Any metal, even plastic that touches the doors (seat belt buckle), pillars, center console, glove box, etc....becomes damaged. The material has no padding under it so there is no absorption and it is "honey comb" design which when scratched breaks the "honey comb" which has a light grey under it. My father bought the same car at the same time and he too has this problem. The car's showing this damage immediately. The dealership has no way of fixing it and the manufacturer is telling us to wait for their solution, many people have been waiting for over a year. Kia has put other 2010 Souls on the lot with completely different material so this should be the solution... chipping paint that has started to rust with 6000 miles [9,650 km] on it. We deserve consumer protection. Please check *www.kiasoulforum.com* for greater awareness of this very public issue. Also, rear view window so small and high it is a danger.

The engine design attracts pools of water.

SERVICE BULLETIN-REPORTED PROBLEMS: Power steering oil pump noise; a fix for excessive brake noise; drivebelt squealing noise remedy and the following warranty extension campaigns allowing for free repairs: rear wiper squeal noise repair (Campaign SA026); crash pad centre tray damper pad (Campaign SA027); manual transmission shifter skirt replacement (Campaign SA015); mood lamp control unit replacement (Campaign SA010); and audio system software update (Campaign SA009).

FORTE, FORTE KOUP ★★★

RATING: Average. Good value for your money. Kia slew the poor-quality dragon last year with its 2011 models; now, Kia's the roomier compact sedan, coupe, and hatchback get the engine, suspension, and equipment refinements the lineup lacked in the past. Among the various models, the hatchback is the most versatile

The Kia Forte.

for access and storage. **Strong points:** Good acceleration; fore and aftcompetent engines at high revs, with plenty of reserve power and a smooth-shifting automatic transmission; sure-footed and precise, confidence-inspiring handling and a comfortable ride; four-wheel disc brakes standard; easily-accessed and intuitive controls; Bluetooth and steering wheel controls with voice activation; nicely bolstered, comfortable front seats; lots of interior room, heated side-view windows; fewer rattles and body glitches (but still too many); a large dealer network with both Kia and Hyundai providing servicing; and a comprehensive base warranty. NHTSA gives the car five stars for front and side crash protection; four stars for rollover resistance. IIHS also gives the car top marks for front, side, rear, and roof crashworthiness. **Weak points:** No problem with acceleration, but the the ride is jittery and stiff; steering wheel tilts but doesn't telescope (EX trim excepted); engine and rtoad noise is pervasive and gets louder as speed increases. Prices will become more negotiable by the end of the year. Overall quality is much improved with zero complaints posted on the NHTSA website. **New for 2012:** 6-speed manual and automatic transmissions.

KEY FACTS

CANADIAN PRICE (NEGOTIABLE): *LX man.:* $15,995, *Auto.:* $17,195, *EX:* $18,495, *SX:* $21,795, *Auto.:* $22,995, *EX Koup:* $18,995, *Auto.:* $20,195, *SX Koup:* $22,295, *Auto.:* $23,495 **U.S. PRICE:** *LX man.:* $14,995, *Auto.:* $15,995, *EX Auto.:* $17,395, *SX auto.:* $18,895, *Forte EX 5d man.:* $16,895, *EX 5d Auto.:* $17,895, *SX 5d man.:* $18,395, *SX 5d Auto.:* $19,395, *EX Koup man.:* $16,995, *Auto.:* $17,995, *SX man.: $18,395,* *Auto.:* $19,395 **CANADIAN FREIGHT:** $1,455 **U.S. FREIGHT:** $695

POWERTRAIN (FRONT-DRIVE)
Engines: 2.0L 4-cyl. (156 hp) • 2.4L 4-cyl. (173 hp); Transmissions: 6-speed man. • 6-speed auto.

DIMENSIONS/CAPACITY
Passengers: 2/3; Wheelbase: 104.3 in.; H: 57.5/L: 176.3/W: 69.4 in.; Headroom F/R: 4.0/2.5 in.; Legroom F/R: 41/27 in.; Cargo volume: 12.6 cu. ft.; Fuel tank: 51.9L/regular; Load capacity: 850 lb.; Turning circle: 33.8 ft.; Ground clearance: 5.5 in.; Weight: 2,707–2,868 lb.

OVERVIEW: All three body styles have what it takes to satisfy the needs of the daily commuter as well as excite the most ardent high-performance fan. Two different 4-cylinder engines deliver more than enough power without wasting fuel. In fact, the SX features an upgraded 2.4L inline 4-banger that delivers 173 hp. Handling is a breeze, thanks to the Forte's front-drive unibody frame and four-wheel independent suspension, which provide a smooth and sporty ride, with a minimum of noise, vibration, and harshness.

COST ANALYSIS: This little econocar has proven its worth. First-year production defects have been minor and most have been corrected. As for buying a Forte south of the border: Is saving $5,000 worth the trouble? **Best Alternatives:** The Ford Focus, Honda Civic, Hyundai Elantra, Mazda3, and Toyota Corolla. **Highway/city fuel economy:** *2.0L:* 5.8/8.3 L/100 km, 49/34 mpg. *2.4L:* 6.2/9.2 L/100 km, 46/31 mpg.

OWNER-REPORTED PROBLEMS: Minor audio and fit and finish complaints.; major paint defects.

SERVICE BULLETIN-REPORTED PROBLEMS: Hard starts; rough idle; power steering oil pump noise; dealing with brake noise; pop noise on 2–3 manual shift; manual transmission 2–3 shift shock (Campaign SA022); sunroof noise (Campaign SA030); automatic transmission shift hesitation (Campaign SA020); replacement of the junction box relay (Campaign SA012); manual transmission inspection of the driveshaft housing seal (Campaign SA011); clock, temperature display locks up (Campaign SA073); seat belt buckle replacement (Campaign SC078); fuel filler cap replacement (Campaign SA023); and a fix for doors rattling as they are closed.

OPTIMA (MAGENTIS) ★★

RATING: Below Average. Vehicle rating has been downgraded due to persistent steering failures (as with the 2011 Sonata) and slow parts delivery. Goodbye, Magentis; hello Optima. Finally, Kia Canada has reverted to calling the Magentis, an Optima, the name used almost everywhere else in the world. **Strong points:** The 2011 Optima/Megantis was completely redesigned, getting a more powerful 200 hp 2.4L 200-hp four4-cylinder engine and an optional 274 hp 2.0L 274-hp turbo- four. Restyled, it now has a longer wheelbase, a roomier cabin, a wider and lower body, and a hybrid variant. Parts availability is helped by sharing the Sonata platform and engine components. The Optima is nicely appointed; has good overall visibility; provides plenty of front headroom; uses firm, supportive front bucket seats with plenty of fore and aft travel; and posts better-than-average fuel economy figures with regular fuel. Other advantages include a comfortable and secure ride and handling; a spacious trunk; and a five-star front, side, and rollover crashworthiness rating. IIHS gives its top, "Good" rating for frontal, side rear, and roof crash protection. Another plus: Servicing can be done by both Hyundai and Kia dealers. The 5-year/100,000 km all-inclusive warranty sweetens the deal. *Hybrid:* Since the Hybrid doesn't use a CVT transmission like the Ford Fusion and Toyota Prius, there's none of the CVT's drone and rpm spiking; minimal body roll when cornering; excellent ride; nicely styled and well-appointed; intuitive, easily accessed controls; and plenty of room in front and back. **Weak points:** Mediocre braking; average rear headroom; considerable body lean when turning; excessive wind and tire noise; trunk has a small opening; stability and traction control are optional on base models and standard only on the higher-end versions; and fit and finish isn't up to Honda's or Toyota's standards. *Hybrid:* Fuel economy is not impressive; repair parts could be hard to find and costly; and the electrically assisted steering is a bit numb. **New for 2012:** Nothing major; Kia plans to stay with the 2011 model redesign for at least the next three years.

OVERVIEW: Kia's mid-sized sedan is essentially a rebadged Hyundai Sonata. All models include front side airbags, side curtain airbags, seat belt pretensioners, ABS, four-wheel disc brakes, and anti-whiplash head restraints that have received IIHS's top safety rating.

KEY FACTS

CANADIAN PRICE (NEGOTIABLE): *LX:* $21,995, *LX+:* $25,595, *EX:* $26,695, *EX+:* $28,095, *EX Luxury:* $30,595, *SX:* $33,695; *Hybrid:* $30,595 **U.S. PRICE:** *LX:* $18,995, *EX:* $22,495, *EX Turbo:* $24,495, *SX:* $25,995, *Hybrid:* $26,500 **CANADIAN FREIGHT:** $1,455 **U.S. FREIGHT:** $750

POWERTRAIN (FRONT-DRIVE)
Engines: 2.4L 4-cyl. (200 hp) • 2.0L Turbo 4 (274 hp) • *Hybrid:* 2.0L 4-cyl (206 net hp); Transmissions: 6-speed man. • 6-speed auto.

DIMENSIONS/CAPACITY
Passengers: 2/3; Wheelbase: 107 in.; H: 58.2/L: 188.9/W: 71 in.; Headroom F/R: 4.5/3.0 in.; Legroom F/R: 41.5/30 in.; Cargo volume: 14.8 cu. ft.; Fuel tank: 62L/regular; Tow limit: *2.4L:* No towing, *2.7L:* 1,000–2,000 lb.; Load capacity: 905 lb.; Turning circle: 35.4 ft.; Weight: 3,157 lb.

DIMENSIONS/CAPACITY (HYBRID)
Passengers: 2/3; Wheelbase: 110.1 in.; H: 57.3/L: 190.7/W: 72.1 in.; Headroom: N. A.; Legroom F/R: 45.5/34.7 in.; Cargo volume: 9.9 cu. ft.; Fuel tank: 62L/regular; Tow limit: *2.4L:* No towing, *2.7L:* 1,000–2,000 lb.; Ground clearance: 5.1 in.; Turning circle: 35.8 ft.; Weight: 3,490 lb.

Optima Hybrid

Kia's Optima Hybrid can be driven on battery power alone, and/or in blended gas-electric mode. When the car is stopped, the engine shuts off to save fuel. It uses a lithium polymer battery that will hold its charge up to 25 per cent longer than hybrids with nickel metal hydride batteries.

The Hybrid also is one of the first full hybrid systems to use a typical automatic transmission—a compact six6-speed automatic that debuted on the 2011 Kia Sorento SUV. An external electrically driven oil pump provides the pressure needed to keep the clutches engaged when the vehicle is in idle stop mode.

In addition to developing the hybrid powerplant, Kia's engineers also addressed other ways to madke itsthe Hybrid more fuel-efficient through better aerodynamics and less rolling resistance. This has resulted in a lower ride height, an active air flap system, lower- drag wheels, and underbody aero tuning (to reduce drag), and low- rolling- resistance tires.

COST ANALYSIS: Save money with a 2011 model, but buy one built as late in the model year as possible. Not only because first-year redesigns are usually problem-prone, but more so because the Sonata's 2011 redesign has wreacked havoc on that car's performance and reliability. Early reports show the Optima has been affected similarly. Be especially wary of the Hybrid. Many hybrid parts plants were destroyed in the recent Fukushima earthquake and this could make for long repair delays and drive uphigher repair costs. Hold out for major discounting and generous rebates to cut the retail price by at least 15 percent. **Best alternatives:** Consider the Chevrolet Cruze, Ford Focus or Fusion, Honda Accord, Kia Rondo, Mazda3, Suzuki Kizachi, and Toyota Camry. **Options:** Save your money. **Rebates:** Look for $2,500 rebates or discounts and low financing rates early in 2012. **Depreciation:** Average for the Megantis; unknown with the Optima. **Insurance cost:** Average. **Parts supply/cost:** Undetermined. In the following incident, mice attacked the wiring harness and repair parts were unavailable:

> On 04/15/2011 our Kia Optima was damaged by mice eating wires in the engine compartment. We need an engine harness replaced. Dealer told us that the part is not in the US. They also tell us that they don't know when it will be found. On 5/3/2011 we were told that it might be available on 6/11/2011. This car has approx. 1050 miles [1,690 km]. The service manager at the dealer has been great in keeping us updated. Our problem is with the lax attitude I received from Kia CS, and the "parts manager of the region" from NJ that called me and told me that we just have to wait. While we make out monthly lease payments to Kia. How is [it] that a company can have no parts to repair a brand new vehicle and still make money from us?

Annual maintenance cost: Average. **Warranty:** Bumper-to-bumper 5 years/100,000 km; powertrain 5 years/100,000 km; rust perforation 5 years/ unlimited km. **Supplementary warranty:** A wise buy for the engine and transmission. **Highway/city fuel economy:** 2.4L man.: 6.2/9.4 L/ 100 km, 46/30 mpg. *2.4L auto.:* 6.2/9.4 L/ 100 km, 46/30 mpg. *2.7L:* 7.0/10.5 L/100 km, 40/27 mpg. *Hybrid:* 4.9/5.6 L/100 km (Natural Resources Canada), 35/40 mpg (EPA).

OWNER-REPORTED PROBLEMS: As with its Sonata cousin, the Optima pulls sharply to one side when accelerating:

> Purchased a 2011 Kia Optima LX on 5/18/11. Car constantly pulled left so bad that you would end up into oncoming traffic on a two-lane road if you didn't continually correct to the right. Had the dealer align vehicle to factory specs with no change. Took car back to dealer who realigned to new specs received from Kia tech support. Vehicle now only has a tendency to pull left but will drift left if you take your hands off of the steering wheel. Dealer test drove the car again and claims the vehicle drives better than a new one on the lot. Dealer said they couldn't do anything else for me and referred me to Kia consumer relations.

Sudden, unintended acceleration; catastrophic transmission failure; parked car will roll down an incline, despite being put in First gear or having the emergency brake engaged; and the rear window is difficult to see through when backing up.

SERVICE BULLETIN-REPORTED PROBLEMS: Power steering oil pump noise; two free service campaigns: one to check accelerator pedal return spring (SA065), and the other to correct an off-centre steering wheel (SA066). The tire monitor system can be affected by radio signals.

SEDONA ★ ★ ★

RATING: Average. In theory, this should be the minivan everyone should buy, but sadly, a good idea has been hobbled by poor execution. **Strong points:** An

KEY FACTS

CANADIAN PRICE (NEGOTIABLE): *LX:* $27,995, *LX Convenience:* $29,945, *EX:* $34,195, *EX Power:* $36,495, *EX Luxury:* $39,995, *EX Navigation:* $40,995 **U.S. PRICE:** *LX auto.:* $24,900, *EX auto.:* $29,190 **CANADIAN FREIGHT:** $1,650 **U.S. FREIGHT:** $800 **POWERTRAIN (FRONT-DRIVE)** Engine: 3.8L V6 (250 hp); Transmission: 5-speed auto.

DIMENSIONS/CAPACITY Passengers: 2/2/3; Wheelbase: 119 in.; H: 69./L: 202/W: 78 in.; Headroom F/R1/ R2: 4.5/2.5/2.5 in.; Legroom F/R1/R2: 37.5/32/28 in.; Cargo volume: 6.5 cu. ft.; Fuel tank: 80L/regular; Tow limit: 3,500 lb.; Load capacity: 1,160 lb.; Turning circle: 43 ft.; Ground clearance: 5.0 in.; Weight: 4,802 lb.

entry-level Sedona will cost about $6,000 less than the equivalent Honda or Toyota minivan. Nevertheless, the Sedona is well-appointed, and stability control is a standard feature. The engine supplies more than enough power in all gear ranges; the automatic transmission shifts smoothly and quietly; the ride is comfortable; and handling is very responsive. Low ground clearance adds stability and helps passengers access the interior. Important interior features include a low step-in; a convenient "walk-through" space between front seats; second-row seats that flip and fold for access to the third row; a split rear bench that folds into the floor (a Honda idea); well laid-out, user-friendly instruments and controls; lots of storage areas; active head restraints; and side curtain airbags for head protection in all three rows. There's also good visibility, minimal engine and road noise, excellent crashworthiness scores; good braking, traction control, stability control; and a comprehensive base warranty. NHTSA gives the Sedona good marks for crashworthiness: five stars for front and side occupant protection; four stars for rollover resistance. IIHS follows with equally good marks: a "Good" rating for front, side, and rear-impact occupant protection. **Weak points:** Reliability, reliability, and reliability. Both the Sedona and the discontinued Hyundai Entourage minivans are riddled with factory-related defects affecting primarily the powertrain, brakes, electronic system, suspension, and fit and finish. Fuel consumption is also much higher than what Kia and Transport Canada represent. **New for 2012:** Nothing important.

OVERVIEW: Sedona leapfrogged over most of the competition when it was restyled and reengineered a few years ago. Only problem is they forgot to improve the quality along with the performance. The latest model refines all the previous changes and offers buyers a minivan that's similar in size to the Honda Odyssey and Toyota Sienna; full of standard safety, performance, and convenience goodies; and backed by a comprehensive warranty. But, on the other hand, who wants a minivan that will spend much of its time in the service bay?

COST ANALYSIS: Without a doubt, this is a cheaper minivan than the Japanese competition, but the money you save may be spent on expensive repairs later on. Take a breather for the rest of 2011 and see how prices and performance shake out early in 2012. **Best alternatives:** Consider the Honda Odyssey, Mazda5, and Toyota Sienna. Chrysler's minivans are good second choices that will become cheaper and more feature-loaded as we approach mid-2012. Their only drawback will be the need for you to buy an extended warranty as protection against tranny failures that usually occur just after the five-year mark. **Options:** The $5,000 EX

Luxury option is a waste of money on nonessentials. Stay away from the power-sliding doors: They open when they should close and close when they should open. **Rebates:** Look for $3,500 rebates, low financing rates, and attractive leases. **Depreciation:** Faster than average. **Insurance cost:** Average. **Parts supply/cost:** Average costs, but availability has been spotty. **Annual maintenance cost:** Higher than average. **Warranty:** Bumper-to-bumper 5 years/100,000 km; powertrain 5 years/100,000 km; rust perforation 5 years/unlimited km. **Supplementary warranty:** A wise buy, considering Kia's past powertrain deficiencies. **Highway/city fuel economy:** 8.8/13.2 L/100 km, 33/22 mpg.

OWNER-REPORTED PROBLEMS: Right door handle broke off when opening the door; erratic opening and closing of the power-sliding door (a common failure with all minivans' power-assisted doors); the Sedona eats brakes and tires; front axle failure due to bearing and seal defect; vehicle rolled back while in Park. Suddenly accelerated to 145–161 km/h when passing another car; chronic stalling while underway or turning into an intersection; engine constantly misfires. Electrical malfunctions:

> With only 700 miles [1,127 km] on Sedona minivan I have had an air bag sensor go bad, a driver-side sliding door sensor go bad, a passenger-side front door sensor go bad, the IP computer (fuse box inside vehicle near drivers side) burned up completely.

SERVICE BULLETIN-REPORTED PROBLEMS: Power-steering oil pump noise; reducing brake noise. Tips on improving rear combination bulb life.

SPORTAGE ★★★★

KEY FACTS

CANADIAN PRICE (NEGOTIABLE): *LX:* $21,995, *EX:* $26,995, *EX Luxury:* $33,695, *SX:* $36,995 **U.S. PRICE:** *Base man.:* $18,500, *LX auto.:* $20,800, *LX AWD:* $22,300, *EX auto.:* $23,900, *EX AWD:* $25,400, *SX auto.:* $26,900, *SX auto.:* $26,900, *AWD:* $28,400
CANADIAN FREIGHT: $1,650 **U.S. FREIGHT:** $800
POWERTRAIN (FRONT-DRIVE/AWD)
Engine: 2.4L 4-cyl. (176 hp), 2.0L 4 cyl. (270 hp); Transmissions: 6-speed man. • 6-speed auto.
DIMENSIONS/CAPACITY
Passengers: 2/3; Wheelbase: 103.5 in.; H: 66.7/L: 171.3/W: 70.9 in.; Headroom F/R: 5.5/4.0 in.; Legroom F/R: 42/29 in.; Cargo volume: 28 cu. ft.; Fuel tank: 58L– 65L/regular; Tow limit: 2,000 lb.; Load capacity: 925 lb.; Turning circle: 38 ft.; Ground clearance: 6.0 in.; Weight: 3,230–3,527 lb.

RATING: Above Average. The Sportage has become a 4-cylinder "crossover" similar to the Tucson. Question: Why not simply buy a Tucson? **Strong points:** A lively 4-banger and a comfortable, quiet ride; dependable handling, thanks to the responsive steering and better-tuned suspension; and standard stability control and curtain airbags. The 4-cylinder is adequate for most chores and is a bit less buzzy this year. NHTSA gives the 2010 Sportage five stars for frontal and side occupant crash protection; rollover protection was given three stars. "Acceptable" IIHS scores. The Sportage is reasonably priced and has a better reliability record than the Sorento does. **Weak points:** On paper, the powertrain setup and suspension system scream performance, but the on the road Sportage takes it down to a whisper. It's neither in the front nor the rear of the performance pack. Roadway feedback is barely noticeable, and the car exhibits excess body roll and pulling. One wishes Kia had chosen Hyundai's more-powerful, direct-injected 4-cylinder engine instead. Styled like a Pontiac Vibe with upscale Audi headlights and LED lighting; interior hard plastic garnishings cheapen the look; the firm leather seats look good, but are hard on the butt. **New for 2012:** All models will use Kia's 176 hp 2.4L engine coupled to a 6-speed tranny, which Kia claims is a more fuel-efficient and powerful setup than the 2.7L V6 and 5-speed team it replaces. Later in the year the high-performance Sportage SX will arrive with its 270 hp 2.0L turbocharged engine and lots of performance enhancements. The boost in power is accompanied by a sport-tuned suspension with more tauter shock and strut valving.

OVERVIEW: The Sportage has been around forever. Now—in its downsized configuration, resting on the Hyundai Tucson's frame, and using Kia's ubiquitous 2.4L 4-cylinder engine—Sportage offers power, car-like handling, and better dependability. Standard equipment for the base LX version, which has a 4-cylinder engine hooked to a manual 5-speed transmission, includes power windows and door locks, cruise control, tilt steering, power side mirrors, and four-wheel disc brakes with ABS.

COST ANALYSIS: Wait a bit before opting for the 2012, and leave the power- and performance-challenged 2011 version alone. **Best alternatives:** The Ford Escape, Honda CR-V, Hyundai Tucson, Kia Rondo, Mazda Tribute, and Toyota RAV4. **Options:** The LX V6; the EX version is padded with nonessentials. Forget the rear spoiler. **Depreciation:** Average. **Insurance cost:** Average. **Parts supply/cost:** Average cost; some delays for parts. **Annual maintenance cost:** Average. **Warranty:** Bumper-to-bumper 5 years/100,000 km; powertrain

5 years/100,000 km; rust perforation 5 years/unlimited km. **Supplementary warranty:** Worth considering. **Highway/city fuel economy (2010):** *2.0L man.: 7.8/10.3 L/100 km, 36/27 mpg. 2.0L auto.: 8.0/10.2 L/100 km, 35/28 mpg. 2.0L AWD: 8.3 10.8 L/100 km, 33/25 mpg. 2.7L: 8.5/11.5 L/100 km, 34/26 mpg. 2.7L AWD: 8.8/11.7 L/100 km, 32/24 mpg.* Owners report they get nowhere near these numbers.

OWNER-REPORTED PROBLEMS: Owner feedback indicates only minor problems with the audio system and fit and finish:

> The steering wheel coating began to peel, which leads to hands slipping on the wheel and the layers continue to peel.

SERVICE BULLETIN-REPORTED PROBLEMS: Troubleshooting power steering oil pump noise; warning that outside radio signals may cause the tire pressure monitoring system to malfunction; and tips for improved rear combination bulb life. Campaign SA060 offers a free navigation upgrade; Campaign SA052 provides for a free Smart Key software update; Campaign SA052 relates to an audio and navigation software upgrade; and Campaign SA062 provides for the free repair or replacement of a leaky or noisy AC unit:

CAMPAIGN SA062—A/C COMPRESSOR NOISE/LEAKS

BULLETIN NO.: 015   DATE: OCTOBER 2010

2011 MY Sportage

This bulletin provides information relating to potential air conditioning compressor noises or leaks on some 2011 Model Year Sportage (SL) vehicles produced from May 2010 (start of 2011 MY production)–July 30, 2010 and in dealer stock at the time of TSB release. A visual inspection will be required to ensure there are no A/C compressor PAG oil leaks Follow the procedure outlined below to check the climate control system for proper operation and any abnormal noises. Kia is requesting the completion of this Service Action on all affected 2011 MY Sportages in dealer stock prior to delivery.

SORENTO ★★

KEY FACTS

CANADIAN PRICE (NEGOTIABLE): *LX:* $23,995, *Auto.:* $26,595, *LX V6:* $29,195, *EX:* $31,695, *EX V6:* $33,695, *EX V6 Luxury:* $37,995, *SX:* $40,895 **U.S. PRICE:** *2.4L LX auto.:* $23,150, *3.5L LX V6:* $24,950, *2.4L LX AWD:* $25,350, *3.5L V6 AWD:* $26,650, *2.4L EX:* $25,950, *2.4L EX AWD:* $27,650, *3.5L EX V6:* $27,950, *3.5L EX V6 AWD:* $29,650, *3.5L V6 SX:* $33,150, *3.5L V6 SX:* $34,850 **CANADIAN FREIGHT:** $1,650 **U.S. FREIGHT:** $800 **POWERTRAIN (REAR-DRIVE/4WD)** Engines: 2.4L 4-cyl. (175 hp) • 3.5L V6 (276 hp); Transmissions: 6-speed man. • 6-speed auto. **DIMENSIONS/CAPACITY** Passengers: 2/3; 2/3/2; Wheelbase: 106.3 in.; H: 68.7/L: 183.9/W: 74.2 in.; Headroom F/R/R1: 5.5/5.5/0.0 in.; Legroom F/R: 41/27/26 in.; Cargo volume: 37.5 cu. ft.; Fuel tank: 80L/ regular; Tow limit: 3,500 lb.; Load capacity: 1,120 lb.; Turning circle: 38 ft.; Ground clearance: 7.5 in.; Weight: 3,571–3,682 lb.

RATING: Below Average. What, $40,895 for this? Poor reliability and future orphanhood make the Sorento's 2011 carryover model a very poor buy. **Strong points:** Okay, it *is* well appointed and you get more SUV for fewer bucks, but what you do get may be all show and no go—and not very reliable, either. (Not really "strong points," eh?) The base engine will do what is required. You also have standard stability control and a fairly roomy interior with good fit and finish. At first glance, this is an off-roader's delight, with low-range gearing and good ground clearance, but there's always that pesky reliability thing. NHTSA gives four stars for front, side, and rollover protection. IIHS says frontal offset crashworthiness and head-restraint protection are "Good." **Weak points:** Your off-roading fun will end as soon as the tranny, steering, or brakes give out. (Did we mention reliability?) Fuel consumption is much higher than represented, and IIHS says side-impact crashworthiness is "Poor." **New for 2012:** Nothing significant; all the upgrades were done last year.

OVERVIEW: The Sorento represents good value in theory, with its strong towing capacity and excellent safety ratings. However, it falls short on reliability, fuel economy, and ride quality. The 2011 redesign adopted a new unibody platform and an additional third-row seat, making the Sorento longer and wider than previous models.

COST ANALYSIS: If you feel lucky, opt for a 2012, but steer clear of the poor-quality 2011 models. **Best alternatives:** The Honda CR-V or Hyundai Tucson. **Options:** The Sport package isn't worth its cost. **Rebates:** Look for $5,000 rebates and low financing and leasing rates in late 2011. **Depreciation:** Faster than average for an Asian make. For example, a 2009 4WD Sorento that originally sold for $27,000 is now worth only $14,000. **Insurance cost:** Average. **Annual maintenance cost:** Higher than average. **Warranty:** Bumper-to-bumper 5 years/100,000 km; powertrain 5 years/100,000 km; rust perforation 5 years/unlimited km. **Supplementary warranty:** A wise buy, considering Kia's previous transmission troubles. **Highway/city fuel economy:** 2.4L man.: 7.4/10.6L/100 km, 38/27 mpg. *Auto.:* 6.9/9.7 L/100 km, 41/29 mpg. 2.4L AWD: 7.4/9.9 L/100 km, 38/29 mpg. *V6 man.:* 7.7/10.3 L/100 km, 37/27 mpg. V6 AWD: 7.4/10.6 L/100 km, 36/25 mpg.

OWNER-REPORTED PROBLEMS: This is a bad car. Normally one would expect to see an average of 50 complaints posted on the NHTSA website for a one-year-old vehicle. The 2011 Sorento has 140 complaints. Here's a summary of the most serious and chronic life-threatening defects. Airbag, steering, and automatic transmission failures:

> Transmission broken for the 4th time. Vehicle towed for 4th time.

·

> The contact stated that the transmission failed to switch gears while driving 55 mph [88 km/h]. The contact had to shut off the engine to allow the vehicle to cool in order to proceed with driving. The vehicle was taken to the dealer for diagnosis where they were unable to diagnose or duplicate the failure. The vehicle was not repaired. The VIN is unavailable. The failure mileage was 3,000 [4,800 km].

·

> On three occasions during the first month I owned the vehicle, I have experienced uncommanded downshift from 6th gear to 4th gear at speed. Transmission then locks in 4th gear until shut down and restarted. Very violent event when it occurs, with an instantaneous bang and corresponding immediate loss of speed.

Vehicle jerks, stutters, and stalls when accelerating:

> Almost immediately started experiencing the occasional hesitation problem when pulling into traffic from a stop. On a couple occasions it put us in a very dangerous situation as we were crossing 2 lanes of traffic. Took the vehicle to dealer 4 times, they could not duplicate the problem. Finally they got us a 2012 near identical Sorento V6, and on the 3rd day had the same experience w/ 50 miles [80 km] on the vehicle. We now have 500+ [800 km] on it and have had a total of 7 similar situations.

Early brake wearout; chrome bezel instrument panel creates a painful and annoying reflection; rear sunroof exploded for no reason; headlight illumination is too short; and sudden tire blowouts:

> My tire went flat. I went to a Kia dealer ins Savannah. They told me the tire could not be repaired and there was no warranty even tho the tire only had 21K miles [33,800 km] on it. I purchased a new tire ($192).

> Approx. 700 miles [1,130 km] later the new tire went flat. I went to another Kia dealer, they told me I needed a new tire ($174) and there was no warranty. They also said they didn't see any road hazard damage. Kia refused to help and referred me to Kumho tires.

> Kumho blamed the dealerships for not following proper procedures. The dealerships referred me back to Kia.

SERVICE BULLETIN-REPORTED PROBLEMS: Campaign SA075 provides the free correction of the engine control module (ECM); Campaign SA060 does the same for the navigation map; Campaign SA055 provides for a Hill Hold assist upgrade;

Campaign SA053 allows for another free ECM upgrade; and Campaign SA031 authorizes a free exterior bulb replacement. Other problem areas: Sunroof chatter, vibration; a plastic tick, snap noise from the centre of the console, and trouble-shooting tips on correcting brake and power steering oil pump noise.

Lexus

The first Lexus, the LS 400, appeared in 1989 and didn't share any major components with previous Toyotas. Equipped with a V8 engine and noted for its outstanding engine performance, quietness, well-appointed interior, and impressive build quality, the car was an immediate success and a feather in Toyota's cap.

No one had heard of Lexus vehicles suffering from sudden, unintended acceleration with attendant brake loss—until a few years ago.

Lexus's impeccable reputation for quality and safety has been hurt by the past several years' news barrage of owner complaints, recalls, and serial mea culpas issued by Toyota's president who admits (rather reluctantly and with tears flowing) that "Ahem, well, you know—the company lost its way."

No, this was no mistake. Toyota simply believed it was above the law—showing the same arrogant attitude it manifested earlier in Canada when it tried to fix new-car prices under an "ACCESS" price scheme. Caught with its pants down by Ottawa anti-competition investigators who were acting on a Lemon-Aid complaint, Toyota paid a $2 million settlement to charity and beat the rap. In the States, the automaker paid much more: $48 million for dragging its feet on recalls and it lost forever the customer goodwill it had won over four decades.

The combination of bad press, an economic recession, and Japan's Fukushima earthquake has seriously hurt sales for both Toyota and Lexus, particularly for hybrid models and replacement parts. Of course sales will slowly climb back, but buyers will no longer say "I'm gonna buy a Toyota or a Lexus." Instead, they will look at vehicles offered in the luxury or family class and then make their choice. To make sure that choice is either a Toyota or Lexus, both automakers will pile on rebates and other sales incentives as we near 2012.

Lexus is a luxury automaker on its own merits, even though many models are mostly dressed-up Camrys. Unlike Acura and Infiniti, Lexus is seen by some as the epitome of luxury and comfort, with a small dab of performance thrown in. Lexus executives know that no matter how often car enthusiast magazines say that drivers want "road feel," "responsive handling," and "high-performance" thrills, the truth of the matter is that most drivers simply want cars that look good and that give them bragging rights for safety, performance, convenience, and comfort; they want to travel from point A to point B, without interruption, in cars that are more than fully equipped Civics or warmed-over Maximas. Lexus executives figure that hardcore high-performance aficionados can move up to its sportier IS models and the rest will stick with the Camry-based "Japanese Oldsmobile" ES series.

Although these imports do, in most cases, set advanced benchmarks for quality control, they don't demonstrate engineering perfection, as proven by a recent spate of engine failures, including sludge buildup and automatic transmissions that hesitate and then surge when shifting. And yes, cheaper luxury cars from Acura, Hyundai, Kia, Nissan, and Toyota give you almost as much comfort and reliability, but without as much cachet and resale value.

Speaking of resale values, don't believe the hype. Used Lexus models aren't impervious to some wallet-busting depreciation hits. Take for example a 2008 entry-level ES 350: New, it sold for $42,900; today you can get one for about $23,000. What? A three-year-old Lexus selling for almost half its original value? Welcome to the real world.

Technical service bulletins show that these cars have been affected mostly by powertrain and electrical malfunctions, faulty emissions-control components, computer module miscalibrations, and minor body fit and trim glitches. Many owners haven't heard of these problems, because Lexus dealers have been particularly adept at fixing many of them before they appear.

Most of the 2012 Lexus models are carryovers from last year, so don't look for sweeping changes apart from new paint colours. Minor trim changes: ES 350, GX 460, IS F, IS 250/350, IS 250C/350C, RX 350. Unchanged: GS 350/460, LFA, LS 600h, LX 570, RX 450h. Gone: GS 350/450h/460.

Toyota/Lexus have sworn to phase in a standard brake override feature on all its models to combat sudden, unintended acceleration. Hold the company to that promise and don't buy any Lexus that doesn't have that life-saving feature.

ES 350 ★★★

RATING: Average; a near-luxury sedan that's really an all-dressed Camry clone. **Strong points:** Good acceleration; pleasantly quiet ride; and excellent quality control and warranty performance. Five-star NHTSA crashworthiness rating for frontal and side impacts, and four-star rollover protection. IIHS gave "Good" ratings for front and side-impact protection. **Weak points:** Dangerous automatic transmission that hesitates and surges when shifting; primarily a four-seater, as three adults can't sit comfortably in the rear; headroom is inadequate for tall occupants; steering feel is muted; manual shifting system isn't very user-friendly and overall handling isn't as nimble as with its BMW or Mercedes rivals; trunk space is limited (low liftover, though); rear-corner visibility is hampered by the high rear end; and head restraints are rated "Marginal" by IIHS. **New for 2012:**

KEY FACTS

CANADIAN PRICE (NEGOTIABLE): *Base:* $42,150, *Navi.:* $46,000, *Premium:* $49,350, *Ultra Premium:* $52,200 **U.S. PRICE:** *Base:* $36,725 **CANADIAN FREIGHT:** $1,950 **U.S. FREIGHT:** $875 **POWERTRAIN (FRONT-DRIVE)**
Engine: 3.5L V6 (268 hp); Transmission: 6-speed auto.

DIMENSIONS/CAPACITY
Passengers: 2/3; Wheelbase: 109.3 in.; H: 57.1/L: 191.1/W: 71.7 in.; Headroom F/R: 2.5/1.5 in.; Legroom F/R: 42/28 in.; Cargo volume: 14.7 cu. ft.; Fuel tank: 70L/regular; Load capacity: 900 lb.; Turning circle: 38.7 ft.; Ground clearance: 4.0 in.; Weight: 3,580 lb.

A low-volume Touring Edition and new paint colours.

OVERVIEW: This entry-level Lexus front-drive carries a 268 hp V6 mated to an electronically controlled 6-speed automatic transmission that handles the 3.5L engine's horses effortlessly, without sacrificing fuel economy. All ES 350s feature dual front and side air-bags, anti-lock brakes, double-piston front brake calipers, an optional Adaptive Variable Suspension, power-adjustable pedals with memory setting, 60/40 split-folding rear seats, a DVD navigation system, a 10-way power-adjustable driver's seat with memory, rain-sensing wipers, and one of the rarest features of all: a conventional spare tire.

COST ANALYSIS: A discounted leftover 2011 model will be cheaper and practically identical to the 2012. Consider getting the usurious freight/PDI fee cut in half. **Best alternatives:** The all-dressed Camry, the Acura TL, the BMW 3 Series, and the Toyota Avalon. **Options:** Don't fall for the frivolous $7,000 Ultra Luxury Package. **Rebates:** Mostly low-cost financing. **Depreciation:** Much lower than average. **Insurance cost:** Much higher than average. **Parts supply/cost:** Good availability, and parts are moderately priced. **Annual maintenance cost:** Below average. **Warranty:** Bumper-to-bumper 4 years/80,000 km; powertrain 6 years/120,000 km; rust perforation 6 years/unlimited km. **Supplementary warranty:** May be needed to cover automatic transmission malfunctions. **Highway/city fuel economy:** 7.2/10.9/L 100 km, 39/26 mpg.

OWNER-REPORTED PROBLEMS: Sudden, unintended acceleration; stuck accelerator; automatic transmission shifts erratically, suddenly accelerates, or slips and hesitates before going into gear; some minor transmission malfunctions; car lurches forward when the cruise control is re-engaged; brake failure and premature wearout; radio system glitches; fit and finish imperfections; tire monitor system malfunctions; Bluetooth cell phone voice distortion; and an inoperative moonroof.

IS 250, IS 350, IS F ★★★★

The Lexus IS 250.

RATING: Above Average. **Strong points:** More standard safety, performance, and convenience features than with the IS 300; the car is wider, longer, and more solid-looking; a competent standard IS 350 3.5L engine; easy handling and effective braking; an upgraded interior; optional navigation screen is user-friendly and easily read; pleasant riding; low beltline provides a great view; and first-class workmanship. NHTSA crashworthiness figures are five stars for side-impact and rollover protection and four stars for front-impact protection. IIHS gives a "Good" rating to frontal offset protection and an "Acceptable" score to head-restraint protection. IS F: Lots of tire-smoking power; high-performance handling; and a relatively quiet, high-quality interior. **Weak points:** The IS 250 feels rather sluggish when pushed. Handling on both the 250 and 350 models doesn't feel as sharp or responsive as with the BMW competition, owing in large part to an intrusive Vehicle Dynamics Integrated Management system that automatically eases up on the throttle during hard cornering. Emergency braking also isn't a confidence-builder. Cramped rear seating. The car requires premium fuel and has outrageously high freight charges. IS F: A bone-jarring, teeth-chattering ride; a too-firm suspension; no manual transmission option; and a tiny cabin. **New for 2012:** Minor trim changes.

KEY FACTS

CANADIAN PRICE (NEGOTIABLE): *IS 250:* $32,900, *Auto.:* $34,500, *AWD:* $38,000, *250C:* $49,100, *350C:* $57,000, *IS C:* $49,000, *IS F:* $69,850 **U.S. PRICE:** *IS 250:* $34,465, *AWD:* $36,925, *RWD MT:* $33,295, *250C RWD:* $42,360, *250C RWD MT:* $41,190, *IS 350:* $39,720, *AWD:* $42,180, *350C:* $46,640, *IS F:* $60,660 **CANADIAN FREIGHT:** $1,895 **U.S. FREIGHT:** $875

POWERTRAIN (REAR-DRIVE/AWD)
Engines: 2.5L V6 (204 hp) • 3.5L V6 (306 hp) • 5.0L V8 (416 hp); Transmissions: 6-speed man. • 6-speed auto.

DIMENSIONS/CAPACITY
Passengers: 2/3; Wheelbase: 107.5 in.; H: 55.7/L: 182.5/W: 70.9 in.; Headroom F/R: 2.0/2.0 in.; Legroom F/R: 41.5/25.5 in.; Cargo volume: 10.8 cu. ft.; Fuel tank: 65L/premium; Tow limit: 1,500 lb.; Load capacity: 825 lb.; Turning circle: 33.5 ft.; Ground clearance: 4.7–5.3 in.; Weight: 3,814 lb.

OVERVIEW: Targeting BMW's 3 Series, Lexus's entry-level IS 250 and IS 350 rear-drive sport-compact sedans come with either a 204 hp 2.5L V6 or a 306 hp 3.5L V6. The F version ups the ante considerably with its 416 hp 5.0L V8 powerplant, which is going into its fourth year on the market. Owner comments have been positive, and the car's residual value has been quite strong.

COST ANALYSIS: Lexus has lost a lot of its lustre after going through two years of safety-related recalls and increased competition from European and Japanese luxury carmakers. Look for prices to soften and discounts in the new year of about 15 percent, plus generous leasing deals by summer's end. **Best alternatives:** Try the Acura TL, BMW 3 Series, and Infiniti G35. Audi's A4 would be a contender, were it not for its poor quality-control history. **Options:** Don't waste money on the sunroof, heated seats, or leather upholstery. **Rebates:** Expect $2,000–$3,000 discounts early in 2012, along with attractive financing and leasing deals. **Depreciation:** Much lower than average. **Insurance cost:** Higher than average. **Parts supply/cost:** Average availability, though parts may be quite expensive because of the lack of independent parts suppliers. **Annual maintenance cost:** Below average. **Warranty:** Bumper-to-bumper 4 years/80,000 km; powertrain 6 years/120,000 km; rust perforation 6 years/unlimited km. **Supplementary warranty:** Not necessary. **Highway/city fuel economy:** *IS 250 man.:* 7.5/11.4 L/100 km, 38/25 mpg. *IS 250 auto.:* 6.8/9.8 L/100 km, 42/29 mpg. *IS 250 AWD:* 7.6/10.5 L/100 km, 37/27 mpg. *IS 350:* 7.8/10.9 L/100 km, 37/27 mpg. *IS 350C:* 7.9/11.5 L/100 km, 36/25 mpg. *IS F:* 8.5/13.0 L/100 km, 33/22 mpg.

OWNER-REPORTED PROBLEMS: Sudden, unintended acceleration:

> On several occasions…the rpms increase randomly after the car has stopped and is stationary. The car inches forward and the driver has to apply more pressure on the brake pedal to make sure the car doesn't lurch forward and hit the car in front. The rpms go up almost 1000 rpms from idling. Happens in D and R. When turning on car, putting the gear [in] R, the car just lurches backwards unless the brake pedal is heavily [depressed]. This seems to be a software/ECM issue.

Many reports of premature brake wear and jerking the car to one side when the brakes are applied, and fit and finish imperfections. Poor instrument visibility:

The visual displays on the center dashboard console indicating HVAC and audio information for the Lexus IS 250 C are so light as to be virtually invisible to the driver, particularly in bright sun and when the driver is wearing sunglasses.

Sunroof shattered while vehicle was underway; excessive window rattling when driving with the top down; loss of transmission fluid; and AC mildew odour (Lexus replaced vehicle).

GS 350, GS 450H, GS 460 ★★★★

The Lexus GS 350.

RATING: Above Average. An exercise in passive driving—an abundance of electronic gadgetry cannot transform these luxury sedans into sports cars. **Strong points:** Good high-performance powertrain set-up; pleasantly quiet ride; acceptable handling and braking; average fuel economy, though premium fuel must be used; and exceptional quality control. IIHS crashworthiness scores are "Good" for frontal and side protection and "Average" for roof strength. **Weak points:** Primarily a four-seater with limited headroom for six-footers; the Audi A6 offers more rear legroom; middle-rear passengers, as usual in rear-drive sedans, get to ride the powertrain hump and thump the low roof with their heads; high window line impedes rear visibility; and some instruments are hidden by the steering wheel. No NHTSA crashworthiness data available. IIHS rates head restraint protection as "Marginal." **New for 2012:** Minor trim changes.

OVERVIEW: The GS 350 luxury sedan comes with a 303 hp 3.5L V6 engine hooked to a 6-speed automatic transmission with sequential manual shift. The GS 460 and the GS 450h gas-electric hybrid are powered by a 342 hp V8 and a 340 hp V6, respectively. The GS 450h can run on one or both of its power sources, uses a CVT, and doesn't need plug-in charging. Standard safety features include traction/anti-skid control, ABS, front knee airbags, front side airbags, side curtain airbags, a rear-view camera, and a Pre-Collision System designed to automatically cinch seat belts and apply the brakes if an unavoidable crash is detected. Other standard features include driver-adjustable shock absorbers (460 and 450h models), leather upholstery, and dual-zone climate controls, plus oodles of other safety, performance, and convenience features.

COST ANALYSIS: Since the 2011s are practically identical to last year's model, why not opt for a "leftover Lexus" and save thousands? **Best alternatives:** Granted, GS models are comfortable, polished luxury sedans, but sporty performers they are not. The Infiniti M, for example, allows for more driver input and is more satisfying to drive, owing mainly to smooth power delivery, crisper shifts, precise steering, more-predictable brakes, and a less-intrusive stability system. The Acura TL and BMW 5 Series are two other models you may consider. **Options:** Lexus has now packaged GS options so that it is almost impossible to get the essential without getting the frivolous or dangerous. Try to stay away from the in-dash navigator; it complicates the calibration of the sound system and climate controls. Other money-wasting options include a power sunshade, moonroof, the Mark Levinson stereo, XM radio, ventilated seats, spoiler, Intuitive Park Assist parking sensors, and rain-sensing wipers with Adaptive Front Lighting swivelling headlights. Be wary of the Dynamic Radar Cruise Control that reduces your speed when cars cut you off; if it malfunctions, as other systems have, you're toast. **Rebates:** By early winter, expect $3,000 rebates, zero percent financing, "giveaway" leasing terms, and discounting on the MSRP by about 10 percent. **Depreciation:** Slower than average. **Insurance cost:** Much higher than average. **Parts supply/cost:** Parts aren't easily found outside of the dealer network, and they're fairly pricey. **Annual maintenance cost:** Much less than average. **Warranty:** Bumper-to-bumper 4 years/80,000 km; powertrain 6 years/120,000 km; rust perforation 6 years/unlimited km. **Supplementary warranty:** Not necessary. **Highway/city fuel economy:** GS 350: 7.4/10.9 L/100 km, 38/26 mpg. GS 350 AWD: 8.0/11.6 L/ 100 km, 35/24 mpg. GS 450h: 7.8/8.7 L/100 km, 35/23 mpg. GS 460: 8.1 /12.4 L/100 km, 36/32 mpg.

OWNER-REPORTED PROBLEMS: Car suddenly accelerated as it was being parked; vehicle wandering at highway speeds requires constant steering corrections; brake failures.

SERVICE BULLETIN-REPORTED PROBLEMS: Front brake squeal or squeak:

BRAKES—FRONT BRAKE SQUEAL/SQUEAK ON LIGHT APPLICATION

BULLETIN NO.: L-SB-0011-11   DATE: MARCH 15, 2011

INTRODUCTION: Some 2WD GS and IS vehicles may exhibit a squeal or squeak noise from the front of the vehicle when lightly applying the brakes. A newbeake pad kit anti-squeal shim kit and disc brake rotors are available to address this condition. Use the following repair procedure to remove and replace the front brake pad kit anti-squeal shim kit and disc brake rotors.

WARRANTY INFORMATION: This repair is covered under the Lexus Comprehensive Warranty. This warranty is in effect for 48 months or 50,000 miles, whichever occurs first, from the vehicle's in-service date.

Notchy steering feel:

NOTCHY FEEL AT HIGHWAY SPEEDS

BULLETIN NO.: L-SB-0016-11   DATE: MARCH 23, 2011

INTRODUCTION: Some Lexus vehicles may exhibit an intermittent non-binding notchy steering feel and/or the steering wheel will not smoothly self-center when driving at highway speeds. This condition may occur when changing lanes or when coming out of long sweeping turns at highway speeds.

YEAR(S)	MODEL(S)	ADDITIONAL INFORMATION
2006	GS300	Drive Type(s): 2WD VDS(s): BH96S
2007–11	GS350, GS450H, GS460	Drive Type(s): 2WD VDS(s): BC1KS, BC96S, BE1KS, BE96S, BL1KS, BL96S
2006–07	GS430	Drive Types(s): 2WD VDS(s): BN96S
2006–10	IS F, 1S250, IS250C, IS350, 1S350C IS350, 1S350C	Drive Type(s): 2WD VDS(s): BE262, BE5C2, BF5C2, BK262, BP262, BP5C2

RX 350, RX 450H ★★★★/★★★

RATING: *RX 350:* Above Average. Lexus invented the luxury crossover segment with the RX series in 1998, and since then it has been a perennial bestseller. *RX 450h:* Average. Some fuel savings, but you will pay a heavy purchase price in Canada (in the States, the car costs much less). Buying the car in mid-2012 should save you about 15 percent in either country. Resale value for the hybrid will drop faster as you get closer to the battery pack's replacement time—around the eight-year mark. **Strong points:** Now in its third generation, the 2012 doesn't disappoint with its attractive styling, great safety ratings, lots of luxury in a spacious cabin, and a smooth, car-like ride. The RX received a "Top Safety Pick" award from IIHS. To earn that status, vehicles must be ranked as "Good"—the institute's top crash rating—in front, side, and rear impacts and be equipped with electronic stability control. Improved braking response and feel; more back-seat legroom; and the backrest's recline lever is more-easily accessible. Also, the RX has excellent gas

The Lexus RX 350.

KEY FACTS

CANADIAN PRICE (NEGOTIABLE): *RX 350*: $47,050, *Premium 1*: $50,500, *Premium 2*: $52,000, *RX 350 Touring*: $55,150, *RX 350 Sport*: $57,550, *Ultra Premium*: $59,450, *RX 450h*: $59,550, *Touring*: $62,750, *Ultra*: $66,700, *Ultra2*: $72,200 **U.S. PRICE:** *RX 350*: $39,075, *350 AWD*: $40,475, *450h FWD*: $44,735, *450h AWD*: $46,325 **CANADIAN FREIGHT:** $1,950 **U.S. FREIGHT:** $875 **POWERTRAIN (FRONT-DRIVE/AWD)** Engines: 3.5L V6 (275 hp) • 3.5L V6 Hybrid (295 hp); Transmissions: 6-speed auto. • CVT

DIMENSIONS/CAPACITY

Passengers: 2/3; Wheelbase: 108 in.; H: 67/L: 188/W: 74.2 in.; Headroom F/R: 3.0/4.5 in.; Legroom F/R: 41.5/28.5 in.; Cargo volume: 40 cu. ft.; Fuel tank: 70L/regular; Tow limit: 3,500 lb.; Load capacity: 825 lb.; Turning circle: 37.1 ft.; Ground clearance: 7.3 in.; Weight: 4,178 lb.

mileage for a luxury crossover. **Weak points:** High, firm prices; the car doesn't feel as agile as its competition (this year's 350 model has 400 more pounds); no third-seat option; expensive options packages; less steering feedback when compared to the RX 450h, although the latter version takes more effort to turn; modest cargo capacity; and excessive road noise. The hybrid's acceleration is slower and its Remote Touch multifunction joystick and screen force you to take your eyes off the road. **New for 2012:** Carried over unchanged.

OVERVIEW: Exterior styling is slightly different in the latest RX. Suspension is independent all around, and the progressive electronic power-steering system is speed-sensing for enhanced control. The front-drive and all-wheel-drive RX models come identically equipped. Rear cargo room has been increased slightly, and anti-lock brakes, stability control, traction control, and 10 airbags are standard.

COST ANALYSIS: Get the cheaper, practically identical 2011 model, but take 7 percent off the list price. **Best alternatives:** The BMW 5 Series, Hyundai Veracruz, and Lincoln MKX. **Options:** Stay away from the moonroof option. Not only is it nonessential and often failure-prone, but it also comes in packages that include other frivolous features. Be wary of the Adaptive Cruise Control; it may behave erratically.

Rebates: Expect $2,000 rebates, zero percent financing, and good leasing terms. Discounting and rebates will become more attractive in the new year. **Depreciation:** Slower than average. **Insurance cost:** Much higher than average. **Parts supply/cost:** Parts are hard to find from independent sources; prices are on the high side. **Annual maintenance cost:** Less than average. **Warranty:** Bumper-to-bumper 4 years/80,000 km; powertrain 6 years/120,000 km; rust perforation 6 years/unlimited km. **Supplementary warranty:** Not needed. **Highway/city fuel economy:** *RX 350:* 8.2/11.6 L/100 km, 3424 mpg. *RX 450h:* 7.2/6.6 L/100 km, 39/43 mpg.

OWNER-REPORTED PROBLEMS: Hybrid suddenly accelerated as it was being parked, brakes were ineffective, and the front tire exploded. Car surges forward when the brakes are applied. RX 450h brake failures are similar to those reported on the Prius:

> I wanted to alert you that other hybrid models that were manufactured with the same braking system as the Prius suffer the same issue. I have a 2010 Lexus 450h RX and its brakes disengage when I am driving on bumpy roads and over pot holes. I live in a northeastern city with many bumps and my brakes stop working often and as a result I have to slam them on much more quickly.

The 4×4 system doesn't perform as advertised:

> The RX450h is downright dangerous. The 4 wheel drive does not switch "on demand" as the advertising says. I live in snowy Massachusetts and do not need permanent 4 wheel drive, but it is essential when the roads are full of snow or ice. I was puzzled at first that the 4 wheel drive only actuated under 25 mph [40 km/h]. I tested it on sharp corners in the snow: the back slid out; and on faster, gradual corners: the car side slipped. Never did the 4 wheel drive switch on and correct the slide. I looked in the manual for the method to manually activate 4 wheel drive but couldn't find it. I contacted Lexus. They said that I should use the snow switch. This is a menu item which annoyingly much be switched on every time you drive. It didn't work, as it only changes the gear and acceleration characteristics like any other winter/summer switch. They also said that it should work at high speeds when more power is needed. I tried that and found that at 60 mph [95 km/h] if I absolutely floored the accelerator on a steep hill the 4 wheel drive would switch on briefly.

Audio system problems and poor fit and finish are other owner grievances. Owners also report excessive dust/powder blows from the AC vents; tire monitor system malfunctions; inoperative moonroof; the vehicle pulls to the right; and the original equipment Firestone Dueler H/L 400 tire having hairline splits along the sidewall.

SERVICE BULLETIN-REPORTED PROBLEMS: Tonneau cover rattle noise.

Mazda

All "Smiles"

Record profits and a popular auto lineup makes for "happy" Mazdas.

Following its debut four decades ago as a marginal automaker selling cheap, hard-to-service, here-today-gone-tomorrow rustbuckets, Mazda has left its unremarkable past behind. Granted, the company did snare the innovative Wankel rotary engine from GM (destined for the Vega and Astre) that had a reputation for being a small, powerful gas-guzzler. Mazda put the Wankel in its RX-7 series of roadsters (1978–2002) and its RX-8 sport cars (2004–2010). The engine is no longer used, partially due to higher fuel prices, but also due to the rotary engine's hard starting, frequent stalling, high emissions, excessive oil consumption, and expensive sojourns to the repair bay.

Ford saved Mazda from bankruptcy in 1994 by purchasing part of Mazda and sharing the production of their cars and trucks. Mazda soon turned profitable through better management and a popular new array of small cars and trucks made in partnership with Ford. The company's sole minivan, the MPV, never got any traction and was taken off the market in 2006.

Mazda has gone downstream this year with its brand-new $13,995 Mazda2, a four-door hatchback that uses a 100 hp 1.5L 4-cylinder engine with a standard 5-speed manual transmission or optional 4-speed automatic. It gets 7.2 L/100 km (39 mpg) in the city and 5.6 L/100 km (50 mpg) on the highway (see the Appendix I for a rating summary).

The Mazda3 does everything the Mazda2 doesn't. There's plenty of interior room, the car has power to spare, and the powertrain performs flawlessly. No wonder the "3" has constantly been on back order for the performance crowd since its debut as a 2004 model. This peppy and fuel-efficient compact takes Mazda back to its compact-car roots and adds some performance thrills to its fuel-saving powertrain. This year the car is restyled, the suspension has been retuned to enhance handling, and a third engine, a 155 hp 2.0L four, debuts.

A bit more upstream, Mazda's mini-minivan, the Mazda5, is revamped this year and has more innovative features to attract the minivan crowd to a smaller conveyance. The Mazda6 returns with a hatchback and a wagon to accompany its sedan version. In March 2012, Mazda will launch the CX-5, its smallest SUV, equipped with an innovative 148–155 hp 2.0L 4-cylinder engine. A 2.2L diesel version is planned for 2013. The CX-7 and CX-9 have weathered the recession relatively well, so they return with few changes. The Tribute (Ford's Escape SUV twin) has been dropped.

MAZDA3 ★★★★★

RATING: Recommended; a fuel-sipper with a performance edge. **Strong points:** Good powertrain set-up, with plenty of reserve power for passing and merging; easy, predictable handling; good steering feedback; small turning radius; rear multi-link suspension gives the car great stability at higher speeds; spacious, easy-to-load trunk; user-friendly instruments and controls; and better-than-average workmanship. NHTSA's front-impact crashworthiness rating is five stars, and roll-over resistance earned four stars. IIHS gives the Mazda3 its top score, "Good," for frontal offset and head-restraint protection. **Weak points:** The Mazda3 has a history of automatic transmission malfunctions (but no more than with Honda or Toyota vehicles) and prematurely worn-out brake rotors and pads. NHTSA gives only two stars out of five for side-impact crashworthiness. A very small trunk; a high deck cuts rear visibility; limited rear footroom; excessive road noise intrudes into the cabin. **New for 2012:** Carried over mostly unchanged.

KEY FACTS

CANADIAN PRICE (NEGOTIABLE): *GX sedan:* $16,295, *Auto.:* $17,495, *GX Sport:* $17,495, *Auto.:* $18,695, *GS sedan:* $19,595, *Auto.:* $20,795, *GS Luxury:* $21,690, *Auto.:* $22,890, *GT sedan:* $24,425, *Auto.:* $25,625, *MazdaSpeed:* $29,695 **U. S. PRICE:** *SV 4d:* $15,800, *Sport:* $16,705, *Touring:* $18,100, *s Sport:* $19,545, *s Grand Touring:* $22,510 **CANADIAN FREIGHT:** $1,495 **U.S. FREIGHT:** $795

POWERTRAIN (FRONT-DRIVE)
Engines: 2.0L 4-cyl. (148 hp) • 2.0L 4-cyl. (155 hp) • 2.5L 4-cyl. (167 hp); Transmissions: 5-speed man. • 6-speed man. • 5-speed auto. • 6-speed auto.

DIMENSIONS/CAPACITY (SEDAN)
Passengers: 2/3; Wheelbase: 104 in.; H: 58/L: 181/W: 69.1 in.; Headroom F/R: 4.5/3.0 in.; Legroom F/R: 41/25 in.; Cargo volume: 12 cu. ft.; Fuel tank: 55L/regular; Load capacity: 850 lb.; Turning circle (hatchback): 34.2 ft.; Ground clearance: 6.1 in.; Weight: 3,065 lb.

OVERVIEW: The Mazda3 is an econobox with flair that pleases commuters and "tuners" alike. The car offers spirited acceleration and smooth, sporty shifting. Handling is enhanced with a highly rigid body structure, front and rear stabilizer bars, a multi-link rear suspension, and four-wheel disc brakes. Interior room is quite ample with the car's relatively long wheelbase, extra width, and straight sides, which maximize headroom, legroom, and shoulder room.

COST ANALYSIS: There is an outrageously high $1,495 freight fee you shouldn't pay. Hell, just across the border Mazda charges Americans only $795. Plus, the base Mazda3 costs $15,800 stateside, while Canadians pay $16,295 for the same car. So, by driving 80 kilometres, smart shoppers can save over $1,000. The cheaper and virtually identical 2011 version is recommended, but it may be hard to find as higher gas prices cause buyers to stampede toward anything that is cheap to buy and fuel. Hatchback models give you the most versatility. **Best alternatives:** A 2011 Honda Civic. **Options:** Don't accept the original Goodyear Eagle RS-A tires; go to *www.tirerack.com* to find some better tires for less money. The 5-speed automatic transmission with AC is a good start, although the 6-speed manual is lots more fun to drive. **Rebates:** Not likely. **Depreciation:** Much less than average. Consider this: A 2009 base Mazda3 sedan that sold for $14,895 is still worth almost $11,000. **Insurance cost:** Average. **Parts supply/cost:** Parts are easy to find. **Annual maintenance cost:** Less than average, so far. **Warranty:** Bumper-to-bumper 3 years/80,000 km; powertrain 5 years/100,000 km; rust perforation 5 years/unlimited km. **Supplementary warranty:** Not needed. **Highway/city fuel economy:** *2.0 man.:* 5.9/8.1 L/100 km, 48/35 mpg. *2.5 man.:* 6.9/10.2 L/100 km, 41/28 mpg.

OWNER-REPORTED PROBLEMS: The Mazda3 rating this year has been upgraded to five stars mainly due to the absence of owner complaints. Nevertheless, some owners have reported premature wearout of brake pads and rotors, accompanied by an annoying grinding sound and pulling to one side when the brakes are applied; brake rotors are easily grooved; rear glass window may explode in chilly weather:

Morning: 16 degrees F [–9°C]. Approached my car in the morning and heard a crackling noise. I thought the sound was ice. I started the car and the rear defogger. As I sat in my driveway...approximately 30 seconds after turning on the defogger... the rear glass exploded with a loud noise. Glass was thrown into the rear passenger seats. The car is 4 months old and under warranty. I took the car to the dealer and they would not repair under warranty. I called Mazda and was told that this is due to outside influence (i.e. the same as if a tree branch fell on the car). He indicated that I should expect that this could happen in the cold weather. I cannot believe that I should expect that my rear window can explode in cold weather.

(Note: in the above-cited incident, the car owner could have easily sought restitution from small claims court on the grounds that the "balance of probabilities" points to a defective rear window.)

Front passenger-side airbag may be disabled even though an average-sized adult is seated; manual transmission clutch failure; and the rear sway bar link nut may loosen, causing a clunking sound to be heard coming from the rear undercarriage when the car passes over bumps or rough roads.

SERVICE BULLETIN-REPORTED PROBLEMS: Troubleshooting inadvertent front passenger-side airbag deactivation; blank navigation system screen; poor AC blower motor performance; AC compressor squeaking; seat heater malfunction; inoperative sunroof; excessive water condensation in front and rear lights; liftgate won't open or close properly; brakes may clunk or bang on initial forward takeoff; and corrective measures to reduce front brake judder, vibration:

BRAKES—FRONT BRAKE JUDDER/VIBRATION ON APPLICATION

BULLETIN NO: 04-003/11   DATE: FEBRUARY 23, 2011

2007–11 Mazda3 vehicles (except Mazdaspeed3) with VINS lower than JM1BL******444805 (produced before January 6, 2011); 2008-2012 Mazda5 vehicles with VINS lower than JM1CW******107306 (produced before January 6, 2011)

DESCRIPTION: Some vehicles may exhibit a vibration in the steering wheel or the vehicle body when the brakes are applied. This is caused by uneven wear on the disc plate, depending on how the brakes are applied. To correct the problem, the production process of the disc plate has been changed.

MAZDA5   ★ ★ ★

RATING: Average. There have been few problems reported with the new engine, which replaced the 2.3L 4-cylinder last year. **Strong points:** All the advantages of a small minivan, without the handling or fuel penalties; reasonably priced; decent fuel economy; adequate 2.5L engine; a comfortable ride; dual sliding rear doors; an easy-access liftgate; and relatively quiet interior (except for omnipresent road noise—a common trait with small wagons). It handles well: Drivers will find this vehicle a breeze to park and easy to manoeuvre with its tight turning radius and direct steering. The cabin is roomy and two wide-opening sliding doors make for easy access and are a great help when installing a child safety seat. Respectable fuel economy. NHTSA's front- and side-impact crashworthiness rating for the 2010 model is five stars, and rollover resistance scored four stars. **Weak points:** The small 4-cylinder engine doesn't have much torque ("grunt," or pulling power)

KEY FACTS

CANADIAN PRICE (NEGOTIABLE): *GS:* $21,795, *Auto.:* $22,995, *GT:* $24,395, *Auto.:* $25,595 **U.S. PRICE:** *Sport:* $19,195, *Touring:* $21,185, *Grand Touring:* $23,875

CANADIAN FREIGHT: $1,695 **U.S. FREIGHT:** $795

POWERTRAIN (FRONT-DRIVE)

Engine: 2.5L 4-cyl. (157 hp); Transmissions: 6-speed man. • 5-speed auto.

DIMENSIONS/CAPACITY (2010)

Passengers: 2/2/2; Wheelbase: 108.2 in.; H: 64.1/L: 181.5/W: 68.7 in.; Headroom F/R1/R2: 4.5/4.5/2.0 in.; Legroom F/R1/R2: 41/29.5/22 in.; Cargo volume: 39 cu. ft.; Fuel tank: 60L/regular; Tow limit: No towing; Load capacity: 1,020 lb.; Turning circle: 37 ft.; Ground clearance: 5.9 in.; Weight: 3,408–3,465 lb.

for heavy loads or hill climbing, and towing isn't recommended. Some body roll when cornering, and steering is somewhat vague. There isn't much room for passengers in the third-row seat and the interior seats may be too firm for some. There's also a history of automatic transmission malfunctions (but no more than with Honda or Toyota vehicles), premature wear-out of brake rotors and pads, and fit and finish deficiencies. **New for 2012:** Repowered with a new 2.5L four-banger and restyled with wavy side panels and that ubiquitous smiley front grille.

OVERVIEW: This small minivan is a relatively tall and narrow car—it looks like a long hatchback—with a thick, obtrusive front A-pillar. It's basically a compact miniwagon that's based broadly on the Mazda3 and carries six passengers in three rows of seats. Used mostly for urban errands and light commuting, the "5" employs a peppy, though fuel-frugal, 157 hp 2.5L 4-cylinder engine hooked to a standard 6-speed manual transmission or a 5-speed automatic.

COST ANALYSIS: Get a 2012 for the upgrades. **Best alternatives:** The Honda Civic (2011), Hyundai Tucson, and Toyota Corolla, Camry, or Matrix. **Options:** Any good tires, instead of Bridgestone or Firestone. **Rebates:** Look for $2,000 discounts as the new year approaches. **Depreciation:** Average. **Insurance cost:** Average. **Parts supply/cost:** Easy to find. **Annual**

maintenance cost: Less than average, so far. **Warranty:** Bumper-to-bumper 3 years/80,000 km; powertrain 5 years/100,000 km; rust perforation 5 years/ unlimited km. **Supplementary warranty:** Not needed. **Highway/city fuel economy:** *Man.:* 7.0/9.6 L/100 km, 40/29 mpg. *Auto.:* 7.2/9.9 L/100 km, 39/ 29 mpg.

OWNER-REPORTED PROBLEMS: Very few owner complaints recorded, except for the suspension, brakes, and fuel system (fuel pumps, mostly):

> The vehicle again suddenly shut down while driving on the highway. During this incident, not only was I about 80 miles [130 km] away from home, but I was traveling with 5 children in the vehicle! At this point, I became very concerned for the safety of my children in the car! The possibility that an accident could occur if my car lost power and another vehicle impacted the rear of the vehicle; or if I wasn't able to properly steer the vehicle was extremely high on such a busy highway!

Fit and finish glitches are quite common. Also, owners report a few automatic transmission failures; transmission gear hunting and fluid leaks; power-steering malfunctions; electrical system shorts; and rapid brake and tire wear. Airbag warning light and Traction Stability Control (TSC) light come on for no reason.

MAZDA6 ★★★★

RATING: Above Average. A car enthusiast's family sedan, although not as refined or as sporty as Honda's Accord. The car stands out for its sharp styling, comfortable ride, and nimble handling. Its score has been upgraded this year due to fewer customer complaints and a softening of the car's actual transaction price. **Strong points:** Good powertrain set-up; very agile, with nice overall handling; responsive, precise steering; a tighter turning circle than with previous versions; all-independent suspension; impressive braking; comfortable seating; and

KEY FACTS

CANADIAN PRICE (NEGOTIABLE): *GS I4:* $23,995, *Auto.:* $25,195, *GS V6:* $31,500, *GT I4:* $29,395, *GT V6:* $37,440 **U. S. PRICE:** *i SV:* $18,600, *i Sport:* $20,240, *i Touring:* $22,885, *i Touring Plus:* $24,490, *i Grand Touring:* $27,070, *s Touring Plus:* $27,330, *s Grand Touring:* $29,570

CANADIAN FREIGHT: $1,695 **U.S. FREIGHT:** $795

POWERTRAIN (FRONT-DRIVE)

Engines: 2.5L 4-cyl. (170 hp) • 3.7L V6 (272 hp); Transmissions: 6-speed man. • 5-speed auto. • 6-speed auto.

DIMENSIONS/CAPACITY

Passengers: 2/3; Wheelbase: 110 in.; H: 58/L: 194/W: 72.4 in.; Headroom F/R: 5/3 in.; Legroom F/R: 40.5/29.5 in.; Cargo volume: 16.5 cu. ft.; Fuel tank: 64L/regular; Tow limit: No towing; Load capacity: 850 lb.; Turning circle: 35.4 ft.; Ground clearance: 5.1 in.; Weight 3,185 lb.

acceptable workmanship. High prices are easily bargained down as the model year plays out. NHTSA gives its top, five-star score to the Mazda6 for front, side, and rollover protection. Also, IIHS gives its top score, "Good," for frontal offset and side occupant protection, while roof strength is rated "Acceptable." **Weak points:** Excessive road noise intrudes into the cabin; unusually low roofline restricts access, and the V6 can cut your fuel economy by almost 20 percent. IIHS rates head-restraint effectiveness as "Marginal." Mazda has a history of automatic transmission and fit and finish deficiencies and scheduled maintenance overcharges. One major Mazda6 drawback may be its price—too high to lure customers away from the competition. **New for 2012:** Carried over unchanged.

OVERVIEW: This mid-sized sporty sedan offers a sweet combination of high performance, a roomy interior, and clean, aerodynamic styling.

COST ANALYSIS: There's no reason to spend more money with the identical 2012; shop for a cheaper 2011. **Best alternatives:** The Ford Fusion, Honda Accord, Hyundai Tucson, Nissan Altima, and Toyota Camry or Matrix. **Options:** The V6 is a better-performing and more-reliable engine; be wary of the Bridgestone and Firestone tires. **Rebates:** $3,000 sales incentives and low-cost leases and financing are most likely. **Depreciation:** Faster than average. A 2009 top-of-the-line GS V6 that sold for $27,695, is now worth only $19,000. **Insurance cost:** Average. **Parts supply/cost:** Easy to find. **Annual maintenance cost:** Average. **Warranty:** Bumper-to-bumper 3 years/80,000 km; powertrain 5 years/100,000 km; rust perforation 5 years/ unlimited km. **Supplementary warranty:** Not needed. **Highway/city fuel economy:** *2.5 man.:* 6.9/10.4 L/100 km, 41/27 mpg. *2.5 auto.:* 6.7/9.7 L/100 km, 42/29 mpg. *3.7:* 8.0/12.1 L/100 km, 35/23 mpg.

OWNER-REPORTED PROBLEMS: Some minor problems with the transmission, electrical, and fuel systems. Many fit and finish deficiencies, particularly with paint delamination and peeling.

SERVICE BULLETIN-REPORTED PROBLEMS: Passenger airbag deactivation alert comes on inadvertently; inoperative sunroof; excessive water/condensation in headlamps; and poor AC blower motor performance. 2009–11 models with front brakes that click or pop during low-speed braking can be silenced by applying a special grease, says Mazda service bulletin No.: 04-005/11.

★★★★★

RATING: Recommended. A time-tested, reasonably priced, exceptional roadster. **Strong points:** Well-matched powertrain provides better-than-expected acceleration and top-end power at the 7000 rpm range; classic sports car handling; perfectly weighted steering with plenty of road feedback; a firm but comfortable suspension; impressive braking; mirrors are bigger and more effective than those found in most luxury sports cars; engine is fairly quiet, and less road noise intrudes into the cabin; instruments and controls are easy to read and access; good fuel economy; user-friendly trunk; manual top is easy to operate; very few safety- or performance-related defects; and a high resale value. The 2005 earned five stars for rollover protection, four stars for frontal crashworthiness, and three stars for side-impact protection, but NHTSA hasn't crash tested the MX-5 since then. **Weak points:** All the things that make roadsters so much "fun": not a car for tall drivers; difficult entry and exit; restricted rear visibility with the top up; and a can of tire sealant is given instead of a spare tire. **New for 2012:** Nothing important. Everything was redesigned or tweaked two years ago, including the engine, suspension, exhaust, exterior styling, and interior trim and fittings.

KEY FACTS

CANADIAN PRICE (FIRM): *GX:* $28,995, *Auto.:* $29,995, *GS:* $33,495, *Auto.:* $33,495, *GT:* $39,995, *Auto.:* $41,195 **U.S. PRICE:** *Sport:* $23,110, *Touring:* $24,450, *Grand Touring:* $26,710, *PRHT Touring:* $27,150, *PRHT Grand Touring:* $28,550 **CANADIAN FREIGHT:** $1,695 **U.S. FREIGHT:** $795

POWERTRAIN (REAR-DRIVE)

Engine: 2.0L 4-cyl. (167 hp); Transmissions: 6-speed man. • 6-speed auto.

DIMENSIONS/CAPACITY

Passengers: 2; Wheelbase: 92 in.; H: 49/L: 157/W: 68 in.; Headroom: 1.5 in.; Legroom: 40 in.; Cargo volume: 5.0 cu. ft.; Fuel tank: 48L/regular; Tow limit: N/A; Load capacity: 340 lb.; Turning circle: 30.8 ft.; Ground clearance: 4.6 in.; Weight: 2,458–2,632 lb.

OVERVIEW: The MX-5 is a stubby, lightweight, rear-drive, two-seater convertible sports car that combines new technology with old British roadster styling reminiscent of the Triumph, the Austin-Healy, and the Lotus Elan. It comes in a variety of trim levels: The three convertibles are the Sport, Touring, and Grand Touring. The fourth model is the Touring (Power-Retractable) Hard Top. The lineup begins with the soft-top-only Sport; a removable hardtop is available as an option. All models come with a heated glass rear window.

It's amazing how well the MX-5 is put together, considering that it isn't particularly innovative and most parts are borrowed from Mazda's other models. For example, the engine is borrowed from the Mazda3 and Mazda6 and the suspension is taken from the RX-8. A 5-speed manual gearbox is standard fare, while the 6-speed manual and automatic are optional. The MX-5 is shorter than most other sports cars; nevertheless, this is a fun car to drive, costing much less than other vehicles in its class.

COST ANALYSIS: Get a discounted 2011, if you can find one; it's identical to the costlier 2012. **Best alternatives:** The BMW Z cars, Chevrolet Camaro, Ford Mustang, Infiniti G37 Coupe, Mercedes-Benz SLK, and Porsche Boxster. **Options:** The 6-speed manual transmission is a toss-up, since the 5-speed is so smooth. **Rebates:** Look for $1,000 discounts by year's end. **Depreciation:** Slower than average: A 2009 Miata GX convertible that sold for $28,495, is now worth $20,000. **Insurance cost:** Higher than average. **Parts supply/cost:** Parts are easy to find, but they often cost more than average. **Annual maintenance cost:** Much less than average, particularly when compared to other roadsters. **Warranty:** Bumper-to-bumper 3 years/80,000 km; powertrain 5 years/100,000 km; rust perforation 5 years/unlimited km. **Supplementary warranty:** Not needed. **Highway/city fuel economy:** *5-speed man.:* 7.1/9.2 L/100 km, 40/31 mpg. *6-speed man.:* 7.1/9.7 L/100 km, 40/29 mpg. *6-speed auto.:* 7.2 /10.1 L/100 km, 39/28 mpg.

OWNER-REPORTED PROBLEMS: Some minor driveline, fuel system, and fit and finish complaints. Headlight beams blind oncoming drivers:

> I have to apply tape over the driver side headlight to "fix" the problem and now I get zero bright beam flashes from oncoming cars. Other auto manufacturers offer the same type of lighting for their products, but they also install a dial that is used to adjust the light beams up and down. This car does not have such a device. Affixing an ugly piece of tape to my car is not what I expected when I paid $34,000 for this automobile.

SERVICE BULLETIN-REPORTED PROBLEMS: Passenger-side airbag is disabled inadvertently; excessive water, condensation in front/rear headlamps; clunk, bang on initial take-off, and AC poor blower motor performance.

CX-7, CX-9 ★★★

The Mazda CX-7.

RATING: Average. **Strong points:** *CX-7*: Well-equipped; turbocharged engine has power to spare; excellent handling, with a relatively tight turning radius and responsive steering; plenty of cargo room; and good all-around visibility. *CX-9*: The only engine offered, a 273 hp 3.7L V6, delivers plenty of power with little noise or delay. Handling is better than average, ride is fairly smooth over irregular terrain, and there is plenty of headroom, legroom, and storage space. Instruments and controls are nicely laid out and not hard to master. **Weak points:** *CX-7*: Base engine is a so-so performer, and the turbocharged version is hampered by considerable "turbo lag," which increases the response time from the throttle to the engine. Both engines are also relatively noisy, with the 2.5L producing a coarse drone and the turbo powerplant emitting an annoying whine. Ride comfort is so-so and may be a bit too firm for some; irregular roadways give occupants a shaky ride; tall occupants may find headroom too limited; rear seating is a bit low and cramped; and interior garnishing seem a bit on the cheap side. Mediocre fuel economy; the turbo-equipped model requires premium fuel. *CX-9*: Third-row seating is mainly for children being punished; rear visibility is limited; and gas consumption is relatively high. **New for 2012:** Nothing significant.

OVERVIEW: *CX-7*: Essentially a small five-passenger front-drive and AWD SUV crossover, the CX-7 debuted as a 2007 model in Canada and has been one

KEY FACTS

CANADIAN PRICE (SOFT): *GX FWD:* $26,495, *GS AWD:* $29,995, *GT AWD:* $36,690, *CX-9 GS:* $36,395, *GS AWD:* $38,395, *GT:* $45,595 **U.S. PRICE:** *GX-7 i SV:* $21,990, *i Sport:* $22,795, *s Touring:* $26,255, *AWD:* $27,955, *s Grand Touring:* $31,640, *AWD:* $33,340, *CX-9 Sport:* $29,135, *AWD:* $30,525, *Touring:* $31,055, *AWD:* $32,445, *Grand Touring:* $33,145, *AWD:* $34,535 **CANADIAN FREIGHT:** $1,695 **U.S. FREIGHT:** $795 **POWERTRAIN (FRONT-DRIVE/AWD)** Engines: 2.5L 4-cyl. (161 hp) • 2.3L 4-cyl. (244 hp); *CX-9:* 3.7L V6 (273 hp); Transmissions: 5-speed auto. • 6-speed auto.; *CX-9:* 6-speed auto. **DIMENSIONS/CAPACITY (CX-7 AND CX-9)** Passengers: 2/3, 2/3/2; Wheelbase: 108.2 in., 113.2 in.; H: 52.7, 68.0/L: 184.3, 200.8/W: 73.7, 76.2 in.; Cargo volume: 29.9 cu. ft., 37.5 cu. ft.; Fuel tank: 69L, 76L/regular or premium; Tow limit: 2,000 lb., 3,500 lb.; Load capacity: 1,190 lb.; Turning circle: 37.4 ft.; Ground clearance: 8.1 in., 8.0 in.; Weight: 3,500–4,007 lb., 4,265–4,585 lb.

of Mazda's best-selling models ever since. Available safety features include ABS, traction control, anti-skid system, side curtain airbags, and front side airbags. *CX-9:* The seven-passenger CX-9 is not an extended CX-7. In fact, it shares its platform with the popular Ford Edge and adds a better interior in the process. Its Ford DNA makes the "9" a quieter-running and more agile performer than its smaller sibling.

COST ANALYSIS: There has been strong demand for these cars and that may be their saving grace, because the more CXs sold, the better servicing and supply should become. **Best alternatives:** The Chevrolet Equinox or Traverse, Ford Flex, GMC Acadia or Terrain, Honda Pilot, Hyundai Tucson or Santa Fe, or the Toyota Highlander. **Options:** Nothing extra is needed. **Rebates:** Look for $2,000 discounts by year's end. **Depreciation:** Faster than average: A 2009 base CX-7 that once sold for $29,995 now sells for $19,000. The CX-9? Not much better. The base model first sold for $36,795; now it's worth only $24,000. **Insurance cost:** Higher than average. **Parts supply/cost:** Parts are easy to find, but they often cost more than average. **Annual maintenance cost:** Average. **Warranty:** Bumper-to-bumper 3 years/80,000 km; powertrain 5 years/100,000 km; rust perforation 5 years/unlimited km. **Supplementary warranty:** Don't drive without one. **Highway/city fuel economy:** CX-7 2.5: 7.2/10.4 L/100 km, 39/27 mpg. 2.3: 8.7/12.2 L/100 km, 32/23 mpg. *CX-9 front-drive:* 9.1/13.4 L/100 km, 31/21 mpg. *AWD:* 9.6 /14.0 L/100 km, 29/20 mpg.

OWNER-REPORTED PROBLEMS: *CX-7:* Drivers have reported minor engine problems in addition to fuel system, brake, and fit and finish deficiencies. Gauges on the instrument panel are hard to read at night and in bright sunlight; excessive condensation in the front headlights; accelerator and brake pedals are mounted too close together; and persistent brake squeaking, groaning. *CX-9:* Among the few registered complaints we find early brake wear; poor fit and finish; and audio system malfunctions.

SERVICE BULLETIN-REPORTED PROBLEMS: *CX-7:* Two bulletins address front brake squeaks and rear brake groan: the solution to the first problem is to apply a special grease. Rear brake groan, however, applies to 2007–2011 CX-7 and CX-9 models and requires the installation of new rear brake pads under warranty (Service Bulletin No.: 04-004/11). Troubleshooting brakes that clunk or bang upon initial takeoff; tips on correcting a passenger-side airbag that is constantly disabled inadvertently; poor AC blower motor performance; inoperative sunroof; and excessive water/condensation in headlamps. How to silence an engine rattle or knock below 2000 RPM (see following page). *CX-9:* Tips on correcting a passenger-side airbag that is constantly disabled whenever a normal-sized adult is seated; troubleshooting brakes that clunk or bang upon initial take-off; left-hand door mirror vibration; inoperative sunroof; excessive water/condensation in headlights; condensation in front and rear lamps; and improving poor AC blower motor performance.

RATTLE NOISE FROM ENGINE DUE TO STRETCHED TIMING CHAIN

2007–11 CX-7 2.3L Turbo vehicles with VINS lower than JM3ER******352482 (prod. before Sept. 29, 2010)

2007–11 Mazdaspeed3 vehicles with VINS lower than JM1BL******398222 (prod. before Sept. 29, 2010)

2006–07 Mazdaspeed6

DESCRIPTION: With the engine warmed up, some vehicles may exhibit a knocking/rattle type noise from the front timing cover and/or valve (cylinder head) cover below 2,000 rpm. The noise is caused by excessive stretching of the timing chain.

Mitsubishi

Strong Cars, Weak Dealers

Mitsubishi has had a rocky road in Canada, particularly since 2003. This is mainly because of its practically nonexistent dealer network, maladministration, and the rise of many Japanese and South Korean makes that are more refined and better accepted by shoppers. The automaker's two redesigned models—the 2007 Endeavor and 2008 Lancer—were expected to showcase the company's engineering and styling prowess, but they floundered in the economic recession that hit in mid-2008 and they have yet to recover. Worse yet, Mitsubishi Canada doesn't seem to give a damn if it sells cars or not. One *Lemon-Aid* correspondent, Donald M, reports this "Mitsu" experience last May in the Ottawa area:

> Early this year I visited one of the two local Mitsubishi dealerships and expressed interest in the Evo 10. They had none in stock but would follow up with me within a month. They never called back. About 2 months later I dropped in and they still had none in stock and did not know when they would get one. So I visited the other local Mitsu dealer. I asked if they had an Evo available. The sales guy just walked into the sales manager's office and did not return.
>
> I e-mailed Mitsubishi Canada asking where was the nearest dealer to Ottawa that has an Evo in stock that I could go test drive. I got no reply. So 2 weeks later I e-mailed pointing out that greater Ottawa is the 4th largest metropolitan population in Canada, and if they wanted to sell cars, couldn't they keep at least 1 Evo in stock here? Again I got no reply. When they are not willing to even reply to an e-mail from an obviously interested customer, maybe your prediction that they are exiting Canada is correct (and deserved).

The RVR Compact Crossover and Electric/Hybrids

Honda's and Toyota's reduced production while they rebuild their factories and renew their supply lines will give Mitsubishi its best chance in years to make a

The RVR's Outlander roots makes it a good performer, but reliability and servicing are still unproven.

profit with new products. One of those "new" models, the RVR, was launched in Canada last year as a 2011 model. It is essentially a compact crossover that has been running on European and Japanese roads for some time. It has a pleasing, simple style and a rigid, lightweight body. The RVR is just over a foot shorter than the Outlander and shares the Outlander's stance and packaging, while giving slightly better fuel economy. Sales of the RVR (Outlander Sport to Americans) have been quite good, pushing the RVR to eleventh overall on total SUV sales in Canada—outpacing the Jeep Grand Cherokee, Subaru Forester, and Nissan Juke. The RVR ES pricing starts at $19,998.

Electric cars and hybrids, sprouting from the company's existing lineup, will be Mitsubishi's main thrust for 2012 when the electric "i car" arrives in November. Known in Europe as the i-MiEV, the Mitsubishi i is expected to sell 20,000 units annually and will be joined by three other electric car or plug-in hybrid vehicles by 2016. The first to follow the i car will be a plug-in hybrid version of the Outlander crossover, due to arrive in the spring of 2012.

If all goes well, Mitsubishi says it should make a profit by March of 2013. But, that's a big "if."

The company candidly admits that the $28,000 i car will sell at a loss in North America for the first few years. However, as fuel prices pick up, Mitsubishi expects better sales, particularly now that the U.S. Environmental Protection Agency rates the i as providing 128 mpg city and 99 mpg highway, and calculated a real-world driving range of 62 miles, just a bit over 100 kilometers.

Mitsubishi also sells the following models in Canada: the compact Lancer ($15,998–$25,198 for the GT), the sporty Eclipse (ranging from $24,498 for the GS coupe man. to $30,498 for the Spyder man), Sportback ($19,998-$25,398), Sportback Ralliart ($31,998), and the Endeavor ($36,998), Outlander ($25,498), and Outlander 4×4 ($27,998–$34,498) sport-utilities.

Should You Buy a Mitsubishi?

It depends on the model. The Chrysler Colt, launched in Japan by Mitsubishi in 1962, was so well-received in foreign markets that Chrysler bought 15 percent of Mitsubishi in 1971 and started selling the popular line of compacts in North America through dual dealerships (Chrysler/Mitsubishi). The Colts were popular small cars that were both reliable and cheap. Then Mitsubishi started getting fancy in its lineup with more technologically advanced turbo and AWD designs and the addition of sporty cars. This resulted in the decline of the cars' reliability (think of the powertrain-challenged 1989–98 Eagle Talon sports coupe, Eclipse, and Laser) and increased prices and servicing costs. Plus, many Chrysler mechanics were ill-equipped to service "foreign" vehicles they hadn't studied and had to wait for parts that were often back-ordered for weeks at a time. Chrysler and Mitsubishi reduced their shared models in 1997, and shortly thereafter parted ways. This has left Mitsubishi struggling with its small Canadian dealer network and little new product.

All things considered, Mitsubishis are reliable, cheap buys—mechanically. However, when you buy the product, you also buy the management, and that part is shaky and dispirited. The purchase of any Mitsubishi product is particularly risky for Canadians because of the company's weak dealer network. Moreover, insiders say that after a quarter-century, the automaker is seriously considering leaving the North American market after going through two recessions in a row.

True, Mitsubishi has bounced back from former North American economic down-turns, but this time, many new small-car automakers have added to the competition and car buyers want fresh product.

RATING: With the exception of the RVR (which is new to the market, though quite similar to the Outlander, all Mitsubishis are rated Average, with easily negotiated base prices. These cars are still fairly reliable; however, servicing continues to be a problem on models with complicated fuel-delivery systems or other high-tech features. Problems they all share include poor original equipment tire traction; sudden loss of brakes; premature replacement of the brake pads and rotors; early clutch failures; and airbags that don't deploy when they should. NHTSA has given these vehicles mostly four- and five-star crash protection scores.

COST ANALYSIS: Although the Endeavor mid-sized SUV is the best of the lot, its maintenance is highly dealer-dependent. When Mitsubishi leaves town, repairs and parts will be hard to find. **Best alternatives:** The 2011 Honda Civic; Hyundai Accent, Elantra, or Tucson 4×4; Mazda3; Nissan Sentra; and Toyota Yaris or Matrix. **Options:** Electronic stability control is recommended, but stay away from any of the models equipped with cash-gobbling turbocharged engines. Turbo repairs will devour your wallet. **Rebates:** Look for $3,000 discounts on the small cars and $5,000 on the SUVs. The Eclipse Spyder sportster, on the other hand, will continue to sell at its full retail price. **Depreciation:** Average. **Insurance cost:** Above average for the SUVs and Spyder. **Parts supply/cost:** Not always easy to find. **Annual maintenance cost:** Average. **Warranty:** Bumper-to-bumper 3 years/80,000 km; powertrain 5 years/100,000 km; rust perforation 5 years/ unlimited km. **Supplementary warranty:** A good idea, if the warranty is sold by an insured independent company.

Nissan

Nissan, Honda, and Toyota were hurt the most from this year's Fukushima earth-quake, tsunami, and nuclear plant meltdowns. Nevertheless, the company should return to normal production by year's end, carrying a lineup of models that covers almost every marketing niche, with a few (like the small Cube and Juke) that are hard to pin down.

While many manufacturers continue to dial back on their product-development activities, Nissan has ploughed ahead into the 2012 model year with the all-new NV full-sized commercial van (Nissan's first entry into the commercial van market), a redesigned Quest minivan, a refreshed Maxima, and more standard features on the Leaf electric car.

Judging by the last three years of complaints registered by *Lemon-Aid* and government/private agencies, Nissan quality control has let its guard down, particularly when it comes to fuel delivery systems, brake and original equipment tire durability, climate controls, and fit and finish. The above-cited problems are seen more often with the Armada, Cube, Pathfinder, Quest, Sentre, Titan, Versa, Xterra. Maximas and Frontier pickups are reasonably reliable, while the Altima, Murano, and Rogue models are relatively trouble-free.

VERSA ★★★

RATING: Average. **Strong points:** Good-quality interior appointments; tilt steering column; and standard side-impact and side curtain airbags. A 6-speed manual transmission is available, whereas most small cars offer only a 4- or 5-speed gearbox. IIHS gives the 2011 model its top, "Good" score for frontal offset crash protection and head-restraint occupant protection; "Acceptable" ratings for the car's roof strength and side crashworthiness. As *Canadian Driver* columnist Paul

Williams put it, the Versa is the "jumbo shrimp" of micro cars. The car's larger wheelbase makes for a smooth ride and creates a lot more interior room than what is offered by other small cars in its class. A tall roofline makes for easy access. Visibility is first rate, and there's minimal road noise. The fuel tank dwarfs the mini-car field, where most tanks are 45L; standard 15-inch wheels are used, versus the competition's 14-inchers; and the Versa carries a 122 hp engine, while the other micro cars get by with 103–110 hp powerplants. The 1.8L 4-cylinder engine provides plenty of power, and handling is responsive and predictable, thanks to the tight, power-assisted steering and independent front suspension. **Weak points:** Engine lacks "grunt" at higher rpms and produces an annoying drone when pushed; the manual 6-speed is a bit clunky; the suspension is tuned more to the soft side; the rear drum brakes are less effective; there is no stability control on some models; and owners say real-world fuel economy is about 20 percent less than what is represented. NHTSA awarded the Versa only two stars for overall occupant crash protection. **New for 2012:** Nissan plans to continue to sell the old Versa hatchback alongside this year's redesigned sedan.

KEY FACTS

CANADIAN PRICE (NEGOTIABLE): *1.6 S Sedan:* $11,798, *SV:* $13,798, *Auto.:* $15,098, *1.8 S Hatchback:* $14,678, *SV:* $15,678, *Hatchback SL:* $17,678, *Auto.:* $18,978 **U.S. PRICE:** *Versa Sedan:* $10,990, *1.6 SV:* $14,560 **CANADIAN FREIGHT:** $1,397
U.S. FREIGHT: $760
POWERTRAIN (FRONT-DRIVE)
Engines: 1.6L 4-cyl. (107 hp) • 1.8L 4-cyl. (122 hp); Transmissions: 5-speed man. • 6-speed man. • CVT • 4-speed auto.
DIMENSIONS/CAPACITY
Passengers: 2/3; Wheelbase: 102.4 in.; H: 60.4/L: 169.1/W: 66.7 in.; Headroom F/R: 5.0/3.5 in.; Legroom F/R: 40/30 in.; Cargo volume: 17.8 cu. ft., 13.8 cu. ft.; Fuel tank: 50L/regular; Tow limit: N/A; Load capacity: 860 lb.; Turning circle: 37 ft.; Ground clearance: 5.0 in.; Weight: 2,538–2,758 lb.

OVERVIEW: The Versa is Nissan's first "micro" car since the Micra was dropped in 1991 and the Sentra became the company's entry-level model.

The all-new, second-generation 2012 Nissan Versa Sedan targets mainly Ford and GM small cars, the Honda Fit, Hyundai Accent, and Toyota Yaris. It's the largest of these. This year's model offers a stylish exterior design, well-appointed interior, many standard features that would cost extra on competing models and exceptional room for five adults.

The Versa sedan starts at $10,990, making it one of the least-expensive 2012 models in the U.S. For around $14,500, it's the least expensive car with an automatic transmission, air conditioning, and power windows. The sedan comes in S, SV, and SL trims. The S is the only model without an automatic transmission. The Versa hatchback carries over from the previous generation for 2012, with a redesign on the way.

COST ANALYSIS: Get the 2011 hatchback coupled to a 6-speed manual transmission for the best overall performance and highest residual value. **Best alternatives:** Honda Fit and Hyundai Accent. Nevertheless, the Versa's relatively strong engine and large body make it stand out. **Options:** The 6-speed transmission is a much better performer than the CVT, and the hatchback has a better reliability record than the sedan. **Rebates:** Not likely. Expect a little discounting by early summer. **Depreciation:** Below average. **Insurance cost:** Average. **Parts supply/cost:** Parts aren't hard to find and are relatively inexpensive. **Annual maintenance cost:** Predicted to be much less than average. **Warranty:** Bumper-to-bumper 3 years/60,000 km; powertrain 5 years/100,000 km; rust perforation 5 years/ unlimited km. **Supplementary warranty:** Not needed. **Highway/city fuel economy:** 1.6: 5.8/7.7 L/100 km, 49/37 mpg. *Auto.:* 6.0/7.9 L/100 km, 47/36 mpg. *1.8:* 6.2/8.5 L/100 km, 45/36 mpg. *Auto. 6-spd.:* 6.3/7.9 L/100 km, 45/36 mpg. *CVT:* 5.7/7.2 L/100 km, 50/39/ mpg.

OWNER-REPORTED PROBLEMS: Brake failures, reduced braking effectiveness, and many complaints of hard starting. Speedometer can't be read in daylight, and only the driver-side door can be unlocked from the outside. Owners also report problems with the fuel and climate systems, paint, and body integrity.

SERVICE BULLETIN-REPORTED PROBLEMS: Diagnosing CVT oil leaks; rear brake squealing; front axle clicking; front-seat creaking; key sticking in the ignition, even though vehicle is in Park and shut off; drive belt noise troubleshooting tips; repair tips for a malfunctioning fuel gauge. There's also a voluntary service program (Campaign #PM053) involving the free replacement of the instrument panel cluster and a free correction for seatbacks that won't recline.

SENTRA ★ ★ ★

RATING: Average. **Strong points:** The 2.5L engine provides lots of power; occupants are treated to a quiet, comfortable, "floaty" ride; easy handling if not pushed hard; plenty of cabin space, and the rear seat cushion can be folded forward, permitting the split rear seatback to fold flat with the floor; a commodious trunk; the locking glove box could house a laptop; and good quality control, with few safety- or performance-related defects. Standard ABS and electronic stability control. NHTSA gives three-star scores for front and side crashworhiness; rollover resistance garnered four stars. IIHS judged frontal offset occupant protection to be "Good," while side, rear, and roof crashworthiness were rated "Acceptable." **Weak points:** The 2.0L engine is underpowered; manual transmission shifter's location may be too high and forward for some drivers; some body lean when cornering under power, and the rear end tends to fishtail; lots of road wander; long braking distances, probably due to the use of rear drum brakes instead of the more-effective disc brakes; and the front side pillar obstructs the view of what lies ahead. Body integrity and paint head the list of fit and finish complaints. **New for 2012:** Carried over with minor trim changes.

OVERVIEW: Unlike many bare-bones economy cars, entry-level Sentras offer dependable motoring with lots of safety, performance, and comfort. Besides making for a roomier interior, the large body produces a quieter, smoother ride. These entry-level small sedans come in three trim levels: a fuel-frugal base 140 hp 2.0L 4-cylinder engine and two 2.5L 4-bangers that produce 177 and 200 horses, respectively.

KEY FACTS

CANADIAN PRICE (NEGOTIABLE): *2.0:* $15,478, *Auto.:* $16,778, *2.0 S:* $18,878, *Auto.:* $20,178, *2.0 SL:* $23,278, *2.0 SE-R:* $22,098, *2.0 SE-R Spec V:* $23,478 **U.S. PRICE:** *2.0:* $16,060, *2.0 S:* $17,990, *2.0 SR:* $17,990, *2.0 SL:* $19,390, *2.0 SE-R:* $20,120, *2.0 SE-R Spec V:* $20,620 **CANADIAN FREIGHT:** $1,467

U.S. FREIGHT: $760

POWERTRAIN (FRONT-DRIVE)

Engines: 2.0L 4-cyl. (140 hp) • 2.5L 4-cyl. (177 hp) • 2.5L 4-cyl. (200 hp); Transmissions: 6-speed man. • CVT

DIMENSIONS/CAPACITY

Passengers: 2/3; Wheelbase: 105.7 in.; H: 59.5/L: 179.8/W: 70.5 in.; Headroom F/R: 6.0/2.0 in.; Legroom F/R: 41/26.5 in.; Cargo volume: 13.1 cu. ft.; Fuel tank: 50L/regular/premium; Tow limit: 1,000 lb.; Load capacity: 850 lb.; Turning circle: 35.4 ft.; Ground clearance: 5.5 in.; Weight: 2,819–3,079 lb.

COST ANALYSIS: Get the practically identical and cheaper 2011. **Best alternatives:** Sentra's engine and body dimension improvements over the past few years have made it a good competitor for the Ford Focus, Honda Civic (2011), Hyundai Elantra, and Mazda3. **Options:** Choose the 177 hp 2.5L 4-cylinder for the best power and fuel economy combination. Keep in mind that the sportier models don't handle much better than the base Sentra. **Rebates:** Expect $1,500 rebates in early 2012. **Depreciation:** Average. **Insurance cost:** Average for the base models. **Parts supply/cost:** Inexpensive parts can be found practically anywhere. Suspension parts and parts needed for recall campaigns are often back ordered. **Annual maintenance cost:** Less than average. **Warranty:** Bumper-to-bumper 3 years/60,000 km; powertrain 5 years/100,000 km; rust perforation 5 years/ unlimited km. **Supplementary warranty:** Not needed. **Highway/city fuel economy:** *2.0:* 6.4/8.4 L/100 km, 44/34 mpg. *2.0 CVT:* 5.8/7.5 L/100 km, 49/38 mpg. *SE-R:* 6.5/8.7 L/100 km, 43/32 mpg. *Spec V:* 7.0/9.8 L/100 km, 40/29 mpg. Again, many owners say they are getting about 30 percent less fuel economy than advertised.

OWNER-REPORTED PROBLEMS: Airbags failed to deploy; rear end of the car caught on fire; gas pedal is mounted too close to the brake pedal; sudden, unintended acceleration; faulty computer module causes the vehicle to shut down; early replacement of Bridgestone Turanza EL400 tires; premature wearout of rear tires due to factory misalignment of the rear suspension; sudden brake loss; engine piston slap; blown engine head gasket; power-steering failure; ABS clanks, grinds and causes excessive vibration when it is active; car can be started without driver's foot on the brake, unlike most other cars; unstable front seats; seat belts snap back so quickly that they can cause injury; driver's sun visor obstructs the rear-view mirror:

> The sun visor on the Nissan Sentra when flipped down causes loss of visibility, which can make it very difficult to see cars ahead and requires adjustments, which can make it very annoying to use and lead[s] to loss of concentration required when driving. It is a bad design and can cause accidents as it did in my case.

Bottom of the windshield may be distorted; tire-pressure indicator malfunctions. Other problem areas include fuel, climate, electrical, and audio systems, in addition to horrendous fit and finish deficiencies that produce excessive rattling and other noises.

ALTIMA, ALTIMA HYBRID ★★★★/★

The Nissan Altima.

RATING: Above Average. *Hybrid:* Not Recommended. The few 2011 Hybrid leftovers may appear to be bargains at first, but long service waits and a low resale value will quickly put a damper on your enthusiasm. **Strong points:** A powerful 4-cylinder engine that delivers good fuel economy, and an even better V6 that provides scintillating acceleration while sipping fuel; flawless automatic transmission shifting; good braking; well laid-out instruments and controls; and better-than-average interior room. The 2.5 S handles well and is relatively soft-sprung, whereas the 3.5 SE corners better but delivers a stiffer, more-jittery ride. Quality problems have abated during the last two model years. NHTSA gave the two-door Altima five stars for side and rollover crash protection; four stars were awarded for front crashworthiness. The four-door version got four stars for front and five stars for side crash protection; rollover protection was also given four-stars. IIHS scored frontal offset and side crash protection as "Good"; roof and rear crashworthiness were judged "Acceptable." **Weak points:** Pricier 3.5 SE models come equipped with a firmer suspension and wider tires that degrade ride comfort. Limited rear headroom; snug rear seating for three adults. All Altimas depreciate quickly, making them poor new car buys, but used car bargains. *Hybrid:* Less fuel savings than advertised; a small trunk; and cycling between gasoline and electric power is a bit rough. As it leaves the marketplace, parts, servicing, and resale value will all be impacted negatively. **New for 2012:** Carried over without any significant changes. There won't be a 2012 Hybrid: Nissan's first gas-electric hybrid, debuted in 2007 and used much of Toyota's hybrid technology, without achieving Toyota's hybrid success. Despite nationwide availability from competing hybrid mid-size sedans like the Ford Fusion Hybrid and the Hyundai Sonata Hybrid, the Altima Hybrid was sold in only a few American states that have stringent emissions standards, like California, New York, and Oregon. All other Altima models return with minor trim changes.

> **KEY FACTS**
>
> **CANADIAN PRICE:** *2.5 S: $23,998, Auto.:* $25,298, *3.5 S: $28,498, 3.5 SR:* $32,098, *Hybrid (2011): $33,398, 2.5 S Coupe: $27,698, Auto.: $28,998, 3.5 SR Coupe: $35,298, Auto.: $36,598* **U.S. PRICE:** *2.5 S: $20.410, Hybrid (2011):* $26,800 **CANADIAN FREIGHT:** $1,595 **U.S. FREIGHT:** $760
>
> **POWERTRAIN (FRONT-DRIVE)**
> Engines: 2.5L 4-cyl. (175 hp) • 2.5L 4-cyl. (198 hp; Hybrid net) • 3.5L V6 (270 hp); Transmissions: 6-speed man. • CVT
>
> **DIMENSIONS/CAPACITY (2.5S)**
> Passengers: 2/3; Wheelbase: 109.3 in.; H: 57.9/L: 190.7/W: 70.7. in.; Headroom F/R: 4.5/2.0 in.; Legroom F/R: 41.5/29 in.; Cargo volume: 7.4–13.1 cu. ft.; Fuel tank: 76L/regular; Tow limit: 1,000 lb.; Load capacity: 900 lb.; Turning circle: 34.6 ft.; Ground clearance: 5.4 in.; Weight: 3,168–3,492 lb.

OVERVIEW: Nissan's front-drive, mid-sized sedan stakes out territory occupied by the Honda Accord, Hyundai Sonata and Elantra, Mazda6, and Toyota Camry. The car's base 4-cylinder engine is almost as powerful as the competition's V6 power-plants, and the optional 270 hp 3.5L V6 has few equals among cars in this price and size class. And, when you consider that the Altima is much lighter than most of its competitors, it's obvious why this car produces sizzling acceleration with little fuel penalty. Four-wheel independent suspension strikes the right balance between a comfortable ride and sporty handling. The 3.5 S, 3.5 SE, and SR models add even more performance and luxury enhancements.

COST ANALYSIS: No need to buy a 2012 model; a discounted 2011 equipped with the V6 engine is just as good—and cheaper, as well. Stay away from the discontinued Hybrid. **Best alternatives:** The Honda Accord, Hyundai Elantra or Sonata, Mazda6, and Toyota Camry. **Options:** Watch out for option loading after you agree to a reasonable base price. Canny Nissan sales agents pretend that some options *must* be purchased, or that some can't be bought without having others included. **Rebates:** $3,000 rebates or discounts and zero percent financing on fully loaded models. Attractive leasing deals are also common. **Depreciation:** Faster than average, especially the much-coveted V6-equipped models. For example, a 2006 SE-R high-performance model that sold new for $36,000 is now worth only $10,500. All Nissan models are affected similarly. **Insurance cost:** Higher than average. **Parts supply/cost:** Slightly higher than average, but most parts are easily found. **Annual maintenance cost:** Average. **Warranty:** Bumper-to-bumper 3 years/60,000 km; powertrain 5 years/100,000 km; rust perforation 5 years/unlimited km. **Supplementary warranty:** Not needed. **Highway/city fuel economy:** *2.5:* 6.2/8.8 L/100 km, 46/32 mpg. *CVT:* 6.0/8.7 L/100 km, 47/32 mpg. *Coupe:* 6.3/9.0 L/100 km, 45/31 mpg. *Auto.:* 6.2/8.9 L/100 km, 46/32 mpg. *3.5 sedan:* 7.2/10.2 L/100 km, 39/28 mpg. *Coupe:* 7.3/11.4 L/100 km, 39/25 mpg. *Auto.:* 7.3/10.2 L/100 km, 39/28 mpg. *Hybrid:* 5.9/5.6 L/100 km, 48/50 mpg.

OWNER-REPORTED PROBLEMS: Only eight safety complaints posted for the 2011 Altima. Sudden, unintended acceleration when the car was started remotely:

> I used my automatic start…the car started and was warming up. As I approached my running car, I walked in front of the car to get around to the driver's side. I opened the driver's side door and the car accelerated and took off moving forward with nobody in it. I was holding onto the door chasing after my car trying to jump in and put my foot on the brake to stop the car. I was unsuccessful as the car ran into another car in the parking lot and came to an abrupt stop. My car was damaged and still running. The parked car that it hit was damaged. Upon impact, I was thrown against the open door and then onto the pavement on my back/right side. Many people were exiting church and gathered around…. It is fortunate that nobody was hit/run over by this "run-away" car.

Continental tire sidewall separation; windshield wipers that don't clear enough of the front windshield. 2010 Altima owners point out these incidents: sudden, unintended acceleration; passenger-side airbags may be disabled even though an average-sized adult is seated; airbags failed to deploy in a frontal collision; a fusible link failure may cause the vehicle to shut down completely; hybrid models also may suddenly lose all power:

> Hybrid suddenly lost all power (both electric and gasoline generated) while moving in traffic. I had to cut across 2 lanes through heavy traffic (while coasting) to get to the curb. After waiting and shutting the car down, I was able to restart it. I took it to the local dealer, which simply said the car "showed no codes" and, therefore, was unable to diagnose the problem or make repairs. I consider this a major safety problem.

Vehicle may jerk when accelerating; while cruising, vehicle suddenly veered to the right as the steering "froze"; transmission popped out of gear; in another transmission-related incident, the car couldn't accelerate adequately and the transmission was replaced, after it was back ordered for several weeks. Owners also report frequent AC, electrical, and fuel system failures. Fit and finish is reportedly still subpar. Hybrid owners complain that the cruise control locks out the regenerative braking system. This makes the brakes less effective, reduces fuel economy, and increases brake wear.

SERVICE BULLETIN-REPORTED PROBLEMS: Steering/suspension drift; door panel looks faded, discoloured; sunroof water leak.

MAXIMA ★★★★

RATING: Above Average. **Strong points:** Competent powertrain performance, decent handling, and a comfortable ride. Last year's redesign didn't degrade quality, as evidenced by the small number of safety- and performance-related complaints reported to public and governmental agencies. The 2010 earned NHTSA's top, 5-star crashworthiness rating. IIHS give the car a "Good" rating for frontal and side occupant protection and an "Acceptable" award for roof strength. **Weak points:** Handling is a bit ponderous when compared with the competition; 18-inch tires produce high-speed tire whine; tall occupants may find rear seating a bit cramped; the latest redesign produced a shorter, though wider, car; small trunk opening limits what luggage you can carry; requires premium fuel; and many incidents of the SkyView roof suddenly shattering. IIHS judged head restraint effectiveness to be "Marginal." **New for 2012:** Not much. The car is slightly restyled with a new front grille, tail light, and wheel designs. The interior will have a new instrument cluster and centre dash.

KEY FACTS

CANADIAN PRICE (NEGOTIABLE): *3.5 SV:* $39,800 **U.S. PRICE:** *3.5 S:* $31,750, *3.5 SV:* $34,450, *3.5 SV with Sport Package:* $36,550, *3.5 SV with Premium Package:* $37,750 **CANADIAN FREIGHT:** $1,620 **U.S. FREIGHT:** $750
POWERTRAIN (FRONT-DRIVE)
Engine: 3.5L V6 (290 hp); Transmission: CVT
DIMENSIONS/CAPACITY
Passengers: 2/3; Wheelbase: 109.3 in.; H: 57.8/L: 190.6/W: 73.2 in.; Headroom F/R: 4.0/2.0 in.; Legroom F/R: 42/30 in.; Cargo volume: 14.2 cu. ft.; Fuel tank: 70L/premium; Tow limit: 1,000 lb.; Load capacity: 900 lb.; Turning circle: 37.4 ft.; Ground clearance: 5.6 in.; Weight: 3,574 lb.

OVERVIEW: After its recent redesign, the front-drive, mid-sized Maxima soldiers on as Nissan's luxury flagship, a competent and roomy sedan that's a mini-step above the bestselling Altima. Its 290 hp 3.5L V6 is coupled to a continuously variable transmission, and the vehicle comes with an impressive array of standard equipment and a host of performance and safety features, such as large front brakes with full brake assist, a power driver's seat, xenon headlights, and 18-inch wheels. Granted, you get plenty of horsepower, comfort, and gadgets, but unfortunately the car isn't backed up with all the technical refinements and quality components provided by its Honda and Toyota rivals.

COST ANALYSIS: The practically identical 2011 is a cheaper choice. **Best alternatives:** The Acura TSX, BMW 3 Series, and automatic versions of the Honda Accord V6, Lexus IS 5-speed Mazda6 GT V6, and Toyota Camry V6. **Options:** Traction control wouldn't be a bad idea if you are lead-footed; otherwise, keep things simple. **Rebates:** $3,500 discounts and low-interest financing and leasing in early 2012. **Depreciation:** Average. **Insurance cost:** Higher than average. **Parts supply/cost:** Moderate parts prices, and some powertrain parts may be back ordered. **Annual maintenance cost:** Average. **Warranty:** Bumper-to-bumper 3 years/60,000 km; powertrain 5 years/100,000 km; rust perforation 5 years/unlimited km. **Supplementary warranty:** Not needed. **Highway/city fuel economy:** 7.7/10.9 L/100 km, 26/37 mpg.

OWNER-REPORTED PROBLEMS: Front airbags failed to deploy; passenger-side airbag is disabled when the seat is occupied; unstable driver's seat rocks back and forth; sometimes vehicle won't shift into Drive; engine surges when brakes are applied; drivers must constantly fight the steering wheel to keep from veering to the left or right; car would not shift out of First as the Check Engine warning light came on; electrical problems knock out the interior lights, door locks, and other controls; headlights may provide insufficient illumination; head restraints obstruct rear visibility, particularly when backing up; and the adjustable steering wheel may stick in its highest position.

SERVICE BULLETIN-REPORTED PROBLEMS: Steering pull/drift; door panel looks faded, discoloured; rear-end squeak, clunk when driving over bumps; driver's seat bottom shifts or rocks slightly.

ROGUE ★★★★

RATING: Above Average. More car than truck. **Strong points:** Standard features abound, with stability control, curtain airbags, active head restraints, and anti-lock brakes. The fuel-thrifty 2.5L 4-banger gets a bit noisy when pushed, but the fuel savings are worth it. The quiet-running CVT transmission smoothes out the power delivery. Handling is a pleasure. Well-crafted interior, comfortable front seating, and impressive braking. Interestingly, fit and finish elicits few complaints, whereas this has been a chronic problem with Nissan's other models. NHTSA gives the 2010 Rogue five stars for side crashworthiness and four stars for front-occupant

crash protection and rollover resistance. IIHS gave its top, "Good," rating for frontal offset, side, and head-restraint protection; roof strength was judged "Acceptable." **Weak points:** Some of the standard features are fairly basic, and those that are in the premium packages should be standard; engine sounds like a diesel when accelerating, and it could use a bit more "grunt"; lacks cargo space and rear-seat versatility; and poor rearward visibility. **New for 2011:** A variety of minor trim changes.

OVERVIEW: This compact SUV is based on the Sentra sedan and gives car-like handling and better fuel economy than the competition that's still wedded to truck platforms. Nevertheless, the Rogue's car DNA becomes all the more evident as the engine protests going through the upper reaches of the CVT when accelerating.

COST ANALYSIS: Go for an almost identical, cheaper 2011 version. **Best alternatives:** The Buick Enclave, GMC Acadia, and Ford Escape/Mazda Tribute. **Options:** Consider getting the top-drawer Bose audio system, but stay away from the failure-prone, expensive, and back-ordered run-flat tires. **Rebates:** $2,500 by late 2011, in addition to low-cost financing and leasing. **Depreciation:** Slower than average: A first-year base 2009 Rogue that sold for $23,798 now goes for about $16,000. **Insurance cost:** Higher than average. **Parts supply/cost:** Parts are easily found in the Sentra bin, and are reasonably priced. **Annual**

KEY FACTS

CANADIAN PRICE (NEGOTIABLE): *S FWD:* 23,648, *S AWD:* $26,448, *SV FWD:* $26,548, *SV AWD:* $28,548, *SL AWD:* $33,848 **U.S. PRICE:** *S FWD:* 21,460, *S V:* $23,900, *S Krome FWD:* $24,430 **CANADIAN FREIGHT:** $1,650 **U.S. FREIGHT:** $760 **POWERTRAIN (FRONT-DRIVE/AWD)** Engine: 2.5L 4-cyl. (170 hp); Transmission: CVT **DIMENSIONS/CAPACITY** Passengers: 2/3; Wheelbase: 105.9 in.; H: 65.3/L: 182.9/W: 70.9 in.; Headroom F/R: 3.5/4.0 in.; Legroom F/R: 42/30 in.; Cargo volume: 28.9 cu. ft.; Fuel tank: 60L/regular; Tow limit: 1,500 lb.; Load capacity: 953 lb.; *AWD:* 1,026 lb.; Turning circle: 37.4 ft.; Ground clearance: 8.3 in.; Weight: 3,315– 3,469 lb.

maintenance cost: Average. **Warranty:** Bumper-to-bumper 3 years/60,000 km; powertrain 5 years/100,000 km; rust perforation 5 years/unlimited km. **Supplementary warranty:** Not needed. **Highway/city fuel economy:** *Front-drive: 7.3/9.2 L/100 km, 39/31 mpg. AWD: 7.8/9.6 L/100 km, 36/29 mpg.*

OWNER-REPORTED PROBLEMS: Only seven 2011 model complaints recorded, but some are deadly serious, like the following:

> I was on my way to work and had entered our parking lot and was ready to pull into a parking space. As I pulled in and was at a stop, my car suddenly accelerated and I was unable to stop it. I started to turn the wheel to the right because there was a 2010 Ford Explorer that was parked in front but unfortunately I hit the back end of the car and pushed it at least 30 ft dead straight. My car continued going to the right and over an island and by the time I got it to stop, the air bag had gone off. I'm not sure how this happened since I was stopped. There were two witnesses that saw my vehicle stopped and the next thing it accelerated. I know my foot was on the brake because I was stopped and ready to exit the vehicle, but it would not stop.

Transmission, steering wheel, gear shifter, and brake failures (brakes may also suddenly lock up):

> Nissan Rogue transmission failure at 16,000 miles [25,750 km]. Transmission began to make strange noises under load from the front end. Dealer replaced transmission and claimed there is no current recall. A check on the internet indicates the problem is pervasive.

Tire-pressure monitoring systems are so sensitive that they often give false alerts, so drivers end up ignoring them. Steering wheel vibrations may numb your hands:

> I think it's absurd my vehicle has 2,100 miles [3,380 km] on it and I've never owned a car that does this. You have to move your hands off the wheel because they go numb. I was told drive faster or take a different route to work.

Driver-side door handle broke and it took over a month to get the part:

> In the meantime, the only way to access my vehicle is by using the passenger side door and climb over the seats. If I were physically unable to climb over the seats, I would not be able to operate my vehicle. Fortunately, I am able, but if a person was not, they would either have to rent a vehicle or use some other means of transportation. I find this problem inexcusable. A simple door handle part must be sent from Japan to fix this problem.

SERVICE BULLETIN-REPORTED PROBLEMS: Steering/suspension pull or drift diagnosis.

MURANO ★★★★

RATING: Above Average. **Strong points:** Nicely equipped with a refined, responsive powertrain that includes a smooth V6 coupled to a quiet CVT transmission; sports-car-like performance; a plush, easily accessed, comfortable, and roomy interior; standard stability control; a comfortable, quiet ride, good fuel economy; no-surprise, responsive, car-like handling; and better-than-average reliability. NHTSA gives the Murano five stars for side crash protection and four stars for frontal crashworthiness and rollover resistance. IIHS gives the Murano a "Good" rating, a perfect score, for frontal offset, side, and head-restraint protection. **Weak points:** There is less cargo space behind the second row than what is available in competing models; limited rear visibility; requires premium fuel. IIHS says the Murano's roof strength is "Marginal." **New for 2012:** A minor restyling and the debut of the Murano CrossCabriolet (convertible).

OVERVIEW: The mid-sized Murano continues to be the car-based "ying" to the Pathfinder's truck-based "yang." Both vehicles embody strong, in-your-face styling and are loaded with many standard safety, performance, and convenience features.

KEY FACTS

CANADIAN PRICE (NEGOTIABLE): *S:* $34,498, *SV AWD:* $37,548, *SL AWD:* $40,648, *LE:* $44,048 **U.S. PRICE:** *S:* $29,290, *SV:* $32,860, *SL:* $36,400, *LE:* $38,300 **CANADIAN FREIGHT:** $1,650 **U.S. FREIGHT:** $760

POWERTRAIN (FRONT-DRIVE/AWD)
Engine: 3.5L V6 (265 hp); Transmission: CVT

DIMENSIONS/CAPACITY
Passengers: 2/3; Wheelbase: 111.2 in.; H: 68.1/L: 188.5/W: 74.1 in.; Headroom F/R: 3.0/3.0 in.; Legroom F/R: 40.5/28 in.; Cargo volume: 31.6 cu. ft.; Fuel tank: 82L/premium; Tow limit: 3,500 lb.; Load capacity: 900 lb.; Turning circle: 39.4 ft.; Ground clearance: 6.5 in.; Weight: 4,034–4,153 lb.

COST ANALYSIS: The 2011 model isn't much different from the 2011 version and it's a lot cheaper. Delay your purchase until mid-2012 so as to take advantage of the inevitable discounts, rebates, and factory quality fixes. It would also be a good idea to buy the second-year Cabriolet to allow for prices to settle and the inevitable factory-related defects to get fixed. **Best alternatives:** The Buick Enclave, GMC Acadia, and Hyundai Santa Fe. **Options:** Don't buy the failure-prone, expensive, and back-ordered run-flat tires. **Rebates:** $3,500 rebate by early 2012. **Depreciation:** Average. **Insurance cost:** Higher than average. **Parts supply/ cost:** Parts are sometimes hard to find and can be costly. **Annual maintenance cost:** Higher than average. **Warranty:** Bumper-to-bumper 3 years/60,000 km; powertrain 5 years/100,000 km; rust perforation 5 years/unlimited km. **Supplementary warranty:** Not needed. **Highway/city fuel economy:** 8.7/11.8 L/100 km, 32/24 mpg.

OWNER-REPORTED PROBLEMS: No 2011 model safety incidents logged by NHTSA. 2010 owners had the following problems: Passenger-side airbag is disabled when a normal-sized occupant is seated. Nissan recalled the 2009s for this defect. Owners also report frequent brake replacements (calipers and rotors) and poor body fit and finish, including paint defects and water/air leaks. Other concerns: Airbag warning light comes on continually, even after multiple resets by the dealer; vehicle rolls down incline when stopped in traffic; Check Engine light comes on after each fill-up (cap must be carefully resealed); faulty transmission body causes the powertrain to vibrate when cruising; headlights may suddenly shut off; the Start/Stop ignition button can be accidently pressed, and this can suddenly shut down the vehicle when it's underway; tilt steering wheel may be unsafe in a crash:

> Unsafe design of tilt steering wheel adjustment lever (SWAL) that will cause a shat-
> tered left knee in a front or rear crash (FORC). The SWAL is positioned on the lower
> left side of the steering column so that the left knee will be shattered in a FORC.
> Other vehicles do not have this design flaw. Nissan maintains that the SWAL design
> has not resulted in problems and therefore nothing will be done.

Remote-controlled door locks operate erratically; inoperative sunroof; faulty sun visors suddenly flop down, completely blocking visibility; and excessive vibration (fixed by reducing tire pressure from 41 psi to 36 psi).

SERVICE BULLETIN-REPORTED PROBLEMS: Intermittent power steering noises; steering/ suspension pull or drift diagnostics; and Bluetooth voice recognition issues.

Nissan/Suzuki

FRONTIER/EQUATOR ★★★★★

The Nissan Frontier.

RATING: Recommended. **Strong points:** Well equipped; carries a powerful V6, with towing horsepower to spare; the 4-cylinder engine is acceptable for light chores; handling is quick and nimble; an accommodating interior, especially with the Crew version; plenty of storage in the centre console; and outstanding reliability. NHTSA gives the Frontier and Equator four stars for frontal crash protection, five stars for side crashworthiness, and three stars for rollover resistance. **Weak points:** Ride is a bit stiff; stability control is optional; rear seatroom is tight in the Crew Cab; and you'll need to eat your Wheaties before attempting to lift the tailgate. **New for 2012:** Returns with minor trim changes. *Equator:* Going, going, gone? Suzuki sold six Equators in Canada in March 2010 but none during the first quarter of 2011. As of July 2011, it's still shown as the $34,995 2010 Suzuki Equator on Suzuki's Canadian website.

OVERVIEW: These are gutsy, reliable pickups that are compact in name only. The PRO-4X model offers

KEY FACTS

CANADIAN PRICE (NEGOTIABLE): *King S 4x2:* $24,398, *SV 4x2:* $28,348, *4x4:* $30,348, *PRO-4X:* $33,298, *Crew SV 4x4:* $34,148, *PRO-4X:* $38,798, *Equator Crew Cab (2010) JX:* $35,000 **U.S. PRICE:** *King S:* $18,200, *SV:* $21,380, *SV V6:* $21,970, *Pro-4X:* $26,620 **CANADIAN FREIGHT:** $1,595 **U.S. FREIGHT:** $820 **POWERTRAIN (REAR-DRIVE/4WD)** Engines: 2.5L 4-cyl. (152 hp) • 4.0L V6 (261 hp); Transmissions: 5-speed man. • 6-speed man. • 5-speed auto.

DIMENSIONS/CAPACITY
Passengers: 2/3; Wheelbase: 126 in.; H: 70/L: 206/W: 73 in.; Headroom F/R: 3.0/3.5 in.; Legroom F/R: 40/27 in.; Cargo volume: 60 cu. ft.; Fuel tank: 80L/regular; Tow limit: 6,100 lb.; Load capacity: 1,160 lb.; Turning circle: 43.3 ft.; Ground clearance: 8.7 in.; Weight: 4,655 lb.

serious off-road features seldom found among compact trucks, like a locking rear differential, Bilstein dampers, and skid plates.

COST ANALYSIS: A cheaper 2011 Frontier will give almost everything that's offered with the 2012 version. Delay your purchase until early 2012 so as to take advantage of the inevitable discounts, rebates, and manufacturing fixes. **Best alternatives:** The 2011 Ford Ranger. Other small pickups like the GM Colorado and Canyon or the Toyota Tacoma are not recommended due to their poor reliability. **Options:** Run away from the failure-prone, expensive, and back-ordered run-flat tires. **Rebates:** *Frontier:* $2,000 by early 2012. **Depreciation:** Average. For example, a 2010 Equator JX 4×4 that sold for $35,000 new is now worth about $12,000 less. A similar Nissan Frontier will fetch a couple of thousand dollars more than the Equator. **Insurance cost:** Higher than average. **Parts supply/cost:** Parts are everywhere, and they don't cost much, since many parts are shared with the Pathfinder, Xterra, and Titan. **Annual maintenance cost:** Average. **Warranty:** Bumper-to-bumper 3 years/60,000 km; powertrain 5 years/100,000 km; rust perforation 5 years/unlimited km. **Supplementary warranty:** Not needed. **Maintenance/repair costs:** Less than average. **Highway/city fuel economy:** 2.5 man.: 8.7/10.7 L/100 km, 32/26 mpg. 2.5 auto.: 9.2/12.6 L/100 km, 31/22 mpg. 4.0 4×2 auto.: 9.2/14.2 L/100 km, 31/20 mpg. 4.0 4×4: 10.4/13.7 L/100 km, 27/21 mpg. 4.0 4×4 auto.: 10.4/14.7 L/100 km, 27/19 mpg.

OWNER-REPORTED PROBLEMS: Only five 2011 model safety-related incidents posted on NHTSA's website. Passenger-side front airbag is disabled when a normal-sized adult occupies the seat; airbags deploy for no reason. Delayed acceleration; faulty fuel-level sending unit sensor:

> I went online to *nissanhelp.com* after performing a search. I came across many others who have experienced the same problem. Apparently it has something to do with the fuel sending unit. A similar problem was found on the 2000–2004 Xterra models and a recall was performed when the vehicle would stop after not getting any fuel.

Electrical short caused all of the lights and gauges to go out and the vehicle stalled.

SERVICE BULLETIN-REPORTED PROBLEMS: Steering/suspension pull or drift diagnostics; fuel cap tether detached from body; low airflow from AC front air vents; front brake noise at low speeds; noise/vibration from front engine mounts:

NOISE/VIBRATION FROM FRONT ENGINE MOUNT(S)

BULLETIN NO.: NTB11-014   DATE: FEBRUARY 16, 2011

2005–11 Pathfinder; Xterra; and Frontier with VQ40 engines.
IF YOU CONFIRM: The front engine mount insulator is leaking or cracked resulting in engine vibration/noise.
ACTION: Replace both front engine mounts, stoppers, and bolts with the ones from the Parts Information table...

Nissan Canada is doing this repair for free on a case-by-case basis. If you are asked to pay, suggest that a "goodwill warranty" be applied. If the claim is again denied, take the above service bulletin to small claims court and sue for the estimated cost, under the principle of "reasonable durability."

Subaru

An Extraordinary Ordinary Car

Even in these hard economic times, buyers are clamouring for Subaru's all-wheel-drive Forester, Impreza, and Legacy. And the company doesn't intend to risk its success with any dramatic changes. Except for a slight freshening of the Impreza, the Subaru's overall product lineup this year stands pat, with most of the redesigns and styling changes scheduled for 2012 and later.

Combined Japanese brand sales in Canada through July 2011 have fallen 10.7 percent to 282,657 units, which has cut market share by 4 points to 29.8 percent—the first time since 2002 when Japanese share has been below 30 percent in Canada. Mitsubishi, Nissan, and Subaru recorded single-digit gains, while all others were lower compared to 2010 (see the "Japanese Car Sales in Canada" chart on p. 418).

Although all Subarus provide full-time AWD capability, studies show that most owners don't need the off-road prowess; only 5 percent will ever use their Subaru for off-roading. The other 95 percent just like knowing they have the option of going wherever they please, whenever they please—and they don't seem to care that an AWD burns about 2 percent more fuel. As one retired Quebec mechanic told me, "All-wheel drive simply means that you will get stuck deeper, further from home. It's no replacement for common sense."

FORESTER, IMPREZA, WRX, STI ★★★★✦★★★✦★★

The Subaru Impreza.

KEY FACTS

CANADIAN PRICE (FORESTER: FIRM; IMPREZA: NEGOTIABLE): *Forester 2.5X:* $25,995, *Convenience Package:* $28,095, *Convenience with PZEV:* $28,795, *Touring Package:* $28,695, *Limited Package:* $32,995, *XT Limited:* $35,495 *Impreza 2.5i:* $20,995, *Auto.:* $22,095, 5d: $21,895, *Touring Package:* $22,495, *Touring Package 5d:* $23,395, *Limited Package:* $26,695, *Auto.:* $23,095, *Limited Package 5d:* $27,595; *WRX Sedan:* $32,495, 5d: $33,395, *Limited 5d:* $36,395, *STI:* $37,995, 5d: $38,895,*Sport-Tech Package:* $41,595, *Sport-Tech Package 5d:* $42,495
U.S. PRICE: *Forester 2.5X:* $20,45, *Premium:* $23,195, *X Limited:* $26,495, *XT Premium:* $26,995, *XT Premium:* $26,995, *Touring:* $29,995 *Impreza 2.5i:* $17,495, *Premium:* $18,495, *Outback Sport:* $19,995, *GT:* $26,995 *WRX Sedan:* $25,495 *Premium:* $27,995, *Limited:* $28,995 *STI:* $33,995, *STI Limited:* $37,345
CANADIAN FREIGHT: $1,525 **U.S. FREIGHT:** $725

POWERTRAIN (AWD)
Engines: 2.5L 4-cyl. (170 hp) • 2.5L 4-cyl. Turbo (265 hp) • 2.5L 4-cyl. Turbo (305 hp); Transmissions: 5-speed man. • 6-speed man. • 4-speed auto.
DIMENSIONS/CAPACITY (FORESTER)
Passengers: 2/3; Wheelbase: 103 in.; H: 66/L: 180/W: 70 in.; Headroom F/R: 6.5/6.5 in.; Legroom F/R: 41/29.5 in.; Cargo volume: 35.5 cu. ft.; Fuel tank: 64L/regular/ premium; Tow limit: 2,400 lb.; Load capacity: 900 lb.; Turning circle: 38 ft.; Ground clearance: 8.9 in.; Weight: 3,064–3,373 lb.
DIMENSIONS/CAPACITY (IMPREZA)
Passengers: 2/3; Wheelbase: 104.1 in.; H: 58/L: 173.8/W: 77.7 in.; Headroom F/R: 6.0/3.5 in.; Legroom F/R: 41.5/28 in.; Cargo volume: 11.2 cu. ft.; Fuel tank: 64L/regular/premium; Tow limit: Not recommended; Load capacity: 900 lb., *WRX, STI:* 850 lb.; Turning circle: 37 ft.; Ground clearance: 6.1 in.; Weight: 3,064–3,384 lb.

RATING: *Forester:* Above Average. *Impreza:* Average. *WRX and STI:* Below Average. **Strong points:** Impressive acceleration with the base 2.5L engine; however, the WRX, STI, and STI Limited models have even more powerful 305 hp engines. But with that power comes complexity—a complexity that requires good access to parts and servicing that is frequently lacking. Competent handling, without any torque steer; Forester passengers are spoiled by agile and secure handling, thanks to a tight turning circle; a roomy cabin; lots of storage space with the wagons; a nice control layout; and average quality control. Better than average NHTSA crash test results: *Forester:* Four stars for front and rollover crash protection, and three stars for side crashworthiness. The Forester also excelled in IIHS crash tests, getting the Institute's top, "Good," mark for frontal offset, side, roof, and head-restraint protection and for roof strength. *Impreza:* The Impreza got five stars for front and side occupant protection and four stars for rollover resistance; its IIHS scores were identical to the Forester rating. WRX would likely post similar results. **Weak points:** Keep in mind, there is nothing remarkable about Subaru's lineup except for the inclusion of AWD in all models. If you don't need the AWD capability, you're wasting your money. Also, your slow base Impreza just got slower for 2012. The car is wimpy enough with 170 horsepower, now it has to split 140 horses between all four wheels. (Yawn.) Some body roll when cornering; the outdated 4-speed automatic transmission shifts roughly and wastes fuel, making the new CVT a must-have. The Outback Sport doesn't ride as comfortably or handle as well as other Imprezas. There's also problematic entry and exit, and the seats require additional lumbar bolstering and more height. WRX and STI require premium fuel. **New for 2012:** *Impreza:* Less performance, but on the other hand, fewer fill-ups. The 2012s will carry a more fuel-efficient 148 hp 2.0L 4-banger engine. It's less powerful than the 2011's 170 hp 2.5 L, but is predicted to be about 30 percent more fuel-efficient. Base models get a 5-speed manual transmission and a CVT automatic is optional. A slightly larger wheelbase also gives a bit more passenger space. The restyled exterior hints of the Mazda3 combined with touches of Honda Civic and Chevrolet Cruze. The new roof antenna looks out of place.

OVERVIEW: The Forester is a cross between a wagon and a sport-utility. Based on the shorter Impreza, it uses the Legacy Outback's 2.5L engine, or an optional turbo-charged version of the same powerplant. Its road manners are more subdued, and its engine provides plenty of power and torque for off-roading. The two "Boxer" 4-cylinder engines are both competitive in terms of power and fuel economy, despite being coupled to an outmoded 4-speed automatic transmission.

The Impreza is essentially a shorter Legacy with additional convenience features. It comes as a four-door sedan, a wagon, and an Outback Sport wagon, all powered by a 170 hp 2.5L flat-four engine or a 224 hp turbocharged 2.5L. The rally-inspired WRX models have a more-powerful turbocharged engine (a 305 hp 2.5L variant), lots of standard performance features, sport suspension, an aluminum hood with functional scoop, and higher-quality instruments, controls, trim, and seats.

COST ANALYSIS: Be wary of Subaru's high-performance WRX and STI models. They require special parts and specialized mechanical know-how that may be hard to find in these troubled economic times. Instead, buy a discounted 2011 Forester or Impreza. Better yet, compare prices with dealers in the States; prices may be $10,000 less on some models bought south of the border. Remember, WRX versions are expensive, problematic Imprezas, but when they run right, they'll equal the sporty performance of most of the entry-level Audis and BMWs—cars that cost thousands of dollars more. **Best alternatives:** If you don't really need a 4×4, there are some front-drives worth considering: the Honda Civic, Hyundai Elantra or Sonata, Mazda6, and Toyota Corolla or Matrix (only with the brake override feature). **Rebates:** $1,500 rebates on the more-expensive models, and low-interest financing. **Options:** Larger tires to smooth out the ride and the CVT automatic transmission to smooth out the gear changes. **Depreciation:** Slower than average, and faster than average. Foresters hold their value best: A 2007 Forester that originally sold for $27,000 is still worth half its original cost. But WRX models lose their value quickly: A 2007 entry-level WRX that sold for $35,500 is now barely worth $14,000. **Insurance cost:** Higher than average. **Parts supply/cost:** Parts aren't easy to find, and they can be costly. **Annual maintenance cost:** Average. Mediocre, expensive servicing is hard to overcome because independent garages can't service Subaru AWD powertrains and turbochargers. **Warranty:** Bumper-to-bumper 3 years/60,000 km; powertrain 5 years/100,000 km; rust perforation 5 years/unlimited km. **Supplementary warranty:** Protect yourself with an extended powertrain warranty. **Highway/city fuel economy:** *2.5 (2011):* 7.5/10.6 L/100 km, 38/27 mpg. *Auto.:* 7.7/10.4 L/100 km, 37/27 mpg. *WRX:* 8.1/11.3 L/100 km, 35/25 mpg. *STI:* 8.7/12.2 L/100 km, 33/23 mpg.

OWNER-REPORTED PROBLEMS: *Forester:* Sudden, unintended acceleration while the vehicle was cruising on the highway; *Impreza:* WRX models have had fewer owner complaints (mostly paint, trim, and body hardware) than the Impreza, which has been afflicted with similar fit and finish deficiencies, plus engine, exhaust, and fuel system complaints. Also, reports of sudden, unintended acceleration:

> While driving approximately 15 mph [24 km/h] on normal road conditions, there was sudden, aggressive, and forceful acceleration. The driver immediately depressed the brake pedal, but there was no response. The driver placed the gear shifter into Park, but the vehicle failed to slow down. The vehicle crashed into a brick wall. The failure occurred without warning. The police and ambulance were called to the scene and a police report was filed. The driver sustained severe back injuries. The vehicle was completely destroyed.

When accelerating, there's also a serious shift lag, then the vehicle surges ahead; defective engine had to be replaced; head restraints push head forward at an uncomfortable angle, causing neck strain and backache; and the moonroof system cavity allows debris and small animals to enter between the headliner and interior walls—the perfect place for fungi and mould to incubate. *STI:* Sudden engine failure due to a failed ringland with piston #4. It took two weeks to rebuild the engine to correct this defect, which is common to 2008–10 Impreza STIs.

SERVICE BULLETIN-REPORTED PROBLEMS: *Forester:* TCM computer re-boot to cure harsh shifting; another service bulletin (#02-113-11R), published January 26, 2011, addresses cold start engine noise and suggests that the timing chain tensioner be changed; excessive oil consumption, white exhaust smoke:

EXCESSIVE OIL CONSUMPTION/WHITE EXHAUST SMOKE

BULLETIN NO.: 02-115-11R   DATE: JANUARY 31, 2011

WHITE SMOKE FROM TAILPIPE AND/OR HIGH OIL CONSUMPTION
2011 MY Legacy/Outback; 2011 MY Impreza; 2010 MY Forester
INTRODUCTION: If you encounter a customer complaint concerning white smoke from the exhaust pipe and / or high oil consumption, it may be the result of the # 1 and/or # 4 intake valve guide insertion hole improperly machined, permitting oil to enter the combustion chamber. To remedy this condition, the cylinder head(s) will need to be replaced.

Impreza: Highway speed, vibration, harshness, and noise diagnostic and correction tips.

LEGACY, OUTBACK   ★★★/★★

RATING: *Legacy:* Average. *Outback:* Below Average; the car's greater number of safety complaints (related almost entirely to hesitation and stalling) shows sloppy assembly and the use of subpar components. Both cars are distinguished by their standard full-time all-wheel-drive drivetrain. This AWD feature handles difficult

The Subaru Legacy.

a comfortable ride; interior materials and fit and finish have been substantially upgraded; standard electronic stability control; the GT version handles best and has power to spare; lots of cargo room. NHTSA gives the Legacy and Outback four stars for front and side protection and five stars for rollover resistance. IIHS gives it its top, "Good," rating for frontal offset, side, roof, and rollover crash protection.

KEY FACTS

CANADIAN PRICE (NEGOTIABLE): *Legacy 2.5i:* $23,995, *CVT:* $25,195, *Convenience:* $26,395, *PZEV:* $27,095, *Sport:* $27,995, *Auto.:* $29,195, *Limited:* $31,995, *Limited with Multimedia Option:* $34,295, *GT:* $38,595, *3.6R:* $31,895, *3.6R Limited:* $34,695, *3.6R Limited with Multimedia Option:* $36,995 *Outback 2.5i Convenience:* $28,995, *CVT:* $25,195, *PZEV:* $30,895, *Sport:* $31,795, *Limited:* $35,795, *Limited with Multimedia Option:* $34,295, *GT:* $38,595, *3.6R:* $31,895, *3.6R Limited:* $34,695, *3.6R Limited with Multimedia Option:* $36,995 **U.S. PRICE:** *Legacy 2.5i:* $19,995, *Premium:* $20,995, *Limited:* $25,295, *GT:* $31,395, *3.6R:* $24,995, *3.6R Premium:* $25,995, *Limited:* $28,295 **CANADIAN FREIGHT:** $1,525 **U.S. FREIGHT:** $725
POWERTRAIN (AWD): Engines: 2.5L 4-cyl. (170 hp) • 2.5L 4-cyl. Turbo (265 hp) • 3.6L V6 (256 hp); Transmissions: 5-speed man. • 6-speed man. • 5-speed auto. • CVT

DIMENSIONS/CAPACITY (LEGACY)
Passengers: 2/3; Wheelbase: 108.2 in.; H: 59.2/L: 186/W: 72 in.; Headroom F/R: 6.0/3.0 in.; Legroom F/R: 43/30 in.; Cargo volume: 15 cu. ft.; Fuel tank: 70L/regular/premium; Tow limit: 1,000 lb.; Load capacity: 850 lb.; Turning circle: 36.8 ft.; Ground clearance: 5.9 in.; Weight: 3,273–3,522 lb.

DIMENSIONS/CAPACITY (OUTBACK)
Passengers: 2/3; Wheelbase: 1,078 in.; H: 65.7/L: 188.1/W: 71.6 in.; Headroom F/R: 4.0/6.0 in.; Legroom F/R: 39.5/29 in.; Cargo volume: 36.5 cu. ft.; Fuel tank: 70L/regular; Tow limit: 2,700 lb.; Load capacity: 900 lb.; Turning circle: 39 ft.; Ground clearance: 8.6 in.; Weight: 3,540 lb.

Weak points: The base 2.5L engine is a sluggish performer, undoubtedly because of the car's heft. On the other hand, the more-powerful GT version is a fuel hog. Fuel economy, trails rivals like the Chevrolet Malibu, Ford Fusion, and Toyota Camry. Another mixed blessing: The stability control feature (VDC) adds exponential complexity to a vehicle that is already complicated to repair. Other minuses: Crosswinds require constant steering correction; excessive engine and road noise; limited rear access; front seats need more padding; interior garnishes look and feel cheap; the Mazda6 and Ford Fusion offer more cargo space; the V6 engine requires premium fuel; and these cars are very dealer-dependent for parts and servicing. God help you if the dealer goes under, or you need parts when dealers are cutting back on inventory. **New for 2011:** Carried over without any significant changes.

OVERVIEW: A competent full-time 4×4 performer for drivers who want to move up in size, comfort, and features. Available as a four-door sedan or five-door wagon, the Legacy is cleanly and conventionally styled.

COST ANALYSIS: Get a nearly identical leftover discounted 2011 model. **Best alternatives:** The Honda CR-V, Hyundai Tucson or Santa Fe, and Toyota RAV4. **Options:** Base models hooked to an automatic transmission are severely performance-challenged. Stay away from the Firestone and Bridgestone original-equipment tires. **Rebates:** $2,000 rebates and low-interest financing. **Depreciation:** Slower than average. **Insurance cost:** Average. **Parts supply/ cost:** Parts aren't easily found, and they can be costly. **Annual maintenance cost:** Average. **Warranty:** Bumper-to-bumper 3 years/60,000 km; powertrain 5 years/100,000 km; rust perforation 5 years/unlimited km. **Supplementary warranty:** A good idea. **Highway/city fuel economy:** *Legacy 2.5:* 7.4/10.6 L/100 km, 38/27 mpg. *Auto.:* 6.5/9.2 L/100 km, 43/31 mpg. *GT:* 8.0/11.5 L/100 km, 35/25 mpg. *3.6R:* 8.2/11.8 L/100 km, 34/24 mpg. *Outback 2.5:* 7.4/10.6 L/100 km, 38/27 mpg. *Auto.:* 6.9/9.5 L/100 km, 41/30 mpg. *3.6:* 8.2/11.8 L/100 km, 34/24 mpg.

OWNER-REPORTED PROBLEMS: *Legacy:* Passenger-side airbags are still disabled when normal-sized passengers are seated (a problem for years); sudden, unintended acceleration when in Park:

> The vehicle was in Park when it accelerated in reverse through a yard, crashing into a retaining wall.

Long delay to get up to speed when accelerating; cruise control and brake failures; steering shimmy and wobbles, and car sways from right to left (partially corrected by replacing the steering column dampening spring and force-balancing the tires). Excessive steering wheel, clutch, and brake vibration; airbag warning light comes on for no reason; head restraints force driver's head into a painful and unsafe chin-to-chest position (worse for short drivers), a problem plaguing all Subarus for several years; running lights do not illuminate high or far enough and headlights have a similar handicap; owners have to pay $50 twice per year to have the federally mandated tire-pressure monitoring system reset when they change tires in the spring and fall; driver-side floor mats "creep" toward the accelerator pedal. *Outback:* Almost four times the number of safety-related complaints registered for the 2010 Impreza and 44 incidences posted for the 2011 model. *2011:* passenger-side airbag is disabled even though an average-sized adult is seated; airbag alert comes on for no reason; defective original equipment Continental tires; when stopped on an incline with the engine running, car will roll back; driving lights illuminate only a small part of the roadway; excessive steering wheel pulsing and shaking. *2010:* Sudden, unintended acceleration:

> Sudden acceleration disabling the cruise control to slow down and then hitting the resume button caused the car to surge. The rpm increased from 2000 to 6000 rpm. This occurs whenever the set speed is 20 mph [32 km/h] greater than the current speed. The dealer could not correct this, claiming that the full acceleration is by design.

Chronic hesitation, stalling; steering shimmy, wobble, and vehicle wander; airbag warning light comes on for no reason; and passenger-side airbag may suddenly disable itself while vehicle is underway.

SERVICE BULLETIN-REPORTED PROBLEMS: *Legacy* and *Outback:* Highway speed vibration, harshness, and noise countermeasures; some vibrations require the installation of a free steering-wheel kit on 2010 and 2011 models says TSB #05-48-10R, published February 3, 2011; the sunroof binds when opening.

Suzuki

Suzuki proves that simply building good, cheap cars and SUVs isn't enough to succeed as an auto manufacturer in North America. You also have to have a large advertising budget and almost perfect timing in your launches and promotion. Suzuki never put much money into advertising, and it has had a revolving door of incompetent executives who have run the company into the ground. Most shoppers don't give the company a second thought, since many of its products were sold under GM's name.

And many of those who do buy what they think is a Suzuki, like the Equator pickup, are actually buying a Nissan Frontier—a good buy, but not a Suzuki. On the other hand, Suzuki's partnership with South Korean Daewoo was a fiasco that resulted in the entry of cheap, unreliable compacts that tarnished the Suzuki brand and have kept Suzuki sales in the basement.

In Canada, Suzuki sells only three models, if you don't include six Equator/Frontier pickups that were sold earlier this year (see page 409). They are the SX4 compact crossover; the Grand Vitara, a small SUV; and the latest arrival, the Kizashi, a sporty all-wheel-drive, mid-sized sedan. The Kizashi retails for $30,000 (plus $1,495 freight and PDI) and carries a 180 hp 2.4L 4-cylinder engine coupled to a continuously variable transmission (see Appendix I for the Kizashi rating).

JAPANESE CAR SALES IN CANADA—JULY 2011

	JULY 2011	JULY 2010	% CHG.	YTD 2011	YTD 2010	% CHG.
HONDA	8,818	11,615	–24.1	67,545	77,886	–13.3
Car	5,550	6,812	–18.5	40,607	46,829	–13.3
Truck	3,268	4,803	–32.0	26,938	31,057	–13.3
TOYOTA	12,167	14,882	–18.2	91,191	108,154	–15.7
Car	6,590	7,792	–15.4	47,210	61,238	–22.9
Truck	5,577	7,090	–21.3	43,981	46,916	–6.3
MAZDA	6,589	7,268	–9.3	41,405	48,127	–14.0
Car	5,475	6,082	–10.0	34,815	40,034	–13.0
Truck	1,114	1,186	–6.1	6,590	8,093	–18.6
NISSAN	7,523	8,318	–9.6	51,101	49,834	2.5
Car	4,614	5,396	–14.5	31,690	33,093	–4.2
Truck	2,909	2,922	–0.4	19,411	16,741	15.9
SUZUKI	460	935	–50.8	3,307	5,277	–37.3
Car	337	604	–44.2	2,186	3,640	–39.9
Truck	123	331	–62.8	1,121	1,637	–31.5
SUBARU	1,916	2,336	–18.0	16,093	15,684	2.6
Car	752	987	–23.8	6,938	6,610	5.0
Truck	1,164	1,349	–13.7	9,155	9,074	0.9
MITSUBISHI	1,682	1,672	0.6	12,015	11,511	4.4
Car	685	1,016	–32.6	4,361	6,595	–33.9
Truck	997	656	52.0	7,654	4,916	55.7
TOTAL	39,155	47,026	–16.7	282,657	316,473	–10.7
Car	24,003	28,689	–16.3	167,807	198,039	–15.3
Truck	15,152	18,337	–17.4	114,850	118,434	–3.0

Source: AIAMC / JAMA Canada (www.jama.ca/aq/news)

SX4 ★★★★

RATING: Above Average. This roomy little car is a winner because of its better-than-average overall performance, low price, and versatile body styles that rival many wagons and hatchbacks. What's worrisome is the company's huge losses and rumours that it will soon quit the North American market, where it has lost millions of dollars over the past decade. If Suzuki does leave, the car's resale value will fall, but servicing shouldn't be a problem. **Strong points:** All models are bargain-priced, and they deliver a lot of content. On the road, the SX4 performs fairly well. Its lightweight and competent engine eventually gets it up to cruising speed; handling is fairly nimble; the automatic transmission shifts smoothly; the ride quality is good; and brakes are adequate, though a bit soft. The tall roofline ensures plenty of headroom for all passengers, makes for easy passenger access, and enhances overall visibility. There's a surprising amount of occupant and cargo room, and legroom is on par with or better than most of its competition. Lots of glass all around, making the cabin appear much larger than it is. ABS and front and side curtain airbags are standard. NHTSA gives the car five stars for side-impact occupant protection and four stars for frontal and rollover crashworthiness. IIHS rates frontal offset and side-impact crashworthiness as "Good." **Weak points:** Acceleration is underwhelming, but acceptable; excessive engine and road noise, and the ride is jarring when passing over small bumps; fuel economy is sharply reduced with the AWD, but not so much with the automatic transmission. IIHS rates roof crashworthiness and head-restraint protection as "Marginal." **New for 2012:** Standard stability control and rear discs will be put on all sedan models and the Crossover's navigation system will be upgraded.

KEY FACTS

CANADIAN PRICE (SOFT): *Base sedan:* $17,835, *Auto.:* $18,795, *Sport:* $19,83, *Auto.:* $20,795, *Hatchback JX:* $20,435, *Hatchback JLX:* $24,835 **U.S. PRICE:** *Base sedan:* $15,195, *Auto.:* $18,795, *Sport:* $16,479, *Auto.:* $20,795, *Sportback:* $16,599, *Crossover AWD:* $16,999, **CANADIAN FREIGHT:** $1,395 **U.S. FREIGHT:** $765
POWERTRAIN (FRONT-DRIVE/AWD)
Engine: 2.0L 4-cyl. (150 hp);
Transmissions: 6-speed man. • CVT
DIMENSIONS/CAPACITY (SEDAN)
Passengers: 2/3; Wheelbase: 98 in.; H: 63/L: 163/W: 69.1 in.; Headroom F/R: 4.5/3.5 in.; Legroom F/R: 40/25 in.; Cargo volume: 16 cu. ft.; Fuel tank: 50L/regular; Tow limit: No towing; Load capacity: 850 lb.; Turning circle: 34.8 ft.; Ground clearance: 6.3 in.; Weight: 29,990 lb.

OVERVIEW: Available in both front-drive and all-wheel-drive trims, the SX4 crossover is a fun-to-drive, inexpensive small SUV-like hatchback with interior features and performance qualities that make it a great alternative to the top-ranked small cars. Practical dimensions, combined with a lengthy list of features and sporty dynamics, make the SX4 a good choice for anyone who's put off by the higher-priced competition. Reliability hasn't been a major issue, but a limited servicing network, less-than-average fuel economy with the AWD, and a cheap-looking plastic-wrapped cabin has turned away many buyers.

COST ANALYSIS: Get the practically identical 2011 model if it's offered with a 20 percent discount/rebate. **Best alternatives:** The Honda Fit or Civic (2011), Mazda3, Nissan Versa or Rogue, and Toyota Yaris or Matrix are affordable alternatives that have more-established reputations. **Options:** Stay away from the Firestone and Bridgestone original-equipment tires. The Garmin GPS option looks like a real bargain. **Rebates:** $2,000 rebates and low-interest financing. **Depreciation:** Average. A 2007 base SX4 that originally sold for $16,000 is now worth $7,500. **Insurance cost:** Average. **Parts supply/cost:** Parts aren't hard to find, and are moderately priced. **Annual maintenance cost:** Average. **Warranty:** Bumper-to-bumper 3 years/60,000 km; powertrain 5 years/100,000 km; rust perforation 5 years/unlimited km. **Supplementary warranty:** It's a good idea to get an extended powertrain warranty. **Highway/city fuel economy:** *Base sedan:* 6.0/9.0 L/100 km, 47/31 mpg. *CVT:* 6.1/8.0 L/100 km, 46/35 mpg. *SP sedan:* 6.2/9.1 L/100 km, 46/31 mpg. *Sport sedan CVT:* 6.7/8.9 L/100 km, 42/32. *Hatchback:* 6.3/9.1 L/100 km, 45/31 mpg. *Hatchback CVT:* 6.4/8.2 L/100 km, 44/34 mpg. *JX:* 6.6/9.3 L/100 km, 42/30 mpg. *JX CVT:* 6.9/8.9 L/100 km, 41/31 mpg.

OWNER-REPORTED PROBLEMS: Only one safety-related complaint for the 2011s: The headlights don't automatically turn on when the dash lights are lit. The 2010 models are also relatively clean of safety defects with only 10 owner comments posted by NHTSA: airbags fail to deploy; vehicle surges forward while cruising; stalling when underway; floor mats interfere with the accelerator and brake pedals; and the tire valve stem pressure sensors corrode and split. These few complaints are all the more surprising because Suzuki is a small player in the automaker game and its vehicles are cheaper than most in the small car category.

Other owner complaints mostly target the fuel system and fit and finish, where water leaks are common, paint is easily chipped, and the unprotected metal is quick to rust.

Toyota

"Blame the Victim"

Granted, Toyota is having a bad year. Through the end of July, its sales in Canada fell 15.9 percent, while the number of Lexus buyers declined by 13.4 percent, according to DesRosiers Automotive Consultants.

Part of this downturn can be blamed on the devastating earthquake and tsunami in Japan, but another reason is that shoppers don't trust Toyota as much as they once did. Owner complaints of sudden, unintended acceleration, brake failures, and no-haggle prices have sent shoppers scurrying to Ford, GM, Hyundai, Kia, and Volkswagen dealers. Camry mid-year sales are off by a third, while Chrysler trucks have been taken off life support.

I have recommended Toyota models since the early '70s, when the company first came to Canada. Their vehicles were reliable and cheap (though rust-prone), and most disputed warranty claims were paid without forcing customers to file small claims court lawsuits.

All this came to an end over a decade ago when bean counters took over the company and adopted the mantra that profit and market share trump quality and fair prices.

Let's look at prices. In my opinion, Toyota and its dealers used the Toyota Access program to keep retail prices artificially high in Canada. *Lemon-Aid* made a formal complaint to Ottawa, alleging Toyota price-fixing, and the next thing we knew, Toyota settled and agreed to give $2 million to a Canadian charity— without admitting guilt. Slick, eh?

Fast-forward to Toyota's sudden-acceleration woes over the past two years. Although NHTSA logged complaints confirm that Toyota reps stonewalled thousands of Toyota car and truck owners, these same Toyota executives and lawyers said they were unaware that the vehicles would suddenly accelerate out of control. Toyota's president cried as he testified before the U.S. Congress in 2010 when confronted with complaint records. Shortly thereafter, Toyota recalled almost its entire lineup to change floor carpets and throttles.

There was no admission of guilt, nor any confirmation by Toyota that its own internal service bulletins (published in *Lemon-Aid*) confirmed that 2002 and 2003 Camrys can suddenly accelerate due to defective computer modules.

And get this: Apple Inc. co-founder Steve Wozniak repeatedly called Toyota over the course of several months to report brake failures with his Prius. Toyota officials ignored him. However, when he mentioned the problem in an aside during an Apple press conference, all hell broke loose. The company fixed his car and recalled thousands of others.

After the congressional hearings the U.S. government fined Toyota $48 million for dragging its feet in implementing the above recalls. In the meantime, owners swear that electronic component failures are the real culprit and Toyota still ignores their pleas. Toyota responds that the problem isn't electronic-based but just in case it's mistaken, a brake override feature has been added. European vehicles have had this safety device as a standard feature for years.

Yes, Toyota has put profit ahead of people's lives. My distrust of the company and its Canadian administration has deepened.

With the redesigned 2012s, Toyota will likely continue with the same cost-cutting, "decontenting" practices that doomed its earlier models and caused a dramatic erosion of Toyota safety and quality. Why? Because it's easy to get away with. Much of the cheapening of Toyota vehicles will go unnoticed in the showroom since lower-quality content and reduced performance isn't seen until you have lived with your car or truck for a few months. Honda, for example, cheapened its redesigned 2012 Civic, forcing *Consumer Reports* to change its "Recommended Buy" rating to "Not Recommended" in the space of a few months.

Smart shoppers should wait until mid-2012 to let the first year of the Yaris and Sienna redesigns go by to avoid spending money on hype and hope.

Toyota's Quality Myth

Toyota's image as a builder of quality vehicles has been legendary, with both J.D. Power and Associates and the Insurance Institute for Highway Safety giving the company high marks for building reliable, crashworthy vehicles. Not so, *Consumer Reports* and the U.S. Department of Transportation's National Highway Traffic and Safety Administration. They found that many Toyota models were unreliable and had serious throttle and brake defects.

Then, in the late '90s, Toyota's reputation took a battering when angry owners refused to pay $6,000–$9,000 to repair the sludged-up engines used on many Toyota and Lexus models. After first blaming the problem on poor owner maintenance, the automaker relented and quietly settled most claims (see *www. oilgelsettlement.com*).

Toyota's also blamed the victim in the first slew of incidents alleging sudden, unintended acceleration and brake failures that surfaced during the past decade. Toyota finally admitted it had a safety-related defect, paid a fine of over $48 million fine, and settled other lawsuits out of court.

One would think Toyota has learned to fess up when it messes up, but recent developments this year show the contrary is the case. Remember the case of Mark Saylor, a California Highway Patrol officer loaned a Lexus ES350 by a San Diego dealer? The Lexus suddenly accelerated, flipped and burst into flames. As the car careened out of control, the occupants dialed 911 and you can hear them screaming in terror.

The dispatcher asks where they are passing, and Lastrella is heard asking someone in the car where they are. He exclaims: "We're going 120 [mph]! Mission Gorge! We're in trouble—we can't—there's no brakes, Mission Gorge...end freeway half mile."

The dispatcher asks if they can turn the car off.

Lastrella doesn't answer and says repeatedly, "We are now approaching the intersection, we're approaching the intersection, we're approaching the intersection."

The last sounds heard on the tape are someone saying "hold on" and "pray." Lastrella says: "Oh shoot...oh...oh." Then a woman screams.

Saylor, 45, his wife, their 13-year-old daughter, and Saylor's brother-in-law, Lastrella, died in the crash on August 28, 2009.

Toyota blamed the driver, denied knowledge of similar incidents reported by other Toyota and Lexus owners, and refused to support its dealer, who claimed Toyota electronics was to blame for the crash, and was sued separately. Bowing to public pressure, the company finally paid $10 million to the officer's estate on February 25, 2011, in an out-of-court settlement. The automaker asked that a gag order be issued to prevent disclosure of the settlement sum. This was refused (*John Saylor v. Toyota Motor Corp.*, 37-2010-00086718, California Superior Court, San Diego County).

But the story doesn't end there.

Last August, Toyota rejected a petition from Phillip Pretty, the owner of a Ford Explorer that was hit by the out-of-control Lexus speeding behind him at more than 160 km/h. Pretty was hospitalized with a concussion and injuries to a shoulder and knee. Toyota denied all responsibility—in the same accident it had paid $10 million a few months earlier to settle.

Oh, what a feeling! Toyota!

Toyota has also systematically rejected owner complaints over dangerously defective drivetrains that possibly affect all of its 1999–2011 lineup. A look at NHTSA's safety complaint database shows a ton of complaints alleging these vehicles have an electronic module glitch that causes a "lag and lurch" when accelerating, decelerating, or turning.

Toyota knows that if it confirms the defect is electronic in nature, the company re-opens the sudden acceleration polemic and could be forced to replace electronic control modules on millions of vehicles—modules that cost far more than a floormat anchor.

Also, perusal of *Lemon-Aid* readers' letters and emails, as well as NHTSA reports, shows that recent-model Toyotas have been plagued by engineering mistakes that put occupants' lives in jeopardy. These include Corollas that wander all over the road, Prius hybrids that temporarily lose the ability to brake, and Tundra trucks with rear ends that bounce uncontrollably over even the smoothest roadways. Other safety failures include engine and transmission malfunctions; fuel spewing out of cracked gas tanks; sudden, unintended acceleration; gauge lights that can't be seen in daylight; and electrical system glitches that can transform a power door into a guillotine. This year's *Lemon-Aid* has lowered the ratings on a number of Toyota's most popular models to reflect these dangers and to warn buyers of the potential for harm.

A quick glance at NHTSA's 2010 safety defects complaint log shows that the Camry, Corolla, and Prius are runaway bestsellers—"runaway" in the sense that you may find yourself an unwilling hostage in a car careening out of control with a stuck accelerator, no brakes, and limited steering.

When running properly, Toyotas do hold up very well over the years, are especially forgiving of owner neglect, and cost very little to service at independent garages. But the kicker for most buyers is how little most Toyotas depreciate: It's not unusual to see a five-year-old Camry or Avalon selling for over half its original selling price (most Detroit Three vehicles sell for half their price after only three years). But this is not the case with Toyota trucks, hybrids, and the Sienna minivan, which depreciate quite rapidly. Evidently word has gotten out that, first, these vehicles have serious performance and quality deficiencies, and second, hybrid fuel economy is not all that impressive when one considers that a $3,000 (U.S.) battery pack replacement can buy a lot of gas.

YARIS ★ ★ ★

RATING: Average. Yaris is a function-over-form classic commuter car, where practicality trumps style and driving pleasure. Not a sporty performer by any stretch. It doesn't feel as refined as a Fiat 500, as powerful as a Volkswagen Golf, or as solid as a Ford Fiesta. **Strong points:** Ride and handling have improved with this year's redesign. Plenty of usable power; better road feel with SE models, thanks to electric power steering; good fuel economy; lots of interior space up front; a nice array of storage areas, including a huge trunk and standard 60/40 split-folding rear seats; well-designed instruments and controls don't look as cheap as last year's version; comfortable, high front seating; easy rear access; and good visibility fore and aft. Yaris passes over uneven terrain with less jarring movements than do other minicompacts, and is quite nimble when cornering. Surprisingly quiet for an economy car. NHTSA gives the Yaris four stars for frontal, side, and rollover crash protection; liftback versions get five stars for front and side protection. IIHS rates frontal offset and side crashworthiness protection as "Good." **Weak points:** Not overly generous with standard features. Car feels underpowered, especially when equipped with the automatic transmission. The same transmission doesn't downshift quickly or smoothly. The 2012's restyling is dull; an example of the bland leading the bland. Interior ergonomics are not the best; rear seating is cramped. Its tall profile and light weight make the car vulnerable to side-wind buffeting; the base tires provide poor traction in wet conditions; there's excessive torque steer (sudden pulling to one side when accelerating); some wind noise from the base of the windshield; and the steering wheel is mounted too far away for some drivers. Plastic trim in L models looks and feels cheap. Gas mileage doesn't match the competition. IIHS rates head-restraint protection as "Marginal." **New for 2012:** Restyled (yes, the instrument panel has been moved from the centre of the dash back to in front of the driver, due to popular demand). The car is 2 inches longer than the previous version, and 3 inches longer overall. Toyota has reserved the sedan version of the Yaris for fleet sales, as buyers chose hatchback versions 70 percent of the time.

OVERVIEW: Positioned just below the Corolla, the Yaris manages to offer about the same amount of passenger space, thanks to a tall roof, low floor height, and upright seating position. The Yaris has a more-modern look with its large windows, additional legroom, and high-quality trim and seats that give it the allure of a much more expensive car.

COST ANALYSIS: Get the 2012 model for the performance upgrades. **Best alternatives:** The Honda Fit is the best of the competition—it's got more room and is a lot more fun to drive. Nevertheless, the Ford Focus, Honda Civic (2011) or Fit, Hyundai Accent, Kia Soul, Rio, or Forte hatchback, Mazda2 or Mazda3, Nissan Versa, and Suzuki SX4 are all worthwhile candidates. **Options:** Consider snow tires and better-quality 14-inch tires for improved traction in inclement weather. Beware of option loading, where you have to buy a host of overpriced, nonessential, impractical features in order to get the one or two amenities you require. **Rebates:** 2011 models will get $1,500–$2,000 rebates early in the new year. **Depreciation:** Much slower than average. **Insurance cost:** Below average. **Parts supply/cost:** Easily found and reasonably priced. **Annual maintenance cost:** Costs over the long term are predicted to be low. **Warranty:** Bumper-to-bumper 3 years/60,000 km; powertrain 5 years/100,000 km; rust perforation 5 years/unlimited km. **Supplementary warranty:** Not needed. **Highway/city fuel economy:** *Man.:* 5.5/6.9 L/100 km, 51/41 mpg. *Auto.:* 5.7/7.0 L/100 km, 50/40 mpg.

OWNER COMPLAINTS: Passenger-side airbag is disabled when an average-sized passenger is seated, requiring that the warning light be constantly reset; airbags did not deploy in a high-speed frontal collision; vehicle wanders all over the road, requiring constant steering corrections; driver-side window spontaneously shattered.

KEY FACTS

CANADIAN PRICE (NEGOTIABLE): *Sedan:* $14,990, *Auto:* $15,990, *CE:* $13,995, *LE:* $15,350, *RS:* $19,530 **U.S. PRICE:** *L:* $14,115, *SE:* $17,200 **CANADIAN FREIGHT:** $1,350 **U.S. FREIGHT:** $760

POWERTRAIN (FRONT-DRIVE)
Engine: 1.5L 4-cyl. (106 hp); Transmissions: 5-speed man. • 4-speed auto.

DIMENSIONS/CAPACITY
Passengers: 2/3; Wheelbase: 100.4 in.; H: 57.5/L: 169.3/W: 66.7 in.; Headroom F/R: 3.5/1.5 in.; Legroom F/R: 40.5/27 in.; Cargo volume: 13.7 cu. ft.; Fuel tank: 42L/regular; Tow limit: 700 lb.; Load capacity: 845 lb.; Turning circle: 30.8 ft.; Ground clearance: 5.5 in.; Weight: 2,315–2,355 lb.

SERVICE BULLETIN-REPORTED PROBLEMS: Troubleshooting a windshield back glass ticking noise.

COROLLA ★★

KEY FACTS

CANADIAN PRICE (NEGOTIABLE): *CE:* $15,450, *S:* $20,815, *XRS:* $23,235
U.S. PRICE: *Base:* $15,900 **CANADIAN FREIGHT:** $1,390 **U.S. FREIGHT:** $825
POWERTRAIN (FRONT-DRIVE)
Engine: 1.8L 4-cyl. (132 hp); Transmissions: 5-speed man. • 4-speed auto.
DIMENSIONS/CAPACITY
Passengers: 2/3; Wheelbase: 102.4 in.; H: 57.7/L: 178.7/W: 69.3 in.; Headroom F/R: 4.0/2.0 in.; Legroom F/R: 41/28 in.; Cargo volume: 12.3 cu. ft.; Fuel tank: 50L/regular; Tow limit: 1,500 lb.; Load capacity: 825 lb.; Turning circle: 37.1 ft.; Ground clearance: 5.8 in., *XRS:* 5.3 in.; Weight: 2,722 lb.

RATING: Below Average. The Corolla has dropped two notches in *Lemon-Aid's* rating due to its large number of safety-related complaints. **Strong points:** The 1.8L engine is a quiet, competent performer noted for its pleasant ride. Handling is responsive and predictable, though a bit slow. The user-friendly interior ergonomics are enhanced by the flat rear floor, which provides more room. High crashworthiness scores and standard electronic stability control add to the car's safety; side and side curtain airbags are standard on the LE and Sport. A high resale value is another plus. **Weak points:** Average acceleration requires constant shifting to keep in the pack; automatic-transmission-equipped versions are slower still; clumsy emergency handling; lots of high-speed wind and road noise; limited front legroom; head restraints block rear visibility; and plastic interior panels and trim look cheap. Reports of airbags deploying inadvertently or failing to deploy. IIHS rates head-restraint protection as "Poor." Overall reliability is average to below average. **New for 2012:** Nothing significant.

OVERVIEW: A step up from the Yaris, the Corolla has long been Toyota's conservative standard-bearer in the compact sedan class. Over the years, however, the car has grown in size and price, to the point where it can now be considered a small family sedan. All Corollas ride on a front-drive platform with independent suspension on all wheels. There are three variants: the value-leader base version and the more-upscale LE and S models. Power is supplied by a torquey 132 hp 1.8L twin-cam 4-cylinder teamed with a standard 5-speed manual gearbox or optional 4-speed automatic.

COST ANALYSIS: Selling prices are firming up as the market turns to smaller cars. **Best alternatives:** Other small cars that are good investments include the 2011 Honda Civic, Hyundai Elantra, and Mazda3 or Mazda6. **Options:** For better steering response and additional high-speed stability, order the optional 185/65R14 tires that come with the LE. **Rebates:** $1,500 rebates, low-interest financing, and modest discounting early in 2012. **Depreciation:** Much slower than average. **Insurance cost:** Average. **Parts supply/cost:** Parts are easily found and reasonably priced. **Annual maintenance cost:** Lower than average. **Warranty:** Bumper-to-bumper 3 years/60,000 km; powertrain 5 years/100,000 km; rust perforation 5 years/unlimited km. **Supplementary warranty:** Not needed. **Highway/city fuel economy:** *1.8 man.:* 5.6/7.5 L/100 km, 50/38 mpg. *2.4 auto.:* 6.7/9.5 L/100 km, 42/30 mpg.

OWNER-REPORTED PROBLEMS: Owners report a major steering defect that makes the Corolla unsafe to drive. Steering tends to allow the vehicle to wander all over the road; car cannot track a straight line on a flat road (alignments and a new steering rack don't help):

> It is very difficult to keep the vehicle within the lane. If it deviates (which is normal) and a correction is made, the car over-reacts and the vehicle veers to the other side of the lane. Another correction puts the vehicle back to the other side. So the vehicle moves side to side.

Sudden acceleration accompanied by total brake failure:

> While driving 50 mph [80 km/h] the vehicle suddenly accelerated. As the vehicle is accelerating, the contact is trying to slow the vehicle down by applying the brakes. At this time the brakes are malfunctioning and increasing in speed. The contact was unable to slow the vehicle down and crashed into another vehicle.

Car speeds up or slows down on its own:

> I see variations of about 500 rpm on the tachometer. Sometimes when letting off the throttle pedal, the car keeps going and doesn't get the message it's supposed to slow down. This is scary, it's almost like the car thinks it's on cruise control when it's not at all (here is a link to a forum where owners of 2011 Toyota Corollas describe exactly the same safety issue with the car: *www.corollaforum.com/showthread. php?p=285#post285*).

Sudden brake failure:

I went over a dip in the road at about 40 mph [64 km/h] and went to hit the brakes while taking a turn that was approaching a stoplight when the brakes would not let me push them down and would give me feedback as if ABS was active. After a couple seconds I was able to reapply pressure to the brakes to stop. This happened a total of eight times in 2,100 miles [3,380 km]. The car has been in some close calls, and all the incidents happened after hitting a dip while trying to reduce my speed from over 50 mph [80 km/h] to the time of hitting the dips.

Driver cannot open the rear window with the other windows closed, as it produces a dramatic vibration and shaking inside the vehicle; car parked on a small hill and with the parking brake applied will still roll away; harsh downshift when stopping; seatbelt warning alarm isn't loud enough; instrument-panel rattling; front-seat squeaking, and the front power seat grinds and groans.

SERVICE BULLETIN-REPORTED PROBLEMS: Engine rattle/knock on startup; steering wheel feels off-centre; premature front brake pad wear; troubleshooting a rear windshield ticking noise.

CAMRY, CAMRY HYBRID ★★

The Toyota Camry.

RATING: Below Average. The Camry is another example of one of Toyota's "good cars gone bad." **Strong points:** Last year's redesign corrected most of the Camry's performance gaps; a retuned SE trim level delivers sporty handling; the base 4-cylinder is a competent, responsive performer; surprisingly, the 3.5L V6 powertrain set-up delivers fuel economy figures that are almost as good as the base 4-banger; there's a nice array of standard safety and convenience features that include a telescoping steering column, 10 airbags, stability control, antilock brakes, and four-wheel disc brakes that are larger than those on the 2011 version. The ride has smoothed out; the interior is quieter; instruments and controls are well laid-out in an interior that has a richer look and feel; interior passenger and storage space is better than average. Unlike the Sienna minivan and Toyota's trucks, the Camry keeps a high resale value. NHTSA gives the Camry and its Hybrid variant four stars for side crashworthiness and rollover resistance and three stars for frontal crash protection. IIHS also gives the Camry its top rating for frontal offset, side, and roof crash protection. **Weak points:** The same safety-related failures are reported year after year and will likely to increase with the 2012 redesign. These defects can be especially lethal to older drivers with slower reflexes. Indeed, probably few Camry drivers have the necessary driving skills to confront sudden engine surging or delayed transmission engagement when accelerating, merging, passing, or turning. No manual transmission is offered. IIHS rates head-restraint effectiveness as only "Marginal." Hybrid fuel economy is overstated by almost 30 percent, says *Consumer Reports* and almost everyone else. **New for 2012:** A quieter 2.5L 4-cylinder engine which features reduced vibration levels and produces 178 horsepower, an increase of nine horses. The new Hybrid engine is quicker, more fuel-efficient, and less polluting. The 6-speed automatic transmission has a taller final drive ratio, which saves fuel, but slows acceleration. There's also an improved suspension (the SE suspension is much stiffer) and an upgraded, slightly roomier interior. The LE and Hybrid return lighter by 150 and 220 pounds, respectively, and the fuel tank holds four litres less fuel. Cabin noise has been reduced by adding more soundproofing to the pillars, doors, and floor.

KEY FACTS

CANADIAN PRICE (NEGOTIABLE): *LE:* $25,310, *Convenience:* $26,700, *SE:* $27,755, *LE V6:* $29,020, *XLE:* $31,235, *SE V6:* $34,255, *XLE V6:* $36,410, *Hybrid:* $31,310 **U.S. PRICE:** *L:* $21,995, *LE:* $22,500, *SE:* $23,000, *SE V6:* $26,640, *XLE:* $24,725, *XLE V6:* $29,845, *Hybrid:* $25,900, *XLE:* $27,400 **CANADIAN FREIGHT:** $1,490 **U.S. FREIGHT:** $760
POWERTRAIN (FRONT-DRIVE)
Engines: 2.4L 4-cyl. Hybrid (200 hp) • 2.5L 4-cyl. (178 hp) • 3.5L V6 (268 hp); Transmissions: 6-speed man. • 6-speed auto. • CVT
DIMENSIONS/CAPACITY
Passengers: 2/3; Wheelbase: 109.3 in.; H: *Camry:* 57.9, *Hybrid:* 57.9/L: 189.2/ W: 71.7 in.; Headroom F/R: 5.0/2.0 in.; Legroom F/R: 42/29 in.; Cargo volume: *Camry:* 15 cu. ft., *Hybrid:* 10.6 cu. ft.; Fuel tank: *Camry:* 66L, *Hybrid:* 65L/ regular/premium; Tow limit: *Camry:* 1,000 lb., *Hybrid:* Not advised; Load capacity: 900 lb.; Turning circle: 36.1 ft.; Ground clearance: *Camry:* 5.3 in., *Hybrid:* 5.9 in.; Weight: *Camry:* 3,190 lb., *Hybrid:* 3,638 lb.

OVERVIEW: The Camry is based on the Avalon platform and is available as a four-door sedan only. Power is supplied by a peppy 178 hp 2.5L 4-cylinder engine, a 187 hp 2.4L gas-electric hybrid 4-cylinder, or a 268 hp 3.5L V6. The base engine can be coupled to a 6-speed manual or a 6-speed automatic, and the V6 uses a 6-speed automatic. Hybrids come with a continuously variable transmission (CVT). There are many standard features available on all Camrys: side airbags, side curtain airbags, a driver's knee airbag, and anti-lock four-wheel disc brakes; stability and traction control can be found on the higher-end models and the Hybrid (traction/ anti-skid control). Rear seats have shoulder belts for the middle passenger; low-beam lights are quite bright; and the headlights switch on and off automatically as conditions change.

COST ANALYSIS: Both the Camry and its main rival, the Honda Accord, have lost considerable sales traction to the Hyundai Sonata, Ford Fusion, and Nissan Altima. Through the first half of this year, Camry sales in Canada were down 38.8 per cent due to the earthquake and tsunami in Japan and press reports in North America that Toyotas were unsafe and had lost their quality edge. Now shoppers are looking for the deal that best suits their pocketbook. In an effort to attract buyers, Toyota says it will hold the line on prices and plans to offer substantial price reductions and rebates before year's end through the fall of 2012. **Best alternatives:** The Honda Accord, Hyundai Elantra, Mazda5 or Mazda6, and Nissan Sentra or Altima. Next year both the Accord and Altima will be redesigned. **Options:** Stay away from the optional moonroof: It robs you of much-needed headroom and exposes you to deafening wind roar, rattling, and leaks. Original equipment Firestone and Bridgestone tires should be shunned in favour of better-performing tires recommended by *thetirerack.com:*

> The car has Bridgestone Turanza EL 400–02 tires, which had 689 miles [1,109 km/h] on them. The rear driver side tire failed at 60 mph [96 km/h] when the tread split. After reading all the similar complaints by other Toyota car owners, I believe these tires are dangerous. After a very ugly discussion with the dealership, the one tire was replaced, but Toyota would not replace the remaining three.

Rebates: $3,000 rebates, plus low-interest financing and very attractive leasing deals in 2012. **Depreciation:** Lower than average; in Canada, safety complaints and slow sales haven't affected the Camry's resale value. For example, a 2007 entry-level Camry LE that sold for $25,800 is still worth $13,000. Most Detroit vehicles lose half their value after three years. **Insurance cost:** Higher than average. **Parts supply/cost:** Owners report long service waits for their Hybrids. Parts are generally moderately priced. **Annual maintenance cost:** Average. **Warranty:** Bumper-to-bumper 3 years/60,000 km; powertrain 5 years/100,000 km; rust perforation 5 years/unlimited km. **Supplementary warranty:** Not needed. **Highway/city fuel economy:** *Hybrid:* Supposedly averages 5.7 L/100 km and 50 mpg for city and highway driving combined, but many owners say their vehicle's real-world fuel consumption is much more. *2.5 SE man.:* 6.1/9.5 L/100 km, 46/30 mpg. *2.4 auto.:* 6.1/9.0 L/100 km, 46/31 mpg. *3.5 V6:* 7.0/10.7 L/100 km, 40/26 mpg. Owners say fuel-economy figures are much lower than advertised:

> Brand new 2011 Camry, 4-cylinder: 19 mpg city, 21 mpg highway after multiple repeated measurements. Driving in manual mode does not help as the manual mode is very misleading on the steptronic as well.

OWNER-REPORTED PROBLEMS: 64 safety-related failures have been reported to NHTSA for the 2011 Camry, and 303 incidences have been reported with the 2010 version. Normally one would expect about 50 complaints a year. As seen with other Toyota models (like the 2010 Prius, which has received 1,700 complaints), sudden, unintended acceleration without any brakes is the top reported problem for Camrys, with an added twist: They still speed out of control after having recall work done:

While depressing the brake pedal and attempting to merge into a parking space at approximately 20 mph [32 km/h] my 2011 Camry suddenly accelerated and crashed into a brick wall. There was damage to the building and to the front end of the vehicle. The air bags did not deploy.

An airline pilot and Camry owner blames electronic computer module programming that overrides driver input:

I was driving my 2010 Camry in the Great Smokey Mountains descending a mountain road. I tested downshifting at several speeds into various gears to determine if it was possible to slow down the car under runaway accelerator conditions. I had wrongly assumed that bad drivers had failed to use the controls of the car to slow down and stop such vehicles. The computer refused to accept my command to downshift into 1st gear at speeds above 25 mph [40 km/h]. I did not try higher speeds into 2nd. Clearly the product manager and program engineers at Toyota do not understand that saving the transmission or engine from stress could lead to destruction of that same car and [its] occupants in their foolish decision to limit driver command and control.

Other safety problems reported: Airbags fail to deploy; when accelerating from a stop, the vehicle hesitates, sometimes to a count of three, before suddenly accelerating; and when decelerating, the vehicle speeds up, as if the cruise control were engaged. The close placement of the brake and accelerator pedals also causes unwanted acceleration due to driver error; however, this cannot explain the large number of incidences of sudden acceleration reported. Frequent failures of the engine cam head, which is often back ordered; transmission shift lever can be inadvertently knocked into Reverse or Neutral when the vehicle is underway; harsh up- and down-shifting; vehicle may roll backwards when parked on an incline; electronic power steering operates erratically and is sometimes unresponsive.

There have also been reports that the steering constantly pulls the car to the left, into oncoming traffic, no matter how many alignments you get; one car caught on fire after being plugged into a block heater; the centre console below the gear shift becomes extremely hot; Hybrid's lower beam lights are inadequate for lighting the highway; excessively bright LED tail/brake lights will impair the vision of drivers in trailing vehicles; inaccurate speedometer readings; gasoline in the fuel tank hits the tank baffle with a loud bang; wheels locked up; driver-seat lumbar support may be painful for some drivers; a strong "out-gassing" odour may permeate the cabin; windows often stick in the up position; rear windshield distortion when viewed through the rear-view mirror during night driving; and head restraints obstruct driver's rearward vision. Reports of the front windshield cracking from the driver-side upper left corner and gradually extended toward the middle of the windshield. Glass sunroof implodes and in one incident the rear window exploded while the vehicle was stopped in traffic.

Passenger-side window fell out; front windshield distortion looks like little bubbles are embedded in the glass; rear window-defrosting wires don't clear the upper top of the windshield; a number of Hybrid AC failures have also been reported. Owners say the Camry is a "rat-hotel":

> While driving 40 mph [64 km/h], the driver noticed a rat crawled from under the passenger seat into the glove compartment and into the air conditioner. The [sight] of the rat almost caused the driver to crash. The contact was able to get the rat out of the vehicle. Two days later the contact took the vehicle to the dealer to repair the back seat and the seat belt that the rat has chewed through and also clean the air conditioner.

SERVICE BULLETIN-REPORTED PROBLEMS: A Toyota secret warranty (Campaign # (LSC) 90K) will cover the cost to replace the VVT-I oil hose in some V6-equipped Camrys. When the oil hose fails, it will cause unusual engine noise and make the engine run hot. This campaign will expire March 31, 2013. Uneven rear brake wear:

UNEVEN REAR BRAKE PAD WEAR

BULLETIN NO.: T-SB-0366-10   DATE: DECEMBER 23, 2010

YEAR(S)	MODEL(S)	ADDITIONAL INFORMATION
2007–2008	Camry	WMI(s): 4T1, 4T4
2007–2011	Camry	WMI(s): JTN

Some 2007–11 Camry vehicles may exhibit uneven rear brake pad wear due to corrosion between the pad backing plate and mounting bracket. The outer pad may wear more at the top of the pad versus the bottom. The vehicle may also exhibit a grinding noise during braking due to metal-to-metal contact between the rotor and the pad backing plate.

This repair is covered under the Toyota Comprehensive Warranty. This warranty is in effect for 36 months or 36,000 miles, whichever occurs first, from the vehicle's in-service date.

Warranty application is limited to occurrence of the specified condition described in this bulletin.

PREVIOUS PART NUMBER	CURRENT PART NUMBER	PART NAME	QTY
47821–06052	Same	Mounting, Rear Disc Brake Cylinder, RH	1
47822–08052	Same	Mounting, Rear Disc Brake Cylinder, LH	1
04466–06090	Same	Pad Kit, Disc Brake, Rear	1
04946–06070	Same	Shim Kit, Anti Squeal (For Rear Disc Brake)	As Needed

1. Confirm the complaint condition (grinding noise from the rear brakes and uneven rear pad wear due to corrosion between the pad backing plate and mounting bracket).
2. Replace the rear brake pads and Caliper/Pad Mounting Brackets (both sides).
3. Machine or replace rear rotors as needed.

Remedy for a front/rear suspension noise that occurs when passing over bumps in the road; a front door trim panel rattle; underbody rattling; and troubleshooting a windshield back glass ticking noise.

PRIUS

bad buy ★

RATING: Not Recommended. Sudden acceleration, no brakes or weak brakes, and a cruise control that doesn't turn off are scary enough. But what about a steering column that becomes unhinged? Bottom line: Don't buy a Prius. **Strong points:** Good fuel economy and acceleration in most situations, and little cabin noise. NHTSA gave Prius a five-star rating for side crash protection, and four stars for front-impact protection and rollover resistance. IIHS gave its top, "Good," rating for frontal offset, side, and head-restraint protection. **Weak points:** The car is too darn dangerous to drive; owners are still reporting that the brakes give out when they pass over a bump in the road:

> I have a 2011 Prius and if while I am braking, I drive over a bump in the road, the brakes release. I must re-apply the brakes to re-engage them. I feel this is very dangerous. There are numerous website references to this problem. When will a recall happen before someone has a serious accident?

It's also pricey; Honda's Insight sells for almost $4,000 less ($27,800 versus $23,900). Poorer performance in cold weather; battery pack will eventually cost about $3,000 (U.S.) to replace; fuel economy may be 20 percent less than advertised; 50 percent depreciation after five years; higher-than-average insurance premiums; dealer-dependent servicing means higher servicing costs; rear seating is cramped for three adults; sales and servicing

KEY FACTS

CANADIAN PRICE (NEGOTIABLE): *Base:* $27,800, *Premium Package auto.:* $30,045, *Premium with Solar Panel Option:* $31,865, *Touring Package:* $31,865, *Technology Package:* $37,395 **U.S. PRICE:** *Prius II:* $22,800, *Prius III:* $23,800, *Prius IV:* $26,600, *Prius V:* $28,070 **CANADIAN FREIGHT:** $1,490 **U.S. FREIGHT:** $760 **POWERTRAIN (FRONT-DRIVE)** Engine: 1.8L 4-cyl. (134 hp); Transmission: CVT **DIMENSIONS/CAPACITY** Passengers: 2/3; Wheelbase: 106.3 in.; H: 58.3/L: 175.6/W: 68.7 in.; Headroom F/R: 4.0/2.0 in.; Legroom F/R: 40.5/30 in.; Cargo volume: 15.7 cu. ft.; Fuel tank: 45L/regular; Tow limit: No towing; Load capacity: 810 lb.; Turning circle: 34.2 ft.; Ground clearance: 5.5 in.; Weight: 3,042 lb.

may not be available outside large urban areas; and the CVT cannot be easily repaired by independent agencies. Owners say the Prius is slow-steering, has lots of body roll when cornering, and is stall-prone. Braking isn't very precise or responsive, and the car is very unstable when hit by crosswinds. Highway rescuers are wary of the car's 500-volt electrical system, and take special courses to prevent electrocution and avoid toxic battery components. Reliability is subpar and performance is summed up quite well by Ontario-based car columnist and editor of *Straight-Six.com* John LeBlanc, who calls the Prius "the worst car of the last decade." **New for 2012:** Delayed until late fall due to the earthquake, the 2012 Prius V five-door wagon will debut. The base models get new headlights and tail lights and a restyled front bumper.

OVERVIEW: This third-generation Prius contains a 1.8L DOHC 16-valve 4-cylinder engine. It may sound hard to believe, but the bigger engine doesn't have to work as hard. So at highway speeds, the lower rpms save about 1.3 km/L (3 mpg). The Prius is now approaching the Camry in size, and its powerplant is more sophisticated, powerful, and efficient than what you get with similar vehicles in the marketplace. Interestingly, because the car relies primarily on electrical energy, fuel economy is better in the city than on the highway—the opposite of what one finds with gasoline-powered vehicles.

An electric motor is the main power source, and it uses an innovative and fairly reliable CVT for smooth and efficient shifting. The motor is used mainly for acceleration, with the gasoline engine kicking in when needed to provide power. Braking automatically shuts off the engine, as the electric motor acts as a generator to replenish the environmentally unfriendly NiMH battery pack. The Solar Panel option uses solar energy to keep the vehicle cool when it's parked.

COST ANALYSIS: Prices are relatively firm due to the 2012 improvements. Wait until the new year to allow prices to settle down a bit. **Best alternatives:** A Honda Civic (2011), Fit, or Insight; Hyundai Accent; and the Nissan Versa. In a Prius-versus-Insight matchup, the Prius gets better fuel economy but is more expensive; the Insight, despite its fewer horses, is more fun to drive, though it's not as fast as the Prius. On the other hand, the Insight won't abduct you at high speed, or send you head-on into a guardrail with no brakes. **Options:** Stability control and the 17-inch wheels will make for quicker steering response and better road feedback. **Rebates:** The Prius's popularity rises and falls in tandem with fuel prices and safety defect horror stories, so $1,500 (maximum) rebates will quickly come and go. **Depreciation:** Unbelievably fast. A 2007 Prius that sold for $31,280 is now worth barely $14,000; a 2007 Honda Accord EX-L sedan, which originally cost $30,500, is now worth $15,000. **Insurance cost:** Higher than average. **Parts supply/cost:** Parts aren't easily found, and they can be costly. **Annual maintenance cost:** Average, so far. **Warranty:** Bumper-to-bumper 3 years/60,000 km; powertrain 5 years/100,000 km; hybrid-related components (battery, battery-control module, inverter with converter) 8 years/unlimited km; major emissions components 8 years/130,000 km; rust perforation 5 years/

unlimited km. **Supplementary warranty:** Not needed. **Highway/city fuel economy:** 4.0/3.7 L/100 km, 71/76 mpg.

OWNER-REPORTED PROBLEMS: Only nine safety-related complaints have been posted against the 2011 Prius, while over 1,800 incidents were reported on the 2010 model; 50 reports would be average. Almost all of the complaints concern sudden acceleration, loss of brakes, and cruise control failures. Sudden acceleration and loss of braking occurs right after passing over uneven terrain. The car is also extremely vulnerable to side winds, and light steering doesn't help much, causing the vehicle to wander all over the road and require constant steering corrections. There is poor braking at both low and high speeds, and often the car accelerates when the brakes are applied:

> While driving 5 mph [8 km/h] into a parking space, the brakes did not work when the pedal was depressed. On two separate occasions, the vehicle struck a garage door and the contact rear-ended another vehicle due to the brake failure.

Car lurches forward when brakes are applied; many reports of loss of braking even after having the recalled ECU replaced:

> Since Toyota updated the software for the recall, I still experience the same problem multiple times, and it is not only [happening] during slow and steady application of brakes, also [happening] when I use the brake in more sudden fashion even at moderate speed (30–40 mph [48–64 km/h]).

Cruise control doesn't disengage quickly enough:

> I have to press the brake harder than any prior vehicles I have owned to kill the cruise control and if I release the brake before the cruise control is released then the car lurches forward. Many other people have experienced this issue and have documented their experiences on the forum *priuschat.com*. They have even fixed the problem themselves by moving the cruise control disengagement closer to the top of the brake pedal.

The steering column may fall out of its mount:

> My wife and 2 daughters were driving on Interstate 90/94 when the entire steering column slowly dropped. I double checked the lever underneath to adjust it, but that was tight. I could see wires and bolts where the column had been dropped several inches. I lifted the column up and thought it would lock in or click back in place. When I did this, the entire column collapsed in my lap. An alarm sounded and I had no control of the steering while going 110 [km/h].

Inaccurate fuel readings; transmission sometimes goes into Reverse when shifted into Drive, or goes into Drive when Reverse is selected; traction control engages when it shouldn't; airbags failed to deploy; headlights go on and off intermittently;

musty AC smell; headlights shut off one at a time without warning; and the driver-side head restraint may slide up and out of the seat while driving; the head restraint also obstructs driver's rearward vision.

SERVICE BULLETIN-REPORTED PROBLEMS: Abnormal noise when brake pedal is released; troubleshooting rear windshield ticking.

AVALON ★★★★

KEY FACTS

CANADIAN PRICE (NEGOTIABLE): *Base:* $41,100 **U.S. PRICE:** *Base:* $32,445, *Limited:* $35,685 **CANADIAN FREIGHT:** $1,490 **U.S. FREIGHT:** $760
POWERTRAIN (FRONT-DRIVE)
Engine: 3.5L V6 (268 hp); Transmission: 6-speed auto.
DIMENSIONS/CAPACITY
Passengers: 2/3; Wheelbase: 111 in.; H: 59/L: 197.6/W: 72.8 in.; Cargo volume: 14.4 cu. ft.; Fuel tank: 70L/regular; Headroom F/R: 3.0/2.5 in.; Legroom F/R: 41/31 in.; Tow limit: Not recommended; Load capacity: 875 lb.; Turning circle: 36.9 ft.; Ground clearance: 5.3 in.; Weight: 3,567 lb.

RATING: Above Average. The Avalon is a relatively reliable luxury sedan that can turn deadly with delayed shifts and engine surging. **Strong points:** Good powertrain performance—when it's working right—and acceptable handling and ride; a roomy, limousine-like interior with reclining backrests and plenty of storage space; large doors make for easy front- and rear-seat access; comfortable seats; a quiet interior; exceptional reliability when compared with some of Toyota's other models; and good resale value. NHTSA gives the car five stars for front and side crash protection and four stars for rollover resistance. IIHS rates frontal offset, side, roof, and rear (head restraint) crash protection as "Good." **Weak points:** Rear-corner blind spots; mushy brake pedal; a "floaty" suspension and ultra-light steering degrades handling; and it's a bit fuel-thirsty. **New for 2012:** Returns relatively unchanged.

OVERVIEW: This five-passenger near-luxury four-door offers more value and reliability than do other, more expensive cars in its class. A front-engine, front-drive, mid-sized sedan, the Avalon is similar in size to the Ford Taurus, yet, despite its generous interior space, the car has a relatively small profile.

COST ANALYSIS: Buying an Avalon means you are getting the equivalent of an entry-level Lexus: It performs well, is loaded with safety, comfort, and convenience features, and costs thousands of dollars less than a Lexus. To save even more money, look for an identical, cheaper 2011 model. **Best alternatives:** The Honda Accord V6, Hyundai Genesis, Mazda6, and Nissan Altima. **Options:** The engine-immobilizing anti-theft system and dealer-installed towing package are worthwhile items. Stay away from the navigation control system; it's still a pain to program. **Rebates:** $3,000+ on the 2011 models and half as much on the 2012s, plus low-interest financing. **Depreciation:** Average. **Insurance cost:** Higher than average. **Parts supply/cost:** Parts are relatively inexpensive and easily found. If the Avalon *is* discontinued, parts still won't be a problem because so many were sold and the model hasn't changed much over the years. **Annual maintenance cost:** Less than average. **Warranty:** Bumper-to-bumper 3 years/60,000 km; powertrain 5 years/100,000 km; rust perforation 5 years/unlimited km. **Supplementary warranty:** Not needed. **Highway/city fuel economy:** 7.0/10.7 L/100 km, 40/27 mpg. Expect actual fuel consumption to be about 20 percent higher than advertised.

OWNER-REPORTED PROBLEMS: There have been only 35 safety-related complaints logged by NHTSA on the 2010 and 2011 Avalon (100 complaints would be expected). Here are some of the failures reported: "lag and lurch" when accelerating; when cruise control is engaged, applying the brake slows the car, but as soon as the foot is taken off the brake, the car surges back to its former speed; vehicle rolls backward when parked on an incline; "chin-to-chest" head restraints; a defective telescopic steering wheel lever may cause the steering wheel to collapse towards the dash when the vehicle is underway; steering column is unusually loose; "outgassing" produces an interior film that coats the inside of the windows, seriously distorting visibility:

> I bought a new 2011 Avalon in May 2010. Within 2 weeks, film from gas vapors formed on interior windows. The film impedes clear vision, which is a safety hazard. The film is so thick, one can write their name. Looking outward it appears you are inside an iridescent bubble. Reflection from sun and headlights worsens the problem to the point that it's difficult to judge the distance between your car and other vehicles.

Newly designed high-intensity discharged headlights only partially illuminate the highway; and electrical shorts may suddenly shut down dash lights.

Practically all owner complaints unrelated to safety concern poor fit and finish and water leaking into the headliner/footwell area. Other concerns include engine and rear windshield/window ticking; a front power-seat grinding, groaning noise; transmission control module (TCM) updates needed to improve shifting; problems with the trunk opener; and sunshade switches that are located too close together.

SERVICE BULLETIN-REPORTED PROBLEMS: Front or rear suspension knocking noise when passing over bumps; underbody rattling noises; windshield or back glass ticking; and inaccurate compass readings.

SIENNA *bad buy* ★

KEY FACTS

CANADIAN PRICE (NEGOTIABLE): *Base:* $27,900, *V6:* $28,900, *LE 8-pass.:* $32,500, *LE AWD 7-pass.:* $35,350, *SE V6 8-pass.:* $36,600, *XLE V6:* $38,700, *Limited AWD:* $49,100 **U.S. PRICE:** *Base:* $24,520, *LE:* $25,545, *SE:* $30,750, *XLE:* $32,375, *Limited AWD:* $40,570 **CANADIAN FREIGHT:** $1,560 **U.S. FREIGHT:** $810 **POWERTRAIN (FRONT-DRIVE/AWD)** Engines: 2.7L 4-cyl. (187 hp) • 3.5L V6 (266 hp); Transmission: 6-speed auto.

DIMENSIONS/CAPACITY
Passengers: 2/3/2; 2/3/3; Wheelbase: 119.3 in.; H: 69.5/L: 200.2/W: 78.2 in.; Headroom F/R1/R2: 3.5/4.0/2.5 in.; Legroom F/R1/R2: 40.5/31.5/2.5 in.; Cargo volume: 39.1 cu. ft.; Fuel tank: 79L/ regular; Tow limit: 3,500 lb.; Load capacity: 1,120 lb.; Turning circle: 36.7 ft.; Ground clearance: 6.2 in.; Weight: 4,189–4,735 lb.

RATING: Not Recommended. Serious safety complaints involving injuries to children and adults combined with an unproven redesigned model adds up to a failing grade for this year's Sienna. There has been a resurgence of safety-related defects since the 2004 model was redesigned. That said, the Sienna's 2011 redesign is worrisome because reworked Siennas have been glitch-prone in the past, at least for the year or two following their redesign—hence, the Not Recommended designation for the 2011 and 2012 versions. **Strong points:** Nicely restyled; smooth (most of the time) 3.5L V6 powertrain; optional full-time AWD; standard stability control; three-row side curtain airbags; a comfortable, stable ride; plenty of standard safety, performance, and convenience features; a fourth door; a tight turning circle; and a good amount of passenger and cargo room. NHTSA awards the Sienna four stars for overall crash protection and IIHS gives the car its top, "Good," rating for frontal offset, side, roof, and head restraint crashworthiness. **Weak points:** An under-powered, noisy, 4-cylinder engine; mediocre handling; recommended options are bundled with costly gadgets; an unusually large number of body rattles and assorted other noises. The 2011s still aren't as versatile or as reasonably priced as Chrysler's vans. How's this for "spin control"? Toyota says slimmer seats and controls add to the feeling of "roominess." No matter how they spin it, the interior looks less luxurious than before, cabin noise levels are higher, and fit and finish is far from acceptable. Be wary of the fast-wearing and expensive-to-replace run-flat tires. **New for 2012:** Returns with no significant changes.

OVERVIEW: Toyota's redesigned, third-generation Sienna has become more car-like than ever in its highway handling and comfort, while offering a larger, restyled interior. It is sold in a broad range of models, and stands out as the only van with an all-wheel-drive option (though this is not recommended). It's available with either a 4- or 6-cylinder engine and as a seven- or eight-passenger carrier.

Toyota built the Sienna for comfort and convenience. If you want more performance and driver interaction, get a Honda Odyssey. Sienna's V6 turns in respectable acceleration times, and the handling is also more car-like, but not as agile as with the Odyssey. However, the spacious interior accommodates up to eight passengers. All models come with standard four-wheel disc brakes, and all-wheel drive is available.

COST ANALYSIS: Toyota is keeping 2012 prices near last year's levels, making this year's model a better buy from a price perspective. As far as quality is concerned, it would be wise to delay your purchase another year to take advantage of more-generous summer and fall 2012 sales incentives and to give Toyota time to "debug" the reworked Sienna. **Best alternatives:** The redesigned 2012 Honda Odyssey or Mazda5 (a mini-minivan). Chrysler's minivans bring up the rear of the pack due primarily to their automatic transmission failures and shaky financial footing. Why not Nissan's Quest? Its serious powertrain and fit and finish deficiencies over the past five years preclude its purchase until we see if the upcoming redesign removes or exacerbates present design flaws. **Options:** Power windows and door locks, rear heater, and AC unit. Be wary of the power-sliding door and power-assisted rear liftgate. The doors can crush children and pose unnecessary risks to other occupants, while the liftgate can "bean" anyone standing under it. Go for Michelin or Pirelli original-equipment tires. Don't buy Bridgestone or Dunlop run-flats. **Rebates:** *2011:* $3,000; *2012:* $2,000 in the new year. **Depreciation:** Faster than average and expected to lose much more value as the discounted 2011 and 2012 models drive prices down. For example, a 2007 CE seven-passenger Sienna that sold for $31,200 now sells for $14,000. **Insurance cost:** Higher than average. **Parts supply/cost:** Excellent supply of reasonably priced parts taken from the Camry's parts bin, but run-flat tire replacements are expensive and hard to find. **Annual maintenance cost:** Less than average. **Warranty:** Bumper-to-bumper 3 years/60,000 km; powertrain 5 years/100,000 km; rust perforation 5 years/unlimited km. **Supplementary warranty:** An extended warranty isn't necessary. **Highway/city fuel economy:** *2.7L:* 7.5/10.4 L/100 km, 38/27 mpg. *3.5L:* 8.1/11.5 L/100 km, 35/25 mpg. *AWD:* 9.0/12.8 L/100 km, 31/22 mpg. The 4-cylinder engine burns almost as much fuel as the V6.

OWNER-REPORTED PROBLEMS: Siennas continue to suddenly accelerate, in Reverse or in Drive especially, when the brakes are applied; cruise control won't turn off; brake failure:

> At around 5 pm on a clear Monday evening I went to turn left into a parking spot. I stepped on the gas and nothing happened, I let up a bit and stepped again and my Sienna shot forward. I slammed on the brake halfway into the parking spot and ran into the tree in front of the van.

Airbags don't deploy when needed; power sliding rear doors and power rear hatch are two options known more for their dangerous malfunctions than their utility:

> My 17 month old's head got jammed between the right rear wheel and the right rear door panel while the electric door slid open. Even though my wife pulled on the door handle the door kept sliding open. My baby's head was crushed between the tire and door panel. This is a very unsafe design as my wife tried to stop the door from sliding back and the door kept moving.

•

> My 2 year old daughter got her leg caught in the back part of the sliding door of a 2011 Toyota Sienna. She was inside the car. The door was opened. Her leg fell into the space while the door was opening. The door opened as far as it could and constricted her leg. Her leg was so constricted we could not reposition her body to open the door.... She was trapped (screaming) for 20–25 minutes. Her leg was cold and turning blue before it was freed.... I'm very concerned about the design of the door. I've looked at other minivans (even the same make and model but different year) and they don't have the gap in the back part of the door like the 2011 Toyota Sienna.

•

> Couple of months after I got the car, there were several incidents [in which] me and family members were hit on our heads and shoulders by self closing liftgate [and we] didn't know what the cause was. After researching about this problem, Toyota had recalled Sienna in the past about this same problem for older models for faulty strut used for power liftgates.

In another reported incident, a driver accelerated to pass another car, and his Sienna suddenly accelerated out of control, while the brakes were useless.

Brakes can take a couple of seconds before they engage; the slightest touch of the gear shifter causes a shift into Neutral or Reverse; airbags fail to deploy; multiple warning lights come on, and the vehicle cannot be shifted; engine ticking; more ticking from the windshield/back glass; transfer-case fluid leaks; sunroof may spontaneously explode; front windshield distortion:

> I noticed a distortion across the lower 3" of the windshield. It is very distracting, as the paint stripes on the road "bend" towards the driver. It's worse at night.

Excessive rear-view mirror vibration; factory-installed TV screen obstructs the field of vision through the rear-view mirror; rear tires quickly wear out; front passenger seatback tilts forward when braking and second-row seats may be unstable; water puddles in the van's rear storage area near the back door.

SERVICE BULLETIN-REPORTED PROBLEMS: Rattle, buzz from driver's side of the dash; squeaky seat; inoperative second-row ottoman seat; and the sliding door rattles while driving.

RAV4 ★★★★

RATING: Above Average. **Strong points:** Base models offer a nice array of standard safety, performance, and convenience features, including electronic stability control and standard brake override; 4-cylinder acceleration from a stop is acceptable with a full load; excellent V6 powertrain performance; precise handling and a comfortable, quiet ride are big improvements over earlier, more firmly sprung models; RAV4 seats five, but an optional third-row bench on Base and Limited models increases capacity to seven; comfortable seats; a quiet interior; cabin gauges and controls are easy to access and read; exceptional reliability; and good fuel economy with the 4-cylinder engine (the V6 is almost as fuel-frugal). NHTSA gives the RAV4 five stars for front and side crashworthiness and four stars for roll-over protection. IIHS says head-restraint protection and frontal offset and side crashworthiness are "Good." Roof strength was judged "Acceptable." **Weak points:** Transmission is hesitant to shift to a lower gear when under load, and sometimes produces jerky low-speed shifts; some noseplow and body lean when cornering under power; and some road and wind noise. Resale value is only average, which is good news only for smart used-car shoppers. **New for 2012:** This year's model is mostly a carryover of the 2011 version.

KEY FACTS

CANADIAN PRICE (NEGOTIABLE): *Base:* $24,595, *Base 4WD:* $27,230, *Base 4WD V6:* $29,845, *Sport:* $28,345, *Sport V6:* $30,100, *Sport 4WD:* $30,540, *Sport 4WD V6:* $32,295, *Limited:* $30,185, *Limited V6:* $32,440, *Limited 4WD:* $32,385 *Limited 4WD V6:* $34,640
U.S. PRICE: *Base:* $22,475, *Base 4WD:* $23,875, *Base V6:* $24,510, *Base 4WD V6:* $25,910, *Sport:* $24,175, *Sport V6:* $26,105, *Sport 4WD:* $25,575, *Sport 4WD V6:* $27,505, *Limited:* $25,465, *Limited V6:* $27,385, *Limited 4WD:* $26,855, *Limited 4WD V6:* $28,785
CANADIAN FREIGHT: $1,560
U.S. FREIGHT: $825
POWERTRAIN (FRONT-DRIVE/AWD)
Engines: 2.5L 4-cyl. (179 hp) • 3.5L V6 (269 hp); Transmissions: 4-speed auto. • 5-speed auto.
DIMENSIONS/CAPACITY
Passengers: 2/3; 2/3/2; Wheelbase: 105 in.; H: 66/L: 181/W: 72 in.; Cargo volume: 39 cu. ft.; Fuel tank: 70L/ regular; Headroom F/R: 6.55/4.0 in.; Legroom F/R: 41.5/29 in.; Tow limit: 1,500lb.; Load capacity: 825 lb.; Turning circle: 37.4 ft.; Ground clearance: 7.5 in.; Weight: 3,590 lb.

OVERVIEW: This SUV crossover combines a car-type unibody platform with elevated seating and optional all-wheel drive. Although classed as a compact SUV, the RAV4 is large enough to carry a kid-sized third-row bench seat, giving it seven-passenger capacity. A powerful V6 makes this downsized SUV one of the fastest crossovers on the market.

COST ANALYSIS: If you can find a discounted 2011, buy it. **Best alternatives:** The Honda CR-V, Hyundai Tucson, or Nissan X-Trail. **Options:** The engine-immobilizing anti-theft system and dealer-installed towing package are worthwhile items. The Sport model has an option that uses run-flat tires and dispenses with the tailgate-mounted spare tire. Stick with the regular tire; it's cheaper and less problematic. **Rebates:** $2,000+ on the 2011s and $1,000 on the 2012s, plus low-interest financing and leasing. **Depreciation:** Average; a 2007 Base 4WD that sold for $29,300 is now worth about $15,000. **Insurance cost:** Higher than average. **Parts supply/cost:** Parts are relatively inexpensive and easily found. **Annual maintenance cost:** Less than average. **Warranty:** Bumper-to-bumper 3 years/60,000 km; powertrain 5 years/100,000 km; rust perforation 5 years/ unlimited km. **Supplementary warranty:** A waste of money. **Highway/city fuel economy:** 2.5L: 6.9/9.4 L/100 km, 41/30 mpg. 2.5L AWD: 7.2/9.7 L/ 100 km, 39/29 mpg. 3.5L: 7.4/10.7 L/100 km, 38/26 mpg. 3.5L AWD: 7.7/11.7 L/100 km, 37/25 mpg. Owners say fuel economy figures are too high by 20 percent.

OWNER-REPORTED PROBLEMS: The 2011 RAV4 has elicited only 12 safety-related complaints, which is impressive for such a popular SUV. Among the incidents reported we find sudden acceleration (even after recall repairs were done) and loss of braking:

> This unintended acceleration occurs randomly when I apply the brakes and is more powerful with each episode. When I depress the brake pedal, the engine revs very loudly and the vehicle feels as though it will speed in whatever gear I am in (i.e., Drive or Reverse). In order to keep the vehicle under control, I have to keep the brake depressed, engage the emergency brake, shift into park and turn off the engine. On the last occurrence—Jan. 2, 2011—the engine revved so strongly the front end shook violently and we could smell the engine overheating.

Other reports: Fire erupted in the engine compartment; steering angle sensor malfunction causes the vehicle to stall out; original-equipment Yokohama tires may blow out their side walls; and the defroster/air circulation system is weak.

Practically all of the owner complaints unrelated to safety concern poor fit and finish and audio system malfunctions. Some drivers say they are sickened by a sulphur smell that invades the interior. Owners also deride the flimsy glove box lid, loose sun visor, constantly flickering traction control light, sticking ignition key, uncomfortable head restraints, squeaks and rattles from the dashboard and rear-seat area, and wide rear roof pillars that obstruct visibility. And, the mice are back! Rodents routinely enter the vehicle at will through the clean-air filter. One dealer suggested owners buy mouse traps or adopt a cat:

> Check Engine light indicated. The car was taken to the dealer, where the dealer mentioned, "Evidence of rodent/small animal has chewed wiring harness at connector completely through." The car will need wiring harness.

SERVICE BULLETIN-REPORTED PROBLEMS: Only the ubiquitous windshield/back glass ticking.

VENZA ★★★

RATING: Average. This combination of a small SUV and a wagon has proven itself to be relatively problem-free and a good highway performer. **Strong points:** Powerful and efficient engines; roomy interior; pleasant driving demeanour; comfy ride; innovative interior storage areas; an automatic headlight dimmer; easy entry and exit; a low rear loading height; and standard stability and traction control. NHTSA gave the Venza a three-star rating for front crashworthiness, five stars for side protection, and four stars for rollover resistance. IIHS rated the vehicle as "Good" for frontal offset, side, roof, and rear occupant protection. **Weak points:** Not an exciting drive; the ride is stiff and there's not much steering feedback; no third-row seat; radio station indicator washes out in sunlight; high-intensity discharge headlights are annoying to other drivers, are often stolen, and are expensive to replace. Resale value is lower than one would expect for a Toyota SUV. **New for 2012:** Minor trim changes.

KEY FACTS

CANADIAN PRICE (NEGOTIABLE): *Base front-drive:* $29,310, *AWD:* $30,760, *V6:* $30,800, *AWD:* $32,250 **U.S. PRICE:** *Base front-drive:* $26,275, *V6 front-drive:* $28,100, *AWD:* $27,725, *V6 AWD:* $29,550 **CANADIAN FREIGHT:** $1,560 **U.S. FREIGHT:** $785
POWERTRAIN (FRONT-DRIVE/AWD)
Engines: 2.7L 4-cyl. (182 hp) • 3.5L V6 (268 hp); Transmission: 6-speed auto.
DIMENSIONS/CAPACITY
Passengers: 2/3; Wheelbase: 109.3 in.; H: 63.4/L: 189/W: 75 in.; Cargo volume: 33 cu. ft.; Fuel tank: 67L/regular; Headroom F/R: 5.0/4.5 in.; Legroom F/R: 41.0/30 in.; Tow limit: 2,500–3,500 lb.; Load capacity: 825 lb.; Turning circle: 39.1 ft.; Ground clearance: 8.1 in.; Weight: 4,125 lb.

OVERVIEW: Toyota's Venza is a five-passenger wagon sold in two trim levels that match the two available engines. Going into its fourth year, the car offers the styling and comfort of a passenger car with the flexibility of a small SUV. A perfect alternative for Toyota customers who need more vehicle than what the Camry offers but not as much as the Highlander.

COST ANALYSIS: Most of the 2011s have been sold; expect to pay almost full list price for a 2012, until competition heats up at year's end. Remember, Toyota is hurting for sales and will sweeten rebates and discounts throughout the year to attract customers. **Best alternatives:** The Ford Edge, Nissan Murano, and Toyota Highlander. **Options:** Stay away from the panoramic roof option and back-up camera; both are expensive gadgets of doubtful utility. **Rebates:** $2,000 on the 2012s later in the new year, plus low-interest financing. **Depreciation:** Faster than average, especially for a Toyota; for example, a 2009 entry-level Venza that sold new for $28,270 is now worth only $19,500. **Insurance cost:** Average. **Parts supply/cost:** Parts are average-priced and easily found. **Annual maintenance cost:** Less than average. **Warranty:** Bumper-to-bumper 3 years/60,000 km; powertrain 5 years/100,000 km; rust perforation 5 years/unlimited km. **Supplementary warranty:** Not needed. **Highway/city fuel economy:** 2.7L: 6.8/10.0 L/100 km, 42/28 mpg. AWD: 7.1/10.2 L/100 km, 40/28 mpg. 3.5L: 7.6/11.0L/100 km, 37/26 mpg. AWD: 7.9/11.5 L/100 km, 36/25 mpg.

OWNER-REPORTED PROBLEMS: Not a single safety-related incident reported on the 2011 Venza; only 29 complaints were filed against the 2010 model. Sudden, unintended acceleration:

> We accelerated our Venza to match ongoing traffic speeds, when the throttle stuck wide open and was increasing in speed. I stepped on the brakes, which failed to respond. I then checked the cruise control, to see if I had inadvertently engaged it, but I had not. I then started to pump the accelerator pedal with extreme force, and after numerous pumps, the throttle disengaged.

Transmission would not go into Reverse; the Hill-Start Assist feature doesn't prevent the car from rolling back when stopped on a hill in traffic:

> I feel Toyota should immediately send out a safety notice requiring all employees be briefed about the Hill-Start Assist feature, how it doesn't activate automatically, and how to activate the feature when stopped on an uphill slope.

Airbags failed to deploy; brakes don't immediately work when slow and steady pressure is applied; sometimes, after the brakes are applied, the car won't accelerate; automatic rear hatch can crush a hand if it is caught when the hatch is closing; seatbelt began strangling a three-year-old, who had to be cut free; sunroof exploded for no reason; radio overheated up to 145 degrees; and chin-to-chest head restraints:

> The head rest on my vehicle pushes my neck forward into an extremely uncomfortable position. This cannot be adjusted. As a 5'4" female, I was having to seek medical treatment for neck and shoulder pain following long trips. I have reversed the head rest so that I can continue to drive my car. I am now concerned about the safety of this in the event of an accident (whiplash), but feel like I have no choice. Severe neck pain was interfering with ability to turn my head while driving.

SERVICE BULLETIN-REPORTED PROBLEMS: Steering column rattling and windshield/back glass ticking.

HIGHLANDER ★★★★

RATING: Above Average. **Strong points:** Powerful engines and a smooth, refined powertrain; the Hybrid can propel itself on electric power alone; a quiet interior enhances the comfortable ride; responsive handling; roomy second-row seating is fairly versatile. NHTSA gives the Highlander and its Hybrid variant four stars for frontal crashworthiness and rollover resistance; five stars were awarded for side impact protection. IIHS rates the vehicle as "Good" for frontal offset, side, roof, and rear occupant protection. **Weak points:** Steering is somewhat vague, there's a high step-in, and the vehicle isn't very agile. The third-row seat is a bit tight and doesn't fold in a 50/50 split. **New for 2012:** Minor styling revisions.

KEY FACTS

CANADIAN PRICE (NEGOTIABLE): *Base:* $31,500, *V6 4WD:* $35,750, *Limited V6 4WD:* $44,900, *Hybrid:* $42,850, *Hybrid Limited:* $51,650 **U.S. PRICE:** *Base:* $28,090, *Limited 4WD:* $37,045, *Hybrid:* $38,140, *Hybrid Limited:* $43,795
CANADIAN FREIGHT: $1,560 **U.S. FREIGHT:** $810
POWERTRAIN (FRONT-DRIVE/AWD)
Engines: 2.7L 4-cyl. (187 hp) • 3.3L V6 (270 hp) • 3.5L V6 (270 hp); Transmissions: 5-speed auto. • 6-speed auto. • CVT
DIMENSIONS/CAPACITY
Passengers: 2/3/2, *Hybrid:* 2/3; Wheelbase: 110 in.; H: 69.3/L: 188.4/W: 75.2 in.; Cargo volume: 37.5 cu. ft.; Fuel tank: 72.5L/regular; Headroom F/R1/R2: 3.5/5.0/0.0 in. (Ouch! Third-row seat is for only the very young or very short.); Legroom F/R1/R2: 41.5/32/23.5 in.; Tow limit: 3,500–5,000 lb.; Load capacity: 1,200 lb.; Turning circle: 38.7 ft.; Ground clearance: 8.1 in.; Weight: 4,050–4,641 lb.

OVERVIEW: A crossover alternative to a minivan, this competent, refined, family-friendly SUV puts function ahead of style and provides cargo and passenger versatility along with a high level of quality. V6-equipped models best represent the Highlander's attributes, as the Hybrid models' higher prices will take years to offset in fuel savings.

COST ANALYSIS: Look for an identical 2011 model discounted by about 10 percent. **Best alternatives:** From the Detroit SUV side: the Buick Enclave, Chevrolet Traverse, Ford Flex, or GMC Acadia. A good Asian SUV is the Honda Pilot. The Honda Odyssey is the only suitable Asian minivan choice. **Options:** Say yes to the engine-immobilizing anti-theft system; no to the failure-prone and costly-to-maintain tire-pressure monitoring system. **Rebates:** $2,500+ on the 2011s; $1,500+ on the 2012s, plus low-interest financing and leasing. **Depreciation:** Faster than average; a Base 2009 AWD version that originally sold for $37,150 can now be picked up for $24,500. **Insurance cost:** Higher than average. **Parts supply/cost:** Parts are relatively inexpensive and easily found. **Annual maintenance cost:** Average. **Warranty:** Bumper-to-bumper 3 years/60,000 km; powertrain 5 years/100,000 km; rust perforation 5 years/unlimited km. **Supplementary warranty:** Not needed. **Highway/city fuel economy:** 7.3/10.4 L/100 km, 39/27, mpg. V6: 8.8/12.3 L/100 km, 32/23 mpg. *Hybrid:* 8.0/7.4 L/100 km, 35/38 mpg.

OWNER-REPORTED PROBLEMS: NHTSA's safety-defect log sheet shows very few complaints registered against the Highlander. *2011 models:* sudden brake failure; brake and steering both went out as driver was making a turn; engine replaced after overheating, due to road debris damaging the radiator; and Bridgestone Dueler HL400 original equipment tire blowouts due to cracks in the sidewall. *2010 models:* sudden, unintended acceleration *after* the recall fix; steering veered to the left and right while brakes went out; a long delay after the brakes are applied; the tire-pressure monitoring system has to be reset by the dealer when the tires are changed ($135 twice a year).

SERVICE BULLETIN-REPORTED PROBLEMS: Windshield/back glass ticking. *Hybrid:* Fuel cap binding and windshield/back glass ticking.

RATING: Average. This cheap and reliable light-duty truck would have been rated higher if it weren't for owner reports that Toyota's infamous, decade-old lag and lurch transmission and sudden acceleration problems have spilling over into the 2011s. **Strong points:** Well-chosen powertrain and steering set-up; ideal for off-road work with the optional suspension; good acceleration; standard electronic stability control; very responsive handling over smooth roads; a well-garnished, roomy interior; plenty of storage space; and good reliability. Given three stars by NHTSA for frontal crashworthiness, five stars for side protection, and four stars for roll-over resistance. IIHS rates front, side, and head-restraint protection as "Good." **Weak points:** The ride can be jolting and lead to loss of steering control, and the driving position seems low when compared with the competition. Delayed transmission engagement is still present. Depreciation during the first three years takes a big bite out of the Tacoma's resale value. IIHS rates the Tacoma's roof strength as "Marginal." **New for 2012:** New hood, grille, headlights, and bumpers, in addition to various interior trim changes.

OVERVIEW: Toyota's entry-level pickup isn't as utilitarian as its predecessors or some of the competition, but it has sufficient power and is

KEY FACTS

CANADIAN PRICE (NEGOTIABLE): *Access Cab 4×2:* $21,895, *4×2 SR5:* $24,085, *4×4:* $25,995, *4×4 SR5:* $28,025, *4×4 V6:* $28,380, *4×4 V6 SR5:* $30,410, *V6 TRD offroad:* $34,585, *Double Cab V6:* $32,645, *Double Cab V6 TRD Sport:* $35,455
U.S. PRICE: *Access Cab 4×2:* $19,655, *Auto.:* $20,555, *4×4:* $24,390, *4×4 V6:* $25,045, *4×4 auto.:* $25,925, *Double Cab V6:* $26,145, *Double Cab auto.:* $27,025
CANADIAN FREIGHT: $1,560 **U.S. FREIGHT:** $825

POWERTRAIN (REAR-DRIVE/AWD)
Engines: 2.7L 4-cyl. (159 hp) • 4.0L V6 (236 hp); Transmissions: 5-speed man. • 6-speed man. • 4-speed auto. • 5-speed auto.

DIMENSIONS/CAPACITY
Passengers: 2/2; Wheelbase: 127.8 in.; H: 70/L: 208.1/W: 75 in.; Fuel tank: 80L/regular; Headroom F/R: 4.0/3.0 in.; Legroom F/R: 42.5/28 in.; Tow limit: 3,500–6,500 lb.; Load capacity: 1,100 lb.; Turning circle: 44.6 ft.; Ground clearance: 8.1 in.; Weight: 4,115 lb.

relatively inexpensive if not too gussied up. If you decide to go for the optional off-road suspension, you will quickly notice the firmer ride and increased road feedback.

COST ANALYSIS: Look for a nearly identical (except for the bumper, grille, hood, and headlights) 2011 model discounted by about 15 percent. **Best alternatives:** The 2010 Mazda B-Series and this year's Nissan Frontier. **Options:** The stiffer suspension for off-roading, an engine-immobilizing anti-theft system, and the dealer-installed towing package are all worthwhile items. **Rebates:** $1,500+ on the 2010s, plus low-interest financing and leasing. **Depreciation:** Faster than average for both front-drives and four-wheel drives; a 2007 front-drive Access Cab that originally sold for $22,635 now fetches barely $9,000. An entry-level 2007 4WD V6 that sold for $29,660 is now worth $13,500. **Insurance cost:** Average. **Parts supply/cost:** Inexpensive and easily found. **Annual maintenance cost:** Average. **Warranty:** Bumper-to-bumper 3 years/60,000 km; powertrain 5 years/100,000 km; rust perforation 5 years/unlimited km. **Supplementary warranty:** Not needed. **Highway/city fuel economy:** 2.7: 7.8/10.5 L/100 km, 36/27 mpg. *Auto.:* 7.9/11.0 L/100 km, 36/26 mpg. *AWD:* 9.1/12.0 L/100 km, 31/24/ mpg. 4.0 4×4: 10.8/14.7 L/100 km, 26/19 mpg. *Auto.:* 9.9/13.4 L/100 km, 29/21 mpg.

OWNER-REPORTED PROBLEMS: Truck accelerated on its own as driver waited for pedestrians to clear the crosswalk; the throttle stuck when passing another vehicle; when brakes were applied, vehicle suddenly accelerated; when cruise control was disengaged, then re-engaged, the vehicle accelerated up to 130 km/h; premature automatic transmission failures; an automatic transmission shift lag and lurch, especially when coming out of a turn; vehicle veers to the left when accelerating (not because of the tires or alignment); serious highway instability:

> My 2011 Toyota Tacoma is very dangerous to drive in windy conditions. At interstate speeds (70 mph [113 km/h]) it loses directional stability. My 2006 Tacoma was solid as a rock in any conditions. I feel that the height of the vehicle causes wind to raise the vehicle ever so slightly, causing a very dangerous drivability situation. Sadly I have spoken to other owners and they experienced the same problems. This is my 12th Toyota of which 6 have been Tacomas. It is my very worst nightmare to drive.

The truck bounces and hops over uneven pavement (a problem owners have been reporting for years); brakes are difficult to modulate; brake rotors and drums may warp or glaze prematurely; history of original equipment Dunlop Grand Trek tires splitting at the edge of the tire.

SERVICE BULLETIN-REPORTED PROBLEMS: Windshield/back glass ticking; manual transmission clutch slips in all gears. Improved low speed Second to First downshift (use a revised electronic control module); bouncy rear suspension ride with a heavy load can be corrected by installing free upgraded rear spring assemblies up to 3 years/36,000 miles. This problem affects 2005–2011 models. Owners who have older vehicles or more mileage than acceptable should make a claim in small claims court, quoting Toyota service bulletin #T-SB-0359-10, published December 21, 2010.

TUNDRA

RATING: Not Recommended. It's an excellent concept that's been poorly executed. The Tundra's lag and lurch transmission/throttle problem and dangerous rear-end bounce make the truck a risky highway traveller. **Strong points:** Strong powertrain performance; a roomy interior with plenty of storage space; large doors make for easy front- and rear-seat access; comfortable seats; and a quiet interior. **Weak points:** Engines are fuel-thirsty due to the Tundra's excess weight, and handling is degraded by excessive rear-end bounce; rear axle shaft bearing growling; low-range gearing is for the most slippery roads; powertrain lag and lurch is hazardous to all; steering needs to be retuned to dial in more road feedback and quicker response; the interior design looks early Paleolithic—not as stylish as Ford and Chrysler, nor as upscale as GM's Silverado and Sierra; and passengers may find headroom a bit tight. **New for 2012:** Styled steel wheels, heated mirrors, and a backup camera on Limited versions.

Double Cabs are Tundra's most popular models. Their 2012 prices have gone up by $1,000, and those prices are expected to hold as fuel prices moderate and Canada's economy keeps the truck segment humming along.

OVERVIEW: A heavy full-sized truck that has more glitches than goodies, this year's freshened Tundra uses an improved V6 that's stronger and more fuel-efficient than the engine it replaced last year. Thanks, Toyota. Now turn your attention to the Tundra's hazardous powertrain and "shake, rattle, and roll" suspension.

KEY FACTS

CANADIAN PRICE (NEGOTIABLE): *4.6 Regular Cab 4×2:* $26,195, *5.7 Regular Cab 4×4:* $29,910, *TRD Package,* $33,895, *5.7 Regular Cab 4x4 Long:* $30,260, *4.6 Double Cab SR5 4x2:* $32,055, *4.6 Double Cab SR5 4x4:* $36,120, *5.7 Double Cab SR5 4x2:* $36,015, *5.7 Double Cab SR5 4x4:* $37,220, *5.7 Double Cab Limited 4x4:* $48,275, *CrewMax SR5 4x2:* $37,630, *CrewMax Limited 4x4:* $51,400, **U.S. PRICE:** Prices start at $27,115 for the 2WD V6 Double Cab and top out at $43,345 for the 4WD Limited CrewMax with a 5.7L V8 and 6-speed automatic transmission. **CANADIAN FREIGHT:** $1,560 **U.S. FREIGHT:** $985
POWERTRAIN (REAR-DRIVE/AWD) Engines: 4.0L V6 (270 hp) • 4.6L V8 (310 hp) • 5.7L V8 (381 hp); Transmission: 6-speed auto.
DIMENSIONS/CAPACITY Passengers: 2/1; 2/3; 3/3 Wheelbase: 145.7 in.; H: 75.6/L: 228.71/W: 79.9 in.; Fuel tank: 100L/regular; Headroom F/R: 5.5/3.5 in.; Legroom F/R: 42.5/28.5 in.; Tow limit: 8,100–10,800 lb.; Load capacity: 1,755–1,900 lb.; Turning circle: 44 ft.; Ground clearance: 10 in.; Weight: 4,830–5,480 lb.

COST ANALYSIS: Go for a cheaper, second-series 2011 model with all its refinements. Consider waiting until mid-2012 for Toyota to iron out its suspension bounce/vibration, growling noise, and transmission lag problems, and for prices to drift downward. **Best alternatives:** Ford's F-Series pickups, or GM's Sierra or Silverado. **Options:** The engine-immobilizing anti-theft system is worthwhile. Stay away from the Bridgestone and Firestone tires, and make sure the spare tire is the same make and size as your regular tire. The TRD package gives a ride that may be too stiff for some. **Rebates:** $4,000+ on the leftover 2011s, plus low-interest financing and various leasing deals. **Depreciation:** Faster than average. Surprisingly, Toyota's bad press as of late has depressed the resale value of its trucks more than one would expect for a Japanese make. For example, a 2007 4×4 5.7 Deluxe Regular Cab that once sold for $34,045 is now worth a bit over $13,000. **Insurance cost:** Higher than average. **Parts supply/cost:** Parts are moderately expensive and sometimes hard to find. **Annual maintenance cost:** Average. **Warranty:** Bumper-to-bumper 3 years/60,000 km; powertrain 5 years/100,000 km; rust perforation 5 years/unlimited km. **Supplementary warranty:** Yes, on the powertrain. **Highway/city fuel economy:** 4.6 4×2: 9.9/14.0 L/100 km, 29/20 mpg. 4×4: 10.5/14.9 L/100 km, 26/18 mpg. 5.7 4×2: 10.9/15.3 L/100 km, 27/19 mpg. 4×4: 11.8/16.8 L/100 km, 24/17 mpg.

OWNER-REPORTED PROBLEMS: Sudden, unintended acceleration; stuck accelerator; vehicle speeds up when coming to a stop; rear wheel came off the vehicle because the lug nuts weren't tightened sufficiently at the factory. Engine lag and lurch when accelerating; engine knocking caused by a piston striking the cylinder wall of the 5.7L V8 engine; engine suddenly self-destructed; repeated failure of the transmission and transfer case; vehicle will stall in any gear. Owners complain the truck is a "Shake-undra" with excessive bed bounce when going over smooth roadways:

I was travelling at about 65 mph [105 km/h] and moved to the number 4 lane, same thing—bed bounce was violent for about 2 miles [3 kilometres]. This is very dangerous because it felt like I had very limited control of the truck while bouncing.

•

On highway this truck shakes uncontrollably. It feels like it is bending in the middle between a cabin and a bed. While driving everyone in the truck keeps bouncing off the seat at times. If this was disclosed as "normal" as a dealer says, I would have never bought this truck.

TCM updates needed to improve shifting; brake pedal slowly goes to the floor when applied with sustained pressure; fuel rail split causing gasoline to leak onto the engine; water leaks into the headliner/footwell area; engine ticking noise; heat/AC/ventilation system is a "rodent lair" (rodents are attracted by the ready-made cubbyholes throughout the vehicle and enjoy snacking on the soya-based electrical wiring coverings; air inside the vehicle may be laced with rodent feces); inoperative instrument lighting for the power-mirror control (must turn on dome light to see); rear windshield ticking noise; shattered rear windshield caused large shards of glass to fly into the cabin; CrewMax windshields are particularly vulnerable to stress cracks; front power-seat grinding, groaning noise; lots of owner complaints relating to poor fit and finish; blue paint is easily scratched and looks bad; and sudden Bridgestone Dueler tire side wall blowout.

SERVICE BULLETIN-REPORTED PROBLEMS: Windshield/back glass ticking.

EUROPEAN VEHICLES

Saab Story

2010 is over. Ford is the champion. Saab isn't.

Granted, Saab only began selling cars in December, but The Good Car Guy spotted new 9-5s at one Saab dealer in a small east coast Canadian city a few weeks back. Yet they only sold 2 in the whole month...in the whole country? That makes two Saabs sold in Canada in 2010, down 99.7% from 2009's totals.

GOOD CAR BAD CAR

Good Year, Bad Year

It doesn't make sense.

We are in a worldwide recession, major European countries like Greece and Spain are threatening to default on their public debt, unemployment is rampant, and European car sales, for the most part, are surging in Canada. That's right. European automakers are returning to profitability thanks to cost-cutting and the surge in demand for German luxury vehicles. Audi, BMW, Mercedes-Benz, and Volkswagen have snagged the top four European car sales spots through August 2011 with double-digit sales gains. Apparently, Canadian buyers are fuelling a flight to luxury with an emphasis on European products.

Take for example Volkswagen, Audi, and Porsche: three corporate powerhouses of German engineering and creative design that have strongly rebounded from the

---

EUROPEAN WINNERS AND LOSERS IN CANADA

RANK	AUTOMAKER	AUGUST 2011	% CHANGE	YEAR TO DATE	YTD % CHANGE
1	Volkswagen	4,302	+27.7	35,766	+18.7
2	BMW	2,442	+4.3	19,300	+10.8
3	Mercedes-Benz	2,170	−3.7	20,043	+4.1
4	Audi	1,466	+6.5	11,655	+16.6
5	Fiat	616	—	3,856	—
6	Volvo	512	−1.7	4,905	+3.0
7	Mini	402	+3.1	3,305	+14.6
8	Land Rover	222	+6.7	1,849	+11.3
9	Porsche	175	+30.6	1,771	+30.8
10	Smart	130	−24.9	1,293	−12.2
11	Jaguar	60	−14.3	531	−2.7
12	Saab	24	—	132	—

Source: Manufacturers, AIAMC, DesRosiers, and *Automotive News* Data Center

recession. Volkswagen has done particularly well because it offers the best mix of fuel savings and high performance. Its North American marketing presence is relatively intact, with minimal dealer attrition, and the company is well positioned to ride the upcoming diesel craze to fatter future profits as hybrids and electric-car sales falter. On the other hand, increased small-car competition from Ford, GM, and the Japanese and South Korean automakers will produce more-refined econocars and cheaper crossovers, eroding some VW and Mercedes small-car and SUV sales. Already, the Mercedes Smart Car is barely hanging on as it tries to compete with cheaper, better-built Asian and American econocars. It's no surprise that VW has purchased a substantial interest in Suzuki—in case the Smart franchise goes belly up.

BMW, the second most popular brand in Canada, is a formidable automaker that beats Audi in world sales, including unexpected strength in North America, China, India, Brazil, Russia, Korea, and Turkey. The company's growth through May 2011 has been an impressive 20.7 percent, which is all the more surprising considering the mediocre quality of its cars and SUVs.

European automakers hard-hit by poor sales a year ago have tried to achieve sustainability by focusing on entry-level econocars and luxury high-performance vehicles, while seeking out investors to buy their companies or make joint production deals.

Who is most likely to succeed? European-American products are a mixed bag. Fiat/Chrysler, for example, is keeping a tight control of costs and has a leaner, back-to-basics administration in the States. Unfortunately, this doesn't address the sad fact that Fiat makes bad cars and will simply replace Chrysler's low-quality cars and trucks with its own problem-plagued lineup; essentially restacking the chairs on Chrysler's *USS Marchionne Titanic*. But there may be time for Fiat to shift gears if we can believe August sales, which show upstart startup Fiat busting MINI's ball-joints after just a few months.

European "Orphans"

Orphans are those vehicles that have been sold by their parent builder, or, as in Volvo's case, sold twice to different automobile manufacturers. Usually when this occurs, the purchased companies dwindle into bankruptcy or irrelevancy after a few years. It happened with American Motors, Bricklin, Chrysler, and Delorean, and will likely happen to Jaguar, Land Rover, Saab, and Volvo.

There are many problems with buying orphan models. First, there's the high cost of servicing, due to increased costs for parts that become rarer and rarer. Second, it's incredibly difficult to find mechanics who can spot the likely causes of some common failures; there isn't a large pool of them who work on those vehicles all the time, and those who can work on them don't have current service bulletins to guide them. There's also an absence of secret ("goodwill") warranties to pay for work outside of the warranty period, because the automaker will have dropped the warranty extensions along with the models. Finally, these unwanted cars suffer from plummeting resale values.

Tata-owned Jaguar and Land Rover are making some money for a change, thanks to better sales in India and Asia and improved sales in North America for Land Rover. On the other hand, Jaguar's North American performance has been poor. Sales of the two prestige brands were severely hit by the global economic slow-down after Tata Motors bought the automakers from Ford for $2.5 billion dollars in 2008.

GM sold Saab in February 2010 to Spyker, a tiny Dutch company that made its name by building luxury high-performance cars that typically go for $1 million apiece. The small automaker had never made a profit and saw a substantial net loss for 2011. Spyker subsequently sold the luxury car business and in June 2011 changed its name to Swedish Automobile while awaiting regulatory approval of its acquisition by Zhejiang Youngman Lotus Automobile Co. and Pangda Automobile Trade Co. Ltd.

The Saab car plant has been shut down since April 2011 because suppliers refused to deliver parts until their bills were paid. In the meantime, Saab has applied for court protection from its creditors while it restructures its operations and seeks a Chinese corporate partner.

Volvo is also on shaky ground now that it has been sold to Geely, a Chinese truck manufacturer that has limited experience in automobile manufacturing and marketing and no experience in North America. The 15-year-old company will face the formidable task of integrating the Swedish and Chinese corporate cultures, with a little Ford thrown into the mix. Its greatest challenge, though, will be to make a profit from what had been a perennial money pit for Ford. Ford even lost money in selling off the dying brand to Geely: originally purchased for $6.45 billion in 1999, Volvo was sold by Ford for a measly $1.5 billion (U.S.). Having lost its quality edge after the Ford purchase over a decade ago, Volvo models will likely show a further decline in quality, plus poor parts supply and spotty servicing support…just before the company closes its doors.

Luxury Lemons

European vehicles are generally a driver's delight and a frugal consumer's nightmare. They're noted for having a high level of performance combined with a full array of standard comfort and convenience features. They're fun to drive, well-appointed, and attractively styled. On the other hand, you can forget the myth about all European luxury vehicles holding their value; most don't. They're also unreliable, overpriced, and a pain in the butt to service.

This last point is important to remember because in hard economic times such as these, cash-strapped dealers do not invest in a large parts inventories or mechanic training to adequately service what they sell. For them, the present is chaotic and the future is unknown and threatening, so you should buy a model that's been sold in relatively large quantities for years and has parts that are available from independent suppliers. If you insist on buying a European make, be sure you know where it can be serviced by independent mechanics in case the dealership's service falters or servicing costs are too high. Interestingly, in my travels across Canada, independent Volkswagen and Volvo garages seem to be fairly well distributed, while BMW, Jaguar, Mercedes, and Saab repairers are found mostly in the larger cities, if at all.

So what's wrong with European cars? First, they can't compare to cheaper Asian competitors in terms of performance and durability. Who wants a Mercedes when offered a Lexus? Why get a dealer-dependent VW Jetta when you can have more fun with a Mazda3 Sport (even with its stupid grin on the front grille)? Second, when times get tough, European automakers get out of town. Remember ARO, Dacia, Fiat, Peugeot, Renault, Skoda, and Yugo? Asians, on the other hand, tough it out. Finally, European vehicles aren't that dependable and tend to be poorly serviced, with maintenance bills that rival the cost of a week in Cannes. Shoppers understandably balk at these outrageously high prices, and European automakers respond by adding nonessential, problem-prone gadgets that drive up costs even more. In effect, they are selling the sizzle because the steak is *pourri*.

British independent automotive journalist Robert Farago, former editor of the *Truth About Cars* website (*www.thetruthaboutcars.com*), writes:

> Once upon a time, a company called Mercedes-Benz built luxury cars. Not elk aversive city runabouts. [An allusion to the Smart Car.] Not German taxis. Not teeny tiny hairdressers' playthings. And definitely not off-roaders…. In the process, the Mercedes brand lost its reputation for quality and exclusivity. In fact, the brand has become so devalued that Mercedes themselves abandoned it, reviving the Nazi-friendly Maybach marque for its top-of-the-range limo. Now that Mercedes has morphed with Chrysler, the company is busy proving that the average of something good and something bad is something mediocre.

You won't read this kind of straight reporting from the cowering North American motoring press, as they fawn over any new techno-gadget-laden vehicle hailing from England, Germany, or Sweden. It's easy for them; they get their cars and press junkets for free.

Lemon-Aid readers who own pricey European imports invariably tell me of powertrains that stall, transmissions that jump out of gear, nightmarish electrical glitches that run the gamut from annoying to life-threatening, and computer malfunctions that are difficult to diagnose and hard to fix. Other problems noted by owners include premature brake wear, excessive brake noise, AC failures, poor driveability, hard starts, loss of power, and faulty computer modules leading to erratic shifting. Interestingly, although Ladas were low-quality Soviet imports, their deficiencies pale in comparison to what I've seen coming out of today's

European luxury corral. Plus, servicing diesels will get costlier and more complicated in the future, now that your diesel's urea tank has to be refilled regularly—only by the dealer. Yikes!

Service, *Nicht Gut*

Have you visited a European automaker's dealership lately? Although poor servicing is usually more acute with vehicles that are new on the market, it has long been the Achilles' heel of European importers. Owners give European dealerships low ratings for mishandling complaints, for inadequately training their service representatives, and for hiring an insufficient number of mechanics—not to mention for the abrasive, arrogant attitude typified by some automakers and dealers who bully customers because they have a virtual monopoly on sales and servicing in their regions. Look at their dealer networks and you'll see that most European automakers are crowded in Ontario and on the West Coast, leaving their customers in eastern Canada or the Prairies to fend for themselves.

Not Recommended European Models

Lemon-Aid cannot recommend vehicles from the following five European automakers because the risks associated with buying them are too great: Jaguar, Land Rover, Saab, Smart, and Volvo. We believe these manufacturers may not remain solvent following the present automotive turmoil. If the companies do survive, buyers risk owning vehicles with plummeting resale values that cannot be serviced due to a shortage of skilled mechanics or underfunded parts inventories. Most of these brands have been disowned by their parent manufacturers and sold for barely a third of their value to Indian, Dutch, and Chinese interests. Their former owners couldn't support the cost of ownership, and neither can you.

Audi

Saddled in the early '80s with a reputation for making poor-quality cars that would suddenly accelerate out of control, Audi fought back for two decades and staged a spectacular comeback with well-built, moderately priced front-drive and AWD Quattro sedans and wagons that spelled "Performance" with a capital "P." Through an expanded lineup of sedans, coupes, and Cabriolets during the last decade, Audi gained a reputation for making sure-footed all-wheel-drive luxury cars loaded with lots of high-tech bells and whistles—and they look drop-dead gorgeous.

Audi now accounts for a quarter of Volkswagen's U.S. sales. Last year, VW ranked third in U.S. sales, about 1.2 million deliveries behind Toyota and General Motors Co. Through the first half of 2011, it trails GM by about 400,000 sales and leads Toyota by about the same amount.

Sure, Audi and VW are seeing profitable times, but many Audi lovers say this has been done through the "gentrification" of the Audi spirit. Says this former

Audi owner (*www.autoweek.com/article/20100420/carnews/100429990#ixzz1XHY0 Oqyk*):

> Audi currently disappoints me. I've owned Audis for the last 15 years. They are going soft. Automatics are taking over the line and Manual transmissions are disappearing. TT sales are alleged to be slow, but you can only get it in an automatic. Paddle Shifters + dual auto clutch is not a manual. No manual is available with Quattro, although it is available in the A3 or the A4 Avant. And no S4 Avant, auto or manual. Non-turbo V6 is gone from the A4. The vibrating and noisy 2.0TFSI that is shared with VW and is awful when paired with an automatic.

Audi's quality control, servicing, and warranty support remain problematic and are not expected to get much better as the company rebounds from the recession. It's no secret that reliability in most Audis declines quickly after a few years of use, causing many owners to walk away when their lease or warranty expires. As used Audis pile up in dealer inventories, resale values take a beating, even among the models that have a relatively clean record. Take, for example, the poor-selling TT: a 2008 TT Quattro Coupe that originally sold for $50,600; it's now worth barely $29,000 after three years—a boon for used car buyers, a bust for owners. The fact that Audi powertrains are covered under warranty only up to 4 years/80,000 km is far from reassuring, since engines and transmissions have traditionally been Audi's weakest components and many other automakers cover their vehicles up to 5 years/100,000 km. This worry is backed up by *Consumer Reports* surveys showing serious powertrain problems with the entire Audi lineup, including the recently launched Q7 SUV and the entry-level A3. The A7, which made its debut in 2011, is rated Not Recommended until it proves its worth.

A3   ★★★

RATING: Average. **Strong points:** The car's a superb highway performer, thanks to its powerful and smooth-running engines and transmissions. Handling is crisp, steering is accurate, and cornering is accomplished with minimal body roll. Lots of safety, performance, and convenience features. Audi rates the A3 as capable of

KEY FACTS

CANADIAN PRICE (NEGOTIABLE): *2.0 TFSI:* $35,750, *Premium:* $37,000, *Quattro:* $38,900, *Quattro Premium:* $41,950, *TDI:* $37,300, *TDI Premium:* $39,000 **U.S. PRICE:** *2.0 TFSI:* $27,270, *Premium:* $28,750, *Premium Quattro:* $30,850, *Premium Plus:* $29,270, *Premium Plus auto.:* $30,750, *Premium Plus Quattro:* $32,850, *TDI Premium:* $32,250 **CANADIAN FREIGHT:** $1,995 **U.S. FREIGHT:** $875 **POWERTRAIN (FRONT-DRIVE/AWD)** Engines: 2.0L 4-cyl. Turbo (200 hp) • 2.0L 4-cyl. Diesel (140 hp); Transmission: 6-speed man. • 6-speed auto. **DIMENSIONS/CAPACITY** Passengers: 2/3; Wheelbase: 102 in.; H: 56/L: 169/W: 69 in.; Headroom F/R: 4.5/2.0 in.; Legroom F/R: 42.0/25.5 in.; Cargo volume: 19.5 cu. ft.; Fuel tank: 55L/premium/diesel; Tow limit: Not recommended; Load capacity: 990 lb.; Turning circle: 35 ft.; Ground clearance: 4.0 in.; Weight: 3,305 lb.

carrying five passengers; however, the three back-seat passengers had better be friends. IIHS rates the A3 as "Good" for head-restraint and roof protection and in protecting occupants in frontal offset and side crashes. **Weak points:** Fairly expensive for an entry-level Audi; on top of that, depreciation will likely be much faster than average, which doubles your losses. Also, a freight fee that nudges $2,000 should be made a felony. Premium gas is required, and insurance premiums are higher than average. Numerous factory-related problems affecting primarily the electrical system, powertrain, brakes, and accessories. Fit and finish are not up to luxury-car standards, either. No NHTSA crashworthiness data. **New for 2012:** Returns relatively unchanged.

OVERVIEW: Based on the redesigned Volkswagen Golf, the A3 is Audi's entry-level, compact, four-door hatchback. It's a well-appointed, generously powered vehicle that arrived in the summer of 2005. The A3 comes in Standard and Premium trim levels, with a choice of two engines: 2.0 T versions have a 200 hp 2.0L turbocharged 4-cylinder engine, available with a 6-speed manual or 6-speed automatic transmission; the 2.0 TDI has a 140 hp 4-cylinder turbodiesel with the automatic only. All A3s are available in front-drive, and Audi's Quattro all-wheel drive is available on automatic transmission 2.0 Ts. Standard safety features include ABS, traction control, an anti-skid system, front side airbags, rear side airbags, and side curtain airbags.

COST ANALYSIS: This four-door hatchback is smaller and less costly than Audi's A4 compacts, and is just as much fun to drive. Since these cars are mostly carryovers from the 2011s, look for a discounted previous model year. **Best alternatives:** Acura TSX, BMW 3 Series, and a fully loaded VW Jetta TDI. **Rebates:** Not likely, though prices will probably soften in late winter. **Depreciation:** Faster than average. A $33,800 entry-level 2008 A3 is now worth only $19,000. Audi values usually nosedive when the base warranty expires. **Insurance cost:** Higher than average. **Parts supply/cost:** Frustrating. Owners report months-long waits for fuel system, powertrain, and electronic components. The present recession is making the problem of limited part supplies and high parts costs untenable—sufficient reason to not buy an Audi this year. Independent suppliers scratch their heads when you ask about Audi parts. **Annual maintenance cost:** A bit higher than average. **Warranty:** Bumper-to-bumper 4 years/80,000 km; rust perforation 10 years/unlimited km. **Supplementary warranty:** Don't leave the dealership without getting at least five-year coverage for the powertrain. **Highway/city fuel**

economy: *2.0 front-drive man.:* 6.7/10.4 L/100 km, 42/27 mpg. *2.0 front-drive auto.:* 6.9/9.4 L/100 km, 41/30 mpg. *2.0 AWD:* 7.5/9.6 L/100 km, 38/29 mpg. *TDI:* 4.7/6.7 L/100 km, 60/42 mpg.

OWNER-REPORTED PROBLEMS: Sudden loss of diesel power when accelerating; the same failure occurs with 2010 models, as well. Transmission engages and then disengages when accelerating from a stop or when parking:

> Purchased a new 2011 Audi A3 TDI last Saturday. The following Friday while pulling out into an intersection the DSG transmission briefly went into neutral and I saw the tachometer needle shoot up and heard the engine whine. I was in manual mode at the time. I down shifted and let off the gas and it re-engaged. The following day (today) the same thing happened again. This time I was also in manual mode and was again pulling out into traffic from an almost complete stop. I have since learned that this is an ongoing and known issue with VW/Audi DSG transmissions. [Author's note: You bet it is.]

Engine, transmission, climate control, fuel pump, and electrical system failures, as well as fit and finish deficiencies. Owners also report blinking headlights and interior lights when the brakes are applied. Premature brake replacements (rotors and calipers) and bad Bridgestone original equipment tires that are shredded by the tire rim.

SERVICE BULLETIN-REPORTED PROBLEMS: Electrical harness damage from animal chewing; higher than normal oil consumption; free O2 sensor replacement or ECM update (Campaign 23F5); steering service bulletin #2022563/4, published April 14, 2011 gives extensive troubleshooting tips to correct steering wheel shimmy, vibration. In some cases, a free tire replacement will be provided through the tire manufacturer and the Audi Tire Assistance Program (not Audi) for eligible 2008–11 models; sound system speakers may cause interior buzzing, vibrating noises on all 2008–11 models; front suspension cracking or rubbing noise on all 2008–11 models; squealing brakes are addressed on Audi's entire lineup for 2008–11 model years in service bulletin #461111, 2017130/9, published March 10, 2011; instrument displays dim or darken and interior lighting flickers; seat heaters don't get enough heat; 2005–11 A3 models may have faulty front windshield wipers; and various fixes for sunroof issues affecting Audi's entire lineup since 2005.

A4, S4, A5, S5	★ ★ ★

RATING: Average. The recession has made Audi quality and servicing problems worse. On the positive side, so many of these vehicles have been sold for so long that sustained digging will usually find you the part and a mechanic who can service the vehicle competently. Plus, there has been a dramatic reduction in safety-related problems reported by owners. **Strong points:** Loaded with safety, performance, and convenience features. Safety-related complaints have dropped

The Audi A4.

considerably. The base 2.0L engine provides gobs of low-end torque and accelerates as well with the automatic transmission as it does with the manual. The turbocharger works well, with no turbo delay or torque steer. The manual gearbox, Tiptronic automatic transmission, and CVT all work flawlessly. Comfortable ride; exceptional handling, though not as sporty as Acura's TSX; impressive braking performance (when the brakes are working properly); and lots of cargo room in the wagon. NHTSA gave both the A4 and the S4 four stars for front crashworthiness and five stars for side and rollover protection; IIHS posted similarly impressive scores, giving a "Good" rating to frontal offset, side, roof, and head-restraint protection. **Weak points:** Although there have been fewer safety complaints reported, overall reliability is unimpressive. Not as fast as its rivals; the

KEY FACTS

CANADIAN PRICE (NEGOTIABLE): *2.0 TFSI:* $39,300, *Quattro:* $40,700, *Quattro Premium:* $44,600, *S4 3.0 TFSI Quattro:* $53,500, *S4 Quattro 7-speed:* $55,100 **U.S. PRICE:** *2.0 TFSI:* $32,500, *Quattro Premium:* $33,300, *Quattro Premium 8-speed:* $34,600, *Premium Plus:* $36,800, *Quattro Premium Plus:* $37,600, *Quattro Premium 8-speed:* $34,600, *Quattro Premium:* $33,300, *Quattro Prestige:* $42,000, *Quattro Prestige 8-speed:* $44,100; *S4 Premium Plus Quattro:* $47,300, *S4 Premium Plus Quattro 7-speed:* $48,700, *S4 Prestige Quattro:* $54,000, *S4 Prestige Quattro 7-speed:* $55,400, *S5 Premium Plus Quattro 6-speed man.:* $53,900, *S5 Premium Plus Quattro Tiptronic:* $55,100, *S5 Prestige Quattro 6-speed man.:* $60,200, *S5 Prestige Quattro*

Tiptronic: $61,400 **CANADIAN FREIGHT:** $1,995 **U.S. FREIGHT:** $875
POWERTRAIN (FRONT-DRIVE/AWD)
Engines: 2.0L 4-cyl. (211 hp) • 3.0L SC V6 (333 hp); Transmissions: 6-speed man. • 8-speed auto. • 7-speed auto. • CVT
DIMENSIONS/CAPACITY (A4 SEDAN)
Passengers: 2/3; Wheelbase: 110.5 in.; H: 56.2/L: 169.5/W: 71.8 in.; Headroom F/R: 3.5/2.5 in.; Legroom F/R: 41.5/24.5 in.; Cargo volume: 16.9 cu. ft.; Fuel tank: 62L/premium; Tow limit: Not recommended; Load capacity: 1,060 lb.; Turning circle: 37.4 ft.; Ground clearance: 4.2 in.; Weight: 3,665 lb.

ride is stiff at low speeds, and a bit firm at other times; some body roll and brake dive under extreme conditions; braking can be a bit twitchy; some tire drumming and engine noise; and limited rear seatroom (the front seatbacks press against rear occupants' knees). Overpriced, with an outrageously high $2,000 freight charge and depreciation that is a wallet-buster. Another expense to consider is the car's high maintenance cost, especially because of its overall poor reliability. **New for 2012:** Minor trim upgrades.

OVERVIEW: This is Audi's bread-and-butter model, probably because it comes in so many variations, including sedans, Avant wagons, and convertibles; the lineup also includes high-performance models that are sold under the S4 and S5 labels. The A4 bills itself as Audi's family sport sedan and targets the BMW 3 Series and Mercedes E Class customer by featuring a roomy interior, an 8-speed automatic transmission, all-wheel drive, independent suspension, low-speed traction enhancement, automatic climate control, and more airbags than you can imagine.

The 2012 Audi A4 lineup also includes a recently restyled and upgraded supercharged S4 sedan model, along with four-door sedans and Avant wagons. The Cabriolet convertible is redesigned and is sold as part of Audi's A5 and S5 lineup. Sedans and wagons continue to offer Audi's Quattro all-wheel drive, and some versions of the sedan are available as front-drives. Sedans and Avants come as the 2.0 T and feature a turbocharged 211 hp 2.0L 4-cylinder engine. A continuously variable automatic transmission is standard on front-drive 2.0 Ts. The S4 sedan and S5 convertible are powered by a powerful 333 hp 3.0L supercharged V6 mated to either a 6-speed manual or an 8-speed automatic; This setup provides impressive torque that kicks in at just 2500 rpm and remains constant through 4850 rpm, making the car especially responsive in everyday driving. Performance buffs will choose the 354 hp 4.2L V8 S5 coupe. All models are loaded with standard high-tech safety and performance features that add to the car's complexity and price.

COST ANALYSIS: Go for a discounted, practically identical 2011. Better yet, buy this model used, and get your servicing from an independent agency with a reputation for performing competent repairs. S5 convertibles cost about $10,000 more than the A5 convertible mainly due to the V8 engine used by the S5. This is too much to pay for what is only a slightly better performer. **Best alternatives:** If you like the S4 or S5 tire-burners, also consider the BMW M3 convertible or 5 Series and the Porsche 911 Carrera. A4 alternatives are the Acura TL or TSX, BMW 3 Series, Hyundai Genesis, Infiniti G37, and Lexus ES 350 or IS series. **Options:** An automatic transmission and all-wheel drive. Think twice about getting the power moonroof if you're a tall driver. **Rebates:** $3,000–$6,000 rebates, and a variety of dealer incentive plans and low-interest financing programs. **Depreciation:** Incredibly fast; a 2008 A4 that sold for $35,350 is now worth $21,000, a 2008 S4 that once cost $74,400 now barely fetches $38,000. Not even high-performance S5 variants can escape value-robbing depreciation: The 2008 V8-equipped S5 coupe that originally sold for $66,000, is now worth $37,000. Worse yet, convertibles are no longer a safe haven: A 2010 S5 convertible that once sold for about

$69,000 is now worth $12,000 less. **Insurance cost:** Higher than average. **Parts supply/cost:** Often back ordered and expensive. Forget about saving money by getting parts from independent suppliers; they carry few Audi parts. **Annual maintenance cost:** Higher than average, but not exorbitant. **Warranty:** Bumper-to-bumper 4 years/80,000 km; rust perforation 10 years/unlimited km. **Supplementary warranty:** Don't leave the dealership without it. **Highway/ city fuel economy:** *2.0 front-drive man.:* 6.5/8.9 L/100 km, 43/31 mpg. *2.0 front-drive auto.:* 7.0/10.0 L/100 km, 43/30 mpg. *2.0 Quattro man.:* 6.5/9.5 L/100 km, 38/28 mpg. *2.0 Quattro auto.:* 7.0/10.0 L/100 km, 38/28 mpg. *A5 convertible:* 7.0/10.0 L/100 km, 35/23 mpg. *A5 coupe man.:* 6.5/9.5 L/100 km, 36/23 mpg. *S4 man.:* 8.1/12.2 L/100 km, 35/23 mpg. *Auto.:* 7.9/12.1 L/100 km, 36/23 mpg. *S5 convertible:* 8.1/12.9 L/100 km, 35/23 mpg. *Coupe man.:* 9.4/15.1 L/100 km, 36/23 mpg. *Auto.:* 9.8/12.8 L/100 km, 36/23 mpg. Remember, AWD models trade fuel economy for better traction.

OWNER-REPORTED PROBLEMS: NHTSA logs show very few safety-related complaints going back to the 2009s and no incidents for the 2011 models. The 2010 reports show continued acceleration while braking; acceleration lag and engine surge; vehicle lunging every time the Tiptronic transmission is downshifted; stalling caused by faulty fuel-injectors; CVT allows the vehicle to roll down an incline when stopped; secondary radiator is easily damaged from road debris; sudden water pump failure; and the windshield wipers stop working when the vehicle comes to a stop. Quality control is far from acceptable. The following problems have all taken these cars out of service for extended periods in the past: airbag fails to deploy; excessive steering shake due to a faulty lower control arm; engine, fuel-system (fuel-injectors, principally), and powertrain component failures; defective brakes; electrical shorts; and abysmal fit and finish. The electrical system is the car's weakest link, and it has plagued Audi's entire lineup for the past decade. Normally, this wouldn't be catastrophic; however, as the cars become more electronically complex and competent mechanics are fired as dealerships open and close, you're looking at a greater chance of poor-quality servicing, long waits for service, and unacceptably high maintenance and repair costs.

SERVICE BULLETIN-REPORTED PROBLEMS: Electrical harness damage from animal chewing; low idle when starting up and ECP light is on; no start after CAN bus silence; steering wheel shimmy, vibration; steering squeaking when turning; suspension shock absorber leaks; AC doesn't cool; AC moisture in driver or front passenger footwell; hard to select First gear when car is cold; partially detached outer door seals; noises from the sunroof area; B-pillar rubbing, squeaking, rattle noises; automatic transmission fluid leaks; 2 TCM computer module updates for smoother shifting; cracking noise when depressing clutch pedal; interior noises when speakers play heavy bass notes; speaker sound is distorted or can't be heard; audio system CD drive malfunctions; flickering MMI screen; MMI screen is blank in hot temperatures; false Low Oil message; false side object warning alert; false Parking Assist System warnings; false Antitheft system alarms; various electrical shorts; satellite radio prematurely deactivates; can't program garage door opener; inoperative door handle Touch Sensor; front door armrest noises; inoperative exterior trunk handle; trunk lining handle hook is mis-positioned; key won't stay in the ignition lock; Remote Control key doesn't work; multiple electrical malfunctions after window tinting (affects all 2005–12 Audis); and navigation joystick is loose or falls off; inoperative daylight running lights. Campaign #44J2 TPMS: software update; Campaign #91G1: software update of MMI 3G.

A6, S6, R8 ★★★

The Audi A6.

RATING: Average. The A6 would have been rated higher if its build quality was better and its residual value were higher. Nevertheless, the new A6 is far better than the car it replaces. The BMW's 5 Series is a worse car than the Bimmer it replaces. **Strong points:** A potent base engine that produces incredible acceleration times and gives excellent gas mileage; predictable handling; good, though mushy braking; comfortable seating; interior includes a user-friendly navigations system and an analog/digital instrument panel that is a joy to behold and use; plenty of passenger and cargo room (it beats out both BMW and Mercedes in this area); easy front and rear access; and very good build quality. Dropping the failure-prone DSG automatic transmission in favour of the 8-speed automatic on the A6 was smart. The Avant wagon performs like a sport-utility, with side airbags, high-intensity discharge xenon headlights, and excellent outward visibility. IIHS considers offset crash protection and head-restraint effectiveness to be "Good." **Weak points:** The restyling looks limp and dated: overdone lights, ho-hum grille, and a painfully boring interior. A6's Servotronic steering is improved, but it is still the car's weakest feature. It is both over-boosted and uncommunicative in "Comfort" mode and ponderous and numb in its "Dynamic" setting. Brakes are mushy compared to the BMW 535i's firm pedal. V8 is a bit "growly" when pushed; no real-world performance or reliability data on the V10 yet; firm suspension can make for a jittery ride; some tire thumping and

CANADIAN PRICE (NEGOTIABLE): *A6 2.0 TFSI:* $58,800, *3.0 TFSI Quattro:* $62,700, *3.0 TFSI Quattro Premium:* $66,900, *A6 4.2 FSI Quattro:* $75,900, *S6 5.2 TFSI Quattro:* $99,500, *R8 4.2T FSI Quattro:* $141,000, *R8 5.2 TFSI Quattro:* $173,000 **U.S. PRICE:** *A6 2.0 TFSI Premium FWD:* $41,700, *2.0 TFSI Premium Plus FWD:* $45,920, *3.0 TFSI:* $49,900, *3.0 TFSI Premium Plus Quattro:* $54,120, *3.0 TFSI Prestige Quattro:* $56,780, S5 *4.2 FSI Quattro:* $55,100, *S6 5.2 FSI Quattro:* $76,100, *R8 4.2L Quattro:* $114,200, *R8 4.2L R tronic Quattro:* $123,000, *R8 5.2L Quattro:* $149,000, *R8 Quattro R tronic Quattro:* $158 **CANADIAN FREIGHT:** $1,995 **U.S. FREIGHT:** $875

POWERTRAIN (FRONT-DRIVE/AWD)
Engines: 2.0L 4-cyl. (211 hp) • 3.0L V6 (310 hp) • • 4.0.L V8 (414 hp) • 4.2L 5.2L (350 hp) • V10 (560 hp); Transmissions: 8-speed auto. • 6-speed man. and S tronic • CVT

DIMENSIONS/CAPACITY
Passengers: 2/3; Wheelbase: 111.9 in.; H: 57.5/L: 193.5/W: 73 in.; Headroom F/R: 3.0/3.0 in.; Legroom F/R: 42/27.5 in.; Cargo volume: 16 cu. ft.; Fuel tank: 80.1L/premium; Tow limit: Not recommended; Load capacity: 1,100 lb.; Turning circle: 40 ft.; R8: 38.7 ft.; Ground clearance: *A6:* 5.0 in.; *S6:* 4.3 in.; *R8:* 4.5 in.; Weight: 4,110 lb.

highway wind noise; uncomfortable centre-rear seating; the wagon's two-place rear seat is rather small; no NHTSA crashworthiness ratings; limited availability of the most popular models; and servicing can be problematic. And, if high servicing costs aren't enough, at the end of four years you may find your Audi is worth only a third of its original value. **New for 2012:** *A6:* Redesigned with a cabin full of borrowed A7 parts, styling borrowed from both the A4 and A8, and two engines: a 211 hp 2.0L turbo-four and an updated supercharged 310 hp V6. AWD is expected to be phased in on the 4-cylinder models in early 2012. The cabin also becomes an Internet hot spot that can provide web access for up to eight devices at a time. *A6 Avant:* Dropped. *S6:* The V10 is replaced by a 4.0L twin-turbocharged 414 hp V8, hooked to a 7-speed S-tronic automatic, it posts a 0–60 mph time of 4.8 seconds and a top speed of 155 mph. Other refinements: upgraded adaptive air suspension, larger disc brakes, and better tires. *R8:* Returns with its V10 boosted to 560 hp.

OVERVIEW: The A6 is a comfortable, spacious front-drive luxury vehicle that comes as a sedan or wagon and offers standard dual front side airbags and head-protecting side curtain airbags; torso side airbags are optional. Also standard are ABS, an anti-skid system, and xenon headlights (thieves love 'em). There's even a multi-tasking joystick control for all the entertainment, navigation, and climate-control functions. It's similar in function to BMW's iDrive system, which has been roundly criticized as being both confusing and dangerously distracting. The A6 sedan comes with a base 211 hp 2.0L four or an optional 310 hp 3.0L V6. Both engines are mated to a CVT or an 8-speed automatic transmission with manual-shift capability; Audi's Quattro all-wheel drive is also available.

The Audi R8 is an all-wheel-drive, two-seat coupe with a mid-mounted engine. The entry-level 4.2L has a 420 hp V8 engine, but the 5.2L has a 525–560 hp V10. Both models are available with an 8-speed Tiptronic automatic transmission or

Audi's R-tronic automated manual. As with other Audis, depreciation is a value-killer. A 2008 (its debut year) top-of-the-line R8 that sold new for $139,000 is now worth about $89,000—$50,000 less—in not quite three years.

COST ANALYSIS: Audi has never been a major player in the global midsize luxury sedan market. For every A6 sold in 2010, Mercedes sold seven E-Series models and BMW moved five 5 Series sedans. That ratio hasn't changed much in 2011. This means you can haggle to your heart's delight because Audi dealers have a substantial profit margin to share and they'll do almost anything to poach buyers from their competitors. For example: this year's $41,700 price for a base A6 is $3,500 less than the 2011's $45,200 MSRP. BMW's 5-Series line starts at $45,050 (U.S.), and Mercedes-Benz E-Class sedans start at $49,400 (U.S.). **Best alternatives:** Although the base A6 2.0T models are cheaper and more fuel-efficient than many competitors, they are also the least powerful cars in the segment. *A6 4-cylinder:* This base model rivals the more-powerful BMW 528i which costs about $3,000 more. On the downside, the 528i's gas consumption can't match the A6. Now, if BMW puts a turbocharged 4-banger into its early 2012 models, then it's back to the drawing boards. The automaker says that the new engine should deliver up to 15 percent better fuel economy. The *A6 3.0T:* Infiniti's M37x is worth test driving. Other vehicles worth taking a look at are the Hyundai Genesis and Lexus GS. **Options:** Think twice about getting the power moonroof if you're a tall driver. **Rebates:** $8,000 rebates and low-interest financing. **Depreciation:** Lightspeed fast: a 2008 A6 Quattro which sold new for $63,600 sells used for barely half that price. **Insurance cost:** Higher than average. **Parts supply/cost:** Very dealer-dependent and expensive. Independent suppliers carry few Audi parts. **Annual maintenance cost:** Low during the warranty period, and then it climbs steadily. **Warranty:** Bumper-to-bumper 4 years/80,000 km; powertrain 4 years/80,000 km; rust perforation 10 years/unlimited km. **Supplementary warranty:** A prerequisite to Audi ownership, and it guarantees a good resale price. **Highway/city fuel economy:** *3.0:* 8.0/12.0 L/100 km, 35/24 mpg. *4.2 Quattro:* 8.6/13.0 L/100 km, 33/22 mpg. *3.0 Avant Quattro:* 8.6/13.0 L/100 km, 33/22 mpg. *R8 4.2 Coupe man.:* 10.2/16.3 L/100 km, 28/17 mpg. *Auto:* 11.4/17.0 L/100 km, 25/15 mpg. *S6 5.2:* 10.0/15.2 L/100 km, 27/19 mpg.

OWNER-REPORTED PROBLEMS: Very few safety-related complaints recorded over the past two model years. Sudden loss of coolant and early wearout of original equipment Continental tires. Non-safety related problems concern mostly the electrical and fuel delivery systems in addition to scads of fit and finish deficiencies (see "Service Bulletin-Reported Problems").

SERVICE BULLETIN-REPORTED PROBLEMS: Electrical harness damage caused by animal chewing; automatic transmission fluid leaks; excessive steering wheel vibration or shimmy; squeaking noise when turning; brakes moan on acceleration or during low-speed turns; AC doesn't cool; cooling fan noise when turning; disc brake squealing; noises from the sunroof area; interior buzzing, vibrating noises when the audio system is playing; inoperative external trunk handle; door handle touch sensor failure; water in fog lamps; key won't stay in the ignition; multiple malfunctions after window tinting; navigation joystick is loose or falling off; MMI screen is blank in hot temperatures; inoperative daytime running lights; satellite radio prematurely deactivates; false Parking Assist alerts; antitheft alarm comes on for no reason; remote control key is inoperative; and the garage opener can't be programmed. Software update Campaign #91G1.

TT, TTS, TT RS COUPE ★★★★

The Audi TT RS Coupe.

RATING: Above Average, due to its nice balance of agility and comfort. Be prepared for a surprisingly low resale value and handling that's not the equal of a Hyundai Genesis, Mazda RX8, or Porsche Boxster. **Strong points:** Acceptable acceleration with the base 211 hp 4-cylinder powerplant, but you will long for the extra grunt found in the up-rated TTS model; good handling and road holding; very well appointed and tastefully designed interior; comfortable, supportive seats; plenty of passenger and cargo space (especially with the rear seatbacks folded); standard ABS; "smart" dual front airbags; and standard stability control. 2006 NHTSA crashworthiness tests awarded the convertible five stars for side occupant protection and rollover resistance. **Weak points:** Base 211 hp engine lacks low-end torque; excess weight limits handling; lacks a 6-speed manual gearbox (S Tronic and DSG aren't the same); poor rear and side visibility; ride may be too firm for some; a useless back seat; difficult rear-seat access; lots of engine and road noise. Hatch is heavy to raise, and a rear windshield wiper would be nice. No recent NHTSA or IIHS crashworthiness tests. **New for 2012:** Nothing significant, except for the late entry of the high-performance RS.

OVERVIEW: These cars, like most Audis, don't hold their value well. Used bargains abound if you are a savvy Audi mechanic or have access to a competent independent repairer. The TT Coupe Quattro debuted in the spring of 1999 as a

$49,000 sporty front-drive hatchback with 2+2 seating, set on the same platform used by the A4 and the VW Golf, Jetta, and New Beetle. The TT's engines are coupled to a manual 6-speed front-drive gearbox. A spoiler and anti-skid system are also standard. Audi's TTS version is an upgraded, more powerful version of the standard car.

More beautifully styled and with better handling than most sporty cars, the TT comes with lots of high-tech standard features that include four-wheel disc brakes, airbags everywhere, stability and traction control, a power top (Quattro), a heated-glass rear window, and a power-retractable glass windbreak between the roll bars (convertible). An alarm system employs a pulse radar system to catch prying hands invading the cockpit area.

TT Coupes carry two variations of the same 2.0L 4-cylinder engine: a 211 hp 2.0L 4-banger and a 265 hp turbocharged version of the same engine. On the safety front, all of the 2011 models have self-supporting run-flat tires; a tire pressure warning system; full-sized two-stage front airbags; and side (head/thorax) and knee airbags. There's also a connection located in the glove box for playing and charging your iPod, which you can control via the radio or the multi-function steering wheel. A Bluetooth mobile telephone feature allows for hands-free operation with voice-controlled capabilities.

TT RS

The series' most powerful model, the RS will appear in early 2012. It is powered by a 360 hp 2.5L 5-cylinder turbocharged engine hooked to a revised 6-speed manual transmission (there is no automatic). This little rocket goes from 0 to 60 mph in just 4.3 seconds with a top speed of 174 mph.

COST ANALYSIS: Buy an almost identical, discounted 2011 TTS, priced thousands of dollars less and powered by a torquier small engine. TT sales have been slow this year, so prices can be haggled down by at least 15 percent. **Best alternatives:** The BMW Z Series, Hyundai Genesis Coupe, Infiniti G37 Coupe, and Mazda Miata. **Options:** Think twice about getting the power moonroof if you're a tall driver. On the other hand, the Audi Magnetic Ride option truly personalizes suspension performance, but its high price ($1,900) is an unexpected jolt. **Rebates:** $6,000 rebates and low-interest financing. **Depreciation:** Surprisingly fast, but slower than other Audi models, like the A5 and A6. **Insurance cost:** Higher than average. **Parts supply/cost:** Very dealer-dependent and expensive. Independent suppliers carry few Audi parts. **Annual maintenance cost:** Low during the warranty period, and then it climbs steadily. **Warranty:** Bumper-to-bumper 4 years/80,000 km; powertrain 4 years/80,000 km; rust perforation 10 years/unlimited km. **Supplementary warranty:** A prerequisite to Audi ownership, and it guarantees a good resale price. **Highway/city fuel economy:** *TT Coupe Quattro 2.0:* 6.4/9.1 L/100 km, 44/31 mpg. *Roadster:* 6.4/9.1 L/100 km, 44/31 mpg. *TTS Coupe:* 7.4/10.7 L/100 km, 38/26 mpg. *Roadster:* 6.4/9.1 L/100 km, 38/26 mpg.

OWNER-REPORTED PROBLEMS: No safety-related incidents reported for the last two model years. 2009 versions suddenly stalled or would not shift into gear (familiar problem with DSG transmissions).

SERVICE BULLETIN-REPORTED PROBLEMS: Steering wheel shimmy, vibration, and brake squealing. *TTS Roadster:* Electrical harness damage caused by animal chewing; brake squealing; front suspension cracking, rubbing; steering squeaks when turning; stripe across instrument cluster display; convertible top alignment issues; multiple malfunctions after window tinting; can't program the garage opener; inoperative daylight running lights; satellite radio prematurely shuts off; and false warnings from the Parking Assist feature.

BMW

From a performance and reliability perspective, BMW is the best of the German brands. That's why it remains one of Canada's favourite luxury car manufacturers, after Volkswagen and Mercedez-Benz.

No Decontenting—Yet

Despite the hard economic times, and unlike Toyota and Honda, BMW has resisted the temptation to keep prices down by decontenting its vehicles. In fact, the company is expected to hold the line on the cost of its 2012s by offering an array of discounts, rebates, and other incentives in the new year to keep its number one spot in Canada's pantheon of luxury cars. Consumers haven't balked at BMW's high prices, yet, inasmuch as they are more attracted by the auto-makers reputation for offering well-built, nicely-appointed cars with excellent handling and superior driving comfort. No matter if fuel prices rise or fall, BMW has a product that will be appropriate for the times. Entry-level shoppers have the 1 and 3 Series; families with more disposable income may opt for the 5 and 6 Series; and for those who have the cash to buy loads of cachet, there's always the flagship 7 Series. Sport-utility fans also have four vehicles to choose from: the just-arrived X1 (a "baby SUV"), the compact X3, and the larger X5 and X6.

BMWs have excellent road manners and shout "I got mine!" Unfortunately, there's barely a whisper to warn you of chronic brake, fuel system, and powertrain problems that can be quite expensive to troubleshoot and repair. Shh... There's also the incredibly complicated centre-console-mounted iDrive feature that some have renamed the "iDie" controller. Lately, BMW has made the iDrive more user-friendly, but the system still takes some getting used to.

Other BMW minuses: limited interior room (except in the high-end models), some quality-control deficiencies (notably the electrical system, brake pads, and fit and finish), and its vehicles can be difficult and expensive to service. A good website that lists BMW problems and fixes is *www.roadfly.com*.

Other than cachet, there are many acceptable reasons for buying a BMW, including fair overall reliability; impressive, high-performance road handling; and a low rate of depreciation. Keep in mind, though, that there are plenty of other cars that cost less, offer more interior room, are more reliable, and perform better.

New Engines, New Problems?

Judging by BMW's history with reworked models, you don't want to be the first on the block to try out new fuel, electrical, or powertrain systems. Stick with the cars that have had the fewest changes, and if that means buying a leftover 2011, then so be it. For example, after a 13-year absence, a new 240 hp 2.0L 4-cylinder turbo-charged aluminum engine makes its debut, replacing the naturally aspirated 3.0L six now found in the Z4, 3, and 5 Series sedan. Prudent buyers would be wise to put off purchasing models equipped with the new engine until the summer of 2012. This will give the factory time to work out the early glitches and ensure that mechanics are more familiar with the new powertrain setup. An additional benefit of waiting: Prices will drift downwards as the competition heats up and more choices are available.

Remember, though, that the entry-level versions of these little status symbols are more show than go, and just a few options can blow your budget. Adding to that, the larger, better-performing high-end models are much more expensive and don't give you the same standard features as many Japanese and South Korean imports do. Also, be prepared to endure long servicing waits and body and trim glitches, as well as brake, electrical, powertrain, and accessory problems.

3 SERIES ★★★✦★

RATING: Average. *M3:* Not Recommended; the transmission hesitation on acceleration or deceleration is too risky. Many competitors deliver more interior room and standard features for less money. Smart BMW buyers will stick with the simple, large-volume, entry-level models until the recession blows over. **Strong points:** Very well appointed; cockpit amenities include a standard tilt/telescope steering wheel, optional power-memory seats, power lumbar adjustments, an in-dash CD player, steering-wheel audio and cruise controls, standard traction and stability control, and rear side-impact airbags. Good acceleration (highlighted by the M3's incredibly fast performance); the 6-cylinder engines and the

The BMW 3 Series.

transmissions are the essence of harmonious cooperation, even when coupled to an automatic transmission—there's not actually that much difference between the manual and the automatic from a performance perspective. Light and precise gear shifting with easy clutch and shift action; competent and predictable handling on dry surfaces; no-surprise suspension and steering make for crisp high-speed and emergency handling; lots of road feedback, which enhances rear-end stability; smooth, efficient braking that produces short stopping distances; and top-notch quality control. NHTSA gives its top crashworthiness score—five stars—for front and side protection; rollover resistance received four stars. **Weak points:**

KEY FACTS

CANADIAN PRICE (FIRM): *323i Sedan:* $34,900, *328i Sedan:* $41,500, *328i Convertible:* $57,300, *328i xDrive Sedan:* $39,950, *328i xDrive Executive:* $46,900, *328i xDrive Touring:* $46,900, *3281 Coupe:* $44,300, *328i xDrive Coupe:* $46,800, *335i Sedan:* $49,900, *335i Coupe:* $53,400, *335i Convertible:* $68,900, *335i xDrive Coupe:* $54,100, *335i xDrive Sedan:* $52,100, *335d Sedan:* $49,900, *M3 Sedan:* $70,300, *M3 Coupe:* $71,700, *M3 Convertible:* $82,300 **U.S. PRICE:** *328i Coupe:* $37,650, *Convertible:* $46,450, *Sedan:* $34,600, *Sports Wagon:* $37,150, *xDrive Coupe:* $39,550, *xDrive sedan:* $36,600, *xDrive Sports Wagon:* $39,150, *335i Coupe:* $44,100, *335is Convertible:* $59,650, *335i Sedan:* $42,050, *335i xDrive Sedan:* $44,050, *335i xDrive Coupe:* $46,000, *335d Sedan:* $44,150, *M3 Sedan:* $55,900, *M3 Coupe:* $58,900, *M3 Convertible:* $67,550 **CANADIAN FREIGHT:** $1,995
U.S. FREIGHT: $875
POWERTRAIN (REAR-DRIVE/AWD)
Engines: 2.0L 4-cyl. (240 hp) • 3.0L 6-cyl. (230 hp) • 3.0L 6-cyl. Turbo (300 hp) • 3.0L 6-cyl. Diesel (265 hp) • 4.0L V8 (414 hp); Transmissions: 6-speed man. • 8-speed auto.

DIMENSIONS/CAPACITY

Passengers: 2/3; Wheelbase: 109 in.; H: 56/L: 178/W: 72 in.; Headroom F/R: 3.5/2.5 in.; Legroom F/R: 40.5/27.5 in.; Cargo volume: 11 cu. ft.; Fuel tank: 63L/premium; Tow limit: No towing; Load capacity: 1,060 lb.; Turning circle: 19.4 ft.; Weight: 3,485 lb.

Seriously overpriced; depreciation is only slightly slower than with Audi's lineup; a somewhat harsh ride (the M3 is harsher than most); insufficient front headroom and seat lumbar support for tall occupants; limited rear-seat room and cargo area; tricky entry and exit, even on sedans; confusing navigation system controls; excessive tire noise, especially with the M3; radio buzz; and requires premium fuel. **New for 2012:** The 2012 BMW 3 Series that arrives in March is powered by two turbocharged engines: a new 240 hp 4-cylinder powerplant and a carried-over inline six. Two transmissions will be available: a 6-speed manual and an 8-speed automatic. Except for the 335d, all 3 Series trims offer an automatic transmission as a no-cost option; the 335d's transmission cost has been lowered. All-wheel-drive models will use new 17-inch all-season tires, and iPod/USB integration is a standard feature for BMW's entire 2012 vehicle lineup. The high-performance M3 sedan and 3 Series wagon have been dropped, while the 3 Series coupe and convertible return with minor trim changes; the 328i should continue to be available with rear-drive or with BMW's xDrive AWD hooked to a 230 hp 3.0L 6-cylinder engine. All the other models will remain powered by a turbocharged 300 hp version of the 3.0L 6-cylinder. The rear-drive 335d will return with its 265 hp 3.0L 6-cylinder turbodiesel powerplant. M3 models return with the 414 hp 4.0L V8.

OVERVIEW: With BMW's recent mechanical upgrades, styling changes, and increased exterior and interior dimensions, the 3 Series has come to resemble its more-expensive big brothers, with super-smooth powertrain performance and enhanced handling.

COST ANALYSIS: Buy the cheaper 2011s, which embody previous upgrades and are practically identical in performance to the early 2012 models. Be wary of the diesel power option; the system is relatively new and much more complicated to service and repair than earlier versions. **Best alternatives:** Other cars worth considering are the Hyundai Genesis Coupe or Sedan and the Lexus IS series. **Options:** If you buy a convertible, invest $1,800 in the rollover protection system that pops up from behind the rear seat. The optional Sport suspension does enhance handling and steering, but it also produces an overly harsh, jiggly ride on rough pavement. Wider tires compromise traction in snow. Stay away from the Turanza run-flats and Bridgestone tires:

> Bridgestone tire exhibits unsafe characteristics in wet weather, with noticeable drift and hydroplaning in any amount of standing water, even as little as 1/16 inch [1.5 mm]. In heavy rains, even with no standing water present, the tire seems incapable of dispersing water as quickly as it falls, again leading to vehicle instability. From a ride quality point of view the tire is also unsatisfactory in that it flat spots every morning, especially in cool weather, but even in warmer weather as well, leading to vibrations in the initial miles of any drive. It is also especially harsh over roadway expansion joints, and is so loud on concrete pavement that it poses a safety hazard due to driver fatigue induced by the continuous noise. I also understand that there may be an issue regarding the rating as an "all season tire" with many owners reporting that this tire is virtually useless in any kind of snow conditions.

Rebates: Not likely. Instead, dealers will push generous leases and low-interest financing. **Depreciation:** The entry-level models keep their value reasonably well, but as you get into the pricier BMWs, the depreciation is mind-spinning. For example, a 2008 BMW 323i that once sold for $35,900 is still worth about $22,000, but a 2008 750i that sold for $108,500 is now worth only $44,000. Ouch! **Insurance cost:** Higher than average. **Parts supply/cost:** Parts are less expensive than those for other cars in this class. Unfortunately, they aren't easily found outside of the dealer network, where they're often back-ordered. That said, parts and repairs are far easier to find than with Audi, Jaguar, Mini, Porsche, and Saab. **Annual maintenance cost:** Average—until the warranty runs out. Then your mechanic starts sharing your paycheque. **Warranty:** Bumper-to-bumper 4 years/80,000 km; rust perforation 6 years/unlimited km. **Supplementary warranty:** Not needed. **Highway/city fuel economy (2011 models):** *323i:* 6.9/11.1 L/100 km, 41/25 mpg. *Auto.:* 6.7/11.2 L/100 km, 42/25 mph. *328i:* 7.0/10.9 L/100 km, 40/26 mpg. *Auto.:* 6.9/11.3 L/100 km, 41/25 mpg. *328i xDrive:* 7.6/12.2 L/100 km, 37/23 mpg. *Auto.:* 7.8/11.9 L/100 km, 36/24 mpg. *335i:* 7.9/11.9 L/100 km, 36/24 mpg. *Auto.:* 7.6/11.9 L/100 km, 37/24 mpg. *335i xDrive:* 7.9/12.2 L/100 km, 36/23 mpg. *Auto.:* 7.9/12.2 L/100 km, 36/23 mpg. *335d:* 5.4/9.0 L/100 km, 52/31 mpg. *M3:* 9.7/15.3 L/100 km, 29/18 mpg. *M3 Cabrio:* 10.1/15.7 L/100 km, 28/18 mpg.

OWNER-REPORTED PROBLEMS: Fire originated in the fog light socket (see *www.bmw-fire.com*); engines, brakes, electrical system (telematics), and some body trim and accessories are the most failure-prone components; engine overheating is a serious problem, and it's most common on past models; premature tire wear, and noisy run-flat tires—and owners are forced to pay for tire failures. *325i:* Excessive hesitation on acceleration:

> When the driver demands a sudden increase in acceleration, the car hesitates any-where from 1.5 to 3 seconds. This is a dangerous condition when someone is making a left turn in traffic, or getting onto a highway, or passing on a 2 lane country road, etc. Other cars traveling at 60 mph [96.5 km/h] are moving at 88 ft./sec. [27 m/s]. The amount of leeway this car needs is much too excessive.

Bridgestone tire-tread separation and side wall buckling:

> Bridgestone Potenza RE050A run-flat tires. The tires buckled on the side wall after less than 8,000 miles [12,870 km]. Out of curiosity I checked the Bimmerfest (*www.bimmerfest.com/forums/showthread.php?t=146728*) forum and discovered this is a widespread problem among BMW owners.

328: Very few 2010 and 2011 model safety-related incidences recorded by NHTSA (12). Some of the failures reported during the past few years: Airbags fail to deploy; underhood fire ignited while car was parked; premature tire failure (bubbles in the tread); sudden acceleration; engine slow surge while idling at a stoplight; when accelerating, engine cuts out and then surges forward (suspected failure of the throttle assembly); severe engine vibrations after a cold start as Check Engine light comes on; poor rain handling; First gear and Reverse are positioned too close together, as are the brake and gas pedals; sunroof spontaneously shattered; a rear-quarter blind spot with the convertibles; seat brails that project a bit into the foot area could catch the driver's feet; and the front passenger head restraint won't go down far enough to protect short passengers. *330i:* Side airbag deployed when vehicle hit a pothole; vehicle overheats in low gears; and vehicle slips out of Second gear when accelerating. *335i:* Delay in throttle engagement when slowing to a roll and then accelerating; frequent false brake safety alerts; sunroof suddenly exploded; tires lose air due to defective tire rims; faulty fuel injectors; and engine stalling and loss of power, which is fixed by replacing the fuel pump: now exhaust is booming, fuel economy has dropped, and there's considerable "turbo lag" when accelerating. Many other cases of loss of power on the highway or the high-pressure fuel pump failing, with some owners having to replace the pump four times. *335d:* After a short downpour, engine started sputtering. Dealer and BMW said there was water in the fuel and held the car owner responsible for the full cost of the repairs. *M3:* Tail light socket overheats, blowing the bulb and shorting other lights: costs $600 to rewire. Vehicle loses power due to faulty fuel pumps; transmission hesitates when accelerating in Second gear (see *www.roadfly.com*).

SERVICE BULLETIN-REPORTED PROBLEMS: Low engine power; loss of power may be caused by an insufficient oil supply to the inlet VANOS adjustment unit; excessive engine vibration when underway; leak from the automatic transmission's selector shaft seal; AC provides insufficient heat; AC airflow may be too strong or too weak; steering column rubbing noises; audio is intermittently inoperative; no audio just after start-up; radio continues to play after ignition is shut off; auto-lamps switch on too early or too late; deteriorated headlight wiring; various electrical failures; inoperative computer controller; door can't be locked or unlocked; check coolant hose and replace if necessary under Service Action Campaign #576; headlight washer nozzle doesn't fully retract; and repair tips for retractable hardtop leaks.

X3, X5, X6 ★★★

RATING: Average; overpriced vehicles that depreciate quickly. The X3 is a small crossover SUV for the upscale crowd that wants a compact five-seater SUV that behaves like a sports sedan. The 2011 version is slightly larger than the 2004–10 model and received the same upgrades as the 3 Series sedan. For example, the 35i xDrive carries a base 240 hp 3.0L powerplant or a 300 hp turbocharged 3.0L inline-six. Engines mate to an 8-speed automatic transmission, increasing fuel economy and low-end torque. The suspension was also updated so that models equipped with the Electronic Damping Control have shock absorbers that can be adjusted to road conditions and driving style. An X5 spin-off, the X6 gives you many of the X5 advantages and disadvantages, but in a larger box. 2012 versions have one turbo less and still unleash 300 horses. Moreover, all models get the 8-speed automatic transmission and an "energy regeneration" system that some

The BMW X6.

owners claim makes gearshifts less than luxurious. The X5, BMW's first crossover SUV, has been on the market since 1999. The X5 mid-sized seven-seater is quick to depreciate and has a spotty reliability record that is worse than what owners have reported on the X3 and X6. **Strong points:** *X3:* Responsive handling; precise, predictable steering; abundant cargo space; good cabin access; and a quiet, nicely appointed interior, with a better integrated centre screen. The second-row seats have much more leg and elbow room than previous models. Also, the vehicle's cargo capacity is an estimated 56.6 cubic feet—the largest in its class. *X5:* The X5 engines deliver plenty of power, and there's a turbocharged diesel option; smooth, responsive power delivery; secure handling; good steering feedback; comfortable first- and second-row seating; and a well-appointed interior. Suspension improvements have smoothed out the ride. NHTSA gives the 2010 X5 five stars for front and side crash protection and four stars for rollover resistance. *X6:* On the market for only five years, the X6 is billed as BMW's "sports activity" coupe because it's loaded with high-performance features. It carries a standard turbocharged 3.0L 6-cylinder engine or a powerful optional 4.4L V8 and is a bit taller than most coupes. The AWD system can vary the torque from side to side to minimize under-steer. **Weak points:** *X3:* This little SUV with its somewhat narrow interior is way overpriced; options are a minefield of inflated charges; and mind-spinning depreciation makes Wall Street look tame. On the road, you will find a stiff and choppy ride that is only a bit better than the previous X3 and jerky stops, caused by the transmission's inherent imprecise shifting, compounded by the standard Brake Energy Regeneration system. Reliability is compromised by powertrain deficiencies, serious fit and finish problems, audio system malfunctions, power equipment failures, and electrical system glitches. Although backseat legroom is adequate, the seat cushions are too low, forcing your knees to your chin. Worse, the 60/40-split backseat Recline button won't help—there isn't

X3

CANADIAN PRICE (SOFT): *28i:* $41,900, *35i:* $46,900
U.S. PRICE: *28i xDrive:* $36,750, *35i:* $41,050 **CANADIAN FREIGHT:** $1,995 **U.S. FREIGHT:** $875
POWERTRAIN (REAR-DRIVE/AWD)
Engines: 3.0L 6-cyl. (240 hp) • 3.0L Turbo. 6-cyl. (300 hp) Transmission: 8-speed auto.

DIMENSIONS/CAPACITY
Passengers: 2/3; Wheelbase: 110.6 in.; H: 67/L: 182.8/W: 74 in.; Headroom F/R: 4.0/3.0 in.; Legroom F/R: 41.5/27.5 in.; Cargo volume: 56.6 cu. ft.; Fuel tank: 67L/premium; Tow limit: 3.500 lb.; Load capacity: 905lb.; Turning circle: 38.4 ft.; Ground clearance: 8.5 in.; Weight: 4,067 lb.

X5

CANADIAN PRICE (NEGOTIABLE): *35d xDrive:* $62,800, *35i xDrive:* $61,800, *50i xDrive:* $75,700 **U.S. PRICE:** *35i xDrive:* $47,200, *35i xDrive Premium:* $54,800, *35i xDrive Sport Activity:* $57,300, *35d xDrive:* $51,800, *50i xDrive:* $63,800 **CANADIAN FREIGHT:** $1,995 **U.S. FREIGHT:** $875
POWERTRAIN (REAR-DRIVE/AWD)
Engines: 3.0L Turbo. 6-cyl. (300 hp) • 4.4L V8 Turbo. V8 (400 hp); Transmissions: 6-speed auto • 8-speed auto.

DIMENSIONS/CAPACITY
Passengers: 2/3/2; Wheelbase: 116 in.; H: 70/L: 191/W: 76.1 in.; Headroom F/R: 3.5/3.0 in.; Legroom F/R: 40.5/26.5 in.; Cargo volume: 36 cu. ft.; Fuel tank: 93L/premium; Tow limit: 6,500 lb.; Load capacity: 1,290 lb.; Turning circle: 42 ft.; Ground clearance: 8.3 in.; Weight: 5,265 lb.

X6

CANADIAN PRICE (NEGOTIABLE): *35i xDrive:* $66,650, *50i xDrive:* $82,850, *Active Hybrid:* $99,900 **U.S. PRICE:** *35i xDrive:* $58,900, *50i xDrive:* $69,500, *Active Hybrid:* $88,900 **CANADIAN FREIGHT:** $1,995 **U.S. FREIGHT:** $875
POWERTRAIN (REAR-DRIVE/AWD)
Engines (Turbo): 3.0L 6-cyl. (300 hp) • 4.4L 8-cyl. (400 hp) • 4.4L 8-cyl. (555 hp) • 4.4L 8-cyl. Hybrid (480 hp); Transmissions: 6-speed auto. • 7-speed auto. • 8-speed auto.

DIMENSIONS/CAPACITY
Passengers: 2/2; Wheelbase: 116 in.; H: 67/L: 192/W: 78 in.; Headroom F/R: 3.5/2.5 in.; Legroom F/R: 40/27.5 in.; Fuel tank: 85L/premium; Tow limit: No towing; Load capacity: 935 lb.; Turning circle: 42 ft.; Ground clearance: 8.5 in.; Weight: 4,895–5,687 lb.

one. Unfortunately, the car's old nemesis—accelerator lag—is still present. Kickdown response suffers from a similar delay. Some help, though, is offered by leaving the transmission setting in Sport mode, which keeps the transmission in lower gear longer. The X3 hasn't yet been crash-tested by NHTSA. *X5:* The X5 has long-standing quality control issues with the fuel system, brakes, powertrain, electrical components, climate control, body integrity, and fit and finish. The complicated shifter and iDrive controls can be hard to master without a lot of patience and frustration; and the third-row seats are a bit cramped. *X6:* Mostly delayed throttle response and fit and finish glitches; seats only four; X6 crashworthiness hasn't yet been tested by NHTSA. **New for 2012:** *X3:* A more forgiving suspension that provides a softer, less choppy ride; more power steering assistance; and minor trim changes. *X5:* Standard roof rails, a power tailgate and a USB port, while all but the 35i xDrive get auto-dimming mirrors and heated front seats. The navigation system is now standard on the 50i xDrive. *X6:* A rear middle seat option that increases capacity to five passengers; upgraded standard equipment like privacy glass, auto-dimming mirrors, heated front seats, BMW Assist with Bluetooth, and a USB port.

OVERVIEW: Here is where BMW took on the Asian automakers and came out second best. Despite BMW's recent sophisticated (and complicated) engineering, mechanical upgrades, styling changes, and increased exterior and interior dimensions, the X3, X5, and X6 SUVs are not very impressive from either a performance or a comfort/convenience perspective. Despite tax credits and superior gas mileage figures, BMW is reportedly having a tough time selling its new diesel-equipped X5 35d xDrive. Last year's X6 35i xDrive and 50i xDrive gasoline engines are rated at 15/21 mpg and 13/18 mpg, respectively. As for replacing the 6-speed transmissions with 8-speeds, BMW says fuel economy is increased by seven percent and 0–60 mph times are shaved by one- to two-tenths of one percent. Big deal, eh?

COST ANALYSIS: Buy an almost identical, cheaper 2011, or wait for the X5's second-series models in mid-2012. The X3 is a better buy as a 2011, but give the car a year or so to shake off its redesign bugs. The X6? A big, brash, and beautiful barge—for potentates and poseurs. **Best alternatives:** Acura RDX and Honda's recently redesigned CR-V. Other worthy contenders: the GM Acadia, Enclave, Escalade, Terrain, or Traverse, and the Lexus RX Series. **Rebates:** $4,000–$7,000 discounts along with low-rate financing and generous leasing terms. Remember, slow sales with the X Series models has created a buyer's market; patience is your ally. **Depreciation:** Faster than a speeding bullet. A 2006 X3 that once sold for $45,000 is now worth only $16,500. Hold on, it gets worse: a 2007 X5 sold for $61,900 new, yet its used value is now barely $33,000—a loss of almost $30,000 in four years. Incidentally, the 2008 X6 (its debut year) sold new for $64,000 may eventually take the crown for "treasure turning to trash." Its value four years later: $34,000—another $30,000 loss. **Insurance cost:** Higher than average. **Parts supply/cost:** Moderately expensive; often on dealer back-order, and they aren't easily found outside the dealer network. **Annual maintenance cost:** Average until the warranty runs out, and then your mechanic gets to know you real well. **Warranty:** Bumper-to-bumper 4 years/80,000 km; rust perforation 6 years/unlimited km. **Supplementary warranty:** A wise decision. **Highway/city fuel economy:** *X3 28i:* 8.3/12.2 L/100 km, 34/23 mpg. *X3 30i:* 8.2/12.5 L/100 km, 34/23 mpg. *X5 30i:* 9.3/13.6 L/100 km, 30/21 mpg. *Diesel:* 7.5/10.7 L/100 km, 38/26 mpg. *X5 48i:* 10.2/15.6 L/100 km, 28/18 mpg. *X5 M:* 11.9/17.2 L/100 km, 24/16mpg. *X6 35i:* 10.0/14.4 L/100 km, 28/20 mpg. *X6 50i:* 11.0/17.1 L/100 km, 26/17 mpg. *X6 M:* 11.9/17.2 L/100 km, 24/16 mpg. *X6 Hybrid:* 10.3/12.6 L/100 km, 27/22 mpg.

OWNER-REPORTED PROBLEMS: Parts are scarce outside of major metropolitan areas, and independent mechanics who can service these vehicles are rare. Servicing deficiencies are accentuated by a weak dealer network and unreliable suppliers. *X3:* Eight safety complaints: The car caught fire while parked; acceleration lag:

> Yesterday, I felt unsafe due to the hesitation. The car didn't move for about a second or two when I tried to make a left turn in an intersection and then again when I was on the highway changing lanes.

Rear main crankcase seal failure; car will roll backwards even if in Park; seal failure; run-flat tires are noted for their short tread life; chronic stalling; and car veers to the right with sudden stops. The few general complaints target the fit and finish, power equipment, audio system, fuel system, and transmission as most in need of special attention. *X5:* Nine safety-related complaints have been logged by NHTSA for the 2010 model: sudden acceleration with loss of brakes; engine surges upon startup; and chronic stalling (see *www.xoutpost.com/bmw-sav-forums/X5-E70-forum/68822-engine-warning-battery-failure-same-time.html*). Owners also complain that the transmission shifts abruptly; the car is very hard-riding; there is no air from AC; there is excessive brake dust; the exhaust system rusts; the leather indents easily and stays indented; and the rear tailgate doesn't always open with key fob. Other problem areas concern the powertrain, electrical system, climate controls, inadequate braking, audio system, body integrity, and fit and finish. The four overhead reading lights don't have protective covers and can seriously burn a child's hand or finger. *X6:* Two safety-related complaints, one of stalling caused by a faulty fuel pump and the other concerning original equipment tires with blown-out sidewalls.

SERVICE BULLETIN-REPORTED PROBLEMS: *X3:* Automatic transmission defaults to limp mode; AC evaporator drain modification; and an incorrect outside temperature display. *X5:* Various Hybrid electrical system faults; transmission defaults to limp mode; shifter knob cover replacement; steering column squeaking noise is heard when turning; upper door frame seal noises; front seat noise heard while vehicle is underway; radio continues playing with the ignition shut off; missing, incorrect road map data; incorrect outside temperature display; Collision Avoidance display flickers; broken or lost fuel cap tether; a creaking from top of window and door frame; wind whistle from door mirrors; rear seat noise from ISOFIX clips; deformed dashboard may cause rubbing noise; rattle from the luggage compartment; clicking or squeaking from rear tailgate area; and various automatic tailgate operation faults.

Jaguar

Not Recommended. Period.

Tata's 2008 acquisition of money-burning Jaguar and Land Rover for $2.5 billion (U.S.) was more a vanity play than a serious investment. After all, Ford bought Jaguar for $2.38 billion (U.S.) about a decade earlier and lost its shirt. How could Tata make money? Well, Tata did make some money by 2010, thanks to cost cutting, a better product mix, and a slowly improving global economy.

Now, we are back to the bad times and things couldn't look bleaker for Tata, its Jaguar Land Rover division, and even Tata's Nano mini-minicar, at $2,100 "the world's cheapest car," which saw sales plunge 85 percent in August.

The Nano's dramatic sales slide means buyers are turned off by tales of fires and other safety defects, no matter how cheap the product.

Tata is facing the challenge of reversing six straight months of declining Jaguar sales even as economies in Europe stall and auto sales from the cheapest to the most luxurious take a pounding. Tata's shares have dropped 44 percent through August, making it the worst-performing stock in the BSE India Sensitive Index.

Can Jaguar Land Rover Be Saved?

Doubtful. The only places where Jaguars have sold well are India, Tata's home base, and Asia, where buyers mistakenly believe these are still quality luxury cars. They'll learn soon enough why North American and European buyers see Jaguar as a doddering old uncle who's had multiple hip replacements, suffers from Alzheimer's, has been thrown out of his American rest home, and is now in intensive care somewhere in India. There, the uncle has found rich benefactors who remember how great he was and are paying his life support. Unfortunately, they'll soon realize that Jaguar is too far gone to be anything but an Asian niche-car invalid.

Jaguar is proof positive that the British can't build quality cars anymore and Ford can't build British cars. When Ford bought Jaguar, it transformed the company's luxury cars into a hodgepodge of Taurus/Sable and Lincoln parts thrown together with a Jaguar badge. No wonder Taurus-sourced powertrain, electronic, and body problems persist—problems such as sudden, unintended acceleration; automatic transmission and brake failures; shimmying; and excessive cabin noise when driving with the rear windows open.

High-end Jaguars have excess weight that makes it necessary to install lots of complicated and difficult-to-troubleshoot devices, as well as larger engines encased in aluminum bodies, in order to make them decent highway performers. Entry-level Jags have a different problem: convincing buyers that the X-Types are more than gussied-up Ford-Tata-Nanos.

Mercedes-Benz

High Profits, Small Lemons

Daimler AG, Mercedes' governing company, made a healthy profit in 2011—mostly generated by strong sales of the lucrative E-Class and S-Class models, a drop in costly sales incentives, and a surprisingly sharp rebound in demand from Chinese and U.S. car buyers.

The company has pulled off this turnaround by increasing sales of smaller and less-expensive cars in the United States, while selling fewer—but larger and more expensive—models in Europe and Asia. This means we'll soon see new subcompacts, electric vehicles, crossovers, and a return to 4-cylinder engines that haven't been offered in years. Most of these front-drive minicars will be based on Daimler's new A/B platform.

Is it "Moose-Proof"?

Mercedes hasn't been vey good at making reliable or well-performing small cars and SUVs over the past few decades. Its first efforts with the C- and M-Class were flops and the jury is still out on the new compact B-Class entrants. Its first effort, the "Baby Benz" 190 was the Mercedes 190. The A-Class overturned in a 1997 test run called the "moose test," a performance exercise used for decades in Sweden that calls for the driver to suddenly change lanes while going 70–80 km/h (45–50 mph), as though trying to avoid hitting a moose. What shocked most the West Germany-based Daimler dignitaries was that the Trabant—a much older, widely mocked car from Eastern Germany—passed the test with flying colours.

New Products

This year, C-Class sedans get a restyling inside and out, while the 2012 coupe version is given a heart transplant with an all-new 201 hp 1.8L turbocharged 4-cylinder that replaces the 228 hp 3.0L V6. The existing V6 will have direct fuel injection. Mercedes is intentionally taking its time in introducing small-car derivatives, mindful, no doubt, of the nightmarish press criticism that followed its disastrous first "mini-Benz" A-car press presentation in 1997.

C250, C300, and C350 models swap the 6-speed manual transmission for a 7-speed automatic; the powerful C63 returns (this may be its last year) with a naturally aspirated 6.2L 451 hp V8 hooked to the new 7-speed automatic and a reworked suspension.

The E-Class wagons and sedans return with direct-injection engines coupled to a 7-speed automatic transmission; E350 models have new 17-inch wheels and Bluetec diesels that are still the fuel-economy leaders; the E63 carries a 518 hp 5.5L twin-turbo V8 featuring the fuel-saving ECO stop/start feature, and a 7-speed gearbox.

The E-Class Coupe and Cabriolet haven't changed much for 2012. They return with a redesigned steering wheel; the media interface has been moved to the centre console; and lane departure and blind spot monitoring systems are now extra-cost items. 2012 will see the appearance of new V6 and V8 engines on the 2013 models.

Quality Concerns

Mercedes' poor quality reputation lingers on.

In a 2007 *Consumer Reports* survey of 36 leading automobile brands, Mercedes-Benz ranked dead last in predicted reliability. In *CR's* April 2010 Auto Guide edition, Mercedes' 2004–08 models have more "Poor Reliability" black spots than Walt Disney's *101 Dalmatians*. Even so, *Consumer Reports'* April edition recommends the C-Class, GLK-Class, M-Class, S-Class, and SLK-Class models. Overall, the company's lineup gets an "Average" rating, except for the R-Class, which underperforms in almost every category.

Way before *Consumer Reports* got involved, everyone (except for some clueless buyers) knew that Mercedes' 1998 M-Class sport-utilities were abysmally bad. You couldn't have made a worse vehicle, judging by the unending stream of desperate-sounding service bulletins sent from head office to dealers after the vehicles' official launch. Two bulletins stand out in my mind. One was an authorization for dry-cleaning payouts to dealers whose customers' clothing had been stained by the dye from the burgundy-coloured leather seats. The other was a lengthy scientific explanation (which the Germans compose so well) as to why drivers were "tasered" by static electricity when entering or exiting their vehicles.

Car columnists have always known that Mercedes has made some bad cars and SUVs, but it took business reporters (not auto beat writers) from the gutsy *Wall Street Journal* to spill the beans. In a February 2, 2002 article titled "An Engineering Icon Slips," the *WSJ* cited several confidential industry-initiated surveys that showed that Mercedes' quality and customer satisfaction had fallen dramatically since 1999—to a level below that of GM's Opel, a brand that had one of the worst reputations for poor quality in Europe.

Industry insiders give different reasons for why Mercedes-Benz quality isn't world class. They say quality control has been diluted by M-B doubling its product lineup since 1997. Helpful, too, were the company's aggressive PR campaigns and the company mindset that blamed the driver rather than the product—both spectacularly successful in keeping the quality myth alive in the media until the *Wall Street Journal* broke its story. Neither mindset nor PR worked to mitigate owners' displeasure over M-B's engine sludge stonewalling, though. It cost Mercedes $32 million (U.S.) to settle with owners of 1998–2001 models after the company denied that there was a factory-related problem.

Although Mercedes sales are on the upswing, its vehicles' residual values have fallen dramatically. At the top end, a 2006 65 AMG that cost $254,500 new is now worth barely $55,000—around 20 percent of its original value. Even the entry-level B-Class models feel the depreciation bite: a 2007 B-Class 200 that originally sold for $31,400 is now worth only $12,500, and a 2007 E-Class E320 BlueTEC sedan, once priced at $67,801, can now be bought for $25,000.

B-CLASS ★★

RATING: Below Average. This is essentially an enlarged A-Class keeping the same engine and suspension system. First launched as a 2006 model, the B200 is sold mainly in Canada and Europe. **Strong points:** It is Mercedes' second-smallest car, following the Smart, and is feature-laden, with four-wheel disc brakes, side airbags, and stability control. **Weak points:** Fuel economy isn't all that impressive, crash-worthiness hasn't yet been tested, and the retail price could be trimmed by at least $3,000, making the car more competitive. Furthermore, the "B" has an unusually large turning circle, which cuts its urban usefulness. Shoppers would be wise to consider the equivalent Mazda or other Japanese or European compacts. **New for 2012:** Restyled and re-engineered, the second-generation B-class uses a new platform that offers greater levels of safety, a larger interior, and 4×4 capability. Power is provided by two 4-cylinder gasoline engines and one diesel engine, hooked to new 6-speed and 7-speed gearboxes. Both transmissions feature a fuel-saving automatic stop/start feature. The front seats are set lower and sit more upright than before, while the lengthened wheelbase provides more rear-seat legroom and luggage space.

OVERVIEW: M-B's latest entry in the North American premium-compact-car market, the B-Class complements the C-Class lineup in the same way that the A3 and A4 models draw less demanding Audi shoppers and the 1-Series and 3-Series bring BMW cars within reach of buyers with fewer dollars to spare. There's also the B's small outside, big inside versatility, and respectable fuel economy. Still, without the Mercedes cachet, this is an ordinary, middle-of-the-pack, overpriced subcompact.

KEY FACTS

CANADIAN PRICE (NEGOTIABLE): *B200:* $31,650 **CANADIAN FREIGHT:** $1,995
POWERTRAIN (FRONT-DRIVE/AWD)
Engines: 1.6L Turbo 4-cyl. (122 hp) • 2.0L Turbo 4-cyl. (156 hp) • 1.8L diesel Turbo 4-cyl. (109 and 136 hp); Transmissions: 6-speed man. • 7-speed auto.

DIMENSIONS/CAPACITY
Passengers: 2/3; Wheelbase: 109.4 in.; H: 61.1/L: 171.7/W: 70 in.; Legroom F/R: 43.0/38.4 in.; Cargo volume: 23.5 cu. ft.; Fuel tank: 54L/premium; Tow limit: No towing; Turning circle: 39.2 ft.; Weight: 2,854 lb.

COST ANALYSIS: Take a pass on this year's redesigned models to give prices a chance to come down and allow first-year redesign problems to be fixed. The popular diesel-equipped models may not be sent to North America. **Best alternatives:** Take a look at the BMW 1 Series, Kia Rondo, Mazda5, or Toyota Matrix. **Options:** Nothing much worth buying; the car comes well-quipped. **Depreciation:** Faster than average; a $30,000 2008 B-Class 200 is now barely worth $17,500. **Insurance cost:** Average. **Parts supply/cost:** Remember, these are Canada-only cars, so parts may not be easily found. Parts are moderately expensive. **Annual maintenance cost:** Average. **Warranty:** Bumper-to-bumper 4 years/80,000 km; powertrain 5 years/120,000 km; rust perforation 5 years/120,000 km. **Supplementary warranty:** A good idea for the new powertrain. **Highway/city fuel economy (2011):** *Man.:* 6.7/9.2 L/100 km, 42/30 mpg. *CVT:* 7.2/9.2 L/100 km, 39/30 mpg. *Turbo and 6-speed man.:* 6.9/10.2 L/100 km, 40/28 mpg. *Turbo with CVT:* 7.4/9.5 L/100 km, 38/30 mpg.

OWNER-REPORTED PROBLEMS: Mostly fit and finish, electrical system shorts, and premature brake wear gripes.

C-CLASS ★★★

RATING: Average. These little entry-level cars lack the sparkling V6 power, simplicity, and popular pricing found with the Japanese luxury competition; save up for an E-Class or a Hyundai Genesis. **Strong points:** Plenty of high-tech performance and safety features; a good powertrain matchup; available AWD; a comfortable ride; easy handling; excellent braking; and an innovative anti-theft system. NHTSA awarded the C-Class five-stars for side impact occupant protection; four stars for rollover protection and three stars for frontal crashworthiness. IIHS crash tests gave top marks ("Good") for frontal offset, side, roof, and head-restraint crash protection. Average reliability. **Weak points:** The light steering requires constant correction; a choppy ride; complicated controls; limited rear-seat and cargo room; tight entry and exit; some tire thumping; and some engine and wind noise. Also, the cars are noted for their weak resale value and for being very dealer-dependent for parts and servicing—a problem likely to worsen with this year's new powertrains. **New for 2012:** A lightly restyled sedan and a new coupe. Also new: a 201 hp 1.8L turbocharged 4-cylinder engine and a V6 with direct injection. C250s get the new 1.8L turbo, C300 4MATICs bring back the 228 hp 3.0L V6, and the 2012 C350 is now powered by M-B's new 302 hp 3.5L V6. A 7-speed automatic transmission is standard. The powerful C63 returns with a naturally-aspirated 451 hp 6.2L V8 hooked to the new 7-speed automatic and a reworked suspension.

OVERVIEW: C-Class cars use a 7-speed automatic, though the C300 is also available with Mercedes' 4MATIC all-wheel drive. All C300 models can run on ethanol-blended E85 fuel. Sport models have a sport suspension and unique interior and exterior styling. Available safety features include a rearview camera, ABS, traction control, and anti-skid systems, front and rear side airbags, curtain side airbags, and front hip-protecting airbags.

COST ANALYSIS: Take a pass on this year's models until mid-2012, when prices come down. **Best alternatives:** Take a look at the BMW 3 Series, or a Hyundai Genesis Coupe. **Options:** The Bose sound system is a good investment. **Rebates:** $5,000 rebates, generous leasing deals, and low-interest financing. **Depreciation:** Faster than average; a $37,000 2006 C-Class Coupe is now barely worth $12,500. **Insurance cost:** Higher than average. **Parts supply/cost:** Limited availability, and parts are expensive. **Annual maintenance cost:** Average. **Warranty:** Bumper-to-bumper 4 years/80,000 km; powertrain 5 years/120,000 km; rust perforation 5 years/120,000 km. **Supplementary warranty:** Extra powertrain coverage would be a good idea. **Highway/city fuel economy (2011):** 3.0L: 7.7/11.7 L/100 km, 37/24 mpg. *Auto.:* 7.8/11.7 L/100 km, 36/24 mpg. *4MATIC:* 8.0/12.0 L/100 km, 35/24 mpg. *3.5L:* 8.0/12.2 L/100 km, 35/23 mpg. *AMG:* 10.4/17.2 L/100 km, 27/16 mpg. Fuel economy on the 2012s as projected by Mercedes (no mpg equivalent given): *1.8L:* 6.4/9.7 L/100 km; *3.0L V6:* 7.7/11.7 L/100 km; *3.5L V6:* 7.0/10.9 L/100 km; *6.2L V8:* 10.4/16.1 L/100 km.

OWNER-REPORTED PROBLEMS: No 2011 model safety-related failures were reported to NHTSA. *Lemon-Aid* readers and *Consumer Reports* subscribers did report problems with the transmission; fuel, electrical, and climate control systems; brakes; power system; audio devices; body hardware and paint; and fit and finish.

KEY FACTS

CANADIAN PRICE (NEGOTIABLE): *C250:* $36,700, *Coupe:* $39,900, *C250 4MATIC:* $39,990, *C300 4MATIC:* $45,200, *C350:* $49,000, *Coupe:* $49,200, *350 4MATIC 7-speed:* $50,800, *C63 AMG:* $65,000, *Coupe:* $66,900 **U.S. PRICE:** *C250 Sport:* $34,800, C250 Luxury: $35,220, C300 4MATIC Sport: $38,020, 4MATIC Luxury: $38,430, C350 Sport Sedan: $40,575 **CANADIAN FREIGHT:** $1,490 **U.S. FREIGHT:** $875

POWERTRAIN (REAR-DRIVE/AWD)
Engines: 1.8L four-cyl. (201 hp) • 3.0L V6 (228 hp) • 3.5L V6 (302 hp) • 6.2L V8 (481 hp); Transmission: 7-speed auto.

DIMENSIONS/CAPACITY
Passengers: 2/3; Wheelbase: 108.7 in.; H: 56.9/L: 182/W: 70.0 in.; Headroom F/R: 2.5/1.5 in.; Legroom F/R: 42/26 in.; Cargo volume: 12.4 cu. ft.; Fuel tank: 62L/premium; Tow limit: Not recommended; Load capacity: 835 lb.; Turning circle: 35.3 ft.; Ground clearance: 4.2 in.; Weight: 3,565 lb.

RATING: Average. Redesigned only a few times during the past decade, these family sedans, wagons, and convertibles manage to hold five people in relative comfort while performing acceptably well. **Strong points:** Solid acceleration in the higher gear ranges; well-appointed with many new safety, performance, and convenience features; good engine and transmission combo; 4MATIC all-wheel drive operates flawlessly; easy handling; good braking; acceptable ride; a relatively roomy interior (except for front headroom); lots of cargo room (with the 4MATIC wagon); an innovative anti-theft system; and acceptable quality control. NHTSA awarded the 2010 models four stars for driver and passenger frontal crash protection, and five stars for rollover resistance and side protection; IIHS designated the 2010 and 2011 model years as "Good" for offset crashworthiness, side-impact protection, roof strength, and head-restraint effectiveness. **Weak points:** The car feels much slower than it actually is and handling is not quite as crisp as with the BMW 5 Series; numb steering; complicated electronic control centre and navigation system controls are a pain to use; overly firm seats; a surprisingly small trunk; and tall drivers may be bothered by the knee bolsters and limited headroom. **New for 2012:** New engines and a 7-speed automatic transmission; sedans and wagons get direct-injection engines.

OVERVIEW: Mercedes' E-Class cars have improved incrementally over the years, but they have also suffered from unreasonably high base prices, some content-cutting, overly-complex electronics and fuel-delivery systems, and poor quality control relative to the automatic transmission, brakes, fuel pump, and electronics. This year, we again rate the E-Class as Average, and shoppers are cautioned to be wary of the latest diesel-equipped models, which may require costly periodic urea fill-ups at the dealership. Try to get your urea off the shelf and pour it yourself.

A few years ago, *Consumer Reports* took its own diesel-powered Mercedes-Benz GL320 BlueTEC to a dealer because a warning light indicated that the SUV was low on AdBlue urea. The fill-up cost? $316.99! The GL needed 7.5 gallons, which accounted for $241.50 of the total bill ($32.20/gallon). Labour (twisting a cap and pouring) and tax accounted for the remaining $75.49.

It took *CR* about 26,660 kilometres (16,565 miles) to run low on AdBlue, which means they'll be spending $1,457.80 on the stuff over 160,935 kilometres (100,000 miles); BMW covers this cost for its diesel-powered vehicles up to 80,470 kilometres (50,000 miles).

Besides adding to the retail cost, the new diesels haven't had the quality or servicing support of gasoline-powered engines. Plus, cautious dealers who are hunkering down during the present economic recession aren't likely to hire specialized mechanics or invest in expensive diesel inventory or diagnostic machines until the present fragile economy strengthens.

COST ANALYSIS: The 2012s' more refined powertrains are an important step in giving these cars additional power and saving fuel. Nevertheless, it would be wise to skip this year's redesigned models and opt for the better-built 2013s. In addition to a $1,995 freight/PDI fee, Mercedes supports an additional $375 dealer administration fee. What a weasel attitude! Again, diesel owners be wary: diesels have radically changed since 2007 and it is much more difficult to find competent, inexpensive servicing by independent agencies. **Best alternatives:** The Hyundai Genesis sedan or high-performance coupe. They both have lower price tags, fantastic interiors, rear-drive power delivery, and powerful V8s. Other choices include the Acura RL, BMW 5 Series, Infiniti M35x, and Lexus GS AWD. Why no Volvo S80? We are waiting for the dust to settle around Geely, Volvo's new China-based owner, to see which models are dropped and which new models will debut. **Options:** Nothing is needed. **Rebates:** $5,000+ rebates/discounts, generous leasing deals, and low-interest rate financing. **Depreciation:** Faster than average. Forget those myths about Mercedes' high resale values: A $74,300 2006 E350 is now worth $17,500—less than a quarter of its original price. **Insurance cost:** Higher than average. **Parts supply/cost:** Hard to find outside the dealer network, and they can be expensive at times (body and electronic parts, especially). **Annual maintenance cost:** Higher than average. **Warranty:** Bumper-to-bumper 4 years/80,000 km; powertrain 5 years/120,000 km; rust perforation 5 years/120,000 km. **Supplementary warranty:** Not needed. **Highway/city fuel economy (2011):** *E350:* 8.3/12.7

KEY FACTS

CANADIAN PRICE (NEGOTIABLE): *E350 coupe:* $59,900, *Sedan:* $62,500, *4MATIC:* $62,500, *4MATIC BlueTEC diesel:* $62,500, *4MATIC wagon:* $66,900, *E350 cabriolet:* $67,900, *E550 coupe:* $69,900, *E550 4MATIC:* $73,200, *E550 cabriolet:* $77,500, *E63 AMG:* $106,900 **U.S. PRICE:** *E350 coupe:* $49,800, *Sedan:* $49,400, *Cabriolet:* $57,720, *E550 coupe:* $55,450, *E550 4MATIC:* $57,100, *E550 BlueTEC sedan:* $50,900, *E550 cabriolet:* $64,800, *E63 AMG:* $87,600 **CANADIAN FREIGHT:** $1,995 **U.S. FREIGHT:** $875 **POWERTRAIN (REAR-DRIVE/AWD)** Engines: 3.0L V6 turbodiesel (210 hp) • 3.5L V6 (302 hp) • 4.7L V8 (402 hp) • 5.5L V8 (518 and 550 hp); Transmission: 7-speed auto. **DIMENSIONS/CAPACITY** Passengers: 2/3; Wheelbase: 113.1 in.; H: 57.7/L: 191.7/W: 71.9 in.; Headroom F/R: 3.0/3.0 in.; Legroom F/R: 44/28.5 in.; Cargo volume: 16 cu. ft.; Fuel tank: 80L/premium; Tow limit: N/A; Load capacity: 960 lb.; Turning circle: 36.2 ft.; Ground clearance: 4.1 in.; Weight: 4,020 lb.

L/100 km, 34/22 mpg. *E550*: 8.6/13.8 L/100 km, 33/20 mpg. *E63*: 10.2/16.5 L/100 km, 28/17 mpg.

OWNER-REPORTED PROBLEMS: Only about a dozen safety-related incidences have been reported to NHTSA during the past two model years. They include inadvertent airbag deployment; airbags failing to deploy in a number of collisions; engine surged as vehicle was being parked and car sped out of control; automatic transmission malfunctions; transmission defaults into Second gear after each start cycle; when the gearshift lever shows the transmission is in Park, it may not be. The same criticism applies to the Drive indicator; a 2010 550 model was parked on a hill with the gearshift lever in Park—it rolled away. Turn signal and cruise control levers are mounted too close together; brake pedal is notchy and sticks during the initial portion of pedal travel (likely cause: a leaking brake booster); premature replacement of brake rotor and pads; a faulty power steering pump; inoperative climate control; body hardware and fit and finish deficiencies; a turn signal light exploded in the rain; impossible to drive comfortably with the window open; wind ear pressure can be intolerable; the horn won't sound if the car has been shut off; early tire blowouts with original equipment tires (said to be caused by defective rims); power equipment and audio system breakdowns; the speedometer is difficult to read during daylight conditions; and the Check Engine light may come on for no reason.

Volkswagen

That Quality "Thing"

How did VW increase market share during a recession? It was a combination of diesel popularity, less exposure to the slumping American market than other automakers, the right mix of vehicles that respond well to up-and-down fuel prices, and a solid international footing. It has profitable operations in Latin America; an expanding presence in China, Russia, and India; and a dominant role in Western Europe, where it also markets its Seat and Skoda brands.

VW's small, fuel-efficient cars and diesel-equipped lineup has touched a nerve with Canadian shoppers in much the same way as the company's first Beetle captured the imagination and support of consumers in the mid-'60s. Building on that support, over the past few years Volkswagen has cut prices and features to keep its small cars affordable.

But, quality has always been the company's Achilles' heel, from no-heat heaters on the first Beetles, to gear-hopping, car-stopping DSG transmissions afflicting Volkswagen's 2007–11 models:

> I own a 2009 Jetta TDI with a DSG transmission. I feel like I am going to get hit when
> I start from a stop. The transmission jumps and hesitates. It has been to the dealer

without being fixed. It is terrifying to drive a car that may or may not accelerate, which also jumps in and out of gear!

We can all agree that Volkswagens are practical drivers' cars that offer excellent handling and great fuel economy without sacrificing interior comfort. But overall reliability goes downhill after the fifth year of ownership and servicing is often more competent and cheaper at independent garages, which have grown increasingly popular as owners flee more expensive VW dealerships. Unfortunately, parts are fairly expensive, and both dealers and independent garages have trouble finding them due to VW's frequent addition of more complex electronic and mechanical components as well as a chaotic parts distribution system, which has resulted from dealer and supplier closures during the on-going recession.

With rare candor Volkswagen now admits that car buyers see its products as failure-prone, and the automaker vows to change that perception by building a more reliable, durable product and providing timely, no-return servicing.

Taking a page out of Toyota's sudden unintended acceleration/brake failure Congressional testimony early last year, Volkswagen says it is now paying more attention, sooner, to problems reported by fleet customers and dealers in order to find and fix problems before they become widespread among individual customers.

A check of the NHTSA owner complaints log at *safercar.gov* does show safety-related incidents have dropped during the last two years, probably as a result of the recall of the DSG transmission and subsequent warranty extension to address DSG claims.

Two years ago, *Lemon-Aid* exposed the DSG problem and rated Audi and VW models equipped with DSG transmission Not Recommended. Since then, VW and Audi have recalled the tranny several times and extended the warranty to 10 years/100,000 miles on 2007–2010 models.

For a copy of VW's extended warranty go to *www.dsgproblems.co.uk/Volkswagen%20 of%20America%20Inc.pdf.*

Now there is fresh evidence that the DSG failures have spread to the 2011 models. Therefore, *Lemon-Aid* maintains and extends its Not Recommended designation to the 2011 and 2012 models as well.

New Products

VW is tinkering with its 2012 lineup by bringing back the retired New Beetle (see Appendix I); introducing a higher-performing Jetta, and presenting a redesigned Passat, Although VW recently bought a major interest in Suzuki to diversify and further venture into the small car and compact SUV markets, Suzuki has balked at

VW's plans. That cooperative arrangement now appears to be headed for the rocks. VW had similar plans for Porsche at the market's high-performance end, however, that deal has encountered German government opposition and may be abandoned.

Diesel Goes "Green"

During the past few years diesel emissions have been cleaned up to the point that environmentalists and economist alike see the increased use of diesel engines as the only way to gain time for the development of cleaner-burning fuel alternatives.

Just don't look for big fuel savings in the interim.

Keep in mind that, unless you travel more than 30,000 km a year, diesel cost savings may be illusory. Granted, there are usually fewer things that go wrong with diesel engines, and their fuel economy is high, but gasoline-powered Asian compacts are much more reliable, their parts are cheaper and more easily found, and they're almost as fuel frugal. And here's the biggest drawback with recently redesigned diesels: They have been completely changed to be as emissions-free as possible. Mechanics aren't yet familiar with them. Backup parts are still "in the pipeline," supposedly, and dealers aren't rushing to buy replacement parts until they can sell their old stock. Therefore, wise shoppers will steer clear of VW's diesel-equipped vehicles, at least until the 2013 model year, when we can hope that servicing know-how and parts distribution will have improved.

GOLF, JETTA, CC ★/★★/★★★

The Volkswagen Golf.

RATING: *Golf* and *Jetta:* Not Recommended, due to reports of serious, life-threatening powertrain and fuel delivery defects. Below Average on cars equipped with the wimpy 115 hp 2.0L 4-cylinder engine. *CC:* Average. **Strong points:** When they are running right, these cars are good all-around front-drive performers when coupled to a manual shifter; the sporty GLI, with its turbocharged 200 hp

CANADIAN PRICE (NEGOTIABLE): *Golf 3d:* $20,475, *5d:* $21,475, *GTI:* $28,875, *Wagon:* $22,975, *Jetta Trendline:* $15,875, Trendline+: $17,275, *Comfortline:* $19,075, *Sportline:* $23,300, *Highline:* $23,980, *2.0 TDI:* $25,275, *2.5 Sportline Tiptronic:* $25,300, *2.5 Highline:* $26,475, *DSG:* $26,675, *2.5 Highline Tiptronic:* $27,875, *2.0 TDI Highline:* $28,775, *2.0 TDI Highline DSG:* $30,175, *Jetta 2.5 Trendline:* $22,175, *Jetta TDI Trendline:* $24,475, *Jetta 2.5 Comfortline:* $24,875, *Jetta TDI Comfortline:* $27,175, *Jetta 2.0 Highline:* $29,075, *Jetta TDI Highline:* $30,875, *Jetta Wolfsburg:* $27,275, *GLI:* $27,475, *CC:* 33,375 **U.S. PRICE:** *Golf two-door:* $17,995, *Golf four-door:* $19,795, *Golf two-door TDI:* $23,995, *Golf four-door TDI:* $24,695, *Jetta S:* $16,495, *Jetta SE:* $18,495, *Jetta SEL:* $23,195, *Jetta TDI:* $22,525, *Jetta TDI Premium:* $23,965, *Jetta GLI:* $23,495, *Autobahn:* $25,545, *CC Sport:* $28,515, *CC Sport auto.:* $29,615, *CC R-Line:* $30,460, *CC Luxury:* $31,420, *CC VR6 4Motion Executive:* $40,390 **CANADIAN FREIGHT:** $1,490 **U.S. FREIGHT:** $770 **POWERTRAIN (FRONT-DRIVE)** Engines: 2.0L 4-cyl. (115 hp) • 2.0L TDI 4-cyl. (140 hp) • 2.0L Turbo 4-cyl. (200 hp) • 2.5L 5-cyl. (170 hp); Transmissions: 5-speed man. • 6-speed man. • 6-speed auto. **DIMENSIONS/CAPACITY (JETTA)** Passengers: 2/3; Wheelbase: 104.4 in.; H: 57.2/L: 182.2/W: 70 in.; Headroom F/R: 4.5/2.5 in.; Legroom F/R: 43/30 in.; Cargo volume: 15 cu. ft.; Fuel tank: 55L/regular; Tow limit: 1,500 lb.; Load capacity: 1,070 lb.; Turning circle: 35.7 ft.; Ground clearance: 5.5 in.; Weight: 3,090 lb.

2.0L 4-cylinder engine, delivers high-performance thrills without much of a fuel penalty. The 170 hp 2.5L 5-cylinder engine is well suited for city driving and most leisurely highway cruising, thanks mainly to the car's light weight and handling prowess. Excellent braking; a comfortable ride; plenty of headroom, legroom and cargo space with the Golf; standard tilt/telescope steering column; a low load floor; and good fuel economy. NHTSA gave the CC, Golf, and Jetta four stars for frontal crash protection and rollover resistance and five stars for side occupant protection. IIHS awarded top marks to all three models. The CC and Golf scored five stars for frontal offset, side, roof, and rear collision crash protection and the Jetta got similar scores, except that it wasn't tested for side crashworthiness. **Weak points:** The DSG powertrains on the 2011s are showing the same "Death Shift" failures as the recently recalled 2007–10 models. Base Jettas come with a 115 hp 4-cylinder engine that is the runt of the litter. It fails to meet the driving expectations of most Jetta buyers, who want both good fuel economy and an engine with plenty of low-end torque and cruising power. Diesel-equipped models with cruise control can't handle small hills very well, and often slow down by 10–15 km/h. Excessive engine and road noise; difficult entry and exit; and restricted rear visibility. Folding rear seats don't lie flat. Maintenance costs increase after the fifth year of ownership. A high number of safety-related complaints have been logged by NHTSA on the 2010 Jetta and an average number (55) on the 2011s. No DSG failures were found, although there were some incidents of airbags deploying for no reason, injuring occupants. Of the 25 owner reports on the 2011 Golf, more than half involved DSG failures. **New for 2012:** The CC, base Golf, GTI, Jetta/Sports Wagon, Routan, and Touareg all return with only minor trim changes. One new addition is the Golf R, a sportier version of the GTI, equipped with a 260 hp 4-cylinder and a 6-speed manual transmission. It's available as a three- and five-door and uses larger brakes with 18-inch wheels. *2012 Jetta:* A sporty GLI will arrive with a 200 hp 2.0L four, independent suspension, 6-speed manual and automatic gearboxes, and a lightly restyled interior and exterior.

OVERVIEW: "Practical and fun to drive" pretty well sums up why these VWs continue to be so popular. Yet they offer much more, including an accommodating interior, plenty of power with the higher-end models, responsive handling, and great fuel economy. Jetta S models use a 115 hp 2.0L 4-cylinder engine. The SE and SEL are powered by the same 170 hp 2.5L 5-cylinder engine from the previous-generation Jetta. The TDI continues with its 140 hp 2.0L turbodiesel 4-cylinder. Interestingly, the GLI will keep its 200 hp turbocharged 2.0L 4-cylinder—the same engine that, in the Audi TTS, produces 265 horses. A 5-speed manual transmission is standard on the S, SE, and SEL. A 6-speed manual is standard on the TDI and GLI. Optional on the S, SE, and SEL is a 6-speed automatic. The GLI and TDI offer a 6-speed dual-clutch automated manual that behaves much like an automatic...when it's not falling into Neutral or simply falling apart.

Again, we raise the caveat that VW's relatively new diesel design will likely have higher servicing costs and parts availability problems. That said, in spite of *Lemon-Aid*'s criticisms regarding how much you really save, other analysts say diesel is the best alternative to paying high fuel prices at the moment. *Autoweek* magazine concluded, "For comfort, quiet, and highway handling, our drivers found the TDI had significant advantages over every other car in the test. It would have been our choice, in other words, for an easy daytrip on the interstates, regardless of fuel economy. And we topped the hybrids by driving with just a little attention to fuel economy, not making it an obsession."

COST ANALYSIS: Before opting for the cheapest 2012 Jetta with its 115 hp 4-cylinder engine, take it for a test drive and see if the reduced power is acceptable. Also, be wary of last-minute $375 "administration" or "processing" fees; they're scams. **Best alternatives:** Other cars worth considering are the Honda Civic or Accord, Hyundai Elantra, Kia Forte, Mazda6, Nissan Sentra, Suzuki Kizashi, and Toyota Corolla or Matrix. **Options:** Stay away from the electric sunroof; it costs a bundle to repair and offers not much more than the well-designed manual sunroof. On top of that, you lose too much headroom. Save $275; the Cold Weather Package doesn't offer much. The $375 Lip Spoiler is another money-waster of doubtful efficacy. **Rebates:** $1,000 rebates on non-diesels, low-interest financing, and attractive leases. **Depreciation:** About average, especially with the Jetta. However, as you approach the end of the four-year warranty, the value drops sharply, even with the popular Jetta. For example, a 2006 Jetta Wagon that first sold for $27,780 is now barely worth $10,500. **Insurance cost:** Higher than average. **Parts supply/cost:** Not hard to find, but parts can be more expensive than for most other cars in this class. Diesel parts may be expensive and harder to find. **Annual maintenance cost:** Less than average while under warranty. After that, repair costs start to climb dramatically. **Warranty:** Bumper-to-bumper 4 years/80,000 km; powertrain 5 years/100,000 km; rust perforation 12 years/

unlimited km. **Supplementary warranty:** A good idea. **Highway/city fuel economy:** *Golf City 2.0L:* 7.0/9.8 L/100 km, 40/28 mpg. *Golf 2.5L:* 7.0/10.4 L/100 km, 40/27 mpg. *Auto.:* 6.9/9.2 L/100 km, 41/31 mpg. *TDI:* 4.7/6.7 L/100 km, 60/42 mpg. *Auto.:* 4.6/6.7 L/100 km, 61/42 mpg. Jetta fuel economy should be similar.

OWNER-REPORTED PROBLEMS: The numbers of reported safety-related incidents range from fewer than normal to about average. Still, those that were mentioned are definitely life-threatening and many of the same failures have been reported since 2007: *CC:* Scattered reports of stalling, hard starts, and premature brake replacements. *Golf:* Diesel-powered Golf suddenly lost power on the highway as diesel fuel started spraying all over the car; the source of the problem was a leaking fuel line at the injector for the number 2 cylinder. Failure of the high-pressure fuel pump is another cause of chronic stalling; cruise control is not always disabled when depressing the brake pedal; various electrical shorts cause the Check Engine and Tire Pressure warning lights to come on for no reason; and the sunroof suddenly exploded.

Has the DSG "Death Shift" returned to dog the 2011s after the 2007–10 models were recalled? The following stories describe exactly the kinds of DSG failure experienced by owners of previous model years:

> I own a 2011 VW GTI 2-door DSG. I have experienced a "false Neutral" about 7 times in the 5+ weeks.... Each time I have been in Manual mode.... It occurs when I am coasting to either slow down or stop...then attempt to accelerate...though the car MFD tells me it is in gear (i.e. 3), the car is in Neutral.... The accelerator does nothing but rev the engine.... The car remains coasting. I have to take the shifter out of Manual mode, and place it into D...and wait about a second or two without touching the accelerator in order for a clutch to engage a gear and allow me to move.

•

> 2011 VW GTI w/ DSG transmission. Vehicle has 12K miles [19,300 km] and requires replacement of mechatronics unit. On two occasions while accelerating from a stop with transmission in Drive, the vehicle failed to accelerate. Engine revved as if in Neutral. After several attempts with throttle input, the transmission slammed into gear. On another occasion while driving at approx 65 mph [105 km/h] with the transmission in Drive, the vehicle revved in Neutral and would not accelerate. This lasted for a duration of at least 5 seconds and caused an extremely dangerous condition. Cars were flying by on both sides and it nearly caused a collision.... There are currently no replacement parts available in the country.

Jetta: Car is not child safety seat friendly; inadvertent airbag deployment; chronic stalling; fuel tank leakage; many complaints of a cracked fuel line from the common rail to injector #2 on diesel-equipped models; drivers complain of both sudden unintended acceleration and chronic stalling:

The clutch response is somehow different than any other car and after adding the "diesel turbo lag," it makes for a dangerous first acceleration. To my salesman's surprise, I did not stall the car when I drove it off the lot. However, I have since stalled it several times in traffic. When the clutch stalls, driver must completely turn off ignition and turn it back on before attempting to clutch-drive again. Some owners on "TDI Club" list server are changing out their own clutches to stay alive.

•

Automatic transmission has extreme hesitation when accelerating from slow speed such as merging with traffic. Dealer says this is normal and finds no fault with the powertrain. When accelerating the car will virtually stall with zero forward movement, then it will finally engage and lunge the car forward very abruptly. Have had three very close calls.

•

The contact rented a 2011 Volkswagen Jetta. The contact states that the gear shifter independently shifted from Park into Reverse while driving. The vehicle then began to reverse uncontrollably and crashed into a small patio but the vehicle did not stop. The contact then jumped from the driver side window and sustained injury. A relative then jumped into the vehicle while still in motion to maintain control of the vehicle. The relative was able to stop the vehicle while on a residential patio. The contact was hospitalized.

Vehicle was idling on an incline with the brakes depressed and it started rolling backwards, even though brakes were continuously applied; when stopped on an incline the automatic transmission holds the car for only a few seconds before the vehicle starts rolling backwards.

While attempting to start the vehicle, the steering wheel locked; premature replacement of the rear brakes; windshield distortion:

Front and rear windshields have a blur, the front windshield extends from the bottom to approximately six inches up the glass and the rear glass has distortion throughout. This causes eye strain, watering, and headache when subjected to for an hour or more of travel and is especially bad in bright sunlight, causing an unsafe driving condition.

Roof design sends excess rainwater to the front windshield and the wipers push large amounts of water into the driver's viewing range; wipers slow down as engine speed decreases; inoperative wiper motor; delayed horn response; premature original equipment tire failures; bubbling in the sidewall of Continental original equipment tires; the muffler extends too far out from the underbody: one woman was burned on the leg while unloading groceries; and heated seats can catch on fire and give occupants much more than a "hot foot," as one owner so succinctly wrote to government investigators:

SERVICE BULLETIN-REPORTED PROBLEMS: *CC:* Fuel system warning light comes on; abnormal vibration when braking could be caused by inadequate removal of disc brake corrosion protection; other causes of brake pulsation, vibration; creaking, popping from rear of vehicle; front suspension knocking; unpleasant odours coming from AC vents; Bluetooth complaints; inoperative rain sensor for intermittent wipers; music skips on iPod; blank radio screen; and under-hood paint doesn't match exterior paint job. *Golf:* Abnormal vibration when braking; other causes of brake pulsation, vibration; unpleasant odours coming from AC vents; Bluetooth complaints; music skips on iPod; blank radio screen; unusual screen colours when cold; under-hood paint doesn't match exterior paint job; and rear lid parcel shelf doesn't open evenly. *Jetta:* Inoperative remote key; abnormal vibration when braking; other causes of brake pulsation, vibration; unpleasant odours coming from AC vents; music skips on iPod; and under-hood paint doesn't match exterior paint job.

EOS ★★★

RATING: Average, as long as you stay away from the unpredictable, failure-prone DSG automated manual transmission. **Strong points:** A more-than-adequate 200 hp 4-cylinder engine; the car is agile, handles well, and provides a comfortable, taut ride; effective, smooth, and easy-to-modulate braking; standard traction and stability control; instruments and controls are intuitive and easily accessed; supportive front seats with plenty of headroom and legroom; rear seats are a bit firmer; acceptable cargo area. Pockets on side doors are handy for storage. IIHS gives Eos its top, "Good," rating for frontal offset and side crashworthiness and head restraint effectiveness. **Weak points:** The triumph of style over practicality; limited interior access, rear legroom, and headroom; and excessive cabin engine noise. The Eos gets none of the Jetta's 2011 upgrades; NHTSA hasn't crash-tested the Eos; and owners give it a below average reliability score. **New for 2012:** A light restyling inside and out.

OVERVIEW: The Jetta-based Eos is a four-seater convertible equipped with a retractable roof and powered by a 200 hp 2.0L turbocharged 4-cylinder engine coupled to either a standard 6-speed manual or an optional 6-speed automatic transmission. The Eos comes with standard head-protecting side curtain airbags. It also handles well, if you can put up with all of the road and wind noise intrusion into the cabin when the top is closed; the noise is practically unbearable when the top is open. Incidentally, the latest research shows that convertibles driven with the top down contribute to premature hearing loss. (SORRY, WHAT WAS THAT? I CAN'T HEAR YOU!)

COST ANALYSIS: Look for a cheaper, leftover 2011 model, and seek a 10 percent discount. Some VW dealers are asking for $300–$400 "administration" or "processing" fees; don't pay them. **Best alternatives:** The BMW 3 Series Cabriolet, Mazda's Miata, the Mercedes-Benz CLK-Class Cabriolet, and Mitsubishi Eclipse Spyder. Of that grouping, the Miata and Spyder are your best bets from a cost/quality standpoint. **Rebates:** Rebates and discounts are quite modest ($1,000–$2,000). **Depreciation:** Fairly steep for a convertible; a 2007 Eos that sold for $36,900 is now worth only $17,500. **Insurance cost:** Higher than average. **Parts supply/cost:** Parts aren't hard to find, since they're taken from the Golf/Jetta parts bin, but they can be costly. **Annual maintenance cost:** Average during the first three years. After this, expect repair costs to climb rapidly. **Warranty:** Bumper-to-bumper 4 years/80,000 km; powertrain 5 years/100,000 km; rust perforation 12 years/ unlimited km. **Highway/city fuel economy:** 6.7/10 L/100 km, 42/28 mpg. *Auto.:* 6.7/9.5 L/100 km, 42/30 mpg.

OWNER-REPORTED PROBLEMS: The Eos uses most of the same components that VW has put into its popular Golf and Jetta, so servicing and parts availability may be less of a problem than with other models (except for roof components and body panels). Nevertheless, short-term reliability reports are negative, reflecting similar deficiencies as noted by Jetta owners. Owners of two- and three-year-old models reports serious problems with fit and finish, body hardware, power equipment, and the audio system, not to mention a deadly "lag and lurch" problem:

> I was making a right turn when the car switched into Neutral causing the car behind me to hit the brakes so as not to hit me. My car then switched into Drive and lurched forward causing me to hit the brakes so as not to hit the car in front of me. This is the third time since I leased the car that it has shifted into Neutral and then into Drive.

2011 Eos has no power from stopped position when on a hill. Vehicle eventually has power after 5–6 seconds. Brakes must be applied and then car surges forward. Vehicle response on level ground varies from non-responsive to irregular to full power. Dealer provided 3-page document entitled "Momentary Delay With DSG Gearbox" outlining steps to take but will not take any corrective action with the vehicle.

SERVICE BULLETIN-REPORTED PROBLEMS: Inoperative remote key; fuel system malfunction light comes on; abnormal vibration when braking; other causes of brake pulsation, vibration; unpleasant odours coming from AC vents; Bluetooth complaints; music skips on iPod; unusual screen colours when cold; and under-hood paint doesn't match exterior paint job.

PASSAT, PASSAT CC ★★

RATING: Below Average. **Strong points:** Well-appointed and holds its value fairly well. Impressive acceleration with the turbocharged engine. Great performance with the manual gearbox; smooth and quiet shifting with the automatic gearbox. The sophisticated, user-friendly 4Motion full-time all-wheel drive shifts effortlessly into gear; refined road manners; no turbo lag; better-than-average emergency handling; quick and predictable steering; handling outclasses most of the competition's; the suspension is both firm and comfortable; quiet-running; plenty of passenger and cargo room; impressive interior fit and finish; and exceptional driving comfort. Good crashworthiness scores from both NHTSA and IIHS. NHTSA gave it five stars for side crash protection and four stars for frontal collision and rollover protection. IIHS gave the vehicle a "Good" rating for head restraint effectiveness and frontal offset and side crash protection. **Weak points:** Function sacrificed to style. Engines hesitate when accelerating; excessive brake fade after successive stops; rear-corner blind spots, and rear head restraints impede rear visibility; many safety and performance complaints after the two-year mark (faulty airbags and transmissions, distorted windshields, and chronic

CANADIAN PRICE (NEGOTIABLE): 2.5L 5-cylinder engine: *Trendline:* $23,975, *Plus:* $24,875, *Comfortline:* $27,975, *Highline:* $31,475; 3.6L V6 engine: *Comfortline:* $33,575, *Highline:* $37,475; 2.0L 4-cylinder TDI diesel engine: *Trendline:* $27,475, *Comfortline:* $30,575, *Highline:* $33,775, *CC:* $33,375, *VR6:* $46,375 **U.S. PRICE:** 2.5L 5-cylinder engine: *S:* $20,765; TDI diesel engine: $26,000, *VR6:* $29,765, *CC:* $28,515, *VR6:* $40,000 **CANADIAN FREIGHT:** $1,365 **U.S. FREIGHT:** $800

POWERTRAIN (FRONT-DRIVE/AWD)
Engines: 2.0L 4-cyl. diesel (140 hp) • 2.5L 5-cyl. (170 hp) • 3.6L V6 (280 hp); Transmissions: 5-speed man. • 6-speed man. • 6-speed auto. • 6-speed manumatic.

DIMENSIONS/CAPACITY
Passengers: 2/3; (CC): 2/2; Wheelbase: 106.6 in.; H: 55.9/L: 188.8/W: 73 in.; Headroom F/R: 4.0/3.0 in.; Legroom F/R: 43/29 in.; Cargo volume: 14.2 cu. ft.; Fuel tank: 70L/premium; Tow limit: 2,000 lb.; Turning circle: 38 ft.; Ground clearance: 4.5 in.; Weight: 3,853 lb.

stalling); plus, these models are expensive to purchase and service. **New for 2012:** All new for 2012. Volkswagen says the redesigned 2012 Passat has tackled the company's well-known quality problems. We hope so: In the 2011 J.D. Power Initial Quality Survey, VW tied with Mini for 29th among 32 brands. Lexus was the best, scoring at 73/100. Dodge was the worst at 137/100. VW's score in 2010 was 135/100.

OVERVIEW: The Passat is an attractive mid-sized car that rides on the same platform as the Audi A4. It has a more-stylish design than the Golf or Jetta, but it still provides a comfortable, roomy interior and gives good all-around performance for highway and city driving. The car's large wheelbase and squat appearance give it a massive, solid feeling, while its aerodynamic styling makes it look sleek and clean. Base 2.0T Passats come with a turbocharged 200 hp 4-cylinder engine and front-drive, while the 3.6L models use a 280 hp V6 harnessed to a front-drive or 4Motion all-wheel-drive powertrain. Passats come fully loaded with anti-lock four-wheel disc brakes, traction and anti-skid control, front side and side curtain airbags, tinted glass, front and rear stabilizer bars, and full instrumentation. In addition to the standard 6-speed manual transmission found on 4-cylinder models, an optional, problem-prone 6-speed Direct Shift Gearbox (DSG) automated manual transmission is available.

COST ANALYSIS: Get an identical 2011 model with a sizeable discount (at least 15 percent) and tell the dealer to take a hike if you are asked to pay a $300–$400 "administration" or "processing" fee. **Best alternatives:** The BMW 3 Series, Ford Fusion, Honda Accord, Hyundai Genesis, and Toyota Camry. **Options:** The AWD will give you the extra sure-footedness and traction when you want it. Not so with the adaptive cruise control; it frequently malfunctions. **Rebates:** $3,000–$5,000. **Depreciation:** Faster than average. How'd you like to lose over half the car's value after barely three years? That's what happened if you bought a 2007 Passat sedan, which originally sold for $29,970. **Insurance cost:** Higher than average. These cars are a favourite among thieves—whether for stealing radios, wheels, VW badges, or entire cars. **Parts supply/cost:** Parts are getting harder to find as dealers and suppliers close. **Annual maintenance cost:** Higher than average. **Warranty:** Bumper-to-bumper 4 years/80,000 km; powertrain 5 years/100,000 km; rust perforation 12 years/unlimited km. **Supplementary warranty:** A must. Maintenance costs are higher than average once the warranty expires. **Highway/ city fuel economy (2011):** *2.0L:* 6.7/10.0 L/100 km, 42/28 mpg. *Auto.:* 6.6/9.6 L/100 km, 43/29 mpg. *3.6L:* 8.3/12.7 L/100 km, 34/22 mpg.

OWNER-REPORTED PROBLEMS: Right front wheel suddenly shattered.

TIGUAN ★ ★ ★

RATING: Average. **Strong points:** Easy handling, a comfortable ride, and a roomy, well-equipped, upscale interior. The small turbocharged engine is an impressive performer, without exacting much of a fuel penalty. Excellent crash scores from both NHTSA and IIHS: five stars for frontal and side crash protection and four stars for rollover protection from NHTSA, and a "Good" rating for frontal offset, side crash protection, roof strength, and head restraint effectiveness from IIHS. **Weak points:** Pricey compared to the competition (did you see that $1,580 freight charge?); limited cargo space; side airbags for rear passengers are optional; and the 998 kg (2,200 lb.) towing limit is about 590 kg (1,300 lb.) less than V6-powered rivals. **New for 2012:** Minor interior and exterior changes; a bit better gas mileage due to some transmission tweaking.

OVERVIEW: Based on the Golf platform, the Tiguan has been a sales success story mainly because it is well-positioned between moderately priced small SUVs, like the Honda CR-V, and more upscale offerings, like the Acura RDX.

COST ANALYSIS: Get a practically identical, cheaper 2011 version. Watch out for VW dealers who tack on a phony $375 "administration" or "processing" fee. **Best**

KEY FACTS

CANADIAN PRICE (NEGOTIABLE): *Trendline:* $27,875, *Comfortline:* $31,275, *Highline:* $37,775 **U.S. PRICE:** *S:* $22,840, *SE:* $28,635, *SEL:* $33,975 **CANADIAN FREIGHT:** $1,580 **U.S. FREIGHT:** $875

POWERTRAIN (FRONT-DRIVE/AWD)
Engine: 2.0L 4-cyl. Turbo (200 hp); Transmissions: 6-speed man. • 6-speed auto.

DIMENSIONS/CAPACITY
Passengers: 2/3; Wheelbase: 102.5 in.; H: 66.0/L: 174.3/W: 71.2 in.; Headroom F/R: 5.0/1.5 in.; Legroom F/R: 42/28 in.; Cargo volume: 23.8 cu. ft.; Fuel tank: 70L/premium; Tow limit: 2,200 lb.; Load capacity: 1,110 lb.; Turning circle: 39.4 ft.; Ground clearance: 6.9 in.; Weight: 3,432 lb.

alternatives: A Honda CR-V or a Hyundai Tucson. **Options:** Be careful of option packages—they are pricey and full of non-essential features. Consider getting a good anti-theft system from an independent agency (they usually offer better selection and cheaper prices). Think twice about the AWD option: It will drive up your fuel consumption and only ensure that you get stuck deeper, farther from home. **Rebates:** No more than $1,000–$2,000 until the "newness" of the light restyling wears off in early 2012. **Depreciation:** Faster than average; a 2009 Highline AWD that once sold for $38,375 is now worth only $23,000. **Insurance cost:** Average. **Parts supply/cost:** Parts are no problem as many components are shared with other models. **Annual maintenance cost:** Predicted to be average. **Warranty:** Bumper-to-bumper 4 years/80,000 km; powertrain 5 years/100,000 km; rust perforation 12 years/unlimited km. **Supplementary warranty:** Always a good idea with cars that are relatively new to the market. **Highway/city fuel economy:** *Manual:* 7.7/12 L/100 km, 37/24 mpg. *Auto.:* 8.0/10.7 L/100 km, 35/26 mpg. *AWD:* 7.9/10.9 L/100 km, 36/26 mpg.

OWNER-REPORTED PROBLEMS: Only one complaint registered with NHTSA, and it concerned coffee spilled into the recessed area housing the electronic parking brake switch, causing the car to suddenly brake and lock up. Other past problem areas have been fit and finish, and to a lesser extent, fuel system and climate controls.

SERVICE BULLETIN-REPORTED PROBLEMS: Inoperative remote key; fuel system malfunction light comes on; abnormal vibration when braking; front brakes squeal when backing up; unpleasant odours coming from AC vents; sunroof, sun shade won't open; complaints regarding Bluetooth; music skips on iPod; unusual screen colours when cold; and under-hood paint doesn't match exterior paint job.

Appendix I

MINI-REVIEWS AND 2013 PREVIEWS

New car prices generally rise in the fall and drop in the winter. Popular vehicles maintain their original value well into the summer, while the average car or truck is discounted by about 10–15 percent in early winter when auto show and media hoopla has subsided.

Two factors that have a huge impact on prices are production delays and the cost of fuel. The first factor affects particular companies, while the second impacts specific models. Honda, Nissan, and Toyota, for example, have been hurt by a series of natural disasters that forced them to curb production by 50 percent this year. Now their plants are re-opening and these automakers are breaking with tradition by using generous rebates, low-interest leases, and special financing programs to capture sales throughout the model lineup.

The price of fuel is another wild card that affects new vehicle prices, depending upon how much fuel each model burns. As gasoline becomes more expensive, large trucks and SUVs become cheaper to buy as compacts and mini-compacts sell at a premium. However, once a barrel of oil goes below $80 U.S., small car sales wane and large cars, trucks, and SUV sales surge.

Yes, these are volatile times; car and truck prices fluctuate dramatically and fuel costs change every day. Still, take your time before choosing a new vehicle. Usually, the longer you wait, the less you will pay. You don't want the economic burden of buying a car that's on the market for the first time or one that has been radically changed this model year—the value of these vehicles is yet unproven. Nor should you invest in a vehicle that merely looks nice or is cheap if it doesn't have a positive reliability history. And you certainly don't want to overpay for a car or truck simply to be the first in your town with something "different" (remember the Chrysler PT Cruiser?). The uniqueness will pass; the repairs will remain constant.

Consider these tips:

1. If you really want to save money, try to buy a vehicle that's leased by a family member. You'll likely get a good buy for half what the vehicle originally cost and with some warranty coverage left. Plus, there won't be any secrets; everyone will know how the vehicle was driven and maintained, and you can use the same repair facilities that have been repairing your family's vehicles for years.

2. Get a fuel-efficient car. Be wary of diesel-equipped or hybrid cars that may require more-expensive dealer servicing that could wipe out any fuel consumption savings. Don't trust hybrid fuel economy hype—sometimes it can be off by 40 percent. Also, don't buy a "lemon" simply because it's touted as being fuel-efficient; a failure-prone Chrysler Sebring/Avenger may cost you more to repair than to fuel, and a 4-cylinder pickup like GM's Canyon and Colorado—though cheap to run—can make highway merging a white-knuckle affair.

3. Use *www.insurancehotline.com* to find out which cars are the cheapest to insure. Remember, having an additional licensed driver in the family places your policy in a higher risk category, with accompanying higher premiums. Not giving that extra driver permission to use the car has little bearing on your rates—you'll still pay more.

4. Crashworthiness *is* important and has nothing to do with how much you paid. Many entry-level vehicles have high crash protection scores given out by both the National Highway Traffic and Safety Administration and the Insurance Institute for Highway Safety. Imports unrated by American agencies will likely have been tested in Europe or Australia (see *www.crashtest.com*).

5. Delay buying a new car until early 2012, when automaker and dealer clearance rebates bring down new prices, and lots of inexpensive trade-ins reduce used prices. Also, refuse all preparation charges, wear and tear insurance, and $375+ "administration" or "processing" fees. It's uncanny how automakers and dealers create problems and then sell you the solution. For example, extended warranties are bought because the car industry rejects so many valid claims. Now, wear and tear insurance, selling for about $700, is used to "protect" those who lease their car and are afraid of the dealer's chargeback for accelerated wear and tear.

6. Buy an entry-level Asian model or Asian/American co-venture from dealer stock for better price leverage.

7. Stay away from superflous fancy options like failure-prone manu-matic transmissions; hard-to-replace, overpriced "run-flat" tires; leak-prone, head-room-robbing sunroofs; and tone-deaf, voice-controlled electronic systems.

8. Be wary of all European models. Even the venerable *Consumer Reports* now agrees with *Lemon-Aid*: European makes are way overpriced, depreciation is head-spinning, parts and servicing can be a problem, and poor quality control will drive you to "speak in tongues"—not necessarily French, German, or Italian.

9. Don't buy "nostalgia" cars; they aren't as good as the memories they evoke. This includes the resurrected Dodge Challenger.

10. Buy in the States, or use lower American prices as leverage with Canadian dealers. It's easy to find fully loaded trucks, sports cars, and luxury vehicles for up to $20,000 less than what you would pay in Canada. Look in Part Three of this guide and compare costs between the two countries.

2012–13 Model Changes

Here are the new cars and trucks that will undergo the most change, mechanical and stylistic, this year and next. Some models are totally "first-timers," others incorporate major redesigns, and a few are gone forever. There are a number of 2013 newbies, like the Kia Credenza, Chevrolet Volt, Ford Taurus/SHO, and Nissan Leaf that may not make it to Canada or will be sold only in limited numbers.

Redesigns are carried out every three years. Remember, never purchase new or redesigned models during the first six months they are on the market. The second series that comes out in late spring will have fewer defects, thanks to assembly-line fixes or a change of suppliers. As for a car or truck that has been dropped, don't automatically draw an X across its name; some can be outstanding buys. It all depends upon which vehicles have a good reliability reputation and whether parts are available from similar models still being built. Among the discontinued models listed below, good buys in this category are marked with an asterisk.

New Models: Audi A7, Buick Sonic and Verano, Chevrolet Spark and Volt, Fiat 500, Ford Focus (EV), Hyundai Velostar, Infiniti M35 Hybrid, Kia Cadenza, Mazda CX-5, Mini Coupe, Mitsubishi I EV, Nissan Leaf and NV, Range Rover Evoque, Subaru Coupe, and Toyota Prius V.

Redesigned Models: Audi A6; BMW 6 Series; Chevrolet Malibu; Ford Focus; Honda Civic, Civic Hybrid, and CR-V; Hyundai Accent and Azera; Kia Rio; Lexus GS; Mercedes-Benz GLS and the ML Series; Nissan Versa; Subaru Impreza; Toyota Camry, Tacoma, and Yaris; and Volkswagen Beetle and Passat.

Discontinued Models: BMW 1 Series M, 3 Series Wagon*, and M3 Sedan; Buick Lucerne; Cadillac DTS and STS; Chevrolet Aveo and HHR; Dodge Dakota, Nitro, and Sebring (renamed the 200); Ford Ranger*; Honda Element*; Lexus GS350, 450h, and 460; Mazda RX8 and Tribute*; Mercedes-Benz G55 AMG; Mitsubishi Endeavor*; Nissan Altima Hybrid; Saab 9-3, 9-4X, and 9-5; Subaru Outback Sport; and Volvo 940, 950, and XC90 V8.

2011–13 Models

Some of the vehicles rated in this section may not be available before early next year, or are relatively new to the market. Others may have been sold in small numbers, just dropped from production, or lack sufficient owner feedback to make a more detailed analysis.

Audi
Q5

RATING: Below Average. Audi's history of factory-related glitches and its "lag and lurch" powertrain are immediate turn-offs. 2011 sees the addition of a base 2.0 T, powered by a 211 hp turbocharged 2.0L 4-cylinder engine used by the Audi A4. Sales of the smaller models and 3.2 Standard upgrade have been quite good. **Price:** *2.0 TFSI Premium:* $41,200 (firm); *2.0 TFSI Premium Plus:* $45,300 (firm); *3.2 FSI Standard:* $45,500 (firm); *3.2 FSI Premium:* $49,900 (soft). The Q7's smaller brother debuted four years ago as a stylish five-passenger luxury crossover compact full of high-tech gadgetry, including an adaptive suspension that allows for firm, sporty handling, if so desired. The Q5 power comes by way of a 270 hp 3.2L V6 and the latest rear-biased version of AWD. **Strong points:** Stylish, luxury appointments; good acceleration; excellent handling; and full of nifty safety, performance, and convenience goodies. **Weak points:** Overpriced; limited rear seat room and cargo space; and, in the best German tradition, controls are needlessly complicated. Servicing is highly dependent upon a weak dealer network and parts are problematic. Unlike the Q7, there is no diesel option. Furthermore, powertrain performance is less than stellar. Owners report hard and delayed upshifts and downshifts between First and Second gear; sometimes, when coming to a stop, the transmission downshifts just as the engine suddenly surges. Excessive wind noise. **Crashworthiness:** NHTSA awarded five stars for front and side crashworthiness and four stars for rollover protection. IIHS gave its top, "Good," rating for frontal offset and side protection. Head restraint effectiveness is also rated "Good."

Q7

RATING: Average. These are complicated five- or seven-passenger machines are made from bits and pieces of VW's other models. The Q7 offers both gasoline and diesel powertrains hooked to an 8-speed automatic transmission, The 2012 3.0L engine gets eight more horses. Past reliability has been poor, the ride is stiff, and handling is mediocre. **Price:** *3.0 TFSI:* $53,900 (firm); *3.0 TFSI Premium:* $59,000 (soft); *3.0 TFSI Sport:* $69,200 (soft); *3.0 TDI:* $58,900 (soft); *3.0 TDI Premium:* $64,000 (soft). **Strong points:** A more-refined powertrain: The new 3.0T Premium and 3.0T Prestige are powered by a supercharged 3.0L V6 engine, putting out 272 and 333 horses, respectively. The 3.0 TDI Premium carries a 225 hp 3.0L turbodiesel V6. Maximum towing capacity is 6,600 pounds. **Weak points:** The Q7 is a VW Touareg/Porsche Cayenne combo with an Audi badge and new powertrains that have yet to be tested. Off-road prowess is not as great as the Touareg's or Cayenne's; fuel economy is not impressive; ride quality is ho-hum; rear visibility is limited; and the third-row entry/exit is problematic. Furthermore, early owner feedback indicates that this large crossover AWD wagon has a host of factory-related defects affecting its fuel and electrical systems, powertrain components, and fit and finish—exactly the problems owners find with Porsche and VW models. Poor servicing and recurring factory glitches are to be expected. **Crashworthiness:** NHTSA gives the Q7 five stars for front and side crash protection and four stars for rollover resistance. IIHS gives its top, "Good," score for frontal offset, side, and head-restraint protection.

BMW

1 Series

RATING: Below Average. Returning with minor trim changes, this little Bimmer is a joy to drive—when the powertrain, fuel, and electrical systems aren't acting up. Fit and finish isn't first-class, either, and servicing requires sustained dealer support. BMW's entry-level 128i and 135i include either a two-door coupe or convertible with a power-folding soft top. A standard 3.0L inline 6-cylinder is shared with the 3-Series. The 128i has 230 hp, while the 135i is turbocharged and has 300 hp. All models carry a 6-speed manual transmission, though the 128i offers an optional 6-speed automatic. This year, the top-end 135i offers an optional 7-speed automated manual transmission; in the past, this has been a problematic transmission. **Price:** *128i Coupe:* $35,800; *128i Convertible:* $41,200; *135i Coupe:* $43,000; *135i Convertible:* $48,500. **Strong points:** Excellent acceleration, steering, and handling; good outward visibility (coupes); average depreciation. **Weak points:** Styling is "unique." Harsh riding—you feel every bump in the road; poor outward visibility with the convertible top up; fuel consumption is a big letdown. Owners also report chronic fuel pump failures covered by a 10-year secret warranty:

> As I pulled out into the road, the Engine light came on and the car had reduced power. The car (with only 5500 miles [8,850 km] or so) was shaking violently when going under 10 miles [16 km] an hour. The RPMs fluctuated at idle to where the car almost stalled several times. I drove the 15 or so miles [24 km] home with my flashers on as the car was having trouble. The above is a description of a HPFP failure on the N54 engine. I would say many, many people get a bad fuel pump. BMW has covered the part for 10 years/120K miles [193,100 km], but it will fail again. There is no fix at this point. Just a new pump that eventually gives way. I know people who are on their 4th pump. Just do a Google search on "BMW HPFP" and see what comes up. The 135I, 335I, 535I [and] Z4 35I all have the N54 engine, and they all suffer from this defect.

ABS malfunctions; early ignition coil, clutch plate, and DTC traction failures; run-flat tire alerts come on for no reason; cramped interior creates awkward entry and exit; and few storage spaces. **Crashworthiness:** No crashworthiness data available.

Mini Cooper

RATING: Average; pain-in-the-butt kind of cute. This eye-catching classic British-*cum*-German car is a good highway performer, but high maintenance bills makes "cute" costly. Although the base Mini has an average reliability rating, the Cooper S has been much less reliable. The newly arrived Coupe will likely have a number of factory-related defects. The Cooper and Clubman return with few changes, a two-seater Coupe makes its debut this year, and a 2013 two-seater Roadster arrives next year. **Strong points:** This is a driver's car, especially when equipped with the 181–208 hp 1.6L turbo four. The car handles well and has exceptionally responsive steering. There is sufficient front legroom but back seat room is quite cramped. Stability and traction control are standard. The car's distinctive styling and slow depreciation add to its popularity. **Weak points:** You will find the base engine adequate, but the Cooper S is more spirited; high freight/PDI fee; mediocre fuel economy, considering the powertrain components; a choppy ride; and limited front and rear visibility. Audio and climate controls aren't intuitive, either. **Crashworthiness:** IIHS rates the Mini as "Good" for offset crash protection and head-restraint effectiveness; side crashworthiness was given an "Average" score. NHTSA says this little tyke merits a four-star rating for its frontal collision crashworthiness and five stars for side occupant protection and resistance to rollovers.

Fiat

500

RATING: Not Recommended during its first year on the market. Fiat's got some nerve. After walking out on its U.S. and Canadian owners in 1984 and leaving them high and dry with worthless warranties and rust-cankered vehicles, Fiat announced a triumphant return to North America as Chrysler's saviour. When Fiat pulled out of North America, I was in the trenches as president of the Automobile Protection Association and remember only too well the many Fiat owners who were stunned that their rusty, unreliable, and unwanted pieces of crap would never be fixed. The CAW, UAW, Ontario provincial government, and Canadian federal government never lifted a finger to help owners of these rust heaps get their money back. Now Mexican workers are getting their salaries underwritten by our unions and governments. **Price:** $17,500–$19,000 for the base model. **Strong points:** Adequate acceleration; fuel frugal; and good steering, handling, and outward visibility. The switch to a new platform for the North American imports is predicted to boost the 500's crashworthiness, reduce cabin noise and vibration, and lower the car's overall weight. **Weak points:** Quality! The May 2009 J.D. Power quality survey put Fiat at the bottom—28th of 28—in U.K. satisfaction rankings. Lexus, Skoda, Honda, Toyota, and Jaguar filled out the top five spots, while Citroen, Kia, Chevrolet, Mitsubishi, and Fiat rounded out the bottom five. Seating is for four only; parts availability and mechanic competency will be built up slowly; and a 100 hp engine is wimpy for a vehicle that is priced a couple of thousand dollars more than the Honda Civic or Fit. Other minuses include a small interior, a harsh ride, and wind buffeting. **Crashworthiness:** Neither NHTSA nor IIHS has tested the 500. European crash-test results don't apply because the North American version will ride on an all-new platform shared with the Panda utility vehicle and the Lancia Ypsilon hatchback.

Ford

Econoline, E-Series

RATING: Average. These gas-guzzling full-sized vans haven't changed for 2012 and quickly lose their value, making them a better deal used. **Price:** *Commercial van:*

$31,299; *Passenger van:* $36,399 (very soft). **Strong points:** Parts are plentiful and repairs aren't dealer-dependent. **Weak points:** Vulnerable to side winds; rapid brake wear; poor-quality original equipment tires; electrical system shorts; excessive steering wander; and surging, power loss, or black/white smoke (6.0L engines). Harsh automatic transmission shifts and automatic transmission converter clutch lockup, causing hesitation and/or lack of power during shift. **Crashworthiness:** NHTSA gives the van three stars for rollover protection.

Edge, MKX

RATING: Above Average. A five-passenger wagon/SUV crossover based on the same platform as the Fusion sedan, the Edge comes in either all-wheel drive (without low-range gearing) or front-drive. The turbocharged four, 285 hp 3.5L V6, and optional 305 hp 3.7L V6 are hooked to a fuel-efficient 6-speed automatic transmission. Standard features include ABS, traction/anti-skid control, and front-side and side-curtain airbags. **Price:** $28,000–$46,500 (soft). **Strong points:** Good acceleration, and handling is better than average for a crossover. Good passenger and cargo room. **Weak points:** There is some hesitation and gear hunting when downshifting. Although softly sprung, the ride is jittery. Mediocre fuel economy, lots of engine noise, and spongy brakes. Parts are a bit scarce and repairs are highly dealer-dependent. Optional equipment you don't need: Ford's Vista Roof (a glass roof with a sliding glass sunroof over the front seats), a navigation system, a DVD entertainment system, leather upholstery, and larger wheels. Lincoln's MKX is a more luxury-laden spin-off. **Crashworthiness:** NHTSA gives the Edge and MKX five stars for front and side protection and four stars for rollover protection. IIHS rated the Edge "Good" in front offset, side, and rear crashworthiness.

Expedition

RATING: Below Average. This gas-guzzling, over-priced full-sized SUV quickly loses its value and, like Ford vans, is a better deal bought used. Expeditions come with standard Trailer Sway Control that works with Ford's AdvanceTrac and Roll Stability Control to enhance safety while towing. An SOS Post-Crash Alert System activates the horn and emergency flashers should the airbags deploy. And, like the rest of Ford's lineup, Sync with available voice-activated navigation features, HD Radio, and Sirius Travel Link offers Expedition customers more choices in information and entertainment, if you can figure it out—many owners can't. The Expedition comes with a 310 hp 5.4L V8 housed in a truck-based chassis. Extended-length versions have more cargo space and seating for up to nine passengers. GM's Suburban, Tahoe, and Yukon represent credible alternatives. **Price:** *XLT:* $47,000 (soft); *Limited:* $58,500 (soft); *4×4 Max Limited:* $61,000 (laughable). **Strong points:** The Expedition has adequate passing/merging power and can tow up to 9,200 pounds. Occupants have a comfortable ride, and interior appointments are exceptional. Most large SUVs have heavy third-row seats that must be manually removed for more cargo space; however, the Expedition has second- and third-row seats that automatically fold flat into the floor. Both seat rows offer plenty of room, and the seats are nicely bolstered. Repairs aren't dealer-dependent and parts can be easily found at discount suppliers. **Weak points:** Powertrain performance is seriously deficient. Owners also say theV8 engine is sluggish and noisy. Ponderous handling is outclassed by GM's Tahoe and Yukon. Rapid depreciation: The $61,899 2010 King Ranch 4×4 model is now worth about $38,000. NHTSA safety-related logs mention rapid brake wear; harsh automatic transmission shifts; water leaks; chin-to-chest head restraints; and electrical malfunctions. **Crashworthiness:** NHTSA gives the Expedition five stars for frontal and side crash protection. Three stars were awarded for AWD rollover resistance, but only two stars were given for front-drive rollover resistance. IIHS hasn't crash-tested the Expedition.

Flex

RATING: Above Average. This boxy front-drive, or AWD four-door wagon seats either six or seven passengers in three rows of seats. Power comes from a 262 hp 3.5L V6 mated to a 6-speed automatic transmission and an optional turbocharged 3.5L that unleashes 355 horses while mated to the same gearbox. Safety features include ABS, traction control, an anti-skid system, front side airbags, and curtain side airbags. Some of the Flex's other features include a rear-view camera, power liftgate, voice-activated navigation system with real-time traffic and weather updates, four-panel glass roof, and refrigerated centre console. Another available feature is Ford's Sync, which is a voice-activated system that controls navigation, communication, and entertainment features. Other vehicles worth considering: The Chevrolet Traverse, GMC Acadia, Honda Pilot, Hyundai Santa Fe, Mazda CX-9, and Toyota Highlander. **Price:** $29,999–$46,599 (soft). **Strong points:** Acceptable acceleration and handling; a roomy interior; comfortable third-row seating; easy entry/exit; a quiet cabin; and a soft, compliant suspension that provides a comfortable ride for seven with car-like handling. Good overall visibility. **Weak points:** Pricey; loses value quickly; and is a gas-burner. The Flex is new to the market, so servicing is very dealer-dependent. Steering is a bit too light; excessive nose dive upon hard braking; a moderate engine noise when accelerating; a harsh, uneven idle; power locks cycle on their own; airbags fail to deploy in a head-on collision; sudden brake failure; and chronic stalling. **Crashworthiness:** NHTSA gave the Flex five stars for front and side protection and four stars for rollover resistance.

Taurus

RATING: *2013 models:* Average. *2012 models:* Below Average. The Taurus will have a shortened 2012 model year. Restyled 2013 versions will be launched early in the new year, offering a more-powerful 237 hp turbocharged 2.0L four to accompany the base 290 hp 3.5L V6. SHO models return with bigger brakes and the same old 365 hp 3.5L V6. The SHO (super high-output) returns with an EcoBoost turbocharged 365 hp 3.5L V6 engine, 6-speed automatic transmission, and AWD. SHO models have performance-oriented steering, suspension tuning, brakes, and 20-inch summer performance tires. **Price:** $28,000–$48,200 (firm). **Strong points:** Highway performance has been cranked up several notches, and the interior is more user-friendly, with better-quality materials and more attention paid to ensuring proper fit and finish. Excellent overall reliability. Good acceleration and steering/handling with the SHO version; the base Taurus does reasonably well. A quiet interior and a comfortable ride. **Weak points:** Automatic transmission performance degraded by frequent gear-hunting (non-SHO), and the SHO ride can be uncomfortably firm. Electrical and suspension glitches reported, and roof pillars obstruct rearward vision. The interior feels closed-in and there's not much rear-seat room. **Crashworthiness:** NHTSA gives the Taurus four stars for overall crash protection. IIHS has awarded the car its top, "Good," rating for front offset, side, and rear collision occupant protection.

Transit Connect

RATING: Below Average. Only two years on the market and sales volume is low. The Transit lineup returns this year unchanged; however, last year it expanded with a new trim level and versions that are capable of running on batteries, compressed natural gas, or liquid petroleum gas. Sold worldwide for the past decade, it can seat two, four, or five passengers. It has minivan-like sliding rear side doors and two rear "barn doors," similar to a commercial van. Powered by a puny 136 hp 2.0L 4-cylinder engine and a rather primitive, fuel-thirsty 4-speed automatic transmission, the Transit is longer, wider, and heavier than a Focus. This vehicle is aimed at the small-business commercial market and fits between the discontinued compact Chevrolet HHR and the recently ditched humongous and problematic Dodge Sprinter. **Price:** $27,000–$29,000 (soft). **Strong points:** An easily accessed, capacious rolling box with traction control; an anti-skid system; a vehicle tracking device; and an Internet connection. Handling is fairly good. Fuel economy is only acceptable. **Weak points:** Lethargic acceleration caused by a sluggish, uncertain transmission (a deal-breaker, for sure); very vulnerable to side winds; cheap interior materials; tall head restraints and closed rear quarter panels limit visibility; drivetrain pedals are too close to each other for such a wide interior, and the pads are unusually small; navigation feature is buggy; and engine and road noise transform the interior into a Jamaican steel drum. Owners can expect problems with premature brake wear and powertrain glitches due to the Transit's heft. Internal service bulletins target various water leaks; excessive steering play and noise; and rear brake thumping or knocking. **Crashworthiness:** Good; NHTSA gives it five stars for protection from frontal- or side-impact injury, while IIHS has yet to test the van.

General Motors

DTS

RATING: Average; dropped this year. It's essentially your father's comfortable, roomy, bouncy, and ponderous Oldsmobile. **Price:** $56,540–$75,880 (very soft). **Strong points:** Good reliability, parts are plentiful, and repairs aren't dealer-dependent. **Weak points:** There have been reports of airbags failing to deploy, loss of braking, and head restraints literally being a pain in the neck (try before you buy):

> Head rest is too far forward for his wife to drive the vehicle...The consumer stated
> when his wife adjusted the seat for driving, the head rest forced her head down. The
> consumer stated all that needed to be done was to have the two head rest supports
> bent down backwards a little to solve the problem.

Other owner complaints concern electrical shorts, premature brake wear, and subpar fit and finish. **Crashworthiness:** Good; four- and five-star protection ratings across the board.

STS

RATING: Below Average; dropped this year. A rear-drive/AWD Seville replacement, the STS is attractively styled and has plenty of power and performance—all available for a premium price. **Price:** $56,540 (soft) for the 255 hp 3.6L V6 with a 5-speed automatic transmission and $64,305 (soft) for the 320 hp 4.6L V8 AWD with a 6-speed automatic. This is a $5,500–$8,000 drop in price from the 2009 models. **Strong points:** Cadillac's switch to rear-drive enhances the STS's balance, handling, overall performance, and reliability. The torquey V6 with 302 horses is impressive and almost eclipses the V8's 320 hp advantage. Think: The V6 has just 18 fewer ponies than the optional 4.6L V8, and the V6 will likely cost some $11,000 less. Eleven grand for 18 horsepower? The STS has had few safety-related complaints posted with NHTSA. Those posted concern the side airbags failing to deploy, the car's poor traction in the snow, sudden rear differential lock-up (also a CTS complaint), and chronic stalling. **Weak points:** Way overpriced. Steering feels a bit vague and over-assisted. Plastic trim pieces have no place in a Cadillac. Sporty front seats may be too firm for some, while rear seats could use more lateral support and a longer seat bottom. Rear legroom and foot space is tight. Interior fit and finish is subpar. Setting the memory functions for the driver's seat, mirrors, radio, and climate control can be confounding, and the blind spot warning icon is washed out by sunlight. Trunk volume is unusually small and restrictive. The predicted reliability rating provided by J.D. Power and Associates is just slightly above average. Internal service bulletins highlight drivetrain chatter and rear axle clunks; lack of Forward or Reverse gear; an automatic transmission grinding sound; upshift/downshift clunks; key sticking in the ignition; airbag warning light staying lit; clicking or ticking after a cold start; side window chipping; and tires that slowly go flat. **Crashworthiness:** NHTSA gave the STS four stars for frontal and side protection and five stars for rollover resistance.

SRX

RATING: Below Average. Base models are front-drive, while Luxury versions include all-wheel drive; both are powered by a new 308 hp 3.6L V6 hooked to a 6-speed automatic transmission, with a maximum towing capacity of 3,500 pounds. Available safety features include ABS, traction control, an anti-skid system, side curtain airbags, and front side airbags. Optional safety features include steering-linked headlights and adjustable pedals. Alternative vehicles are the Lexus RX or Acura RDX. **Price:** *Base FWD: $41,780 ; AWD (entry-level):*

$48,000. Prices are negotiable. **Strong points:** Sporty handling when the tranny and engine are in sync. **Weak points:** Overpriced; quickly loses resale value; slow acceleration; the AWD model is slower to accelerate than the rear-drive, and the transmission often hesitates before downshifting. Insufficient rear passenger room; poor fit and finish; costly, dealer-dependent servicing; and suspension may be too firm for some. Owners report the following safety related glitches, no doubt related to the SRX's redesign: chronic stalling (the vehicle then proceeds to roll downhill); electrical malfunctions that knock out instruments and gauges as the car automatically switches to Neutral; automatic transmission sticks in low gear (vehicle has to be brought to a stop and restarted); hood release is located too close to driver's left foot; brakes grind as pressure is slowly lifted off the brake pedal; hard to get a spare tire. **Crashworthiness:** NHTSA has given its five-star rating for front and side crash protection; rollover resistance received four stars.

Express, Savana

RATING: Recommended. These full-sized, rear-drive vans have been around forever. **Price:** *Express:* $31,460; *Savana:* $31,460 (soft). **Strong points:** An easily accessed, capacious van. With fuel prices going higher and the economy softening, these vehicles are turning into "blue-light specials" and are discounted by up to 25 percent. Both vans are perfect recession buys because any independent garage can repair them, and most of their reliability issues aren't expensive to correct. **Weak points:** Fuel-thirsty, mediocre handling, and water leaks. **Crashworthiness:** NHTSA gives the Express 1500 cargo van five stars for frontal protection; the 1500 passenger van gets five stars for frontal protection and three stars for rollover resistance. The 2500 and 3500 12-passenger vans and the 3500 15-passenger van earned three stars each for rollover resistance. But, as *Lemon-Aid* has reported before, 15-passenger vans can be killers due to their high propensity to roll over.

HHR

RATING: Not Recommended; dropped this year. The HHR (Heritage High Roof) is a mini version of GM's 1949 Suburban, but it's equipped with many of the latest safety, performance, and convenience features. This five-passenger crossover compact wagon uses GM's Cobalt/Pursuit platform and a 4-cylinder engine. HHR's entry-level LS and 1LT models use a 155 hp 2.2L 4-cylinder engine, while a 172 hp 2.4L 4-cylinder is optional with the 1LT and standard with the 2LT. The high-performance, turbocharged SS has a 250–260 hp 2.0L 4-cylinder engine. It's not offered with the panel model. A mediocre 5-speed manual transmission is standard and a primitive 4-speed automatic is optional. **Price:** $20,395–$22,040 (soft). **Strong points:** Small-statured drivers moving from a minivan or SUV will appreciate the HHR's high seating position. There's also adequate rear legroom and storage space, and the vehicle's interior is easily accessed through wide-opening doors and easy-entry seats. It handles quite well and steering is accurate and responsive. **Weak points:** Woefully underpowered without the turbocharged engine option; the better-performing 2.4L powerplant makes passing and merging almost acceptable. Expect a bouncy ride; tire thump, engine buzz, and turbo whine; mushy brakes; thinly padded seats; and front seatbacks that are too upright for some. Drivers over six feet tall will likely find their heads grazing the headliner, especially if a sunroof is installed. The under-floor storage bins are too shallow. Thick pillars block the view fore and aft, especially on the windowless side panels. Forward view is impeded by the low roof design. Owners report electrical, suspension, and brake system failures in addition to a slap-dash fit and finish. A Honda Element, also to be dropped this year, would be a good alternative choice. **Crashworthiness:** NHTSA gives the HHR five stars for frontal- and side-impact occupant protection; rollover protection scored four stars.

Orlando

RATING: Not Recommended during its first year on the market, particularly in view of GM's less-than-stellar history of bringing poor-quality European imports into Canada. Scheduled to arrive in 2012 as a 2013 model. Whether you call the Orlando a crossover SUV or a minivan, the truth is that Chevrolet is all set to build an Opel-inspired seven-seat people mover; it will combine reasonable fuel economy with a minivan passenger load in much the same way as the Mazda5, Kia Rondo, and my old favourite, the long-gone, greatly lamented Nissan Axxess. Its basic layout and underpinnings will closely mirror the Chevrolet Cruze, GM Volt, and Opel Zafira. In GM's lineup, it will fit beneath the Chevy Equinox, Terrain, and Traverse (a mid-sized crossover that shares GM's Lambda platform with the Buick Enclave) and GMC Acadia. **Price:** $22,000 (estimated). **Strong points:** Thanks to its European DNA, the Orlando will likely ride and handle well and be reasonably fuel-efficient. Its wheelbase will be about three inches longer than the Cruze's, and it will have wider front and rear tracks than the Cruze, giving buyers a larger interior. **Weak points:** Minivans equipped with small, fuel-saving engines do less for less. Merging and hill-climbing with a full load will be patience-building exercises. A 6-speed manual tranny will be a plus. Reliability will likely be below average during the Orlando's first year on the market. **Crashworthiness:** No crashworthiness data yet available.

Spark

RATING: Not Recommended during its first year on the market, especially because it's a Daewoo tadpole that's best used only in the city. The Spark is a front-drive four-door hatchback that's smaller than Chevy's Aveo subcompact. Since it's built by Daewoo, think of it as Aveo's smaller brother. Yikes! This minicar has been kicking around the world for many years since it replaced the Daewoo Matiz. **Price:** $12,500 (estimated). **Strong points:** Light, direct steering is useful in the city; you can count on almost 50 mpg, no matter which engine you choose. **Weak points:** Accept the fact that this is a four-passenger urban econocar and you won't be disappointed. Five TV's *Fifth Gear* in Britain clocked the acceleration time for 0–100 km/h (0–62 mph) with the 1.0L and 1.2L engines. The results? 15.5 and 12.1 seconds, respectively, so bring along a good book. Some may find steering too light for highway driving; gear shifts are a bit clunky; a harsh ride when going over uneven terrain; and refinement isn't what the Spark is best known for. **Crashworthiness:** The Spark (called the Matiz in South Korea) received the maximum five stars in South Korea's KNCAP's frontal crash test, offset frontal crash test, and side crash test. It earned a four-star rating from the European New Car Assessment Program in November 2009.

Honda
CR-Z Hybrid

RATING: Below Average. Choose a cheaper second-series Hyundai Velostar instead. CR-Z is a sporty ("sporty" by hybrid standards, I suppose) two-passenger hybrid coupe equipped with a manual shifter; however, it doesn't come with the rev-happy performance we enjoyed with earlier sporty, fuel-frugal Honda runabouts, like the little CRX. A spin-off from Honda's "born again" Insight, the CR-Z has a shorter wheelbase, shorter length, and wider front and rear tracks than its cousin. Nevertheless, the Insight DNA is found everywhere in this little coupe. It's equipped with a 122 hp 1.5L 4-cylinder engine and uses the same hybrid system as the Insight, which manages to produce only 98 horses with its 1.3L 4-banger. A 6-speed manual transmission is standard, and a continuously variable transmission with steering wheel paddle shifters is optional. Drivers can dial in the car's highway performance electronically by choosing Sport, Normal, or Economy mode. As with the Insight, an electric motor is used to augment the gasoline engine. **Price:** $23,490; $19,200 in the States. **Strong points:** Fuel-efficient: EPA mileage figures will be 36 mpg in the city and 38 mpg on the highway. With the manual gearbox, predicted mileage falls to 31 mpg in the city and—thanks to the CVT—37 mpg on the highway. **Weak points:** The CR-Z fuel economy numbers aren't all that impressive. Stylistically, this is not a pretty car. Its extremely short rear end and long front overhang are somewhat jarring, and the rear tail lights and liftgate window are Insight derivatives. The wheels need to be upsized to fill in the wheelwells. **Crashworthiness:** NHTSA gives the car three stars for overall crash protection and five stars for rollover resistance.

Hyundai
Veloster

RATING: Not Recommended during the Veloster's first year on the market. **Strong points:** Surprisingly fuel-efficient; fuel economy rivals the Honda CR-Z Hybrid. A four-seater hatchback, this two-door sports coupe actually has a hidden rear passenger-side third door that gives access to the two rear seats. Parts and servicing won't likely be a problem since the Veloster shares most of the Accent's hardware and electronics, notably the 138 hp 1.6L 4-cylinder engine coupled to a 6-speed manual or automatic transmission. If its reliability matches the Accent, this $21,000 small hatchback has lots of potential. **Weak points:** At $22,000 for the base vehicle you are in Honda CR-Z range. Wait six months for Veloster prices to settle lower (by about $1,500) and for the initial first-year production snafus to be corrected. **Crashworthiness:** No crashworthiness data from NHTSA or IIHS is expected before early 2012.

Kia

Borrego

RATING: Below Average; the Borrego is selling poorly and may not make it through the 2012 model year. It lacks the refined ride comfort and easy handling found in other luxury three-row SUVs, due to its truck-like body-on-frame construction. Look to the Nissan Pathfinder and Toyota 4Runner for truck-like attributes. Vehicles with more car-like qualities are the Chevy Traverse, Ford Flex, Honda Pilot, and Mazda CX-9. **Strong points:** The V6 performs quite well in all driving situations and can handle heavy loads with ease. The V8 cranks up the towing capability to 7,500 lb., with plenty of power in reserve. There's also a smooth-shifting automatic transmission, a quiet interior, user-friendly controls, ample third-row seating, a standard trailer hitch and electric harness, and standard stability control. NHTSA gives the Borrego five stars for frontal and side occupant crash protection. Rollover protection was given four stars. Few owner complaints over reliability, so far. **Weak points:** A hard, jolting ride; poor emergency handling; head restraints are too close to the back of the head; lacks a power tailgate; and fuel consumption is much higher than represented. Owners claim the Borrego sticks in Drive once underway; suddenly accelerates in Drive; wanders along the road, requires constant steering correction; and constantly pulls to the right. **Crashworthiness:** No crashworthiness data available.

Land Rover

RATING: Not Recommended (all models). Land Rover sells four SUV models in Canada that cost between $45,000 (LR2) to $102,000 (Range Rover Sport Autobiography). They are the LR2, LR4, Range Rover, and Range Rover Sport, all of which return for 2012 with minimal changes. A fifth "Baby Rover," the Evoque, will debut at year's end and sell for $50,000. Land Rover has also had one too many owners, which clouds its future prospects. Both Rover and Jaguar are owned and built by India's Tata Motors, who purchased the companies in March of 2008. The $2.3 billion (CDN) purchase price is about a third of what Ford originally paid for the luxury nameplates. Nevertheless, Tata's "bargain" contributed to the company's first loss in eight years of $520 million (up to March 2009). Since then, Land Rover has had respectable sales, while being dragged through a sea of red ink due to Jaguar losses. Tata is looking for a white knight to take one or both companies off its hands.

Mazda

Mazda2

RATING: Average. This subcompact five-seater (really, it's a four-seater) comes only as a four-door hatchback equipped with a 100 hp 1.5L 4-cylinder engine. The engine can be paired to either a 4-speed automatic transmission or a 5-speed manual gearbox. A success in Europe where it was known as the Demio, the Mazda2—like the Honda Fit (Jazz)—has proven itself in other countries. **Price:** GX: $13,995; GS: $18,195. **Strong points:** Roomier in the rear than the Ford

Fiesta and costs less. Highway/city fuel economy is quite good: *Man.*: 5.6/7.2 L/100 km, 50/39 mpg; *Auto.*: 5.8/7.3 L/100 km, 49/39 mpg. Highway and city driving is a breeze due to the car's superb handling and comfortable ride. Mazda's new vehicle launches have produced fewer first-year factory defects than Detroit-based and some Japanese and South Korean automakers like Daewoo/GM, Kia, Nissan, and Toyota. The 2008 Mazda2 garnered the highest rating of five stars for adult protection, a class-leading four stars for child protection, and a respectable two stars for pedestrian protection from the EuroNCAP ADAC-administered crash testing. Standard safety features include electronic stability control and curtain airbags. **Weak points:** Slow when carrying a full load; transmission needs more gears; and the interior is rather Spartan when compared with the competition. **Crashworthiness:** IIHS frontal offset and roof crash protection is rated "Good," while side and rear crashworthiness is judged "Acceptable." NHTSA gave the car a combined crashworthiness score of four stars.

Mercedes-Benz

ML 350

RATING: Not Recommended. In the past, these luxury SUVs weren't recommended due to their low quality and high cost. This year, 2012s aren't recommended for a different reason: they have been totally redesigned, and past experience tells us that M-B redesigns are usually accompanied by serious engineering faults and poor quality control. Plus, the ML Series is still way overpriced and loses its value quickly. In 2010 the Mercedes-Benz M-Class ranked 8th out of 15 luxury midsize SUVs in the *U.S. News and World Report*'s analysis of 64 published reviews and test drives, which included checks on reliability and safety data. This year's ML adopts the Grand Cherokee/Dodge Durango platform, which has been problem-prone on past Jeeps and Dodges. It will be powered by a new 302 hp 3.5L V6 or a 240 hp 3.0L V6 diesel. **Price:** $58,900 (ML350 BlueTEC) to $97,500 (ML63). Imagine spending that amount of money for an SUV that places in only the middle of the pack. By the way, these same two models can be found in the States for $50,490 and $92,590, respectively. **Strong points:** A luxurious interior; the ride is comfortable and quiet; handling is responsive and fairly predictable. Good off-road performance. **Weak points:** Not worth the asking price; quality will likely worsen with this year's redesign, and powertrain parts will be harder to find. The V6 is a competent but fuel-thirsty powerplant and the 7-speed gearbox may be rough-shifting. **Crashworthiness:** NHTSA gives the M-Class five stars for front and side crash protection and four stars for rollover resistance, while the IIHS ranked the 2010 and 2011 M-Class "Good" for frontal offset, side, and head restraint protection.

Smart

RATING: Below Average; this subcompact is highly dealer-dependent and seriously outclassed by the Ford Fiesta and Focus, Honda Fit, Hyundai Accent, Mazda2, and Nissan Versa. **Price:** *Fortwo Coupe:* $13,990; *Passion:* $17,500; *BRABUS:* $20,900; *Passion Cabriolet:* $20,500; *BRABUS Cabriolet:* $23,900. **Strong points:** Once the car gets up to highway speeds (which may seem like it takes forever), it manages to keep up with traffic; fuel-frugal; highly practical for city driving and parking; good reliability reports; distinctive styling; its engine bay isn't as crammed as small cars' often are; responsive steering and transmission performance; and the ride is almost comfortable. Standard stability control, side airbags, and ABS. **Weak points:** You pay a maxi price for a mini vehicle that's less refined than cheaper Honda, Hyundai, Kia, Mazda, Nissan, Suzuki, or Toyota minicars; dealer-dependent servicing (trips must be planned carefully for servicing accessibility); slow acceleration from a stop; the automated manual shifter is annoyingly slow and rough; and you must use premium fuel. **Crashworthiness:** NHTSA gives the 2010 Smart four stars for frontal collision occupant protection, five stars for side protection, and three stars for rollover resistance. It also received "Good" ratings for front offset, side, and rear crash protection in IIHS tests.

Nissan

Cube

RATING: Above Average. This is the five-passenger front-drive's fourth year on the Canadian market, and so far it has proven to be a reliable, though odd-looking, small car. The Cube is essentially a box on wheels that has plenty of room, but no personality. It is ugly stylistically and induces a feeling of instant claustrophobia. No 2012 changes are expected for this 122 hp 1.8L 4-cylinder-powered people-mover. **Price:** *Cube S:* $17,398; *Auto.:* $18,698; *SL:* $20,898; *Krom Edition:* $23,098. **Strong points:** The small number of complaints posted by NHTSA is surprising considering Nissan's history of churning out new and redesigned models before they have been "debugged." In comparison with the Kia Soul, the Cube is a better buy. Although the Kia is cheaper, neither the ride nor the handling can touch the Nissan. Then add the fact that the Cube has been proven in other countries (it's in its third generation), is highly reliable, and offers a high level of quality. As for the initial cash savings with the Soul, they will be wiped out by the Kia's higher rate of depreciation. **Weak points:** A wimpy engine and subpar fuel economy complement what *Motor Trend* calls "awkward proportions and asymmetric styling." **Crashworthiness:** Ratings have been quite positive. NHTSA gave the Cube five stars for side crash protection and four stars for frontal crashworthiness and roll-over resistance. IIHS awarded the Cube "Good" marks in frontal offset, side, and rear occupant protection.

Juke

RATING: Average. This funky-looking small wagon crossover makes no attempt to blend into the crowd; it also makes no attempt to provide an outstanding driving experience or offer good fuel economy, unlike the Mini Cooper. No, the Juke takes a cheap shot and targets young consumers who want a well-performing car with a unique look that will be a conversation starter and an attention-getter. *Car and Driver* believes the car's unique styling resembles a frog. Others say it looks like a crocodile. Esthetics aside, this front-drive, five-door compact crossover uses a direct-injection, turbocharged 188 hp 1.6L 4-cylinder engine coupled to a 6-speed manual or hooked to an optional CVT automatic transmission. All-wheel-drives use only an automatic shifter that splits engine power 50/50 between the front and rear wheels or the left and right sides. **Price:** *SV FWD:* $19,998; *Auto.:* $21,298; *SV AWD auto.:* $23,098; *SL FWD:* $23,548; *SL FWD auto.:* $24,848; *SL AWD auto.:* $26,648. **Strong points:** A reasonable front-drive price, without much difference in pricing between Canada and the States; excellent acceleration (hitting 62 km/h in 7.5 seconds—over a second quicker than the Honda CR-V); agile, with steering that is quick and sensitive; a comfortable ride; decent seating in front and back, complemented by reasonable storage space; a well-appointed interior; and Reliability hasn't been a problem during the Juke's first year. **Weak points:** Styling is weird (*autoblog.com* says it has a "Baby Predator" front end), and traction is quickly lost in fast starts or on wet highways. A recommended optional "integrated control" system can render the car more stable by uniformly setting the throttle, transmission, and steering response settings to Normal, Sport, or Eco modes. Rear seatroom is decidedly on the skimpy side, meaning anyone over six feet will feel cramped. **Crashworthiness:** An unknown, inasmuch as neither NHTSA nor IIHS has crash-tested this car.

Leaf

RATING: Not Recommended during its first year on the Canadian market, which is expected to start in January 2012. Nissan's first all-electric car (no, it doesn't have a tailpipe). **Price:** No Canadian price has been provided, but the car sells for $33,600 in the States, minus a $7,500 federal rebate. If it sells for the same price in Canada, the Leaf will likely cost about $5,600 more than the $28,000 Prius and $7,400 less than the $41,000 Chevrolet Volt. Incidentally, the list price doesn't include freight and preparation charges for any of the above cars. **Strong points:** Good acceleration in city traffic; comfortable seats, with an interior about the size of a Toyota Prius; quiet running; great navigation feature that computes how far you can travel on a map of your current location. **Weak points:** Lethargic steering, excessive leaning when cornering, and a few, *ahem*, electrical problems. The Leaf is advertised as being able to travel up to 160 kilometres without stopping to recharge—a process the automaker tells us would normally take "only" eight hours on a 220-volt circuit (wink, wink; nudge, nudge). But, just after reassuring us with the above claims, Nissan then adds this caveat (i.e., don't believe what we just said): "Battery capacity decreases with time and use. Actual range will vary depending upon driving/charging habits, speed, conditions, weather, temperature, and battery age." Age, weather, temperature, speed? Yikes! **Crashworthiness:** No crashworthiness data available.

NV

RATING: Not Recommended during its first year on the market. The 2013 NV (Nissan Van) represents Nissan's first attempt at breaking into the lucrative full-sized commercial van market monopolized by Ford and General Motors. There are two engines available: a 4.0L V6 and a 5.6L V8, both coupled to a 5-speed automatic transmission. Standard features include 17-inch steel wheels, fold-down passenger seatback, flat cargo floor, wide-coverage cargo area lighting system, water-repellent fabric on main seating surfaces, multifunction front layout and storage, multiple power outlets, cargo area side metal inner panels, multiple weld-nut attachment points for shelving and rack systems, recessed tie-down rings, a sliding passenger-side door, and wide-opening front and rear doors. **Price:** Nissan plans to sell these vans as 2013s early next year. **Strong points:** These vans combine convenience and utility, as well as roominess and comfort. There's a full-length cargo area inner panel to protect the outer walls from dents and dings from the inside, and there are multiple weld-nut attachment points for shelving and racks—again, requiring no sheet metal drilling. In addition, the NV's nearly vertical sidewalls maximize the usable cargo space. From the seats forward, the NV looks, acts, and feels like a pickup. You don't have to take apart the interior to access the engine and you don't have to worry about tucking your work boots into a cramped footwell. The U.S. EPA says gas consumption figures should average 21 mpg on a good day. **Weak points:** Since it is so new to the market, factory-related defects will likely be a problem and servicing will be slow due to back-ordered parts and mechanics' lack of familiarity with this new model. **Crashworthiness:** No crashworthiness data yet.

370Z, GT-R

RATING: Recommended. Nissan does have a couple of sports cars that are worth considering, although they have yet to be crash-tested. The 350hp V6-equipped 370Z is available as a $40,898 coupe or a $47,400 roadster. Is either model worth the price? Yes: both are speedy and attractive alternatives to the Chevrolet Corvette, which costs much more. The Nissan GT-R ($99,500) is the first AWD sports car to be fitted with an independent rear axle and is powered by a 530 hp twin-turbo V6.

Porsche

RATING: *Boxster and 911:* Below Average; *Cayenne:* Average; *Cayman and Panamera:* Not rated. Of these five cars, the Boxster and 911 owe their low rating to their high frequency of repairs and greater need for dealer servicing. The Panamera is too new to the market to recommend. **Price:** *Boxster:* $58,000–$73,000; *911:* $94,100–$118,500; *Cayenne:* $58,3000–$152,200; *Cayman:* $65,300–$77,500; *Panamera:* $115,100–$137,550. Shop in the States and you will see savings of up to $40,000 (CDN). Porsche was forced to cut its Canadian prices by almost 10 percent when the Canadian dollar increased value in September 2007. Now that the dollar is stronger once again, look for further price cuts. Adroit haggling should get you 20 percent off the suggested retail price. **Strong points:** A legendary racing cachet and excellent road manners. **Weak points:** Outrageously overpriced and a source of worry regarding service, repairs, theft, depreciation, high insurance costs, and premature wear and tear from cold and snow. Recent consumer complaints show that even the entry-level Boxster hasn't escaped the typical Porsche factory-induced defects affecting the engine, transmission, electrical system, brakes, and fit and finish. On the 911 and Cayenne, the powertrain, climate system, suspension, and fit and finish should be your main concerns. Making the reliability failings hurt more is the company's attitude that its cars are perfect, and what problems do occur are caused mainly by "driver abuse." Much to most owners' surprise and contrary to what Porsche dealers will tell you, Porsches *do* depreciate quickly. For example, a 2009 Boxster that originally sold for $58,400 is now worth about $38,000. All of the other Porsche models also lose much of their value during the first few years on the road. **Crashworthiness:** Not tested.

Saab

RATING: *9-3, 9-4X, 9-5, and 9-7X:* Not Recommended "distressed merchandise." With Saab thrown into bankruptcy by its creditors and union last September, it is doubtful any Saab models will be built in 2012. Saab dealers know this and they are cutting their ties with the automaker as they liquidate leftover Saabs at fire sale prices. Of course, no discount can compensate for poorly made cars hobbled by non-existent parts and servicing. Think Bricklin, Delorean, and Fiat. The 9-3 is the automaker's entry-level model and represented 81 percent of the company's North American sales, while the 9-4X is a spin-off of the Cadillac SRX with different sheet metal, a 265 hp 3.0L V6, front-drive or all-wheel-drive power, and an Aero option that offers a 300 hp turbocharged 2.8L V6 AWD drivetrain. Saab prices for Canada are almost unobtainable and depreciation is cataclysmic. For example, a 2009 9-7X AWD sold originally for $49,300 and is now worth barely $15,000. All models suffer from an abundance of defective components that imperil the cars' reliability and your own financial solvency. Be especially wary of powertrain, electrical, and fuel system breakdowns; brake failures; and poor fit and finish. **Crashworthiness:** NHTSA has given the 9-3 four stars for frontal crashworthiness and rollover resistance; side crash protection was awarded five stars. The 9-4X has shown good rollover resistance, while the 9-5 and 9-7X AWD remain untested by NHTSA. IIHS rated the 9-3's frontal offset, side, and rear crash protection as "Good." The 9-5's frontal offset crash protection was given a "Good" rating and side impact protection scored "Average." Head restraints were rated "Average." The 9-7X models got the worst scores among the Saabs tested by the IIHS; frontal offset protection was given an "Average," side crashworthiness was judged to be "Marginal," and restraints were rated "Poor."

Suzuki

Kizashi

RATING: Below Average. This mid-sized front-drive is more sizzle than steak and offers nothing exceptional for a $30,000 Suzuki. What's new for 2012? Mostly a rejigging of trim options and the promise of a hybrid and V6 for 2013. This front-drive, five-door compact crossover comes with a 180 hp 2.4L 4-cylinder engine coupled to a 6-speed manual. The all-wheel-drive SX version carries the same engine hooked to a continuously variable transmission. Highway/city fuel economy is 6.8/9.3 L/100 km, 42/30 mpg. **Price:** *SX AWD:* $29,995. Some good alternatives: the Acura TSX ($33,000) or the Subaru Legacy (*2.5i Sedan:* $24,000; *Sedan Sport:* $28,000). **Strong points:** The Kizashi is a relatively well-equipped family sedan with standard electronic stability control. Handling is better than average, especially with the Sport model's precise steering. The trunk has a useful pass-through to the folded rear seats. A perusal of NHTSA owner-safety complaints and Suzuki's internal service bulletins shows no evidence of any quality problems. **Weak points:** Insufficient power, a firm ride, and a narrow interior that's invaded by engine noise (especially with the Sport version). And speaking of the "sportier" Sport model, since when do a spoiler and five more horses (185) make a sports car? Furthermore, the 6-speed manual's long throws are annoying and the "gentle" gearing favours fuel economy over a sporty driving experience. The sunroof cuts into headroom, and rear seating is cramped. The 18-inch tires rumble on some road surfaces. **Crashworthiness:** NHTSA gives the car its top, five-star rating for front and side crashworthiness; four stars were awarded for rollover resistance. IIHS rated head restraints as "Good" and roof crashworthiness as "Acceptable."

Toyota

FJ Cruiser

RATING: Not Recommended for general use; Average for off-roading. **Price:** $31,900–$37,500 (negotiable). The same vehicle sells for between $25,290 and $26,880 in the States. FJs are powered by a competent 258 hp 4.0L V6 that can be used for either two- or four-wheel drive. A 5-speed automatic transmission comes with both versions, and a 6-speed manual gearbox is available with the all-wheel drive. **Strong points:** The Cruiser competes especially well off-road against the Ford Escape, Honda Element, Jeep Liberty or Wrangler, and Nissan Xterra. Off-roading should be a breeze if done carefully, thanks to standard electronic stability control, short overhangs, and better-than-average ground clearance. **Weak points:** The FJ's turning circle is larger than those of similar-sized SUVs, making for limited maneuvrability in close quarters. The rear side doors are taken from the Honda Element, which means rear and side visibility are severely restricted. There is also some side-wind vulnerability; a jiggly, busy ride; and annoying wind noises generated by the large side mirrors. Although touted as a five-passenger conveyance, a normal-sized fifth passenger in the back seat may consider litigation for cruel treatment. Plus, the rear seats are hard to access, forcing front occupants to unbuckle every time a rear occupant gets in or out. Front-seat headrests may be uncomfortably positioned for short occupants. Another minus is that premium fuel must be used to obtain mediocre gas mileage. **Crashworthiness:** A big surprise. Although NHTSA crashworthiness scores for front and side impacts are five stars, rollover protection merits only three stars. This is disappointing and is almost never seen with vehicles that are equipped with electronic stability control.

Volkswagen

The "new" New Beetle

RATING: Below Average. Volkswagen has taken the familiar Beetle design and literally flattened it to increase cabin and cargo space and add 3.5 inches to the car's length. We'll also see a more upright windshield, a wider track, and a reduced front overhang this year. **Price:** *Hatchback:* $24,175; *Convertible:* $29,175. **Strong**

points: Easy handling; a sure-footed and comfortable, though firm, ride; impressive braking; standard traction and stability control; most instruments and controls are user-friendly; comfortable and supportive front seats with plenty of headroom and legroom up front; cargo area that can be expanded by folding down the seats; upgraded head-protecting airbags and front head restraints. **Weak points:** An underwhelming, noisy 2.5L engine (a turbocharged variant is available); steering is over-assisted; the use of the failure-prone DSG dual-clutch automatic transmission doesn't bode well for long-term reliability; although diesel fuel economy is good, it's not as good as VW claims; the car is easily buffeted by crosswinds; large head restraints and large front roof pillars obstruct front visibility; limited rear legroom and headroom; and skimpy interior storage and trunk space. **Crashworthiness:** NHTSA gives the 2010 models five stars for side occupant crash protection and four stars for frontal and rollover protection. Interestingly, rear-seat passengers would not do as well in a side collision: The five-star side rating for front-seat passengers drops to only three stars for rear-seat occupants. Something to think about. IIHS gives the 2010 New Beetle a "Good" rating for frontal offset crash protection and head restraint effectiveness, but cites side crashworthiness as "Poor."

Touareg

RATING: Not Recommended. **Price:** $45,300–$61,800 (very soft). Redesigned last year, this new SUV offers a 3.0L turbocharged V6 diesel mated to an 8-speed automatic transmission, in addition to the carried-over base 280 hp 3.6L V6. Next year's models will be equipped with a 380 hp 3.0L V6 hybrid powerplant that will cruise at 100 km/h on electric power alone. **Strong points:** Volkswagen's third-generation, mid-sized Touareg comes with lots of style, a plush and comfortable cabin, and some of the most impressive off-road capabilities in its class. **Weak points:** For those benefits, you pay an outrageously high price to get an SUV that doesn't offer third-row seating, has a pitifully poor reliability record, and has sky-high maintenance costs. Its problem areas include the powertrain, fuel, and electrical systems; brakes; and fit and finish. **Crashworthiness:** NHTSA gives the Touareg five stars for front and side crashworthiness and four stars for rollover resistance.

Volvo

Volvo is a car company without a country and with a limited future, like Saab, Jaguar, Land Rover, Smart, and, to a lesser extent, Chrysler LLC. The once-Swedish automaker is now owned by the Chinese firm Geely after living through a decade of "benign neglect" at Ford. Geeley wants Volvo's new models to cater to luxury-car buyers while the company's North American advisors want it to remain for mostly middle-class owners.

Geely's voice has prevailed; Volvo's future will mirror Saab's present.

The Chinese takeover will annihilate what's left of the Volvo legacy. Innovation and product improvements will be starved from underfunding, and quality control will continue to decline because the Beijing mindset will be to "move the metal" and worry about quality after gaining market share (also called TQSD: Toyota Quality Decline Syndrome). Furthermore, additional performance features will price most Volvos out of reach for the average car buyer and make the cars almost impossible to service for the average mechanic. When it is found that a part is defective, its replacement may be back ordered for weeks—if it can be found in Beijing, Detroit, or Sweden.

Recession-ravaged dealers have lost confidence in Volvo and don't have the money to invest in a well-stocked parts inventory. Also, loyal Volvo customers have lost confidence in a brand they once believed in; they don't want to buy a car that can't be serviced, with a residual value that flows faster downhill than the Yangtze river.

In the meantime, Volvo dealers are closing their doors, mechanics have turned off the lights, and Volvo owners have fewer places that will service their cars or honour their warranties.

Bottom line: Don't buy any Volvo until we see where the company's headed.

Some Final Precautions

Here's how to check out a new or used vehicle without a lot of hassle. But if you are deceived by a seller despite your best efforts, don't despair. As discussed in Part Two, Canadian federal and provincial laws dish out harsh penalties to new- and used-car dealers who hide or embellish important facts. Ontario's *Consumer Protection Act* (*www.e-laws.gov.on.ca/html/statutes/english/elaws_statutes_02c30_e. htm*), for example, lets consumers cancel a contract within one year of entering into an agreement if a seller makes a false, misleading, deceptive, or unconscionable representation. This includes using exaggeration, innuendo, or ambiguity about a material fact, or failing to state a material fact, if such use or failure deceives or tends to deceive.

Just keep in mind the following points:

- Dealers are *presumed* to know the history, quality, and true performance of what they sell.
- Even details like a vehicle's fuel economy can lead to a contract's cancellation if the dealer gave a higher-than-accurate figure. In *Sidney v. 1011067 Ontario Inc. (c.o.b. Southside Motors) 15*, the plaintiff was awarded $11,424.51 plus prejudgment interest. The plaintiff claimed the defendant advised him that the vehicle had a fuel efficiency of 800–900 km per tank of fuel when, in fact, the maximum efficiency was only 500 km per tank.

Appendix II
INTERNET INFO

Recent surveys show that close to 80 percent of car buyers get reliability and pricing information from the Internet before visiting a dealer or private seller. This trend has resulted in easier access to confidential price margins, secret warranties, and lower prices—if you know where to look.

Getting the Lowest Price

If you want a low price and abhor dealership visits and haggling, search out a reliable new- or used-car broker. For years, *Lemon-Aid* has recommended Dealfinder, an Ottawa-based auto broker that helps clients across Canada. Go to *www.dealfinder.com* for all of the particulars. Ottawa-based Bob Prest, a small broker who believes in big discounts, has helped many people find great deals:

> To: Bob Prest <dealfinder@magma.ca>, August 30, 2010.
>
> Thank you so much! We picked up our new RAV4 today and are happy with the process. The salesman we had talked to previously took care of the details and we were pleased that he was not cut out of the transaction. Yet I know from past experience that we could never have negotiated such a good price... Thanks to Phil as well. His book was a big help.

For those readers who feel comfortable negotiating all of the transaction details with the dealer themselves, here's what to do: First, compare a new vehicle's "discounted" MSRP prices published on the automaker's website with invoices downloaded from the Automobile Protection Association (*www.apa.ca*), the Canadian Automobile Association (*www.caa.ca*), and a host of other agencies. Second, check the prices you find against the ones listed in this book. Third, pay particular attention to the prices charged in the States by accessing the automaker's U.S. website—just type the company name into Google and add "USA." For example, "GM USA" will take you directly to the automaker's American website, whereas "GM Canada" gives you the Canadian headquarters, models, and prices. If you find the U.S. price is substantially lower than what Canadian dealers charge, take your U.S. printout to the Canadian dealers and ask them to come closer to the American price. There is no reason why you should pay more in Canada. And this includes freight and pre-delivery inspection fees.

Real Trade-in Values

If you have a trade-in, it's important to find out its true value to decide whether selling it privately would put more money in your pocket than selling it to the dealer.

Right now, there is a shortage of good three- to five-year-old used cars on the market and private buyers are paying a premium for them.

Problem is, how do you find how much your trade-in is worth? In the past dealers had a monopoly on this information because only they could afford the hundreds of dollars in annual subscription fees charged by the "Black Book" and "Red Book" publishers. That has now changed with the advent of the Internet.

Carmakers are now using these price guides as a tool for new car shoppers who wish to configure the total cost of their purchase. Simply click on, for example, Chrysler Canada or Toyota Canada and the website will produce the figures for the make, model, and year of the trade-in. Or you can access the *Canadian Black Book*, or *Red Book* through Google.

Confidential Reliability Info

Unearthing reliability information from independent sources on the Internet takes a bit more patience. You should first wade through the thousands of consumer complaints logged in the NHTSA database at *www.safercar.org*. Next, use the NHTSA and ALLDATA service bulletin databases to confirm a specific problem's existence, find out if it's caused by a manufacturing defect, and learn how to correct it. Augment this information with tips found on car forums and protest/information sites. *Lemon-Aid* does this for you in its guides, but you can stay current about your vehicle's problems or research a particular failure in greater depth on your own by using the above search methods.

Automobile companies have helpful—though self-serving—websites, most of which feature detailed sections on their vehicles' histories and research and development, as well as all sorts of information of interest to auto enthusiasts and bargain hunters. For example, you can generally find out the freight fee before you even get to the dealership; sales agents generally prefer to hit you with this charge at the end of the transaction when your guard is down. Manufacturers can easily be accessed through a search engine like Google or by typing the automaker's name into your Internet browser's address bar followed by ".*com*" or ".*ca*". Or for extra fun and a more balanced presentation, type the vehicle model or manufacturer's name into a search engine, followed by "lemon," "problems," or "lawsuits."

Appendix III
CROSS-BORDER SHOPPING

Who would have thought the Canadian loonie would be worth more than $1.05 American? Certainly not automakers. They have been ripping us off for years with car prices 15 to 20 percent more than the American price.

But Canadians aren't as dumb as the automakers think.

Every time the loonie goes up in value, thousands of Canadians buy their new or used car across the border in the United States, where vehicles are 10 to 25 percent cheaper. For example, the Canadian dollar traded at par with the U.S. dollar in July 2008, and that year Canadian shoppers imported a record 240,000 vehicles from the United States into Canada. Imports slowed to a trickle in the first quarter of 2009 when the dollar dropped well below 90 cents (U.S.) (then, only 18,800 vehicles were imported). But, now with the Canadian dollar's value once again flying high, Canadian buyers are again flocking to dealer showrooms in the States.

Furthermore, dealers on both sides of the border are hungry for sales and aren't likely to knuckle under automaker pressure to refuse warranty repairs or service on cars purchased in the States, as they attempted to do a few years ago. Also, Transport Canada has made it easier to import new and used cars from the States, and businesses on both sides of the border have sprung up to facilitate purchases for Canadians. It's clear that getting a cross-border bargain is easier than ever. And most of us live within an hour's drive of the border,

Shopping Tips

Reported savings range from around 10 percent for subcompact and compact vehicles, compact SUVs, and small vans, to over 25 percent in the luxury vehicle segment. Most manufacturers honour the warranty, and many dealers and independent garages will modify cars to Canadian standards, including speedometer and odometer labels, child tether anchorage, daytime running lights, French airbag labels, and anti-theft immobilization devices. Some will complete the import paperwork for you. Again, whether it's worthwhile importing a car from the U.S. is a personal decision. Keep in mind that there may be a few extra costs to consider. For instance, if the vehicle was not made in North America, you have to pay duty to bring it into Canada. Normally, the duty for cars is 6.2 percent of the value of the vehicle. There are also excise taxes on vehicles weighing more than 2,007 kg (4,425 lb). A listing of Canadian border crossing spots where you can bring in a just-purchased new or used car can be found at *www.ucanimport. com/Border_Crossing_Info.aspx*.

Consumer groups like Montreal-based Cars Without Borders and the Automobile Protection Association (*www.apa.ca*) say buying a car in the States as part of your vacation trip and driving it back to Canada or using an auto broker is a sure money-saver and easy to do. Canadian dealers say it's unpatriotic and not fair to dealers, and that U.S. cars have softer paint and weaker batteries.

Canadian independent new- and used-car dealers aren't buying that argument; they are some of the biggest buyers of used cars in the States. For example, Advantage Trading Ltd. in Burnaby, B.C. (one of the largest importers on the West Coast) says they can get U.S. cars so cheaply that they can offer discounts to Canadians and still make a handsome profit. The only downside is that there is a shortage of some popular makes and models.

If you do decide to import a vehicle on your own, Transport Canada suggests you use the Registrar of Imported Vehicles' comprehensive and easy-to-follow checklist of things you must do (*www.riv.ca/ImportingAVehicle.aspx*).

- What to do before importing a vehicle
- What to do at the border
- What to do after the vehicle enters Canada
- What RIV fees will be applied
- Who to contact for vehicle import questions, including contact information for the Canada Border Services Agency (CBSA)

This list is all you need to import almost any car and get big savings. There are also independent resources listed at *www.riv.ca/HelpfulLinks.aspx* and *www.importcarto-canada.info/category/faq*.

MODEL INDEX

Recommended

Above Average

Average